독해·문법·작문을 한 번에 완성하는

NEXUS
영문
독해연습
501 +플러스

ENGLISH READING PRACTICE

4th Edition

독해 · 문법 · 작문을 한 번에 완성하는
NEXUS 영문독해연습 501 플러스 (4th Edition)

지은이 김일곤
펴낸이 임상진
펴낸곳 (주)넥서스

초판 10쇄 발행 2004년 2월 20일
2판 22쇄 발행 2014년 2월 5일
3판 16쇄 발행 2020년 3월 23일

4판 1쇄 발행 2020년 9월 14일
4판 7쇄 발행 2024년 2월 15일

출판신고 1992년 4월 3일 제311-2002-2호
주소 10880 경기도 파주시 지목로 5
전화 (02)330-5500 팩스 (02)330-5555
ISBN 979-11-9092-748-2 13740

www.nexusbook.com

독해·문법·작문을 한 번에 완성하는

NEXUS
영문
독해연습

김일곤 지음

+ 플러스

501

ENGLISH READING PRACTICE

4th Edition

넥서스

개정 4판 출간에 붙여 …

이 책《NEXUS 영문독해연습 501 플러스》의 전신인《영문독해연습 501》초판 1쇄가 출간된 것은 1999년 3월이었다. 그러니까 이 책도 출간된 지 벌써 20년이 넘었다. 그동안 초판은 10쇄, 제2판은 22쇄, 제3판이 16쇄가 발간된 것은 오로지 독자 여러분의 호응이 있었기 때문이다. 성원해주신 모든 분께 진심으로 감사의 말씀을 올린다.

초판에는 501개의 영어 지문들이 수록되었었다. '501개'에서 '1'의 의미는 향후 더 많은 지문이 보충될 수 있음을 전제로 한 것이었다. 초판은 5년 동안 10쇄가 발행되어 독자 여러분의 신망을 얻게 되었고, 이에 힘입어 제2판이 출간되었다. 제2판에서는 상당수의 지문이 추가되었고 22쇄가 발행되었다. 2014년 4월에 출간된 제3판은 초판과 제2판에서 15과로 되어 있었던 Part 1의 문법 설명을 17과로 늘림과 동시에 170개의 지문을 200개로 확장하였다. 또한 Part 5를 새로이 추가하여 기출문제와 실전대비 문제를 수록하였다. 그리고 총 지문 수를 540개로 늘렸다. 명실상부한《NEXUS 영문독해연습 501 플러스》의 모습을 갖춘 것이었다.

제3판 1쇄가 출간된 후 지금까지 6년 동안 16쇄가 발행되었는데, 지문 수를 늘리고 교체하는 과정에서 아직 완전하게 잡히지 않은 몇 군데의 오타와 부드럽지 않은 우리말 표현 등을 바로잡아 이제 제4판을 내놓는다. 판을 바꾸는 것은 보통 책의 내용을 바꾸는 것을 전제로 하는 것이지만, 미비점 보완도 판을 바꾸는 것이므로 이번에는 지문의 교체, 추가 등은 하지 않았으며 새로운 내용의 추가는 제5판으로 기약한다.

개정 4판의 특징은 다음과 같다. 이 책은 5개의 주요 Part와 Appendix로 구성되어 있다.

Part 1 : Grammar & Reading
핵심 문법 사항을 17과로 정리하고 이와 관련된 지문을 단·중문 중심으로 200개를 수록하였다 .

Part 2 : Reading & Composition
지문 번호 201−300까지가 수록된 Part 2는 중문 중심으로 구성이 되었는데, 각 독해 지문마다 영작 연습을 넣어 독해로 쌓은 실력이 독자 여러분의 영작 실력으로 이어지도록 하였다. 꼭 학습하고 넘어가길 바란다.

Part 3 : Advanced Reading

지문 번호 301~380까지가 수록된 Part 3는 장문을 통한 독해 실력 연마를 기하는 한편 이 글들을 통하여 영어를 모국어로 하는 사람들의 세상을 보는 눈을 이해하고자 하는 데에도 그 목적이 있다. 그들의 정치, 경제, 문학, 문화, 과학, 철학, 사상 등에 관한 생각들을 깊숙하게 접할 수 있는 지문들이다.

Part 4 : Sentence Completion

Part 4는 문장완성 문제 지문 121개가 수록된 part로 지금까지 연마해온 영어 독해력을 가늠해볼 수 있는 중요 Part이다. 120이 아닌 121의 숫자는 초판에서 의도하였던 [501]의 의미를 유지하고자 함이다. 〈기출문제〉에는 대학 편입학 시험에 출제되었던 문제를 중심으로 60지문을 수록하였고 〈연습문제〉에는 61지문을 수록하였다.

Part 5 : Reading Comprehension

Part 5는 제3판에서 새로이 들어간 Part로, 10개의 〈어법 문제〉 지문과, 10개의 〈내용 흐름 파악 문제〉 지문, 〈장문 독해 기출문제〉 지문 11개, 그리고 〈장문 독해 연습문제〉 지문 8개로 구성되어 있다. 이 책에 수록된 독해 지문 수는 총 540개이지만 문항수로 계산하면 이보다 훨씬 늘어난다. 한 가지 더 특기할 사항은 이 책 전체를 통하여 지문들의 하단 여러 곳에 꼭 알아야 할 영어 속담을 넣어 학습에 도움이 되도록 하였다.

Appendix : Translation & Key

540개 지문 전체의 〈우리말 번역〉과, Part 2의 Composition에 대한 모범 영작문, 그리고 Part 4-5의 문제들에 대한 〈정답〉과 〈해설〉을 수록하여 독자 여러분의 정확한 독해 능력 향상에 도움을 주려고 하였다.

이 책을 공부할 때, 처음에는 지문의 전체적인 뜻을 파악하는 데에 중점을 두고 공부하고, 두 번째 학습 시에는 사전과 Appendix 부분을 이용하여 구문과 어휘 의미 파악 등에 중점을 두고 정독(Intensive Reading)을 하기를 권한다. 시간적인 여유가 있으면 3독도 하도록 권하고 싶다. 아무쪼록 이 책을 이용하여 독자 여러분 모두가 독해력의 높은 수준에 이르기를 기원하며, 끝으로 제4판 출간에 도움을 주신 ㈜넥서스에 깊은 감사의 말씀을 올린다.

2020년 가을, 운중동 우거에서

저자 김일곤

PART 1

독해에 꼭 필요한 17가지의
핵심 문법을 정리하여
Part 1에서 다루는
200개의 지문을 효율적으로
학습할 수 있도록 도와준다.

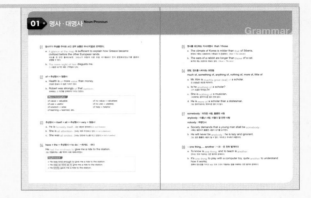

200개의 지문마다 상세한
구문 풀이 설명과 주요 어구를 제공하여
단문 독해 연습을 돕는다.
놓치기 쉬운 중요한 문법 사항들은
70개의 **플러스 문법 정리**로
꼼꼼하게 정리할 수 있다.

PART 2

Part 1에서 익힌 핵심 문법을 토대로
본격적인 단문 독해 연습을 할 수 있다.
Composition에서 주요 구문을 이용한
작문 연습을 하면서 독해와 작문을
함께 학습해 보자.

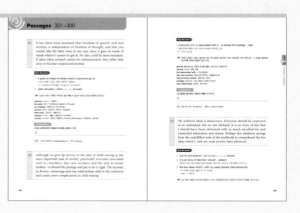

PART 3

Part 3에는 장문 독해 연습을 위한
80개의 지문이 수록되어 있다.
각 지문의 핵심이 되는 주요 구문 설명과
어구 풀이를 참고하여 장문 독해를
차근차근 연습할 수 있다.

PART 4

주요 대학 편입 시험과 대학원 입시 시험,
각종 고시에서 출제된 기출문제 중 핵심이
되는 지문 60개를 엄선했다. 더 나아가
61개의 연습문제를 추가하여 독해력과
실전 감각을 기를 수 있다.

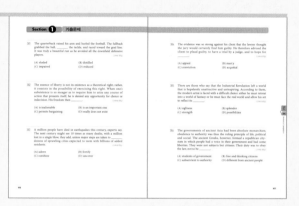

PART 5

Part 4에서 단문 문제를 연습했다면,
Part 5에서는 39개의 중장문 지문을
통해 장문 독해 문제를 연습해 보자.
어법 문제, 내용 흐름 파악 문제 및
종합 독해 문제 등 다양한 유형의 문제를
수록하여 어떤 시험이든 대비할 수 있다.

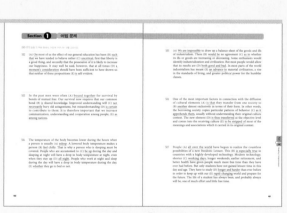

Appendix

540개 지문에 대한 우리말 번역과
정답을 제공하며, Part 4와 5에서
본문에 담지 못한 구문 설명과
어구 풀이가 수록되어 있다.

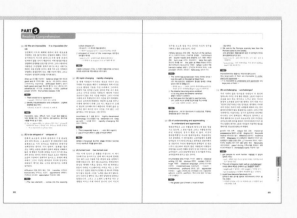

PART 1

Grammar & Reading

문법은 독해력 향상의 밑바탕이다!

01 · 명사 · 대명사 Noun·Pronoun

01 명사구가 무생물 주어로 쓰인 경우 보통은 부사구(절)로 번역한다.

  a. A glance at the map is sufficient to explain how Greece became civilized before the other European lands.
지도를 한 번만 들여다보면, 그리스가 어떻게 다른 유럽 국가들보다 먼저 문명화되었는가를 충분히 설명할 수 있다.

  b. The mere sight of him disgusts me.
그 사람은 보기만 해도 구역질이 난다.

02 of + 추상명사 = 형용사

  a. Health is of more value than money.
건강은 돈보다 더 많은 가치가 있다.

  b. Robert was strongly of that opinion.
로버트는 그 의견을 강력하게 가지고 있었다.

> **More Examples**
>
> of value = valuable   of no value = valueless
> of use = useful   of no use = useless
> of wisdom = wise   of help = helpful
> of learning = learned   etc.

03 추상명사 + itself = all + 추상명사 = very + 형용사

  a. He is honesty itself. 그는 대단히 정직하다. (= very honest)

  b. She is all attention. 그녀는 매우 주의하고 있다. (= very attentive)

  c. She was all smiles. 그녀는 만면에 미소를 띠고 있었다. (= full of smiles)

04 have + the + 추상명사 + to do : ～하게도 …하다

He had the kindness to give me a ride to the station.
그는 친절하게도 나를 역까지 차로 데려다주었다.

> **Rephrased**
>
> = He was kind enough to give me a ride to the station.
> = He was so kind as to give me a ride to the station.
> = He kindly gave me a ride to the station.

05 명사를 대신하는 지시대명사 **that / those**

  a. The climate of Korea is milder than that of Siberia.
  한국의 기후는 시베리아의 기후보다 더 온화하다. (that = the climate)

  b. The ears of a rabbit are longer than those of a cat.
  토끼의 귀는 고양이의 귀보다 길다. (those = the ears)

06 분량, 정도를 나타내는 표현들
much of, something of, anything of, nothing of, more of, little of

  a. Mr. Kim is much[a great deal] of a scholar.
  김 선생님은 대단한 학자이다.

  b. Is he anything of a scholar?
  그가 조금은 학자입니까?

  c. She is nothing of a musician.
  그녀에게는 음악가다운 점이 전혀 없다.

  d. He is more of a scholar than a statesman.
  그는 정치가보다는 학자다운 점이 더 많다.

07 **somebody** : 의젓한 사람, 훌륭한 사람

anybody : 이름난 사람, 이렇다 할 만한 사람

nobody : 무명인사

  a. Society demands that a young man shall be somebody.
  사회는 젊은이가 훌륭한 사람이 되기를 요구한다.

  b. He will never be anybody: he is lazy and ignorant.
  그는 결코 훌륭한 사람이 될 수 없다. 게으르고 무식하기 때문이다.

08 **~ one thing, … another** : ～과 …은 전혀 별개이다

  a. To know is one thing, and to teach is another.
  안다는 것과 가르치는 것은 별개의 문제이다.

  b. It's one thing to play with a computer toy, quite another to understand how it works.
  컴퓨터 장난감을 가지고 노는 것과 그것이 작동하는 법을 이해하는 것은 별개의 문제이다.

001

A glance at the map is sufficient to explain how it was that Greece became civilized before the other European lands. It is nearest to those countries in which civilization first arose. It is the borderline of the East and West.

Key Structure •

1 A glance at the map is sufficient to explain ~
   = If we take a glance at the map, we are able to explain ~
   • 무생물 주어 구문.

2 how it was that Greece became civilized ~
   • how Greece became civilized에서 how의 뜻을 강조하기 위하여 it ~ that 강조 구문에 넣은 구조.

내용 그리스가 다른 유럽 국가들보다 먼저 문명화한 이유는 지리적인 것이다.

glance [glæns] 일견, 얼핏 보기(= quick look, peep, scan) ⓥ 일견하다, 흘끗 보다
sufficient [səfíʃənt] 충분한, 충족한(= adequate, enough, satisfactory)
civilized [sívəlàizd] 문명화된, 교양 있는
borderline [bɔ́ːrdərlàin] 국경선, 국경 지방(= boundary, rim, fringe, periphery)

플러스 문법정리 1

부사구, 부사절을 대신하는 명사(구) 표현
영어에는 우리말과 달리 명사(구) 표현을 빌어 부사구 또는 부사절의 의미를 나타내는 경우가 많다. 특히 명사(구)가 주어로 쓰일 때 그러한데, 이를 **무생물 주어 구문**이라고 한다.

a. The year 2005 saw the publication of the book.
= The book was published in 2005.

b. The following morning found him dead in his bed.
= He was found dead in his bed the following morning.

c. A little more humility will earn him respect and fame.
= If he has a little more humility, he will earn respect and fame.

d. A little more effort would have led him to success.
= If he had made a little more effort, he would have succeeded.

해석 a. 그 책은 2005년에 출간되었다. b. 그는 다음날 아침, 침대에서 죽은 채로 발견되었다.
      c. 그가 조금만 더 겸손하다면 존경과 명성을 얻을 것이다. d. 그가 조금만 더 노력했다면 성공했을 텐데.

002 Luck or the grace of Heaven may seem to take part in many happenings in life, but **a little deeper looking into the causes of them** reveals that one's own efforts were by far more responsible for them than most people imagine.

Key Structure ▸

1 a little deeper looking into the causes of them reveals that…
   = If we look into the causes of them a little more deeply, it reveals that…
   그 원인들을 조금 깊게 조사해 보면 …을 보여 준다 (무생물 주어 구문)

2 **one's own efforts were ~ imagine**
   자기 자신의 노력이 대부분의 사람들이 상상하는 것보다는 그것들에 훨씬 더 책임이 있었다
   • be responsible for ~에 대하여 책임이 있다
   • by far는 비교급, 최상급을 꾸며 주는 부사적 기능을 지닌 전치사구로 '훨씬', '단연'이라는 뜻.
   [e.g.] This car is by far the better than that one.
          이 차는 저 차보다 훨씬 좋다.
          He is by far the handsomest man she has ever seen.
          그는 그녀가 지금까지 본 중에서 단연 잘생긴 사람이다.

   내용 인생사에서는 운보다는 자신의 노력이 훨씬 더 중요하다.

   grace [greis] 은총, 고상, 우아, 매력(= beneficence, benevolence, favor, mercy)
   heaven [hévən] 하늘, 창공 *cf.* Heaven 신
   take part in 참여하다, 참가하다(= participate in)
   responsible [rispánsəbl] 책임이 있는, ~의 원인이 되는(= accountable, answerable)

003 The watch was by no means low-priced, and was too expensive for a person **of my limited means**; still it was cheap at the price asked, for as to its action it defied all comparison.

Key Structure ▸

1 The watch was too expensive for ~ means
   그 시계는 나같이 한정된 수입을 가진 사람에게는 너무나 비쌌다

2 **a person of my limited means** 나처럼 (적은 수입으로) 옹색한 생활을 하는 사람

3 **as to its action** = concerning its action
   = with regard to its action = as far as its action is concerned
   그 성능에 관한 한

내용 그 시계는 비싼 것은 아니었지만 나처럼 옹색한 사람에게는 비싼 편이었다.

by no means 결코 ~이 아니다(= never, in no way, under no circumstances, not at all)
limited [límitid] 제한된, 한정된(= finite, restricted)
means [miːnz] 재산, 부, 수단, 방법(= wealth, method)
defy [difái] 무시하다, 거부하다, 반대하다(= challenge, confront, disobey, face up to)
comparison [kəmpǽrisən] 비교, 견줌, 유사(점)(= contrast, likeness)

플러스 문법정리 2

전체 부정을 나타내는 표현들

전체 부정(전혀 ~이 아니다)을 나타내는 다음 표현들은 사용 빈도가 높으므로 꼭 기억해 두어야 한다.

by no means, in no way, not (in) the least, under no circumstances, etc.

a. It is by no means easy to satisfy everybody.
b. This problem is in no way easy to solve.
c. He was not satisfied with the result in the least.
d. In summer there isn't the least rain in that part of the country.
e. You must under no circumstances approve of his offer.

해석 a. 모두를 만족시키는 것은 결코 쉬운 일이 아니다.   b. 이 문제는 풀기가 결코 쉽지 않다.
c. 그는 그 결과에 결코 만족하지 않았다.   d. 그 지역은 여름에 비가 전혀 오지 않는다.
e. 어떤 경우라도 그의 제안에 찬성해서는 안 된다.

004

As a matter of fact, every book worth reading ought to be read in precisely the same way that a scientific book is read—not simply for amusement, and every book worth reading should have the same amount of value in it that a scientific book has, though the value may be **of a totally different kind.**

Key Structure

1 **every book** (that is) **worth reading**   읽을 가치가 있는 모든 책

2 **in precisely the same way that ~**   ~과 정확히 같은 방식으로
   • that은 관계부사로 how와 같은 뜻임.

3 **of a totally different kind**   전혀 다른 종류인
   • 'of+추상명사'는 be동사의 보어로 쓰여 성질, 종류 등을 나타냄.

내용 읽을 만한 가치가 있는 책은 과학 서적을 읽듯 (세세하게) 읽어야 한다.

precisely [prisáisli] 정확히, 명확히(= accurately, correctly, exactly)
amusement [əmjúːzmənt] 즐거움, 오락, 취미(= delight, enjoyment, fun, pleasure, entertainment)
amount [əmáunt] 양, 액수, 금액, 총계
totally [tóutəli] 전부, 전혀(= completely, entirely, fully)

005 Washington was **discretion itself** in the use of speech, never taking advantage of an opponent, or seeking a short-lived triumph in a debate.

Key Structure ▸

1 Washington was discretion itself
= Washington was all discretion / very discreet
워싱턴은 매우 신중하였다

2 seek a short-lived triumph in a debate
논쟁에서 일시적인 승리를 추구하다
• short-lived 짧은 생애의

내용 워싱턴은 언어의 사용에 매우 신중하였다.

discretion [diskréʃən] 신중, 분별(= prudence, circumspection) ⓐ discreet 신중한
take advantage of 이용하다, 활용하다, 속이다(= utilize, make use of)
opponent [əpóunənt] 대항자, 반대자(= adversary, antagonist, challenger, contestant)
seek [siːk] 찾다, 추구하다
triumph [tráiəmf] 승리, 정복, 위업(= victory, conquest, accomplishment)
debate [dibéit] 논의, 논쟁, 토론(= argument, dispute, polemic)

플러스 문법정리 3

all+추상명사 = 추상명사+itself = very+형용사
'all+추상명사'는 '매우 ~하다'의 뜻으로 '추상명사+itself' 또는 'very+형용사'로 바꾸어 쓸 수 있고, 가끔 'all+복수명사' 표현이 쓰이기도 한다.

a. She was all kindness to me then.
= She was kindness itself to me then.
= She was very kind to me then.

b. She was all smiles to hear the news.
= She was full of smiles to hear the news.

해석 a. 그때 그녀는 나에게 매우 친절하였다. b. 그 소식을 듣고 그녀는 활짝 웃었다.

006

When I was a boy, I knew an old gentleman who used to say the most ferocious things about his landlady behind her back, but who was **all smiles and obeisance** as soon as she came into the room.

Key Structure

1 behind her back 그녀의 등 뒤에서

2 who was all smiles and obeisance = who was full of smiles and very obeisant
만면에 미소를 짓고 경의를 표했던 (늙은 신사)

내용 한 늙은 신사의 집주인 마님에 대한 이중적 태도.

ferocious [fəróuʃəs] 사나운, 포악한(= bestial, brutal, cruel, fierce, merciless)
landlady [lǽndlèidi] (하숙집 등의) 여주인, 여지주
obeisance [oubéisəns] 경의, 존경(= respect, homage)

007

Nothing can be more touching than to behold a soft and tender female, who has been **all weakness and dependence**, and alive to every trivial roughness, while treading the prosperous paths of life, suddenly rising in mental force to be the comforter and supporter of her husband under misfortune, and abiding with unshrinking firmness the bitterest blasts of adversity.

Key Structure

1 than to behold a soft and ~ female, ~ suddenly rising...
부드럽고 연약한 여성이 갑자기 일어나서 …을 견뎌 내는 것을 바라보는 것보다
• than 이하는 'behold+목적어+목적격보어' 5형식 구문. who절과 while절은 삽입절.

2 a female, who has been all weakness and dependence
지금까지 연약하고 남에게 의지만 해 온 여성

3 be alive to ~에 민감하다

4 while (she was) treading ~ life (자신이) 성공적인 삶의 길을 걷는 동안에는

5 rise ~ to be the comforter and ~ misfortune
정신적으로 분연히 일어서서 불행에 처한 남편을 위로하고 지지하는 자가 되다

6 abide ~ the bitterest blasts of adversity
가장 험난한 역경을 견디다

18

내용 연약한 여성이 분연히 일어서서 어려움에 처한 남편을 돕고 역경을 헤쳐 나가는 것을 보는 것만큼 감동적인 일은 없다.

touching [tʌ́tʃiŋ] 감동적인, 마음을 움직이는(= moving)
behold [bihóuld] 주시하다, 지켜보다(= look at, see, view, set eyes on)
tender [téndər] 부드러운, 약한, 온화한(= affectionate, warm-hearted, humane)
female [fíːmèil] 여성, 여자
trivial [tríviəl] 사소한, 하찮은(= inessential, insignificant, unimportant)
roughness [rʌ́fnis] 비정함, 난폭함
tread [tred] 밟다, 걷다
prosperous [práspərəs] 번영하는, 성공하고 있는(= successful, affluent, flourishing)
abide [əbáid] 견디다, 저항하다(= stand, bear, endure, brook, put up with)
unshrinking [ʌnʃríŋkiŋ] 움츠리지 않는, 단호한
firmness [fə́ːrmnis] 확고함, 단호한 태도
bitter [bítər] (맛이) 쓴, 견디기 어려운
blast [blæst] 돌풍, 폭발
adversity [ædvə́ːrsəti] 역경, 불운, 재난(= misfortune, uncongeniality)

008

Let your company be always, where possible, better than yourself and when you **have the misfortune to move** amongst your inferiors, bear in mind this seriously, that if you do not seize the apt occasion to draw them up to your level—which requires wisdom as well as love—they will certainly not be slow to drag you down to theirs.

Key Structure

1 **Let your company be ~** 너의 친구가 ~이 되게 하라(~한 친구를 사귀어라)

2 **when you** have the misfortune to **move ~**
= **when you** are so unfortunate as to **move ~**
불행히도 ~와 어울리게 될 때에

3 **bear in mind this seriously, that ~** ~을 진지하게 마음에 새겨라[명심하라]
• this는 bear의 목적어로 that 이하를 받음.

4 **they will certainly ~ theirs**
그들은 틀림없이 너를 그들의 수준으로 끌어내리는 데에 지체하지 않을 것이다

내용 가능하면 자신보다 더 나은 사람을 친구로 사귀어라.

company [kʌ́mpəni] 친구, 동료, 모임, 일행, 친교, 회사(= friend, associate, society, firm)
inferior [infí(ː)əriər] 열등한 사람, 손아랫사람(= lower, subordinate | ≠ superior) ⓐ 하위의, 열등한
bear in mind 명심하다
seriously [sí(ː)əriəsli] 심각하게, 진지하게

seize [siːz] 잡다, 쥐다, 파악하다, 이해하다
apt [æpt] 적절한, 어울리는, ∼하기 쉬운(= adequate, proper)
draw up to (∼로) 끌어올리다
drag down to (∼로) 끌어내리다

플러스 문법정리 4

have+the+추상명사+to부정사
'∼할 만큼 충분히 …하다'의 뜻으로 'be+형용사+enough+to부정사' 또는 'be+so+형용사+as+to부정사'로
바꾸어 쓸 수 있다.

a. She had the kindness to show me the way to the city hall.
= She was kind enough to show me the way to the city hall.
= She was so kind as to show me the way to the city hall.
= Kindly she showed me the way to the city hall.

b. He had the bravery to challenge his boss.
= He was brave enough to challenge his boss.
= He was so brave as to challenge his boss.

해석 a. 그녀는 친절하게도 시청으로 가는 길을 안내해 주었다.   b. 그는 감히 사장에게 대들었다.

---

009 Privacy is one of the necessities of human life, and to lose one's privacy makes life difficult to bear. This is the reason why people who **have had the misfortune to be born** royal sometimes make frantic efforts to break their way out into private life. To be born royal means being condemned in advance to live one's life in public, and this is an almost intolerable servitude.

Key Structure ▸

1 people who have had the misfortune to be born royal
   = people who have been unfortunate enough to be born royal
   = people who have been so unfortunate as to be born royal
   불행히도 왕족으로 태어난 사람들

2 make frantic efforts ~ life
   자신들이 처한 상황을 뚫고 사적인 삶을 가지려고 정신없는 노력을 하다
   • make ~의 주어는 윗줄의 people.

3 being condemned in advance to live one's life in public
   공적으로 자신의 삶을 살도록 미리 운명지어짐

20

내용 사생활은 인간 삶의 필수 요건 중의 하나이다.

privacy [práivəsi] 사생활, 비밀
necessity [nəsésəti] 필요성, 필수적인 일
be born royal 왕족으로 태어나다
frantic [frǽntik] 정신없는, 광란적인(= furious, hectic, panicky, violent)
be condemned to (~하도록) 운명지어지다(= be doomed to, be destined to)
in advance 미리, 앞서서
intolerable [intálərəbl] 참을 수 없는, 견딜 수 없는(= unbearable, unendurable, insufferable, excruciating)
servitude [sə́:rvitʃùːd] 노예 상태, 예속(= slavery)

010 No matter what other conquest a human being makes, he stands a defeated man if he fails to bring himself into subjection. No other case demonstrates this truth more tragically than **that** of Alexander. Conqueror of the Mediterranean world at the age of thirty-two, he failed in the greatest conquest, **that** of self.

Key Structure

1 No matter what other conquest a human being makes
인간이 다른 어떠한 정복을 이룩한다고 하더라도

2 he stands a defeated man
그는 패배한 사람으로 남아 있다[서게 된다]

3 bring himself into subjection
자신을 정복하다

4 that of Alexander = the case of Alexander

5 that of self = the conquest of self
자아[자신]의 정복

내용 자신을 잘 다스리지 못하면 다른 어떤 큰일을 하여도 패배자로 남는다.

conquest [kánkwest] 정복, 점령(지)(= subjection, subjugation) ⓥ conquer 정복하다
defeated [difíːtid] 패배한, 좌절한
subjection [səbdʒékʃən] 정복하기, 지배하에 두기, 복종(= subjugation, submission)
demonstrate [démənstrèit] 논증하다, 증명하다, 시위하다(= exemplify, show, prove, expound)
tragically [trǽdʒikəli] 비극적으로, 애처롭게
Alexander the Great(356-323 B.C.) 알렉산더 대왕(고대 마케도니아 왕)
the Mediterranean world 지중해 주변 세계 *cf.* 지중해 the Mediterranean Sea

21

플러스 문법정리 5

지시대명사 that과 those

that, those는 앞에 나온 명사를 대신하는 지시대명사로서 'the+명사'로 바꾸어 쓸 수 있다.
(앞에 온 명사가 단수이면 that, 복수이면 those를 씀)

a. The climate of Korea is milder than that of Siberia.
b. The ears of a rabbit are longer than those of a cat.
c. The population of Seoul is more than two times that of Busan.

해석 a. 한국의 기후는 시베리아의 기후보다 더 온화하다. b. 토끼의 귀는 고양이의 귀보다 더 길다.
     c. 서울 인구는 부산 인구의 2배가 넘는다.

011
The methodology of social science is inevitably different from **that** of natural science. It is different and must be different for one basic reason—the investigator is inside instead of outside his material. Man cannot investigate man by the same methods by which he investigates external nature.

Key Structure ▸

1 different from that of natural science
   자연과학의 방법론과 다르다
   • that = the methodology

2 the investigator is inside instead of outside his material
   조사자는 그가 다루는 자료의 외부가 아닌 내부에 있다
   • instead of는 not으로 바꾸어 보면 됨.

내용 사회과학의 방법론은 자연과학의 방법론과 다르다.

methodology [mèθədάlədʒi] 방법론
social science 사회과학 *cf.* 인문과학 liberal science / humanities
inevitably [inévitəbli] 필연적으로(= inescapably, surely, unavoidably)
natural science 자연과학
investigator [invéstəgèitər] 조사원, 연구원
external [ikstə́ːrnəl] 외부의, 바깥의(= exterior, outer, outward | ≒ internal)

012 The child who is placed in a foreign language environment attains a satisfactory competence in the new language with amazing speed not only because he is linguistically more flexible and without restraint and self-consciousness, but also because his language needs are much less than **those** of an educated adult. His experience and his vocabulary are much limited in his own language and it takes him comparatively little time to gain control of an equivalent vocabulary in the new language.

Key Structure •

1 not only **because** ~, but also **because**...
   ~라는 이유뿐만 아니라 …라는 이유로도
   • without restraint and self-consciousness는 앞의 he is로 연결됨.

2 those of an educated adult
   • those는 지시대명사로 the language needs를 가리킴.

3 it takes him comparatively little time to gain...
   그가 …을 얻는 데 비교적 시간이 안 든다

   내용 어린이는 새로운 언어 환경에 어른보다 훨씬 빨리, 더 잘 적응한다.

   environment [inváiərənmənt] 환경, 주위(의 상황)(= circumstances, conditions, surroundings)
   competence [kámpitəns] 능력, 역량, 적성(= capability, efficiency, adequacy)
   linguistically [liŋgwístkli] 언어적으로, 언어학적으로
   flexible [fléksəbl] 휘기 쉬운, 융통성 있는, 유연한(= pliable, accommodating)
   restraint [ristréint] 억제, 구속력(= constraint)
   self-consciousness [selfkánʃəsnis] 자의식
   comparatively [kəmpǽrətivli] 비교적, 어느 정도(= relatively)
   equivalent [ikwívələnt] 동등한, 등가의, 등량의

Liberty often degenerates into lawlessness.
자유는 자칫하면 방종으로 흐른다.

013 Your mind, like your body, is a thing whereof the powers are developed by effort. That is a principal use of hard work in studies. Unless you train your body you cannot be an athlete, and unless you train your mind you cannot be **much of** a scholar. The four miles an oarsman covers at top speed is in itself nothing to the good, but the physical capacity to hold out over the course is thought to be of some worth.

Key Structure ▸

1 a thing whereof the powers are developed by effort
그 힘이 노력에 의해서 개발되는 일
• whereof = of which (whose의 뜻을 갖는 관계부사)

2 you cannot be much of a scholar 대단한 학자는 될 수 없다

3 nothing to the good 이익에 도움이 안 되는 것

4 is thought to be of some worth 약간의 가치가 있다고 생각된다

내용 정신도 육체처럼 노력에 의해 그 힘이 개발된다.

athlete [ǽθliːt] 운동선수, 육상 선수(= sportsman)
oarsman [ɔ́ːrzmən] 노 젓는 사람
physical [fízikəl] 신체의, 육체의
capacity [kəpǽsəti] 능력, 용적, 수용력(= ability, capability)
hold out 견디다, 저항하다(= endure, tolerate, stand)

플러스 문법정리 6

somebody, something 등의 의미
somebody, something 등은 막연히 '어떤 사람, 어떤 물건'을 지칭하는 것뿐만 아니라 '중요한 인물, 물건' 등의 뜻으로도 쓰이므로 문맥을 잘 살펴야 한다.

a. She tried to look somebody. (훌륭한 인물)
b. I think he is something. (대단한 녀석)
c. Money is everything to him. (모든 것, 중요한 것)
d. He says that he is much of a scholar, but I think he is nothing of a scholar.
   (대단한 학자 / 전혀 학자가 아님)
e. I know that she is something of a singer. (상당한 가수)
f. I think they start something. (말썽)
g. It's a pity that he has been something of a laughingstock. (약간의 웃음거리)

해석 a. 그녀는 훌륭한 인물로 보이려고 노력하였다. b. 나는 그가 대단한 녀석이라고 생각한다.
     c. 돈은 그에게 전부다. d. 그는 자기가 대단한 학자라고 말하지만, 나는 그가 전혀 학자가 아니라고 생각한다.
     e. 나는 그녀가 상당한 가수라고 알고 있다. f. 나는 그들이 뭔가 일을 꾸미고 있다고 생각한다.
     g. 그가 약간의 웃음거리가 된 것은 유감이다.

014 When I had last seen Amabel, she was full of ambition because a girl she was at school with, quite an ordinary kind of girl too—in fact she had been **something of a laughingstock**—told her, when they had met by chance at a theater, that she was making quite a nice little income by contributing short stories to magazines. "If she can," said Amabel, who was full of false logic, "why can't I?"

Key Structure

1 a girl (whom) she was at school with 그녀와 같은 학교에 다니는 여학생
• a girl ~은 told her로 연결되는 주어임.
2 something of a laughingstock 약간은 남의 웃음거리

내용 자신보다 떨어지던 친구가 늘 거기 머물러 있으리라고 생각하는 착각.

ambition [æmbíʃən] 야망, 대망, 포부
laughingstock [lǽfiŋstɑ̀k] (남의) 웃음거리
by chance 우연히, 어쩌다가(= by accident | ≒ by design, on purpose)
contribute [kəntríbjuːt] 투고하다, 기증하다
false [fɔːls] 잘못된, 그릇된(= wrong, erroneous, erratic)
logic [ládʒik] 논리(학), 조리(= reasoning)

015 With regard to theory and practice there are two opinions. Some say that theory is **one thing** and practice **another**, so that they cannot necessarily go together. Others are again of opinion that it is because of the inaccuracy of theory that the two does not agree.

Key Structure

1 theory is one thing and practice (is) another 이론과 실제는 전혀 별개의[다른] 것이다
2 Others are again of opinion that it is because of ~ that...
또 다른 사람들은 역시 …라는 의견을 갖고 있다
• 두 번째 that은 it is ~ that 강조 구문. because of ~ theory 부분이 강조된 것.

내용 이론과 실제에 대한 두 가지 견해.

with regard to (~과) 관련하여(= with respect to, in regard to, concerning)
theory and practice 이론과 실제
opinion [əpínjən] 의견, 견해
go together 같이 가다, 조화를 이루다
inaccuracy [inǽkjərəsi] 부정확, 잘못(= error, impreciseness, untruth)

01 **what with ~ and what with... : 한편 ~하고, 또 한편 ...하여**

a. What with **hunger** and what with **fatigue**, **I could not walk any further.**
한편으로는 굶주리고 또 한편으로는 피곤하기도 하여, 나는 더 이상 걸을 수가 없었다.

b. What by **policy** and what by **force, he always accomplishes his purpose.**
지모를 이용하기도 하고 강압을 가하기도 하여, 그는 항상 목적을 달성한다.

c. What between **drink** and **fright, he did not know much about the facts.**
취하기도 하고 겁을 먹기도 해서, 그는 사실에 대해 잘 모르고 있었다.

partly ~, and partly... : ~하기도 하고 ...하기도 하고

d. I employed him partly **out of compassion,** and partly **because I was short of hands.**
그가 불쌍하기도 하고 또 일손도 달려서, 나는 그를 고용하였다.

e. We must sail sometimes **with the wind** and sometimes **against it.**
우리는 가끔은 바람을 등에 지고, 또 가끔은 바람을 안고서 항해 해야만 한다.

02 **what he is : 현재 그의 모습, 인간 됨됨이**
what he was : 과거 그의 모습
what he will be : 앞으로 그의 모습

a. Man is happy by what he is.
인간은 그 사람됨에 따라 행복하게 된다.

b. What I am is not what I was.
오늘날의 나는 지난날의 내가 아니다.

c. I owe to my parents the man I am now.
오늘의 내가 있게 된 것은 부모님 덕택이다.
• the man I am = the man (that) I am = what I am

03 **what we call / what is called / so called : 소위, 이른바**

a. He has had no regular education: he is what you call **a self-made man.**
그는 정상적인 교육을 받지 못했다. 그는 이른바 자수성가한 사람이다.

b. He is what is called **a grown-up baby.**
그는 이른바[소위] 다 큰 어린애이다.

04 **A is to B what C is to D** : A가 B에 대해 갖는 관계는 C가 D에 대해 갖는 관계와 같다

It is with A as with B : A의 경우도 B의 경우와 마찬가지이다

   a. Reading is to the mind what food is to the body.
     독서가 정신에 필요한 것은 음식이 육체에 필요한 것과 같다.

   b. No one can be disagreeable with sunny days. It is with manners as with the weather.
     햇빛 비치는 날을 싫어하는 사람은 아무도 없다. 예절도 날씨와 마찬가지이다.

05 복합관계대명사 **Whatever**

   a. Whatever may happen, I am prepared for it.
     어떠한 일이 일어나든, 나는 준비가 되어 있다.

   b. In a trying situation you must look for whatever element of humor may be present.
     괴로운 입장에 처하게 되면, 있을 수 있는 모든 유머를 찾아보아야 한다.
     • whatever는 복합관계대명사로 element of humor를 수식하는 형용사 기능 보유.

> **More Examples**
>
> Whatever may happen = No matter what may happen
> _cf._ Choose whatever you like. = Choose anything that you like.
>
> whatever element of humor may be present
> = any element of humor that may be present

06 유사관계대명사 (Quasi Relative Pronoun)

as   **a.** As many members as were present agreed on the plan.
      참석한 사람들 모두가 그 계획에 찬성하였다.
      • as는 유사관계대명사로서 주어 역할.

but   **b.** There is no child but likes playthings.
      장난감을 좋아하지 않는 어린이는 없다.
      • but likes playthings = that does not like playthings

than   **c.** He spent more money than was necessary.
      그는 필요 이상의 돈을 사용하였다.
      • than은 유사관계대명사로서 주어 역할.

Passages 016~027

016

What with the joy of seeing her son back safe and sound, **and what with** their good fortune, the boy's mother got well in a few days. She began to be very proud of her son, and she was never tired of talking about his adventures to her visitors.

Key Structure

What with **the joy ~**, and what with **their good fortune**
한편으로는 아들이 안전하고 정상적인 모습으로 돌아온 것을 보는 즐거움이 있고, 또 한편으로는 운이 좋아서
• What with **A**, and what with **B** 한편 A하고, 또 한편 B하여
• (be) back safe and sound 안전하고 건강한 모습으로 돌아오다

내용 아들이 안전하게 살아 돌아온 것을 본 어머니의 기쁨.

sound [saund] 정상의, 건전한(= healthy, fit, in good shape)
get well 건강해지다
adventure [ədvéntʃər] 모험(= venture, exploit)

플러스 문법정리 7

what with ~, and what with와 **what by ~, and what by**
두 표현 모두 '한편 ~하고, 또 한편 …하여'의 뜻이나, 쓰이는 용법이 약간 다르다. 전자는 원인이 되는 경우에 자주 쓰이고 후자는 수단·방법을 나타낼 때 쓰인다. with / by 대신에 between이 쓰이기도 한다.

a. What with **drink** and (what with) **fright**, he did not know much about the facts.
b. What by **hard work** and (what by) **good fortune**, he passed the test with ease.
c. What between **disappointment at the result** and **scold from his wife**, he left his home.

해석 a. 한편으로는 취기도 있고 또 한편으로는 두렵기도 하여 그는 그 사실들을 잘 알지 못하였다.
　　　 b. 한편으로는 열심히 노력하고 또 한편으로는 운도 따라서, 그는 시험을 쉽게 통과하였다.
　　　 c. 한편으로는 그 결과에 실망하고 또 한편으로는 아내로부터 질책도 받아 그는 집을 떠났다.

017

The aim of science is to foresee, and not, as has often been said, to understand. Science describes facts, objects and phenomena minutely, and tries to join them by **what we call** laws, so as to be able to predict events in the future.

Key Structure

1 The aim of science is ~, and not, as has often ~, to understand.
과학의 목적은 종종 이야기된 것처럼 이해하는 것이 아니고 예견하는 것이다.
- as has often been said 종종 이야기된 것처럼 (as는 유사관계대명사)

2 join them by what we call laws
우리가 법칙이라 부르는 것으로 그것들을 묶는다
- what we call laws = so-called laws 소위 법칙들

3 so as to be able to ~할 수 있도록 하기 위하여

내용 과학의 목적은 미래에 일어날 일을 예측하는 것이다.

aim [eim] 목표, 목적, 조준(= purpose, end, object, target)
foresee [fɔːrsíː] 예견하다, 미리 알다(= forecast, envisage, picture)
describe [diskráib] 기술하다, 묘사하다
object [ábdʒikt] 물건, 대상, 목표
phenomenon [fənámənàn] 현상, 사건 pl. phenomena
minutely [mainútli] 자세하게, 상세히(= in detail)
predict [pridíkt] 예언하다, 예보하다(= foretell, forecast, prophesy)

---

018 There is no one of us who has not wondered how the universe came into being. This world, with its flowers, rivers, roads, sky, stars, sun, and moon, all did not come about by mere chance, we reason. All that we see around us, and all that we know of, must have become **what it is today** by some process. If we could understand this process, we would understand the nature of the universe.

Key Structure

1 This world, ~ , we reason. = We reason that this world ~.
- 주절에 해당하는 we reason을 문장 끝으로 보내어 자신의 뜻을 밝히는 형태임.

2 All that ~ must have become what it is today by some process.
~한 모든 것은 어떤 과정에 의해 오늘의 그런 모습이 되었음에 틀림없다.
- All that ~에서 that은 관계대명사. / all that we know of 우리가 알고 있는 모든 것
- must have become 되었음에 틀림없다
- what it is today 오늘날의 그것의 모습, 현재의 모습

3 If we could ~, we would ~. (가정법 과거 구문)

내용 우주는 우연히 생겨난 것이 아니라 그 발생의 원인이 있다.

universe [júːnəvə̀ːrs] 우주, 전세계, 전인류(= world, cosmos)
come into being 생겨나다, 존재하게 되다(= come into existence)
by mere chance 순전히 우연하게
reason [ríːzən] 생각하다, 결론을 내리다, 추론하다(= think, conclude)

플러스 문법정리 8

조동사+have+과거분사

'can/may/must+have+과거분사' 구문은 과거에 있었던 일에 대한 추측을 나타낸다.
그리고 should, ought to가 have+과거분사와 합쳐질 때에는 과거의 있었던 일에 대한 반대의 유감을 나타낸다.

a. He may have said so. (가능성이 있는 추측)
= It is probable that he said so. / Probably he said so.

b. He cannot have said so. (가능성이 없는 추측)
= It is impossible that he said so.

c. He must have said so. (확실성의 추측)
= It is certain that he said so.

d. You should have followed his advice. (과거에 있었던 일에 대한 반대의 유감)
= It is a mistake that you didn't follow his advice.

e. He ought not to have said so. (과거에 있었던 일에 대한 반대의 유감)
= It is a pity that he said so.

해석 a. 그가 그렇게 말했을지도 모른다. b. 그가 그렇게 말했을 리가 없다. c. 그는 그렇게 말했음에 틀림이 없다.
d. 너는 그의 충고를 따랐어야 했다. e. 그는 그렇게 말하지 말았어야 했다.

---

019 Society is like a building, which stands firm when its foundations are strong and all its timbers are sound. The man who cannot be trusted **is to** society **what** a bit of rotten timber **is to** a house.

Key Structure ▸

The man who ~ is to society what a bit of rotten timber is to ~
신용할 수 없는 사람이 사회에 대해 갖는 관계는 썩은 목재가 가옥에 대해 갖는 관계와 같다
• A is to B what C is to D A 대 B의 관계는 C 대 D의 관계와 같다 (what은 관계대명사)

내용 사회는 건축물과 같아서 기초가 튼튼하고 목재가 견고할 때 굳건히 선다.

stand firm 굳건히 서다, 단단하게 서다
foundation [faundéiʃən] 기초, 밑바탕(= base, basis)

timber [tímbər] 목재, 삼림
trust [trʌst] 신뢰하다, 확신하다, 맡기다(= count on, depend on, rely on)
rotten [rátən] 썩은, 부패한, 역겨운(= decayed, corroded)

---

020 If bad manners are infectious, so also are good manners. There is no one who can be disagreeable with sunny people. **It is with manners as with** the weather. "Nothing clears up my spirits like a fine day," said Keats, and a cheerful person descends on even the gloomiest of us with something of the blessing of a fine day.

Key Structure •

1 **be disagreeable with sunny people**
   웃는 사람에게 기분 나쁘게 대하다

2 **It is with** manners **as with** the weather.
   = What is true of **the weather** is true of **manners.**
   날씨의 경우처럼 예절도 또한 마찬가지이다.

3 **even the gloomiest of us** 우리들 중 가장 우울한 사람조차도

   내용 명랑한 사람의 태도는 맑게 갠 날의 축복처럼 다른 사람에게 전염된다.

bad manners 나쁜 예절, 무례함
infectious [infékʃəs] 전염성의, 전염병의(= contagious, catching)
disagreeable [dìsəgríː(:)əbl] 불쾌한, 싫은(= distasteful, disgusting, nasty, offensive)
clear up 깨끗이 치우다, 정돈하다, 설명하여 풀다
descend on ~에게 내려오다, 다가오다
blessing [blésiŋ] 축복, 은혜, 예배
cf. Keats, John 존 키츠 (1795~1821, 영국의 시인)

---

021 Children readily understand that an adult who is sometimes a little stern is best for them: their instinct tells them whether they are loved or not, and from those whom they feel to be affectionate they will put up with **whatever strictness results from sincere desire** for their proper development. Thus in theory the solution is simple: let educators be inspired by wise love, and they will do the right thing.

Key Structure ▸

1 **from those whom they feel to be affectionate**
   (자신들에게) 애정을 가지고 있다고 느끼는 사람들로부터는
   • whom(관계대명사)은 feel의 목적어임.

2 **they will put up with** whatever **strictness ~**
   그들은 ~에서 나오는 어떠한 엄함도 참아 낼 것이다
   • whatever strictness results from ~ = any strictness that results from ~
   • whatever는 형용사적으로 쓰인 복합관계대명사로 any ~ that의 뜻이며 strictness를 꾸밈.

3 **let educators be ~, and they...**
   교육자들에게 현명한 사랑을 불어넣어 주어라, 그러면 그들은 …할 것이다
   • 명령문+and ~해라, 그러면 …한다

   내용 어린이들은 자신들을 사랑하는 어른이 보여 주는 것이면 어떠한 엄함도 참아 낸다.

readily [rédəli] 곧, 즉시, 쉽사리(= soon, at once, easily)
stern [stəːrn] 엄한, 엄정한, 준엄한(= strict, austere, rigorous, stringent)
instinct [instíŋkt] 본능, 재능, 충동
affectionate [əfékʃənit] 애정이 넘치는, 따뜻한(= loving, caring, tender)
put up with 참다, 견디다(= endure, tolerate, bear, stand)
strictness [stríktnes] 엄함
sincere [sinsíər] 진지한, 참된, 거짓 없는(= candid, earnest, heartfelt, truthful)
solution [səljúːʃən] 해결책
inspire [inspáiər] 고무하다, 영감을 주다

플러스 문법정리 9

관계형용사로 쓰인 관계대명사 what / whatever / whichever
관계대명사 what, whatever, whichever 등은 명사 앞에서 그것을 꾸며 주는 형용사 역할도 한다.
이것을 관계형용사라 부른다.

a. I gave him what money I had.
= I gave him all the money that I had.

b. Try to endure whatever hardships you may come across in your life.
= Try to endure any hardships that you may come across in your life.

c. I am in a difficult position whichever way I turn.

해석 a. 나는 내가 가진 모든 돈을 그에게 주었다. b. 살아가면서 어떠한 어려움을 만나더라도 참도록 해라.
      c. 어느 길을 가더라도 나는 어려운 입장에 있다.

022 In a trying situation you can also look for **whatever element of humor may be present**. The ability to laugh things off has saved many an awkward situation in the classroom and social life. The world is thankful to the person who can create laughter. There is something about it which sweeps away worry, jealousy, and even disgust. Laughing is mutually stimulating. Your laughter will start that of the other person. His laughter in turn will make your laughter the more hearty.

Key Structure ▸

1 whatever element of humor may be present
= any element of humor that may ~ = all the elements of humor that may ~
있을 수 있는 모든 유머 요소

2 Your laughter will start that of the other person.
당신의 웃음은 상대방의 웃음을 유발할 것이다.
• that = the laughter

내용 웃음, 유머에는 힘든 상황을 극복하게 하는 숨은 힘이 있다.

trying [tráiiŋ] 괴로운, 시련의, 쓰라린
look for 찾다, 기다리다(= seek, search for, wait for)
laugh off 웃어넘기다
awkward [ɔ́:kwərd] 서투른, 미숙한(= clumsy, embarrassing, tricky)
sweep away 쓸어가다, 털다
jealousy [dʒéləsi] 질투, 선망(= envy)
disgust [disgʌ́st] 혐오, 반감(= aversion, distaste, abhorrence, sickness)
mutually [mjú:tʃuəli] 상호간에, 공통으로(= commonly, reciprocally, jointly)
stimulate [stímjəlèit] 자극하다, 격려하다(= activate, encourage, excite, incite, inspire, instigate)
in turn 교대로, 차례로

A stitch in time saves nine.
제때의 한 바늘이 훗날 아홉 바늘 꿰매는 수고를 덜어 준다. (호미로 막을 걸 가래로 막으랴.)

023 Among writers who have left behind them works sufficient to keep their memory alive, one here and there has also had the peculiar power to impress his personality, not only upon his contemporaries, but upon posterity likewise, which accordingly thinks of him with the kind of interest usually reserved solely for the living. The mere sight or sound of his name brings with it a train of attractive association and arouses the same sort of pleasure **as** we feel at the unexpected reappearance of an old friend.

Key Structure

1 impress his personality upon ~
~에게 개성에 대한 인상을 남기다

2 which accordingly thinks of him ~
따라서 그들은 그를 생각한다
• which의 선행사는 앞의 posterity.

3 The mere sight or sound of his name brings ~
그의 이름을 보거나 듣기만 하여도 ~이 나타난다
• 무생물 주어 구문.

4 arouses the same sort of pleasure as we feel ~
우리가 ~에 느끼는 것과 같은 종류의 즐거움을 불러일으킨다
• as는 유사관계대명사로 쓰였으며 feel의 목적어 역할.

내용 동시대인뿐만 아니라 후세에도 이름을 남기는 작가는 그 이름만 보고 들어도 즐거운 연상을 가져다준다.

sufficient [səfíʃənt] 충분한, 자격이 있는
impress [imprés] 인상을 남기다, 감동시키다
contemporary [kəntémpərèri] 동시대의 사람
posterity [pɑstérəti] 후대, 후세, 자손(= offspring, descendant)
likewise [láikwàiz] 또한, 마찬가지로(= too, as well)
reserved [rizə́ːrvd] 예비된, 유보된
association [əsòusiéiʃən] 연상, 의미, 회사
unexpected [ʌ̀nikspéktid] 예기치 않은, 뜻밖의

024

Our humanity is by no means so materialistic as foolish opinion is continually asserting it to be. Judging by what I have learned about men and women, I am convinced that there is far more in them of idealistic power **than** ever comes to the surface of the world.

Key Structure •

1   Our humanity is ~ so materialistic as ~ asserting it to be.
우리 인간은 어리석은 견해가 계속해서 주장하는 만큼 그렇게 물질적인 것은 결코 아니다.
   • by no means ~ so materialistic as ~ 부정의 표현을 이용한 비교 구문.
   • it = our humanity / by no means = never

2   there is far more ~ of idealistic power than ~ world
그들에게는 세상의 표면으로 드러나는 것보다 훨씬 더 많은 이상적인 힘이 있다
   • more (in them) of idealistic power than   ~보다 더 많은 이상적인 힘
   • than ever comes to ~ world   조금이라도 세상의 표면으로 드러나는 ~
     than은 유사관계대명사로 주어 역할을 하고 있음. / in them에서 them은 men and women을 지칭.

내용 인간에게는 물질적인 힘보다는 이상적인 힘이 더 많다.

humanity [hju(:)mǽnəti] 인간, 인간성, 인간애
by no means 결코 ~이 아니다(= never, not ~ at all, not ~ in the least, not ~ by any means)
materialistic [mətìəriəlístik] 물질적인, 유물론의
opinion [əpínjən] 판단, 개인적 의견
assert [əsə́ːrt] 주장하다, 옹호하다(= claim, contend, maintain, affirm)
be convinced that (~을) 확신하다
idealistic [aidì(:)əlístik] 이상적인, 이상주의자의
surface [sə́ːrfis] 표면, 수면

025

If much education is apparently wasted, so is much of turnip seed that the farmer sows in the field. It is necessary for the farmer, one might say, to sow more seed **than** is necessary if he wishes to get a first-rate crop.

Key Structure •

1   so is much of turnip seed 많은 무씨도 마찬가지이다[낭비되고 있다]
2   more seed than is necessary 필요한 것보다 더 많은 씨앗
   • than은 유사관계대명사로 주어 역할을 하고 있음.

내용 훌륭한 교육 효과를 얻기 위해서는 꼭 필요한 것 이상의 교육을 해야 한다.

apparently [əpǽrəntli] 분명히, 외관상(= surely, evidently, seemingly)
turnip [tə́:rnip] 무, 순무, 바보, 시시한 일
sow [sou] (씨를) 뿌리다, 심다(= seed, plant, disseminate, spread)
crop [krɑp] 농작물, 수확물(= harvest, produce, yield)

플러스 문법정리 10

So am I.와 So I am.
주어와 동사가 도치되어 있는 전자는 also의 뜻을 지니고 있으며, 정치로 되어 있는 후자는 really의 뜻을 지니고서 상대방의 말을 긍정으로 다시 인정하는 표현이다.
So do I. / So have I. / So will I. 등도 So am I.처럼 also의 뜻을 갖는 표현이며, So I do. / So I have. / So I will. 등은 So I am.처럼 '정말 그렇다'는 뜻을 갖는다.

a. A : I am hungry now, Bill.
　 B : So am I. (나도 그렇다.)

b. A : You must be hungry now, Bill.
　 B : So I am. (정말 그렇다.)

c. A : I have passed the English test.
　 B : So have I. (나도 그렇다.)

d. A : You have passed the English test, haven't you, Bill?
　 B : So I have. (정말 그렇다.)

그러나 부정의 경우에는 도치 구문만이 가능하다.

e. A : I have not passed the English test.
　 B : Neither have I. (나도 그렇다. Neither I have.는 틀린 표현임.)

026 You will all find that a time comes in every human friendship, **when** you must go down into the depths of yourself, and lay bare what is there to your friend, and wait in fear for his answer. A few moments may do it; and it may be that you never do it but once. But done it must be, if the friendship is to be worth the name. You must find what is there, at the very root and bottom of one another's hearts.

Key Structure

1 a time comes ~ when... …할 때가 온다
　• when은 a time을 선행사로 갖는 관계부사.

36

2 **lay bare what is there** 그곳에 있는 것을 적나라하게 드러내 보이다
- what is there가 lay의 목적어, bares는 목적격보어.

3 **wait in fear for his answer** = wait for his answer in fear

4 **A few moments may do it** 몇 분이면 충분하다
- do it = be sufficient

5 **it may be that ~** = perhaps ~ 아마도 ~일 것이다

6 **You never do it but once.** 한 번밖에는 그 일을 하지 못한다.
- but = except

7 **be worth the name** 이름값을 하다

내용 진정한 우정은 속마음을 털어놓고 보여 줄 때 가능하다.

depth [depθ] 깊이, 깊은 곳(= heart, bottom)
lay bare 드러내다, 폭로하다(= expose, reveal)
bottom [bátəm] 바닥, 최저부(= depth, base, nadir)

---

027 A knowledge of grammar can be of considerable help to us; for it will usually enable us to understand the reason why certain ways of expressing ourselves are right and others wrong, and to correct any errors we may have made. Further, a firm grasp of the rules of grammar will also enable us to understand the meaning of the great English writers far better **than** would otherwise be possible, and thus more fully to appreciate their work.

Key Structure ▸

1 **a firm grasp of the rules of grammar**
문법 규칙에 대한 확고한 이해

2 **far better** than **would otherwise be possible**
그렇지 않은 경우에[문법 규칙을 몰랐을 경우에] 가능한 것보다 훨씬 더 잘 ~
- than은 유사관계대명사로 주어 역할을 하고 있음.
- otherwise = if we did not have a firm grasp of the rules of grammar 그렇지 않은 경우에

내용 문법 규칙을 잘 아는 것은 외국어를 배우거나 외국 문학을 이해하는 데 상당한 도움이 된다.

considerable [kənsídərəbl] 상당한, 주목할 만한(= fairly important, large, significant)
firm [fəːrm] 굳건한, 견고한(= sound, rigid, solid)
grasp [græsp] 움켜쥠, 이해(= understanding)
appreciate [əprí:ʃièit] 이해하다, 감상하다(= understand, comprehend, apprehend)

03 · 동사구 Verb Phrase

01 제거, 탈락을 나타내는 동사구들 (전치사 of가 쓰이고 있음에 유의)

a. He managed to break himself of that bad habit.
그는 그럭저럭 그 나쁜 버릇을 끊을 수 있었다.

b. He tried to clear himself of the suspicion.
그는 자신에게 씌워진 혐의를 씻으려고 노력하였다.

c. The doctor cured him of rheumatism.
의사는 그의 류머티즘을 치료해 주었다.

d. The envious person deprives others of their advantages.
시기심이 많은 사람은 다른 사람이 지닌 이점을 빼앗는다.

e. He eased me of the burden.
그는 나의 짐을 덜어 주었다.

f. He emptied the closet of all its things.
그는 벽장에 들어 있는 물건을 모두 끄집어내었다.

g. That relieved him of all responsibility.
그 일로 그는 모든 책임을 면하였다.

h. Rid yourself of jealousy.
시기심을 떨쳐 버려라.

i. A highwayman robbed the traveler of his money.
노상강도가 여행자에게서 돈을 강탈하였다.

j. The wind stripped the trees of all their leaves.
바람이 불어 잎이 떨어졌다.

k. They swept the seas of the enemy fleets.
그들은 해상에서 적군의 함대를 일소하였다.

02 공지 사항 · 내용 전달 등을 나타내는 동사구들 (전치사 of가 쓰이고 있음에 유의)

a. She accused him of stealing her car.
그녀는 그가 자신의 차를 훔쳤다고 고발하였다.

b. He assured me of his hearty assistance.
그는 나를 진심으로 도와주겠다고 확약하였다.

c. He tried to convince me of his innocence.
그는 나에게 자신이 죄가 없음을 확신시키려고 하였다.

d. She informed her parents of her safe arrival.
그녀는 부모님께 자신이 안전하게 도착했음을 알렸다.

e. How can I persuade you of my plight?
어떻게 하면 너에게 나의 곤궁을 설득시킬 수가 있을까?

f. You remind me of your father.
너를 보면 네 아버지 생각이 난다.

g. I suspected him of the murder.
나는 그에게 살인 혐의를 두었다.

03 one's way를 이용한 특수한 동사구들

a. She saw him elbowing his way through the crowd.
그녀는 그가 군중을 헤집고 나오는 것을 보았다.

b. The party managed to find its way out of the jungle.
그 일행은 마침내 정글을 겨우 빠져나올 수 있었다.

c. He forced his way into the crowd.
그는 군중 속을 힘으로 밀치고 들어갔다.

d. He wants to go his own way.
그는 자신의 길을 가고자 한다.[마음대로 하고 싶어 한다.]

e. We made our way through the forest.
우리는 숲을 뚫고 나아갔다.

f. He paid his way through college.
그는 고학을 하여 대학을 나왔다.

04 뜻이 없는 상황의 it을 사용하는 동사구들

a. The Nixon Administration didn't try to fight it out in Vietnam.
닉슨 행정부는 베트남에서 끝까지 싸우려 하지 않았다.

b. He made up his mind to have it out with her.
그는 그녀와 담판하여 끝장을 내리라 결심하였다.

05 설득하여 어떤 일을 하도록 하는 동사구들

a. Her parents persuaded her into marrying him.
그녀의 부모는 그녀를 설득하여 그와 결혼하게 하였다.

b. Can you persuade her out of wearing that queer dress of hers?
그녀를 설득하여 그 이상한 옷을 못 입게 할 수는 없나?

c. He tried to reason me out of my obstinacy.
그는 나를 타일러서 고집을 버리도록 하려고 하였다.

028
When a man or woman of ordinary appearance and uninteresting speech comes into our presence, we say 'How do you do!' and turn away; but when we are informed that this same person has written a novel, immediately we become interested and turn again to him or her in the expectation that something profoundly illuminating will be said to us. Experience does not **cure** us **of** that delusive hope.

Key Structure ●

1 **in the expectation that ~**
   ~라는 기대감을 갖고
   • that절은 exception과 동격절.

2 **Experience does not** cure **us of that delusive hope.**
   경험도 우리에게서 그러한 속임수의 희망을 치료하지 못한다[제거하지 못한다].
   • cure A of B A에게서 B를 치료해 주다

내용 사람의 겉모습과 실제 모습이 별로 다르지 않지만, 우리는 그렇지 않을 것이라는 희망을 버리지 않는다.

appearance [əpí(:)ərəns] 외관, 용모, 출현(= look, demeanor, mien)
immediately [imí:diətli] 곧, 즉시, 당장에(= at once)
profoundly [prəfáundli] 깊이, 충심으로(= deeply, thoroughly, perfectly)
illuminate [iljú:mənèit] 비추다, 조명하다, 계몽하다(= brighten, enlighten, explicate)
delusive [dilú:siv] 남을 속이는, 가공적인, 망상적인(= illusive, misconceived, deceiving)

플러스 문법정리 11

동격명사절을 인도하는 접속사 that
접속사 that은 명사절, 형용사절, 부사절 등을 이끌 뿐만 아니라 동격명사절을 이끄는 기능이 있다. 이 경우 번역은 '~라는 ~'이다. 동격절의 that은 관계대명사 that과 혼동하기 쉬우므로 주의해야 한다. 관계대명사는 반드시 격(Case)이 있지만 동격접속사는 격이 없는 접속사 기능만 있다.

a. The rumor that he killed himself has turned out false.
b. There is a possibility that we may not be on time.
c. Your idea that we resign in a body cannot be supported.

동격절에는 그 외에도 the belief[thought/notion/expectation] that 등이 있다.

해석 a. 그가 자살하였다는 소문은 거짓으로 드러났다.   b. 우리가 제시간에 도착하지 못할 가능성이 있다.
　　　　c. 함께 사직하자는 너의 생각은 지지할 수 없다.

029 One of the most difficult things to make up our minds about is in what freedom consists. I once met a woman who, having been left with a fortune, said that she would never feel free till she had **got rid of** her property. Possessions, she maintained, made one a slave, and one became their servant and not their master; and the only hope of recovering one's liberty was to **disburden** oneself **of** them somehow or other and to live a propertyless life, like Thoreau or an Indian saint.

Key Structure ▸

1 **in what freedom consists** = what freedom consists in
   자유는 어디에 존재하는가

2 **having been left** with a fortune = when she had been left with a fortune
   유산을 물려받았을 때에
   • 완료분사 구문.

3 **till she** had got rid of her property
   자신의 재산을 처분해 버릴 때까지는
   • had got rid of는 원래는 미래완료를 대신하는 현재완료형이 시제의 일치 때문에 과거완료형으로 변한 것임.
      e.g. A woman said, "I will never feel free till I have got rid of my property."
                                             (미래완료를 대신하는 현재완료)
         ⇒ (간접화법) A woman said that she would never feel free till she had got rid of her property.

4 **disburden** oneself of them
   자신에게서 그것들을 덜어내다[없애다]

내용 자유가 어디에 있는가를 결정하는 것은 힘든 일이다.

make up one's mind about (~에 대하여) 결심하다(= determine, decide)
consist in (~에) 존재하다(= lie in)   *cf.* consist of (~로) 구성되다(= be made up of, be composed of)
get rid of (~을) 제거하다(= do away with, remove)
possessions [pəzéʃənz] 재산, 소유물
maintain [meintéin] 주장하다(= assert, argue, claim)
recover [rikʌ́vər] 회복하다, 되찾다
disburden [disbə́:rdən] 짐을 내리다, 부담을 덜다
somehow or other 어떻게 해서든, 이 방법 저 방법으로
propertyless [prápərtilis] 재산이 없는
cf. Thoreau, Henry David 헨리 데이비드 소로 (1817~1862, 미국의 자연주의자, 수필가, 시인)

030 Of all the characteristics of ordinary human nature envy is the most unfortunate; not only does the envious person wish to inflict misfortune and do so whenever he can with impunity, but he is also himself rendered unhappy by envy. Instead of deriving pleasure from what he has, he derives pain from what others have. If he can, he **deprives** others **of** their advantages, which to him is as desirable as it would be to secure the same advantages himself.

Key Structure

1 Of all ~ = Among all ~
모든 ~ 중에서

2 not only does the envious person wish ~, but he is...
시기심 많은 사람은 ~을 희망할 뿐만 아니라, 또한 그는 …이다 (도치 구문)

3 do so whenever he can with impunity
벌 받지 않고 할 수 있을 때는 언제나 그렇게 한다

4 he deprives others of their advantages
그는 다른 사람에게서 이득[이익]을 빼앗는다

5 which to him is ~ himself
그런데 그것은 그 스스로 같은 이득을 확보하는 것만큼 그에게는 바람직한 일이다
• which는 관계대명사로 계속적 용법으로 쓰였음.
• as it would be to secure~에서 it은 가주어, to secure 이하가 진주어, would be는 가정의 뜻을 가진 동사.

내용 시기심은 인간 본성 중에서 가장 불행한 특성이다.

characteristic [kæ̀riktərístik] 특징, 성질(= attribute, feature, quality)
envy [énvi] 시기, 질투(= covetousness, jealousy) ⓥ 시기하다
        ⓐ envious 시기심 많은 enviable 시기심을 살 만한
inflict [inflíkt] (불행을) 가하다, 입히다
impunity [impjúːnəti] 무책임, 무사 cf. with impunity 벌 받지 않고
render [réndər] ~되게 하다, 마치다, 양도하다, 제출하다(= make)
deprive A of B A에게서 B를 빼앗다
secure [sikjúər] 확보하다, 획득하다, 보증하다(= acquire, obtain, procure, come by)

A little pot is soon hot.
작은 냄비는 쉬 뜨거워진다. (소인은 금방 화를 낸다.)

031　The kind of boredom which the person accustomed to drugs experiences when **deprived of** them is something for which I can suggest no remedy except time. Now what applies to drugs applies also, within limits, to every kind of excitement. A life too full of excitement is an exhausting life, in which continually stronger stimuli are needed to give the thrill that has come to be thought an essential part of pleasure.

Key Structure

1　The kind of boredom which the person (who is) accustomed to drugs experiences
약물에 중독된 사람이 경험하는 권태의 종류

2　when (he is) deprived of them
그가 그것들을 빼앗겼을 때[투여 받지 못했을 때]

3　what applies to drugs applies ~ to...
약물에 적용되는 이야기는 …에도 적용된다
　• what은 관계대명사.

4　A life (which is) full of excitement is an exhausting life
흥분으로 가득 찬 삶은 심신을 지치게 한다

5　in which ~ needed
그런데 그러한 삶에서는 계속해서 강한 자극제가 필요하다

6　the thrill that ~ pleasure
쾌락의 필수 부분으로 생각하는 전율

내용　약물 중독에는 시간밖에 치료책이 없고, 이것은 모든 쾌락에도 마찬가지이다.

boredom [bɔ́ːrdəm] 권태, 지루함
remedy [rémədi] 치료, 개선 방법, 치료약(= cure, treatment, relief)
within limits 한계는 있지만
exhausting [igzɔ́ːstiŋ] 소모적인, 심신을 지치게 하는(= tiring, wearying, fatiguing, grueling)
stimulus [stímjələs] 자극(제)(= incentive, stimulant)　*pl.* stimuli
thrill [θril] 전율, 진동(= frisson, shiver)

A rolling stone gathers no moss.
구르는 돌에는 이끼도 끼지 않는다.

exhausting과 exhausted
현재분사(exhausting)는 능동의 뜻을, 과거분사(exhausted)는 수동의 뜻을 갖는다.

(1) a. He has led so far an exhausting life.
    b. He is exhausted with hard work.

(2) c. This is a very interesting story.
    d. The boy is interested in the story.

(3) e. The result was very satisfying to us.
    f. We are satisfied with the result.

(4) g. It was a boring lecture.
    h. We were bored with his lecture.

(5) i. Today is a very tiring day.
    j. I am very tired today.

(6) k. The news that our team had won the game was exciting to us.
    l. We were excited at the news that our team had won the game.

해석 a. 지금까지 그는 소모적인 삶을 살아왔다. b. 그는 힘든 일로 지쳐 있다. c. 이것은 매우 재미있는 이야기이다.
d. 소년은 그 이야기가 재미있다. e. 결과는 우리에게 매우 만족스러웠다. f. 우리는 그 결과에 만족하였다.
g. 그것은 지겨운 강의였다. h. 우리는 그의 강의가 지겨웠다. i. 오늘은 매우 피곤한 날이다. j. 나는 오늘 매우
피곤하다. k. 우리 팀이 이겼다는 소식은 우리에게 즐거웠다. l. 우리 팀이 이겼다는 소식에 우리는 즐거웠다.

032 Lack of rain is perhaps the most harmful of all weather conditions, as it **robs** future generations, as well as the present one, **of** huge amounts of food and creates the prospect of turning large areas of good ground into deserts. The challenge of man-made rain is therefore a serious one.

Key Structure ▸

1   as it robs future generations, as well as the present one, of huge amounts of food
왜냐하면 그것은 현 세대뿐만 아니라 미래 세대들에게서 엄청난 양의 식량을 빼앗기 때문이다
- rob A of B A에게서 B를 빼앗다
- the present one = the present generation

2   the challenge of man-made rain 인공 비를 만드는 과제

3   a serious one = a serious challenge

내용 강수량의 부족은 기후 조건 중 가장 해로운 상황이다.

lack [læk] 결핍, 부족(= absence, dearth, deficiency, shortage)
harmful [há:rmfəl] 해로운, 유해한(= baleful, dangerous, pernicious)
prospect [práspèkt]] 전망, 가망, 기대(= likelihood, possibility, probability)
ground [graund] 땅, 토양
desert [dézərt] 사막 ⓥ [dizá:rt] 버리다, 포기하다(= give up)

033

Does history give us any information about our own prospects? And, if it does, what is the burden of it? Does it spell out for us an inexorable doom, which we can merely await with folded arms— resigning ourselves, as best we may, to a fate that we cannot avert or even modify by our own efforts? Or does it **inform** us, not **of** certainties, but **of** probabilities, or bare possibilities, in our own future?

Key Structure ▸

1   **if it does** = if it gives us any information about our own prospects

2   **with folded arms**
    팔짱을 낀 채로(소극적으로)

3   **resigning ourselves, as best we may, to a fate**
    충분하지는 못하나 할 수 있는 데까지 우리 자신의 운명을 감수하면서
    • as best we may = to the best of our ability = so far as we can do

4   **does it inform us, not of A, but of B ~?**
    그것은 우리에게 A가 아닌 B를 알려 주는가?
    • inform A of B A에게 B를 알려 주다

내용   역사는 우리에게 우리의 장래에 대한 어떠한 정보를 제공하고 있는가?

prospect [práspèkt] (장래에 대한) 전망, 예상(= expectation, anticipation, likelihood, probability)
spell out 완전히 철자하다, 상세히 설명하다, 모두 적다
inexorable [inéksərəbl] 불변의, 냉혹한(= unchangeable, cold, relentless)
merely [míərli] 단지, 오직(= only, simply)
fold [fould] 접다, 포개다, (손·팔·다리를) 끼다
resign [rizáin] 사임하다, 감수하다
fate [feit] 운명, 숙명, 죽음
avert [əvá:rt] 돌리다, 피하다(= change, modify, turn away, turn aside, deflect)
modify [mádəfài] 수정하다, 한정하다, 완화하다(= adjust, alter, revise, transform)

probability와 possibility / appointment와 engagement
probability나 possibility는 우리말로는 '가능성', '실현성'으로 번역되나, 전자는 실현 가능성이 있는 경우에 쓰이고, 후자는 막연히 '가능성'만을 나타내는 경우에 쓰인다.

a. There's a strong probability that he will succeed.
b. It is probable that he is sick in bed.
c. There's a possibility that he will come.
d. It is probable for him to swim across the river. (×)
   It is possible for him to swim across the river. (○)

appointment나 engagement도 '약속'이라는 뜻이지만, 전자는 특별한 목적을 가진 약속(의사, 교수, 상사와의 약속)을, 후자는 동료, 애인 간의 격의 없는 약속에 쓰인다.

e. I have an appointment with Dr. Kim at 11 o'clock.
f. I have a previous engagement tonight.
g. She broke off her engagement with him.

해석 a. 그가 성공할 가능성이 많다. b. 그는 아파서 누워 있을 것 같다. c. 그가 올 가능성이 있다. d. 그는 강을 헤엄쳐 건널 수 있다. e. 나는 김 박사와 11시에 약속이 있다. f. 나는 오늘 밤 선약이 있다. g. 그녀는 그 남자와 한 약혼을 파기하였다.

034

You are mistaken if you think that luxury, neglect of good manners, and other vices **of** which each man **accuses** the age in which he lives, are especially characteristic of our own epoch; no era in history has ever been free from blame.

Key Structure

1 luxury, ~ vices of which each man accuses the age in which he lives, ~
모든 사람이 자신들의 시대에 대하여 비난하는 사치, 예의범절의 경시, 그리고 다른 악덕들
　cf. Each man accuses the age in which he lives of luxury, neglect of manners, and other vices.

2 no era in history ~ blame 역사의 어느 시기도 비판을 면한 적은 없었다
　• be free from blame 비난을 면하다

내용 역사상 모든 시대가 사치, 예의범절 없음 등으로 비난을 받았다.

luxury [lʌ́kʃəri] 사치(품), 호사, 쾌적함(= extravagance, indulgence, sumptuousness, voluptuousness)
neglect [niglékt] 무시, 태만, 무관심(= inattention, negligence, oversight, dereliction) ⓥ 무시하다
manners [mǽnərz] 예절, 몸가짐, 태도, 풍습
vice [vais] 악덕, 부도덕(= badness, corruption, evil-doing, venality)
accuse A of B A를 B라는 이유로 비난하다, 고소하다
especially [ispéʃəli] 특별히, 두드러지게

characteristic [kæ̀riktərístik] (~에) 독특한, 특유한 ⓝ 특징
epoch [épək] 시대, 시기, 신기원(= age, era, period)
blame [bleim] 비난, 책망(= accusation, charge, criticism, condemnation, reproach) ⓥ 비난하다

035

I hope that no one present will **suspect** me **of** expressing my personal criticism of the Western system in order to suggest socialism as an alternative. No, with the experience of a country where socialism has been realized, I shall certainly not speak for such an alternative.

Key Structure •

1 **no one (who is) present will** suspect **me** of ~
여기에 참석하신 누구도 내가 ~할 것이라고 의심하지 않을 것이다
• suspect A of B A가 B할 것이라고 의심하다

2 **speak for such an alternative**
그러한 대안을 찬성하여[옹호하여] 말하다
• such an alternative = socialism

내용 내가 서구 제도를 비판하는 것은 사회주의를 대안으로 제시하고자 해서가 아니다.

suspect [sʌ́spekt] 수상히 여기다, 알아채다, 추측하다(= distrust, disbelieve)
criticism [krítisìzəm] 비평, 비판 ⓥ criticize ⓐ critical
suggest [səgdʒést] 제안하다, 암시하다
socialism [sóuʃəlìzəm] 사회주의(운동 · 정책)
alternative [ɔːltə́ːrnətiv] 대안, 양자택일(= choice, option, selection, substitute)
speak for 찬성하여 말하다

It is no use crying over spilt milk.
엎질러진 우유에 대하여 울어 보아도 소용이 없다.

036 For three years he **worked his way through** school. Then in 1890 he enrolled at Iowa State College. Four years later he took his degree in agriculture, having earned every penny of his expenses. His work had been so outstanding that the college authorities asked him to remain as a teacher.

Key Structure

1 **he** worked his way through **school**
그는 일하면서 학교를 마쳤다

2 **His work had been so outstanding** that ~ **teacher.**
학업 성적이 대단히 출중하여 학교 당국은 그가 선생으로 남도록 제안하였다.
• so ~ that... 대단히 ~하여 …하다 (that은 결과의 부사절)

내용 그는 고학으로 고등학교와 대학을 마쳤으며 성적이 아주 출중하였다.

enroll [inróul] 등록하다, 입학하다
expense [ikspéns] 비용, 경비(= cost, expenditure)
outstanding [àutstǽndiŋ] 특출난, 현저한, 뛰어난(= distinguished, excellent, exceptional, remarkable, prominent, unrivalled, conspicuous)
authorities [əθɔ́ːrətiz] 당국, 관계자

037 He sat in silence, and when spoken to answered in monosyllables. He was making up his mind to **have it out** with Rose when they were alone.

Key Structure

1 **when spoken to** = when he was spoken to =when somebody spoke to him
(누군가가) 말을 걸어 왔을 때

2 **answered in monosyllables**
단음절어(yes, no 등)로 대답하였다[무뚝뚝하게 간단히 대답하였다]
• answered의 주어는 문장 처음의 He.

3 **to** have it out **with Rose**
로즈와 담판을 하기로
• it은 뜻이 별로 없는 상황의 it임.

내용 로즈와 결판을 내고자 하는 그의 마음의 상태.

in silence 조용히(= silently)
monosyllable [mάnəsìləbl] 단음절어(yes, no 등)
make up one's mind 결심하다, 결정하다(= determine, decide)
have it out 담판하다, 결판을 내다(= determine)

---

038 The human being seems to be a person who jumps mystically to conclusions, yet who never loses hope of being able to **reason** others **into** the same conclusions.

Key Structure ▸

1 **jumps mystically to conclusions** 이상하게도 성급하게 결론을 내리다

2 **reason** others **into** the same conclusions
다른 사람들을 설득하여 같은 결론을 내리게 하다
 • reason ~ into / out of... ~를 설득하여 …시키다 / 못하게 하다
 e.g. I reasoned him into marrying her. 나는 그를 설득하여 그녀와 결혼하게 했다.
  I reasoned him out of marrying her. 나는 그를 설득하여 그녀와 결혼을 못하게 했다.

내용 인간은 자기 결론을 쉽게 내리고 다른 사람에게도 전파하려는 이상한 존재이다.

mystically [místikəli] 신비하게, 불가사의하게(= mysteriously, arcanely)
conclusion [kənklúːʒən] 결말, 결론, 결정
reason [ríːzn] 설득하다(= persuade), 추론하다

Life is short, art is long.
인생은 짧고 예술은 길다.

It의 5가지 용법

대명사 it은 앞에 나온 명사를 지칭하는 경우 외에도 다음의 여러 가지 용법으로 쓰인다.

1. **실질대명사 it** : 앞에 나온 명사를 대신하는 경우

    a. I bought an umbrella yesterday, but it doesn't work.

2. **예비의 it** : 가주어, 가목적어로 쓰이는 경우

    b. It is wrong to break your promise. (가주어)

    c. I think it wrong to break your promise. (가목적어)

3. **비인칭 it** : 시간, 날씨, 거리, 명암 등을 나타내는 경우

    d. It is already 11 o'lock; let's go home. (시각)

    e. It was fine yesterday in Boston. (날씨)

    f. It is 20 miles from here to the school. (거리)

    g. How long does it take to go there? (시간)

    h. It is very dark outside. (명암)

4. **상황의 it** : 특별한 뜻 없이 상황만을 나타내는 경우

    i. It had gone well up to that time.

    j. It's all over with me.

    k. How is it with your mother?

    l. Let's fight it out.

5. **강조 구문의 it** : It is ~ that

    m. It is you that are to blame.

    n. How is it that you are here now, not in Busan?

    o. It is not until we fall ill that we realize how valuable our health is.

해석 a. 어제 우산을 하나 샀는데, 그것이 잘 작동이 되지 않았다.   b. 약속을 어기는 것은 잘못된 일이다.
c. 약속을 어기는 것은 잘못된 일이라고 생각한다.   d. 벌써 11시야. 집에 가자.   e. 어제 보스턴은 날씨가 좋았다.
f. 여기서 학교까지 20마일이다.   g. 그곳까지 가는 데 얼마나 걸리느냐?   h. 밖은 지금 매우 어둡다.
i. 그때까지는 일이 잘 되어 갔다.   j. 이제 나는 끝장이다.   k. 어머님 근황은 어떠신가?
l. 끝까지 싸워 보자.   m. 비난 받을 자는 너다.   n. 지금 부산에 있지 않고 여기에 있는 것은 어떻게 된 일이나?
o. 우리는 아프고 나서야 비로소 건강이 얼마나 중요한지를 깨닫는다.

Love me, love my dog.
아내가 귀여우면 처갓집 말뚝 보고도 절한다.

039 The country was full of snakes and other dangerous creatures, and the jungle was so thick that one would be able to advance only slowly, **cutting one's way** with knives the whole way.

Key Structure

cutting one's way with knives the whole way
칼로 온 정글 숲을 자르며 나아가다
• the whole way 온 정글 숲을(부사구 역할을 함)

내용 정글의 험한 모습.

creature [kríːtʃər] 생명체, 창조된 물건, 인간, 피조물(= being, organism) *cf.* creation 창조
advance [ədvǽns] 나아가다, 진보하다(= go forward, make headway, progress, push on)

Like father, like son.
그 아버지에 그 아들.

04 ▶ 부정사·분사 Infinitive·Participle

01 부정사의 명사적 용법

a. To love **and** to be loved **is the greatest happiness of man.** (주어)
사랑을 주고받는 것은 인간이 누리는 최대의 행복이다.

b. In writing, the first problem is to clarify our ideas. (보어)
글을 쓸 때 첫째 문제는 우리의 생각을 분명히 하는 것이다.

c. I make it a rule not to eat anything between meals. (목적어)
나는 간식을 하지 않는 것을 규칙으로 삼고 있다.

d. How to spend money **is harder than** how to earn it. (의문사+to부정사)
돈을 쓰는 것은 버는 것보다 더 힘들다.

02 부정사의 형용사적 용법

a. Young men have a passion to meet the celebrated. (명사 수식)
젊은이들은 저명인사를 만나는 것을 매우 좋아한다.

b. The old man finally found a chair to sit on. (명사 수식. 전치사 on에 유의)
그 노인은 마침내 앉을 의자를 발견하였다.

c. She appears to have been satisfied with the result. (보어)
그녀는 그 결과에 만족한 것처럼 보인다.

03 be + to부정사의 형용사적 용법

a. You are to obey your parents. (의무)
부모님 말씀을 따라야 한다.

b. I am to build a house of my own. (예정)
내 소유의 집을 한 채 지으려 한다.

c. He was never to see his home again. (운명)
그는 다시는 고향에 돌아오지 못했다.

d. Not a stone was to be seen at his grave. (가능)
그의 무덤에는 비석 한 개 보이지 않더라.

e. If you are to succeed, be more patient. (의도)
성공하고자 한다면 좀 더 인내심을 가져라.

Rephrased

a. = You <u>should</u> obey your parents.
b. = I <u>will</u> build a house of my own.
c. = He <u>was doomed</u> never to see his home again.
d. = Not a stone <u>could</u> be seen at his grave.
e. = If you <u>wish</u> to succeed, be more patient.

04 부정사의 부사적 용법

a. He worked day and night to make both ends meet. (목적)
그는 수지를 맞추기 위해 밤낮으로 일했다.

b. She fainted to see her lost child dying by the roadside. (원인)
행방을 몰랐던 아이가 길 옆에서 빈사 상태에 빠져 있는 것을 보고 그녀는 기절하였다.

c. He must have managed well to have made such a success. (이유, 판단)
그가 그렇게 큰 성공을 한 것을 보면 운영을 잘 했나 봐.

d. They tried again only to fail. (결과)
다시 해 보았으나 실패뿐이었다.

e. You will do well to accept his proposal. (조건)
그의 청혼을 받아들이면 좋을 거야.

f. They came to love each other. (방향)
그들은 서로 사랑하게 되었다.

05 지각동사, 사역동사의 목적격보어는 원형부정사

a. We saw her dance to the music.
= She was seen by us to dance to the music.
우리는 그녀가 음악에 맞추어 춤추는 것을 보았다.

b. He made me drink another glass of beer.
= I was made by him to drink another glass of beer.
그는 나에게 맥주 한 잔을 더 억지로 마시게 했다.

과거의 상황만을 기술하는 단순부정사

c. He intended to go to the concert with her.
그는 그녀와 함께 음악회에 가려고 했다.

과거에 이루어지지 못한 일을 기술하는 완료부정사

d. He intended to have gone to the concert with her.
그는 그녀와 함께 음악회에 가고자 했는데 그러지 못했다.

06 부정사의 기타 용법

a. To do him justice, he is not an ill-mannered man.
공정하게 평한다면, 그가 예절이 없지는 않다.
- 독립부정사로 문장 전체를 수식하며 의미를 한정함.

b. His new novel will sell well; it's bound to.
그의 새 소설은 잘 팔릴 것이며, 또 그래야 한다.
- 대부정사(Pro-Infinitive) : to는 to sell well을 대신함.

c. He failed to entirely understand what I said.
그는 내가 하는 말을 전적으로 이해하지는 못했다.
- 분할부정사 : to와 동사 사이에 부사를 넣어 동사의 의미를 한정함.

d. Oh, to be young again!
청춘이여, 다시 한 번!
- 감탄 · 원망 부정사 : 부정사 생략의 한 표현으로 감탄조의 to부정사만 남아 있음.

e. It is kind of you to help her.
그녀를 도우시다니 친절하시네요.
- 인품, 특징, 성질 등을 나타내는 형용사가 온 경우 to부정사의 의미상의 주어는 'of+목적격'.

f. It is necessary for us to be up and doing.
지금은 우리가 분발하여 행동할 필요가 있다.
- 형용사가 기능, 당연 등을 나타낼 때 to부정사의 의미상의 주어는 'for+목적격'.

07 부정사를 그대로 목적어(구)로 하는 동사 표현들

agree to	attempt to	care to	dare to	endeavor to	fail to
hope to	intend to	learn to	like to	long to	manage to
need to	pretend to	try to	want to	wish to	

a. I cannot afford to buy such a luxury car.
나는 그런 비싼 차를 살 능력이 없다.

b. Can you arrange to be here at 10 o'clock sharp?
10시 정각에 이곳에 도착하도록 할 수 있겠소?

c. He endeavored to reform the educational system.
그는 교육제도를 개혁하려고 애썼다.

08 분사의 형용사적 용법

a. Here comes a girl carrying a bouquet.
꽃다발을 든 한 소녀가 이리로 온다.
- 현재분사가 앞에 나온 명사를 수식함.

b. His husband is a man descended from a noble family.
그녀의 남편은 귀족 가문의 후손이다.
- 과거분사가 앞에 나온 명사를 수식함.

c. You look dazzling this evening.
오늘 저녁 당신은 눈부시도록 예쁘군요.
- 현재분사가 동사의 보어로 쓰임.

d. He remained perfectly composed.
그는 그대로 태연자약했다.
- 과거분사가 동사의 보어로 쓰임.

09 분사가 다른 품사로 바뀌는 경우

the + 현재분사 = 복수 보통명사

a. The battlefield was covered with the dying.
전쟁터는 죽어가는 군인들로 덮여 있었다.

the + 과거분사 = 복수 보통명사

b. The deceased tell no tales.
죽은 자는 말이 없다.
- 현재분사, 과거분사에는 형용사 기능이 있으므로 'the+형용사 = 복수 보통명사'가 되는 경우와 같다.
  cf. the uneducated 교육을 받지 못한 사람들   the suffering 가난한 사람들

the + 과거분사 = 추상명사 또는 단수 보통명사

c. The unexpected always happens.
뜻밖의 일은 언제나 일어난다.
  cf. the accused 피고   the condemned 죄인   the undersigned 서명자   the betrothed 약혼자

전치사 기능을 가진 현재분사

d. They had long talks concerning the domestic political situations.
그들은 국내 정치 상황에 관하여 오랫동안 이야기하였다.
  cf. regarding ~에 관하여   according to ~에 따라서

접속사 기능을 가진 현재분사

e. Supposing that you were dismissed, what would you do?
만약에 실직하신다면 어떻게 하시겠어요?

부사 기능을 가진 현재분사

f. It is boiling hot today.
오늘은 찌는 듯이 덥다.
cf. freezing[piercing / biting] cold 살을 에이듯 추운

10 분사구문의 의미

시간
a. Going downtown, I met an old friend of mine.
= While I was going downtown, ~
시내 중심가로 가다가 옛 친구 한 사람을 만났다.

이유
b. (Being) Warm and full, he soon fell asleep.
= As he was warm and full, ~
따뜻하고 배가 부르니, 그는 곧 잠들었다.

조건·가정
c. Born in better times, he would have been a free citizen.
= If he had been born in better times, ~
더 좋은 시절에 태어났더라면, 그는 자유 시민이 되었을 것이다.

양보
d. Knowing the danger ahead, they pushed on.
= Though they knew the danger, ~
앞의 위험을 알면서도 그들은 밀고 나갔다.

부대상황
e. We took a walk together, enjoying the fine view around.
= We took a walk together, and enjoyed the fine view around.
주위의 아름다운 경치를 구경하면서 우리는 함께 걸었다.

독립분사구문 (주절과 종속절의 주어가 다른 경우, 종속절의 주어를 없애지 않고 만드는 분사구문)

f. It being cloudy, she took her umbrella with her.
= As it was cloudy, ~
날씨가 흐려서, 그녀는 우산을 들고 나갔다.

11 준분사 : 동사의 과거분사형처럼 -ed형을 지닌 명사로 흔히 형용사 역할을 함.

a. He was a good-humored man.
그는 명랑한 사람이었다.

b. He was a success as a left-handed pitcher.
그는 왼손잡이 투수로 성공하였다.

12 have + 목적어 + 과거분사 : 이득(~시키다), 손해(~당하다)

a. He had his trousers lengthened by an inch. (이득)
그는 바지를 1인치 길게 해 달라고 부탁하였다.

b. She had her wallet stolen in a crowded bus. (손해)
그녀는 만원 버스 안에서 지갑을 도난당하였다.

13 분사구문의 강조

a. Living as he does in the country, he has few visitors.
사실 그는 시골에 살고 있어서 찾아오는 사람이 드물다.
• 현재분사가 쓰인 경우 : 'as+주어+do'를 분사 뒤에 오게 함.

b. Tired as he was, he fell into a sound sleep without himself.
사실 피곤하여 그는 자신도 모르게 곤한 잠에 빠졌다.
• 과거분사가 쓰인 경우 : 'as+주어+be'를 분사 뒤에 오게 함.

040 Our civilization, if it is **to endure**, must have a star on which to fix its eyes—something distant and magnetic **to draw** it on, something **to strive** towards, beyond the shifting needs and passions and prejudices of the moment. Those who wish to raise the dignity of human life should try to give civilization that star, **to equip** the world with the only vision which can save it from ill will and the crazy competitions which lead thereto.

Key Structure •

1 **if it** is to endure 만약 그것이 지속되려면

2 **a star on which to fix its eyes** 그 눈을 고정시킬 별
  • fix A on B B에 A를 고정시키다

3 **equip the world with ~** 세상을 ~의 장비로 채비하다

내용 문명이 살아남기 위해서는 순간적인 욕구나 편견을 넘어 추구해 갈 수 있는 목표가 필요하다.

endure [indʒúər] 견디다, 지탱하다(= continue, carry on, persist, prevail, bear, put up with, tolerate, stand)
magnetic [mæɡnétik] 자석의, 매력 있는, 최면술의
draw [drɔː] 잡아당기다, 끌다
strive [straiv] 노력하다, 분투하다(= endeavor, strain, struggle)
shifting [ʃíftiŋ] 바뀌기 쉬운, 이동하는(= altering, changing)
prejudice [prédʒədis] 편견, 선입관(= bias, bigotry, predilection)
dignity [díɡnəti] 위엄, 존엄, 장중(함)(= elegance, decorum, grandeur)
equip [ikwíp] 장비를 갖추어 주다, 설비하다(= furnish, provide, accouter)
crazy [kréizi] 미친, 제정신이 아닌(= mad, demented, frantic, insane, lunatic, delirious)
competition [kàmpitíʃən] 경쟁, 시합(= contention, emulation)
thereto [ðɛ̀ərtúː] 그곳으로, 그밖에

플러스 문법정리 15

be+to부정사의 5가지 뜻
be동사가 to부정사와 합쳐져서 특수한 뜻을 갖는다. 보통 학교 문법에서는 to부정사의 형용사적 용법으로 분류한다.

a. He is to arrive **here tomorrow.** (예정)
= He will arrive **here tomorrow.**

b. You are to finish **the work by tomorrow.** (의무)
= You should finish **the work by tomorrow.**

c. If you are to succeed, **work harder.** (의도)
= If you would succeed, **work harder.**

d. Nothing was to be seen **there and then**. (가능)
= Nothing could be seen **there and then**.

e. He was never to recover **from his illness**. (운명)
= He was doomed never to recover **from his illness**.

해석 a. 그는 내일 이곳에 도착할 것이다.   b. 내일까지는 그 일을 끝내야 한다.   c. 성공하고 싶으면 더 열심히 노력해라.
　　 d. 그때 그곳에서는 보이는 것이 없었다.   e. 그는 다시 건강을 회복하지 못하는 운명이 되었다.

041
If we are **to find** the best books for children, we need standards for judging them. But two facts we need **to keep** constantly before us: a book is a good book for children only when they enjoy it; a book is a poor book for children, even when adults rate it a classic, if children are unable **to read** it or are bored by its content. In short, we must know hundreds of books in many fields and their virtues and limitations, but we must also know the children for whom they are intended—their interests and needs.

Key Structure •

1 But two facts we need to keep ~ us
　 = But we need to keep two facts ~ us

2 we must also know the children for whom they are intended
　 우리는 그 책들이 대상으로 삼고 있는 어린이들을 또한 알아야 한다
　 • they = (hundreds of) books

내용 어린이용 책들은 어린이들이 읽고 즐겨야 진정한 양서 노릇을 한다.

constantly [kánstəntli] 끊임없이, 자주(= continually, frequently)
rate [reit] 평가하다, 등급을 매기다(= evaluate, grade, rank)
classic [klǽsik] 고전(작품), 대문호 ⓐ 고전의, 제1류의
be bored 지루해 하다, 싫증을 느끼다
content [kəntént] 내용(물) *pl.* 차례, 순서
virtue [vɔ́ːrtʃuː] 미덕, 선행, 고결(≒ vice)
be intended for (~를 위하여) 의도되다, 대상으로 삼다

042

There is something hoggish in sitting down to good food alone. One might as well be an animal, eating merely **in order to keep** alive. **To eat** in company helps **to conceal** the baseness of our appetites.

Key Structure

1 sitting down to good food alone
좋은 음식을 혼자 먹기 위해 앉아 있다

2 **One** might as well **be an animal**
= **One** had better **be an animal**
차라리 동물이 되는 것이 낫다

3 **To eat in company**
여럿이 모여 함께 식사하는 것

내용 식사는 혼자 하는 것보다 여럿이 하는 것이 낫다.

hoggish [hɔ́(ː)giʃ] 돼지 같은, 탐욕스러운, 불결한(= greedy, untidy, unclean)
might as well (~하는 것이) 낫다
in company 여러 사람이 함께 *cf.* company 교제, 동료, 회사
conceal [kənsíːl] 숨기다, 비밀로 하다(= hide, disguise, keep secret │ ≒ reveal)
baseness [béisnes] 비천, 비열, 조악(= meanness, shame, indignity, sordidness)
appetite [ǽpətàit] 욕망, 식욕, 욕구(= desire, greed, longing, hankering)

플러스 문법정리 16

may as well과 might as well
둘 다 '~하는 편이 낫다'의 뜻을 가지나, 후자는 전자보다 정중한 표현으로, 실현 가능성이 낮은 경우에 쓰인다.

a. You may as well go at once.
b. You might as well talk to your son. (정중한 표현)
One might as well be an animal. (실현 가능성이 희박한 경우)

'~하느니 차라리 …하는 편이 낫다'는 may as well ~ as…, 또는 might as well ~ as…로 표현하고, 이 경우에도 후자는 전자보다 실현 가능성이 떨어지는 일에 표현된다.

c. You may as well confess as remain in silence.
d. You might as well try to turn a stone into butter as try to persuade him.

해석 a. 너 지금 당장 가는 게 좋을 거야. b. 아드님한테 주의를 주시는 게 좋겠습니다. / 차라리 동물이 되는 게 낫다.
c. 침묵을 지키느니 속마음을 털어놓는 게 더 낫다. d. 그를 설득하려고 하느니 차라리 돌멩이를 버터로 바꾸려고 하는 것이 나을 것이다.(그를 설득하는 일이 거의 불가능에 가까울 정도로 어렵다는 뜻)

043 Without this liberal spirit, social progress would be slow—perhaps **too** slow **to meet** the rapidly expanding demands of a world in which technological capacities are accelerating at a frightening rate. The liberal approach, I feel, is the only hope for preserving the kind of free, democratic society we believe in. Perhaps it is the only hope for preserving any form of human society.

Key Structure •

1 Without this liberal spirit, social progress would be slow
   = If it were not for this liberal spirit
   = Were it not for this liberal spirit
   = But for this liberal spirit ~
   • 가정법 과거 구문

2 ~ too slow to meet ~
   = ~ so slow that it might[could] not meet ~

3 the kind of free, democratic society (which) we believe in
   우리가 가치를 믿는 자유롭고 민주적인 사회의 종류(민주적인 유형의 사회)

내용 자유정신은 민주적인 사회를 보존하는 유일한 희망일지도 모른다.

liberal spirit 자유정신
progress [prágres] 진보, 발전 ⓥ [pragrés] 진보하다
demand [dimǽnd] 요구, 청구(= requirement, need, claim) ⓥ 요구하다
technological [tèknəládʒikəl] 과학 기술의
capacity [kəpǽsəti] 능력, 재능, 용량(= capability, competence, potential, talent)
accelerate [əksélərèit] 가속하다, 촉진하다(= quicken, go faster, do a spurt)
frighten [fráitən] 놀라게 하다, 놀라다(= agitate, daunt, intimidate)
preserve [prizə́ːrv] 보존하다, 보호하다(= conserve, guard, lay up, maintain)

A watched pot never boils.
냄비를 자꾸 들여다보면 결코 끓지 않는다. (서둔다고 일이 되는 것은 아니다.)

044 As matters stand today, many teachers are unable **to do** the best of which they are capable. For this there are a number of reasons, some more or less accidental, others very deep-seated. **To begin with** the former, most teachers are overworked and are compelled **to prepare** their pupils for examinations rather than **to give** them a liberalizing mental training.

Key Structure ·

1 As matters stand today
   = As it stands today 오늘날의 상태로서는
   cf. as the case stands 사정이 이러하므로

2 do the best of which they are capable
   = do the best which they are capable of
   그들이 할 수 있는 최선을 다하다

3 To begin with **the former** 전자를 먼저 이야기하자면
   • the former = some more or less accidental (reasons)

내용 현재의 상황으로 보면 교사들은 그들이 할 수 있는 최선을 다할 수가 없다.

accidental [æ̀ksidéntəl] 비본질적인, 우연의(= casual, adventitious, inadvertent)
deep-seated 뿌리 깊은, 고질적인(= deep-rooted, chronic)
         cf. a deep-seated disease 만성병(= a chronic disease)
be overworked 과로하다
be compelled to (~하도록) 강요받다(= be forced to, be obliged to)
liberalize [líbərəlàiz] 자유화하다, 너그럽게하다

플러스 문법정리 17

독립부정사 to begin with, to tell the truth 등
독립부정사는 보통 절의 앞머리에 놓여 문장을 이끌며, 기능상으로는 문장 전체의 의미를 한정하는 부사구 기능을 갖고 있다. 몇 개의 예를 들면 다음과 같다.

a. To begin with, he is not a reliable man.
b. To tell the truth, I don't believe him.
c. To make a long story short, we are in the woods.
d. To make matters worse, it began to rain heavily.
e. To be frank with you, I dislike such a behavior of yours.
f. To do him justice, he is not cut out for a teacher.

해석 a. 우선 첫째로, 그는 신뢰할 만한 사람이 아니다.   b. 진실을 말하자면, 나는 그(의 말)를 믿지 않는다.
   c. 줄여서 이야기하자면, 우리는 오리무중 속에 있다.   d. 설상가상으로, 비가 몹시 퍼붓기 시작하였다.
   e. 솔직히 말해서, 나는 너의 그런 행동이 싫다.   f. 정당하게 평가해서, 그는 교사로서 적격자가 아니다.

045 'Please' and 'Thank you' are the small change with which we pay our way as social beings. They are the little courtesies by which we keep the machine of life **oiled** and **running** sweetly. They put our intercourse upon the basis of a friendly cooperation, an easy give-and-take, instead of on the basis of superiors **dictating** to inferiors. It is a very vulgar mind that would wish to command where he can have the service for the asking, and have it with willingness and good feeling instead of resentment.

Key Structure

1 the small change with which we pay our way as social beings
우리가 사회적 존재로서 빚지지 않고 살아나가는 잔돈(잔돈을 지불함으로써 빚지지 않고 살아나갈 수 있다는 뜻)

2 keep the machine of life oiled and running sweetly
인생이라는 기계에 기름을 치고 그것이 부드럽게 움직이도록 유지하다
• oiled and running sweetly는 목적격보어로 쓰인 분사.

3 instead of on the basis of superiors dictating to inferiors
윗사람이 아랫사람에게 명령을 하는 기초 위에서가 아니라
• dictating은 superiors를 의미상의 주어로 하는 동명사.

4 have the service for the asking
요청만 하면 봉사를 얻다

내용 'Please'와 'Thank you'는 인생을 부드럽게 이끌어 주는 잔돈과 같은 것이다.

change [tʃeindʒ] 거스름돈, 잔돈
courtesy [kə́ːrtisi] 예의, 친절(= civility, politeness, good-manners)
intercourse [íntərkɔ̀ːrs] 교제, 교류(= interaction, communication)
cooperation [kouὰpəréiʃən] 협력, 협동(= coordination, collaboration)
give-and-take (공평하게) 주고받기
superior [sju(ː)pí(ː)əriər] 상관, 선배, 윗사람
dictate [díkteit] 명령하다, 지배하다(= command, direct, order)
inferior [infí(ː)əriər] 아랫사람, 후배
vulgar [vʌ́lgər] 천한, 야비한, 서민의(= coarse, crude, impolite, churlish)
resentment [rizéntmənt] 원한, 분개(= animosity, grudge, discontent, malice, rancor, spite)

046 Ranke was strongly of this opinion. "Ambitious, warlike, **incited** by national pride, the French have kept their neighbors in constant excitement, sometimes **liberating** the oppressed, more often **oppressing** the free."

Key Structure ▸

1 Ambitious, ~ pride,
- 이 부분은 the French의 속성을 나타내는 형용사구로서, 그 앞에 Being을 넣어 분사구문의 형태로 분석할 수 있으나 반드시 그러할 필요는 없음. (Being ambitious, ~ pride, = As they were ambitious, ~ pride,)

2 sometimes liberating ~
= and they sometimes liberated the oppressed and more often oppressed the free
- 주어인 the French의 행동의 일면을 보여 주는 분사구문으로, '동시 동작'을 나타냄.

내용 프랑스 사람들에 대한 랑케의 견해.

ambitious [æmbíʃəs] 야망을 품은, 열망하는(= assertive, energetic)
warlike [wɔ́ːrlàik] 호전적인, 도전적인(= aggressive, bellicose, belligerent)
incite [insáit] 자극하다, 선동하다, 고무하다(= excite, inflame, inspire, stimulate, stir)
liberate [líbərèit] 해방하다, 자유롭게 하다(= emancipate, free, disenthral)
the oppressed 억압받는 자들[민족]
the free 자유로운 자들[민족]

플러스 문법정리 18

분사구문과 그 뜻
현재분사나 과거분사를 이용하여 부사절을 구로 바꾼 것이 분사구문으로 그 의미는 다음과 같이 분류할 수 있다.

a. Walking along the street, I found a strange-looking coin. (시간)
= While I was walking along the street, ~

b. Having been exhausted, I went to bed early. (이유)
= As I had been exhausted, ~

c. Following his advice, you will surely win the game. (조건)
= If you follow his advice, ~

d. Admitting what you say, I still think that your way of talking is not right. (양보)
= Though I admit what you say, ~

e. They left the town early in the morning, arriving in Seoul on time. (부대상황)
= They ~ morning, and arrived in Seoul on time.

주절과 종속절의 주어가 다른 경우, 종속절의 주어를 그대로 놔둔 채 분사구문을 만드는데, 이것을 **독립분사구문**이라 부른다.

f. The weather being **fine**, we went on a picnic.
= As the weather was **fine**, ~

해석 a. 길을 따라 걷다가 이상한 모양의 동전 한 닢을 발견하였다. b. 완전히 기진맥진하여 나는 일찍 잠자리에 들었다.
c. 그의 충고를 따르면 너는 틀림없이 경기에 이길 것이다. d. 네가 하는 말은 인정을 하지만, 나는 아직도 네가
말하는 방식이 좋지 않다고 생각한다. e. 그들은 아침 일찍 마을을 떠나 서울에는 정시에 도착하였다. f. 날씨가
좋아서 우리는 소풍을 갔다.

---

047 Health is a priceless treasure but its value is rarely **appreciated** until it is lost. On the basis of personal experience Thomas Carlyle wrote: "The healthy know not of their health but only the sick." Youth especially tend to take good health for **granted** and squander it thoughtlessly, little **realizing** that future success and happiness, and even life itself, are largely **influenced** and in many instances actually **determined** by the habits of living **acquired** during one's developmental years.

Key Structure

1 its value is rarely appreciated until it is lost
그것을 잃을 때까지 그것의 가치를 좀처럼 깨닫지 못한다

2 The healthy know not of their health but only the sick (do).
건강한 사람은 그들 건강에 대하여 (가치를) 모르고 단지 아픈 사람들만이 안다.
• the healthy = healthy people / the sick = sick people

3 little realizing that ~
~을 거의 인식하지 못하고서

4 the habits of living acquired during one's developmental years
자신의 성장기에 얻은 생활 습관들

내용 사람들은 건강을 잃을 때까지는 건강의 가치를 깨닫지 못한다.

priceless [práislis] 매우 귀중한(= invaluable, incalculable, precious)
treasure [tréʒər] 보물, 귀중품
rarely [réərli] 좀처럼 ~ 않다(= seldom)
appreciate [əpríːʃièit] 올바로 평가하다, 감사하다(= value, thank)
take ~ for granted ~을 당연히 여기다
squander [skwándər] 낭비하다, 헤프게 쓰다(= waste)
developmental years 성장기

048

I am for the synthetical method on a journey, in preference to the analytical. I am content to lay in a stock of ideas then, and to examine and anatomize them afterwards. I want to see my vague notions **float** like the down of the thistle before the breeze, and not have them **entangled** in the briars and thorns of controversy. For once I like to have it all my own way; and this is impossible unless you are alone, or in such company as you do not covet.

Key Structure •

1 I am for A in preference to B.
나는 B보다 A를 찬성한다.
• the synthetical method 종합적인 방식 / the analytical (method) 분석적인 방식

2 lay in a stock of ideas 여러 가지 생각을 모으다

3 see my vague notions float like ~
나의 흐릿한 생각들이 ~처럼 떠다니는 것을 보다
• see는 지각동사이므로 float가 원형동사로 나옴.

4 not have them entangled in ~
그것들이 ~에 뒤얽히게 하고 싶지 않다
• have는 사역동사이고 목적격보어가 과거분사 entangled로 나온 구조.
• them = my vague notions

5 in such company as you do not covet
내가 탐내지 않는 사람과 같이 있을 때에는
• as는 유사관계대명사로 covet의 목적어이며 such company를 선행사로 갖고 있음.

내용 나는 여행을 함에 있어서 하나하나 따지고 조사하는 분석적인 방식보다는 전체적인 모습을 즐기는 종합적인 방식을 선호한다.

synthetical [sinθétikəl] 종합의, 통합적인, 인조의(= synthetic, comprehensive, man-made)
in preference to (~보다) 우선적으로
lay in (사)모으다, 비축하다
anatomize [ənǽtəmàiz] 해부하다, 분해하다(= dissect)
vague [veig] 희미한, 막연한(= ambiguous, ambivalent, equivocal, unclear)
float [flout] 떠돌다, 표류하다
down [daun] (새의) 솜털, (식물의) 깃털
thistle [θísl] 엉겅퀴
breeze [bri:z] 미풍, 산들바람
entangle [intǽŋgl] 뒤얽히게 하다, (함정에) 빠뜨리다
briar [bráiər] 가시나무, 브라이어(남유럽산 관목)(= brier)
thorn [θɔ:rn] 가시, 바늘
controversy [kántrəvə̀:rsi] 논쟁, 논전, 토론(= argument, contention, altercation, dispute)
covet [kʌ́vit] (턱없이) 탐내다, 갖고 싶어하다(= long to possess)

플러스 문법정리 19

지각동사, 사역동사의 용법과 뜻

지각동사에는 see, hear, watch, feel 등이 있고, 사역동사에는 make, have, let, bid 등이 있다. 이 동사들은 보통 5형식 구문을 이루며 목적어가 능동의 역할을 할 때에는 목적격보어로 원형동사가, 수동의 역할을 할 때에는 목적격보어로 과거분사가 온다.

(1) a. I saw the girl dance to the music.
     b. I heard the lady weep alone in the room.

(2) c. He made me finish the work at once.
     d. I had him carry the box for me.
     e. He let me do as I please.

지각동사, 사역동사 구문이 수동태로 바뀔 때에는 원형동사 앞에 to가 나온다.

(3) f. The girl was seen to dance to the music.
     g. I was made to finish the work at once.

have+목적어+과거분사가 이득의 뜻을 나타낼 때에는 '～시키다', 손해의 뜻을 나타낼 때에는 '～당하다'로 해석한다.

(4) h. I had my picture taken. (이득)
     i. I had my purse stolen. (손해)

help는 목적격보어로 원형동사 또는 to부정사가 올 수 있는데, 이것은 help가 아직은 준사역동사의 기능이 강하고 사역동사로 변하는 과정에 있음을 보여 준다.

(5) j. He helped me carry the box to the fifth floor.
     k. He helped me to carry the box to the fifth floor.

지각동사의 경우 목적격보어로 원형동사 대신 현재분사가 쓰이는 경우가 있는데, 이것은 목적어가 어떤 동작을 계속하고 있는 상황을 자세하게 묘사하기 위함이다.

(6) l. I saw her dancing to the music.
     m. They watched the enemy soldiers crawling over the slope.

have는 사역의 의미가 강한 동사지만, 사역의 의미가 없는 불가항력적인 경우에도 쓰인다.

(7) n. He had his wife die in the car accident.
     o. He had his only son die in the war.

해석 a. 나는 그 소녀가 음악에 맞추어 춤추는 것을 보았다.   b. 나는 그 부인이 방에서 홀로 흐느끼는 소리를 들었다.
     c. 그는 나에게 그 일을 즉시 끝내게 하였다.   d. 나는 그에게 내 대신 상자를 운반하도록 (부탁)하였다.
     e. 그는 내가 하고 싶은 대로 하도록 허용하였다.   f. a와 동일   g. c와 동일   h. 나는 사진을 찍었다.   i. 나는 지갑을
     도둑맞았다.   j. k. 그는 내가 상자를 5층으로 옮기는 것을 도왔다.   l. a와 동일   m. 그들은 적군이 언덕을 기어
     올라오는 것을 보았다.   n. 그는 자동차 사고로 아내를 잃었다.   o. 그는 전쟁에서 외아들을 잃었다.

049　Among the many problems **facing** our modern civilization, the fate of the aged is certainly one of those foremost in the public mind, **judging** by the number of articles on this subject **carried** by magazines and newspapers. Over the past century, in fact, the average life span in industrialized countries has increased by leaps and bounds until it has now reached 73 years.

Key Structure

1　one of those foremost (problems)
　　가장 주요한 문제점들 중의 하나

2　judging by ~
　　= when we judge by ~
　　~으로 판단해 볼 때

3　carried by magazines and newspapers
　　잡지나 신문에 실리는

　내용　현대 문명사회가 직면한 주요 문제들 중의 하나는 노령화의 문제이다.

the aged 나이 든 사람들, 노인들
foremost [fɔ́ːrmòust] 맨 먼저의, 처음의, 주요한(= leading, main, primary, supreme)
average life span 평균 수명
by leaps and bounds 급속도로, 비약적으로(= very rapidly)

050　Our modern system of popular education was indeed indispensable and has conferred great benefits on the country, but it has been a disappointment in some important respects. **Generally speaking**, it has produced a vast population able to read but unable to distinguish what is worth reading, an easy prey to sensations and cheap appeals. Consequently both literature and journalism have been to a large extent debased since 1896, because they now entertain millions of **half-educated** and **quarter-educated** people.

Key Structure ▸

1 has conferred great benefits on the country
우리나라에 많은 이득을 가져다 주었다

- confer A on B = bestow A on B = give A to B

2 what is worth reading 읽을 가치가 있는 것

3 an easy prey to sensations and cheap appeals
선풍을 일으킨 작품들과 값싼 마음에 호소하는 작품들에 빠진 사람들

- 이 구절은 a vast population~과 동격으로 쓰인 명사구임.

4 half-educated and quarter-educated people
교육을 절반 또는 1/4밖에 받지 않은

내용 현대의 대중교육이 만들어 낸 약점으로, 훌륭한 작품을 선별하여 읽을 줄 아는 사람이 적다.

popular education 대중교육
indispensable [ìndispénsəbl] 필수불가결한, 없어서는 안 될(= imperative, mandatory, required)
confer [kənfə́ːr] 수여하다, 의논하다(= bestow, give, present, award)
vast [væst] 광대한, 막대한(= huge, enormous)
distinguish [distíŋgwiʃ] 구별하다, 구분하다
sensation [senséiʃən] 큰 평판, 대 인기(의 것)
appeal [əpíːl] 호소, 간청, 호소력이 있는 것
debase [dibéis] 가치를 저하시키다, 품위를 떨어뜨리다(= degrade, depreciate, devaluate, belittle)
entertain [èntərtéin] 즐겁게 하다, 대접하다(= amuse, delight, please)

플러스 문법정리 20

무인칭 독립분사구문
분사구문은 주절과 종속절이 같을 때 종속절의 주어를 제거하고 동사를 분사로 바꾸는 것이 일반적인데, 주어의
일치와 상관없이 독립적으로 쓰이는 분사구문이 있다. 이것을 **무인칭 독립분사구문**이라 한다.

a. Generally speaking, Koreans are diligent.
b. Frankly speaking, he is not trustworthy.
c. Judging from his accent, he is not from America.
d. Granting that he was drunk, that is no excuse for his rude behavior.
e. Considering his age and education, he is really a smart man.

이외에도 Supposing that ~ (가령,만약에), Talking of ~ (~에 대해 말하자면), Strictly speaking (엄격히 말해서)
등이 있다.

해석 a. 일반적으로 이야기해서 한국인들은 근면하다.   b. 솔직히 말해서 그는 믿을 만하지 않다.   c. 그의 어투로 판단해
보건대, 미국 출신이 아니다.   d. 그가 술에 취했다는 것을 인정한다고 해도, 그것이 그의 거친 행동에 대한 변명이
되지는 못한다.   e. 그의 나이와 교육 배경을 고려해 볼 때, 그는 정말 똑똑한 사람이다.

05 · 동명사 Gerund

01 동명사의 역할

a. Early rising makes a man healthy. (주어)
일찍 일어나는 것은 건강에 좋다.

b. His chief delight is playing golf on weekends. (보어)
그의 주된 기쁨은 주말마다 골프를 치는 것이다.

c. I prefer traveling by sea to by air. (목적어)
나는 비행기보다는 배로 여행하기를 좋아한다.

d. You can't go without paying. (전치사의 목적어)
돈을 내지 않고는 못 갑니다.

02 동명사의 시제

a. 단순 동명사

We don't like being seen in shabby clothes.
우리는 허름한 옷차림으로 나타나고 싶지 않다.

b. 완료 동명사

He is ashamed of having never been abroad while young.
그는 젊었을 때 외국에 가 보지 않은 것을 부끄러워한다.

03 동명사를 이용한 관용어구

a. There is no accounting for tastes.
= It is impossible to account for tastes.
사람의 취미란 설명하기가 불가능하다.

b. I could not help laughing at the sight.
= I could not but laugh at the sight.
= I could not choose but laugh at the sight.
= There was no other way but for me to laugh at the sight.
그 광경을 보고 나는 웃지 않을 수 없었다.

c. It is no use crying over spilt milk.
= It is of no use to cry over spilt milk.
엎질러진 우유에 대하여 울어 보아야 소용없다.

d. It goes without saying **that health is above wealth.**

= It is needless to say **that health is above wealth.**

건강이 부보다 중요하다는 점은 두말할 필요도 없다.

e. This book is worth **read**ing.

= It is worthwhile to **read this book.**

이 책은 읽을 만한 가치가 있다.

f. His English is far from **be**ing **perfect.**

= **His English is** not **perfect** at all.

그의 영어는 결코 완벽하지 않다.

g. I feel like **cry**ing.

= I feel inclined to **cry.**

울고 싶은 심정이다.

h. His is a profession of his own **choos**ing.

= **His is a profession** which **he himself has chosen.**

그의 직업은 스스로가 택한 것이다.

> **Cf.** 주어 His는 His profession을 나타내는 독립소유대명사. 보어에 같은 낱말이 오므로 중복을 피하기 위한 것임.

i. She makes a point of **answer**ing **every letter she receives.**

= **She** makes it a rule to **answer every letter she receives.**

그녀는 받은 편지에 꼭 답장을 한다.

j. He was on the point of **go**ing **out then.**

= **He** was about to **go out then.**

그는 그때 막 외출하려는 참이었다.

> **Cf.** point 대신 edge, verge, brink 등을 사용할 수 있음.

k. What do you say to **go**ing **out for a walk?**

= What about **going out for a walk?**

산책 나가시는 게 어떻겠습니까?

l. He is above **tell**ing **a lie.**

= **He is** far from **tell**ing **a lie.**

= **He is** the last person to **tell a lie.**

= **He** knows better than to **tell a lie.**

그는 거짓말을 할 사람이 아니다.

051 **I cannot help wishing** sometimes that English people had more theories about conversation. Really good talk is one of the greatest pleasures there is. And yet how rarely one comes across it!

Key Structure ▸

1 I cannot help wishing ~ = I cannot but wish ~
   ~을 희망하지 않을 수 없다
   • wish that English people had ~ : wish+가정법 구문.

2 **one of the greatest pleasures (that) there is**
   있을 수 있는 가장 큰 즐거움 중의 하나

내용 영국 사람들은 대화에 관한 이론[원칙]이 부족하다.

theory [θí(:)əri] 이론, 학설(= argument, idea, notion, principle)
rarely [rɛ́ərli] 드물게, 좀처럼 ~ 않다(= uncommonly, scarcely)
come across 우연히 만나다(= meet by chance, happen to meet, chance upon)

---

052 **There was no denying** that China was the cradle of civilization in the Far East, a far older and greater country than Japan, and that Japan was no more than a small and, for long, a backward branch of Chinese civilization.

Key Structure ▸

1 There was no denying that ~ = It was impossible to deny that ~
   ~을 부인하는 것은 불가능하였다

2 **a far older ~ than Japan** 일본보다 훨씬 더 오래되고 위대한 나라로서
   • 바로 앞의 the cradle ~ East와 동격관계에 있는 명사구.

3 **and that Japan was ~**
   • 글 첫머리의 and there was no denying으로 연결됨.

내용 중국은 극동 지역에서 문명의 요람이었고, 일본은 중국 문명의 후미진 지류였다.

deny [dinái] 부인하다, 취소하다(= contradict, negate, dispute, repudiate)
cradle [kréidl] 요람, 발상지 *cf.* from the cradle to the grave 태어나서 죽을 때까지
the Far East 극동 (지역) *cf.* the Middle East 중동 (지역), the Near East 근동 (지역)
no more than 단지 ~인(= only)
for long 오랫동안(= for a long time)
backward branch 뒤처진 가지, 후진 지류(= division, offshoot, sprig, bough)

053

There is no returning on the road of life. The frail bridge of Time, on which we tread, sinks back into eternity at every step we take. The past is gone from us for ever. It is gathered in and garnered. It belongs to us no more.

Key Structure ▸

1 There is no **return**ing on ~
   = It is impossible to **return** on ~
   인생길에서는 돌아오는 법이 없다

2 at every step (that) we take
   우리가 발걸음을 옮길 때마다

3 It belongs to us no more.
   = It is no longer ours.
   그것은 더 이상 우리의 것이 아니다.

내용 인생길에서 돌아오기란 불가능하다.

frail [freil] 허약한, 연약한(= weak, feeble, fragile, brittle)
tread [tred] 밟다, 걷다(= step on, walk on, trample)
sink [siŋk] 가라앉다, 서서히 내려가다
eternity [i(:)tə́ːrnəti] 영원, 영겁, 불멸(= infinity, perpetuity, immortality)
gather [gǽðər] 모으다, 모이다, 추측하다(= accumulate, amass, pile up, collect)
garner [gɑ́ːrnər] 저장하다, 축적하다(= store up, pile up)
belong to (~에) 속하다

플러스 문법정리 21

관계대명사의 생략
관계대명사가 생략되어 나타나는 경우는 목적격 관계대명사와 here is, there is 구문 등에 나타나는 주격 관계
대명사이다. 아래에서 괄호 속에 들어 있는 관계대명사는 생략될 수 있다.

a. This is the boy (whom) I want to strongly recommend.
b. The house (which) he was born in is almost cracked up.
c. This is all the money (that) I have now.
d. Here is a boy (who) wants to see you.
e. Having someone to love and to be loved by is one of the great pleasures (that) there is.

해석 a. 이 아이는 내가 강력히 추천하고 싶은 소년이다. b. 그가 태어난 집은 거의 망가졌다.
      c. 이것이 지금 내가 가진 돈의 전부이다.   d. 여기 당신을 보고 싶어하는 소년이 있다.
      e. 사랑하고 사랑받을 사람이 있다는 것은 있을 수 있는 커다란 기쁨 중 하나이다.

054 In youth, we are impatient of those who are indifferent to our own tastes. As a boy, **I could scarcely help feeling** hostile to any one who was indifferent to the things about which I was enthusiastic in politics and literature.

Key Structure

1 In youth = When we are young

2 As a boy = When I was a boy

3 I could scarcely help feeling ~ = I could not but feel ~

4 the things about which I was enthusiastic
  = the things which I was enthusiastic about
  내가 알고자 열성을 보이는 것들
  • in politics and literature 정치와 문학에서

내용 젊은 시절에 나는 나의 의견에 무관심한 사람을 참지 못하였다.

be impatient of (~을) 참지 못하다 *cf.* impatient (= intolerant)
be indifferent to (~에) 무관심하다 *cf.* indifferent (= uninterested, incurious, uncaring, unenthusiastic)
hostile [hάstəl] 적의를 가진, 대립하는 (= unfriendly, inimical, aggressive, antagonistic, bellicose)
be enthusiastic about (~에 대하여) 열성이다
                    cf. enthusiastic 열성적인 (= committed, energetic, passionate, zealous)

플러스 문법정리 22

be+형용사+of = 동사

a. I am impatient of his bad manners. = I can't tolerate his bad manners.

b. I am fond of classical music. = I like classical music.

c. Urban people are often ignorant of farm life.
= Urban people often do not know about farm life.

d. Poverty is productive of crimes. = Poverty produces crimes.

e. The total amounts are 500,000 won, inclusive of expenses.
= The total amounts are 500,000 won, including expenses.

f. be destructive of = destroy (파괴하다)
  be constructive of = construct (건설하다)
  be indicative of = indicate (가리키다)
  be exclusive of = exclude (제외하다)
  be expressive of = express (표현하다)
  be comprehensive of = comprehend (이해하다)
  be doubtful of = doubt (의심하다)
  be possessed of = possess (소유하다)

be desirous of = desire (갈망하다)
be suggestive of = suggest (암시하다)

해석 a. 나는 그의 무례함을 참을 수 없다. b. 나는 고전음악을 좋아한다. c. 도시인은 종종 농촌생활을 알지 못한다. d. 가난은 범죄를 낳는다.(가난이 유죄다.) e. 전체 금액은 비용을 포함하여 50만 원에 달한다.

055 **It goes without saying** that sometimes we have to turn to some amusement or other to refresh ourselves. At the same time, however, we should reflect upon our own station in life, for an amusement or pleasure, harmless as it may be in itself, will prove a misfortune to us, should we take to it without regard to our means and capacities.

Key Structure

1 It goes without saying that ~ = It is needless to say that ~
　~은 두말할 필요도 없다

2 turn to some amusement or other
　이런저런 오락에 의지하다

3 harmless as it may be in itself = though it may be harmless in itself
　그것 자체가 해롭지 않더라도

4 should we take to it = if we should take to it
　만약 우리가 그것에 빠지게 되면
　• 가정법 미래 구문.

5 without regard to our means and capacities
　우리의 수단과 능력을 고려함 없이

내용 오락은 우리의 수단과 능력을 고려하여 즐겨야 한다.

turn to (~에) 의지하다, ~로 눈길을 돌리다
amusement [əmjúːzmənt] 흥겨움, 오락, 취미(= entertainment, distraction, pleasure)
refresh [rifréʃ] 상쾌하게 하다, 새롭게 하다(= enliven, invigorate, renew, revitalize)
reflect upon (~을) 심사숙고하다
harmless [háːrmlis] 해롭지 않은
take to (~에) 빠지다, 좋아하다
means [miːnz] 수단, 방법
capacity [kəpǽsəti] 능력, 재능, 수용력(= capability, ability, competence, potentiality)

플러스 문법정리 23

양보의 뜻을 나타내는 접속사 as

as가 양보의 뜻을 나타내는 경우 보통은 강조 구문에 많이 나타난다.

a. Young as he is, he is very prudent.
= Though he is young, he is very prudent.

b. Hero as he was, he was not loved by his people.
= Though he was a hero, he was not loved by his people.

강조 구문에 쓰인 as가 모두 양보의 뜻을 갖는 것은 아니다. 아래의 예문처럼 이유를 나타낼 때도 있다.

c. Hero as he was, he was loved by his people.
= Since / Because he was a hero, he was loved by his people.

해석 a. 그는 젊지만, 매우 신중하다. b. 그는 영웅이었지만 국민들의 사랑을 받지 못했다. c. 그는 영웅이었으므로 국민들의 사랑을 받았다.

056

Turner, the famous British painter, had no conventional education **worth mentioning**, and all his life remained an illiterate—a fact which may have sharpened his visual sensibility.

Key Structure ▸

1 conventional education (which is) worth mentioning
이렇다 할 공(公)교육[언급할 가치가 있는 공교육]

2 remained an illiterate
무식한으로 머물렀다
• an illiterate은 보어로 쓰였음.

3 a fact which ~
• Turner ~ an illiterate을 다시 받는 명사구.

내용 문맹이었으나 날카로운 시각의 소유자인 화가 터너.

conventional [kənvénʃənəl] 틀에 박힌, 상투적인(= traditional, customary, formal)
mention [ménʃən] 언급하다, 거론하다(= remark, speak about, say)
illiterate [ilítərit] 무학자 ⓐ 무학의, 문맹의(= uneducated, unlettered, ignorant, unable to read and write)
sharpen [ʃɑ́ːrpən] 날카롭게 하다, 깎다
visual [víʒuəl] 시각의, 시력의
sensibility [sènsəbíləti] 감각, 감성, 예민한 의식

057 Our everyday speech is a thing that we are apt to take for granted without **stopping** to reflect about it, but when we do begin to think about language, we soon realize that **far from being** a commonplace thing, it is a mystery—mysterious in its origin and mysterious in its infinite potentialities.

Key Structure ▸

1   a thing that we are apt to take for granted
우리가 당연하게 여기기 쉬운 일
• that은 관계대명사로서 원래는 take의 목적어.

2   when we do begin ~
• do는 동사를 강조할 때 쓰이는 조동사

3   far from being a commonplace thing   평범한 일이기는커녕
• (be) far from   ~과는 거리가 멀다

내용   우리가 매일 사용하는 언어는 그 기원과 잠재력에서 신비스러운 것이다.

be apt to (~하기) 쉬운, ~할 것 같은(= be likely to, be liable to, be prone to)
take ~ for granted ~을 당연하게 여기다
reflect [riflékt] 곰곰이 생각하다, 반사하다(= ponder on, brood over, think about)
commonplace [kámənplèis] 보통인, 평범한(= mediocre, plain, standard, trite)
mystery [místəri] 신비(스러운 일) ⓐ mysterious 신비스러운
infinite [ínfənit] 무한한, 막대한(= countless, boundless, immense | ≒ finite)
potentiality [pətènʃiǽləti] 잠재 상태, 잠재적 가능성(= possibility, capacity, capability)

Time and tide wait for no man.
세월은 사람을 기다리지 않는다.

058 You hear everyday greater numbers of foolish people speaking about liberty, as if it were such an honourable thing; **so far from being** that, it is, on the whole, and in the broadest sense, dishonorable, and an attribute of lower creatures.

Key Structure ▶

1   as if it were ~ thing
    그것이 마치 명예로운 것인 것처럼

2   so far from being that   그것이기는커녕
    • that = an honorable thing

내용   자유는 불명예스러운 일로, 하등 동물의 속성이다.

honourable [ɑ́nərəbl] 올바른, 훌륭한, 명예로운(= admirable, decent, noble)
on the whole 대체로, 전체로 보아서(= in general)
in the broadest sense 가장 넓은 의미로 보아
attribute [ǽtrəbjùːt] 특성(= characteristic, feature, property)
                    ⓥ [ətríbjuːt] *cf.* attribute A to B A를 B의 탓으로 돌리다
creature [kríːtʃər] 동물, 생명체, 피조물, 창조물

플러스 문법정리 24

부정 · 반대의 뜻을 나타내는 접두사 in-, il-, ir-, dis-, un- 등
명사, 형용사, 부사, 동사 등을 부정하는 접두사에는 기본형으로 in-이 있고, 변형된 형태로 il-, ir-, im-과 그 외에 ab-, de-, dis-, un-, mal-, mis-, non- 등이 있다.

ab-	: **ab**irritate, **ab**normal
de-	: **de**base, **de**bility, **de**crease, **de**compose, **de**contaminate
dis-	: **dis**honest, **dis**obey, **dis**like, **dis**able, **dis**agree, **dis**appoint
il-	: **il**legal, **il**literate, **il**legible, **il**logical
im-	: **im**patience, **im**movable, **im**modest, **im**penetrable
in-	: **in**capable, **in**competent, **in**dependent, **in**dispensable, **in**finite
ir-	: **ir**regular, **ir**relevant, **ir**responsible, **ir**respective
mal-	: **mal**nutrition, **mal**evolent, **mal**treatment
non-	: **non**admission, **non**essential, **non**productive, **non**sense, **non**stop
op-	: **op**pose, **op**ponent
un-	: **un**able, **un**likely, **un**happy, **un**certain, **un**check, **un**conscious
extra-	: **extra**ordinary, **extra**curricular
anti-	: **anti**war, **anti**communism, **anti**pathy

059 Today we are all in a state of dreadful apprehension. We are frightened—**it is no use pretending** that we are not—about the future. What we are afraid of is not so much bold danger of destruction for ourselves, or for our friends, as danger and death to the ideals by which the best of us have always lived.

Key Structure •

1 **We are frightened ~ about the future**
우리는 ~ 미래에 대해 두려워한다
• frightened는 삽입절 뒤의 about으로 연결됨에 유의할 것.

2 **it is no use pretending that ~** = it is of no use to **pretend that ~**
~인 체해 봐야 소용없다

3 **What we are afraid of**
우리가 두려워하는 것

4 **not so much bold danger ~ as danger and death to the ideals ~ lived**
우리나 우리의 친구들을 무모하게 파괴하는 위험이라기보다는 우리들 중 뛰어난 인물들이 의지하여 살아 온 이상에 다가오는 위험과 죽음이다
• not so much A as B = B rather than A A라기보다는 오히려 B이다
• the ideals which the best of us have lived by 우리의 뛰어난 인물들이 근거로 하여[의지하여] 살아 온 이상들

내용 오늘날 우리가 두려워하는 것은 위대한 인물들이 지켜 온 이상에 닥치는 위험과 죽음이다.

dreadful [drédfəl] 굉장히 무서운, 지독한(= appalling, awful, fearful, horrible)
apprehension [æprihénʃən] 걱정, 두려움, 이해력(= fear, fright) *cf.* comprehension
frighten [fráitən] 몹시 놀라게 하다, 소름 끼치게 하다(= horrify, intimidate, daunt, menace)
pretend [priténd] ~인 체하다(= make believe, make out)
bold [bould] 거침없는, 강한, 용기 있는, 대단한(= brave, courageous)
the best of us 우리들 중 가장 뛰어난 인물들

Every dog has his day.
쥐구멍에도 볕 들 날 있다.

060 Instruction is sterile if it is considered as a goal in itself, dangerous if it is subordinated to selfish sentiments or to the interest of one group. No matter how considerable it is, the accumulation of knowledge does not confer any superiority on man if he utilizes it only outwardly and if he reaches the end of his life **without having deeply evolved** as a responsible element of humanity.

Key Structure ▸

1 if it is subordinated to ~ = if it is subject to ~
   ~에 예속되면, ~을 따르게 되면

2 No matter how considerable it is
   = However considerable it is = Be it ever so considerable
   = Let it be ever so considerable = Though it is very considerable
   그것이 상당한 수준의 것이라고 하더라도

3 confer any superiority on man
   인간에게 우월감을 선사하다

4 without having deeply evolved as ~
   ~으로서 많은 발전을 해 오지 않은 채로

   내용 교육은 인간이 책임 있는 인간 사회의 구성원으로 발전했을 때 그 가치가 있다.

instruction [instrʌ́kʃən] 교육, 가르침, 지시(= teaching, lesson, education, schooling)
sterile [stéril] 무익한, 결실이 없는, 살균한(= barren, fruitless, unproductive | ≒ fertile, useful)
subordinate [səbɔ́ːrdənit] ~에 종속시키다, 따르게 하다(= subject)
sentiment [séntəmənt] 감정, 심정(= emotion, feeling)
accumulation [əkjùːmjəléiʃən] 축적, 적립(= build-up, conglomeration, gathering)
superiority [sju(ː)pìəriɔ́(ː)rəti] 우월, 우세(= seniority | ≒ inferiority)
outwardly [áutwərdli] 외적으로, 표면상
evolve [iválv] 발전하다, 진화하다(= develop)

Too many cooks spoil the broth.
요리사가 많으면 수프를 망친다. (사공이 많으면 배가 산으로 올라간다.)

플러스 문법정리 25

양보절을 이끄는 No matter+의문사

'아무리 ~라고 하더라도'의 뜻을 나타내고자 할 때 No matter+의문사로 표현한다.
이것을 복합관계대명사 · 부사라고 부른다.

a. No matter what happened, he remained calm.
= Whatever happened, he remained calm.

b. No matter where you may go, you will be welcome.
= Wherever you may go, you will be welcome.

c. No matter how poor it is, there is no place like home.
= However poor it is, there is no place like home.
= Be it ever so poor, there is no place like home.
= Let it be ever so poor, there is no place like home.

d. No matter what may come, I will not change my mind.
= Whatever may come, I will not change my mind.
= Come what may, I will not change my mind.

e. No matter how hard you try, you won't succeed.
= However hard you try, you won't succeed.
= Try as you may, you won't succeed.

해석 a. 어떤 일이 일어나도 그는 침착하였다. b. 넌 어디를 가든 환영을 받을 거야.
c. 아무리 누추해도 내 집만 한 곳은 없다. d. 무슨 일이 생겨도 내 마음은 변치 않을 거야.
e. 아무리 열심히 노력해도 성공하지는 못할 것이다.

Fair-weather friends are not worth having.
좋을 때만 친구가 되는 사람은 사귈 가치가 없다.

06 가정법 Subjunctive Mood

01 **but for / without : ~이 없(었)다면**

a. But for the sun, nothing could live on the earth.
만약 태양이 없다면 지구상의 어떤 것도 살지 못할 것이다.

b. But for your help, I could not have succeeded in carrying out the project.
만약 당신의 도움이 없었다면 나는 그 계획을 실행하는 데 성공하지 못했을 것이다.

c. Without water, nothing could live.
만약 물이 없다면 아무것도 살지 못할 것이다.

d. Without his advice, I should have failed then.
만약 그의 충고가 없었다면 나는 그때 실패했을 것이다.

> **Rephrased**
>
> a. = If it were not for the sun, nothing could live on the earth.
>   = Were it not for the sun, nothing could live on the earth.
>   = Without the sun, nothing could live on the earth.
> d. = But for his advice, I should have failed then.
>   = If it had not been for his advice, I should have failed then.
>   = Had it not been for his advice, I should have failed then.

02 **if it were not for / if it had not been for : ~이 없다면 / ~이 없었다면**

a. If it were not for your help, he should fail.
= Were it not for your help, he should fail.
만약 당신의 도움이 없다면 그는 실패할 것이다.

b. If it had not been for her kind care, the baby would not have survived.
= Had it not been for her kind care, the baby would not have survived.
만약 그녀의 친절한 보살핌이 없었다면 그 애는 살아남지 못했을 것이다.

03 **if의 생략과 동사의 도치**

a. If he should fail to come, he would be punished.
= Should he fail to come, he would be punished.
만일 그가 오지 않는다면 그는 벌을 받을 것이다.

b. If he arrived later than expected, he might be scolded.
= Did he arrive later than expected, he might be scolded.
예상보다 늦게 도착한다면 그는 꾸지람을 들을지도 모른다.

04 I wish / as if / It is (high) time + 가정법 동사

  a. I wish she were alive now. 그녀가 지금 살아 있다면 얼마나 좋을까!

  b. He acts as if he were somebody. 그는 마치 자신이 대단한 사람인 것처럼 행동한다.

  c. It is (high) time you went to bed. 지금쯤 잠자리에 들었어야 할 시간이다.

> **Rephrased**
>
> a. = Would that she were alive now.
> = I am sorry that she is not alive now.

> **More Examples**
>
> a. I wish she had been alive then. = I am sorry that she was not alive then.
> b. I wished she were alive. = I was sorry that she was not alive.
> c. I wished she had been alive = I was sorry that she had not been alive.

05 but that + 직설법 동사 (의미는 가정법)

  I would help you but that I am short of money.

  = I would help you if I were not short of money.
    만약 돈만 달리지 않는다면 당신을 도울 텐데.

06 if절을 대신하는 명사(구), 부정사, 부사구

  a. A true friend would behave differently.
    진정한 친구라면 달리 처신할 텐데.

  b. To hear him talk, you would take him for a fool.
    그가 말하는 것을 들으면 그를 바보로 여길 것이다.

  c. With good luck, I might succeed.
    행운만 따라 준다면 성공할 수도 있는데.

> **Rephrased**
>
> a. = If he were a true friend, he would behave differently.
> b. = If you were to hear him talk, you would take him for a fool.
> c. = If I were given good luck, I might succeed.
> = If I were lucky, I might succeed.

    cf. 이 밖에 동명사, 관계대명사절 등도 if절을 대신할 수 있음.

061 Our modern world is in many ways a continuation of the world of Greece and Rome. Other influences joined to make us what we are, but the Greco-Roman element is one of the strongest and the richest. **Without it**, our civilization **would** not merely **be** different but less worthy to be called a civilization, because its spiritual achievements **would be** less great.

Key Structure ▶

1 **Other influences joined to make us** what we are
다른 영향력들이 합쳐져서 우리들을 오늘의 우리로 만들었다
• what we are 우리의 현재 모습

2 **Without it** = But for it = If it were not for **it**
그것이 없다면
• 가정법 과거 구문의 부사절에 해당되는 표현.

3 not merely **be different** but less worthy to ~
다를 뿐만 아니라 문명이라고 불리기에는 덜 가치가 있을 것이다
• not merely A but B = not only A but (also) B

내용 오늘의 세계는 여러 면에서 그리스와 로마 세계의 연속이다.

continuation [kəntìnjuéiʃən] 계속, 연속, 연장(= extension, succession)
influence [ínfluəns] 영향(력), 세력, 위신
Greco-Roman 그리스와 로마의(= Greek and Roman)
spiritual [spíritʃuəl] 영혼의, 정신의(= sacred, holy, inspired, divine)
achievement [ətʃí:vmənt] 업적, 성취(= accomplishment, attainment, acquisition)

플러스 문법정리 26

and라는 뜻을 가진 -o
영어에는 and의 뜻을 지니고서 단어와 단어를 연결하는 어미 -o가 있다. 원래 라틴어에서 유래한 것으로 다음과 같은 표현에서 종종 볼 수 있다.

a. Indo-European = Indian and European 인도 - 유럽어족
b. Greco-Roman style = Greek and Roman style 그리스 - 로마 유형(레슬링)
c. alveolo-palatal sound = alveolar and palatal sound 치경 - 구개음
d. activo-passive verb = active and passive verb 능동형이 수동의 뜻을 나타내는 동사
   e.g. This book sells well. 이 책은 잘 팔린다.

062 The greater part of our knowledge and beliefs has been communicated to us by other people through the medium of a language which others have created. **Without** language our mental capacities **would be** poor indeed, comparable to those of the higher animals; we have, therefore, to admit that we owe our principal advantage over the beasts to the fact of living in human society.

Key Structure •

1 **The greater part of** ~의 대부분
   • of 다음에 나오는 명사에 따라 단수나 복수 동사가 결정됨.
   • our knowledge and beliefs를 단수로 취급하여 has been으로 씀.

2 **Without language ~**
   = But for **language** = If it were not for **language** = Were it not for **language**

3 **comparable to those of the higher animals**
   고등동물의 그것과 비교할 만큼
   • those = the mental capacities

4 **we** owe **our principal advantage ~** to **the fact...**
   우리가 짐승보다 월등히 나은 것은 인간 사회에 살고 있다는 사실에 힘입고 있다
   • owe A to B A가 있는 것은 B 덕분이다

내용 언어가 없었다면 인간의 정신 능력은 보잘것없는 것이 되었을지도 모른다.

communicate [kəmjúːnəkèit] 전달하다, 연락하다
medium [míːdiəm] 매체, 매개, 수단(= means, channel, vehicle) *pl.* media
capacity [kəpǽsəti] 능력, 재능(= ability, capability, talent)
comparable [kámpərəbl] 비교할 만한
owe A to B A를 B에게 빚지다[힘입다]

Necessity is the mother of invention.
필요는 발명의 어머니.

063 Habits are both useful and necessary. Life with its many demands upon our time and attention **would** be painfully difficult **were it not for** the habits which release us from the mental and emotional strain of making and carrying out decisions.

Key Structure

1 **Life with its many** demands upon ~ **attention**
우리에게 시간을 들이고 주의를 기울이도록 많은 요구를 하는 인생
• demand upon ~에 대한 요구, 수요

2 were it not for **the habits**
= if it were not for **the habits** = but for **the habits** = without **the habits**
습관이 없다면

내용 습관은 정신적, 정서적 긴장으로부터 우리를 해방시켜 준다.

demand [diménd] 수요, 요구(≠ supply 공급)
release [rilíːs] 해방하다, 자유롭게 하다(= liberate, emancipate, free)
mental [méntəl] 정신의, 정신적인(≠ material, physical)
emotional [imóuʃənəl] 감정의, 정서의
strain [strein] 긴장, 중압, 큰 부담(= stress, worry, tension)
carry out 실천하다(= execute, fulfill, accomplish)

플러스 문법정리 27

가정법 구문의 if절에서 if 생략
영어 문장을 읽다 보면 가정법 구문의 조건절에서 접속사 if가 생략된 표현을 종종 보게 된다. 이때 주의할 점은 도치가 이루어지고, 일반동사가 쓰인 경우 did를 이용한다는 것이다.

a. If I were you, **I would not behave in such a way.** = Were I you, ~
b. If I knew that, **why wouldn't I tell it to you?** = Did I know that, ~
c. If he had been diligent, **he would not have been fired.** = Had he been diligent, ~
d. If we could know **what may happen tomorrow, life would become monotonous.**
= Could we know **what may happen tomorrow, ~**
e. If it were not for water, **nothing could live.** = Were it not for water, ~
f. If you should fail again, **what would you do?** = Should you fail again, ~

해석 a. 만일 내가 너라면 그런 식으로 처신하지는 않을 것이다. b. 만일 내가 그것을 알고 있다면 왜 너에게 이야기하지 않겠는가? c. 만일 그가 부지런했더라면 해고되지 않았을 것이다. d. 만일 우리가 내일 무슨 일이 생길지 알 수 있다면 삶은 단조로워질 것이다. e. 물이 없다면 아무것도 살 수 없을 것이다. f. 만일 네가 또 떨어지면 어떻게 할래?

064   It is not well for any one to be serious all the time. For one who is
       so the strain of life is often too hard. President Lincoln was very
       fond of a funny story. He felt the strain and the burden of the war
       so strongly that, **if it had not been for** this relief, he **would have
       broken down** long before the war was over.

Key Structure •

1 **For one who is so** = For one who is serious all the time 언제나 심각한 사람에게는

2 if it had not been for **this relief**
   = had it not been for **this relief** = but for **this relief** = without **this relief**
   이러한 구제책이 없었더라면
   • this relief는 a funny story를 가리킴.

내용 언제나 심각한 것은 건강에 좋지 않다.

serious [sí(:)əriəs] 진지한, 엄숙한(= grave, grim, solemn, somber)
strain [strein] 긴장, 중압(감)(= burden)
burden [bə́:rdən] 짐, 부담
relief [rilí:f] 완화, 안심, 구원, 기분 전환
break down 무너지다, 고장 나다, 쇠약해지다(= collapse)

065   We can be but partially acquainted even with the events which
       actually influence our course through life and our final destiny.
       There are other events, if such they may be called, which come
       close upon us, yet pass away without actual results, or even
       betraying their near approach, by the reflection of any light or
       shadow across our minds. **Could we know** all the vicissitudes of
       our fortunes, life **would be** too full of hope and fear to afford us a
       single hour of true serenity.

Key Structure •

1 **be** but **partially acquainted even with** ~ ~을 단지 부분적으로만 알다 (but = only)

2 if such **they may be called** = if **they may be called** such
   만약에 그것들이 그렇게 불릴 수 있다면 (such = events)

3 without ~ **betraying their near approach** 자신들이 가까이 다가왔음을 드러내지 않고서

4 Could we know ~ = If we could know ~

5 life would be too full of hope and fear to afford ~
   = life would be so full of hope and fear that it could not afford ~
   인생은 희망과 두려움으로 너무나 가득 차서 ~을 제공할 수 없을 것이다

   내용 인생과 운명에 영향을 미치는 사건을 모두 알 수 있는 것은 아니다.

destiny [déstəni] 운명, 숙명(= lot, doom, fate, kismet, karma)
come close upon us 우리에게 가까이 다가오다
betray [bitréi] 배신하다, 배반하다, 폭로하다, 속이다(= disclose, expose, indicate, reveal)
approach [əpróutʃ] 접근, 다가옴 ⓥ 접근하다
reflection [riflékʃən] 반사, 반영
shadow [ʃǽdou] 그림자, 그늘
vicissitude [visísitʃùːd] (인생, 운명의) 변천, 부침(= change, alteration, up and down, uncertainty, flux)
afford [əfɔ́ːrd] 주다, 제공하다, ~할 여유가 있다(= give)
serenity [sərénəti] 평온, 안정, 차분함(= calmness, composure, tranquility)

플러스 문법정리 28

but의 여러 가지 용법과 뜻
but은 원래 접속사이지만 부사, 전치사 등 여러 가지 품사의 기능을 가지고 있다.

1. **접속사**
   a. He is rich but not happy. (= yet)
   b. No one is so old but he may learn. = No one is so old that he may not learn.
   c. I do not deny but that he is crooked. = I do not deny that he is crooked.
   d. Life would be short, but that hope prolongs it. ('but that +직설법'에 유의할 것)

2. **부사**
   e. She is but a child. (= only)
   f. He is all but dead. (= almost)

3. **전치사**
   g. They are all gone but him. (= except)
   h. He is anything but a scholar. (= far from)
   i. Nothing but peace can save the world. (= Only)
   j. But for your help, he should fail. (= Without)

4. **관계대명사**
   k. There is no rule but has exceptions.
   = There is no rule that doesn't have exceptions.

해석 a. 그는 재산은 있지만 행복하지는 않다. b. 배우지 못할 만큼 나이가 든 자는 없다. c. 그가 마음이 비뚤어진 자임을 나는 부인하지 않는다. d. 희망이 그것을 연장해 주지 않으면 인생은 얼마나 짧을까?(희망이 없다면 인생은 끝이다.) e. 그녀는 어린아이에 불과하다. f. 그는 죽은 것이나 다름없다. g. 그를 빼고는 모두가 가버렸다. h. 그는 결코 학자가 아니다. i. 평화만이 세상을 구할 수 있다. j. 너의 도움이 없다면 그는 실패할 것이다. k. 예외가 없는 규칙이란 없는 법이다.

066   The laws of any civilized country are so numerous and so complicated that no one man can ever be fully acquainted with all of them. Every man, however, is supposed to know the law, and if he breaks it he cannot be free from punishment by saying that he was ignorant. This, of course, is mere common sense, since the whole system of government **would break down, could a man escape** the consequences of his wrongful act by asserting that he did not know that he was breaking the law.

Key Structure •

1   Every man is supposed to know the law 모든 사람은 법을 알 것이라고 생각된다
2   could a man escape ~ = if a man could escape ~ 어떤 사람이 ~을 피할 수 있다면

내용 법을 몰랐다는 이유를 내세워 자신의 잘못된 행위를 정당화할 수는 없다.

numerous [njúːmərəs] 다수의, 수많은(= abundant, myriad, multitudinous)
complicated [kámpləkèitid] 복잡한, 뒤얽힌(= complex, intricate, sophisticated, tricky)
be acquainted with (~과) 친숙하다, 정통하다
be supposed to (~하기로) 되어 있다, 생각되다
be free from (~을) 면하다, 벗어나다
punishment [pʌ́niʃmənt] 처벌, 형벌
escape [iskéip] 달아나다, 도망하다, 탈출하다
consequence [kánsəkwèns] 결과, 결론, 중요성(= result, conclusion, importance)
assert [əsə́ːrt] 단언하다, 주장하다, 옹호하다(= claim, argue, contend, asseverate)

067   Poetry moves us to sympathy with the emotions of the poet himself or with those of the persons whom his imagination has created. We witness their struggles, triumphs and failures. We feel their loves and hates, their joys and sorrows, hopes and fears, somewhat **as if** these **were** our own. And still while we suffer with their anxieties and sorrows we get a pleasure out of the experience.

Key Structure •

1   those of the persons ~
• those는 앞에 나온 명사를 대신하는 지시대명사로, 여기에서는 the emotions를 대신함.

2 **somewhat** as if **these** were **our own** 이것들이 어느 정도는 우리의 것인 양

- somewhat은 as if절의 '정도'를 나타내는 문장부사임.
- as if 다음에는 가정법 동사가 옴에 유의할 것.

내용 시를 읽음으로써 우리는 시인 자신의 감정이나 시 속의 인물의 감정에 공감한다.

sympathy [símpəθi] 동정, 연민, 공감(= compassion, affinity, fellow-feeling)
witness [wítnis] 목격하다, 증거가 되다(= behold, notice, observe, watch) ⓝ 목격자, 증거
struggle [strʌ́gl] 몸부림, 노력, 투쟁(= difficulty, problem, exertion)
triumph [tráiəmf] 개선, 승리(= victory, accomplishment, achievement) ⓥ 성공하다
somewhat [sʌ́mʰwʌ̀t] 약간, 다소(= a little, a bit, fairly, sort of)
suffer [sʌ́fər] (고통을) 경험하다, 괴로워하다
anxiety [æŋzáiəti] 걱정, 염려, 불안(= distress, dread, fear, misgiving, nervousness)
sorrow [sárou] 슬픔, 비애, 후회, 고난(= anguish, affliction, despair, desperation)

---

068 **I wish I could impress** upon your minds the immense importance of improving your opportunities, and the bitterness of the unavailing regret with which you will look back on the neglect of them; or convey to you some adequate idea of the price at which such opportunities would be purchased by some of us, for whom they are long since past and over.

Key Structure •

1 impress upon **your minds the immense importance of ~**
~의 커다란 중요성을 여러분의 마음에 인상지어 놓다
- impress A upon B의 구문에서 A에 해당하는 부분이 뒤로 이동한 구조임.

2 **the bitterness of the unavailing regret ~** 쓸모없는 후회의 쓰라림
- 이 구절은 또한 1의 동사구에서 A에 해당하는 부분임.

3 **the unavailing regret with which you will ~ them**
(나중에) 그것들을 소홀히 하였음을 회상할 때 느끼는 쓸모없는 후회의 쓰라림
- you will look back on the neglect of them with the unavailing regret이라는 표현에서 with 이하가 선행사인 regret으로 연결되기 위해 with which로 바뀌어 나간 형태임.

4 **convey to you some adequate idea of ~**
~에 대한 적절한 생각을 여러분에게 전하다
- convey는 첫 줄의 I could로 연결되고, convey의 목적어는 some 이하임.

5 **the price at which such ~ by some of us**
우리가 그러한 기회를 살 때 지불하는 가격

6 **for whom they are long since past and over**
그들에게는 그것들[그 기회들]이 사라지고 끝난 지 오래되었다
- be long since past and over 사라지고 끝난 지 오래되다

90

내용 기회를 소홀히 하고 나중에 후회해 봐야 아무 소용없다.

impress [imprés] (~에게) 깊은 인상을 주다, 감동시키다
immense [iméns] 엄청난, 커다란(= enormous, vast, huge)
improve [imprúːv] 개량하다, 개선하다, 진보시키다(= advance, better, enhance, refine, upgrade)
bitterness [bítərnis] 씀, 쓴맛, 비통(= acrimony, cruelty, harshness, hostility)
unavailing [ʌ̀nəvéiliŋ] 무효의, 쓸데없는(= useless)
neglect [niglékt] 소홀, 경시(= indifference, negligence, slackness, dereliction) ⓥ 소홀히 하다, 무시하다
convey [kənvéi] 전하다, 나르다, 시사하다(= impart, disclose, tell, transmit)
adequate [ǽdəkwit] 적절한, 충분한(= fitting, satisfactory, sufficient, acceptable)
purchase [pə́ːrtʃəs] 사다, 구입하다(= buy, procure, secure) ⓝ 구입, 취득

---

069 Memory-training courses are much in vogue nowadays, and it seems to be taken for granted that the more things we remember the happier we are. The pleasures of memory must certainly be rated high, but I am sure forgetfulness also plays a part in making human beings happy. Macbeth and Lady Macbeth **would have given** a good deal **to be** able to forget the murder of Duncan, and many a politician has longed to be allowed to forget his election pledges.

Key Structure ▸

1 it seems to be taken for granted that ~
   ~은 당연한 것으로 받아들여지는 것 같다
   • take ~ for granted ~을 당연히 받아들이다

2 the more things we remember the happier we are
   우리가 더 많은 것들을 기억하면 할수록 우리는 더욱더 행복하다

3 would have given a good deal to be able to ~
   ~할 수만 있었더라면 많은 것을 주었을지도 모른다
   • 가정법 과거완료 구문 (to be able to forget ~ = if they had been able to forget ~)

4 many a politician has ~ = many politicians have ~
   • 'many+a+단수명사+단수동사' 구조에 유의할 것.

내용 기억이 주는 기쁨도 크지만, 잊음도 인간을 행복하게 하는 데 일익을 담당한다.

be in vogue 유행하다, 성행하다(= be fashionable)
rate [reit] 평가하다, 등급을 정하다(= estimate, evaluate, grade, rank, value, weigh)
forgetfulness [fərgétfəlnis] 망각, 건망증, 소홀(= oblivion, absent-mindedness)
long [lɔ(ː)ŋ] 간절히 바라다, 열망하다(= yearn, crave, desire, wish)

플러스 문법정리 29

very와 much가 꾸미는 말들

very는 보통 형용사·부사의 원급, 현재분사, 완전히 형용사가 된 과거분사를 꾸며 주고, much는 형용사·부사의 비교급, 최상급, 과거분사 그리고 부사구 등을 꾸며 준다.

a. We had a very hot summer this year.
b. The summer this year is much hotter than that of last year.
c. This book is very exciting to me.
d. I am much excited at this book.
e. He has a very frightened face. (형용사화된 과거분사)
f. Your idea is much better than his.
g. Your idea is much the best of all.
h. His explanation is much to the point.
i. His plan is much like mine.

해석 a. 금년 여름은 유난히도 더웠다. b. 금년 여름은 작년보다 훨씬 더웠다. c. 이 책은 매우 재미있다. d. 이 책이 아주 재미있다. e. 그는 매우 놀란 얼굴이다. f. 너의 생각은 그의 생각보다 훨씬 낫다. g. 너의 생각은 모든 생각 중에서 월등하게 최고이다. h. 그의 설명은 매우 요령이 있다. i. 그의 계획은 나의 계획과 매우 흡사하다.

070

Aristotle **could have avoided** the mistake of thinking that women have fewer teeth than men, **by the simple device** of asking Mrs. Aristotle to keep her mouth open while he counted. He did not do so because he thought he knew. Thinking that you know when in fact you don't is a fatal mistake, to which we are all prone.

Key Structure

1 by the simple device of ~
= if he had adopted the simple device of ~
= if he had simply adopted the device of ~
~라는 단순한 방법만 생각하였어도
• 위의 부사구는 가정법 구문의 if절을 대신하는 것임.

2 a fatal mistake, to which we are all prone
우리가 저지르기 쉬운 치명적인 실수[치명적인 실수인데, 우리는 모두 이것을 저지르기 쉽다]
• to which ~는 관계대명사의 계속적 용법.

내용 모르는 것을 안다고 생각하는 것은 모두가 저지르기 쉬운 치명적인 실수이다.

avoid [əvɔ́id] 피하다, 비키다, 무효로 하다(= escape, evade, dodge)
device [diváis] 계획, 고안, 장치(= invention, scheme, tactic) ⓥ devise 고안하다
fatal [féitəl] 치명적인, 중대한, 결정적인, 피할 수 없는(= mortal, important, decisive, inevitable)
prone [proun] (~의) 경향이 있는, 하기 쉬운(= liable, apt, inclined, disposed, tending)

플러스 문법정리 30

관계대명사의 두 가지 용법

관계대명사는 앞에 오는 선행사를 뒤에서 꾸며 주는 부가적(제한적) 용법의 기능을 가질 수도 있고, 선행사 다음에
쉼표가 오고 그 뒤에 관계대명사절이 나오는 계속적 용법으로 쓰일 수 있다.

a. He wore nothing which distinguished him from the others.
b. He wore nothing, which distinguished him from the others.

참고) 관계부사의 부가적 용법과 계속적 용법

c. He went to America where his brother lived.
d. He went to America, where his brother lived.

해석 a. 그는 다른 사람들과 구별되는 옷을 전혀 입지 않았다.(부가적 용법) b. 그는 옷을 전혀 입지 않아서 다른
사람들과 구별되었다.(계속적 용법) c. 그는 형이 살고 있는 미국에 갔다.(부가적 용법) d. 그는 미국에 갔는데,
그곳에 그의 형이 살고 있었다.(계속적 용법)

---

071 Genius is only the power of making continuous efforts. The line
between failure and success is so fine that we scarcely know when
we pass it: so fine that we are often on the line and do not know it.
How many a man has thrown up his hands at a time when **a little
more effort, a little more patience, would have achieved** success.
As the tide goes clear out, so it comes clear in.

Key Structure

1 The line ~ is so fine that we ~ it
   실패와 성공의 갈림길은 너무 가늘어 우리가 언제 그것을 지나치는지 거의 알지 못한다

2 at a time when a little more effort, ~ , would have achieved success
   = if he had had a little more effort, ~ , he would have achieved success
   조금만 더 노력하고 조금만 더 참아 내었더라면 성공을 얻어낼 수도 있었을 때에

3 so it comes clear in = so it comes in clear 그것은 뚜렷이 다시 (들어)온다

내용 실패와 성공의 경계선은 너무 가늘어 그것을 모를 수 있다.

genius [dʒíːnjəs] 천재(자질), 특수한 재능 *pl.* geniuses 천재들, genii 수호신
continuous [kəntínjuəs] 끊임없는, 연속적인(= ceaseless, constant, incessant, uninterrupted, persistent)
fine [fain] 가느다란, 예민한, 훌륭한(= narrow, thin, slim, slender, delicate, subtle, skillful, fair, nice)
patience [péiʃəns] 인내(력), 끈기, 견인불발(= composure, endurance, forbearance, fortitude, leniency,
                    perseverance, persistency)
tide [taid] 조수, 영고, 경향, 계절, 호기(= ebb and flow, drift, rise and fall, current)

01 **등위[대등]접속사 and, but, or, for**

a. The coed drove slowly and carefully.
그 여대생은 차를 천천히 조심스럽게 몰았다.

b. To grow old, but to be able to learn is the privilege of man.
나이를 먹어도 배울 수 있음은 사람의 특권이다.

c. Let me pass, or I'll call out.
지나가게 해 주오, 아니면 소리를 지르겠소.

d. It must be false, for everyone says so.
그것은 거짓일 거야, 모두가 그렇게 말하니까.

02 **종속접속사**

명사절을 이끄는 that

a. That he has won the fame is no proof of his merit.
그가 명성을 얻었다고 그것이 그의 공이라는 것을 보여 주는 것은 아니다. (그가 명성을 얻은 것은 전혀 우연인 것 같다.)

명사절을 이끄는 if (선택을 내용으로 함)

b. Nobody can tell if it is genuine.
그것이 진짜인지를 누가 알아낼 수 있겠소?

시간의 부사절을 이끄는 when, while, as, whenever, after, before, until

c. When he was asked his opinion, he cleared his throat.
그에게 의견을 묻자 그는 헛기침을 했다.

장소의 부사절을 이끄는 where, wherever

d. Things are never where one wants them.
흔한 물건도 어쩌다 필요해서 찾으면 없다.

목적의 부사절을 이끄는 that (뒤에 may, can 등의 조동사가 쓰임)

e. Let your dog loose that he may run about for a while.
잠시 뛰어다니도록 개를 놓아 주어라.

부정의 목적을 나타내는 부사절 lest[for fear that] ~ (should)

f. She turned her head away lest he should see her tears.
그가 자신의 눈물을 볼 것이 두려워 그녀는 얼굴을 돌렸다.

이유의 부사절을 이끄는 **because, as, since, now that**

g. My work in French is poor because I don't like the subject.
프랑스어를 좋아하지 않아, 성적이 좋지 않습니다.

결과의 부사절을 이끄는 **(so) that**

h. He spoke so rapidly that we could not understand him clearly.
하도 말이 빨라 그의 말을 제대로 알아듣지 못했다.

방식의 부사절을 이끄는 **as** (미국 영어에서는 **like**를 쓰기도 함)

i. Take things as they are.
세상사를 있는 그대로 받아들이게.

조건의 부사절을 이끄는 **unless[if ~ not], if, only (that), in case, suppose**

j. He will come unless he hears to the contrary.
오지 말라는 통지가 없으면 그는 옵니다.

양보의 부사절을 이끄는 **though, although, even if[though], as**

k. Though he scolds me, yet will I like him.
그가 나를 꾸짖는다 해도, 나는 그가 좋다.

제한의 부사절을 이끄는 **as far as, so far as, as, but (that)**

l. As far as I know, there is no such a nice man as he.
내가 아는 한 그처럼 멋진 사나이는 없다.

가정의 부사절을 대신하는 접속사 **otherwise**

m. He worked hard; otherwise he would have failed.
그는 열심히 일했다. 그렇지 않았더라면 실패했을지도 모른다.
   • otherwise = if he had not worked hard

03 등위상관접속사

either A or B : A 아니면 B

a. Either do not attempt it at all, or go through with it.
아예 그 일을 시도하지 말거나, 아니면 철저히 일을 끝내라.

both A and B / at once A and B / alike A and B : A이기도 하고 동시에 B이기도 하다

b. She can both sing and dance.
그녀는 노래도 춤도 다 할 줄 안다.

c. He was at once surprised and troubled by the news.
그는 그 소식에 놀라기도 하고 걱정도 되었다.

d. This book is alike agreeable and instructive.
이 책은 재미도 있고 유익하기도 하다.

not[neither] A nor B : A도 아니고 B도 아니다

e. She cannot sing nor dance.
그녀는 노래도 춤도 다 못한다.

not only A but (also) B = B as well as A : A뿐만 아니라 B이다

f. Sports are not only good for the health, but (also) helpful in promoting good morals.
스포츠는 건강에 좋을 뿐만 아니라 미덕을 조장하는 데에도 도움이 된다.

04 종속상관접속사

no sooner ~ than = hardly[scarcely] ~ when[before] : ~하자마자 곧 …하다

a. No sooner had he stood up than he began to shout to the audience.
그는 일어서자마자 청중들을 향해 외치기 시작했다.

where ~ there : ~하는 곳에 …이 있다

b. Where your treasure is, there will your heart be also.
보물이 있는 곳에 마음도 가느니라.

the + 비교급, the + 비교급 : ~할수록 …하다

c. The happier we are, the longer we live.
즐거우면 즐거울수록 사람은 장수한다.
  • 앞의 the는 정도의 부사 기능을 갖고, 뒤의 the는 지시의 부사 기능을 가지며, 두 개가 합쳐져서 종속상관접속사 역할을 함.

as ~ so... : ~하는 것처럼 …하다

d. As you make your bed, so you must lie on it.
자기가 뿌린 씨는 자기가 거두어야 한다.

05 종속접속사를 대신하는 표현들

명사구

a. Every time he coughed, he felt a good deal of pain.
기침을 할 때마다 그는 매우 괴로웠다.

b. The moment the button was pressed, the rocket shot up.
단추를 누르자 로켓이 솟아올랐다.

부사

c. Once she consents, we have her.
그녀가 일단 승낙하면 우리 편이야.

d. Now (that) you have packed up your things, you had better start.
이제 짐을 꾸렸으니 너는 떠나는 것이 좋을 거야.

전치사구

e. In case I am prevented from coming, please excuse me.
내가 참석하지 못하게 되면 용서해 주세요.

현재분사

f. Supposing he is absent, what excuse will he make?
그가 참석하지 않는다면 무엇이라 변명할까?

과거분사

g. Provided (that) you bear the expense, I will consent.
당신이 비용을 담당한다면 내가 승낙하겠소.

072 From whatever side Nature is approached obstacles arise which prevent a clear vision of her; and persistent labor **as well as** strong desire is necessary for every step of advance **whether** the motive is purely the pursuit of natural knowledge **or** profitable advantage.

Key Structure

1 From whatever side ~ approached 어느 쪽에서 자연에 접근하든
   • whatever는 복합관계대명사로, 이 문장에서는 side를 꾸며 주는 형용사적 기능을 함.

2 persistent labor as well as strong desire
   = not only strong desire but (also) persistent labor

3 whether the motive is A or B 동기가 A이든 B이든

내용 자연을 정확하게 보는 것을 막는 장애물은 강한 의지와 꾸준한 노력으로 극복할 수 있다.

obstacle [ábstəkl] 장애(물), 방해(= obstruction, hindrance, impediment)
prevent [privént] 막다, 방해하다(= hamper, hinder, impede)
vision [víʒən] 시각, 자태, 시야, 통찰력(= sight, eyesight, perception, insight)
persistent [pərsístənt] 끈덕진, 지속하는(= ceaseless, constant, continuous)
motive [móutiv] 동기, 유인, 목적(= aim, cause, incentive, motivation)
pursuit [pərsjúːt] 추적, 추구, 연구(= chase, tracking) ⓥ pursue
profitable [práfitəbl] 이익이 되는, 유익한(= beneficial, advantageous)

073 Most of the luxuries, and many of the so-called comforts of life are **not only** not indispensable, **but** positive hindrances to the elevation of mankind. With respect to luxuries and comforts, the wisest have lived a more simple and meagre life than the poor.

Key Structure

1 With respect to ~ = In respect of ~ ~에 관련하여서는

2 the wisest / the poor 가장 현명한 사람들 / 가난한 사람들 (the+형용사 = 복수 보통명사)

내용 사치와 안락은 인간성 향상에 장애물이 된다.

luxury [lʌ́kʃəri] 사치, 호사 *cf.* luxuries 사치품들
so-called 소위, 이른바
indispensable [ìndispénsəbl] 불가결의, 없어서는 안 될(= essential, imperative, mandatory, unavoidable)
   ⓥ dispense 분배하다, 베풀다 *cf.* dispense with ~없이 지내다

hindrance [híndrəns] 방해, 장애(= obstacle, obstruction, impediment) ⓥ hinder
elevation [èləvéiʃən] 높임, 향상, 높이
meagre,-ger [mí:gər] 빈약한, 여윈(= insufficient, mean, unsatisfying)

074 The sporting spirit means that one must never forget that the whole of life is only a game, which must be played keenly, according to the rules, but without taking the whole thing too seriously, and that its greatest moments should be lived **not only** with a sense of the game, **but** with a sense of the sports of the field.

Key Structure ●

1 **without taking ~ seriously** 전체를 너무 심각하게 받아들이지 않고
2 not only A but (also) B = B as well as A

내용 인생은 하나의 게임이며 규칙에 따라 행하는 스포츠 정신으로 살아야 한다.

sporting spirit 스포츠 정신, 정정당당한 정신
keenly [kí:nli] 열심히, 빈틈없이(= intensely, anxiously, sharply)

플러스 문법정리 31

상관접속사 (Correlative Conjunction)
접속사는 그 기능에 따라 등위접속사와 종속접속사로 분류하고, 또한 그 형태에 따라 단일접속사, 구접속사, 상관접속사로 분류한다. 상관접속사는 양쪽 말이 서로 연관되어 접속사 기능을 하는 것으로, 양쪽 모두 접속사인 경우도 있고, 한쪽이 형용사 또는 부사인 경우도 있다.

1. 등위상관접속사 (Coordinate Correlative Conjunction)
   a. She can both sing and dance.
   b. He was at once surprised and troubled by the news.
   c. Either do not attempt it at all, or go through with it.
   d. She cannot sing nor dance.
   e. This book is alike agreeable and instructive.
   f. Read not for others but for yourself.
   g. He is not only diligent but (also) smart.
   h. He had neither father nor mother, nor any relatives.

2. 종속상관접속사 (Subordinate Correlative Conjunction)
   i. I am not so strong as I once was.
   j. He is such a fool as he looks.
   k. As a man sows, so he shall reap.
   l. No sooner had he seen me than he ran away.
   m. Where your treasure is, there will your heart be also.
   n. The happier we are, the longer we live.

075 Literature can be no substitute for religion, **not merely because** we need religion **but because** we need literature as well as religion. And religion is no more a substitute for drama than drama is a substitute for religion.

Key Structure

1 **not merely because A but because B** A라는 이유뿐만 아니라 B라는 이유 때문에
   • not merely ~ but (also)는 상관접속사로 두 개의 because절을 연결하고 있음.
   • not merely ~ but = not only ~ but also

2 **religion is no more a substitute ~ than drama is ~ religion**
   드라마가 종교의 대치물이 아니듯 종교도 드라마의 대치물이 아니다 (양자 부정의 비교 구문)

내용 문학과 종교는 서로의 대용물이 아니다.

literature [lítərətʃùər] 문학, 문필업
substitute [sʌ́bstitjùːt] 대용물 (= alternative, deputy, replacement, surrogate) ⓥ 대치하다

플러스 문법정리 32

no more ~ than과 no less ~ than
둘 다 부정 비교를 나타내는 것으로, 전자는 비교가 되는 대상인 양자를 부정하는 것이고, 후자는 둘 다를 긍정하는 것이다. more는 긍정적인 의미가 있는데 그것을 전적으로 부정하는 것이므로 둘 다 부정하는 것이 되고, less는 부정적인 의미가 있는데 그것을 전적으로 부정하는 것이므로 둘 다 긍정하는 것이 된다.

a. A whale is no more a fish than a horse is.
= A whale is not a fish any more than a horse is.

b. He is no more mad than you are.
= He is not mad any more than you are.

c. She is no less beautiful than her mother.
= She is as beautiful as her mother.

d. He is no less diligent than you are.
= He is as diligent as you are.

해석 a. 말이 물고기가 아닌 것처럼 고래도 물고기가 아니다.(양자 부정) b. 그도 너처럼 미치지 않았다.(양자 부정)
c. 그녀는 어머니 못지않게 예쁘다.(양자 긍정) d. 그도 너만큼 근면하다.(양자 긍정)

076 All of us are poets in a measure because all of us have feelings, and power to communicate what we feel to others; but those we call poets are **at once** more sensitive, with a wider range of feelings, **and** better able to express what they feel and move others to share their feelings.

Key Structure

1 at once **more sensitive ~, and better able to express**
보다 민감하기도 하고, ~을 더 잘 표현할 수도 있다
  • at once A and B = both A and B = at the same time A and B A이기도 하고 동시에 B이기도 하다

2 **move others to share their feelings** 다른 사람들을 감동시켜 자신들의 감정을 나누어 갖도록 하다

내용 시인은 보통 사람들보다 더 뛰어난 감수성을 가지고 있다.

in a measure 어느 정도는, 다소간(= to some degree)
communicate [kəmjúːnəkèit] 전달하다, 의사소통하다
sensitive [sénsətiv] 민감한, 예민한(= affected, receptive, susceptible)
range [reinʤ] 범위, 구역, 줄, 산맥(= diversity, selection)
share [ʃɛər] 나누어 가지다, 분할하다

---

077 The scientific attitude is **at once** a way of thought, a way of conduct **and** a way of life. It is an attitude that has been found essential for constructive scientific progress—an attitude which, if it were to be more widely spread, accepted, appreciated and used, would go a long way toward helping mankind resolve the many dilemmas that now confront it. A scientific attitude has many component parts, the most important of which are straightforward and easy to understand.

Key Structure

1 at once A and B **= both A and B = at the same time A and B**
A이기도 하고 동시에 B이기도 하다

2 **if it were to be ~** 그것이 ~된다면 (가정법 과거 구문)

3 **go a long way toward ~** ~하는 데 크게 이바지하다
  • A little effort would go a long way toward(s) settling the dispute.
  조금만 노력하면 그 분쟁을 해결할 수 있을 텐데.

4   **the most important of which are ~**
- 관계대명사의 계속적 용법. which는 component parts를 선행사로 갖고 있음.

내용   과학적인 태도는 사고와 행동과 삶의 방식으로, 건설적인 과학의 진보에 필수적이다.

constructive [kənstrʌ́ktiv] 건설적인, 발전적인(= productive, creative, valuable)
spread [spred] 펴다, 퍼뜨리다, 보급시키다   *cf.* spread-spread-spread
appreciate [əprí:ʃièit] 이해하다, 진가를 인정하다(= esteem, prize, value)
resolve [rizálv] 해결하다, 제거하다, 결정하다(= solve, clear up, work out, determine)
dilemma [dilémə] 딜레마, 궁지, 난국(= predicament, plight, problem, quandary)
confront [kənfrʌ́nt] 마주 보다, 직면하다
component part 구성 성분, 부품
straightforward [strèitfɔ́:rwərd] 수월한, 정직한(= easy, simple, direct, uncomplicated)

---

078   It was not long, however, **before** I found that this pleasant young fellow could do practically anything in the carpentry or mechanical field. **When** it came to repairing or building, he knew **not** the word **but** the action.

Key Structure

1   **It was not long before ~**   얼마 되지 않아 곧 ~하였다

2   **When it came to ~**   ~라는 일에 관한 한
e.g.   When it comes to playing golf, you cannot beat Seri Pak.
골프에 관한 한 박세리를 이길 수는 없다.

내용   그 젊은이는 말보다는 행동을 앞세우는 (실용적인) 사람이었다.

practically [prǽktikəli] 실제로, 실용적으로(= virtually, nearly, almost)
carpentry [ká:rpəntri] 목공일, 목수직
mechanical [məkǽnikəl] 기계의, 기계로 만든
repairing [ripɛ́əriŋ] 수선, 수리(= mending, putting right)

---

079   This has been a year of long sunshine. Month has followed upon month with little unkindness of the sky; I scarcely marked **when** July passed into August, August into September. I should think it summer still, **but that** I see the lanes yellow-purified with flowers of autumn.

Key Structure •

1 This has been ~ = This year has been ~
   • Ours is a trial age. = Our age is a trial one. 우리 시대는 시련의 시대이다.

2 with little unkindness of the sky = with much kindness of the sky
   하늘도 많은 친절을 베풀고[날씨가 좋았고]

3 I scarcely marked when ~ September. 7월이 8월로, 8월이 9월로 변함을 거의 몰랐다.

4 I should think ~, but that ~ autumn.
   아직은 여름인가 했더니 오솔길이 가을 꽃으로 노랗게 순화되어 있음을 본다.
   • but that+주어+직설법 동사 : 가정법 구문과 함께 자주 쓰이며, 직설법 동사가 나옴에 주의할 것.
     but that은 'that 이하의 사실만 없다면'의 뜻을 갖고 있음.

내용 금년은 유난히 날씨가 좋아 계절이 바뀌는 것도 잘 모르겠다.

mark [mɑːrk] 주목하다, 생각하다(= notice, think)
lane [lein] 골목길, 오솔길, 차로
purify [pjú(ː)ərəfài] 정화하다, 청결하게 하다(= cleanse, depurate, refine, sanitize)

---

080 Much **as** I once loved Thoreau, I confess I have never looked on money as a cause of enslavement. I have always felt free **when** I had a pound than **when** I had only a shilling in my pocket. To be able to treat someone to lunch and not to have to worry about **whether** one has enough money in one's pocket to pay for the dishes and the drinks that one has pressed him is one of the freedoms after which many a poor man must have often aspired.

Key Structure •

1 Much as I once loved Thoreau = Though I once loved Thoreau much

2 treat someone to lunch 누군가에게 점심을 대접하다

3 the dishes and the drinks that one has pressed him 자신이 그에게 들도록 권한 요리와 음료

4 one of the freedoms after which many a ~ aspired
   많은 가난한 사람들이 종종 갈망해 왔음에 틀림없는 자유 중의 하나
   • aspire after ~ ~을 열망하다, 갈망하다
   • must have+p.p. ~했음에 틀림없다

내용 나는 돈을 인간 노예화의 원인이라고 생각하지 않는다.

confess [kənfés] 고백하다, 자인하다(= acknowledge, admit, own up)
enslavement [insléivmənt] 노예화함, 노예 상태
aspire [əspáiər] 열망하다, 동경하다(= crave, desire, hope (for), long (for), strive (after))

플러스 문법정리 33

동사형을 파생시키는 파생접사 en-/-en
명사나 형용사에 접두사 en-, 또는 접미사 -en, 또는 접두사 및 접미사를 동시에 붙여 동사를 이끌어 낼 수 있다.

1. 접두사가 붙은 단어들
   en+명사 : **en**courage, **en**chant, **en**act, **en**force, **en**slave, **en**danger 등
   en+형용사 : **en**large, **en**rich, **en**sure, **en**able, **en**dear 등

2. 접미사가 붙은 단어들
   명사+en : height**en**, strength**en** 등
   형용사+en : deep**en**, wid**en**, gladd**en**, weak**en**, broad**en** 등

3. 접두사, 접미사가 다 붙은 단어들
   en+명사+en : **en**light**en** 등
   en+형용사+en : **en**liv**en** 등

4. 변형된 형태의 동사들(주로 발음의 편이성 때문임)
   imprison, **im**press, **im**print, **in**sure 등

081

Man's youth is a wonderful thing; it is so full of anguish and of magic and he **never** comes to know it as it is, **until** it has gone from him forever. It is the thing he cannot bear to lose, it is the thing whose passing he watches with infinite sorrow and regret, it is the thing whose loss he must lament forever, and it is the thing whose loss he really welcomes with a sad and secret joy, the thing he would never willingly relive again, could it be restored to him.

Key Structure

1 he never comes to ~ until... ···할 때까지는 결코 ~을 하지 못한다
  • as it is 있는 그대로

2 It is the thing (which) he cannot bear to lose 그것을 잃는 것을 결코 참지 못하는 일이다

3 the thing (which) he would ~ again 결코 다시 기꺼이 살지는 않을 일

4 could it be restored to him = if it could be restored to him
  그것이 그에게 다시 되돌려진다고 하더라도
  • 가정법 과거 구문의 종속절에서 if가 생략된 구조.

내용 인간은 젊음의 상실을 슬퍼하기도 또는 내밀히 환영하기도 한다.

anguish [ǽŋgwiʃ] 격통, 고뇌(= agony, anxiety, distress)
bear [bɛər] 참다, 견디다, 열매를 맺다(= stand, tolerate, endure, put up with)
infinite [ínfənit] 무한의, 끝없는(= endless, countless, inestimable)
lament [ləmént] 슬퍼하다, 애석해하다(= bemoan, bewail, deplore, mourn)
relive [riːlív] 다시 살다
restore [ristɔ́ːr] 제자리로 되돌리다, 복구하다

---

082 A study of human history and prehistory shows that there has been a wonderful development of ethics and of religion. There is no satisfactory evidence **that** these were handed down from heaven in perfect form, but there is abundant evidence **that** they, in common with all other things, have been evolving and **that** this process has not yet come to an end. Some of the ethical codes and religious practices current today will probably be considered barbarous in times to come.

Key Structure •

1 **A study of human history and prehistory shows that ~**
   = Through a study of human history and prehistory we know that ~
   인간의 역사와 선사시대의 연구를 통하여 우리는 ~을 안다

2 **There is no satisfactory evidence that ~** ~라는 만족스러운 증거는 없다
   • satisfactory evidence that ~의 that, 그 다음 줄 there is abundant evidence that ~의 that, 다음 줄 and that ~의 that은 모두 동격의 명사절을 이끄는 종속접속사로서 바로 앞에 놓인 evidence의 내용을 나타냄.

3 **the ethical codes and religious practices** (which are) **current today**
   오늘날 시행[유행]되는 윤리규범과 종교의식들

4 **in times to come** 앞으로 다가올 시기[미래]에
   • to come은 times를 꾸며 주는 형용사구 역할.

내용 윤리와 종교의 규범은 변하는 것이고 오늘날 유행하는 것이 미래에는 야만적인 것으로 여겨질 수도 있다.

prehistory [prìːhístəri] 유사 이전, 선사(학)
ethics [éθiks] 윤리학, 도덕 ⓐ ethical
evidence [évidəns] 증거, 증언(= proof, attestation, testimony)
hand down 물려주다
heaven [hévən] 하늘, 창공, 천국
abundant [əbʌ́ndənt] 풍부한, 남아돌아갈 만한(= ample, bounteous, copious, plentiful, plenteous)
evolve [iválv] 발전하다, 진화하다, 방출하다(= develop)
come to an end 끝나다(= come to a stop, finish)
practice [prǽktis] 연습, 실제 pl. 예배(의)식
current [kə́ːrənt] 유행하는, 현재의(= prevalent, ongoing, existing)
barbarous [báːrbərəs] 야만의, 미개한(= barbarian, savage)

08 ▸ 비교구문 | Comparison

01 as ~ as를 이용한 동등비교 구문

a. This portrait is as large as life.
이 초상화는 실물 크기와 같다.

b. She is as bright as fair.
그녀는 예쁘기도 하고 총명하기도 하다.

c. Get up as early as possible.
가능한 한 일찍 일어나시오.

d. She is as happy as can be.
= She is as happy as happy can be.
그녀는 더할 나위 없이 행복하다.

02 동등비교 구문의 부정

a. Fortune is **not** so blind as men are.
행운은 인간만큼 눈이 멀지는 않았다.

b. Life is **seldom** as exciting as we think.
인생이 생각만큼 재미있는 경우는 드물다.

c. **Nothing** is so precious as time.
시간만큼 귀중한 것은 없다.

d. There is **no** love so generous as parental love.
부모의 사랑만큼 관대한 사랑은 없다.

03 배수사를 이용한 비교 구문 : 배수사 + as + 원급 + as

a. He reads twice as fast as an ordinary reader.
그는 보통 독자보다 두 배나 빨리 책을 읽는다.

b. This hotel has two-thirds as many rooms as that one.
이 호텔의 방 수는 저 호텔 방 수의 2/3이다.

c. He is not half so wise as his brother.
그는 형의 절반만큼도 현명하지 않다.

04 as ~ as any + 단수 명사 = 최상급

as ~ as (any that) ever + 과거 동사 = 최상급

a. Koreans are as peace-loving a people as any in the world.
한국인은 이 세상 어느 민족 못지않게 평화를 애호하는 민족이다.

b. He is as great a scholar as ever lived.
그는 지금까지 살아온 누구 못지않은 위대한 학자이다.

05 A as well as B / not only B but (also) A : B뿐만 아니라 A도 ~하다

a. He can speak French as well as English.
그는 영어뿐만 아니라 프랑스어도 할 줄 안다.

b. He can speak English and French as well.
그는 영어뿐만 아니라 프랑스어도 또한 할 줄 안다.

c. Labor is not only a necessity but (also) a pleasure.
노동은 필수적인 일일 뿐만 아니라 또한 하나의 즐거움이다.

both A and B : A이기도 하고 동시에 B이기도 하다

(= at once A and B / at the same time A and B)

d. This book is both interesting and instructive.
이 책은 재미있기도 하고 유익하기도 하다.

083   Surely every man deserves the study of a biographer. At least **as much**, perhaps even more, is to be learned from the ordinary **as** from the extraordinary. If the physician were to confine his attention to exceptional persons, he would learn very little of the nature of man.

Key Structure

1 as much, ~ , is to be learned from A as from B
   A에게서도 B에게서만큼 많은 것을 배울 수 있다
   • 동등비교 구문.

2 confine A to B   A를 B에 국한시키다

내용   평범한 사람에게서도 비범한 사람들에게서만큼 많은 것을 배울 수 있다.

deserve [dizə́:rv] (~할 만한) 가치가 있다(= be worthy of, merit)
biographer [baiágrəfər] 전기 작가
the ordinary 평범한 사람들(= common, average)
the extraordinary 비범한 사람들(= uncommon, unusual)
confine [kɑnfáin] 국한하다, 제한하다(= limit, restrict, restrain)
exceptional [iksépʃənəl] 예외적인, 보통이 아닌

플러스 문법정리 34

the+형용사의 3가지 의미
'the+형용사'는 아래의 3가지 뜻을 지니고 있다.

a. 복수 보통명사 : The rich are not always happier than the poor.
b. 단수 보통명사 : The unexpected sometimes happens.
c. 추상명사 : The beautiful is one of human ideals.

해석   a. 부자들이라고 가난한 사람들보다 언제나 더 행복한 것은 아니다.   b. 불의의 사고가 때때로 발생한다.
     c. 미는 인간이 가지고 있는 이상 중의 하나이다.

084   Poetry must be heard through the ear **as well as** read with the eye. Unless we read a poem aloud, we cannot appreciate the rhythm and the music of words. These are just **as** important for the full understanding of the poem **as** the meaning of the words themselves.

1 Unless we read a poem aloud = If we don't read a poem aloud
만약 우리가 시를 소리 내어 읽지 않으면

2 as important for the full understanding of A as B
B를 충분히 이해하는 것만큼 A의 이해에도 중요하다

내용 시어 자체만큼 시의 리듬도 중요하다.

aloud [əláud] 큰 소리로, 소리 내어(= audibly, clearly, out loud)
appreciate [əprí:ʃièit] 감상하다, 느끼다(= apprehend, comprehend, understand)
rhythm [ríðəm] 리듬, 운율(= metre, tempo, time)

---

085 If he himself rose out of poverty, and filled a great position before he died at the age of forty-three, this was not, I fancy, due to that ambition to which most poor boys who afterwards achieve eminence owe their success. He was, so far as I could judge, **as** free from ambition in the ordinary sense of the word **as any** man who **ever** lived.

Key Structure •

1 that ambition to which ~ success
나중에 유명해지는 대부분의 가난한 소년들이 신세를 지게 되는 그 야망
• owe A to B A를 B에 힘입다

2 as free from ambition ~ as any man...
…한 사람 누구에게 못지않게 ~로부터 자유롭다
e.g. He is as brave as any man alive. 그는 살아 있는 어느 남자보다 용감하다.
He was as brave a soldier as ever shouldered a gun. 그는 총을 든 어느 군인보다 용감했다.

내용 그가 야망 때문에 명성을 얻은 것은 아니다.

rise out of poverty 가난에서 벗어나다
be due to (~에) 기인하다
fancy [fǽnsi] 생각하다, 상상하다(= think, imagine)
ambition [æmbíʃən] 야망, 포부
eminence [émənəns] (지위, 신분의) 고귀, 탁월(= renown, prominence, exaltation)

free from과 free of의 차이

둘 다 '〜이 없는', '〜으로부터 벗어난'의 뜻이지만, 전자는 '바람직하지 못한 사람·물건·걱정·고통이 없는'의 뜻으로 주로 쓰이고 후자는 '세금·요금·제약 등이 없는'의 뜻으로 주로 쓰인다. 간단히 말해 추상적인 명사의 경우 from을, 구체적인 명사의 경우 of를 쓴다고 보면 된다.

a. He lived a life free from blemish.
b. Nobody can be free from care and anxiety.
c. The road was free of snow then.
d. The dinner show was free of charge.

해석 a. 그는 흠 없는 삶을 살았다.   b. 근심과 걱정에서 벗어나는 사람은 아무도 없다.   c. 그때 그 길은 눈이 치워져 있었다.   d. 그 디너쇼는 무료였다.

---

086 It can be said that among the men whose genius enriched and deepened human knowledge by creative achievements in the area of exact science there is hardly one who enjoys the sympathy of **as** many **as** does Kepler, despite the facts that his principal field of activity is unfamiliar to most and the result of his labors is difficult to understand.

Key Structure

1 there is hardly one who ~ Kepler
   케플러만큼 많은 사람들의 호응을 누리는 사람도 거의 없다
   • sympathy of many (people) 많은 사람의 공감, 호응
   • as does Kepler = as Kepler does[enjoys] 케플러가 누리는 만큼

2 unfamiliar to most 대다수의 사람들에게 낯선
   • most = most people

내용 케플러가 과학에서 이룩한 업적은 많은 사람의 공감을 사고 있다.

genius [dʒíːnjəs] 천재성, 비범한 재능(= gift, talent, intelligence)
enrich [inrítʃ] 부유하게 하다, 향상시키다
deepen [díːpən] 깊게 하다, 짙게 하다
sympathy [símpəθi] 공감, 호응, 동정(= compassion, commiseration, fellow-feeling)
despite [dispáit] 〜에도 불구하고(= in spite of, with all, for all)

087 Life is **seldom as** exciting **as** we think it ought to be. It is the other fellow's life which seems full of adventure. No matter what your profession, or how happy you may be in it, there are moments when you wish you had chosen some other career.

Key Structure •

1 as we think it ought to be
    마땅히 그래야 한다고 우리가 생각하는 만큼

2 It is **the other** ~ which
    • It ~ that 강조 구문에서 that 대신 which가 쓰인 것임.

3 No matter what **your profession, ~ may be**
    = Whatever **your profession, ~ may be**
    당신의 직업이 무엇이든지 간에

4 how happy ~ in it
    • how 앞에 no matter를 넣어 볼 것.

    내용 인생은 우리가 생각하는 것만큼 그렇게 재미있지는 않다.

adventure [ədvéntʃər] (뜻하지 않은) 사건, 모험(= venture, incident, event)
profession [prəféʃn] (지적) 직업(= job, occupation, career, calling, trade)
career [kəríər] 생애, (전문적) 직업, 경력

플러스 문법정리 36

I wish+가정법 과거/과거완료, as if+가정법 과거/과거완료
I wish / as if 다음에는 가정법 과거나 과거완료 동사가 나올 수 있다.

a. I wish I were in my hometown.
b. He wished he had not spoken so.
    위의 두 문장에서 wish, wished는 직설법 동사이며, 그 다음에 오는 절의 동사가 가정법 동사임에 유의할 것.

c. He talks as if he were a native speaker of English.
d. He talks as if he had been to America.

해석 a. 지금 내 고향에 있다면 좋을 텐데. b. 그는 그렇게 말하지 않았더라면 하고 희망하였다. c. 그는 자신이 마치 영어의 모국어 화자인 것처럼 이야기한다. d. 그는 자신이 마치 미국에 가 본 것처럼 이야기한다.

088 **No** man is **so** foolish **but** he may give another good counsel sometimes; and **no** man is **so** wise **but** he may easily err, if he will take
no other's counsel but his own. But very few men are wise by their
own counsel, or learned by their own teaching. For he that was
only taught by himself had a fool to his master.

Key Structure •

1 No man is so foolish but he may give ~ sometimes
    = No man is so foolish that he may not give ~ sometimes
    때로는 남에게 훌륭한 조언을 하지 못할 만큼 어리석은 바보는 없다

2 no man is so wise but he may easily err
    = no man is so wise that he may not easily err
    누구도 쉽게 실수를 저지르지 않을 만큼 현명하지도 않다

3 if he will take ~ his own 만약에 자신의 지혜밖에는 다른 사람의 지혜를 빌리지 않는다면

4 had a fool to his master 바보를 자신의 스승으로 삼다

내용 혼자 힘으로 학문을 한 자는 바보가 되기 십상이다.

counsel [káunsəl] 조언, 권고, 지혜(= advice)
err [əːr] 실수하다, 잘못 생각하다(= be mistaken, go wrong)
learned [lɔ́ːrnid] 학문[학식]이 있는, 박식한(= educated, academic)

089 There is **nothing so** degrading **as** the constant anxiety about one's
means of livelihood. I have nothing but contempt for the people
who despise money. They are hypocrites or fools. Money is like a
sixth sense without which you cannot make a complete use of the
other five. Without an adequate income half the possibilities of life
are shut off.

Key Structure •

1 There is nothing so ~ as... …만큼 ~한 것은 없다

2 without which ~ five 그것이 없으면 다른 오감을 완벽하게 이용할 수 없다

3 make a complete use of ~ ~을 완벽하게 이용하다

내용 돈은 인간의 다른 오감을 잘 이용할 수 있게끔 해 주는 육감이라고 할 수 있다.

degrading [digréidiŋ] 품위를 떨어뜨리는, 저급한(= shameful, ignoble, dishonorable | ≒ honorable, graceful)
constant [kánstənt] 끝없는, 변함없는
anxiety [æŋzáiəti] 고민, 불안, 걱정(= worry, care)
means [mi:nz] 수단, 방법
livelihood [láivlihùd] 생계(의 수단), 살림
nothing but 단지, 오직(= only)
contempt [kəntémpt] 경멸, 멸시
despise [dispáiz] 경멸하다, 얕보다(= condemn, deride, disdain, look down on)
hypocrite [hípəkrit] 위선자 *cf.* hypocracy 위선
sixth sense 육감
be shut off 차단되다

플러스 문법정리 37

all, both, half, double의 위치
all, both, half, double 등의 대명사나 형용사는 관사 앞에 온다.

a. All the boys were for the proposal.
b. Both the sisters lived single.
c. He wasted half the money he had.
d. I paid double the price for the camera.
e. The little boy walked half a mile this morning.

해석 a. 모든 소년들이 그 제안에 찬성하였다. b. 자매는 둘 다 홀로 살았다. c. 그는 가진 돈의 절반을 허비하였다.
　　　d. 나는 그 카메라 값으로 두 배를 지불하였다. e. 그 작은 소년은 오늘 아침 반 마일을 걸었다.

---

090 The most important thing for you to do as a student of literature is to advise yourself to be an honest student, for in the intellectual sphere at any rate honesty is definitely the best policy. If you prefer the poetry of a third-rate poet to that of Shakespeare it is a most regrettable thing, but **not so** regrettable **as** your doing so and saying you do just the opposite.

Key Structure ▸

1 **in the intellectual sphere at any rate** 어쨌든 지적 영역에서는
  • intellectual 지력의 활동을 요하는

2 **prefer the poetry of ~ to that of Shakespeare**
  셰익스피어의 시보다 삼류 시인의 시를 더 좋아하다
  • that = the poetry

3 **not so regrettable as ~** ~만큼 유감스럽지는 않다

4 **your doing so and ~ opposite** 그렇게 하면서 반대의 일을 한다고[그렇지 않다고] 말하는 것

내용 문학을 공부할 때에는 정직이 최상의 방책이다.

sphere [sfiər] 범위, 영역, 분야(= field, range, realm)
at any rate 어쨌든, 적어도
definitely [défənitli] 틀림없이, 단호히(= clearly, surely, beyond doubt, indubitably)
prefer A to B B보다 A를 더 좋아하다(= like A better than B)
opposite [ápəzit] 반대쪽의, 정반대의 *cf.* the opposite 반대의 일

---

091 **Nothing** can be **more** unjust and ridiculous **than** to be angry with another because he is not of your opinion. The interest, education, and means by which men attain their knowledge, are so different that it is impossible that they should all think alike; and he has at least **as** much reason to be angry with you **as** you with him.

Key Structure •

1 because he is not of your opinion
   그가 당신의 견해와 같지 않다는 이유로
   • of your opinion은 be동사의 보어 역할을 하는 형용사구임.

2 as much reason ~ as you with him
   당신이 그에게 화를 낼 만큼의 충분한 이유
   • as you with him = as you have reason to be angry with him

내용 자신의 의견과 다르다는 이유로 남에게 화를 내는 것은 정당하지 못한 일이다.

unjust [ʌndʒʌ́st] 부정한, 불공평한(= unreasonable, wrong, wrongful)
ridiculous [ridíkjələs] 웃기는, 어리석은(= absurd, illogical, nonsensical, preposterous)
attain [ətéin] 획득하다
alike [əláik] 한결같이, 동등하게

플러스 문법정리 38

떠다니는 양화사 (Floated Quantifier)
원래 대명사와 함께 쓰인 양화사 all, both 등이 마치 혼자 떠다니는 것처럼 단독으로 쓰여 부사적 기능을 갖는다.

a. All of them should think alike.
= They should all think alike.

b. Both of them were disheartened at the news.
= They were both disheartened at the news.

해석 a. 그들 모두는 똑같은 생각을 한다.   b. 그들 둘 다 그 소식을 듣고 낙심하였다.

092 Of all the will for the ideal which exists in mankind only a small part can be manifested in action. All the rest is destined to realize itself in unseen effects, which represent, however, a value exceeding **a thousandfold and more** that of the activity which attracts the notice of the world. Its relation to the latter is like that of the deep sea to the waves which stir its surface.

Key Structure ▸

1 a thousandfold and more = more than a thousand times 천 배 이상으로

2 that of the activity ~
  • 이때의 that은 a value를 대신하는 지시대명사임.

3 that of the deep sea to ~
  • 이때의 that도 지시대명사로서 relation을 대신하고 있음.

내용 이상을 향한 인간의 의지 중에서 일부분만이 행동으로 나타난다.

will [wil] 의지, 소망, 의도(= desire, wish, longing)
manifest [mǽnəfèst] 명시하다, 분명히 나타내다(= make visible, exhibit, reveal, uncover) ⓐ 명백한, 분명한
be destined to ~할 운명에 처하다(= be doomed to)
realize itself 실현되다(= be realized)
exceed [iksíːd] (한계, 범위 등을) 넘다, 초과하다(= outnumber, outshine, transcend)
a thousandfold 천 배의(= a thousand times)
stir [stəːr] 휘젓다, 부추기다(= stimulate, excite, exhilarate, agitate)

All is well that ends well.
끝이 좋으면 다 좋은 법.

01 the + 비교급, the + 비교급 : ~하면 할수록 점점 더 ~해진다

a. The higher up you go, the colder it becomes.
높이 올라가면 올라갈수록 점점 더 추워진다.

b. The less I eat, the better I feel.
음식을 덜 먹으면 덜 먹을수록 기분은 점점 나아진다.

02 all the + 비교급 + │ for + 명사(구) │ : ~이기 때문에 (그만큼) 더욱더 ~하다
                     │ because 절 │

not[none] the less + │ for + 명사(구) │ : ~이라고 해서 결코 덜 ~하는 것은 아니다
                       │ because 절 │

a. I love him all the better for his faults.
= I love him all the better because he has faults.
그에게 결점이 있으므로 나는 그를 더욱더 좋아한다.

b. I do not love him the less for his faults.
= I love him none the less because he has faults.
그에게 결점은 있지만 그래도 나는 그를 좋아한다.

c. We are all the richer under the industrialization movement.
산업화 운동이 있어서 우리는 더욱더 부유하다.

d. He has some faults, but I love him none the less.
그에게 약간의 결점이 있지만, 그래도 나는 그를 마찬가지로 좋아한다.

03 much more : ~은 두말할 필요도 없다 (앞에 긍정의 표현이 올 때)
much less : 하물며 ~할 리는 없다 (앞에 부정의 표현이 올 때)

much more, much less는 공히 다음 어구와 바꾸어 쓸 수 있다.
즉 still more (less), let alone, to say nothing of, not to speak of, not to mention

a. You should welcome a stranger, much more[= still more] a friend.
낯선 사람도 반겨야 하는데 친구야 두말할 필요가 있는가.

b. They rarely cheat, much less[= still less] rob, each other.
그들은 서로를 속이는 법이 거의 없다. 하물며 서로를 강탈하는 것이야 두말할 필요도 없다.

04 최상급의 표현이 양보의 뜻을 소유한 구문

 a. The wisest man cannot know everything.
  제아무리 현명한 사람이라고 해도 모든 것을 다 알 수는 없다.

 b. Time and thinking tame the strongest relief.
  시간이 가고 생각을 많이 하면 제아무리 센 위안도 누그러지는 법이다.

05 (Just) as ~, so... : ~한 만큼 …하다, ~하듯 …하다 (양태의 상관관계)

 a. As rust eats iron, so care eats the heart.
  쇠에 녹이 슬 듯 마음에도 걱정이 깃드는 법이다.

 b. Just as you sow, so will you reap.
  뿌린 대로 거두리라.

Passages 093~103

093

There are various ways we can set about acquiring a foreign language. One way is to get somebody who talks the language, and work with them, imitating and learning the language from them; of course, **the more** like a native speaker that person is, **the better**. The other way is to get a book and sit down with it, alone or in a group, with more or less speaking of the foreign language, but trying to get it by reading rather than by speaking.

Key Structure ▸

the more like ~, the better
그 사람이 모국어 화자에 가까우면 가까울수록 더욱더 좋다

내용 외국어 습득의 두 방법.

set about 착수하다, 시작하다(= start, begin)
imitate [ímitèit] 모방하다, 본받다(= mimic, copy)
native speaker 원어민, 모국어 화자(話者)
more or less 다소간(의)

플러스 문법정리 39

주의해야 할 부정대명사의 용법

one ~, the other(s) ~ : 두 사람, 물건이 있을 때 그중의 하나는 one, 나머지 하나는 the other를 사용하여 부른다. 셋 이상의 정해진 수에서 하나는 one, 나머지가 복수일 경우는 the others를 사용한다. (the의 쓰임에 유의)

a. I have two brothers : one is a singer, the other an actor.
b. There were three participants in the debate : one was for the plan, the others against it.

the one ~, the other ~ : 전자, 후자를 가리킬 때 사용한다.

c. Drinking and smoking are both injurious : the one, however, less than the other.
   (the one = the former, the other = the latter)

one thing, ~ another : 'A와 B는 전혀 별개이다'는 뜻으로 쓰이는 부정대명사.

d. Knowing is one thing, and teaching is quite another.

one ~, another ~ : 정해지지 않은 수에서 막연히 '하나는 ~, 또 하나는 ~'의 뜻을 표현할 때 쓰이는 부정대명사.

e. There were many disabled men. One was blind, another was deaf, a third was lame.

해석 a. 나에게 두 형이 있는데 한 분은 가수이고 또 한 분은 연기자이다. b. 그 토론에 세 명이 참가했는데 한 사람은 그 계획에 찬성하였고, 나머지 두 사람은 반대하였다. c. 음주도 흡연도 해로운데, 전자는 후자보다는 덜 해롭다. d. 아는 것과 가르치는 것은 전혀 별개의 문제이다. e. 불구자가 많이 있었는데 한 사람은 눈이 멀었고, 또 다른 사람은 귀가 먹었고, 또 다른 사람은 다리를 절었다.

094 Language erects as many barriers as bridges. There is a deep-rooted tendency to dislike, to distrust, and to regard as inferior individuals or groups speaking a language different from one's own, just as one considers the monkey a lower animal because it has no language at all. Culture now is transmitted largely by language; **the greater** the language difference, **the greater** the cultural distance.

Key Structure •

1 to dislike, to distrust, and to regard ~
   자신의 언어와 다른 언어를 말하는 사람들이나 집단들을 싫어하고 불신하며 열등한 것으로 여기다
   • 동사 모두 individuals or groups를 목적어로 가짐.

2 regard as inferior individuals or groups ~
   = regard individuals or groups ~ as inferior

3 the greater **the language difference** (is), the greater **the cultural distance** (is)
   언어의 차이가 크면 클수록, 문화적 거리[차이]도 그만큼 커진다

내용 언어는 인간을 이어 주는 교량 역할도 하지만 장벽 역할도 한다.

erect [irékt] 세우다, 만들다(= build, construct, set up)
barrier [bǽriər] 장애물(= bar, drawback, handicap, impediment)
distrust [distrʌ́st] 의심을 품다, 수상히 여기다(= doubt, disbelieve, suspect, question)
inferior [infí(:)əriər] 하위의, 하등의(≒ superior)
transmit [trænsmít] 보내다, 옮기다, 송신하다(= convey, pass on)

Birds of a feather flock together.
깃털이 같은 새는 같이 모인다. (끼리끼리 모인다.)

095 With most men the knowledge that they must ultimately die does not weaken the pleasure in being at present alive. To the poet the world appears still more beautiful as he gazes at flowers that are doomed to wither, at springs that come to too speedy an end. It is not that the thought of universal mortality gives him pleasure, but that he embraces the pleasure **all the more closely because** he knows it cannot be his for long.

Key Structure ▸

1 With most men ~
   • 주어는 knowledge, 동사는 does not weaken이며, that ~ die는 knowledge의 내용을 나타내는 동격명사절.

2 springs that ~ end
   너무 일찍 끝나 버리는 봄철
   • come to an end 끝나다

3 It is not that ~, but that... ~라는 이유에서가 아니라 …라는 이유에서

4 all the more closely because ~ ~이기 때문에 그만큼 더욱더 가까이[꼭]

5 it cannot be his for long 영원히 자신의 것이 될 수는 없다

내용 쾌락과 아름다움은 영원히 존속하지 않는다는 점에서 소중하다.

ultimately [ʌ́ltimitli] 최후로, 마침내(= finally, at last, in the end)
weaken [wíːkən] 약하게 하다(= diminish, enervate, enfeeble, lessen)
gaze at[on, upon] 응시하다
be doomed to (~할) 운명에 처하다
wither [wíðər] 시들다, 말라죽다
mortality [mɔːrtǽləti] 죽을 운명
embrace [imbréis] 안다, 껴안다, 포함하다(= hug, cling to)

096 **The more commonplace** a person is, **the more** will his language bear the stamp of the community in which he lives; the more unique his nature, the more peculiarly his own will be the colouring of his language. He will not only be easily recognized by his voice, but his particular individuality will be recognized in his words and phrases, even through the medium of writing.

Key Structure •

1 bear the stamp of ~ ~의 색조[특징]를 띠다

2 even through the medium of writing 글이라는 매개물을 통해서도

> **내용** 평범한 사람의 언어는 그 사람이 살고 있는 사회의 색조를 띠고, 독특한 사람의 언어는 자신의 개성을 더 잘 나타낸다.

commonplace [kámənplèis] 평범한, 진부한(= ordinary, plain, routine, standard)
bear [bɛər] 지니다, 나르다, 열매를 맺다
unique [juːníːk] 유일한, 독특한, 보통이 아닌(= extraordinary, uncommon)
peculiarly [pikjúːljərli] 특히, 특별히, 기묘하게(= especially, particularly)
coloring, colouring [kʌ́ləriŋ] 색조, 착색
individuality [ìndəvìdʒuǽləti] 개성, 특질
medium [míːdiəm] 매개(물), 매체, 수단(= means)

---

097 It would be unreasonable to suppose that the books that have meant a great deal to me should be precisely those that will mean a great deal to you. But they are books that I feel **the richer for having read,** and I think I should not be quite the man I am if I had not read them.

Key Structure •

1 It would be unreasonable (if we were) to suppose ~
   • 가정법 과거 구문으로 to suppose는 if절을 대신하고 있음.

2 those that will ~ = the books that will ~
   • those는 지시대명사로 that의 선행사로 쓰이고 있음.

3 books that I feel the richer for having read 내가 읽었기 때문에 더욱더 풍요로움을 느끼는 책들
   • that은 read의 목적어로 쓰인 관계대명사.
   • feel (all) the richer for ~ ~했기 때문에 더욱더 풍요로움을 느끼다

4 the man I am = the man that[which] I am = what I am
   현재의 나의 모습
   • 이때 주의할 것은 보어로 쓰인 관계대명사 that이나 which 대신에 who는 쓸 수 없음. who는 주어로만 쓰임. 즉, the man who I am은 올바른 표현이 아님.

> **내용** 사람에 따라 책이 갖는 의미는 다르다.

unreasonable [ʌnríːzənəbl] 비합리적인, 부당한(= irrational, absurd, senseless)
precisely [prisáisli] 틀림없이, 정확히(= accurately, unambiguously, definitely)

플러스 문법정리 40

all the+비교급+for[because]와 none the+비교급+for[because]

all the+비교급+for[because] : 〜이기 때문에 더욱더 …하다
none the+비교급+for[because] : 〜임에도 불구하고 마찬가지로 …하다

a. I love him all the better for his faults.
b. I love him all the better because he has faults.

위와 같은 예문에서 주의할 점은 all the better는 '잘못이 있는 만큼 더욱더~'라는 뜻이므로, all은 생략할 수 있지만 정도를 나타내는 the는 생략할 수 없다는 점이다.

c. I love him none the less for his faults.
d. I love him none the less because he has faults.

이 예문들은 '약점이 있음에도 불구하고 결코 덜 ~하지 않는다'의 뜻을 지니며 none이나 the를 전혀 생략할 수 없다. 이탤릭체 부분은 'all the same for / because'의 뜻으로 바꾸어 쓸 수도 있다.

해석 a. b. 나는 그가 잘못이 있기 때문에 그만큼 더 좋아한다.   c. d. 나는 그가 잘못이 있지만 마찬가지로 좋아한다.

098

The decline of the village is one of the tragedies of English history, **no less tragic because** it is largely unrecognized. Now that this decline is stopped, and there are prospects of revival, it is essential to comprehend the new situation and to revive the village in a manner that is consistent with modern conditions and trends.

Key Structure

1 no less tragic because ~
   〜이라는 이유로 결코 덜 비참한 것이 아닌

2 Now that ~   이제 〜한 이상
   • Now that = Since (이유를 나타내는 접속사)

3 in a manner that is consistent with ~
   〜과 일치하는 방식으로
   • that은 주격 관계대명사.

내용 시골의 복구는 현대 상황에 맞게끔 이루어져야 한다.

decline [dikláin] 쇠퇴, 퇴보, 하락(= falling off, deterioration)
tragic [trǽdʒik] 비극적인, 비참한
prospect [práspèkt] 가망, 예상, 기대(= expectation, likelihood, probability)
revival [riváivəl] 재생, 부활
comprehend [kàmprihénd] 이해하다, 깨닫다(= understand, recognize)
consistent [kənsístənt] 일치하는, 조화를 이루는(= be in harmony with)
trend [trend] 경향, 추세(= mode, fashion, tendency)

122

099 They had never known defeat, **much less** occupation. The people, then, had really no idea as to how they should conduct themselves in a situation that lacked all precedent.

Key Structure •

1 much less ~
~은 두말할 필요도 없고
• much less = let alone = to say nothing of = not to mention = not to speak of

2 as to ~ = concerning ~
~에 관하여

내용 전례가 없는 상황에 처해서 어찌할 바를 모르는 국민들.

defeat [difíːt] 패배, 실패(= failure, conquest)
occupation [àkjəpéiʃən] 점령, 직업, 거주(= conquest, job)
lack [læk] 결여되다, 부족하다(= be lacking in, be devoid of, be short of)
precedent [présədənt] 선례, 전례, 관례 ⓥ precede

플러스 문법정리 41

much more와 much less

A, much more B는 'B는 두말할 필요도 없이 A도 ~한다'라는 뜻의 긍정의 표현이고(즉, A도 하지만 B는 더 잘한다), A, much less B는 'B는 고사하고 A도 ~하지 못한다'라는 부정의 뜻을 갖는 표현이다(즉, A도 못하지만 B는 더 못한다). 두 표현 모두 not to speak of, not to mention, to say nothing of, let alone 등으로 바꾸어 쓸 수 있다.

a. He can speak German, much more English.
= He can speak German, let alone English.

b. He cannot speak English, much less German.
= He cannot speak English, not to mention German.
not to say(~라고까지는 (말) 못해도)와 혼동해서는 안 된다.

c. She is a good actress, not to say an excellent actress.

해석 a. 그는 독일어를 말할 줄 안다. 영어는 두말할 것도 없고. b. 그는 영어를 말할 줄 모른다. 독일어는 고사하고.
　　 c. 그녀는 특출난 배우라고까지는 말 못해도 우수한 배우이다.

100

To think of the future in relation to the present is essential to civilization. **The commonest workman** in a civilized country does this. Instead of spending all the money he earns as fast as he earns it, he will, if an intelligent man, save a large part of it as a provision against future want.

Key Structure

1 **The commonest workman ~**
   제아무리 평범한 일꾼이라도 ~
   • 최상급에 '양보'의 뜻이 들어 있는 표현.
      e.g. The wisest man cannot know everything.
         아무리 현명한 사람도 모든 일을 다 알 수는 없다.

2 **does this** = thinks of the future in relation to the present

3 **if (he is) an intelligent man**

내용 미래를 현재와 관련시켜 생각하는 것은 문명에 필수적이다.

in relation to (~과) 관련하여(= with respect to, in terms of)
provision against (~에 대한) 대비, 준비
want [wɑnt] 필요, 소용(= need)

101

The soul of a journey is a liberty, perfect liberty, to think, feel, do, just as one pleases. We go on a journey chiefly to be free of all impediments and of all inconvenience; to leave ourselves behind, **much more** to get rid of others.

Key Structure

1 **to think ~**
   • liberty를 꾸며 주는 형용사적 역할을 하는 부정사.

2 **chiefly to be free of ~** 주로 ~을 벗어나기 위하여

3 **to leave ~**
   • to be free of처럼 부사적 역할을 하는 부정사로서 동사 go on a journey로 연결됨.

4 **much more ~** = still more = let alone ~은 두말할 필요도 없고

내용 여행의 본질은 완벽한 자유를 얻는 것이다.

soul [soul] 영혼, 정수, 핵(= essence, core)
impediment [impédəmənt] 장애(물), 장벽(= obstacle, obstruction, hindrance)
inconvenience [ìnkənvíːnjəns] 불편(한 것), 부자유
get rid of 제거하다, 없애다(= remove, do away with, abolish)

102 **Just as** it is impossible to see the shape of a wood when you are journeying through the middle of it, **so** it is really impossible for us to see what our age is like. Till we have got out of the wood, and can see it as a whole, we cannot judge which of its trees are most essential to its general shape.

Key Structure

1 **Just as ~, so...**
~인 것처럼 (마찬가지로) …이다

2 **what our age is like**
우리 시대가 어떠한 모습인지를
• what은 원래 like의 목적어로 쓰인 의문사.

3 **Till we have got ~**
• 이 절의 동사 현재완료형은 원래는 미래완료형이지만, 시간을 나타내는 부사절에서는 미래완료가 쓰일 수 없으므로 현재완료로 나타냄.

내용 숲속에서 숲의 전체를 볼 수 없듯이 우리 시대 속에서 그 전체를 보는 것은 불가능하다.

journey through (~을) 통해 여행하다, 나아가다
as a whole 전체로(서)
essential [əsénʃəl] 본질적인, 필수의(= indispensable, distinctive)

플러스 문법정리 42

미래를 대신하는 현재와 미래완료를 대신하는 현재완료
시간이나 조건을 나타내는 부사절에서는 미래 대신 현재, 미래완료 대신 현재완료를 사용한다. 그러나 명사절에서는 그렇지 않음에 유의하자(예문 c. 참조).

a. If he comes back now, I will pardon him.
b. When you have finished the work, you may go home.
c. I don't know clearly when he will come back. (명사절)
d. I will tell him so when he comes back. (부사절)

해석 a. 그가 지금 돌아오면 그를 용서하겠다. b. 그 일이 끝나면 집에 가도 좋다. c. 그가 언제 돌아올지 잘 모르겠다. d. 그가 돌아오면 그렇게 말해야지.

103   Ambition may be a very good or a very bad thing, according to its object. **As** it is the powder in the gun that sends the ball whizzing on its way for good or for evil, **so** it is ambition that gives energy and movement to the life. It is **as** important to have ambition directed rightly **as** it is to have a loaded gun pointed in the right way; but a life without ambition is of little more use than a gun without powder.

Key Structure ▸

1   As it is ~, so it is... = Just as it is ~, so it is...

2   it is the powder in the gun that ~
   - it ~ that 강조 구문으로 the powder in the gun이 강조되었음.

3   It is as important to ~ as it is...
   ~하는 것은 …하는 것만큼 중요하다
   - 동등비교 구문.

4   to have ambition directed rightly
   야망을 올바른 방향으로 잡다
   - have+목적어+p.p. 구조로 have는 사역동사 역할을 함.
   - **cf.** I had my picture taken yesterday.

5   is of little more use than ~
   ~보다 별로 더 유용하지도 않다
   - of use = useful, of no use = useless
   - of more use = more useful, of little more use = little more useful

내용   야망은 그 목적에 따라 좋은 것일 수도 있고 나쁜 것일 수도 있다.

ambition [æmbíʃən] 야망, 야심, 큰 뜻
powder [páudər] 화약(= gun powder)
ball [bɔːl] 탄환
whiz [hwiz] (탄환이) 핑하고 날다
loaded gun 장전된 총, 탄환을 넣은 총

플러스 문법정리 43

It is ~ that 강조 구문에 의한 강조

아래의 예문 a.에서 동사를 제외한 밑줄 친 부분은 It is ~ that 표현을 이용하여 각각 b.~e.처럼 강조 구문으로 바꾸어 쓸 수 있다.

a. I met her in the library yesterday.
b. It was I that[who] met her in the library yesterday.
c. It was her that I met in the library yesterday.
d. It was in the library that I met her yesterday.
e. It was yesterday that I met her in the library.

동사의 강조는 'do'를 이용한다.

f. I did meet her in the library yesterday.

해석 a. 나는 그녀를 어제 도서관에서 만났다.   b. 어제 도서관에서 그녀를 만난 것은 나였다.
      c. 내가 어제 도서관에서 만난 사람은 그녀였다.   d. 내가 어제 그녀를 만난 곳은 도서관에서였다.
      e. 내가 도서관에서 그녀를 만난 것은 어제였다.   f. 나는 어제 도서관에서 그녀를 정말 만났다.

Care killed the cat.
근심이 고양이를 죽였다. (근심은 몸에 해롭다.)

10 · 부정비교구문 Negative Comparison

01 no more ∼ than… = not ∼ any more than… :
∼이 아닌 것은 …이 아닌 것과 마찬가지이다 (양자 부정)

  a. A whale is no more a fish than a horse is.
= A whale is not a fish any more than a horse is.
고래가 물고기가 아닌 것은 말이 물고기가 아닌 것과 마찬가지이다.(말이 물고기가 아니듯 고래도 물고기가 아니다.)

  b. I am no more mad than you are.
= I am not mad any more than you are.
내가 미치지 않은 것은 당신이 미치지 않은 것과 마찬가지이다.

  c. He can no more swim than a hammer can.
= He cannot swim any more than a hammer can.
그가 헤엄을 치지 못하는 것은 망치가 헤엄을 치지 못하는 것과 마찬가지이다.

02 no less ∼ than… = as ∼ as… : …과 마찬가지로 ∼하다 (양자 긍정)

She is no less attractive than her sisters.
= She is as attractive as her sisters.
= She is at least as attractive as her sisters.
그녀는 언니들만큼 매력이 있다.
> *cf.* She is not less attractive than her sisters. 그녀는 적어도 언니들만큼 매력이 있다.

03 no more than = only

  a. She has no more than 5 million won.
= She has only 5 million won.
그녀는 500만 원밖에 가지고 있지 않다.

not more than = at most

  b. She has not more than 5 million won.
= She has 5 million won at most.
그녀는 기껏해야 500만 원을 가지고 있을 뿐이다.

no less than = as much[many] as

c. She has no less than 5 million won.
= She has as much as 5 million won.
그녀는 500만 원이나 가지고 있다.

not less than = at least

d. She has not less than 5 millon won.
= She has at least 5 million won.
그녀는 적어도 500만 원은 가지고 있다.
• (a), (b)는 생각보다 적다는 뜻이고 (c), (d)는 생각보다 많다는 뜻임.

04 **no + 비교급 + than... = as + 반대의 원급 + as**

a. He is no wiser than his wife.
= He is as foolish as his wife.
그는 아내만큼 어리석다.

b. He is no better than yesterday.
= He is as bad as yesterday.
그는 어제와 마찬가지로 좋지 않다.

104 Again and again I find myself arguing passionately with men who are not open to argument and whom I know I could **no more** convert by argument **than** I could turn a stone into butter.

Key Structure

men ~ whom I know I could no more ~ than ~
돌을 버터로 바꿀 수 없는 것처럼 논쟁으로 변화시킬 수 없음을 내가 아는 사람들
• no more ~ than 구문. (양자 부정)

내용 논쟁에 의해 변화될 수 없는 사람과 다툴 때가 자주 있다.

again and again 반복해서(= repeatedly, over and over again)
argue [áːrgjuː] 주장하다, 논하다(= debate, dispute, fight)
passionately [pǽʃənitli] 열렬히, 열의에 차서(= ardently, eagerly, vehemently)
convert [kánvəːrt] 바꾸다, 개조하다(= change, fashion)

105 We are **no more** responsible for the evil thoughts which pass throughout our minds **than** a scarecrow for the birds which fly over the seed-plot he has to guard; the sole responsibility in each case is to prevent them from settling.

Key Structure

1 We are no more responsible ~ than ~
   허수아비가 자신이 지켜야 하는 묘상 위에 날아드는 새들에 대해 책임이 없는 것처럼, 우리도 우리 마음에 생기는 나쁜 생각에 책임이 없다
   • no more ~ than 구문. (양자 부정)

2 prevent them from settling
   그것들이 자리 잡는 것을 막다
   • them은 evil thoughts와 birds를 각각 지칭.

내용 인간의 주된 임무는 나쁜 생각이 정신 속에 자리 잡지 않도록 하는 것이다.

be responsible for (~에 대하여) 책임을 지다
scarecrow [skέərkròu] 허수아비
seed-plot 묘상, 모판(= seedbed)
guard [gɑːrd] 보호하다, 지키다(= defend, protect, keep watch on)
sole [soul] 유일한(= only)
settle [sétl] 자리 잡다, 내려앉다, 놓다, 해결하다

106 If a man writes a diary which he feels sure that nobody will ever see except himself, he is probably perfectly truthful. There is no motive for being otherwise. He is **no more** ashamed of recording his actions, good and bad, just as they happened, **than** of seeing himself in the bath.

Key Structure ▸

1 **There is no motive for being otherwise.**
달리 행동해야 할 동기가 없다.
• being otherwise = being other than perfectly truthful = being not perfectly truthful

2 **He is no more ashamed of ~ than of...**
그는 …하지 않는 것처럼 ~을 부끄러워하지 않는다
• than of seeing = than he is ashamed of seeing

내용 비밀스럽게 쓰는 일기에는 모든 일을 그대로 기록한다.

motive [móutiv] 동기, 원인(= reason)
record [rikɔ́ːrd] 기록하다, 녹음하다, 녹화하다 ⓝ [rékɔːd] 기록, 음반

플러스 문법정리 44

otherwise의 여러 가지 뜻
otherwise의 원래의 뜻은 in other ways이나, 오늘날에는 형용사, 대명사, 부사 등의 기능을 가진 단어로 쓰이고 있으며 이에 따라 그 뜻도 차이가 난다.

1. 형용사로 쓰인 경우 : 보통은 서술적 용법으로 쓰여 보어 역할을 한다.
   a. Some are wise and some are otherwise. (= not wise)
   b. Some things can't be otherwise.

2. 대명사로 쓰인 경우 : 앞의 명사의 의미와 반대적인 내용을 나타내며 '~이나 그 밖의 것'이라는 뜻을 가진다.
   c. There are friendly people and otherwise. (= unfriendly people)

3. 부사로 쓰인 경우 : in a different way의 뜻을 지닌다.
   d. I think otherwise.
   e. How can I do otherwise?

4. 가정법절에서 접속부사로 쓰인 경우 : 앞에 나온 절의 뜻을 반대로 가정한다.
   f. He worked hard, otherwise he would have failed.
   • otherwise ┌ = or / or else
               └ = if he had not worked hard

해석 a. 어떤 자들은 현명하고 어떤 자들은 그렇지 않다. b. 그렇게 될 수밖에 없는 일도 있다. c. 친절한 자들도 있고, 그렇지 않은 자들도 있다. d. 나는 달리 생각한다. e. 내가 어찌 달리 행한단 말인가? f. 그는 열심히 공부하였다. 그렇지 않았더라면 그는 떨어졌을지도 모른다.

107 Thinking is a natural thing, just as natural as breathing or nutrition. This means that one does **not** learn to think **any more than** he learns to breathe or to assimilate food. No one can learn to live; he can only learn to live well. The same is true of thinking. You do not learn to think; what you learn to do is to improve your thinking.

Key Structure

1 **one does** not **learn** ~ any more than **he learns...**
    사람이 …을 배우지 않는 것처럼 ~을 배우지 않는다

2 **The same** is true of **thinking.** = **The same** applies to **thinking.**
    생각에도 똑같은 이야기가 적용된다.

  내용 우리가 배우는 것은 생각하는 것이 아니라, 생각을 개선하는 방법이다.

nutrition [njuːtríʃən] 영양, 영양 공급, 자양물
assimilate [əsíməlèit] 흡수하다, 동화시키다(= digest)
be true of (~에도) 같이 적용되다(= apply to)

108 Resignation, however, has also its part to play in the conquest of happiness, and it is a part **no less** essential **than** that played by effort. The wise man, though he will not sit down under preventable misfortunes, will not waste time and emotion upon such as are unavoidable.

Key Structure

1 **it is a part** no less **essential** than ~
    ~만큼 필수적인 역할이다
    • no less ~ than = as ~ as (양자 긍정)
    • no more ~ than과 반대로 양쪽의 비교 대상을 모두 긍정하는 비교 구문.
    e.g. She is no less beautiful than her sister. = She is as beautiful as her sister.
        그녀는 언니 못지않게 미인이다.

2 **than that played by effort** 노력이 행하는 역할보다
    • that = the part

3 **such as are unavoidable** 피할 수 없는 것들
    • as는 유사관계대명사로 주어로 쓰였음.
    • such = such misfortunes

내용 행복의 정복에는 단념도 일익을 담당한다.

resignation [rèzignéiʃən] 사직, 포기, 체념(= giving up, abandonment)
conquest [kánkwest] 정복, 획득(= triumph, subjugation, occupation) ⓥ conquer 정복하다
preventable [privéntəbl] 막을 수 있는(= avoidable, conquerable)

플러스 문법정리 45

유사관계대명사 as
유사관계대명사 as는 the same, such가 쓰인 구문에 주로 쓰이고, 주어나 목적어로 쓰인다.

a. Keep such company as will benefit you. (주어)
b. This is the same watch as I have lost. (목적어)
cf. This is the same watch that I have lost. (이 예문의 that은 as와 의미 차이가 있는 관계대명사임.)

해석 a. 너에게 도움이 되는 친구를 사귀어라. b. 이것은 내가 잃어버린 것과 같은 종류의 시계이다.
    cf. 이것은 내가 잃어버린 바로 그 시계이다.

---

109 Thinking is as unnatural and laborious an activity for human beings as walking on two legs is for monkeys. We seldom do more of it than we have to; and our disinclination to think is generally greatest at the times when we are feeling the most comfortable. Since this human antipathy to the labor of thought is **no less** manifest in public life **than** it is in private affairs, mankind does not do very much of its historical thinking in easy and prosperous times.

Key Structure ▸

1 Thinking is as ~ as... 생각하는 것은 …만큼 ~하다 (동등비교 구문)

2 we have to = we have to do it (대부정사 구문)

3 no less ~ than...
   …에서만큼 마찬가지로 ~하다 (양자 긍정)

내용 생각하는 것은 인간에게 부자연스럽고 힘이 드는 일이다.

laborious [ləbɔ́ːriəs] 힘든, 어려운, 성가신(= hard, tough, strenuous)
disinclination [disìnklənéiʃən] 싫증, 싫음(= disliking, abhorrence)
antipathy [æntípəθi] 반감, 혐오(≒ sympathy 공감, 동정) cf. apathy 냉담, 무관심(= abhorrence)
manifest [mǽnəfèst] 명백한, 분명한(= evident, clear) ⓥ 분명하게 하다
prosperous [práspərəs] 부유한, 성공한, 번영하는(= thriving, affluent, wealthy)

110 The first subject that attracted my attention was religion. For it seemed to me of the greatest importance to decide whether this world I lived in was the only one I had to think about or whether I must look upon it as **no more than** a place of trial which was to prepare me for a life to come.

Key Structure ▸

1 **For it seemed ~**
   • for는 이유를 나타내는 등위접속사

2 **of the greatest** importance
   = the most important; of importance = important

3 **this world** (which) **I lived in**   내가 사는 세상
   • lived를 현재시제인 '사는'으로 번역함에 유의.

4 **look upon it as ~**
   그것을 ~으로 여기다
   • look upon A as B = think of A as B = regard A as B = consider A (to be) B
   • no more than ~ = only ~

5 **a place of trial which was to ~ come**
   나에게 앞으로 다가올 삶에 대한 준비를 해 주게끔 할 시련의 장소

   내용 내가 종교에 관심을 가진 이유.

trial [tráiəl] 시련, 고생, 시험, 재판(= affliction, hardship, attempt, case)
no more than 단지(= only)
a life to come 앞으로 다가올 삶

플러스 문법정리 | 46

of+추상명사 = 형용사

of wisdom = wise	of use = useful
of help = helpful	of no use = useless
of service = serviceable	of kindness = kind
of importance = important	of consequence = consequent
of essence = essential	of benefit = beneficial

a. He is a man of wisdom. = He is a wise man.
b. I would be glad to be of service to you.
= I would be glad if I were serviceable to you.

'of+형용사'는 부사 기능을 가진다.

of old = in the past   of late = lately, recently

해석 a. 그는 지혜로운 사람이다.   b. 당신께 도움이 된다면 기쁘겠습니다.

111 Friendship is above reason, for though you find virtues in a friend, he was your friend before you found them. It is a gift that we offer because we must; to give it as the reward of virtue would be to set a price upon it, and those who do that have no friendship to give. If you choose your friends on the ground that you are virtuous and want virtuous company, you are **no nearer** to true friendship **than** if you choose them for commercial reasons.

Key Structure ▸

1 **be above reason** 이성[논리]을 초월하다

2 **to give it as ~ would be ~** = if we were to give it as ~, it would be ~
우정을 미덕에 대한 보답으로 주는 것은 그것에 값을 매기는 것이 될 것이다 (가정법 과거 구문)

3 **on the ground that ~** = for the reason that ~ ~라는 이유로

4 **you are no** nearer ~ than... = you are as far away from ~ as...
…만큼 ~에서 멀어진다
• than if you ~ = than you are near to true friendship if you ~
• than 이하에서는 if절만이 나와 있고 주절은 생략되어 있음.

내용 우정은 이성을 초월하는 것이며, 친구의 미덕에 대한 보답으로 주는 것이 아니다.

reason [ríːzn] 이성, 이치, 사려, 논리(= logic, argument)
virtue [vəːrtʃuː] 미덕, 덕행(= decency, rectitude, goodness | ≒ vice) ⓐ virtuous
reward [riwɔːrd] 보수, 보상
set a price upon ~에 값을 매기다
company [kʌ́mpəni] 동료, 교제, 회사
commercial [kəmə́ːrʃəl] 상업적인, 영리적인

플러스 문법정리 47

가정법 구문의 if절을 대신하는 to부정사
to부정사가 가정법 구문의 if절을 대신하는 경우가 종종 있는데, 주절의 동사 시제를 보고 가정법 과거나 가정법 과거완료 중 어느 것으로 바꾸어 쓸 것인가를 판단해야 한다.

a. To hear him talk, you would be greatly surprised.
= If you heard him talk, you would be greatly surprised.

b. To say so would subject you to public ridicule.
= If you were to say so, it would subject you to public ridicule.

c. You would have done the same thing to be in my place.
= You would have done the same thing, if you had been in my place.

해석 a. 그가 말하는 것을 들으면 매우 놀랄 것이다. b. 그렇게 말하면 사람들의 웃음거리가 될 것이다.
c. 내 입장이었더라면 당신도 똑같이 했을 것이다.

112 The man who is contented to be only himself, and therefore less a self, is in prison. Literary experience heals the wound, without undermining the privilege, of individuality. In reading great literature I become a thousand men and yet remain myself. Here, as in worship, in love, in moral action, and in knowing, I transcend myself; and am **never more** myself **than** when I do.

Key Structure ▶

1 be less a self
   자기 이하이다

2 Literary experience heals the wound, ~ privilege, of individuality.
   문학 서적을 읽는 경험은 개성의 특권을 손상시키지 않고 개성의 상처를 고쳐 준다.
   • wound와 privilege는 둘 다 of individuality로 연결됨.

3 I become a thousand men and yet remain myself.
   나는 천 명의 (다양한) 사람이 되지만, 나 자신인 것에는 변함이 없다.

4 Here, as in worship, ~
   신앙에 있어서처럼 이것에서
   • Here = In reading great literature

5 I am never more myself than when I do.
   = I am never more myself than I am myself when I do.
   내가 이렇게 할 때보다 더 나 자신이 되는 경우는 결코 없다.
   • when I do = when I transcend myself

내용 위대한 문학 작품을 읽을 때 사람은 자신을 초월하고, 이때에야 진정한 자신이 될 수 있다.

contented [kənténtid] 만족한(= satisfied, pleased)
literary [lítərèri] 문학의, 저작의, 문필업의
heal [hi:l] (병을) 고치다, 치유하다(= cure, nurse, rejuvenate, revitalize, treat)
wound [wu:nd; waund] 상처, 부상
undermine [ʌndərmáin] 토대를 허물다, 몰래 해치다(= destroy, dig under, ruin, burrow under)
privilege [prívəlidʒ] 특권, 명예, 특전(= advantage, prerogative, entitlement)
worship [wɔ́:rʃip] 숭배, 예배(= adoration, deification, reverence, veneration)
transcend [trænsénd] 초월하다(= surpass, rise above, outdo)

113 In the earlier days of the world human beings, **little better than** wild animals, lived for themselves alone, in the caves and forests, fighting with nature and other human beings and animals for their existence. Their wants were few, **little more than** food for the day, and a safe place in which to sleep at night.

Key Structure •

1 little better than wild animals

= no better than wild animals = as good as wild animals

야생 동물이나 거의 다름없는

2 Their wants were few

그들이 필요로 하는 것[부족한 것]은 별로 없었다

• their wants 그들이 필요로 하는 것들, 그들에게 부족한 것들

내용 원시시대의 인간은 생존을 위해 야생 동물이나 다른 인간과 싸우며 살았다.

wants [wɑnt] 결핍, 부족, 필요
little better than (~이나) 다름없는
food for the day 하루 먹을 식량

After a storm (comes) a calm.
폭풍 후에 고요가 온다. (고생 끝에 낙이 온다.)

11 부정구문 | Negation

01 not ~ but... : ~가 아니라 …이다

a. He is not a scholar but a politician.
그는 학자가 아니라 정치가이다.

b. It is not helps but obstacles, not facilities but difficulties that make men.
인간을 만드는 것은 도움이 아니라 역경이고, 편익이 아니라 어려움이다.

02 부정의 뜻이 들어 있는 표현

a. No information has been obtained so far.
지금까지 어떠한 정보[소식]도 얻어진 게 없다.

b. A wild rumor appeared from nowhere.
뜬소문이 난데없이 나타났다.
• from nowhere 난데없이

c. She will get nowhere, if she continues doing so.
그녀가 그런 식으로 일을 계속하면 아무런 효과도 얻지 못할 것이다.
• get nowhere 아무런 효과도 얻지 못하다

03 all / every / both + not : 부분 부정 (partial negation)

a. All that glitters is not gold.
반짝인다고 모든 것이 금은 아니다.

b. Every man cannot be a poet.
누구나가 다 시인이 되는 것은 아니다.

c. Both of his parents were not interested in his education.
부모가 다 그의 교육에 관심을 갖지는 않았다.

04 not + always / necessarily / altogether / quite : 반드시 ~은 아니다 (부분 부정)

a. To be successful does not always mean to get riches, honors, and power.
성공한다는 것이 반드시 부와 명예와 권력을 얻는 것을 의미하지는 않는다.

b. It does not necessarily follow that honesty is the best policy.
정직이 꼭 최상의 방편이라는 이야기는 아니다.

c. She is not altogether happy.
그녀가 전적으로 행복한 것은 아니다.

05 not at all / not in the least / by no means / not by any means / under no circumstances / in no way : 전혀 ~ 않다 (전체 부정)

a. She is not at all happy.
그녀는 전혀 행복하지 않다.

b. He is not in the least satisfied with the result.
그는 그 결과에 대해 전혀 만족하고 있지 않다.

c. This problem is by no means worth a meticulous research.
이 문제는 꼼꼼하게 연구할 만한 가치가 전혀 없다.

• not at all = not in the least = by no means = never

114 The truly rich society is **not** the one that goes on piling up economic wealth as an end itself, **but** the one that uses its wealth as the foundation on which to build a rich and many-sided culture. From this point of view, a country like ancient Greece, in which hardly anybody could afford more than one good meal a day, was richer than the United States at the height of its prosperity.

Key Structure

1 the foundation on which to build ~ = the foundation on which we can build ~
   그 위에 우리가 ~을 세울 수 있는 기초

2 hardly **anybody could afford** ~
   거의 누구도 ~할 여유가 없었다
   • afford more than one good meal a day 하루에 충분한 식사 한 끼를 먹을 여유가 있다

3 **at the height of its prosperity**
   번영[부]의 절정에 선

   내용 진정으로 부유한 사회는 부를 풍요롭고 다양한 문화를 건설하는 기초로 사용하는 사회이다.

pile up 쌓다, 쌓아 올리다(= accumulate, store up)
foundation [faundéiʃən] 기초, 근거(= base, basis, cornerstone)
many-sided 다양한, 다방면에 걸친(= various, varied)
afford [əfɔ́ːrd] ~할 여유가 있다, 공급하다
height [hait] 정상, 꼭대기, 높이(= summit, top)
prosperity [prɑspérəti] 번영, 부(= affluence, wealth, success)

플러스 문법정리 48

명사가 과거분사화된 준분사(유사분사)
명사가 과거분사화되어 다른 명사를 꾸미거나 보어로 쓰이는 경우, 이것을 준분사라 부른다.

a. He is a very-talented man. (재능이 많은)
b. She was suffering from one-sided love. (짝사랑)
c. Have you ever seen a two-headed snake? (머리가 둘인 뱀)

이 밖에 다음의 표현들이 있다.

d. a salaried man (월급쟁이)   a bald-headed man (대머리)
    a one-eyed cat (애꾸눈 고양이)   a red-haired girl (빨간머리 소녀)
    a bare-footed boy = a barefoot boy (맨발의 소년)

해석 a. 그는 재능이 매우 많은 사람이다.   b. 그녀는 짝사랑으로 앓고 있었다.   c. 머리가 둘 달린 뱀을 보신 적이 있나요?

115 If you find yourself bored by a book that well-informed people regard as important and readable, be honest with yourself and confess that probably the difficulty is **not** in the book **but** in you. Often a book which now seems dull or difficult will prove easy to grasp and fascinating to read when you are more mature intellectually.

Key Structure ▸

1 a book that well-informed people regard as important and readable
박식한 사람들이 중요하고 읽을 만하다고 여기는 책

2 **prove easy to grasp** 이해하기가 쉬운 것으로 판명되다

3 (prove) **fascinating to read** 읽기에 흥미진진한 것으로 판명되다

내용 훌륭한 책이 재미없다고 느끼는 것은 아직 지적으로 덜 성숙했기 때문이다.

well-informed people 많이 배운 사람들, 박식한 사람들
confess [kənfés] 고백하다, 실토하다(= own up, make a clean breast of)
grasp [græsp] 이해하다, 포착하다(= understand)
fascinating [fǽsənèitiŋ] 매혹적인, 흥미진진한(= attractive, captivating, enticing, mesmerizing)
mature [mətʃúər] 성숙한, 어른다운(= mellow, well-developed, grown-up, nubile, of age)
intellectually [intəléktʃuəli] 지적으로, 지적인 면에서

116 Nowadays the only news was that which passed from mouth to mouth. Short of paper, short of ink, short of men, the newspapers had suspended publication after the siege began, and the wildest rumors appeared from **nowhere** and swept through the town.

Key Structure ▸

1 the only news was that which ~ 유일한 뉴스는 ~였다 (that = the news)

2 Short of paper, ~ = As they were short of paper, ~ 종이가 부족하여

3 the wildest rumors ~ town 아주 엉뚱한 소문이 난데없이 나타나 마을을 휩쓸고 다녔다

내용 신문 발행이 중단된 상황에서 출처를 알 수 없는 뜬소문의 위력.

from mouth to mouth 입에서 입으로
suspend [səspénd] 중지하다, 연기하다, 매달다(= discontinue, freeze, postpone, hang)
publication [pʌ̀bləkéiʃən] 출판, 발행

siege [siːdʒ] 포위, 공격(= blockade)
wild rumors 뜬소문, 헛소문
from nowhere 난데없이, 출처를 알 수 없는 곳에서
sweep through (~을) 휩쓸고 다니다

플러스 문법정리 49

관사가 생략된 표현

보통명사는 그 앞에 관사를 붙여서 사용해야 하지만 밀접한 관계를 이루는 어휘들 간에는 관사가 흔히 생략된다.

a. They were living from hand to mouth. (하루 벌어 하루 먹다)
b. He was begging from door to door. (이 집에서 저 집으로)
c. We must live with others hand in hand. (손에서 손잡고)
d. They were walking along the street shoulder to shoulder. (어깨를 맞대고)
e. The couple were seated arm in arm. (팔짱을 끼고)
f. Read through the book from cover to cover. (철저히)
g. She was shivering from top to bottom. (머리끝부터 발끝까지)
h. This treasure has been handed down from generation to generation. (먼 옛날부터)

해석 a. 그들은 하루 벌어 하루 먹고 있었다. b. 그는 문전걸식을 하였다. c. 우리는 서로 손잡고 (협력하여) 살아가야 한다. d. 그들은 어깨를 맞대고 거리를 걷고 있었다. e. 그 한 쌍은 서로 팔짱을 끼고 앉아 있었다. f. 그 책을 철저히 읽으시오. g. 그녀는 온몸을 와들와들 떨고 있었다. h. 이 보물은 먼 옛날부터 전해 내려오고 있다.

---

117 **No** book will teach you how to write. **No** amount of reading will teach you how to write. Reading is essential, and a practical book can help; but unless you have the germ of the writer in you, the unbreakable will to write, you will get **nowhere**. What is more, if you are to make a success of writing, you will have to work.

Key Structure ▸

1 unless **you have** ~ = if you do not have ~

2 **the germ of the writer** 작가로서의 싹, 기초
   • the writer 작가 기질[소질]
   cf. the patriot 애국심(= patriotism), the beggar 거지 근성, the poet 시심(詩心) 등

3 **What is more** = Moreover
   더군다나, 게다가

4 **if you are to make a success of writing**
   만약 당신이 글 쓰는 것으로 성공하고자 바란다면
   • are to make ~ '의도를 나타내는 'be+to부정사' 구문.
   • make A of B B에서 A를 만들어 내다

내용 작가로서 성공은 글을 쓰려는 의지와 노력에 달려 있다.

germ [dʒəːrm] 싹, 근원, 병균(= basis, root, embryo, source)
unbreakable [ʌnbréikəbl] 깨어지지 않는, 무너뜨릴 수 없는(= indestructible, ineradicable, strong)
will [wil] 의지, 결심(= determination, commitment, resolution, volition)
get nowhere 성공하지 못하다, 효과가 없다

---

118 Travelling is always a great joy to everyone. A walk through the suburbs, a trip to the country by train, a voyage by sea or by air to a distant land, each in its own way brings its own particular pleasure to us human beings. We are **not all** lucky enough to be able to visit other countries; some of us have not the time, others of us have not the money.

Key Structure ▸

1 **each** in its own way brings ~
  • each는 앞의 a walk, a trip, a voyage를 가리키는 주어.

2 **We are** not all lucky enough ~
  우리 모두가 ~할 정도로 행운이 있는 것은 아니다 (부분 부정)

내용 여행은 모든 사람에게 항상 기쁨을 준다.

suburbs [sʌ́bəːrb] 교외, 주변(= outskirts, suburbia, fringes)
voyage [vɔ́iidʒ] 배 여행, 항해(= journey, cruise)
in its own way 그 나름대로

플러스 문법정리 50

부분 부정
전체를 나타내는 대명사, 형용사, 부사 등에 not을 붙이면 부분 부정의 뜻을 갖고, '반드시[모두가] ~은 아니다'로 번역한다.

• not + ┌ all, both, every, absolute
　　　　├ completely, perfectly
　　　　└ always, necessarily

a. The rich are not always happy.
b. Both of them are not smart.
c. All that glitters is not gold.
d. Not everybody came to the party.
e. Being rich does not necessarily mean being happy.

해석 a. 부자라고 언제나 행복한 것은 아니다.　b. 그들 둘 모두 명석하지는 않다.　c. 반짝이는 것이라고 다 금은 아니다.
　　 d. 모두가 다 파티에 온 것은 아니었다.　e. 부유함이 반드시 행복함을 뜻하는 것은 아니다.

119 We cannot train ourselves to bear disaster by thinking of all the particular disasters that might happen to us. To do that produces a habit of panic, not of preparation; and we ca**nnot** prepare in detail for **every** disaster that may come. **Nor** can we steel ourselves against a possible sorrow by refusing to enjoy any actual joy. For joy increases the health of the mind, and so strengthens it against the attacks of sorrow.

Key Structure

1 to bear disaster by thinking of ~   ~을 생각함으로써 재해를 참다

2 we cannot prepare ~ for every disaster that may come
우리는 다가올지 모르는 모든 재해를 다 자세히 준비할 수는 없다 (부분 부정)

3 Nor can we steel ourselves against ~   또한 ~에 대하여 견고하게 대비할 수도 없다

4 joy ~ strengthens it against the attacks of sorrow
즐거움은 슬픔의 공격에 대항하여 그것을 강화시킨다 (it = the health of the mind)

내용 닥쳐오는 재난을 미리 걱정하지 말고 현실의 기쁨을 잘 살려 슬픔을 막아 내야 한다.

bear [bɛər] 참다, 견디다, 출산하다(= endure, stand, put up with, tolerate)
disaster [dizǽstər] 천재(지변), 재해, 큰 불행(= calamity, catastrophe, crash, mishap)
panic [pǽnik] 공포, 허둥대기(= alarm, consternation, horror, terror)
preparation [prèpəréiʃən] 준비, 대비
in detail 자세하게, 항목마다
sorrow [sárou] 슬픔, 비애, 비탄(= affliction, anguish, dejection, despondency, grief)

120 If there is one thing that everybody wants to get, it is success. To be successful does **not always** mean to get riches, honors, and power. Some of the richest and most praised and powerful men are perhaps the greatest failures, since they have got what they wanted at the cost of a clean conscience.

Key Structure

1 the most praised men 최고로 칭찬을 받는 사람들

2 at the cost of a clean conscience
= at the expense of a clean conscience = sacrificing a clean conscience
깨끗한 양심을 팔아서

성공한다는 것이 항상 부와 명예와 권력을 얻는 것을 의미하는 것은 아니다.

the greatest failures 최대의 실패자들
at the cost of (~을) 희생하여, (~을) 잃고
conscience [kάnʃəns] 양심 ⓐ conscientious

---

121   Just as good fortune is **not necessarily** all gain, so ill fortune is **not necessarily** all loss. Rome conquered Greece, but Greek civilization overcame Roman civilization and, as a great writer said, "Nothing moves today in Europe which is not Greek in origin."

Key Structure

1   **Just as ~, so...** 마치 ~인 것처럼 …이다
   • 종속상관접속사.

2   **good fortune is not ~ gain** 행운이 모두 다 이득은 아니다

3   **ill fortune is not ~ loss** 불운이 모두 다 손해는 아니다

4   **Nothing ~ which is not Greek in origin.**
   유럽에서 움직이는 것치고 그 기원이 그리스가 아닌 것은 아무것도 없다
   • which 이하는 nothing으로 연결되는 관계대명사절.

내용 행운이 언제나 이득은 아니듯이, 불운이 언제나 손실은 아니다.

gain [gein] 이득, 이익, 증가(= profit, benefit)
loss [lɔ(:)s] 손실, 손실액, 분실, 패배(= deficit, defeat, damage)
conquer [kάŋkər] 정복하다, 극복하다, 이기다(= defeat, get the better of) ⓝ conquest
overcome [òuvərkʌ́m] 극복하다, 압도하다(= overthrow, get over)
origin [ɔ́(:)ridʒin] 근원, 기원, 출처, 원인

---

122   There is much to support the belief that there is a struggle for existence among ideas, and that those tend to prevail which correspond with the changing conditions of humanity. But it does **not** follow **necessarily** that the ideas which prevail are better morally, or even truer to the laws of Nature, than those which fail.

Key Structure •

1 those tend to ~ which... …하는 것은 ~하는 경향이 있다
   • which는 those를 선행사로 갖는 관계대명사. / those = those ideas

2 it does not follow necessarily that ~
   반드시 ~라는 이야기가 뒤따르는 것은 아니다(반드시 ~라는 이야기는 아니다)

3 truer to ~ ~에 더 충실한
   e.g. This picture of his is true to life. 이 그림은 그의 실물 크기 그대로이다.
   This translation is true to the original. 이 번역은 원문에 충실한 번역이다.

내용 힘을 떨치는 생각이 반드시 자연 법칙에 더 충실한 것은 아니다.

struggle for existence 생존 경쟁
prevail [privéil] 유행하다, 유력하다. 효과가 있다(= predominate, preponderate)
correspond with[to] 부합하다, 일치하다, 통신하다
humanity [hju(:)mǽnəti] 인류, 인간성
morally [mɔ́(:)rəli] 도덕적으로, 사실상

플러스 문법정리 51

외치 (Extraposition)
주어가 길거나, 독자의 시선을 끌기 위해 구나 절을 뒤쪽으로 옮기는 형태를 외위치/외치 구조라 한다.

a. It is true that he has failed in the exam.
b. The rumor turned out false that he had killed himself.
c. Nothing can satisfy me that you suggest.
d. He is really a nice man, the man you have talked about.

해석 a. 그가 시험에 떨어진 것은 사실이다.   b. 그가 자살했다는 소문은 거짓으로 드러났다.
c. 당신이 제안하는 어느 것도 나에겐 만족스럽지 않다.   d. 당신이 언급한 그 사람은 진정으로 멋진 사람이다.

---

123 The best way to read fiction is to mix one's reading, **neither** to
favor the present at the expense of the past **nor** to favor the past
at the expense of the present. And do not think that if this policy
is pursued, contemporary work will appear thin and trivial beside
the great work of the past. It is **not necessarily** so at all.

Key Structure •

1 neither to favor A nor to favor B A를 편애하지도 않고 또한 B를 편애하지도 않고

2 appear thin 얄팍하게[사소하게] 보이다

3 beside ~ = compared with ~ ~과 견주어 볼 때

4 It is not necessarily so at all. 상황이 반드시 그런 것은 아니다. (부분 부정)

내용 훌륭한 독서 방법은 고전과 현대 소설을 섞어 읽는 것이다.

fiction [fíkʃən] 소설(문학), 꾸며낸 이야기(= novel)
favor [féivər] 편애하다, 편들다(= go for, like, opt for, think well of) ⓝ 친절한 행위
at the expense of (~을) 희생하여(= at the cost of, sacrificing)
pursue [pərsjú:] 추구하다, 추적하다(= follow, go after, seek) ⓝ pursuit
contemporary [kəntémpərèri] 현대의, 동시대의(= modern)
trivial [tríviəl] 사소한, 평범한, 흔해 빠진(= unimportant, trifling, trite, worthless)

124 Language **never** stands still. Every language, until it dies, that is, until it ceases to be spoken at all, is in a state of continual change. The English which we speak and write is **not** the same English that was spoken and written by our grandfathers, **nor** was their English precisely like that of Queen Elizabeth's time. The farther back we go, the less familiar we find ourselves with the speech of our ancestors, until finally we reach a kind of English which is quite as strange to us as if it were a foreign tongue.

Key Structure

1 until it ceases to be spoken at all = until it is no longer spoken

2 nor was their English precisely like that ~ time
그들이 사용했던 영어도 정확히는 엘리자베스 여왕 시대의 영어가 아니었다

3 The farther **back we go,** the less familiar ~ ancestors
과거로 거슬러 올라갈수록 우리와 우리 조상의 언어와 더 낯설어짐을 알게 된다

4 as if it were a foreign tongue 마치 그것이 외국어인 것처럼

내용 언어는 계속해서 변화한다.

cease [si:s] 중지하다, 그만두다(= desist, discontinue, terminate)
precisely [prisáisli] 정확히, 바로(= exactly, definitely, distinctly)
farther [fá:rðər] 더 멀리, 더 저쪽으로 (far의 비교급)
ancestor [ǽnsestər] 조상, 선조(= forefather, predecessor)
foreign tongue 외국어(= foreign language)

12 · 부정구문 II Negation

01 not so much A as B / B rather than A : A라기보다는 오히려 B이다

  a. He is not so much unintelligent as uneducated.

  = He is uneducated rather than unintelligent.
    그는 머리가 둔하기보다는 교육을 받지 못했다.

  b. Happiness depends not so much on circumstances as on one's way of
    looking at one's lot.
    행복은 환경에 달려 있다기보다는 오히려 우리가 자신의 운명을 어떻게 보느냐에 달려 있다.

  not so much A but B

  c. The greatness of Schweitzer is not so much what he has done for others
    but what others have done because of him.
    슈바이처가 위대한 것은 그가 다른 사람들을 위해 봉사한 일 때문이라기보다는, 오히려 다른 사람들이 그를 본받아
    무엇인가를 행한 것 때문이다.

  not A, so much as B

  d. His talk is not witty, so much as charming.
    그의 이야기는 기지가 있다기보다는 재미가 있다.

  e. He loves wisdom not for its own sake, so much as for the sake of its
    uses.
    그는 학문을 애호하되, 학문 그 자체가 좋아서가 아니라 그것의 이용 가치 때문에 좋아한다.

02 not so much as + 동사 : (심지어) ~조차 못하다

  without so much as -ing : (심지어) ~조차 하지 않고

  a. He cannot so much as write his own name.
    그는 자신의 이름조차도 쓰지 못한다.

  b. He left the room without so much as saying good-bye to me.
    그는 나에게 작별 인사도 하지 않고 방을 떠나 버렸다.

03 cannot ~ too : 아무리 ~해도 지나치지 않다, 아무리 ~해도 오히려 부족하다

a. You cannot praise him too much.
그를 아무리 칭찬해도 지나침이 없다.

b. I can never be sufficiently grateful to you.
당신에게 아무리 감사를 드려도 오히려 부족합니다.

c. We cannot exaggerate the value of literature as a medium for cultivating our minds.
우리가 우리의 정신을 가꾸는 하나의 매개물로서 문학의 가치를 아무리 높이 평가해도 지나침이 없다.

It is not saying too much to + 동사 : ~라고 해서 지나친 이야기는 아니다

d. It is not saying too much to suggest that unrest in this world is mostly caused by the problem of food.
이 세상의 불안이 식량 문제 때문에 야기된다고 해도 지나친 말이 아니다.

04 no ~ but / not ~ that ... not / never[not] ~ without : ~하지 않는 …은 없다

a. There is no rule but has exceptions.
예외가 없는 규칙은 없다.

b. Not a day passes that he does not write to me.
그가 나에게 소식을 주지 않고 지나가는 날은 없다.[그는 매일 나에게 편지를 쓴다.]

c. They never meet without quarreling.
그들은 만나기만 하면 싸운다.

125 We often perceive that very strong and durable friendships often exist between men who are not of the same nation, and that the chief obstacle of the formation of these is **not so much** nationality **as** difference of language.

Key Structure •

1 men who are not of the same nation
국적이 같지 않은 사람들

2 not so much nationality as difference of language
국적이라기보다는 오히려 언어의 차이이다
• not so much A as B = B rather than A A라기보다는 오히려 B이다
 ex He is not so much a scholar as a politician.
  그는 학자라기보다는 정치가이다.

내용 국적이 다른 사람들 사이에 우정을 형성함에 있어서 장애물은 언어의 차이이다.

perceive [pərsíːv] 인지하다, 이해하다(= appreciate, understand, comprehend)
durable [djú(ː)ərəbl] 오래가는, 영속적인(= enduring, long-lasting, permanent)
obstacle [ábstəkl] 장애(물), 방해(물)
formation [fɔːrméiʃən] 구성, 형성, 조성
nationality [næ̀ʃənǽləti] 국적, 국민성

126 If you would learn where true happiness is, you have only to watch the life of those who are in really narrow circumstances, and seek consolation. Happiness depends **not so much** on circumstances **as** on one's way of looking at one's lot.

Key Structure •

1 you have only to ~
당신은 ~하기만 하면 된다

2 those who are in ~ circumstances
정말로 궁핍한 상황에 처한 사람들

3 depends not so much on A as on B
A에 달려 있기보다는 오히려 B에 달려 있다

내용 행복은 인간이 처한 환경보다는 오히려 자신의 운명을 보는 관점에 달려 있다.

narrow circumstances 궁핍한 상황
seek [siːk] 찾다, 구하다(= look for, search for, strive after)
consolation [kɑ̀nsəléiʃən] 위안, 위로(= comfort, encouragement, solace, relief)
lot [lɑt] 운, 운수(= fortune, destiny)

127   The individual, if left alone from birth, would remain primitive and beast-like in his thoughts and feelings to a degree that we can hardly conceive. The individual is what he is and has the significance that he has, **not so much** in virtue of his individuality, **but** rather as a member of a great human society, which directs his material and spiritual existence from the cradle to the grave.

Key Structure ▸

1   if (he were) left alone from birth
    출생할 때부터 홀로 남겨지면

2   to a degree that ~
    ~할 정도로

3   what he is
    현재 자신의 모습[됨됨이]

4   has the significance that he has
    현재 자신이 가진 중요성을 갖고 있다

5   not so much **in virtue of** ~ but rather as...
    ~ 덕택이라기보다는 오히려 …로서

6   from the cradle to the grave = from birth to death
    • the cradle, the grave : the+보통명사 = 추상명사.

내용   인간은 커다란 인간 사회의 구성원으로 존재할 때 가치가 있다.

individual [ìndəvídʒuəl] 개인, 사람
primitive [prímitiv] 원시의, 유치한
conceive [kənsíːv] 생각하다, 상상하다(= imagine, think)
significance [signífikəns] 중요(성), 의미, 뜻깊음(= importance, consequence)
in virtue of (~의) 덕택으로, ~의 힘에 의해(= by virtue of)
spiritual [spíritʃuəl] 정신의, 영적인(= mental)
cradle [kréidl] 요람, 발상지
grave [ɡreiv] 묘소, 무덤, 파멸

what he is와 what he has

what he is는 '그의 인물 됨됨이', '현재의 모습'이라는 뜻이고, what he has는 '그가 가진 재산'이라는 뜻이다. 이때 what은 관계대명사이다.

a. He is not what he was before.
b. No one knows exactly what he will be in the future.
c. A man's worth lies not in what he has but in what he is.

관계대명사 what이 쓰인 기타 표현들

d. He is what we call a grown-up baby.
e. What makes matters worse, they have no intention of reconciling with each other.
f. Reading is to the mind what food is to the body.
g. What with good fortune and what with hard work, he got promoted.

해석 a. 그는 예전의 그가 아니다.   b. 그가 앞으로 무엇이 될지 정확히 아는 자는 없다.   c. 사람의 가치는 그가 가진 재산에 있는 것이 아니라 그 사람 됨됨이에 있다.   d. 그는 소위 다 큰 아이이다.   e. 설상가상으로 그들은 서로 타협하려는 의지가 없다.   f. 독서와 정신의 관계는 음식물과 신체의 관계와 같다.   g. 한편으로 운도 따르고, 또 한편으로 열심히 노력하여 그는 승진되었다.

128

In the affairs of life or of business it is **not** intellect that tells **so much as** character—**not** brains **so much as** heart—**not** genius **so much as** self-control, and patience, directed by judgment.

Key Structure

1 it is not intellect that tells so much as character

= it is not intellect so much as character that tells

중요한 것은 지력이라기보다는 인품이다

• it is ~ that tells 중요한 것은 ~이다 (강조 구문)

• tell 중요하다, 효과가 있다 (자동사로 be effective / important라는 뜻을 가짐)

e.g. Money is bound to tell. 돈의 효과는 반드시 나타난다.

His age is beginning to tell upon him. 그도 나이 드는 것에는 어쩔 수 없게 되어 간다.

2 not brains so much as heart—not genius so much as ~

• it is ~ that 강조 구문에 연결되는 구조임. 또한 not A so much as B의 구조임.

내용 인생과 사업에서는 성격, 마음씨, 자제심과 인내심이 효력이 있다.

affair [əfɛ́ər] 일, 사건(= event, business)
intellect [íntəlèkt] 지력, 지성
character [kǽriktər] 특징, 인격, 인물
brain [brein] 두뇌, 지력
genius [dʒíːnjəs] 천재(성), 비범한 재능

self-control 자제(력), 극기
patience [péiʃəns] 인내, 끈기, 견인불발(= forbearance, fortitude, endurance, composure)

129

Being a good wife, a good mother, in short, a good homemaker, is the most important of all the occupations in the world. It, surely, **cannot** be **too** often pointed out that the making of human beings is a far more important vocation than the making of anything else and that in the formative years of a child's life the mother is best equipped to provide those firm foundations upon which one can subsequently build.

Key Structure ·

1 It cannot be too often pointed out that ~
   ~라는 점은 아무리 자주 지적해도 오히려 부족하다

2 the formative years of a child's life
   어린아이의 삶의 형성[발달]기

3 foundations upon which one can subsequently build
   나중에 자립할 수 있는 기초

내용 훌륭한 아내, 어머니가 되는 것은 세상의 모든 직업 중에서 가장 중요하다.

in short 간단히 말해서(= shortly speaking)
homemaker [hóummèikər] 가정주부(= housekeeper)
occupation [àkjəpéiʃən] 직업, 업무(= vocation, profession, job, career)
be equipped to (~할) 준비가 되다, 소양을 갖추다
firm [fəːrm] 견고한, 단단한(= solid, sound, rigid, stable, compact) ⓝ 회사
subsequently [sʌ́bsəkwəntli] 그 후에, 다음에(= consequently, successively, in the future)

플러스 문법정리 53

cannot ~ too의 의미
'아무리 ~해도 지나치지 않다[오히려 부족하다]'의 표현을 나타내는 것으로, cannot ~ enough / cannot ~ sufficiently 등 변형된 표현도 있다.

a. I cannot thank you too much.
b. I cannot thank you enough.
c. I can never be sufficiently grateful to you.
d. We cannot respect our elders too highly.
e. We cannot exaggerate the value of health.

해석 a, b, c. 어떻게 감사의 말씀을 드려야 할지 모르겠습니다.   d. 노인들을 아무리 존경해도 지나치지 않다.
      e. 건강의 가치는 아무리 강조해도 오히려 부족하다.

130

It has often been said, and most wisely, that **no man** in trade, whether in a large or a little way of business, **can** know **too much** about the habits, the manners, and the wants of his customers.

Key Structure •

1 **most wisely**
   • 앞의 said로 연결되는 부사구이며, 의미상으로 다시 반복하는 기능이 있음. 즉 It has often been said, and most wisely said, that ~의 구문이 축약된 것으로 봄.

2 no man ~ can **know** too **much about...**
   누구도 …에 대해 아무리 많이 알아도 오히려 부족하다
   • cannot ~ too에서 not의 의미가 주어(no man)로 전이된 구조.

3 **whether** (he is) **in a ~ business**

내용 장사꾼은 고객의 습관, 요구 사항을 잘 알아야 한다.

trade [treid] 장사, 직업, 무역, 매매(= business, commerce, merchandising, career)
manners [mǽnərz] 풍습, 습관(= customs, habits)
want [wɑnt] 원하는 것, 부족한 것
customer [kʌ́stəmər] 고객, 단골 *cf.* client 법률적 문제의 의뢰인

131

We **cannot** know **too** much about the language we speak every day of our lives. Most of us, it is true, can get along fairly well without knowing very much about our language and without even taking the trouble to open a volume of *The Oxford English Dictionary*. But knowledge is power. The power of rightly chosen words is very great, whether those words are intended to inform, to amuse, or to move.

Key Structure •

1 We cannot **know** too much about ~
   ~에 대해 아무리 많이 알아도 오히려 부족하다

2 **The power of rightly chosen words**
   = The power of the words which are rightly chosen
   올바르게 선택된 어휘의 힘

내용 우리가 사용하는 언어에 대해 많은 것을 알아야 한다.

get along 지내다, 살아가다
fairly [fέərli] 꽤, 상당히(= pretty, moderately, rather)
take the trouble to (~하는) 수고를 하다
volume [válju:m] 책, 권, 용적, 부피
amuse [əmjú:z] 즐겁게 하다, 웃기다(= entertain, interest, please) ⓝ amusement

132

Food for all is the crucial problem of the world today for several reasons. A hungry world is never likely to be a peaceful world. **It is not saying too much to** suggest that unrest throughout the world most frequently has its root cause in dissatisfaction with that part of the standard of living concerned with food. As Le Gros Clark has put it, a stable civilization will be built only on the foundations of the farm and the kitchen.

Key Structure

1 Food for all 모두를 먹일 수 있는 식량
   • all = all people

2 A hungry world is never likely to ~ world.
   = It is never likely that a hungry world will be a ~ world.

3 It is not saying too much to ~
   ~라고 말한다고 해서 지나친 말은 아니다
   • It = to suggest (it은 가주어)

4 As Le Gros Clark has put it = As Le Gros Clark has said

내용 식량 문제가 해결된 뒤에야 진정한 평화가 가능하다.

crucial [krú:ʃəl] 결정적인, 중대한(= decisive, important, critical)
unrest [ʌnrést] 불안, 불온, 걱정(= unstability, unreliability)
frequently [frí:kwəntli] 자주, 흔히(= repeatedly, reiteratively, very often)
root cause 근본 원인
dissatisfaction [dissὰtisfǽkʃən] 불만, 불평(= disappointment, dismay, discontentment)
put it 말하다(= say)
stable [stéibl] 안정된, 흔들리지 않는(= balanced, firm, solid, sound, constant)
the farm 농업
the kitchen 부엌살림

155

플러스 문법정리 54

the+보통명사 = 추상명사
보통명사가 정관사 the와 함께 쓰여 추상명사의 뜻을 나타내는 경우가 많다.

a. I felt the patriot rise in my heart. (애국심)
b. You can see the woman in the little girl. (여자다운 점)
c. The pen is mightier than the sword. (글의 힘[문력] / 무력)
d. When one is reduced to poverty, the beggar will come out. (거지 근성)
e. The poet in him moved at the beautiful scene. (시적 감흥)

해석 a. 나는 애국심이 가슴에서 솟아오르는 것을 느꼈다. b. 그 조그마한 소녀에게서 여자다운 점을 볼 수 있다.
c. 글의 힘은 무력보다 더 세다. d. 사람이 가난해지면 거지 근성이 나타나는 법이다. e. 그 아름다운 광경을 보고
그에게 시적 감흥이 일어났다.

133 So far am I from feeling satisfied with any explanation, scientific or other, of myself and of the world about me, that **not** a day goes by **but** I fall marvelling before the mystery of the universe. To trumpet the triumphs of human knowledge seems to be worse than childishness; now, as of old, we know but one thing—we know nothing.

Key Structure

1 So far am I from ~ that... = I am so far from ~ that...
나는 ~과는 거리가 너무 멀어서 …한다
• far from -ing ~과는 거리가 멀다, ~을 하지 않다

2 not a day goes by but ~
~하지 않고 지나가는 날은 하루도 없다
• fall marvelling ~에 경탄을 금하지 못하다

3 now, as of old, ~
예전처럼 지금도
• of old = in the past 옛날에 / of late = lately, recently 최근에

내용 나는 우주의 신비에 경탄을 금치 못한다.

explanation [èksplənéiʃən] 설명, 해석
marvel [máːrvəl] 놀라다, 경탄하다(= be amazed by, be astonished at)
mystery [místəri] 신비, 비밀, 추리소설(= miracle, riddle)
trumpet [trʌ́mpit] 멀러 퍼뜨리다, 칭찬을 하고 다니다
triumph [tráiəmf] 승리, 대업적, 큰 공훈(= victory, achievement)
childishness [tʃáildiʃnis] 유치함(= babyishness, foolishness) cf. childlikeness 순진함

134 To you, my dear mother, I know that I **can never** be **sufficiently** grateful, not only for the common kindness of a mother, but for the unceasing watchfulness with which you strove to put virtuous principles into my young mind.

Key Structure •

1 I can never **be** sufficiently **grateful to you.**
= I cannot **be grateful to you** too much.
당신께 아무리 감사드려도 오히려 부족합니다.

2 not only **for A** but (also) **for B**
A에 대해서뿐만 아니라 B에 대해서도

3 **the unceasing watchfulness with which you strove to ~**
당신께서 ~하고자 힘들이신 끊임없는 경계심[마음 씀]
• with which ~는 '~하고자 힘들이셨을 때 가진 ~'이라는 뜻으로 아래의 예문을 참고하기 바람.
e.g. You strove to put virtuous principles into my young mind with unceasing watchfulness.

내용 어머님께서 보여 주신 사랑과 보살핌에 대한 감사의 정.

sufficiently [səfíʃəntli] 충분히(= enough, satisfactorily)
grateful [gréitfəl] 감사하는, 쾌적한(= thankful, pleasant)
unceasing [ʌnsíːsiŋ] 끊임없는, 쉴 새 없는(= ceaseless, endless, incessant, never-ending, interminable)
watchfulness [wátʃfəlnes] 신중, 경계(= attention, heedfulness, vigilance)
strive [straiv] 노력하다, 분투하다(= endeavor, strain, struggle, try)
virtuous [vɜ́ːrtʃuəs] 덕이 있는, 고결한(= blameless, high-principled, chaste, upright)

135 If it were not for literature, our life would be as dry as a desert. We **cannot exaggerate** the value of literature as a medium by which to cultivate our minds. But literary works are too many, while our time for reading is much too limited. Our disappointment becomes the more bitter when we read dull literature. It is the safest way, therefore, to read classics as they have stood the test of time.

Key Structure •

1 If it were not for **literature**
= Were it not for **literature** = But for **literature**
문학이 없다면

157

2 We cannot exaggerate the value of literature
= We cannot estimate the value of literature too highly
문학의 가치를 아무리 높이 평가해도 지나치지 않다

3 a medium by which to cultivate our minds
= a medium by which we can cultivate our minds
우리의 정신을 계발하는 매체로서

4 as they have stood the test of time
그것들이 시간이라는 시험을 견디어 냈으므로
• stand[bear] the test of ~의 시험을 통과하다

내용 문학의 가치는 매우 크나, 시간은 한정되어 있으므로 고전을 읽는 것이 좋다.

literature [lítərətʃùər] 문학, 문필업
desert [dézərt] 사막, 황야(= wasteland, wilderness, dust bowl) ⓥ [dizə́:rt] 버리다
exaggerate [igzǽʤərèit] 과장하다, 떠벌리다(= amplify, embellish, inflate)
medium [mí:diəm] 매개물, 수단(= means), 중간
cultivate [kʌ́ltəvèit] 경작하다, 양식하다, 배양하다(= develop, enrich)
literary work 문학 작품
bitter [bítər] 쓴, 잔인한, 통렬한
dull [dʌl] 재미없는(= uninteresting), 무딘(= not sharp), 우둔한
classics [klǽsik] 고전 (작품)

플러스 문법정리 55

가정법 과거 구문과 if it were not for ~
가정법 과거는 현재 사실의 반대를 가정할 때 쓰인다. if절에는 과거 동사(were), 주절에는 would / should / could / might+동사를 쓴다.

a. If he were honest, I could employ him.
= As he is not honest, I cannot employ him.

b. If it were not for your help, he would not succeed.
= Were it not for your help, he would not succeed.
= But for your help, he would not succeed.
= Without your help, he would not succeed.

해석 a. 그가 정직하다면 그를 고용할 텐데. b. 너의 도움이 없다면 그는 성공하지 못할 텐데.

136

No book is worth anything which is **not** worth much; nor is it serviceable, until it has been read, and reread, and loved, and loved, again; and marked, so that you can refer to the passages you want in it.

Key Structure ▸

1 No book is worth anything which is not worth much.
   = No book which is not worth much is worth anything.
   어떠한 책도 상당한 가치가 있지 않으면 전혀 가치가 없다
   • No book에 연결되는 관계대명사절이 뒤로 옮겨진 외치된(extraposition) 문장.

2 the passages (which) you want in it
   그 속에 들어 있는 당신이 원하는 구절
   • it = the book

　내용　책은 읽고 또 읽고 주석을 달아 놓아 다음에 참조할 수 있을 정도가 될 때 존재 가치가 있다.

serviceable [sə́:rvisəbl] 쓸모 있는, 오래 가는(= usable, durable, dependable)
be marked 주석이 달리다
refer (to) 참조하다, 위탁하다(= consult, go to, look up, turn to)

플러스 문법정리 56

형용사 worth, worthy, worthwhile의 차이
worth는 보어 기능을 하는 형용사로 그 뒤에 목적어를 갖고, worthy는 명사를 꾸미거나 보어로 쓰이는데, 후자의 경우 보통은 of를 동반한다. worthwhile도 명사를 꾸미거나 보어로 쓰일 수 있다. 보어로 쓰일 때에는 worth와 while을 떼어서 쓴다.

(1) a. How much is it worth?
     b. Rome is a city worth visiting.

(2) c. He is a worthy gentleman.
     d. He is a poet worthy of the name.

(3) e. You have to spend your time on worthwhile reading.
     f. It is worth (your) while to see the museum.

해석　a. 그것은 얼마의 가치가 있나요?　b. 로마는 가 볼 만한 도시이다.　c. 그는 이름값을 하는 신사이다.　d. 그는 이름값을 하는 시인이다.　e. 가치 있는 독서에 시간을 써야 한다.　f. 박물관에 가 볼 가치가 있다.

137 It was even suggested that the university as such should be dissolved, to be replaced by three special types of school: institutes for professional training, institutes for general education and research institutes. In the idea of the university, however, these three are indissolubly united. One can**not** be cut off from the others **without** destroying the intellectual substance of the university and **without** at the same time crippling itself. All three are factors of a living whole. By isolating them, the spirit of the university perishes.

Key Structure

1 to be replaced by ~
= and (be) replaced by ~
그래서 ~로 대치되어야 한다
• 부정사 부사적 용법 중 '결과'의 뜻

2 One cannot be cut off from the others without ~
하나를 나머지 둘에게서 분리하면 반드시 ~한다

내용 직업 교육, 교양[일반] 교육, 연구 기능의 세 가지가 하나로 통합될 때 대학의 본질이 유지된다.

as such 그 자체로서, 그 나름대로(= in itself)
dissolve [dizálv] 해체하다, 녹이다, 취소하다(= decompose, break up, split up)
replace [ripléis] 대신하다, 대치하다(= substitute)
institute [ínstitjùːt] 전문학교[대학], 학회
professional [prəféʃənəl] 직업의, 전문의
research [risə́ːrtʃ] (학술) 연구, 탐색, 조사
indissolubly [ìndisáljubli] 분리할 수 없게, 희미하게
be cut off from (~로부터) 차단되다
substance [sʌ́bstəns] 실질, 본질, 물질, 자산(= essence, matter)
cripple [krípl] 마비시키다, 병신으로 만들다(= disable, paralyze, lame)
a living whole 살아 있는 전체(의 물건)
perish [périʃ] 사라지다, 멸망하다(= pass away, die, expire)

All work and no play makes Jack a dull boy.
공부만 시키고 놀게 하지 않으면 아이를 바보로 만든다.

플러스 문법정리 57

not ~ without / not ~ but의 용법

'~하면 반드시 ~한다'의 뜻을 지니는 구문으로 without 다음에는 명사 또는 동명사가 오며, but 다음에는 절(주어+동사)이 온다.

a. It never rains without pouring.
= It never rains but it pours.

b. He never visits me without bringing some problems.
= He never visits me but he brings some problems.
= When he visits me, he always brings some problems.
= Whenever he visits me, he brings some problems.

해석 a. 비가 왔다 하면 쏟아진다.   b. 그는 나를 보러 올 때마다 문젯거리들을 가져온다.

Make hay while the sun shines.
햇볕이 날 때 풀을 말려라. (좋은 기회를 놓치지 마라.)

13 · 부정구문 III Negation

01 양보의 뜻을 지닌 축약절을 동반한 부정구문 : 설사 ~라고 해도, 설사 있다고 해도

a. There are **few**, if any, such men.
= There are few such men, if there are any such men.
그러한 사람은, 있다고 해도, 거의 없다.

b. There is **little**, if any, hope of his recovery from the illness.
그가 병을 떨치고 일어날 가망은, 있다고 해도, 거의 없다.

c. Such a thing occurs **seldom**, if ever.
그러한 일은, 설사 일어난다 해도, 거의 일어나지 않는다.

d. The Chinese are **little**, if at all, inferior to the Japanese.
중국인은 일본인에 비해, 설사 뒤진다 하더라도, 거의 뒤지지 않는다.

e. This event will bring about **bad**, if not fatal, results.
이 사건은, 치명적인 결과는 아니라 하더라도, 나쁜 결과를 초래할 것이다.

02 강조에 의한 도치 구문

a. **Little** did I dream that I should never see him again.
그를 다시 보지 못하게 될 줄이야 꿈에도 생각하지 못했다. (부정어의 강조)

b. **Never in my life** have I seen such a dreadful sight.
그렇게 무서운 광경은 지금까지 결코 보지 못했다. (부정어의 강조)

c. **Full well** do I know that I should not marry her.
내가 그녀와 결혼해서는 안 된다는 점을 충분히 알고 있다. (부사어의 강조)

03 not ~ until... : …하고 나서야 비로소 ~한다

People do not know the blessing of health until they lose it.
= It is not until they lose it that people know the blessing of health.
= Not until they lose it do people know the blessing of health.
사람들은 건강이 주는 축복을 건강을 잃을 때까지는 알지 못한다.

04 not ~ (long) before... : 얼마 ~하지 않아 곧 …하다

a. I had not waited long before he appeared.
얼마 기다리지 않아 그가 나타났다.

b. It was not long before he showed up.
얼마 되지 않아 그가 나타났다.

c. It will not be long before we graduate.
우리가 졸업을 할 날도 얼마 남지 않았다.

cf. It will be some time before he appears.
그가 나타나려면 얼마 동안 시간이 걸려야 할 것이다.

05 too ~ to... : 너무 ~해서 …하지 못하다

a. You are too young to understand such things.
= You are so young that you cannot understand such things.
당신은 너무 어려 그러한 일을 이해하지 못한다.

b. He is too wise not to know it.
= He is so wise that he cannot but know it.
그는 매우 현명하여 그것을 알 수밖에 없을 것이다.

c. He is not too old to learn.
= He is not so old that he cannot learn.
그가 배우기에 너무 늙은 것은 아니다.(배우기에 지금도 늦지 않다)

06 only too = exceedingly : 더할 나위 없이, 기꺼이

a. I am only too glad to accept it.
기꺼이 그것을 받아들이겠다.(그것을 받아들이게 되어 더할 나위 없이 기쁘다)
> *cf.* It is only too true. 그것은 유감스럽게도 사실이다.

too + (ready, eager, anxious, inclined 등의 형용사) + to부정사

b. He is too ready to speak.
= He is too talkative.
그는 말이 많다.

07 최상급이 부정의 뜻 소유

He is the last man to tell a lie.
= He is above telling a lie.
= He knows better than to tell a lie.
그는 거짓말을 할 사람이 결코 아니다.

138 People divide off vice and virtue as though they were two things, neither of which had with it anything of the other. This is not so. There is no useful virtue which has not some alloy of vice, and **hardly** any vice, **if any**, which carries not with it a little dash of virtue.

Key Structure •

1   as though **they were two things**
    = as if **they were two things**
    • as though[if]+가정법 구문임에 유의할 것.

2   **neither of which had ~ the other**
    둘 중의 어느 하나도 나머지 다른 하나의 성질을 갖지 않은
    • had도 가정법 과거의 형태임.

3   **and (there is)** hardly **any vice, if any, which ~ virtue**
    그 자체에 약간의 미덕이 가미되지 않은 액[악덕]은 있다고 해도 거의 없다
    • if any 있다고 해도 (양보를 나타내는 절이 축약된 구문)
    e.g. He has few, if any, friends to love him.
        그는 그를 좋아하는 친구가 있다고 해도 거의 없다.

내용 미덕과 악덕이 따로 있는 것이 아니다.

divide off 나누다, 구분하다, 구별하다(= break up, halve, sunder)
alloy [ǽlɔi] 합금, 혼합물(= mixture, amalgam, blend)
dash [dǽʃ] 소량의 가미 *cf.* a little dash of = a little bit of

플러스 문법정리 58

if any와 if ever
if any와 if ever 양자는 모두 양보절이 축약된 형태로, if any는 명사 표현에, if ever는 동사 표현에 관련된다.

a. There are few, if any, things for us to do now.
    • if any = (even) if there are any things

b. He seldom, if ever, smokes.
=   He rarely, if ever, smokes.
    • if ever = (even) if he ever smokes

해석 a. 지금 우리가 할 수 있는 일은, 있다고 해도 거의 없다.   b. 그가 담배를 피운다고 해도 거의 피우지 않는다.

139 Another question which metaphysics discusses is that of cosmic purpose. Can the universe as a whole be said to have a purpose? If so, **what** part, **if any**, have we to play in its promotion? Further, in what terms is the purpose to be conceived? As a greater moral perfection? A higher degree of consciousness? Or a more intimate communion with God? It is clear that the answers which we give to these and similar questions will have a profound effect upon our ethical views.

Key Structure •

1 **that of cosmic purpose** 우주가 존재하는 목적의 문제 (that = the question)

2 **what part,** if any, **have we to play ~** 우리가 할 역할은 만약에 있다면 무엇인가?
  • if any = if there is any (part) : if any는 조건을 나타냄 / what part는 to play의 목적어임.
  • have we to play = do we have to play

내용 형이상학[철학]이 다루는 문제 중의 하나는 우주의 목적이 무엇인가 하는 문제이다.

metaphysics [mètəfíziks] 형이상학, 순정 철학
cosmic [kázmik] 우주의, 광대무변의(= universal, of cosmos) ⓝ cosmos
promotion [prəmóuʃən] 증진, 장려, 승진(= advancement, elevation)
conceive [kənsíːv] 상상하다, 생각을 품다, (아이를) 배다(= think, imagine, devise)
perfection [pərfékʃən] 완전, 완성, 원숙, 극치(= completion, consummation, fulfillment)
consciousness [kánʃəsnis] 자각, 의식
intimate [íntəmit] 친밀한, 상세한(= friendly)
profound [prəfáund] 심오한, 겸손한(= deep, humble)
ethical [éθikəl] 도덕상의, 윤리적인(= moral)

플러스 문법정리 59

term, terms의 여러 가지 뜻
term, terms에는 여러 가지 뜻이 있으므로 그 사용에 주의하여야 한다.

term :	말, 술어	a. He is employing a quite intelligible term.
	학기	b. The spring term is near at hand.
	기간	c. He deposits a lot of money at The Long-term Trust Bank.
terms :	용어	d. He employs too many technical terms.
	교제, 관계	e. We are on speaking terms with him.
	조건, 요금	f. I bought the refrigerator on deferred terms.
	화해	g. I have come to terms with him at last.
	표현	h. He bowed to me in terms of respect.

해석 a. 그는 매우 알기 쉬운 말을 쓰고 있다. b. 봄 학기가 가까이 다가왔다. c. 그는 장기신용은행에 많은 돈을 저축하고 있다. d. 그는 너무 많은 전문 용어를 사용한다. e. 우리는 그와 말을 하고 지내는 사이이다. f. 나는 냉장고를 할부로 샀다. g. 나는 마침내 그와 화해하게 되었다. h. 그는 존경의 표현으로 나에게 고개를 숙여 인사하였다.

140 Many people, **if not** most, look on literary taste as an elegant accomplishment, by acquiring which they will complete themselves, and make themselves finally fit as members of correct society.

Key Structure ▸

1 **if not most**
대부분은 아니라고 하더라도

2 **by acquiring which ~**
그것을 얻음으로써
• 관계대명사 which는 accomplishment를 가리키며, 계속적 용법으로 쓰이고 있음.

내용 문학 취미는 자신을 완벽하게 하고 올바른 사회의 구성원이 되게끔 하는 우아한 재능이다.

look on A as B A를 B로 여기다(= regard A as B, think of A as B, consider A B)
elegant [éləgənt] 고상한, 품위 있는(= graceful, refined)
accomplishment [əkámpliʃmənt] 예능, 업적, 성취(= talent, gift, skill, attainment)
fit [fit] 알맞은, 적합한(= suitable, adequate, befitting, appropriate)

141 Leisure as we know it today in the United States is a new phenomenon. **Never before** have so many people had so much free time and so much money with which to enjoy it.

Key Structure ▸

1 **Leisure as we know it**
우리가 알고 있는 바의 여가

2 **Never before have so many people had ~**
= So many people have never had ~ before

내용 오늘날 미국에서 여가는 새로운 현상이다.

leisure [líːʒər, léʒər] 여가, 한가한 시간(= free time)
phenomenon [finámənàn] 현상, 사건, 경이(적인 인물, 일)(= happening, incident, occasion)

142

I do not know why a man who writes books should regard himself as a better man than one who makes butter. **Far less do I know** why the man who makes butter should consent to believe that he is less worthy than the man who makes books. But undoubtedly some such superstition fills the minds of most of us.

Key Structure ▸

Far less do I know ~ = I know far less ~

~은 더더욱 모른다

• 강조에 따른 도치 구문

내용 책을 쓰는 작가나 버터를 만드는 사람이나 인간으로서 같은 가치를 갖는다.

regard A as B A를 B로 여기다(= look on[upon] A as B)
consent [kənsént] 동의하다, 승낙하다(= agree)
worthy [wə́ːrði] (~할) 가치가 있는, 덕망 있는
superstition [sjùːpərstíʃən] 미신(행위) ⓐ superstitious

플러스 문법정리 60

부사의 강조와 도치

시간·정도를 나타내는 부사를 강조할 경우 문장 머리에 내세우는 것이 보통인데, 이때 일반적으로 주어와 동사가 도치된다.

a. I little dreamed that she would marry him.
= Little did I dream that she would marry him.

b. I know full well that he is a crooked person.
= Full well do I know that he is a crooked person.

c. I have never seen him before.
= Never have I seen him before.
= Never before have I seen him.

주의) 장소를 나타내는 부사를 강조할 때에는 do 동사를 이용하지 않고 도치가 이루어진다.

d. The rain came down in torrents.
= Down came the rain in torrents.
cf. Down did the rain come in torrents. (×)

해석 a. 그녀가 그와 결혼하리라고는 거의 꿈꾸지도 못했다. b. 그가 마음씨가 비뚤어진 사람임을 나는 아주 잘 알고 있다. c. 나는 그를 전에 본 적이 없다. d. 비가 억수같이 쏟아졌다.

143 **Not until** we had assured Kate that the animal was now really dead and could hurt nobody any more, **did she come** to have a short, very short look at the visitor who had given her such a terrible shock.

Key Structure ▶

1 Not until ~ did she come to... = She did not come to... until ~
   ～할 때까지는 …하지 못하였다

2 come to have a short look at ~
   ～을 잠시 동안 쳐다보다

내용 케이트는 갑자기 나타난 무서운 동물에 충격을 받았다.

assure [əʃúər] 안심시키다, 확실히 하다, 보장하다(= ensure, make sure)
hurt [həːrt] 아프게 하다, 불쾌하게 하다(= harm, afflict, cause pain to, torture)
have a look at (～을) 바라다보다
terrible [térəbl] 무서운, 겁나는(= awful, appalling, frightening) cf. terrific 최고의, 놀라운

플러스 문법정리 61

until 구문의 강조와 도치
not ~ until 구문에서 until 이하를 강조하는 경우 until과 부정어 not은 문두로 보내고 주절의 주어와 동사는 도치시키는 것이 보통이다.

a. We do not realize the value of health until we become sick.
= Not until we become sick do we realize the value of health.
= It is not until we become sick that we realize the value of health.

b. He did not pay attention to what I said until then.
= Not until then did he pay attention to what I said.

해석 a. 우리는 병이 들 때까지는 건강의 가치를 깨닫지 못한다.   b. 그때까지 그는 내가 한 말에 주의를 기울이지 않았다.

144 Another reason for the Declaration's emphasis on education is that education, as recent history shows, is **all too likely to be** subjected to attack in these times, and the educational freedoms are particularly vulnerable. Moreover, the Declaration is concerned with education because the teacher is also a citizen, and like other citizens, has rights and responsibilities which need to be affirmed.

Key Structure •

education is all too likely to ~ 교육이 너무나도 ~되기 쉽다
• be likely to ~할 가능성이 있다
• all too 너무나도 ~한 (이것을 too ~ to...와 혼동하지 말 것)

내용 세계인권선언이 교육을 강조하는 이유는 교육이 너무 많은 공격을 받고 교육의 자유가 침해받기 때문이다.

the Declaration 세계인권선언(= the Declaration of Human Rights)
emphasis [émfəsis] 강조, 역설(= stress, weight) ⓥ emphasize ⓐ emphatic
be subjected to (~을) 받기 쉽다, ~을 당하다
vulnerable [vʌ́lnərəbl] 상처를 입기 쉬운, 공격받기 쉬운(= easily hurt, unguarded, open to attack)
be concerned with (~과) 관련되다
affirm [əfə́:rm] 단언하다, 확인하다(= confirm, attest, assert, avow)

---

145 The political freedom we have today will never be **too easy to preserve**. It came out of struggle, and it may still demand struggle. It came out of wisdom and patience. We may honor the fathers of the Declaration all the more because now that we ourselves live in a time of peril we can understand their danger and their courage.

Key Structure •

1 **be too easy to preserve**
   보존하기에 너무 쉽다

2 **We may honor ~ all the more because...**
   ...하기 때문에 우리는 ~를 더욱더 존경할 수 있다
   • all the more because ~하기 때문에 더욱더
   e.g. I love him all the more because he has faults.
   나는 그가 잘못이 있기 때문에 더욱더 사랑한다.

3 **now that ~ = since ~**
   ~이기 때문에

내용 정치적 자유는 투쟁 끝에 얻은 것이고, 그래서 보존하기가 결코 쉽지 않다.

political freedom 정치적 자유
preserve [prizə́:rv] 보존하다, 보호하다(= conserve, keep, maintain, sustain, uphold)
struggle [strʌ́gl] 노력, 경쟁(= challenge, fight)
honor [ánər] 존경하다(= respect, admire, glorify, pay homage to, pay tribute to, venerate)
the Declaration (미국의) 독립선언문(1776. 7. 4)(= the Declaration of Independence)
peril [pérəl] 위험, 모험(= danger, risk, jeopardy, insecurity)

146 We should **be the last persons** on earth **to** approve the belief that a manual laborer who is educated is fitted for something better than manual labor. It is not so much what a man has to do that degrades him as what he is in habit and association.

Key Structure ◦

1 be the last persons to ~
~할 사람이 결코 아니다

2 It is not so much what a man has to do that ~ as what he is ~
그의 품위를 떨어뜨리는 것은 그가 무슨 일을 하느냐라기보다는 오히려 그가 습관과 교제의 면에서 어떠한 인간이냐 하는 점이다
  • not so much A as B A라기보다는 오히려 B이다
  • It is ~ that degrades him 그의 품위를 떨어뜨리는 것은 ~이다 (It is ~ that 강조 구문)

3 what he is (in ~)
(~점에서) 그의 인간 됨됨이

내용 교육을 받은 사람이라고 해서 육체노동에 어울리지 않는 것은 아니다.

approve [əprúːv] 시인하다, 찬성하다(= admit, assent to, accede to)
manual laborer 육체노동자 *cf.* manual labor 육체노동
be fitted for ~에 어울리다
degrade [digréid] 품위를 떨어뜨리다, 타락하다(= downgrade, demote, debase)
association [əsòusiéiʃən] 교제, 공동생활, 협회(= company, affiliation, society)

Do not count your chickens before they are hatched.
부화되기도 전에 병아리를 세지 마라. (떡 줄 사람은 생각도 않는데 김칫국부터 마신다.)

147 A sharp, clever criticism on any individual is often the cause of later repentance. We are liable to say something rather amusing but perhaps rather unkind and our words leave a sting. The words may **hardly** have left our lips **before** we secretly wish we had not spoken in that way.

Key Structure

1 We are liable to say ~
우리는 ~라는 말을 하기 쉽다

2 The words may hardly have left our lips before ~ way.
그 말이 우리의 입에서 떨어지기가 무섭게 우리는 그렇게 말하지 말았어야 했는데라고 남몰래 바란다.
• hardly[scarcely] ~ when[before]

내용 남을 비난하기는 쉽고 그것은 상대방에게 상처를 남긴다.

criticism [krítisìzəm] 비판, 비난, 비평(= condemnation, reproach)
repentance [ripéntəns] 후회, 유감, 양심의 가책(= contrition, regret, remorse, self-accusation)
be liable to (~하기) 쉽다(= be apt to, be likely to)
sting [stiŋ] 쏘인 상처, 고통, 가시 돋친 말(= bite, prick, stab)
secretly [síːkrətli] 남몰래, 비밀스럽게

Don't put off till tomorrow what you can do today.
오늘 할 수 있는 일을 내일로 미루지 마라.

14 · 양보구문 Concession

01 be it A or B (or C) = whether it be[is] A or B (or C) : 그것이 A이든, B이든 (또는 C이든)

Everybody in practice worships something, be it only himself or money or dog-racing.
실제로 누구나 뭔가를 숭배한다. 그것이 자기 자신이든 돈이든 또는 개를 경주시키는 일이든.

02 복합관계부사절과 간접명령문 : Let + 목적어 + 동사 원형

However healthy a man may be, he must expect to endure a great deal of pain in the course of his life.
= No matter how healthy a man may be, ~
= Let a man be ever so healthy, ~
= Be a man ever so healthy, ~
= Be a man as healthy as he will, ~
어떤 사람이 제아무리 건강하다 해도, 그는 자신의 인생 과정에서 상당한 고통을 이겨 내야 하는 것쯤은 예상하고 있어야 한다.
• 복합관계부사절은 주어가 3인칭일 때 'Let+목적어+동사 원형'의 간접명령문의 형태나 'Be+주어+ever so ~'로 바꾸어 쓸 수 있으며 뜻은 양보를 나타낸다.

03 명령문과 복합관계대명사[부사]절

a. Whatever may come, you must be prepared.
= Come what may(= will), ~
무슨 일이 일어난다 하더라도 당신은 준비가 되어 있어야 한다.

b. Go where you will, you will be welcome.
= No matter where you go, ~
어디를 가든 환영을 받을 것이오.
• 명령문의 형태로 나타난 양보절은 복합관계대명사절이나 복합관계부사절로 바꾸어 쓸 수 있다.

04 as를 이용한 양보절

a. Try as you may, you will not succeed.
= However hard you may try, ~
아무리 열심히 노력해도 성공할 수 없을 것이다.

b. Woman as I am, I may be of help in time of need.
= Though I am a woman, ~
내가 여자이기는 하지만, 필요한 때에는 도움이 될 수 있을 것이다.

c. Young as he is, he has much sense.
그는 젊지만 분별력이 좋다.

d. The insight into the mystery of life, coupled as[though] it be with fear, has given rise to religion.
= ~, though it (may) be coupled with fear, ~
인생의 신비를 꿰뚫어 보는 통찰력은, 그것이 두려움과 결부되기는 하지만, 종교가 생겨나게 하였다.

05 for all / with all / notwithstanding / in spite of : 양보의 뜻을 나타내는 전치사(구)

a. For all his wealth, he is not happy at all.
그는 재산이 많음에도 불구하고, 결코 행복하지 않다.

b. With all his faults, I love him.
그에게 결점이 많지만, 나는 그를 사랑한다.

c. They started yesterday notwithstanding the snow.
눈이 옴에도 불구하고, 그들은 어제 출발하였다.

d. Tears will often flow in spite of our efforts to conceal them.
눈물은, 그것을 감추려는 우리의 노력에도 불구하고, 종종 흘러내린다.

06 최상급이 양보의 뜻을 지닌 경우

The wisest man in the world does not know what is in store for him.
세상에서 제아무리 현명한 사람이라도 자기 앞에 무슨 일이 닥칠지는 모르는 것이다.

148 The manners of a child are of more or less importance, according to his station in life; his morals cannot be attended to too early, **let his station be** what it may.

Key Structure ▸

1 be of more or less importance = be more or less important
다소간 중요하다

2 his morals cannot be ~ too early
어린이의 도덕은 제아무리 일찍 주의를 기울여 주어도 지나치지 않다
• cannot ~ too 아무리 ~해도 지나치지 않다

3 let his station be what it may
= whatever[no matter what] his station may be
그가 어떠한 위치에 있다고 하더라도

내용 어린이의 예절은 어릴 때부터 주의를 기울여 보살펴야 한다.

manners [mǽnərz] 예절, 예의범절(= behavior, conduct, etiquette)
station [stéiʃən] 위치, 신분, 직업(= post, position, situation)
moral [mɔ́(:)rəl] 도덕, 윤리(= lesson, maxim)
attend to (~에) 주의를 기울이다(= heed to)

플러스 문법정리 62

양보절을 이끄는 명령법 let
let는 보통 3인칭 목적어를 동반하여 명령문을 이끌며 양보의 뜻을 지닌다.

a. Let him be ever so rich, he is not satisfied at all.
= Be he ever so rich, he is not satisfied at all.
= However rich he may be, he is not satisfied at all.
= No matter how rich he may be, he is not satisfied at all.

b. Let it be ever so poor, there is no place like home.
= Be it ever so poor, there is no place like home.
= However poor it may be, there is no place like home.
= No matter how poor it may be, there is no place like home.

c. Let him be what he may, I don't mind it.
= Be he what he may, I don't mind it.
= Whatever he may be, I don't mind it.
= No matter what he may be, I don't mind it.

해석 a. 제아무리 부자라고 해도 전혀 만족을 모른다. b. 아무리 가난하다 해도 집만 한 곳이 없다. c. 그가 무엇이 되든 나와는 상관없다.

149 The most important fact about any man is what God he worships—what he really lives for. That reveals the hidden springs of character. That is the true measure of a man as he is at the inner core of his being. People may protest that they have no religion, yet everybody in practice worships something, **be** it only himself **or** money **or** dog-racing.

Key Structure •

1 **what he really lives for**
그가 진정으로 무엇을 위해 사는가

2 **a man as he is at ~ being**
인간 존재 내부의 중심에 있는 사람의 (진정한) 모습

3 **be it only himself or ~ dog-racing**
= whether it be[is] only himself or ~ dog-racing
그것이 단지 자기 자신이든 돈이든 또는 개를 경주시키는 것이든

내용 인간은 누구나 무엇인가를 숭배하며 산다.

worship [wə́ːrʃip] 숭배하다, 경배하다(= pray to, admire, adore, deify)
reveal [rivíːl] 드러내다, 누설하다, 폭로하다(= betray, expose, denude, let on)
hidden [hídən] 숨겨진, 비밀의(= concealed, disguised, enclosed, invisible, secret)
spring [spriŋ] 샘, 원천, 근원, 튐, 봄(= source, fount, fountain)
character [kǽriktər] 인격, 품성, 특징, 명성(= disposition, personality, figure)
measure [méʒər] 평가 척도[기준], 정량(= criterion, standard, test) ⓥ 평가하다
inner [ínər] 내부의, 내면의
core [kɔːr] 핵심, 속, 근성(= center, nucleus)
being [bíːiŋ] 존재, 생존, 인간
protest [prətést] 주장하다, 단언하다(= appeal, argue, object, assert, declare, insist on) ⓝ [próutest] 단언
in practice 실제로, 사실상

Even Homer sometimes nods.
호머(같은 대시인)도 졸 때가 있다. (원숭이도 나무에서 떨어질 때가 있다.)

150 Regardless of what Africa has been in truth or in myth, she will be that no longer. Call it nationalism, call it anticolonialism, **call it what you will**, Africa is going through a revolution.

1 Regardless of ~ **myth** = Irrespective of ~ **myth**
아프리카가 실제나 신화적인 면에서나, 무엇이었든지 관계없이

2 **she will be that no longer**
아프리카는 그러한 모습이 더 이상 아닐 것이다

3 **call it what you will** = whatever[no matter what] you may call it
그것을 무엇이라고 부르든지

내용 아프리카는 과거의 모습에서 벗어나 커다란 변혁을 겪고 있다.

regardless of (〜에) 관계없이, 무관하게(= irrespective of)
myth [miθ] 신화, 전설(= legend, mythology, symbolism)
nationalism [nǽʃənəlìzəm] 민족주의, 국수주의
anticolonialism [æ̀ntikəlóuniəlizm] 반식민주의
revolution [rèvəljúːʃən] 혁명, 대변혁(= revolt, reformation, transformation)

플러스 문법정리 63

국가를 나타내는 대명사 she와 it
국가를 지칭하는 대명사로는 she와 it이 있는데, she는 일반적으로 정치적 상황을 나타내는 경우에, it는 지리적 상황을 나타내는 경우에 쓰인다.

a. The Industrial Revolution has made England what she is now.
b. Africa is no longer what she used to be.
c. Kenya is famous for its beautiful scenery.

해석 a. 산업혁명 때문에 오늘의 영국이 있게 되었다. b. 아프리카는 더 이상 지금까지의 아프리카가 아니다.
  c. 케냐는 아름다운 경치로 유명하다.

151 **Notwithstanding** all the boy's mischiefs, the poor old soul, his mother, loved her boy. It seemed as though she loved him the better the worse he behaved, and that he grew the more in her favor the more he grew out of favor with the world.

Key Structure •

1 Notwithstanding **all the boy's mischiefs** = With[For] all the boy's mischiefs
자식의 모든 비행(非行)에도 불구하고

2 she loved him the better the worse he behaved
= the worse he behaved, the better she loved him
그가 더 형편없이 행동하면 할수록 그녀는 그를 더욱더 사랑하였다

3 he grew the more in her favor the more he ~ world
= the more he ~ , the more in her favor he grew
그가 세상의 미움을 사면 살수록 그는 더욱더 그녀의 눈에 들었다

내용 잘못이 있음에도 불구하고 어머니가 자식에 대해 갖는 무조건적인 사랑.

notwithstanding [nɑ̀twiðstǽndiŋ] (~에도) 불구하고(= with all, for all)
mischief [místʃif] 손해, 해독, 장난(= misconduct, devilry, naughtiness, damage)
soul [soul] 영혼, 기백, 사람
behave [bihéiv] 처신하다, 행동하다(= conduct oneself, act)
favor [féivər] 호의, 친절(= benefit, courtesy, approbation)

---

152 The production of a work of art is not the result of a miracle. It requires preparation. The soil, **be it ever so rich**, must be fed. By taking thought, by deliberate effort, the artist must enlarge, deepen and diversify his personality. Then the soil must lie fallow. Like the bride of Christ, the artist waits for the illumination that shall bring forth a new spiritual life.

Key Structure •

1 be it ever so rich
= let it be ever so rich = however[no matter how] rich it may be
그것이 제아무리 비옥하다고 해도

2 lie fallow 묵혀 있다(경작하지 않은 채로 놓여 있다)

3 the bride of Christ
그리스도의 신부 즉, 교회를 지칭 (여기서는 교회에서 메시아의 구원을 기다리는 크리스천을 지칭한다고도 볼 수 있음)

내용 예술 작품을 만들어 내는 데는 준비와 기다림이 필요하다.

miracle [mírəkl] 기적, 경이(= wonder, mystery) ⓐ miraculous
require [rikwáiər] 요구하다, 명령하다(= demand, call for)
preparation [prèpəréiʃən] 준비, 채비
feed [fi:d] 음식[먹이]을 주다, 공급하다

deliberate [delíbərit] 신중한, 사려 깊은(= careful, cautious, circumspect)
enlarge [inláːrdʒ] 크게 하다, 확대하다
deepen [díːpən] 깊게 하다, 심각하게 하다
diversify [divə́ːrsəfài] 변화시키다, 각양각색으로 하다(= broaden out, extend, vary)
fallow [fǽlou] 경작하지 않은, 묵혀 둔(= uncultivated, unsown, dormant)
bride [braid] 신부, 새색시
illumination [iljùːmənéiʃən] 조명, 해명, 계몽(= clarification, elucidation, enlightening)
bring forth 가져오다
spiritual [spíritʃuəl] 정신의, 성령의, 숭고한, 영적인(= divine, heavenly, holy, inspired)

153

Perhaps the most obvious way in which birds differ from men in their behavior is that they can do all that they have to do, including some quite complicated things, without ever being taught. Flying, to start with, is an activity which, **for all** its astonishing complexity of balance and aeronautical adjustment, comes untaught to birds.

Key Structure ▶

1   without ever being taught
    한 번도 배우지 않고서도

2   for all ~ adjustment
    몸의 균형과 비행상의 조절이 놀라울 정도로 복잡함에도 불구하고
    • aeronautical adjustment 비행시 (몸의) 조절

3   comes untaught to birds
    새들에게는 배우지 않고도 (~이) 온다

내용   새는 인간과 달리 가르쳐 주지 않아도 여러 가지 복잡한 비행상의 일들을 한다.

obvious [ábviəs] 분명한, 명백한(= apparent, clear-cut, distinct, evident)
complicated [kámpləkèitid] 복잡한, 뒤얽힌(= complex)
to start with 우선 첫째로(= to begin with, in the first place)
for all (~에도) 불구하고(= with all, notwithstanding)
astonishing [əstániʃiŋ] 놀라운, 눈부신
complexity [kəmpléksəti] 복잡성, 복잡함
balance [bǽləns] 평형, 균형, 예금 잔고, 천칭
aeronautical [ɛ̀ərənɔ́ːtikəl] 항공의, 비행(술)의
adjustment [ədʒʌ́stmənt] 조정, 조절

플러스 문법정리 64

양보를 나타내는 for all, with all

for all과 with all은 양보를 나타내는 전치사구로서 despite, in spite of와 같은 뜻을 갖는다.

a. **For all** his efforts, he failed to pass the test.

b. **With all** her riches, she was not proud.
= **Despite** her riches, she was not proud.
= **In spite of** her riches, she was not proud.
= **Though** she was rich, she was not proud.

해석 a. 그의 노력에도 불구하고 그는 시험에 실패하였다.   b. 재산이 많지만 그녀는 자랑하지 않았다.

---

154 Lincoln's ideal of 'Government of the people, by the people, for the people,' noble **as** it is, and heroically **as** he himself believed in it, is nevertheless only a splendid abstraction, very advantageously presented to the world, but, so far as political government is concerned, beyond exact realization in practice.

Key Structure ▸

1 noble as it is = though it is noble

2 heroically as he himself believed in it
 = though he himself believed in it heroically
 물론 그가 그것을 과감하게 믿기는 하였지만

3 is nevertheless only ~ abstraction
 그럼에도 불구하고 (역시) 훌륭한 추상(화 된) 개념이다
 • is의 주어는 Lincoln's ideal of ~에서 ideal.

4 so far as political government is concerned
 정치적 관리[통치]에 관한 한(통치라는 면에서 보면)

5 is beyond exact realization in practice
 실제로는 정확하게 실현하기가 어렵다 (beyond ~ ~하기가 어려운)
 e.g. The scenery was so beautiful that it was beyond description.
 그 경치는 너무 아름다워 형용하기가 어려웠다.

내용 링컨의 '국민의, 국민에 의한, 국민을 위한 정부[통치]'는 실제로는 실현하기가 어렵다.

heroically [hiróuikəli] 영웅적으로, 과감하게(= audaciously, bravely, valiantly)
splendid [spléndid] 빛나는, 화려한, 웅장한(= brilliant, dazzling, glorious, imposing, magnificent, inspiring)
abstraction [æbstrǽkʃən] 추상 개념[작용]
advantageously [æ̀dvəntéidʒəsli] 유리하게, 형편에 맞게(= favorably, gainfully)

present [prizént] 제시하다, 선물하다
exact [igzǽkt] 정확한, 엄격한(= accurate, precise, meticulous, rigorous)
realization [rì(:)əlizéiʃən] 실현, 현실화, 인식
in practice 실제로(= in fact), 실제 문제로서

플러스 문법정리 65

부정 · 초월의 뜻을 가진 beyond와 above

beyond와 above는 '~할 수 없는'의 뜻을 지니며, 부정 또는 초월의 의미를 나타낸다. above는 흔히 그 뒤에 동명사를 동반한다.

a. The scene was so beautiful that it was beyond description.

b. He is above telling a lie.

= He is the last person to tell a lie.

= He knows better than to tell a lie.

해석 a. 그 경치는 매우 아름다워서 표현하기가 어려웠다.   b. 그는 거짓말을 할 사람이 아니다.

---

155 Unlettered as he was and unpolished, he was still in some most important points a gentleman. He was a member of a proud and powerful aristocracy, and was distinguished by many both of the good, and of the bad qualities which belong to aristocrats.

Key Structure

1 Unlettered as he was and unpolished
= Though he was unlettered and unpolished
그가 교육을 받지 못하고 세련되지는 못하였지만 (양보 구문)

2 was distinguished by ~ ~으로 (다른 사람과) 구별되었다

3 by many both of the good, and of ~ aristocrats
귀족들이 가지고 있는 많은 좋고 나쁜 자질들에 의해
• many of the good and of the bad qualities의 구조에서 of the good (qualities)를 A로, of the bad qualities를 B로 보고, 'both A and B'의 상관접속사 구조로 연결시킨 특이한 구문.

내용 그는 교육 받지 못하고 세련미는 없었으나 아직은 귀족다운 점을 가지고 있었다.

unlettered [ʌ̀nlétərd] 무식한, 문맹의(= uneducated, illiterate)
unpolished [ʌnpáliʃt] 세련되지 않은, 때를 벗지 못한
aristocracy [æ̀ristákrəsi] 귀족사회(정치) cf. aristocrat [ərístəkræt] 귀족(= nobleman)
quality [kwáləti] 특질, 소질, 자질

156 The most beautiful thing we can experience is the mysterious. It is the source of all true art and science. He to whom this emotion is a stranger, who can no longer pause to wonder and stand rapt in awe, is as good as dead : his eyes are closed. This insight into the mystery of life, **coupled though it be with fear**, has also given rise to religion.

Key Structure •

1 The most beautiful thing (that) we ~ the mysterious
우리가 경험할 수 있는 가장 아름다운 일은 신비이다
   • the mysterious = mystery ('the+형용사'는 추상명사의 뜻을 가짐.)
   e.g. He has an eye for the beautiful. 그는 심미안이 있다. (= beauty)

2 He to whom this emotion is a stranger
이 감정을 전혀 느끼지 못하는 사람

3 He who can no longer ~ awe
하던 일을 멈추고 경탄을 자아내며 외경심에 빠져 황홀함을 느끼며 서 있지 못하는 사람

4 He (to whom ~, who ~) is as good as dead
그는 죽은 것이나 다름없다
   • is as good as dead = is no better than dead = is almost dead

5 coupled though it be with fear
   = though it may be coupled with fear
그것이 두려움과 관련되어 생각되기는 하지만(두려움과 쌍을 지어 나타나지만)

내용 신비를 느끼는 것은 진정한 예술과 과학과 종교의 근원이다.

experience [ikspí(:)əriəns] 경험[체험]하다, 느끼다
pause [pɔːz] (~을 위하여) 잠시 중단하다, 한숨 돌리다(= stop, break off)
rapt [ræpt] (~에) 몰두한, 황홀해 있는(= delighted, exalted, thrilled)
awe [ɔː] 두려움, 외경(= amazement, apprehension, reverence, wonder, veneration)
give rise to (~을) 야기시키다, 가져오다(= bring about, cause)

First catch your hare, then cook him.
우선 토끼를 잡고 요리해라. (일을 하기 전에 우선 사실을 확인하라.)

157

The history of a language largely reflects that of the people who speak it. **The most superficial study** of French shows it to be almost entirely of Latin origin, from which it can be inferred that France was for a long time a province of the Roman Empire.

Key Structure •

1   reflects that of the people who speak it
    그 언어를 사용하는 민족의 역사를 반영한다
    • that = the history

2   The most superficial study ~ origin
    프랑스어를 피상적으로만 연구해도 그것이 거의 전적으로 라틴어에 기원을 두고 있음을 알게 된다
    • shows it to be ~에서 it은 목적어로 French를 지칭하고 to be of Latin origin은 '라틴어에 기원을 두다'라는 뜻으로 목적격 보어.

3   from which it can be inferred that ~
    그 사실로부터 ~을 추론해 낼 수 있다
    • which는 계속적 용법의 관계대명사.

내용   한 언어의 역사는 그 언어를 사용하는 민족의 역사를 반영한다.

reflect [rif/ lékt] 반영하다, 나타내다, 반사하다, 반향하다(= demonstrate, exhibit, reveal, show, evidence, bear witness to)
superficial [sjùːpərfíʃəl] 피상적인, 허울 좋은, 면적의(= unimportant, casual, frivolous)
entirely [intáiərli] 완전히, 오로지(= completely, fully, totally, wholly)
infer [infə́ːr] 추론하다, 추정하다(= assume, conclude, deduce, draw a conclusion, extrapolate)
province [právins] 지역, 분야, 활동 영역
empire [émpaiər] 제국, 통치권

Give a dog a bad name and hang him.
한 번 쓴 누명은 벗기 어렵다.

158 Since he is the only one who has a real history, man is the only creature who has a face. Every face is a present witness to the fact that its owner has a past behind him which might have been otherwise, and a future ahead of him in which some possibilities are more probable than others. To 'read' a face is to guess at what might have been and what may still be. **The noblest** face reveals potential evil overcome, **the vilest** potential good suppressed.

Key Structure •

1 Every face is a present witness to ~
  모든 (사람의) 얼굴은 ~에 대한 현재의 증거이다

2 its owner has a past behind him ~, and a future ahead of him...
  그 주인은 그의 뒤에 ~한 과거를 가지고 있고, 그의 앞에 …한 미래를 가지고 있다

3 a past which might have been otherwise
  다른 모습이었을 수도 있는 과거
  • 가정법 과거완료의 구문으로 otherwise는 보어로 쓰였음. ☞ Part I '플러스 문법정리' 44 참조 (131쪽)

4 a future in which some possibilities ~ others
  어떤 가능성들이 다른 것들보다 더 있을 수 있는 미래

5 guess at what might have been and what may still be
  과거에 그러했음직하고, 아직도 그럴 법한 것에 대하여 추측하다
  • what은 관계대명사.

6 The noblest face ~ overcome.
  가장 고상해 보이는 얼굴도 극복된 잠재적 악을 드러내 보여 준다.

7 the vilest (face reveals) potential good suppressed
  가장 사악해 보이는 얼굴도 억압되어 있는 잠재적 선을 보여 준다

내용 사람의 얼굴에는 그의 과거와 미래의 모습이 새겨져 있다.

creature [krí:tʃər] 창조된 것, 피조물, 생물(= being, organism)
witness [wítnis] 증인, 증거, 목격자(= evidence, observer, bystander)
guess [ges] 추측하다, 어림짐작을 하다
reveal [rivíːl] 드러내다, 폭로하다(= show, exhibit, expose, betray)
potential [pəténʃəl] 잠재적인, 가능성 있는 ⓝ 가능성
evil [íːvəl] 악, 사악, 해악
vile [vail] 몹시 나쁜, 역겨운, 상스러운, 빈약한(= vicious, wicked, sinful, horrible, filthy)
suppress [səprés] 진압하다, 저지하다, 억제하다

15 · 전치사 Preposition

A 주요 전치사의 쓰임새

영어에는 45개 정도의 **단순 전치사**(simple preposition)가 있고, 다른 품사의 말과 합쳐져 구를 이루어 사용되는 **구 전치사**(phrase preposition)가 30개 정도가 있으며, 분사가 전치사로 사용되는 **분사 전치사**(participle preposition)도 몇 개가 있다.

> **단순 전치사** : in, at, on, for, to, from, about, into, above, over, until, by, during 등
> **구 전치사** : as to, as for, according to, out of, up to, by means of, in spite of 등
> **분사 전치사** : concerning, regarding, notwithstanding 등

전치사는 기본적으로 공간을 나타내는 명사와 어울린다(a 예문들). 그러나 전치사는 많은 경우에 시간(b 예문들)이나 추상영역(c 예문들)의 명사들과도 어울리는데, 이것은 그 쓰임새의 확장이라고 볼 수 있다.

01 at

- **a.** He is at London now. 그는 지금 (다른 곳이 아닌) 런던에 있다.
- **b.** The final examination takes place at the end of June.
  학기말 시험은 6월 말에 실시된다.
- **c.** He was at the noon of his career. 그는 자기 생애의 전성기에 있었다.

02 in

- **a.** He is in London now. 그는 지금 런던(안)에 있다.
- **b.** In the afternoon the children will give a play. 오후에는 아이들이 연극을 합니다.
- **c.** They were in great economic difficulty. 그들은 커다란 경제적 어려움에 처해 있었다.

03 on

- **a.** London is situated on the Thames. 런던은 템스 강에 임해 있다.
- **b.** He is not a man to sell his hens on a rainy day. 그가 밑지는 장사를 할 사람이 아니지.
- **c.** He has written a book on Korean economy. 그는 한국경제에 관한 책을 저술하였다.

04 with

- **a.** He came to the party with his wife. 그는 파티에 아내와 함께 왔다.
- **b.** With night coming on, we started home. 밤이 되자 우리는 집으로 향했다.
- **c.** She is now occupied with translation of a Korean novel into English.
  그녀는 지금 한국 소설을 영어로 번역하는 데에 여념이 없다.

05 to

a. Mr. Johnson came to Seoul last Sunday. 존슨 씨가 지난 일요일에 서울에 왔다.

b. It is five minutes to twelve. 12시 5분 전입니다.

c. This is a nice answer to the question. 이것은 그 문제에 대한 멋진 해답이다.

06 for

a. Mr. De Orio took the bus for Busan. 데 오리오 씨가 부산행 버스를 탔다.

b. Mr. De Orio traveled to Busan for three hours.
데 오리오 씨는 부산까지 3시간을 여행하였다.

c. There can be no reason for complaints. 불평할 하등의 이유가 있을 수 없다.

07 from

a. He traveled from London to Prague in 1999.
1999년에 그는 런던에서 프라하까지 여행하였다.

b. There will be another meeting a week from today. 다음 주 오늘 모임이 또 있습니다.

c. Skill comes from practice. 숙련은 연습으로부터 온다.

B 전치사 of의 쓰임새

01 본질적이며 제한적인 속성 · 부분을 나타냄

a. We were impressed by the size of the building. 우리는 그 건물의 크기에 압도되었다.

b. The neck of the jar was easily broken. 그 단지의 목은 쉽게 부러졌다.

02 소유 · 부분 · 분량 등을 나타냄

a. This building is the property of the government. 이 건물은 정부 소유이다.

b. Of all the applicants only three were accepted. 지원자 중에서 3명만이 살아남았다.

03 재료 · 유래 · 구성 관계를 나타냄

a. Don't make a fool of me any more. 저를 더 이상 비웃지 마세요.

b. This gentleman is of noble birth. 이 신사분은 명문 출신이다.

c. The committee consists of eleven members. 위원회는 11명의 위원으로 구성되어 있다.

04 원인 · 저술 관계를 나타냄

   a. My grandfather died of heart attack.   할아버지께서는 심장 마비로 돌아가셨다.

   b. These are the plays of Harold Pinter.   이것들은 해럴드 핀터가 쓴 연극들이다.

05 다른 사람 · 물체의 성질에 견줌

   a. She was an angel of a wife.   그녀는 천사 같은 아내였다.

   b. A mountain of a wave was overwhelming the sailboat.
      산 같은 파도가 그 범선을 집어삼키고 있었다.

06 동격 관계를 나타냄

   a. The State of California became part of the United States of America in September, 1850.
      캘리포니아 주는 1850년 9월에 미합중국의 일원이 되었다.

   b. She is not aware of the fact of my having seen him a week ago.
      그녀는 내가 일주일 전에 그를 만났다는 사실을 모르고 있다.

07 제거 · 탈락 동사 구문에서   ☞ Part I '03 동사구' 참조 (38쪽)

   a. The tall building deprives us of sunlight.   그 높은 건물이 우리에게서 햇볕을 빼앗고 있다.

   b. Why don't you rid yourself of the bad habit of excessive drinking and smoking?
      어째서 너는 과음과 흡연의 나쁜 습관을 떨치지 못하니?

08 공지 · 정보 동사 구문에서   ☞ Part I '03 동사구' 참조 (38쪽)

   a. Please remind me of my appointment with her once again.
      그녀와의 약속을 내게 다시 한 번 상기시켜 주세요.

   b. The man could not convince the jury of his innocence.
      그 사람은 배심원들에게 자신의 무죄를 확신시키지 못하였다.

09 때를 나타내는 구문을 형성할 때

   a. Of late the prices have been on constant rise.   최근 들어 물가가 꾸준히 오르고 있다.

   b. My friend called on me of an evening.   내 친구는 저녁이면 나를 찾아왔다.

C 구 전치사

01
a. Let's have a talk as to who will bell the cat.
누가 고양이 목에 종을 달 것인가에 관해 이야기해 보자.

b. He has succeeded gloriously by means of great exertion.
많은 노력을 통하여 그는 영광스러운 성공을 이룩하였다.

c. She went to Italy for the purpose of studying music.
음악을 공부하러 그녀는 이탈리아에 갔다.

d. Some thinkers live in advance of their age.
어떤 사상가들은 그들의 시대를 앞서 가는 삶을 산다.

e. In place of the typewriter, we commonly use personal computers these days. 타자기 대신에 우리는 오늘날 보통 개인용 컴퓨터를 사용하고 있다.

f. The company arrived late on account of heavy snow.
폭설로 인해 대원들은 도착이 늦었다.

g. I advised him to work hard, but to no purpose.
나는 그에게 열심히 일하라고 충고하였으나 (그 결과는) 허사였다.

h. They did evil things under the cloak of patriotism.
그들은 애국심이라는 미명 아래 비열한 짓들을 하였다.

02
a. They suddenly appeared from behind the curtain.
그들이 커튼 뒤에서 갑자기 나타났다.

b. Aside from his salary, he receives his pension every month.
월급 외에도 그는 매달 연금을 받는다.

D 전치사의 생략과 전치사 상당어

01
a. Stop (for) a moment. 잠시 멈추세요.
b. He is busy (with) preparing for the new business. 그는 새로운 사업 준비에 바쁘다.

02
a. Come see me next Monday, please. 다음 주 월요일에 저를 보러 오세요.
b. There was a big fire in downtown last night. 간밤에 시내에 큰 화재가 있었다.
cf. (×) on next Monday, (×) on last night

03
a. No student answered correctly but him. 그 말고는 어떤 학생도 정답을 말하지 못했다.
b. They are making a law concerning public welfare.
그들은 공공복지에 관한 법률을 만들고 있다.

Passages 159~175

159

The conception of taboo plays a great part **in** the life of primitive peoples. Taboo means that something must be avoided because it will bring misfortunes and death. How these taboo ideas originated lies buried **in** obscurity.

Key Structure •

1 play a great part in ~ ~에서 커다란 역할을 하다

2 How these taboo ideas originated
   이 금기 사항들이 어떻게 유래하였는지는
   • 주어로 쓰인 의문사절.

3 lies buried in obscurity 어둠 속에 묻혀 있다
   • buried는 bury의 과거분사형으로 lies의 보어 역할을 함.

> **내용** 금기는 불행이나 죽음을 가져올 수 있는 말이나 물건을 뜻하나 그것이 어떻게 유래하였는지는 불명확하다.

conception [kənsépʃən] 개념(= idea), 생각, 임신 ⓥ conceive
taboo, tabu [təbúː] (종교나 사회적 관례로서) 금기(하는 말[물건])
primitive [prímitiv] 원시의, 소박한, 야만의 cf. primitive people 원시인
originate [ərídʒənèit] (~에서) 시작하다, 근원이 되다
obscurity [əbskjú(ː)ərəti] 불명료함, 모호함, 어두컴컴함(= unclearness, darkness) ⓐ obscure

---

160

If an opinion contrary **to** your own makes you angry, that is a sign that you are subconsciously aware of having no good reason for thinking as you do. So whenever you find yourself getting angry about a difference of opinion, be **on** your guard; you will probably find, **on** examination, that your belief is going **beyond** what the evidence warrants.

Key Structure •

1 an opinion (which is) contrary to your own
   당신 자신의 의견과 반대되는 의견
   • your own = your own opinion
   > **cf.** He said nothing to the contrary. 그는 반대되는 말을 하지 않았다.
   > 전치사구 to the contrary는 nothing을 꾸미는 형용사 기능을 함. 따라서 **To the contrary** he said nothing.으로 바꾸면 잘못된 표현이 됨. 그러나 on the contrary는 부사 기능을 하므로 He said nothing **on the contrary**.(반대로, 그는 아무 말도 하지 않았다.)를 **On the contrary**, he said nothing.으로 바꾸어 써도 됨.

2 be aware of having no good reason for thinking as you do
당신이 생각하듯이 생각할 하등의 이유가 없음을 알아채다
- have no good reason for -ing (또는 to ⓥ) ~할 이유가 없다
- as you do = as you think (do는 대동사(pro-verb))

3 whenever you find yourself getting angry about ~
~에 대하여 당신이 화를 내고 있음을 알 때에는 언제나

4 on examination = when[after] you examine
(당신이) 검토해 보면

5 what the evidence warrants
증거가 보증하는 것
- 관계대명사절로 전치사 beyond의 목적어 역할을 함.

내용 자신의 의견과 다른 의견에 화가 난다는 것은 자신의 의견이 잘못된 것일 수도 있다는 증거이다.

contrary [kántreri] 반대의, 서로 용납하지 않는
subconsciously [sʌbkánʃəsli] 잠재의식 속에서, 어렴풋이
aware [əwɛ́ər] (…을) 의식하고 있는(= conscious)
guard [gɑːrd] 경계, 감시, 조심 *cf.* be on one's guard 경계하다
beyond [bijánd] ~ 너머에, ~ 저편에
warrant [wɔ́rənt] 보증하다(= justify, prove) ⓝ 보증(서)

---

161 Birds are able sometimes to discriminate **between** protectors and persecutors, but seldom very well, I should imagine; they do not view the face only, but the whole form, and our frequent change of dress must make it difficult for them to distinguish the individuals they know and trust **from** strangers. Even a dog is occasionally **at** fault, when his master, last seen **in** a black suit, reappears **in** white **with** a straw hat on.

Key Structure •

1 seldom very well, I should imagine
= they are seldom able to discriminate very well, I should imagine
좀처럼 썩 잘 구별하지는 못한다고 나는 생각한다
- I should imagine 감히 그렇게 생각해 봅니다(정중한 표현)

2 they do not view the face only, but the whole form
= they view not only the face, but (also) the whole form
- not only A but (also) B 구문

189

3 last seen in a black suit = who was seen in a black suit last time
지난번에는 검정 옷을 입었던 (주인이)

4 with a straw hat on 밀짚모자를 쓰고

- on = on his head: 의미가 분명하여 목적어를 빼고 단독으로 쓰였음. (전치사가 부사 기능을 하는 것으로 볼 수 있음)

내용 새들도 사람을 알아보지만, 사람의 전체 모습을 보기 때문에 옷을 갈아입고 나타나는 경우 누가 누군지 구별을 잘 못한다.

discriminate [diskrímineit] 구별하다, 구분하다 (~ A from B, ~ between A and B)
protector [prətéktər] 보호자 ⓥ protect
persecutor [pə́ːrsəkjùːtər] 괴롭히는 자, 박해하는 자 ⓥ persecute *cf.* persecution 박해
frequent [fríːkwənt] 빈번한, 잦은
occasionally [əkéiʒənəli] 가끔, 이따금씩
fault [fɔːlt] 잘못, 실수 *cf.* be at fault 실수를 하다
straw hat 밀짚모자

플러스 문법정리 66

공간 전치사의 의미와 쓰임새 (1)
전치사는 기본적으로 공간(space)에 존재하는 두 물체 사이의 관계(relation)를 나타내는 품사이다.

(1) a. He is in London now.　　　　　　b. He is at London now.
(2) a. Lots of snow was still on the earth.　b. The earth lay beneath a blanket of snow.
(3) a. The cat came into the room.　　　　b. The cat went out of the room.
(4) a. He took the train for Busan.　　　　b. He came up from Busan.
(5) a. He was walking to the river.　　　　b. He was walking along the river.
　　c. He was walking across the street.　d. He was driving through the tunnel.

위 공간 전치사의 기본적인 의미는 다음과 같이 정의할 수 있다.

in : 한 물체가 다른 물체의 안에 포함되어 있음을 묘사
at : 한 물체가 '지리적인 한 점(geometric point)'에 있음을 묘사 (대조적이고 선택적인 의미가 짙음.)
on : 한 물체가 다른 물체의 위에 놓여 접촉하면서 지탱(support)을 받고 있음을 묘사
beneath : 한 물체가 다른 물체와 접촉한 상태로 그 아래에 붙어 있는 것을 묘사
into : 한 물체가 다른 물체 안으로 들어감을 묘사
out (of) : 한 물체가 다른 물체 밖으로 나옴을 묘사
for : 한 물체가 어떤 행선지로 향함을 묘사 (행선지가 반드시 목적지는 아님: 방향을 강조)
from : 한 물체가 다른 물체·지점으로부터 나온 것임을 묘사 (출처)
to : 한 물체가 다른 물체를 향하여 가거나 그 방향으로 면하고 있음을 묘사 (방향, 목적지)
along : 한 물체가 다른 물체의 옆을 따라감을 묘사
across : 한 물체가 다른 물체를 가로질러 감을 묘사
through : 한 물체가 다른 물체의 속을 뚫고 나아감을 묘사

주요 공간 전치사의 의미를 이미지로 나타내면 다음과 같다.

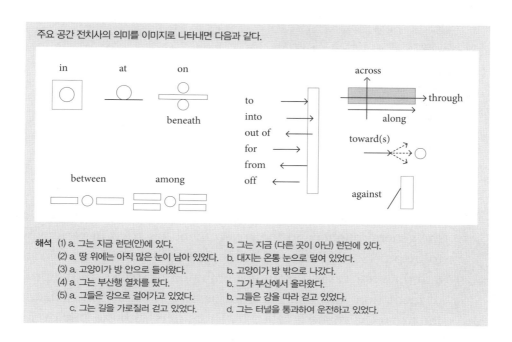

해석 (1) a. 그는 지금 런던(안)에 있다.   b. 그는 지금 (다른 곳이 아닌) 런던에 있다.
(2) a. 땅 위에는 아직 많은 눈이 남아 있었다.   b. 대지는 온통 눈으로 덮여 있었다.
(3) a. 고양이가 방 안으로 들어왔다.   b. 고양이가 방 밖으로 나갔다.
(4) a. 그는 부산행 열차를 탔다.   b. 그가 부산에서 올라왔다.
(5) a. 그들은 강으로 걸어가고 있었다.   b. 그들은 강을 따라 걷고 있었다.
   c. 그는 길을 가로질러 걷고 있었다.   d. 그는 터널을 통과하여 운전하고 있었다.

162 The relation **between** art and religion is one of the most difficult questions that we have to face. We look back **into** the past and see art and religion emerging hand **in** hand **from** the dim recesses of prehistory. For many centuries they seem to remain indissolubly linked; and then, **in** Europe, about six hundred years ago, the first signs of breach appeared. And finally **with** the Renaissance we came to have an art essentially free and independent, individualistic **in** its origins, and aiming to express nothing **beyond** the artist's own personality.

Key Structure

1 see art and religion emerging hand in hand
예술과 종교가 손을 맞잡고 나오는 것을 보다
• 5형식[주어(we) + 동사(see) + 목적어(art and religion) + 목적격보어(emerging ~)] 문장

2 aiming to express nothing beyond ~
~을 넘어서는 것은 어느 것도 표현하지 않는 것을 목표로 하는

내용 중세 이전에는 예술과 종교가 구분이 안 되었으나 문예부흥기 이후 예술가의 진정한 개성만을 표현함으로써 종교로부터 독립되고 독창성을 지닌 예술이 등장하였다.

face [feis] (곤란한 문제에) 직면하다, 부딪히다
emerge [imə́:rdʒ] (어두운 곳에서) 나타나다
dim [dim] 희미한, 침침한
recesses [risés] 후미진 곳, 구석진 곳
prehistory [prì:hístəri] 선사(시대)
indissolubly [ìndisáljubli] 불가분하게, 단단히 ⓥ dissolve 풀다, 분리되다
breach [bri:ʧ] 단절, 불화 ⓥ breach (break와 어원이 같음)
the Renaissance 르네상스, 문예부흥 (14~17세기 유럽에서 나타난 (고대 그리스의) 예술, 문화, 학문의 부흥)
individualistic [ìndəvìdʒuəlístik] (사상, 행동이) 독립적인, 개성적인 cf. individual 개인적인

---

163 Strikes and labor wars are expensive **to** workers, employers, and the general public; and the government has tried **in** various ways to help preserve industrial peace **through** mediation, arbitration, and, **in** a few cases, **through** prohibition of strikes. In the process of mediation, an impartial third party, known as the mediator or impartial chairman, is called in. He confers **with** the employer and labor representatives **in** a friendly, informal way, and tries tactfully to get them together. If he is unable to do this, he is not expected to render any decision **in** the dispute.

Key Structure •

1 **help preserve industrial peace** 산업 평화를 유지하도록 돕다
   • help는 바로 뒤에 to 없는 동사를 가질 수 있음. (직접적인 도움을 준다는 의미가 강함)

2 **get them together** 그들을 한 자리에 모으다

3 **he is not expected to ~ = it is not expected that he will ~**
   그는 ~하지 않으리라고 기대된다(그는 ~하여서는 안 된다)

내용 동맹파업이나 노동전쟁은 값비싼 대가를 치러야 하는 행위이므로 중재나 조정을 통해서 가급적이면 막아야 하고, 이 과정에는 공평한 제3자가 조정자로 나서야 한다.

strike [straik] 동맹파업, 스트라이크
labor war (고용자와 피고용자 간의) 노동전쟁
the general public 일반대중
various [vέəriəs] 다양한 ⓥ vary ⓝ variation, variety
mediation [mì:diéiʃən] 조정(調停) ⓥ mediate cf. mediator 조정자
arbitration [ɑ̀:rbitréiʃən] 중재 ⓥ arbitrate cf. arbitrator 중재자
prohibition [pròuhəbíʃən] (특히, 법에 의한) 금지 ⓥ prohibit ⓐ prohibitive
impartial [impɑ́:rʃəl] 공평한, 공정한
a third party 제3자
call in (조언을 구하려고) 불러들이다
confer [kənfə́:r] 협의하다, 상의하다(with) ⓝ conference

labor representative 노동자 대표
tactfully [tǽktfəli] 요령 있게, 재치 있게
render [réndər] 만들다(= make), 되게 하다
dispute [dispjú:t] 분쟁(하다), 논쟁(하다) *cf.* 여기서는 labor dispute(노동분쟁).

---

164   The wind was blowing sweetly **from over** the hill into my room. On a sudden I wanted to be out in the meadow. Out in the meadow, I found the sun was shining brightly **over** my head. And the earth **beneath** my feet was warm enough to sleep **under** blankets. I picked a wild sunflower, and as I looked into its golden heart such a sudden wave of homesickness came upon me that I almost wept. I wanted mother, with her gentle voice and quiet firmness; I longed to hear father's jolly songs and to see his twinkling blue eyes; I was lonesome for my sister with whom I used to play in the meadow picking daisies and wild sunflowers until the sun went down **below** the horizon.

Key Structure ▸

1   from over **the hill** 언덕 너머로부터
- 소위 이중전치사 구문이나, from이 over the hill이라는 전치사구를 목적어로 갖는 구조. 다시 말해, over the hill은 over라는 전치사가 the hill을 목적어로 취한 전치사구이고 이것이 여기에서 명사처럼 쓰여 또 다른 전치사인 from의 목적어가 됨.

2   **I was lonesome for my sister** 누이가 (그 자리에) 없어서 허전한 마음이었다

> 내용   향기로운 바람이 불어오고 햇볕이 좋은 날 초원에 나가 야생 해바라기 한 송이를 꺾어 냄새를 맡다가 갑자기 어머니, 아버지, 누이가 보고 싶은 향수에 젖어들었다.

on a sudden 갑자기(= (all) of a sudden, suddenly)
meadow [médou] 초원, 목초지
homesickness [hóumsìknes] 향수(병)
come upon[on] ~에게 갑자기 다가오다, 엄습하다
firmness [fə́ːrmnes] 견고함, 단단함
long [lɔ(ː)ŋ] (애타게) 바라다, 갈망하다
jolly [dʒáli] 쾌활한, 즐거운
twinkle [twíŋkl] 반짝거리다
lonesome [lóunsəm] 허전한, 외로운
horizon [həráizən] 지평선, 수평선

플러스 문법정리 67

공간 전치사의 의미와 쓰임새 (2)

앞에서 설명한 주요 공간 전치사 외에 다음의 공간 전치사도 그 쓰임에 유의하여야 한다.

(1) a. They climbed up the hill.
   b. They ran down the hill.

(2) a. Birds were flying high above the trees.
   b. The sun went down below the horizon.

(3) a. There was a bridge over the river.
   b. Several boys were sitting under the willow tree.

(4) a. The boat sank beneath the waves.
   b. There is a village beyond the pass.

(5) a. Don't leave this within the reach of children.
   b. Leave this out of the reach of children.

위 공간 전치사의 기본적인 의미는 다음과 같이 정의할 수 있다.

up : 한 물체가 다른 물체를 따라 위로 올라감을 묘사
down : 한 물체가 다른 물체를 따라 아래로 내려감을 묘사
above : 한 물체가 다른 물체와 거리를 두고 위에 있음을 묘사
below : 한 물체가 다른 물체와 거리를 두고 아래에 있음을 묘사
over : 한 물체가 다른 물체와 떨어져서 위에 있되 넓은 범위에 걸친 덮개의 개념을 묘사
under : 한 물체가 다른 물체와 떨어져서 아래에 있되 넓은 범위에 걸쳐 있음을 묘사
beneath : 한 물체가 다른 물체와 접촉한 상태로 그 아래에 붙어 있는 것을 묘사
beyond : 한 물체가 다른 물체의 저편 너머에 있음을 묘사
within : 한 물체가 일정 지역 안에 있음을 묘사
out of : 한 물체가 일정 영역 밖에 있음을 묘사

위의 공간 전치사의 의미를 이미지로 나타내면 다음과 같다.

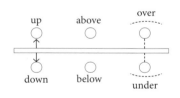
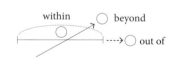

해석 (1) a. 그들은 언덕을 올라갔다.   b. 그들은 언덕을 달려 내려갔다.
  (2) a. 새들이 나무 위 높은 곳에서 날고 있었다.   b. 태양이 지평선 너머로 졌다.
  (3) a. 강 위로 다리 하나가 놓여 있었다.   b. 소년 몇 명이 버드나무 아래에 앉아 있었다.
  (4) a. 그 배는 파도 아래로 가라앉았다.   b. 고개 너머에 마을이 하나 있다.
  (5) a. 이것을 아이들 손이 닿는 곳에 두지 마시오.   b. 이것을 아이들 손이 닿는 곳 밖에 두시오.

165 **On** pleasant afternoons, when he was off duty, he liked to have a ramble **for** some time by himself about the fields and lanes. **In** solitude he was never dull; had you met him **during** one of these afternoon walks, more likely than not you would have seen a gentle smile on his face as he walked. His thoughts were definitely of agreeable things. He liked the sunshine and country quiet, and above all the sense of momentary independence.

Key Structure

1 have a ramble about ~
 ~ 부근을 산책하다
 • about은 '부근'을 뜻하는 전치사.

2 had you met him = if you had met him
 당신이 그를 만났더라면
 • 가정법 과거완료 구문으로 과거 사실의 반대를 나타내며, 접속사 if를 생략으로써 조동사 had가 앞으로 나온 도치 구문.

3 His thoughts were of agreeable things
 그의 생각은 즐거운 일에만 머물렀다
 • of는 성질을 나타내는 전치사이며, of agreeable things는 were의 보어 기능을 함.

내용 일과에서 벗어난 맑은 날 오후에 그는 주변의 들과 오솔길로 산책하기를 좋아하였는데, 그것은 홀로 있는 것이 주는 독립감 때문이었다.

be off duty 비번이다, 일과에서 벗어나 있다(≒ be on duty)
ramble [rǽmbl] (전원 속의) 산책, 거닐기
lane [lein] (시골의) 좁은 길, 오솔길
solitude [sάlitjùːd] 홀로 있음, 고독
dull [dʌl] 지루한(= boring)
more likely than not 아마도(= probably)
definitely [défənitli] 틀림없이(= surely)
country quiet 시골의 고요, 정적 *quiet는 명사로 쓰임
momentary [móuməntèri] 찰나의, 순간의 cf. momentary independence 찰나의 독립감

166 **During** the Middle Ages, architecture, painting, and sculpture were used almost entirely in the service of the Church. Church architecture was the central art of the period, and the other arts were used to embellish, or beautify, it. The building and beautifying of a church was considered a community project **during** the Middle Ages. In their churches, medieval people expressed both religious feeling and local pride.

Key Structure

1 be used in the service of ~ ～을 위하여 쓰이다

2 the building and beautifying of a church
   교회당 하나를 짓고 아름답게 꾸미는 일
   • 동명사 building과 beautifying 앞에 the가 붙음으로 인하여 두 단어는 완전히 명사화됨. the building and beautifying of a church는 이 문장의 주어로 쓰였고 동사는 was임.

내용 중세에는 건축, 그림, 조각 등의 예술이 교회만을 위해 존재하였고, 사람들은 교회당을 짓고 아름답게 꾸미는 일에서 종교적 느낌과 지역의 자존심을 표현하였다.

the Middle Ages 중세 (유럽사에서 보통 5세기부터 1350년경까지를 가리킴)
architecture [ɑ́ːrkitèktʃər] 건축(물), 건축학 cf. architect 건축가
sculpture [skʌ́lptʃər] 조각(품) cf. sculptor 조각가
entirely [intáiərli] 전적으로, 완전히
embellish [imbéliʃ] 장식하다(= beautify)
a community project 한 지역 공동체가 함께 성취해야 할 일
medieval [mìːdíːvəl] 중세의
local pride 지역의 자존심

167 In September, 1773, the East India Company planned to ship 500,000 pounds of tea to their American agents in ports along the Atlantic coast. When the colonists learned about the East India Company's plan, local tea merchants in American ports from South Carolina to Maine took steps to meet this attempt to drive them out of business. The Boston Tea Party was the most violent of these steps. **After** this act of rebellions, Governor Hutchinson called it "the boldest stroke which had been struck in America."

Key Structure

1 drive them out of business
그들을 (장사를 못하게 하여) 폐업으로 몰고 가다

2 the boldest stroke which had been struck in America
아메리카 대륙에 지금까지 있었던 타격 중에서 가장 대담한 타격
• strike a stroke 타격을 가하다 → (수동문) a stroke is struck 타격이 가해지다

내용 1773년 9월에 보스턴 차 사건이 있었고, 이것은 미국 독립의 주요한 계기 중의 하나가 되었다.

the East India Company (영국) 동인도 회사(東印度會社)
ship [ʃip] 선적하다, 배로 보내다
port [pɔːrt] 항구, 항만
the Atlantic coast (미국의) 대서양 연안 (미국의 동쪽 연안)
colonist [kálənist] 식민지 주민
South Carolina 사우스캐롤라이나 (미 남동부 대서양 연안의 주(州)로, 위로는 노스캐롤라이나, 아래로는 조지아 주와 접함)
Maine 메인 (미국 북동부 대서양 연안의 주(州)로, 위로는 캐나다, 아래로는 매사추세츠 주, 서쪽으로는 뉴햄프셔 주와 접함)
take steps 조처를 취하다
the Boston Tea Party 보스턴 차(茶) 사건 (1773년 매사추세츠 주의 수도 보스턴에서 일어난 사건)
violent [váiələnt] 격렬한, 과격한, 난폭한 cf. violence 폭력, 과격함
rebellion [ribéljən] 반란, 모반 ⓥ rebel
bold [bould] 용감한, 대담한 cf. bald [bɔːld] 대머리의
stroke [strouk] 타격, 일격

플러스 문법정리 68

시간 전치사의 의미와 쓰임새

시간을 나타내는 전치사로는 at, on, in, for, during, to, by, until 등이 주로 쓰이고, after, from, between, through, within, since 등도 많이 쓰인다. 여기서 한 가지 특이한 점은, 이 시간 전치사도 사실은 앞에서 설명한 공간 전치사들이 시간이라는 의미장(semantic space)을 빌려 차용된 것일 뿐, 공간 전치사와 그 사용 면에서 큰 차이가 없다는 점이다. 따라서 공간 전치사의 쓰임을 잘 알아 두면 시간 전치사의 사용도 잘 이해가 된다.

(1) a. Trains roared in and out at all hours.
  b. The new semester starts on Monday next week.
  c. The Korean war broke out in June, 1950.
  d. My grandfather passed away in 2010.

(2) a. During the war we couldn't eat for a week.
  b. I stayed at my uncle's through the vacation.

(3) a. Please come back after a week.
  b. Please come back within a week.
  c. Please come back in a week.

(4) a. Please wait here till noon. b. I will be back by noon.

(5) a. We lived here from 2000 to 2005. b. We have lived here since 2000.

(6) a. He is in the prime of life. b. He is past the prime of his life.

(7) a. He has lived in Seoul over ten years.
  b. Boys and girls under age are not allowed in.

시간 전치사 쓰임새의 차이

1) **at, on, in** : at은 여러 개의 점 중에서 하나를 선택하는 의미이고, on은 접촉과 지탱이므로 특정한 요일이나 시각에 일어난 일을 나타낼 때에 쓰이고, in은 container의 개념이 있으므로 그 안에 여러 개의 개체를 지니는 달(month), 계절(season), 연(year)에 쓰인다.

2) **during, for, through** : during은 시간 개념보다는 사건(event) 개념을 나타낸다. (e.g. during the war, during the vacation) 따라서 during two hours라는 말은 잘못된 영어이다. 그러나 '그 두 시간이 지나가는 중에'라는 뜻인 during the[those] two hours는 바른 표현이다.
  for는 지속되는 시간 개념을 나타내므로 시간의 양을 나타내는 말과 함께 쓰여야 한다. (e.g. for three days, for a week, for a moment)
  through는 '~동안 줄곧(처음부터 끝까지)'의 의미이다.

3) **after, within, in** : after는 '~ 후에', within은 '~ 이내에', in은 '(현재로부터) ~의 말미에', '~이 지나서'라는 뜻으로 쓰인다.

4) **till/until, by** : till/until은 동작이나 상태가 어느 시점까지 계속될 때 쓰이고, by는 어느 시점까지 상황이 완료되는 경우에 쓰인다.

5) **from, since** : from은 단순히 '어느 때를 시작으로 하는 기점'을 나타내므로, 현재·과거·미래 동사와 함께 자유롭게 쓰이고, since는 '과거 어느 시점부터 현재까지'라는 의미를 지니므로 주로 현재완료 동사와 함께 쓰인다.

6) **past, over, under** : past는 pass의 과거분사 passed가 변하여 전치사가 된 것으로 '~이 지난'의 뜻을 갖고, over는 일정 시간을 넘는 경우에, under는 그 반대의 경우에 쓰인다.

해석 (1) a. 열차는 밤낮없이 마을을 굉음을 내며 드나들었다. b. 새 학기는 다음 주 월요일에 시작한다.
    c. 한국전쟁은 1950년 6월에 발발하였다. d. 할아버지께서는 2010년에 돌아가셨다.
  (2) a. 전쟁 중에 우리는 일주일 동안을 먹지 못하였다. b. 방학 내내 삼촌 집에 머물렀다.
  (3) a. 일주일 후에 다시 오세요. b. 일주일 안에 다시 오세요. c. 일주일쯤 있다가 다시 오세요.
  (4) a. 정오 때까지 (줄곧) 여기에서 기다리세요. b. 내가 정오 때까지는 돌아오리다.
  (5) a. 우리는 2000년부터 2005년까지 이곳에서 살았다. b. 우리는 2000년 이래로 계속하여 이곳에서 살아왔다.
  (6) a. 그는 인생의 절정기에 있다. b. 그는 인생의 절정기를 지났다.
  (7) a. 그는 서울에서 10년 넘게 살아왔다. b. 미성년자는 입장이 안 됩니다.

168 The anxieties of childhood are **of** shorter term, so to speak, than those which afflict us adults, but fundamentally they are very similar to ours, and in particular these troubles resemble ours in that they are so often wholly imaginary and so often suffered in secret.

Key Structure •

1 **be of shorter term than ~** ~보다 지속되는 기간이 더 짧다
  • of는 본질적인 성질을 나타내는 전치사이고, of 이하는 be동사의 보어 역할을 함.

2 **resemble ours** = resemble our anxieties
  우리의 걱정거리들과 닮았다

3 **in that + 절** ~라는 점에서
  • 전치사는 그 뒤에 명사(구)를 목적어로 갖지만, 가끔 절(clause)이 나오기도 함.
  except that ~ (~을 제외하면), except when ~ (~ 경우를 제외하면), but that ~ (~이 없(었)다면).
  모두 전치사 뒤의 명사가 생략된 경우라고 보면 됨.
  except that ~ = except the fact that ~
  except when ~ = except the time when ~
  but that ~ = but for the fact that ~

4 **they are ~ so often suffered in secret**
  이것으로 남몰래 매우 자주 고통을 받는다
  • they = these troubles
  • suffer these troubles 이 어려움들을 겪다

내용 어린아이 시절의 걱정거리들은 어른의 걱정거리들에 비해 지속되는 기간은 짧지만, 많은 경우 공상에서 나오며 또 남몰래 혼자 겪는 경우가 매우 자주 있다는 점에서 서로가 유사하다.

anxiety [æŋzáiəti] 걱정(거리), 근심(거리) *cf.* anxious [ǽŋkʃəs] 걱정하는, 열망하는
term [təːrm] (지속되는) 기간, 학기
so to speak 말하자면
afflict [əflíkt] 괴롭히다, 피해를 입히다
fundamentally [fʌ̀ndəməntǽli] 근본적으로, 기본적으로
in particular 특히(= particularly)
resemble [rizémbl] 닮다(= take after), 비슷하다
imaginary 상상에서 나오는(= coming from imagination)
  cf. imaginative 상상력이 풍부한(= full of imagination)
  imaginable 상상해 볼 수 있는(= can be imagined)

169   To the average Westerner, East has always been the land **of** mystery, and though modern means **of** communication and modern methods **of** transmitting information, especially the camera, the cinema, the internet, the smart phone, and so on, are making him familiar with the external features **of** Oriental civilization, its inward spirit still remains strange and remote.

Key Structure ▶

1   modern means of communication and modern methods of transmitting information, ~ , are making him familiar with ~
     현대의 통신 수단과 정보 전달방식들로 인해 서양인은 ~과 친숙해지고 있다
     • him = the average Westerner
     • means of communication의 of, methods of transmitting의 of, 또한 land of mystery의 of는 모두 성질 · 속성을 나타내는 전치사임.

2   its inward spirit still remains strange and remote
     그것[동양 문명]의 내적 정신은 아직도 낯설고 먼 곳에 머무르고 있다
     • its = of Oriental civilization

     내용   동양 문명의 외적인 것들이 옛날보다는 더 가까워졌으나 그 내적인 진수는 평범한 서양인에게는 아직 낯설고 멀리에 있다.

mystery [místəri] 신비, 불가사의
communication [kəmjùːnəkéiʃən] 통신, 의사소통
transmit [trænsmít] 전송   *cf.* radio transmission 무선 통신
information [ìnfərméiʃən] 정보, 지식
external feature 외적 특성
inward spirit 내적 정신[영혼]
remote [rimóut] 먼 곳에 있는

170 The story **of** the Tower of Babel appears in the Old Testament. In an attempt to understand mysteries **of** God, men tried to build a tower that would reach to heaven. As a punishment for their pride, the tower collapsed and the language **of** the workers became confused. This is an allegorical explanation **of** the origin **of** the various languages that are spoken throughout the world. Today more than three thousand languages are spoken in the world, many **of** which stem from a common source. The Roman languages, such as French, Spanish, and Italian are all derived from Latin. English, on the other hand, belongs to the Germanic languages, but has borrowed many elements from other languages like Greek, Latin, French, etc. for various reasons.

Key Structure •

1 many of **which stem from** ~ = and many of **them stem from** ~
　(그리고) 그것들 중 많은 것들은 ~에서 유래한다
　• which = more than three thousand languages that are spoken in the world (which는 관계대명사)

2 of의 의미
　The story of the Tower of Babel 동격관계　　　mysteries of God 소유관계
　the language of the workers 소유·소속관계　　an explanation of the origin 목적관계
　the origin of the various languages 주격관계　　many of which 부분·분량관계

　내용　세계에는 3천 개 이상의 언어가 존재하는데, 프랑스어, 스페인어, 이탈리아어 등은 고대 로마의 라틴어에서 갈라져 나온 언어들로 로만스어군에 속하고, 영어는 게르만어군에 속하는 언어이다.

the Tower of Babel 바벨탑(구약 성경 창세기(Genesis)에 나오는 이야기. 하나님의 권위에 도전한 인간을 징벌하기 위해 언어를 혼잡하게 하고 사람들을 온 세상에 흩어지게 한 곳이 바로 바벨이며, 바벨탑은 헬라어로 '혼돈'이라는 뜻이 있음.)
the Old Testament 구약 성경　*cf.* the New Testament 신약 성경
heaven [hévn] 하늘나라, 천국
punishment [pʌ́niʃmənt] 처벌, (형)벌
collapse [kəlǽps] 붕괴(하다)
allegorical [æ̀ləgɔ́(ː)rikəl] 우의(寓意)적인, 비유적인　*cf.* allegory 우화(寓話), 풍자
the Roman languages 로만스어군(群)　*cf.* 고대 로마에서 사용된 라틴에 기원을 둔 언어들을 묶어서 부르는 말. 이탈리아어(Italian), 프랑스어(French), 스페인어(Spanish), 포르투갈어(Portuguese), 루마니아어(Romanian), 카탈로니아어(Catalan) 등이 이에 속함.
Latin 라틴어 (고대 로마에서 사용된 언어로 현재는 기록만으로 존재함.)
the Germanic languages 게르만어군　*cf.* 영어의 기원이 되는 언어군으로 영어 외에, 독일어(German), 네덜란드어(Dutch), 벨기에어(belgic), 덴마크어(Danish), 스웨덴어(Swedish), 노르웨이어(Norwegian), (고대의) 고딕어(Gothic) 등이 이에 속함. 스칸디나비아 3국어 중 핀란드어(Finnish)는 그 기원이 아시아 계통으로 게르만어가 아님.
for various reasons 여러 가지 이유로

전치사 of의 의미와 쓰임새

영어에서 가장 많이 쓰이는 전치사 중의 하나가 of이다. in, at, on 등의 전치사들이 기본적으로 공간을 배경으로 쓰이고 있어서 그 뜻을 이해하는 데에 어려움을 주지 않는 반면에, of는 공간에 기초를 두고 있지 않아서 그 쓰임새를 잘 파악하여 사용하는 데에 어려움이 있다. 그러나 of의 기본적인 의미가 '한 물체의 본질적이며 제한적인 부분 또는 속성'을 뜻하는 것이라는 점을 알면, of 사용에 대한 이해가 훨씬 빨라진다. '본질적이며 제한적인 부분 또는 속성'이라는 말은 of가 연결하는 두 명사의 관계가 불가분의 관계로서 하나가 다른 하나의 본질적인 진부분이라는 말이다. 여기에 of 사용의 포인트가 있다.

(1) a. the neck of the bottle   b. the top of the mountain
    c. the lid to[on] the bottle   d. the label on the bottle

(2) a. The solution of the problem is not easy.
    b. The solution to[for] the problem is satisfactory.
    cf. Proper planning is the key to success.
       Take good care of that brown spot in the lawn.

(1) a.에서 neck는 bottle과 떨어질 수 없는 본질적인 부분이어서 of를 사용한다. (1) b.도 마찬가지.
(1) c.와 d.에서 lid나 label은 bottle의 비본질적인 부분으로 떼어놓을 수 있는 부분이어서 방향의 to나 접촉의 on을 사용한다. of를 사용하면 매우 어색해진다.
(2) a.의 The solution of the problem에서 of는 solve the problem을 명사 표현으로 바꾸면서 삽입된 것으로, solve는 반드시 목적어를 취하는 동사이므로 solution과 problem은 본질적으로 밀접한 관계를 지니는 것이 되어 of를 사용한다. 이때 the를 a로 바꿀 수 없다.
(2) b.에서 solution은 원래부터 존재하는 명사로 '해결책'을 의미하고 보통명사 역할을 한다. the를 a로 바꿀 수 있고 복수도 가능하다. two solutions to the problem 문제에 대한 두 가지 해결책.
cf. success와 key는 본질적으로 떨어진 별개의 추상적 물체이다. 따라서 of를 쓰면 안 된다.
     잔디가 죽어서 갈색으로 변한 부분(spot)은 원래 잔디가 지니는 성질로서 본질적인 부분이 아니다. 따라서 of는 사용이 불가하다.

해석 (1) a. 병목   b. 산정(山頂)   c. 병뚜껑   d. 병에 붙은 라벨
      (2) a. 문제의 해결이 쉽지 않다.(해결하는 행위)   b. 문제에 대한 해결책이 만족스럽다.(하나의 해결책)
      cf. 적절한 계획을 세우는 것이 성공의 열쇠이다. / 저 잔디의 갈색으로 변색된 부분을 잘 돌보세요.

---

171   **In the course of** your formal schooling, it is very important to bring an element of curiosity to the classroom. A desire to learn makes the act of studying and learning a delight. Too many of your fellow students are too busy complaining about the teachers and the system to tend to their studies, which, after all, are the primary reason for being in school. The system has not changed much in the thirty years since I was at college and it probably won't alter much over the next thirty years. So **instead of** complaining about it, why not just get on with beating the system?

Key Structure •

1 Too many of your fellow students are too busy ~ to tend to their studies
= Too many of your fellow students are so busy ~ that they cannot tend to their studies
여러분들 중 너무나 많은 학생들이 선생님들과 학교교육체제에 대해 많은 불평을 하기 때문에 공부에 전념하지 못하고 있다
• too ~ to Ⓥ = so ~ that ~ cannot Ⓥ

2 which, after all, are the primary reason for being in school
그런데 그것[공부]은 결국 학교에 다니는 주된 이유이다
• which는 바로 앞의 their studies를 가리키고, 뒤에 나오는 동사 are의 주어로 쓰인 관계대명사임. 계속적 용법
으로 쓰였으므로(앞에 쉼표에 유의) 접속사 '그런데'를 넣어서 번역하는 것이 좋음.

3 why not just get on with ~ = why don't you just get on with ~
~하려고 해 보는 것이 어떤가

내용 학교교육체제에 대해 불평을 하기보다는 차라리 공부를 붙잡고 이겨 보려고 노력하는 것이 학생들이 해야 할
일이다.

formal schooling 공교육, 정규 교육
curiosity [kjùəriásəti] 호기심
complain about 불평하다
tend to 전념하다
primary [práimeri] 근본적인, 주된, 주요한
be in school 학교에 다니다
alter [ɔ́:ltər] 바뀌다, 바꾸다
get on with (일을) 진행하다
beat the system 제도와 힘을 겨루어 이기다

172　Boys and girls often ask me if I don't think it is a bad thing for
them to be compelled to memorize poetry in school. The answer
is—Yes, and No. If you've got into the way of thinking that poetry
is stupid stuff, or useless, or beneath your dignity, then you
certainly won't get much **out of** learning it by heart. But remember
that it is a good thing to train your memory, and learning a poem
is at least a much more pleasant way of training it than learning,
say, twenty lines **out of** the telephone directory. What is more
important, to learn poetry is to learn a respect for words, and
without this respect for words, you will never be able to think
clearly or express yourself properly.

Key Structure ▶

1 be compelled to memorize poetry
   시를 암기하도록 강요를 받다

2 get into the way of thinking ~
   ~라고 생각하는 길에 들어서다

3 get much out of ~
   ~에서 많은 것을 얻어내다

4 learning, say, twenty lines ~ directory
   예를 들어 전화번호부에서 20개의 번호를 외우는 일
   • say = for example (say는 원형동사 형태로 쓰인 명령형 동사임: '말해 보라' ⇒ '말하자면', '예를 들어')

5 what is more important = the thing which is more important
   더욱 중요한 것은
   • what은 관계대명사.
   • 여기에서는 부사절 역할을 함.

내용 학교에서 시를 암기하도록 하는 것은 기억력 훈련에도 좋고, 더욱이 어휘에 대한 존경심을 배우는 것이므로
      반드시 나쁜 일만은 아니다.

stupid stuff 어리석은[재미없는, 한심한] 물건
be beneath one's dignity 자신의 권위 아래에 있다, 권위에 어울리지 않다
learn by heart 암기하다(= memorize)
telephone directory 전화번호부

플러스 문법정리 70

주격관계의 of와 목적격관계의 of
(1) a. The sudden death of his father was a great shock to all his family.
    b. The love of his parents for him was beyond imagination.

(2) a. The destruction of the city by the tsunami was a great calamity to its people.
    b. The 911 Ambulances hurried to the rescue of the casualties.

구조적인 관점에서 볼 때, 전치사 of 뒤에 나오는 명사는 of 앞의 명사가 나타내는 행위나 상태의 주체가 될 수도
있고 그 대상이 될 수 있다. (1) 문장들에서는 of 뒤의 명사인 his father와 his parents가 각각 death나 love의
주체로 쓰였으며, (2) 문장들에서는 the city와 the casualties가 각각 destruction과 rescue의 대상으로
목적어처럼 쓰였다. 전자를 '주격관계의 of', 후자를 '목적격관계의 of'라고 부른다.

cf. The sudden death of his father → His father suddenly died...
     The destruction of the city by the tsunami → The tsunami destroyed the city...

해석 (1) a. 아버지의 갑작스러운 죽음은 그의 가족 모두에게 큰 충격이었다.
           b. 그에 대한 부모의 사랑은 상상을 초월하는 것이었다.
       (2) a. 지진 해일에 의한 도시의 파괴는 시민들에게 커다란 참화였다.
           b. 911 구급차들이 사상자들을 구조하기 위해 서둘러 왔다.

173 A story that comes **from behind** the Iron Curtain tells of some films that were run one morning in a motion picture theater. It was in a small town in East Germany. The films were in the nature of propaganda and showed some Russian soldiers unloading food supplies from a Russian river boat **onto** a dock in a German city.

Key Structure •

1 **A story that comes** from behind **the Iron Curtain** '철의 장막' 뒤에서 나온 한 이야기
   - from behind 두 개의 전치사로 된 구 전치사(phrase preposition)
   - the Iron Curtain 1989년에 소련연방(USSR)이 붕괴되기 이전의 러시아 중심의 구소련과 미국 중심의 서방측을 분리했던 정치, 군사, 사상적인 벽을 일컫는 표현. (당시 독일은 서방권의 서독(West Germany)과 구소련권의 동독(East Germany)으로 분단되어 있었음.)
     cf. the Bamboo Curtain 죽의 장막 (중국이 개방되기 전의 중국과 다른 나라들 사이의 정치, 군사, 사상적 장벽)

2 **be in the nature of ~** ~의 성격을 띠다

3 **showed some Russian soldiers unloading food supplies from ~** onto...
   몇몇 러시아 군인들이 러시아 강(江) 배로부터 한 독일 항구 도시의 부두에다 식량 공급분을 내리는 것을 보여 주었다
   - some Russian soldiers는 showed의 목적어, unloading은 목적격보어로 쓰인 5형식 동사 구문
   - unload ~ from A onto B : A에서 B 위로 ~을 내리다
   - onto는 on과 to가 합쳐진 전치사

   내용 소련이 붕괴되기 전, 소련연방의 한 국가인 동독의 한 작은 마을에서 러시아가 동독에게 많은 식량을 원조하는 것처럼 보여 주는 영화들이 상영되었는데, 이것은 정치적 선전의 목적을 가진 의도된 내용의 영화들이었다.

motion picture theater 영화관 *cf.* motion picture 활동사진, 영화
propaganda [prὰːpəgǽndə] (정치적인 허위, 과장) 선전
unload [ʌnlóud] (자동차 · 선박 등에서 짐을) 내리다, 하역하다
dock [dɑːk] 부두, 선창, 선거(船渠)

174 It is no exaggeration to say that the English Bible is, **next to** Shakespeare, the greatest work in English literature, and that it will have much more influence than even Shakespeare upon the written and spoken language of the English race. For this reason, to study English literature without some general knowledge of the relation of the English Bible **to** that literature would be to leave one's literary education very incomplete.

Key Structure •

1 next to Shakespeare 셰익스피어 다음으로

2 and that it will have ~
- that 이하는 첫 줄의 say로 연결되는 목적어 기능의 명사절.

3 to study English literature ~ would be to leave...
= if one were to study English literature ~ , it would be to leave...
~ 영문학을 공부한다는 것은 …하게 되는 일인 셈이다
- would는 이 문장이 가정법 구문임을 보여 주는 가정법 과거 동사형.

4 leave one's literary education very incomplete
자신의 문학 교육을 매우 불완전한 상태로 남겨놓다
- '동사(leave) + 목적어(one's literary education) + 목적격보어(very incomplete)' 구문.

내용 영문학을 제대로 하기 위해서는 영어 성경이 영문학사에서 차지하는 위치를 전체적으로 잘 알아야 한다.

exaggeration [igzædʒəréiʃən] 과장
influence [ínfluəns] 영향(력), 영향을 미치다
for this reason 이런 이유로 인하여, 이 이유 때문에

175 To stop science would create more problems than solutions. **Aside from** military considerations, it would be disastrous to freeze culture at its present high point. The highly technical civilization of the late 20th and early 21st century is like an airplane in flight, supported by its forward motion. It cannot stop without falling. If all the world's inhabitants, for instance, learn to use natural resources as fast as Americans do now, many necessary substances will be exhausted. Scientists should confidently count on improvements, including atomic energy, to provide ample substitutes. Present techniques won't do it.

Key Structure •

1 To stop science would create more problems than solutions.
= If we were to stop science, it would create ~ solutions.
과학을 중단시키면 해결책들보다는 문제들을 더 많이 만들어 낼 것이다.
- 가정법 미래 구문: 현재 또는 미래의 일에 대한 강한 의심, 부정적 견해를 나타냄.

2 it would be disastrous (if we were) to freeze
문화를 (현 상태에서) 얼린다는 것은 재앙을 초래하는 일이 될 것이다
- 가정법 미래 구문

3 It cannot stop without falling.

그것을 멈추면 반드시 추락하게 되어 있다. (직역: 추락함이 없이는 멈추지 않는다.)

4 use ~ as fast as Americans do 미국인들이 사용하는 만큼 빠른 속도로 ~을 사용하다

- do = use (대동사 (pro-verb))

내용 과학을 현 수준에서 멈춰 버리게 하는 것은 문제를 해결하기보다는 더 많은 문제를 야기할 것이다.

exhaust [igzɔ́:st] 고갈시키다 ⓝ exhaustion
count on improvements 개선책들에 의존하다
atomic energy 핵에너지
ample [ǽmpl] 충분한, 풍만한

플러스 문법정리 **71**

구 전치사 (Phrase preposition)

구 전치사는 전치사와 다른 품사의 말(들)이 합쳐져서 구(phrase)를 이루고 그것이 마치 하나의 단순 전치사처럼 사용되는 것을 말한다.

(1) a. The ship was at the mercy of the waves.
  b. He failed in his new business for lack of fund.

(2) a. What appeared from behind the cupboard was a big rat.
  b. The Korean emigrants in Hawaii worked without rest from before sunrise till after sunset.

(3) a. Aside from the sandwich, he had eaten half a loaf of the bread.
  b. There is some doubt as to whether the information is totally accurate.

(1)은 '전치사+명사+전치사'로 된 구 전치사이다.
실제로는 '전치사 구(preposition phrase)'라고 말할 수 있고, 다음과 같은 것들이 있다.

at the cost of, by means of, by way of, by dint of, for lack of, for want of, for fear of,
for the sake of, for the purpose of, in need of, in search of, instead of, in terms of, in want of,
in view of, in the light of, on account of, on behalf of, etc.

(2)는 '전치사+전치사'로 구성된 구 전치사이다.
(1)과 달리 전치사가 두 개 엮인 '이중 전치사(double preposition)'라고 말할 수 있으며, 이때 두 번째의 전치사는 그 뒤의 명사와 직접 연결되어 전치사 구를 이루고 이 구가 앞의 또 다른 전치사의 목적어처럼 쓰이는 경우이다. 그다지 숫자가 많지 않다.

from among, from above, from behind, etc.

(3)은 '형용사/부사/접속사 등+전치사'가 구를 이루는 경우이다.
전치사 앞에 형용사, 부사, 접속사, 또는 분사 등이 쓰여 구 전치사를 이룬다.

apart from, because of, but for, due to, except for, next to, owing to, out of, second to, etc.

해석 (1) a. 그 배의 운명은 파도에 달려 있었다. b. 그는 자금 부족으로 인하여 새 사업에 실패하였다.
  (2) a. 찬장 뒤로부터 나타난 것은 큰 쥐 한 마리였다. b. 하와이의 한국 이민자들은 해가 뜨기 전부터 해가 진 후까지 쉬지도 못하고 일을 하였다.
  (3) a. 샌드위치 말고도 그는 그 빵을 절반이나 먹어 버렸다. b. 그 정보가 전적으로 정확한 것이냐에 대해서는 약간의 의심이 존재한다.

16 · 도치, 강조, 생략, 삽입, 공통 구문

A 강조 구문(Emphasis), 도치 구문(Inversion)

강조는 거의 늘상 도치와 함께 다닌다.

01 목적어 등을 문두에 내세워 강조 : 도치 현상 없이

a. The faculty of drawing he inherited from his mother.
= He inherited the faculty of drawing from his mother.
그림 그리는 재주는 그가 모친에게서 이어받은 것입니다.

b. Anything else I would willingly agree to.
= I would willingly agree to anything else.
이것만 빼고 다른 일은 기꺼이 찬성하겠네.

c. Of political sagacity he had very little.
= He had very little of political sagacity.
정치적 지모(智謀)에 관해서는 그는 부족한 바가 매우 많았다.

02 연결동사(be, get, become 등)의 보어를 문두에 내세워 강조 :
동사와 어순이 바뀌는 도치가 이루어지는 경우가 많음

a. Inscrutable **are** the ways of Heaven.
= The ways of Heaven are inscrutable.
알 수 없을지라, 하늘이 하시는 일을. (인간사 새옹지마.)

b. Blessed **are** the children who live in peaceful places.
= The children who live in peaceful places are blessed.
복되도다, 평화로운 곳에서 살아가는 어린이들은.

c. Young as he was, he was very prudent.
= As[Though] he was young, he was very prudent.
나이는 젊었지만 그는 매우 신중한 사람이었다.

03 부사(구)나 접속사를 앞으로 내세워 강조 : 흔히 도치가 이루어짐 ☞ Part I '플러스 문법정리 60' 참조 (167쪽)

a. Never **did I see** such a beautiful sight.
= I never saw such a beautiful sight.
그렇게 멋진 광경을 예전에 보지 못했다.

b. Hardly[Scarcely] **had** she **seen** him when[before] she turned away.
= She had hardly seen him when she turned away.
그를 보는 순간 그녀는 등을 돌려 버렸다.

c. I am not rich now, nor **do I wish** to be.
나는 지금 부자가 아니며, 또 그렇게 되고 싶지도 않소.

04 장소부사를 앞으로 내세워 강조 : 도치는 이루어지되 조동사 **do**는 이용되지 않음

 a. Down **came** the rain in torrents.
 = The rain came <u>down</u> in torrents.
  비가 억수처럼 쏟아져 내렸다.
   cf. (×) Down <u>did</u> the rain come in torrents.

 b. Away **went** Tom to find the boy in question.
 = Tom went <u>away</u> to find the boy in question.
  톰은 길을 나섰던 것이다. 문제의 소년을 찾아보려고.
   cf. (×) Away <u>did</u> Tom go to ~.

B 생략 구문(Ellipsis)

 a. Some find happiness **in money**, some **in fame**, and some **in knowledge**.
  혹자는 돈에서, 혹자는 명예에서, 혹자는 지식에서 행복을 찾는다.

 b. I will not be idle, not if you pay me well.
  게으름을 피우지 않겠소. 보수만 톡톡히 준다면 말이요.
  • not = I will <u>not</u> be idle

 c. Poverty is not a shame, but the being ashamed of it is.
 = Poverty is not a shame, but the being ashamed of it is <u>a shame</u>.
  가난은 수치가 아닙니다. 가난을 수치스러워 하는 것이 수치지요.

C 삽입 구문(Insertion)

 a. Education, it is true, begins in the cradle. 교육이란. 사실 말이지, 유년기부터 시작된다.

 b. Standing, as it does, on a hill, the church commands a fine view.
  교회당이 이렇게 언덕 위에 자리 잡고 있으니, 내다보이는 전망이 좋습니다.

 c. There are very few, if any, trees in that region.
  그 지역에는 나무가 있다고 하더라도 거의 없다.

 d. He seldom, if ever, goes out for walk after dinner.
  그는 저녁 식사 후에 산보 나가는 법이 있다고 하더라도 거의 없다.

D 공통관계 구문(Common Relation)

 a. He will **demand** and probably **receive**, twice the editor-in-chief's salary.
  그는 편집장의 봉급의 갑절은 요구할 것인데, 또 어쩌면 그만큼 받을 게다.

 b. Passions **weaken**, but habits **strengthen**, with age.
  나이가 들어가면서 열정은 식어 가지만 타성은 강해진다.

 c. A man **of words** and not **of deeds** is like a garden full of weeds.
  말만 앞세우고 실천력이 없는 위인은 잡초가 만연한 정원과도 같다.

176   **Deep in the tiny atom lies** hidden a tremendous force. This force has entered the scene of our modern world as a most frightening power of destruction.

Key Structure ▸

Deep in the tiny atom lies hidden a tremendous force.
= A tremendous force lies hidden deep in the tiny atom.
아주 작은 원자 깊숙한 곳에 무시무시한 힘이 숨겨져 있다. (도치 구문)
• hidden은 lies의 보어임.

내용 원자 폭탄에 들어 있는 원자가 가지는 무시무시한 힘에 대한 이야기.

tiny [táini] 조그마한, 아주 작은.
tremendous [triméndəs] 무시무시한, 거대한
enter the scene 등장하다
frightening [fráitəniŋ] 놀라게 하는, 무서운 ⓥ frighten

---

177   **Scarcely** had the ship been out of the harbor **when** the wind began to blow, and the sea to rise in a most frightening manner, and as I had never been at sea before, I was almost inexpressibly sick in body and terrified in mind.

Key Structure ▸

1   Scarcely **had** the ship **been** out of the harbor when the wind began to blow
    = Hardly **had** the ship **been** out of the harbor when the wind began to blow
    = No sooner **had** the ship **been** out of the harbor than the wind began to blow
    = As soon as the ship **was** out of the harbor, the wind began to blow
    배가 항구를 벗어나자마자 바람이 불기 시작하였고
    • As soon as 절에는 과거 동사가 옴에 주의.

2   the sea to rise ~ = the sea began to rise ~ (동사의 생략)
      • 이 절도 the wind began to blow와 같은 역할을 함.

내용 나는 전에 바다에 나가 본 적이 없어서 바람이 불고 파도가 높이 일자 심신에 고통을 느꼈다.

be at sea 바다[해상]에 나가 있다, 선원이 되다   *cf.* be at the sea 바닷가에 있다
inexpressibly [iniksprésəbli] 말로 표현할 수 없을 정도로

178 **Little as he was**, he understood that his big, handsome young papa would not come back any more; that he was dead, as he had heard other people saying that, although he could not comprehend exactly what strange thing had brought all this sadness about.

Key Structure

1 Little **as he was** = Though he was little
그는 어린아이였지만~ (little을 강조)
• 양보절(concession clause)에서 as는 though의 의미를 가짐.

2 **that he was dead** = he understood that he was dead
• 이 절은 understood의 또 다른 목적어절임.

내용 그는 어린아이였지만, 체격이 크고 잘생기고 젊은 아빠가 더 이상 이 세상 사람이 아니라는 점을 이해하고 있었다.

comprehend [kàmprihénd] (충분히) 이해하다, 눈치채다
bring about 가져오다, 야기하다(=cause)

179 I have no desire to impart any knowledge I have to others, **nor do I feel** the need to correct them if they are wrong. **Out of tedious people you can** get a great deal of entertainment if you listen with care. I remember being taken for a drive in a foreign country by a kind lady who wanted to show me around. Her conversation was composed entirely of truism and she had so large a vocabulary of hackneyed phrases, but there was something worth remembering in them.

Key Structure

1 impart any knowledge (that) I have to others
내가 가진 어떤 지식을 남에게 전하다
• impart A to B : B에게 A를 전하다[나누어 주다]

2 nor **do I feel** the need to correct them
그들을 고쳐 줄 필요성도 또한 느끼지 않는다
• 부정접속사 nor로 인한 도치 구문
• them = others

3　Out of tedious people **you can get** ~
　　= You can get ~ out of tedious people
　　지루한 사람들에게서도 ~ 얻을 수 있다

4　**be composed of** ~　~으로 구성되다

5　something (which was) **worth remembering**
　　기억할 만한 가치가 있었던 무엇

내용　지루한 사람들에게서도 잘 듣고 있으면 상당한 양의 즐거움을 얻을 수 있다.

tedious [tíːdiəs]　지루한, 싫증나는　ⓝ tediousness, tedium
entertainment [èntərtéinmənt]　즐거움, (특히 영화·음악 등의) 오락(물)
show me around　나에게 주위를 구경시켜 주다
truism [trú(ː)izəm]　지루한 이야기, 뻔히 아는 이야기
hackneyed phrases　진부한[평범한] 어구

180　Our age began as the age when man seemed to be coming finally into his own. **Never before** in the history of civilization **had** it **been** so generally taken for granted that man's freedom, his dignity, his happiness, even what we call his "prosperity," were the only things that count. **Never before had statesmen and philosophers laid** so much stress on the importance of any and all men.

Key Structure

1　come into his own
　　자신의 본래의 위치 속으로 들어오다(자신의 정당한 권리를 얻다)
　　• his own은 his own self를 의미하는 것으로 생각할 것.

2　Never before in the history of civilization had it been so generally taken for granted that ~
　　= It had never before in the history of civilization been so generally taken for granted that ~
　　문명의 역사 그 어느 시기에도 ~이 널리 당연하게 받아들여진 적이 없었다
　　• it는 that~을 진주어로 하는 가주어
　　• be taken for granted 당연한 것으로 받아들여지다

3　even what we call his "prosperity" = even what is so-called his "prosperity"
　　심지어 우리가 그(인간)의 "번영"이라 부르는 것
　　• what은 관계대명사.

4　the only things that count　중요하게 여겨지는 유일한 일들
　　• count = are important (count는 자동사로 쓰임)

5 Never before **had** statesmen and philosophers **laid** so much stress on ~
= Statesmen and philosophers <u>had</u> never before <u>laid</u> so much stress on ~
그전에는 어느 때에도 정치가들과 철학자들이 ~을 그렇게 강조한 적이 없었다

내용 우리 시대는 인간이 마침내 자신의 정당한 권리를 얻어서, 자유, 존엄, 행복, 심지어 우리가 "번영"이라 부르는 것들이 중요하게 받아들여지게 되었다.

dignity [dígnəti] 존엄(성)
lay stress on 강조하다(= emphasize)
any and all men 어떤 사람이든 구별 없이 모두(= any men and all men)

---

181 Language is a means of communication. Primarily it is something that is spoken; the written form is only a substitute, **though a useful**, and in the modern world an **indispensable**, **substitute** for the spoken form. Without language, there could be no community or society in any meaningful sense of the words, for no one would be able to make contact, even on the lowest intellectual level, with anyone else.

Key Structure •

1 **though (it is) a** useful ~ , **substitute** for the spoken form
(그것이) 말로서의 언어에 대한 유용한 대체물이기는 하지만 (생략절이면서 공통관계 구문을 나타냄)
• though절에서 주어와 동사 it is가 생략된 표현이며, useful은 뒤의 substitute로 연결됨.
• substitute는 또한 바로 앞의 형용사 indispensable과도 연결되는 공통어임.
즉, 절의 골격은 though it is a useful, and ~ indispensable, substitute for the spoken form임.

2 **Without** language there **could** be no community or society ~
= If it were not for language, there ~
= Were it not for language, there ~
= But for language there could ~
• 가정법 과거 구문: 주절의 조동사 could가 그 점을 보여 줌.

3 **in any meaningful sense of the words**
그 단어들이 갖는 어떠한 진지한 의미에서도
• words : community와 society

4 **make contact, ~ , with anyone else**
다른 사람과 접촉하다

5 **even on the lowest intellectual level** (삽입구)
가장 낮은 지적 수준에서조차도(가령 하등 동물의 경우처럼 매우 낮은 수준에서도)

내용 언어는 의사소통의 한 수단으로 기본적으로 글이 아닌 말로 표현되는 것이며, 언어가 없다면 누구도, 아주 낮은 지적 수준에서조차도 다른 사람과 접촉을 할 수 없을 것이기 때문에, 진정한 의미의 공동체나 사회는 없을 것이다.

communication [kəmjùːnəkéiʃən] 의사소통, 통신
primarily [praimérəli] 주로, 기본적으로
substitute [sʌ́bstitjùːt] 대용물, 대체물 ⓥ substitute 대체하다 ⓝ substitution 대체
indispensable [ìndispénsəbl] 없어서는 안 될, 필수적인

182

The valley was now getting broader; bare rocky mountains were giving place to hills covered with pines; then **these to** the plain with its vineyards, farms and fields with ripening corn. What surprised me most was the small amount of land kept for pasture; almost all of it was cultivated.

Key Structure

1 these (were giving place) **to the plain ~**
이 소나무 언덕들은 ~ 평지에 자리를 내주고 있었다 (생략 구문)
• these = these hills covered with pines

2 **What surprised me most** = What was most surprising to me
나를 매우 놀라게 한 것
• 관계대명사절로 was의 주어 절

내용 계곡이 점점 넓어지면서 벌거벗은 바위산들이 소나무로 덮인 언덕들로 바뀌고, 이 소나무 언덕들은 포도원과 농장과 익어가는 옥수수 밭이 있는 평지에 자리를 내주고 있었으며, 더욱 놀랍게도 조그마한 넓이의 목초지가 거의 다 경작이 되고 있었다.

give place to 자리를 내주다
plain [plein] 평지, 평원
vineyard [vínjərd] 포도원, 포도밭
ripen [ráipən] 익다, 익히다 ⓐ ripe 익은
pasture [pǽstʃər] 초원, 목초지
cultivate [kʌ́ltəvèit] 경작하다, (작물을) 재배하다

183 Many remedies are suggested for the avoidance of worry and mental overstrain by persons who, over prolonged periods, have to bear exceptional responsibilities and discharge duties on a large scale. Some advise exercise, and **others, repose**. Some counsel travel, and **others, gaiety**. No doubt all these may play their part according to the individual temperament. But the element which is constant and common in all of them is Change.

Key Structure ▸

1 others, repose = others advise repose 다른 이들은 휴식을 권한다 (생략 구문)

2 others, gaiety = others counsel gaiety 다른 이들은 쾌활해지도록 조언한다 (생략 구문)

내용 오랜 시간 동안 특별한 책임을 떠맡고 있어서 걱정과 정신적인 과도한 긴장을 하는 사람들에게 그것을 피하는 치료책(운동, 휴식, 여행, 또는 쾌활함 등)이 권해지고 있지만, 이 모든 조언들에 늘 공통으로 들어 있는 요소로 중요한 것은 기분 전환이다.

remedy [rémidi] 해결책, 치료법
overstrain [óuvərstrèin] 과도한 긴장, 과로
over prolonged periods 장기간에 걸쳐 *cf.* prolong 늘어지게 하다, 연장하다
bear [bɛər] 참다, 책임을 떠맡다
discharge [distʃá:rdʒ] (직무를) 이행하다
on a large scale 대규모로
counsel [káunsəl] 조언(하다)
gaiety [géiəti] 쾌활함 *cf.* gay ⓐ 쾌활한, 명랑한 ⓝ (특히 남성 간의) 동성애자(↔ lesbian)
play one's part ~의 역할을 하다
temperament [témpərəmənt] 기질
Change [tʃeindʒ] 기분 전환, 변화 (강조하는 의미로 대문자로 시작)

184 In all ages the eccentric—perhaps **because of**, and not **in spite of, his nonconformity**—has furthered the development of science, built great empires, improved the public welfare, and created memorable works of art. In their own time such men as Kant, Thoreau, Paganini, Pascal, Disraeli, Poe, Whitman, and Heine were considered eccentric. History has recorded countless other names of rare individuals—**among them are the poet Charles Baudelaire** and the millionaire businessman Russell Sage.

Key Structure •

1 perhaps because of, and not in spite of, his nonconformity
   = perhaps because of his nonconformity and not in spite of his nonconformity
   (당시 존재하던 사회 상황들에) 그가 '순응하지 못했다는 사실에도 불구하고'가 아니라 아마도 그 '불순응성 때문에'
   (공통 구문)

2 among them are the poet Charles Baudelaire ~
   = the poet Charles Baudelaire ~ are among them
   시인 샤를 보들레르와 백만장자 사업가 러셀 세이지도 그들 중의 하나이다 (도치 구문)

   내용 모든 시대를 통틀어 과학 발전을 촉진하고, 대 제국을 건설하고, 공공복지를 향상시키고, 또한 기억될 만큼 특출
   난 예술 작품들을 만들어 내었던 자들은 사회상에 순응하지 못한 괴짜인 사람들이었다.

   further [fə́ːrðər] 촉진시키다, 더 멀리 가게 하다
   empire [émpaiər] 제국   *cf.* emperor 황제 empress 여제, 황후   ⓐ imperial 제국의
   public welfare 공공복지
   memorable [mémərəbl] 기억될 만한, 현저한, 특출 난
   cf. Kant, Immanuel 칸트(1724~1804, 독일의 철학자)
        Paganini, Nicoló 파가니니(1782~1840, 이탈리아의 작곡가)
        Pascal, Blaise 파스칼(1623~1662, 프랑스의 수학자, 물리학자, 철학자)
        Disraeli, Benjamin 디즈레일리(1804~1881, 영국의 정치가, 소설가)
        Poe, Edgar Allan 포(1809~1849, 미국의 시인, 단편 · 추리소설 작가)
        Whitman, Walt 휘트먼(1819~1892, 미국의 시인)
        Heine, Heinrich 하이네(1797~1856, 독일의 시인)
        Baudelaire, Charles Pierre 보들레르(1821~1867, 프랑스의 시인, 비평가)

---

185 In the near distance **wound that deep treacherous, golden river**, the Yangtse, and some of the most **terrifying** and **sinister**, as well as the most **delightful** and **exciting moments** of that child's life, were spent beside the river.

Key Structure •

1 In the near distance wound that deep treacherous, golden river
   = That deep treacherous, golden river wound in the near distance
   가까이에서는 저 깊고 위험한 황금색 강이 굽이굽이 흐르고 있었다
   • 장소를 나타내는 전치사구 in the near distance가 문두로 나가며 동사가 주어보다 앞에 위치한 도치 구문임.

2 that deep treacherous, golden river, the Yangtse
   저 깊고 위험한 황금색 강인 양쯔강
   • 주어인 that deep treacherous, golden river 다음에 동격 명사 the Yangtse를 놓은 동격 구문임.

3 the most terrifying and sinister, as well as the most delightful and exciting moments 가장 즐겁고 재미있는 순간들이면서도 가장 무섭고 불길한 순간들

- the most terrifying and sinister moments, as well as the most delightful and exciting moments
  A ─────────────────────── B

'A as well as B' 구조에서 A와 B에 공통으로 쓰인 명사 moments를 A에서는 생략하고 B의 뒤에만 남겨 공통관계로 만든 구조

내용 한 사람이 어린 시절에 깊고 위압적인 양쯔강 가에서 살면서 느꼈던 인상을 피력한 글.
(출처: 중국을 배경으로 한 소설, Pearl Buck의 〈대지 The Good Earth〉. 1931년 발표. 1938년 노벨문학상 수상.)

wind [waind] 굽이쳐 흐르다 (wind-wound-wound)
treacherous [trétʃərəs] 변덕스러운, 기만적인, (날씨, 기억 등이) 믿을 수 없는
terrifying [térəfàiiŋ] 놀라게 하는, 무서운 ⓥ terrify 무섭게 하다
sinister [sínistər] 사악한, 불길한

---

186 In the sweet silence of the twilight, the new couple honey-mooned upon the beach. "Dearest," the bride murmured, tremblingly, "now that we are married, I have a secret to tell you!" "What is it, sweetheart?" **asked the bridegroom**, softly. "My... my left eye is made of glass!" "Never mind, lovebird," he whispered, gently, "**so are the diamonds** in your engagement ring."

Key Structure ▸

1 now that we are married 이제 우리가 결혼한 사이니까 말인데요
- now that = since ('이유'를 나타내는 종속접속사)

2 so are the diamonds in your engagement ring
당신의 약혼반지에 들어간 다이아몬드들도 마찬가지이다
- So am I. / So I am. ☞ Part I '플러스 문법정리 10' 참조 (36쪽)

내용 갓 결혼한 신혼부부의 신혼여행 중에 일어난 이야기 하나.

twilight [twáilàit] 땅거미, 황혼
honey-moon [hʌ́nimuːn] 신혼여행을 보내다
murmur [mə́ːrmər] 중얼거리다, 속삭이다
tremblingly [trémbliŋli] 떨리는 목소리로 ⓥ tremble 떨다
lovebird [lʌ́vbəːrd] 열애 중인 남녀, 잉꼬
engagement ring 약혼반지

187 **Looking back** now, after all these years, and knowing **as I do** the terrible difficulties of making a living by writing, and the small chance **there is** of being successful, I realize that I was taking a fearful risk. It never occurred to me then.

Key Structure

1 Looking back = Looking back on my past
   = When I look back on my past
   옛날을 회고해 보니

2 as I do ☞ Part I '04 부정사 · 분사' 참조 (54~57쪽)
   실인즉, 정말로, 사실상
   • 분사구문에서 분사를 강조하기 위해 삽입된 표현. 의미상으로는 없어도 관계없음.
   • do = know

3 the small chance (that) there is of being successful
   (있을 수 있는) 희박한 성공의 가능성
   • (that) there is는 삽입된 절로 볼 수 있으며, 이를 빼도 문맥상 아무 문제가 없음.
     there is 구문에서 흔히 나타나는 (주격)관계대명사 that이 생략된 것.
     cf. This is the most beautiful dress (that) there is in the world.

4 It never occurred to me. 나에게 그런 생각은 들지 않았다.
   • It = That I was taking a fearful risk

   내용 글을 써서 먹고사는 것이 얼마나 어려운 일인지 젊은 시절에는 몰랐다.

terrible [térəbl] 끔찍한, 무시무시한
make a living 생계를 꾸리다, 살아가다
take a risk 위험을 무릅쓰다
fearful [fíərfəl] 무서운, 무시무시한

188

Finally I came in sight of the House of Usher. I do not know **how it was,** but **the moment I** had a look at the house, my heart was seized with a sense of gloom. The feeling was more than I could bear. I could have never borne it, even if I had been in a poetic mood which enables one to face the most desolate or terrible images of nature. I looked **upon the scene before me**—**upon** the house, and the view around it, **upon** the bleak walls, **upon** the vacant eye-like windows, **upon** a few thick growths of sedge, and **upon** some white trunks of decayed trees. As I looked, I sank into utter depression as if I were under the lingering **effect** of opium eating, **a bitter sensation** felt in the awakening from opium dream. It was a hideous feeling aroused with the unveiling of reverie.

Key Structure •

1 I do not know how it was 어찌된 영문인지는 모르겠으나
   • it은 문법적으로는 '상황의 it'로 볼 수 있지만, 내용적으로는 뒤에 나오는 절인 the moment I had a look at the house, my heart was seized with a sense of gloom을 나타냄.

2 the moment I had a look at the house
   = as soon as I had a look at the house
   그 집을 보는 순간

3 I could have never borne it 나는 그 모습을 도저히 참아 낼 수가 없었을 것이다
   • 가정법 과거완료 구문의 주절.
   • it = the feeling

4 as if I were under ~ 마치 ~의 영향력 하에 있는 것처럼

내용 몰락한 어셔 가의 모습이 시야에 들어왔을 때 아편 효과에서 벗어나지 못하는 것처럼 절망 속으로 주저앉았다.

come in sight of ~ 시야에 들어오다
be seized with ~에 사로잡히다
bear [bɛər] 참다, 이겨 내다(= stand; endure; put up with) cf. bear-bore-born/borne
desolate [désəlit] 적막한, 황량한
bleak [bli:k] 황량한
vacant eye-like 멍한 눈초리 모습을 한
sedge [sedʒ] 사초(莎草)
the lingering effect of opium eating 사라지지 않고 있는 아편 효과
hideous [hídiəs] 흉측한, 소름 끼치는
the unveiling of reverie 망상이 베일을 벗는 것

01 **It may be that ∼ = Perhaps : 아마 ∼**

a. It may be that he will come tomorrow. 아마도 그가 내일 올 것이다.

It (so) happened that ∼ : 우연히도 ∼하다

b. It happened that we were in London at that time.
= We happened to be in London at that time.
그때 우리는 우연히도 런던에 있었다.

it follows that ∼ : ∼라는 이야기가 된다[뒤따른다]

c. From this evidence it follows that he is not the murderer.
이 증거로 미루어 볼 때 그는 살인자가 아니라는 결론이 뒤따른다.

The chances[Chances] are that ∼ : 아마도 ∼하다
The odds are that ∼ = It is odds that ∼ : 아마도 ∼하다

d. The chances are that the bill will be rejected.
아마도 그 법안은 통과되지 않을 것이다.

e. The odds are that he will not pass the exam.
아마도 그는 시험에 합격하지 못할 것이다.

02 접속사 as로 이끌어지는 관용적인 표현들

as matters stand (today) = as the matter stands (today) : 현재의 상태로서는

a. As matters stand today, many teachers are unable to do the best of
which they are capable.
현 상태로는, 많은 교사들이 그들이 할 수 있는 최선을 다할 수 없다.

as the case may be : 상황에 따라, 사정에 맞게

b. Do what you think to be the most appropriate, as the case may be.
사정에 맞게, 최선이라고 생각하는 것을 행하시오.

as chance would have it : 우연히(= by chance), 공교롭게도

c. As chance would have it, I met her there.
우연히도 나는 그곳에서 그녀를 만났다.

03 **It behoves[behooves] : ∼할 필요[의무]가 있다**

  a. It behoves a child to obey his parents.
  = A child must obey his parents. 어린이는 부모님의 말씀에 복종해야 한다.

It is not for nothing that ∼ : ∼은 헛된 일은 아니다

  b. It is not for nothing that he went to college.
    그가 대학에 다닌 것이 헛된 일은 아니었다. (for nothing 쓸데없는, 헛된)

04 **may as well = had better : ∼하는 것이 낫다**

  a. You may as well go at once.
    너는 즉시 가는 게 낫다.
    Cf. You may well do so. = You have good reason to do so. 네가 그렇게 하는 것은 당연하다.

may as well A as B : B하느니 차라리 A하는 게 낫다

  b. One may as well be hanged for a sheep as a lamb.
    새끼 양 한 마리 훔친 죄로 교수형 당하느니 차라리 큰 양을 훔치는 것이 낫다. (이왕 손댄다면 철저히 해 버려라)

might as well A (as B)

  c. You might as well talk to your son.
    아드님한테 주의를 주는 게 좋을 것 같군요.
    • may as well과 거의 같은 뜻이나 might as well은 부정적인 뜻이 더 들어 있음.

  d. You might as well throw money away as spend it gambling.
    노름으로 돈을 쓸 바에야 던져 버리는 것이 낫다. (may as well보다 공손한 표현)

05 **의도를 나타내는 if절의 be + to부정사**

Our civilization, if it is to endure, must have a star on which to fix its eyes.
우리의 문명은, 살아남고자 한다면, 그 눈을 고정시킬 수 있는 별[목표]이 있어야 한다.

06 **be given to ∼ : ∼하게끔 되다**

I am given to understand that he has been a faithful friend.
그가 충실한 친구라고 나는 이해하게 되었다.
• 원래 'give+목적어+to부정사(…가 ~하게끔 만들다)'에서 수동형으로 바뀐 형태.

189 We all know what it is to feel hurt and angry, to feel that no one loves us. At such times **it may be that** we long to die so that those who do not love us may be sorry. But these feelings do not come often and they soon pass. We cry ourselves to sleep perhaps and wake up to find that evil thoughts are gone.

Key Structure ▸

1 **what it is to feel hurt and angry**
   마음이 상하고 화가 나는 것이 어떠한 것인지
   • it은 가주어, to feel ~ angry가 진주어임.

2 **it may be that ~ = perhaps ~**
   아마도 ~일 것이다

3 **We cry ourselves to sleep**
   우리는 울다가 지쳐 잠이 든다

4 **wake up** to find ~
   눈을 떠서 ~을 알게 된다
   • to find는 부사적 용법(결과).
   e.g. He left his hometown never to return.
   그는 고향을 떠나 다시 돌아오지 못했다. (운명)

내용 사랑을 받지 못할 때 느끼는 감정은 그렇게 오래 가지는 않는다.

long [lɔ(ː)ŋ] 간절히 바라다, 열망하다, 동경하다(= yearn, desire)
wake up 잠에서 깨다
evil [íːvəl] 사악한, 나쁜(= bad, vicious, malignant)

플러스 문법정리 66

결과의 뜻과 연결되는 재귀대명사
재귀대명사가 동사의 목적어로 쓰여 의미상 그 동작의 결과로 연결되는 경우가 있다.

a. She cried herself to sleep.
b. He overate himself to illness.
c. He overworked himself to damaging his health.

해석 a. 그녀는 울다 지쳐 잠이 들었다.   b. 그는 과식하여 병이 났다.   c. 그는 과로하여 건강을 해쳤다.

190 **It often happens that** a grand attempt, although it may fail—miserably fail—is fruitful in the end and leaves a result, not the hoped-for result, it is true, but one which would never have been attained without it. A youth strives after the impossible and he is apt to break his heart because he has never even touched it, but nevertheless his whole life is the sweeter for the striving.

Key Structure

1 **It often happens that ~** 종종 ~한 일이 발생한다

2 **the hoped-for result** = the result which has been hoped for 바라던 결과

3 **one which would never have been attained without it**
   그것이 없었더라면 결코 얻어질 수 없었던 결과 (one = a result)
   • without it = but for it = if it had not been for it 그것이 없었더라면 (it = the attempt)

4 **strives after the impossible** 불가능한 일을 얻으려 노력한다
   • the impossible = impossible things

5 **his whole life is the sweeter for the striving**
   그의 전 생애는 노력을 했으므로 그만큼 더 달콤하다
   • the sweeter의 the는 '노력한 만큼'을 나타내는 '정도'의 부사로 쓰였음.
   e.g. I like him (all) the better for his faults. 나는 그의 잘못 때문에 더 그를 좋아한다.

내용 어떤 시도에 실패가 있다고 해도, 시도한 만큼 인생은 더 달콤하다.

grand [grænd] 웅대한, 당당한(= magnificent, majestic, stately)
miserably [mízərəbli] 불쌍하게, 초라하게, 비참하게(= pitifully, lamentably, shamefully, deplorably)
fruitful [frú:tfəl] 열매가 많이 열리는, 비옥한, 수익이 많은(= bountiful, productive, copious, fecund)
strive [straiv] 노력하다, 분투하다(= struggle, endeavor)
break one's heart 상심하다, 낙심하다(= be disappointed)

플러스 문법정리 67

지시부사 역할을 하는 the
흔히 the가 비교급을 이끌 때 '~한 만큼 더'의 뜻을 지니며, 이때 the는 정도를 나타내는 지시부사 역할을 한다.

a. I love her the better for her good manners.
b. He is a little awkward in his manners, but I cannot praise his wisdom the less.
c. I love him none the less because he has faults.
d. The sooner, the better.
e. The higher we go up, the thinner the air becomes.

해석 a. 나는 그녀의 좋은 예절 때문에 그녀를 그만큼 더 좋아한다. b. 예절은 조금 서투르지만 그의 지혜를 그만큼 깎아내릴 수는 없다. c. 그가 단점이 있음에도 불구하고 나는 그를 좋아한다. d. 빠르면 빠를수록 더 좋다. e. 높이 올라갈수록 공기는 그만큼 희박해진다.

191 Anyone who learns to know and like the works of good writers will not be satisfied with the cheap magazines and newspapers that flood the newsstands. If a person takes the troubles to learn to appreciate the music of Mozart and Brahms, **the chances are that** he will not be so enthusiastic about the vulgar popular music of the present day.

Key Structure ▸

1 the cheap magazines and newspapers that flood the newsstands
신문 판매대에 범람하는 싸구려 잡지와 신문

2 takes the trouble(s) to ~
~하는 수고를 하다(일부러 수고하여 ~하다)

3 (the) chances are that ~ = it may be that ~ = perhaps ~
아마도 ~일 것이다

내용 고전음악가를 좋아하게 되면 저속한 대중음악에 열정을 느끼지 않을 것이다.

work [wə:rk] 작품, 일
cheap [tʃi:p] 싼, 값이 싼(= inexpensive)
flood [flʌd] 범람시키다, 넘쳐흐르다 ⓝ 홍수
appreciate [əpríːʃièit] 감상하다, 음미하다, 인식하다(= comprehend, acknowledge, realize)
enthusiastic [inθjùːziǽstik] 열심인, 열광적인(= ambitious, ardent, fervent, ebullient)
vulgar [vʌ́lgər] 저속한, 대중의, 자국(自國)의(= common, popular, crude, churlish, uncouth)
cf. vulgar music 대중음악

192 If some refreshment is served, do not hesitate, but help yourself as soon as your host asks you to or as soon as he begins to eat or drink. If you allow the food or drink to remain on the table too long untouched, it looks as if you do not appreciate his efforts to serve it hot or cold, **as the case may be.**

Key Structure ▸

1 help yourself (to ~) 마음껏 들다

2 as soon as your host asks you to (do so)
• 이때의 to는 앞에 나온 동사구를 대신하는 대부정사(Pro-infinitive)로 쓰인 것임.

3 untouched 손도 대지 않은 채

4 as the case may be 경우에 따라서, 그때그때

내용 다과가 제공될 때 망설이지 말고 마음껏 들어라. 주인의 접대에 잘 응하는 길이다.

refreshment [rifréʃmənt] 다과, 음식물, 원기회복(= drink, eatable)
hesitate [hézitèit] 주저하다, 망설이다(= be indecisive, hang back)
host [houst] (연회 등의) 주인, 다수
appreciate [əpríːʃièit] 진가를 인정하다, 고맙게 여기다(= thank for)

---

193 At the outset let it be acknowledged that freedom in reading is a fine thing. However, if it has not been prepared for, it is more likely to lead to indifference and perplexity than to pleasure. **It behoves parents to** accept responsibility in this area just as they accept responsibility in matters relating to health, dress, and politeness.

Key Structure ·

1 let it be acknowledged that ~ = acknowledge that ~
~을 인정하라 (명령문 구조)
• it은 that 이하를 지칭하는 가목적어.

2 it is more likely to lead to ~
~으로 이끌어질 가능성이 더 많다
• it는 진주어로서 freedom in reading을 가리킴.
e.g. It is more likely that he will not show up tonight. = He is more likely not to show up tonight.
그가 오늘 밤 나타나지 않을 가능성이 더 많다.

3 It behoves parents to ~
부모들이 ~하는 것은 의무이다
• behove는 반드시 it을 주어로 하며 to부정사의 의미상의 주어를 목적어로 취함.
e.g. It behoves me to do my duty. = I must do my duty.

내용 독서에서는 우선 읽을 자유가 중요하지만 독서지도에 부모의 책임이 따른다.

outset [áutsèt] 착수, 시작(= beginning) *cf.* at the outset 최초에(부터)
acknowledge [əknálidʒ] 인정하다, 자인하다(= accede, admit, concede)
indifference [indífərəns] 무관심, 냉담(= aloofness, apathy, disinterest, nonchalance)
perplexity [pərpléksəti] 당혹, 난처한 일(= confusion, bewilderment)
politeness [pəláitnis] 공손, 예의 바름(= courtesy, good manners, civility, discretion)

194

It is his nature to create as it is the nature of water to run down hill. **It is not for nothing that** artists have called their works the children of their brains and likened the pains of production to the pains of childbirth.

Key Structure •

1 It is his nature to create as it is ~ hill.
물의 본성이 언덕을 흘러 내려가는 것인 것처럼 예술가의 본성은 창작이다. (his = the artist's)

2 It is not for nothing that ~ ~은 헛된 것이 아니다

3 liken the pains of production to the pains of childbirth
생산의 고통을 출산의 고통에 비유하다
• liken A to B = compare A to B A를 B에 비유하다

내용 창작은 예술가의 본성이다.

brains [breinz] 두뇌
liken [láikən] 비유하다, 견주다(= compare)
pains [peinz] 고통, 수고(= suffering, agony, affliction)
childbirth [tʃáildbə̀ːrθ] 출산, 분만

플러스 문법정리 68

단수 · 복수의 의미가 다른 분화복수
복수형은 보통 단수명사의 복수 개념을 갖지만, 복수형이 복수 개념이 아닌 다른 뜻을 갖는 경우가 많은데, 이러한 명사의 복수형을 분화복수(Differentiated plural)라고 부른다.

a. They walked arm in arm. (팔)

b. They finally laid down their arms. (무기)

c. His study has many books stamped with the college arms. (문장(紋章))

d.
advice 충고	advices 통지	water 물	waters 바다
air 공기	airs 점잔을 빼는 태도	number 숫자	numbers 곡조, 시가
brain 뇌	brains 두뇌, 지력	paper 종이	papers 서류
color 색	colors 기, 깃발	pain 고통	pains 수고
custom 습관	customs 세관	quarter 1/4	quarters 숙소, 지역
effect 효과	effects 동산	spectacle 광경	spectacles 안경
force 힘	forces 군대	provision 준비	provisions 식량
letter 글자	letters 문학	measure 측정	measures 수단
manner 방법	manners 예절	authority 권위	authorities 당국
sand 모래	sands 사막		

해석 a. 그들은 팔짱을 끼고 걸었다.   b. 그들은 마침내 무기를 내려놓았다.   c. 그의 서재에는 대학의 문장이 찍힌 책들이 많다.

195 There is one fact that you **may as well** face now, namely, that the easiest things are rarely the best for you. Trouble has been one of the great blessings to mankind. To overcome disease, famine, poverty, and other misfortunes, mankind has been actually forced by them into thinking out remedies.

Key Structure ▸

1 namely = that is to say = in other words
다시 말하면

2 be forced by them into thinking out remedies
그들에 의해 해결책을 생각해 내도록 강요받다

내용 고통은 오히려 인간에게 커다란 축복 중의 하나이다.

face [feis] 직접 부딪치다, 직면하다
overcome [òuvərkʌ́m] 극복하다, 압도하다(= overthrow, get over, conquer)
famine [fǽmin] 기근, 굶주림, 기아(= hunger, dearth, starvation)
poverty [pávərti] 가난, 빈곤, 결핍
remedy [rémidi] 치료, 구제(책), 의약품(= cure, solution, therapy, treatment)

플러스 문법정리 69

may well과 may as well
may well은 '~하는 것도 당연하다'라는 표현이고, may as well은 '~하는 것이 더 낫다'라는 표현이다. 둘 다 조동사처럼 본동사 앞에 오지만 뜻이 다름에 유의하자.

a. He may well be proud of his son, since he has won the prize in the speech contest.
= He has good reason to be proud of his son, ~
= It is natural that he should be proud of his son, ~

b. He may as well try not to do so, since it will waste his time and money.
= He had better try not to do so, ~
= It would be better for him to try not to do so, ~

해석 a. 아들이 웅변대회에서 상을 탔으니 그가 아들 자랑을 할 만하다. b. 시간과 돈을 낭비하게 될 것이므로 그가 그렇게 하지 않는 것이 나을 것이다.

196 We cannot get rid of noise in any case, so that we **may as well** learn to enjoy it. In order to think well of noise, indeed, one has only to imagine what a modern city would be like if all noise were totally abolished. After a week of it we should weep tears of joy if all the dogs suddenly began to bark again and all the sirens in the docks and factories to make a hideous hooting.

Key Structure •

1 we may as well learn ~
   = we had better learn ~ = we will do well to learn ~

2 what a modern city would be like
   현대의 도시가 어떠한 모습일까를

3 all the sirens in the docks and factories (began) to make ~
   선창과 공장의 사이렌이 몹시 듣기 싫은 경적 소리를 내기 시작하다

   내용 소음은 듣기 싫은 것이지만, 없앨 수 없으므로 즐기는 것을 배우는 것이 낫다.

get rid of (〜을) 제거하다(= do away with, remove, abolish)
may as well (〜하는 것이) 낫다(= had better, do well to)
think well of (〜을) 좋게 생각하다
abolish [əbáliʃ] 폐지하다, 없애다(= exterminate, get rid of) ⓝ abolition
tear [tiər] 눈물, 한탄 ⓥ [tɛər] 찢다
dock [dɑk] 선창, 부두
hideous [hídiəs] 무서운, 몹시 추한(= appalling, beastly, disgusting, macabre, gruesome, grotesque)
hoot [hu:t] 고함치다, 외치다

Good medicine is bitter in the mouth.
좋은 약은 입에 쓰다.

197 If you come to a stream five feet wide and jump four and a half feet, you fall in and get drowned. You **might as well** have tumbled in from the other side and saved yourself the exertion of the jump.

Key Structure ▸

1 might as well
- may as well보다는 가능성이 약화된 내용을 나타낸다.
  e.g. You may as well give up the attempt. 너는 그 시도를 포기하는 게 낫겠다.
  You might as well block the flow of the river. 너는 차라리 강의 흐름을 막는 게 나을 거다.
  ('그 시도를 포기하다'는 충분히 가능한 일이나 '강물의 흐름을 막는다'는 것은 거의 가능성이 없는 일이다.)

2 save yourself the exertion of the jump
   스스로 점프하는 노력을 덜다
- save+O+O : 4형식 구문과 비슷한 구조

내용 불가능한 일을 하는 데 들어가는 수고를 덜어라.

get drowned 물에 빠지다 *cf.* drown oneself 투신 자살하다
might as well (~하는 것이) 낫다
tumble [tʌ́mbl] 쓰러지다, 구르다 *cf.* tumble in 뛰어들다
exertion [igzə́ːrʃən] 격심한 활동, 진력, 고된 일 (= endeavor, strain, striving, struggle)

플러스 문법정리 70

cost, envy, forgive, save의 쓰임새
위 동사들은 흔히 4형식 동사와 비슷하게 쓰이나, 전치사구를 동반하는 3형식 형태로 바꾸어 쓸 수 없음에 유의해야
한다. 특히 직접목적어, 간접목적어라는 용어보다는 제1목적어, 제2목적어라는 용어를 사용하여 부른다.

(1) a. The book costs $50. (○)
    b. The book cost me $50. (○)
    c. The book costs $50 to me. (×)

(2) a. I envy you. (○)
    b. I envy your success. (○)
    c. I envy you your success. (○)
    d. I envy your success from you. (×)

(3) a. Forgive me please! (○)
    b. Forgive my rudeness please! (○)
    c. Forgive me my rudeness. (○)
    d. Forgive my rudeness from me. (×)

(4) a. This machine saves time and money. (○)
    b. This machine saves us time and money. (○)
    c. This machine saves time and money from us. (×)

해석 (1) 이 책은 50달러다. (2) 너의 성공이 부럽다. (3) 나의 무례를 용서해 줘! (4) 이 기계는 시간과 돈을 절약해 준다.

198　The very abundance of books in our day has made it more important to know how to choose promptly and judiciously among them **if one is not to spend** as much time in the mere choice as in the use.

Key Structure ▸

1　The very abundance of books has made it more important to know ~
책이 너무 많아서 ~을 아는 것이 더 중요하게 되었다
• has made가 it을 가목적어, more important를 목적격보어, to know를 진목적어로 갖는 5형식 구문.

2　if one is not to spend ~
만약 사람[우리]이 ~을 사용하지 않으려면
• if절 속의 be+to부정사는 흔히 '~하려면'이라는 의도의 뜻을 가짐.
e.g. If you are to succeed, you'd better work harder.
만약 네가 성공하려 한다면 더 열심히 일하는 게 좋을 거다.

3　spend as much time in the mere choice as in the use
(책을) 사용하는 데 드는 만큼의 시간을 단지 선택하는 데 들이다

내용　책의 양이 너무 많아 빠르고 현명한 선택이 중요한 문제로 대두되었다.

abundance [əbʌ́ndəns]　다량, 다수, 풍부(= ampleness, amplitude)
promptly [prʌ́mptli]　즉시, 즉석에서, 정확히(= at once, swiftly, instantaneously)
judiciously [dʒuːdíʃəsli]　신중하게, 판단력 있게(= wisely, carefully, cautiously, astutely)

199　**If any progress is to be made** with any of the problems that cause East-West tension, negotiators must meet, not in the hope of unwitting each other, but with an absolute determination that agreement shall be reached.

Key Structure ▸

1　If any progress is to be made with ~ = If they are to make any progress with ~
~에 관련하여 어떠한 진보가 이루어지려면 (they = negotiators)

2　not in the hope of ~, but with...
~의 희망을 가지고서가 아니라 …의 결심을 가지고서

내용　동서 양 진영의 긴장을 해결하기 위해서는 협상자들이 마음을 터놓고 만나야 한다.

progress [prɑ́grəs] 진보, 발전 ⓥ [prəgrés] 발전하다(= advance, development)
tension [ténʃən] 긴장, 불안, 압력(= strain, tightness, suspense)
negotiator [nigóuʃièitər] 협의자, 협상자, 교섭자
unwit [ʌnwít] 혼란스럽게 하다(= derange), 미치게 하다
absolute [ǽbsəlùːt] 절대적인, 완전무결한
determination [ditə̀ːrmənéiʃən] 결심, 결의, 판결(= decision, resolution, will-power)

---

200   A fundamental source of knowledge in the world today is the books found in our libraries. Although progress has been made in America's system of libraries, it still falls short of what is required **if we are to maintain** the standards that are needed for an informed America.

Key Structure

1   fall short of what is required
요구 조건에 미치지 못하다

2   if we are to maintain ~
만약에 ~을 유지하고자 바란다면

3   an informed America
박식한 미국

내용   도서관은 오늘날 이 세상 지식의 근원이다.

fundamental [fʌ̀ndəméntəl] 기본의, 중요한(= basic, important, underlying)
source [sɔːrs] 근원, 원인(= origin, spring, head)
fall short of ~에 미치지 못하다
maintain [meintéin] 유지하다, 주장하다(= keep up, perpetuate, retain, contend, assert)

Half a loaf is better than no bread.
반쪽이라도 없느니보다 낫다.

Reading & Composition

독해와 영작 두 마리의 토끼를 잡아라!

201
It has often been assumed that freedom of speech, oral and written, is independent of freedom of thought, and that you cannot take the latter away in any case, since it goes on inside of minds where it cannot be got at. No idea could be more mistaken. If ideas when aroused cannot be communicated, they either fade away or become warped and morbid.

Key Structure •

1 **it goes on inside of minds where it cannot be got at**
그것은 도달할 수 없는 마음의 내부에서 진행된다
• it = freedom of thought / be got at = be reached

2 **when (they are) aroused** 삽입절 역할

[내용] 사상의 자유가 언론의 자유와는 달리 뺏을 수 없다는 생각은 대단히 잘못된 생각이다.

assume [əsjúːm] 가정하다
the latter 후자 *여기에서는 freedom of thought
be mistaken 잘못이다(= be wrong)
arouse [əráuz] 일으키다, 깨우다(= awaken)
fade away 사라지다, 시들어가다
warped [wɔːrp] 뒤틀린, 비뚤어진(= twisted)
morbid [mɔ́ːrbid] 병적인, 우울한(= morose, pathological, unhealthy, dismal)

Composition 《

아내는 남편으로부터 독립하여 재산을 소유할 수 있다.

[Key] ~로부터 독립하여 **independently of** | 재산 **property**

202
Although we give lip service to the idea of child rearing as the most important task of society, practically everyone associated with it—teachers, day-care workers and the stay-at-home mother—is denied the prestige and pay to do it right. The increase in divorce, remarriage and step relationships adds to the confusion and creates more complications in child rearing.

~ everyone (who is) associated with it ~ is denied the prestige ~ right
그 일을 올바로 행할 수 있는 위신과 보상을 부인당하고 있다
• it = child rearing

내용 어린이 교육이 사회가 짊어져야 할 가장 중요한 일이라고 입이 마르도록 이야기하면서도, 그 교육을 담당하는
당사자를 제대로 대접하지 않고 있다.

give lip service to 말로만 호의를 베풀다, 실속 없는 칭찬을 하다
rearing [ríəriŋ] 양육, 교육
(be) associated with (~과) 관련되다
day-care workers 탁아소에 근무하는 사람들(보모 등)
stay-at-home mother 집에 있는 어머니
prestige [prestíːʤ] 위신, 명성(= credit, honor)
step relationship 양부모 · 양자 관계

Composition ❰❰

그는 말로만 봉사하는 사람이지 행동가가 아니다.

Key 말로 하는 봉사 lip-service | 행동가 a man of action

---

203 My political ideal is democracy. Everyone should be respected as an individual, but no one idolized. It is an irony of fate that I should have been showered with so much uncalled-for and unmerited admiration and esteem. Perhaps this adulation springs from the unfulfilled wish of the multitude to comprehend the few ideas which I, with my weak powers, have advanced.

Key Structure ▶

1 but no one (should be) idolized

2 It is an irony of fate that I should ~ esteem.
원하지도 않고 분에 넘치는 찬양과 존경을 그렇게 많이 받았다는 것은 운명의 아이러니다.

3 the few ideas which I, with my weak powers, have advanced
나의 미약한 힘으로 내놓은 몇 가지 생각들
• with my weak powers는 삽입구

내용 나는 모든 사람은 개인으로 존경받고 누구도 우상화되어서는 안 된다는 민주주의 이념을 가지고 있다.

idolize [áidəlàiz] 우상시하다
irony [áiərəni] 반어, 풍자, 아이러니
be showered with (~이) 쏟아지다
uncalled-for 바라지도 않는(= unasked)
unmerited [ʌ̀nméritid] 분에 넘치는, 부당한
admiration [æ̀dməréiʃən] 찬탄, 찬양(= appreciation, commendation, praise)
esteem [istíːm] 존중, 존경(= regard, respect)
adulation [æ̀dʒuléiʃən] 아첨, 추종(= flattery)
unfulfilled [ʌ̀nfulfíld] 이루어지지 않은, 실현되지 않은(= unaccomplished)

Composition

그가 시험에 떨어졌다니 대단히 놀라운 일이다.

Key ~하다니 놀라운 일이다 **It's surprising that ~ should** | 시험에 떨어지다 **fail in the examination**

---

204 The most important task of life is to preserve what is left of civilization, and out of this to build something "nearer to our heart's desire." Education is of small value if it cannot help us in the most important of all tasks. That we can state its purpose in a thousand definitions does not alter the fact that it has a supreme purpose, and that all the other definitions depend on this.

Key Structure

1 what is left of civilization
   문명에서 남아 있는 것(남아 있는 문명)
   • what은 관계대명사.

2 is of small value = is of little value
   거의 가치가 없다
   • of+추상명사 = 형용사

3 the most important of all tasks
   모든 과업 중에서 가장 중요한 과업(문명을 보존하고, 우리가 바라는 무엇을 만드는 일)

4 depend on this
   • this는 a supreme purpose를 가리킴.

내용 삶의 가장 중요한 과업은 문명에서 남아 있는 것을 보존하고 그것에서 우리가 마음속으로 바라는 무엇을 만들어 내는 것이며, 이것이 바로 교육이 해야 할 일이다.

preserve [prizə́:rv] 보존하다, 보호하다(= conserve, defend, guard, lay up)
state [steit] 진술하다, 공표하다(= declare, proclaim, voice) ⓝ 상태, 국가, 주
alter [ɔ́:ltər] 바꾸다(= change, amend, modify)
supreme [səprí:m] 최고의, 최후의(= best, choicest, consummate, culminating)

Composition 《

교육은 그것이 행해지는 사회의 발전에 기여할 때 커다란 가치가 있다.

Key ~에 기여하다 **contribute to** │ 커다란 가치가 있다 **be of great value**

---

205 Books can take us out of ourselves. None of us has had enough personal experience to know other people—or, indeed, himself—thoroughly. We all feel lonely in this vast, irresponsive world. We suffer because of it; we are shocked by the injustice of the world and the hardships of life. But from books we learn that others—greater men than we—have suffered and have sought as we have.

Key Structure •

take us out of ourselves
우리를 자신(에 대한 몰입)에서 빼내다

내용 책을 통해 우리는 다른 사람들이 겪고 추구한 것을 배울 수 있다.

thoroughly [θə́:rouli] 철저히(= completely)
irresponsive [ìrispánsiv] 반응이 없는(= unanswering, unresponding)
suffer [sʌ́fər] (고통을) 입다, 고생하다
seek [si:k] 찾다, 조사하다 *cf.* seek-sought-sought

Composition 《

여행은 우리가 친숙해져 있는 세계에서 우리를 벗어나게 한다.

Key ~와 친숙하다 **be familiar with** │ ~에서 벗어나게 하다 **take ~ out of...**

206　The question of chemical residues on the food we eat is a hotly debated issue. The existence of such residues is either played down by the industry as unimportant or is flatly denied. Simultaneously, there is a strong tendency to brand as fanatics or cultists all who are so perverse as to demand that their food be free of insect poisons. In all this cloud of controversy, what are the actual facts?

Key Structure ▸

1 **brand A as B** A에게 B의 낙인을 찍다

2 **all who are so perverse as to ~** ~할 정도로 고집이 센 모든 사람들 (brand의 목적어)

3 **demand that their food be free of ~**
　• be(동사 원형)는 앞의 demand 때문에 쓰인 가정법 현재형.

내용　우리가 먹는 음식 속에 남아 있는 화학적 찌꺼기는 오늘날 많은 논란이 되는 문제이다.

chemical residue 화학 잔류물[찌꺼기]
play down 경시하다, 무시하다(= look down upon, neglect)
flatly [flǽtli] 단호히, 딱 잘라서
simultaneously [sàiməltéiniəsli] 동시에(= at the same time)
fanatic [fənǽtik] 광신자, 열광적인 지지자
cultist [kʌ́ltist] 예찬자, 이교도
perverse [pərvə́ːrs] 심술궂은, 고집 센(= adamant, obstinate)
insect poison 살충제(= insecticide)

Composition ◀

그는 우리가 매일 먹는 음식에 화학 잔류물이 남아 있을 가능성을 단호히 부인하였다.

Key　화학 잔류물 **chemical residue**　｜　단호히 **flatly**　｜　부인하다 **deny**

207　If our original assumption is true and human nature has in fact remained fundamentally changeless throughout the historical period, then we should expect to find the contemporary world as full of superstitions as the world of the past. For superstitious beliefs and practices are the expressions of certain states of mind, and if the states of mind exist, so ought the practices and beliefs.

so ought the practices and beliefs
의식과 믿음들도 마찬가지일 것이다[마찬가지로 존재할 것이다]

내용 인간의 본성이 예나 지금이나 변함이 없다면, 현대 세계는 과거 세계처럼 미신으로 가득 차 있을 것이다.

assumption [əsʌ́mpʃən] 가정, 전제(= guess, conjecture, hypothesis)
fundamentally [fʌ̀ndəméntəli] 근본적으로(= primarily, essentially, underlyingly)
contemporary [kəntémpərèri] 현대의(= modern)
superstition [sjùːpərstíʃən] 미신, 미신적 행위 ⓐ superstitious
practice(s) [prǽktis] 예배(의식)

Composition 《

현대 세계가 미신으로 가득 찬 세계라고 가정한다면 근본적으로 잘못된 것이다.

Key 현대 세계 **the contemporary world** │ ~로 가득 차다 **be full of** │ 미신 **superstition** │ 가정 **assumption** │
근본적으로 **fundamentally** │ 잘못된 **wrong**

---

208 The aim of literary study is not to amuse the hours of leisure; it is to awake oneself, it is to be alive, to intensify one's capacity for pleasure, for sympathy, and for comprehension. It is not to affect one hour, but twenty-four hours. It is to change utterly one's relations with the world. An understanding appreciation of literature means an understanding appreciation of the world, and it means nothing else.

An understanding appreciation of literature
문학을 이해하면서 바로 평가하는 것

내용 문학을 이해하는 것은 세상을 이해하는 것이다.

amuse [əmjúːz] 즐겁게 하다, 기분전환 시키다(= entertain)
intensify [inténsəfài] 강하게 하다(= strengthen)
affect [əfékt] 영향을 미치다
utterly [ʌ́tərli] 완전히, 철저히(= fully, absolutely, completely, entirely)
appreciation [əprìːʃiéiʃən] 바로 평가하기, 감사

Composition 《

문학을 공부하는 주된 목적은 문학 작품의 이해에 따른 바른 평가를 통해 세상을 바로 보는 것이다.

Key 주된 목적 the main purpose ┃ 이해에 따른 바른 평가 an understanding appreciation

209
Change in the whole social system is inevitable not merely because conditions change—though partly for that reason—but because people themselves change. We change, you and I, we change and change vitally as the years go on. New feelings arise in us; old values go down and new values arise. Things we thought we wanted most intensely we realize we don't care about. The things we built our lives on crumble and disappear.

Key Structure ▸

1 though partly for that reason 부분적으로는 그 이유 때문이기는 하지만

2 Things we thought ~ care about.
   = We realize we don't care about things (which) we thought we wanted most intensely.
   우리가 매우 강력하게 원한다고 생각한 것들에 관심을 두지 않는다는 것을 우리는 깨닫게 된다
   • we thought는 삽입절.

3 The things we built our lives on = The things on which we built our lives
   우리 삶의 토대가 되었던 것[기초]들

내용 전 사회조직에서 변화는 필연적인 것이다.

inevitable [inévətəbli] 피할 수 없는 (= unavoidable, inescapable, ordained)
vitally [vàitəli] 절대로, 불가결하게 (= compulsorily, crucially)
go down 허물어지다 (= crumble)
care about 신경을 쓰다, 걱정하다
crumble [krámbl] 부서지다, 허물어지다 (= break up, crush, break into pieces)

Composition 《

그녀는 아름다울 뿐만 아니라 재능도 있어서 나는 그녀를 좋아한다.

Key 재능이 있다 be talented ┃ A뿐만 아니라 B도 not merely [simply / just] A but (also) B

210 Along with the possibility of the extinction of mankind by nuclear war, the central problem of our age has therefore become the contamination of man's total environment with such substances of incredible potential for harm—substances that accumulate in the tissues of plants and animals and even penetrate the germ cells to shatter or alter the very material of heredity upon which the shape of the future depends.

Key Structure ▸

the very material of heredity
바로 그 유전 물질[형질]
• very는 명사를 강조하는 부사로서 여기에서는 형용사 역할을 함.

내용 핵전쟁으로 인한 인류 종말의 가능성과 더불어 우리 시대의 중대한 문제는 환경 오염이다.

extinction [ikstíŋkʃən] 멸종, 소멸 ⓥ extinguish ⓐ extinct
contamination [kəntæ̀mənéiʃən] 오염(물질)(= pollution)
incredible [inkrédəbl] 믿을 수 없는, 엄청난(= unbelievable, implausible)
potential [pəténʃəl] 가능성, 잠재력(= possibility, capacity, capability)
accumulate [əkjúːmjulèit] 축적되다, 쌓이다
penetrate [pénətrèit] 침투하다, 스며들다
germ cell 생식세포
shatter [ʃǽtər] 분쇄하다, 파괴하다(= destroy, blast, crush)
heredity [hərédəti] 유전, 세습

Composition ◀

우리의 미래는 믿지 못할 만큼 큰 해악의 잠재력을 지닌 물질로부터 인간의 환경을 보호하는 데 달려 있다.

Key 믿지 못할 incredible | 큰 해악의 잠재력 incredible potential for harm | ~로부터 보호하다 protect ~ against

Beggars must not be choosers.
거지가 이것저것 선택할 처지가 아니다. (찬밥 더운밥 가릴 형편이 아니다.)

211
A man is not a fool because he does not understand your technical language any more than an American is a fool because he does not understand Persian. In a mixed audience of both specialists and laymen, the speaker must decide, of course, to which group he shall primarily address himself. There is no fixed principle involved, only a general admonition to talk to the people one is talking to, rather than to oneself.

Key Structure

1 not ~ because...
　…이라고 해서 ~은 아니다

2 ~ not a fool any more than... = no more a fool than...
　…이 바보가 아닌 것처럼 ~도 바보가 아니다 (양자 부정)

　내용 전문가와 비전문가가 섞인 관중을 상대로 이야기할 때에는 어느 그룹을 대상으로 이야기할지를 결정해야 한다.

layman [léimən] 문외한, 비전문가, 아마추어(≒ professional)
address oneself to ~에게 자신의 의견을 전하다
admonition [æ̀dməníʃən] 충고, 훈계(= advice, caution)

Composition

내가 그녀와 결혼하는 것은 그녀를 정말로 사랑해서가 아니다.

Key • not ~ because 구문을 이용한다.

212
If a nation is essentially disunited, it is left to the government to hold it together. This increases the expense of government, and reduces correspondingly the amount of economic resources that could be used for developing the country. And it should not be forgotten how small those resources are in a poor and backward country. Where the cost of government is high, resources for development are correspondingly low.

Key Structure ▸

it is left to the government to hold it together
국가를 단합시키는 것은 정부가 할 일이다

내용 국가를 단합시키는 것은 정부가 할 일이고, 이 경우 정부의 비용 소모가 늘어나고 결과적으로 국가 발전에 필요한
자원은 줄어들게 된다.

hold together 단합시키다(= unite)
correspondingly [kɔ̀(ː)rispándiŋli] 상응하여, 부수적으로(= equivalently, therefore)
resource [ríːsɔ̀ːrs] 원천, 공급원 *pl.* resources 자원, 자산
cost [kɔ(ː)st] 비용, 경비, 값(= expense, expenditure)

Composition ◁

의지가 있는 곳에 길이 있다.

Key ~ 있는 곳에 **where there is ~**

---

213 Language is so much part of our lives that we seldom stop to think about it. We take it for granted that our words are mere passive tools, means of self-expression and of communication. But there is another way of looking at language. Words certainly are the vehicles of our thoughts, but they may be far more than that; they may acquire an influence of their own, shaping and pre-determining our processes of thinking and our whole outlook.

Key Structure ▸

1 we seldom stop to think about it
하던 일을 멈추고 그것을 생각하는 법이 거의 없다

2 We take it for granted that ~ 우리는 ~을 당연시 여긴다
• it은 that절을 받는 가목적어.

3 they may be far more than that
그것들은 훨씬 그 이상일 수도 있다

내용 언어는 의사소통의 수단일 뿐만 아니라 그 자신의 힘을 얻어 우리의 사고와 관점을 미리 결정하는 일도 한다.

take ~ for granted (~을) 당연시하다
vehicle [víːikl] 전달 수단, 매체, 탈것
predetermine [príːditə́ːrmən] 미리 결정하다
outlook [áutlùk] 전망, 견해, 관점

Composition

부자들이 가난한 사람들보다 더 행복할 것이라고 당연시하지 마시오.

〰〰

Key 부자들 **the rich** | 가난한 사람들 **the poor** | 당연시하다 **take it for granted that ~**

---

214 It is almost universally recognized that the West shows all the world the way to successful economic development, even though in past years it has been sharply offset by chaotic inflation. However, many people living in the West are dissatisfied with their own society. They despise it or accuse it of no longer being up to the level of maturity attained by mankind. And this causes many to sway towards socialism, which is a false and dangerous current.

Key Structure

They accuse it of no longer being ~ mankind
그들은 그것[서구 사회]이 인류가 이룩한 성숙도의 수준에 더 이상 미치지 못한다고 비난한다
• accuse A of B A를 B의 죄로 고소하다, A를 B의 명목으로 비난하다

내용 많은 서구 사람들이 자신의 사회에 불만을 느껴 사회주의 쪽으로 눈을 돌리지만, 이것은 바람직한 일은 아니다.

be offset by (~에 의해) 상쇄되다
chaotic [keiátik] 혼돈의, 무질서한(= confused, disordered, anarchic)
despise [dispáiz] 경멸하다, 멸시하다(= scorn, look down on | ≒ admire)
current [kə́ːrənt] 흐름, 경향(= drift, flow, trend, tide)

Composition

나의 자식들은 내가 그들 세대의 생각이나 요구에 따라오지 못한다고 나를 나무란다.

〰〰

Key 요구 **need** | ~에 따라오다 **be up to** | A를 B의 이유로 나무라다 **accuse A of B**

215 We acquiesce in the loss of freedom every time we are silent in the face of injustice. The more we insist that it is not our concern, the easier we make the demagogue's task. For it is of the essence of liberty that it should depend for its maintenance upon the respect it can arouse in humble men. Their power to maintain it lies in their willingness to organize themselves for its maintenance. It has no foe more subtle than their sense of apathy or helplessness.

Key Structure •

1 it is of the essence of liberty that ~ ~은 자유의 본질이다
   • it(가주어) ~ that(진주어) 구문.

2 it should depend for its maintenance upon ~
   그것[자유]은 자신을 유지해 나가기 위해 ~에 의존한다(자유의 수호는 ~에 달려 있다)

내용 자유는 관심을 갖고 그것을 지키려고 노력해야 하며, 무관심과 무기력은 자유에 대한 아주 교활한 적이 된다.

acquiesce [æ̀kwiés] 묵인하다, 동의하다
in the face of (~에) 직면하여, (~을) 눈앞에 보고서도
demagogue [déməgɑ̀g] 선동자, 선동 연설가[정치가]
maintenance [méintənəns] 유지, 보수(= upkeep, looking after) ⓥ maintain
foe [fou] 적, 적병, 상대(= enemy, opponent)
subtle [sʌ́tl] 교활한, 교묘한, 섬세한(= clever, arcane, elusive)
apathy [ǽpəθi] 무관심(= indifference)

Composition ‹

우리가 더 많은 일에 관심을 가지면 가질수록 더욱더 행복해진다.

Key ~에 관심을 갖다 **be interested in** │ ~할수록 더욱더 …하다 **the+비교급, the+비교급**

216 Personality was once regarded as an indefinable something which certain people had and others lacked. Psychologists have now discovered that personality can be developed by training, just as the mind can. Its development depends on learning to do an increasing number of things with and for other people. By personality we mean the extent to which one is able to interest and serve other people. This ability is made up of habits and skills acquired by practice.

Key Structure

1 **just as the mind can** (be developed by training)
 • 반복된 동사구 be developed by training이 생략됨.

2 **with** (other people) **and for other people**
 • other people은 with와 for의 공동 목적어.

3 **By personality we mean the extent ~**
 개성이라는 말로 우리가 뜻하는 것은 ~하는 정도[수준]이다
 • mean A by B B로서 A를 의미하다
 • the extent to which ~ other people 우리가 다른 사람에게 흥미를 주고 봉사할 수 있는 정도

4 **is made up of habits and skills** (which are) **acquired by practice**
 습관과 연습에 의해 얻어지는 기술로 이루어져 있다

내용 개성은 우리가 다른 사람에게 관심을 갖게 하고 또 그들에게 봉사할 수 있는 것으로, 훈련을 통하여 개발할 수 있다.

indefinable 정의 내릴 수 없는, 불가사의한
lack [læk] (~을) 결여하다
psychologist [saikάləʤist] 심리학자, 정신분석 의사
extent [ikstént] 범위, 정도

Composition

행복이라고 할 때 우리가 뜻하는 바는 우리가 <u>스스로를 통제할 수 있는 범위</u>를 말한다.

Key B로서 A를 의미하다 **mean A by B** | ~의 범위 **the extent to which ~**

217 There are no peoples however primitive without religion and magic. Nor are there, it must be added at once, any savage races lacking either in the scientific attitude or in science, though this lack has been frequently attributed to them. In every primitive community, studied by trustworthy and competent observers, there have been found two clearly distinguishable domains, the Sacred and the Profane; in other words, the domain of Magic and Religion and that of Science.

Key Structure ·

1 **There are no peoples however primitive without ~**
아무리 원시적인 민족도 ~이 없는 민족은 없다
 • however primitive = however primitive they may be (축약된 삽입절 역할을 함)

2 **Nor are there, it must be ~, any savage races lacking either in A or in B**
A 또는 B가 부족한 야만족도 없다
 • it must be added at once 즉시 덧붙여져야 할 사실은
 • there are nor any savage races ~에서 부정어 nor로 인해 도치된 구문.

3 **though this lack ~ to them**
종종 이러한 결핍[과학적 태도나 과학이 부족한 것]이 종교나 주술에 기인한 것으로 여겨져 왔지만
 • them = religion and magic
 • A is attributed to B = attribute A to B A를 B의 탓으로 돌리다, A가 B에 있다고 여기다

내용 아무리 원시적인 종족이라 하더라도 종교와 과학을 지니고 있다.

savage race 야만족
(be) lacking in (~을) 결여하다
frequently [frí:kwəntli] 자주, 빈번하게(= often, customarily, usually)
trustworthy [trʌ̀stwə́:rði] 신뢰할 수 있는(= reliable, truthful | ≒ deceitful)
competent [kámpitənt] 능력 있는(= able, capable, skillful, expert)
domain [douméin] 분야, 영역(= field)
the Sacred 신성한 영역
the Profane 불경한 영역

Composition 《

아무리 힘들고 괴롭더라도 삶을 포기해서는 안 된다.

....

Key 힘든 tough │ 괴로운 displeasing │ 포기하다 give up

218 Most of the work that most people have to do is not in itself interesting, but even such work has certain great advantages. To begin with, it fills a good many hours of the day without the need of deciding what to do. Most people, when they are left free to fill their time according to their own choice, are at a loss to think of anything sufficiently pleasant to be worth doing. And whatever they decide on, they are troubled by the feeling that something else would have been pleasanter.

Key Structure ▶

1 **when they are left free to ~**
그들이 ～하도록 자유롭게 놓여 있을 때(자유를 부여받을 때)

2 **the feeling that something else** would have been **pleasanter**
그 밖의 다른 일이 더 즐거웠을지도 모른다는 느낌
  • 가정법 과거완료(조동사 과거+have+p.p.) 구문. that절은 the feeling과 동격.

내용 그 자체로서는 재미가 없는 일이라도 상당한 이점을 가지고 있다.

in itself 그 자체가, 그 자체로는
advantage [ədvǽntidʒ] 이점, 이익 (≒ disadvantage)
be at a loss 어찌할 바를 모르다, 당황하다
sufficiently [səfíʃəntli] 충분히
be worth -ing ～할 가치가 있다
decide on 선택하다, 결정하다

Composition ◀◀

대부분의 학생들은 그들이 하고 싶은 대로 내버려두면 결코 열심히 공부하지 않는다.

Key 하고 싶은 대로 **as they please** │ ～하도록 내버려두다 **be left free to**

Do in Rome as the Romans do.
로마에서는 로마인들이 하는 것처럼 행동하라. (다른 고장에 가면 그 고장 풍속을 따르라.)

219 Bravery, honesty, strength of character are the stuff for hero-worship. At the boy's level, this worship gravitates toward the doer of spectacular deeds; on the average adult level, toward the wielder of power; and in the eye of a more critical judgment, toward idealism and moral qualities. The most universal hero is he who can fill all these specifications. This, by the many shapes of their courage, integrity, and strength, Washington and Lincoln and Lee are able to do.

Key Structure ▸

1 on the average adult level, (this worship gravitates) toward ~; and in the ~ critical judgment, (this worship gravitates) toward ~
 • 괄호 안의 표현을 넣어 생각할 것.

2 a more critical judgment
 보다 비판적인 판단의 소유자

3 This, by the many shapes of ~ are able to do.
 • this는 ~ able to do의 목적어.

내용 영웅 숭배의 요소들.

stuff [stʌf] 자료, 소질(= material)
hero-worship 영웅 숭배
gravitate [grǽvitèit] 인력에 끌리다
doer [dú(:)ər] 행위자, 실행가(= actor)
spectacular [spektǽkjələr] 눈부신, 화려한(= breathtaking, impressive, magnificent)
wielder [wíːldər] (권력을) 휘두르는 자
specification [spèsəfəkéiʃən] 상술한 내용, 특징
integrity [intégrəti] 고결, 청렴(= decency, honesty, rectitude, righteousness, sincerity)
cf. Washington, George 조지 워싱턴 (1732~1799, 미국의 초대 대통령)
　　Lee, Robert Edward 로버트 에드워드 리 (1807~1870, 미국 남북전쟁 때 남군의 총 지휘자)
　　Lincoln, Abraham 에이브러햄 링컨 (1809~1865, 미국의 제16대 대통령. 미국 남북전쟁 시 Gettysburg Address
　　　　("Government of the people, by the people, for the people")로 유명)

Composition ◁

어린이들은 어떤 사람의 눈부신 행동을 보면 그를 영웅으로 떠받드는 경향이 있다.

Key 눈부신 행동 **spectacular deeds** | 떠받들다 **respect** | ~하는 경향이 있다 **be liable to**

220

One of the most conspicuous traits of the human mind, and perhaps more particularly the educated human mind, is indecision. The more one knows, the harder the task to "make up his mind," as the quaint idiom puts it. Many people struggle with indecision throughout life; many end, as Queen Elizabeth is said to have done, by adopting indecision as a settled policy; only a few naturally possess or are able to develop the capacity for coming to quick and positive conclusions.

Key Structure

1 The more one knows, the harder the task to "make up his mind"
   사람이 많이 알면 알수록 결정을 내리는 일이 점점 더 어려워진다

2 as the quaint idiom puts it
   별난 표현에 이르기를
   • puts it = says

3 many end by adopting ~
   많은 사람들이 ~을 택함으로써 (일을) 끝낸다

4 as Queen Elizabeth is said to have done
   엘리자베스 여왕이 그렇게 했다고 이야기되듯이

내용 인간 정신의 가장 뚜렷한 특징 중의 하나는 우유부단함이다.

conspicuous [kənspíkjuəs] 눈에 잘 띄는(= outstanding, marked, prominent)
trait [treit] 특징, 특색(= quality, peculiarity)
indecision [ìndisíʤən] 우유부단, 망설임(= hesitation)
make up one's mind 결심하다(= determine)
quaint [kweint] 별나고 아름다운
settled [sétld] 확정된(= fixed)
a few 소수의 사람들
come to a conclusion 결론에 이르다

Composition

우유부단이란 큰일을 함에 있어서 빠르고 적극적인 결론을 내리지 못하는 무능력함이다.

Key 우유부단 **indecision** │ 큰일을 하다 **do a great task** │ 빠르고 적극적 결론을 내리다 **come to quick and positive conclusions**

221 If history is to be more than just an annalistic record of the past, some subjective judgment is inevitable in the ordering and in the interpretation of events; hence the classic statement that there can be no unbiased history. In the history of a science, and in the present case in the history of linguistics, there is the additional subjective element involved in determining what activities and aims on the part of earlier workers shall be deemed to fall within its sphere and so to belong to its history.

Key Structure ▸

1 **If history is** to be **~ past**
역사가 과거의 단순한 연대기적[역사적] 기록 이상의 것이 되고자 한다면
• is to be는 부정사의 형용사적 용법.(의도)

2 **hence the classic ~**
따라서 ~라는 고전적인 진술이 가능하다
• hence가 나오면 종종 동사의 생략이 가능함.

3 **there is the additional subjective element involved in ~**
= the additional subjective element is involved in ~

내용 역사가 단순히 과거에 대한 연대기적 기록 이상이 되기 위해서는, 사건을 해석하고 순서를 정하는 데 있어서 주관적인 판단이 필연적으로 요구된다.

annalistic [ǽnlístik] 연대기의, 역사의(= historical)
subjective [səbdʒéktiv] 주관적인(≒ objective)
inevitable [inévitəbl] 피할 수 없는, 필연적인(= unavoidable | ≒ dispensable)
interpretation [intə̀ːrpritéiʃən] 해석, 설명
unbiased [ʌnbáiəst] 공평한, 선입견이 없는(= impartial, unprejudiced | ≒ prejudiced)
be deemed 생각되다, 여겨지다(= be considered, be thought)
sphere [sfiər] 영역, 범위(= realm, class, rank)

Composition ≪

대학이 단지 학위를 취득하는 곳 이상이 되기 위해서는 학생들 편에서 무엇을 어떻게 공부할 것인가에 대한 진지한 고려는 피할 수 없는 일이다.

Key 학위 **an academic degree** | 학생들 편에서 **on the part of the students** | 진지한 고려 **sincere consideration** | 피할 수 없다 **be inevitable**

222 It is too much to say that practical-minded America has consciously followed the example set by Franklin. It is nearer to the truth to say that the shrewd and sensible Franklin of all Americans first trod the path that the entire nation was destined later to travel. With his interest in practical mechanics and invention, his insistence upon progress and public improvements and his desire to get along with his neighbors, Franklin was the forerunner of all the nation that he helped found.

Key Structure ▶

all the nation that he helped found
그가 건국에 공헌한 전 미국(민)

• that은 관계대명사로 found의 목적어 역할.
cf. he helped (to) found the nation. 그는 국가 건설에 도움을 주었다.

내용 프랭클린은 미국민들의 국가 건설에 초석이 된 선구자였다.

practical-minded America 실용주의 정신의 미국(인)
consciously [kánʃəsli] 의식적으로, 자각하여 *cf.* subconsciously 잠재의식적으로, unconsciously 무의식적으로
shrewd [ʃruːd] 영리한, 예민한(= clever, astute)
be destined to (~의) 운명이 지워지다(= be doomed to)
insistence [insístəns] 고집, 주장
forerunner [fɔ́ːrrʌ̀nər] 선구자, 선조(= ancestor, pioneer)
found [faund] 설립하다, 창건하다(= establish) *cf.* found-founded-founded
cf. Franklin, Benjamin 벤저민 프랭클린 (1706~1790, 미국의 정치가, 발명가, 저술가)

Composition ◀◀

그가 우리나라 경제 위기의 주범이라고 말하는 것이 지나친 것은 아니다.

∼∼

Key ~의 주범 **author of** | 경제 위기 **economic crisis** | 지나친 것은 아니다 **not too much**

Hunger is the best sauce.
시장이 반찬이다.

223 I believe the first test of a truly great man is his humility. I do not mean by humility, doubt of his own power, or hesitation of speaking his opinion, but a right understanding of the relation between what he can do and say, and the rest of the world's sayings and doings. All great men not only know their business, but usually know that they know it; and are not only right in their main opinions, but they usually know that they are right in them; only they do not think much of themselves on that account.

Key Structure •

1 I do not mean by humility, doubt of his own power
겸손이라는 말로서 내가 말하고자 하는 바는 자신의 능력에 대한 불신이 아니다

2 only they do not ~ account
단지 그들은 그 이유로 자신을 대단하게 여기지는 않는다

내용 진정한 위인을 측정하는 척도는 그 사람이 겸손한가 하는 것이다.

humility [hju:mílǝti] 겸손, 비하(= humbleness, modesty)
hesitation [hèzitéiʃǝn] 망설임, 주저(= indecision, diffidence, dithering, wavering)
think much of (~을) 높이[대단하게] 생각하다(= value highly)
on that account 그 이유로(= for that reason, on that ground)

Composition 《

그는 자신을 대단하게 여기는데, 겸손이 부족하기 때문이다.

Key 대단하게 여기다 **think much of** │ 겸손 **humility** │ 부족하다 **lack**

Ill news runs apace.
나쁜 소식이 빨리 퍼진다.

224 The mistake of making the records and remains of the past the main material of education is that it cuts the vital connection of present and past, and tends to make the past a rival of the present and the present a more or less futile imitation of the past. Under such circumstances, culture becomes an ornament and solace; a refuge and an asylum. Men escape from the crudities of the present to live in its imagined refinements, instead of using what the past offers as an agency for ripening these crudities.

Key Structure ▸

1 **The mistake of making ~ education** 과거의 기록과 유물을 교육의 주된 재료로 삼는 실수

2 **make the past a rival of the present** 과거를 현재의 경쟁자로 만들다 (S+V+O+O.C. 5형식 구문)

3 **make the present a more ~ of the past** 현재를 다소간 쓸모없는 과거의 모방으로 만들다

4 **Men escape from ~ to live in ~ refinements**
인간은 현재의 조잡한 세계에서 벗어나 상상된 근사한 세계 속에 살게 된다

5 **instead of using ~ crudities**
과거가 제공하는 것[역사]을 이러한 조잡성을 원숙시키는 힘으로 이용하지 않고

내용 과거를 교육의 주된 재료로 삼는 것은 현재와 과거의 극히 중요한 관계를 끊어 버리는 맹점을 갖는다.

remains [riméinz] 유물, 유적, 나머지
vital [váitəl] 중요한, 씩씩한, 생명의(= crucial, important, dynamic)
more or less 다소간
futile [fjú:təl] 소용없는, 쓸데없는(= useless, vain, ineffectual)
circumstance [sə́:rkəmstæns] 사정, 상황
solace [sáləs] 위로, 위안(= comfort, consolation)
refuge [réfju:dʒ] 피난(처), 도피처(= asylum, haven, sanctuary)
asylum [əsáiləm] 보호수용소, 피난처(= sanctuary)
crudity [krú:dəti] 미숙, 조잡(= untidiness)
refinement [rifáinmənt] 세련(미), 고상함, 우아
agency [éidʒənsi] 대리(점), 힘, (정부 기관의) ~청 · ~국
ripen [ráipən] 익히다, 원숙시키다

Composition ⟪

돈을 삶의 유일한 목표로 삼는 실수는 그것이 우리에게 인생의 다른 좋은 면을 보지 못하게 한다는 것이다.

Key 유일한 목표 **the only aim** | 좋은 면 **good facets** | ~을 보지 못하다 **be blind to**

225 A person reading a great novel or biography lives a great adventure without disturbance to his peace of mind. In the words of Santayana, art brings before our eyes what we cannot find in action—the union of life and peace. To read history is good for our health of mind; it teaches us moderation and tolerance, and shows us that the terrible disputes over which civil wars or world wars were once fought are now mere wrangles, dead and buried. And that is a lesson in wisdom and in the relativity of values.

Key Structure

1 **lives a great adventure**
모험이 많은 삶을 살다
• adventure는 동족목적어(cognate object) 역할을 하는 명사.

2 **the terrible disputes over which ~ fought**
그것 때문에 한때 큰 내란이나 세계대전이 일어났던 무서운 논쟁거리들

내용 위대한 소설이나 전기를 읽을 때 우리는 마음의 평화를 방해받지 않고 모험을 할 수 있다.

disturbance [distə́ːrbəns] 불안, 방해(= interference, disruption)
moderation [màdəréiʃən] 중용, 절제(= balance, reticence, temperance)
wrangle [rǽŋgl] 말다툼(= dispute, quarrel)
relativity [rèlətívəti] 상대성 (이론)
cf. Santayana, George 조지 산타야나 (1863~1952, 스페인 태생의 미국 철학자, 시인)

Composition

고전 작품을 읽는 사람은 우리가 행동에서 얻을 수 없는 마음의 평화를 얻게 된다.

Key 고전 작품 a classical literary work │ 마음의 평화 the peace of mind

It is a bad action that success cannot justify.
아무리 나쁜 행위도 승리하면 정당화된다. (이기면 충신이요, 지면 역적이다.)

226　Speech is so familiar a feature of daily life that we rarely pause to
define it. It seems as natural to man as walking, and only less so
than breathing. Yet it needs but a moment's reflection to convince
us that this naturalness of speech is but an illusory feeling. The
process of acquiring speech is, in sober fact, an utterly different
sort of thing from the process of learning to walk. In the case of
the latter function, culture, in other words, the traditional body of
social usage, is not seriously brought into play.

Key Structure •

1　only less so than breathing
　　숨 쉬는 것에 비하면 단지 조금만 덜 자연스러울 뿐이다

2　it needs but ~ / ~ but an illusory feeling
　　• but = only

3　culture ~ is not seriously brought into play
　　문화는 심각[진지]하게 이용되지 않는다

　　내용　언어는 우리 일상생활에서 아주 친근하게 보이기 때문에 자연스러운 것처럼 보이나 사실은 그렇지 않다.

feature [fíːtʃər] 특징, 특색(= attribute, facet, characteristic)
reflection [riflékʃən] 심사숙고, 반성
illusory [iljúːsəri] 착각에 의한, 실체가 없는(= delusive, chimerical, unreal)
sober [sóubər] 냉정한, 술 취하지 않은(= calm, composed, solemn)
utterly [ʌ́tərli] 아주, 완전히(= completely)
bring ~ into play 이용하다

Composition 《

잠시만 숙고하면 말하는 것이 인간에게 걷는 것만큼 자연스럽지는 않다는 것을 틀림없이 확신하게 된다.

Key　잠시만 숙고하면 **a moment's reflection**　│　~만큼 자연스럽지 않다 **not so natural as**　│　확신시키다 **convince**

It is an ill wind that blows nobody good.
아무에게도 이득이 되지 않는 바람은 나쁜 바람이다. (갑의 손해는 을의 이득이다.)

227 The person who has a rich store of knowledge and a variety of interests has the foundation for interesting conversation. Sentences that sparkle cannot spring from an empty person any more than milk can be poured from an empty pitcher. The person who has absorbed ideas from books and from people is listened to with respect. The inner richness which develops from study and reading and keen observation breeds quiet confidence. And confidence is the seed of personality and eloquence.

Key Structure •

1 Sentences that sparkle cannot ~ any more than...
빈 주전자에서 우유를 따를 수 없는 것처럼 빈 사람에게서 번득이는 문장이 나올 수 없다
• '양자 부정'의 부정비교 구문.

2 The person ~ is listened to with respect.
= We listen to the person ~ with respect.

내용 연구와 독서 및 날카로운 관찰력으로 인해 갖게 되는 풍부한 지식과 여러 가지 흥미는 재미있는 대화의 기초가 된다.

a variety of 다양한(= various)
sparkle [spάːrkl] 번득이다, 빛나다
spring from 유래하다(= originate from)
pitcher [pítʃər] 주전자, 투수
absorb [əbsɔ́ːrb] 흡수하다 ⓝ absorption
keen [kiːn] 날카로운, 예민한(= sharp, acute, clever)
breed [briːd] 낳다, 기르다(= arouse, cause, engender, generate)
eloquence [éləkwəns] 웅변, 능변

Composition 《

고래가 물고기가 아닌 것은 말이 물고기가 아닌 것과 마찬가지이다.

Key 고래 **whale** | …이 아니듯 ~도 아니다 **no more ~ than...**

Ill weeds are sure to thrive.
잡초는 빨리 자란다. (이 세상에 악인이 판친다.)

228 During the greater part of our lives, we accept our use and understanding of our native language without awareness, comment, or questioning. Memories of early childhood and experience in bringing up young children may cause us temporarily to ponder the complexity of every normal person's linguistic ability, and the learning of one or more foreign languages after mastering one's first or native tongue reveals just how much is involved in mankind's faculty of communication through language.

Key Structure ▸

just how much is involved in ~ language
언어로 인간이 의사소통을 하는 데에는 얼마나 많은 것[노력]이 들어가는가를

내용 언어를 통해 의사전달 능력을 얻는 데에는 많은 노력이 필요하다.

the greater part 대부분
native language 모국어(= mother tongue[language])
bring up 기르다, 교육하다(= rear, foster, educate)
temporarily [tèmpərέ(:)rəli] 일시적으로(= for the time being)
ponder [pándər] 곰곰이 생각하다, 숙고하다(= think deeply about)
reveal [rivíːl] 폭로하다, 밝히다

Composition ⟪

단기간에 외국어를 완전히 습득하는 것은 생각처럼 쉬운 일이 아니다.

Key 단기간에 **in a short period of time** │ 생각처럼 쉽다 **as easy as we think**

It is dark at the foot of a candle.
등잔 밑이 어둡다.

229 Napoleon restored the respect for authority in France. He found chaos and left order, inherited mutiny and created discipline. For ten years the passions which rent the social fabric had raged unchecked, while those moral forces which helped to strengthen it had suffered a disastrous eclipse. The sentiment of reverence had been laughed away. Religion, antiquity, the long descended traditions of France, even the common decencies of life, had been made to appear as absurd and irrational survivals from a tyrannical past.

Key Structure •

1 the passions which rent the social fabric
   사회 조직을 분열시켰던 열정들

2 had raged unchecked
   제지받지 않은 채 날뛰었다

3 The sentiment of reverence had been laughed away.
   = People laughed away the sentiment of reverence.

내용 나폴레옹은 권위에 대한 존경심과 혼돈 대신 질서를, 항명 대신 규율을 프랑스에 확립해 놓았다.

restore [ristɔ́:r] 회복시키다, 되돌리다
inherit [inhérit] 물려받다, 상속하다(= take over | ≒ hand over)
mutiny [mjú:təni] 반항, 폭동(= revolt, rebellion, sedition, uprising)
discipline [dísəplin] 규율, 질서, 수양(= control, management, orderliness)
rend [rend] 잡아 찢다, 분열시키다 *cf.* rend-rent-rent
fabric [fǽbrik] 직물, 구성, 조직(= structure, framework, make-up)
rage [reidʒ] 사납게 날뛰다, 격해지다
eclipse [iklíps] 소멸, 실추
reverence [révərəns] 존경, 숭배(= respect)
antiquity [æntíkwəti] 고대(의 유물, 제도)
decency [dí:sənsi] 예의 바름, 고상함
absurd [əbsə́:rd] 모순된
tyrannical [tirǽnikəl] 독재(정치)의

Composition 《

사회 조직을 잡아 찢어 놓았던 열정들을 잠재우고 규율을 만들어 내려는 나폴레옹의 노력을 국민들은 비웃었다.

⸳⸳⸳

Key 사회 조직 **the social fabric** | 잡아 찢어 놓다 **rend** | 잠재우다 **calm down** | 규율 **discipline** | 비웃다 **laugh away**

230 Among the natural resources which can be called upon in national plans for development, possibly the most important is human labor. Since the English language suffers from a certain weakness in its ability to describe groups composed of both male and female members, this is usually described as "manpower." Without a productive labor force, including effective leadership and intelligent middle management, no amount of foreign assistance or of natural wealth can ensure successful development and modernization.

Key Structure ▸

1 groups (which are) composed of both male and female members
남성과 여성 회원으로 구성된 집단
• both A and B 구문

2 no amount of ~ can ensure...
외국 원조나 천연자원이 아무리 많아도 …할 수가 없다
• 부정 주어 구문

내용 국가 발전 계획을 짜는 데 있어서 이용할 수 있는 가장 중요한 자원은 인력이다.

natural resources 천연자원
call upon 요구하다, 호소하다
manpower [mǽnpàuər] 인력
middle management 중간 경영진
ensure [inʃúər] 확실하게 하다, 보증하다(= confirm, guarantee)

Composition ❰

재산이 아무리 많았어도 교통사고로 아내와 두 자식을 잃어버린 그의 슬픔과 외로움을 달랠 수는 없었다.

Key 재산이 아무리 많았어도 No amount of wealth로 시작할 것. │ 교통사고 car accident │ 슬픔과 외로움 sorrow and loneliness │ 달래다 soothe

231 One of the difficulties that a man has to cope with as he goes through life is what to do about the persons with whom he has once been intimate and whose interest for him has in due course subsided. If both parties remain in a modest station the break comes about naturally, and no ill feeling subsists, but if one of them achieves eminence the position is awkward. He makes a multitude of new friends, but the old ones are inexorable; he has a thousand claims on his time, but they feel that they have the first right to it.

Key Structure

1　the persons with whom he ~ intimate
한때는 친숙했던 사람들
• be intimate with ~과 친숙하다

2　the old ones are inexorable
옛 친구들도 움직일 수 없는 존재들이다
• ones = friends

3　he has a thousand claims on his time
그에게 시간 좀 내달라는 부탁이 엄청나게 많다

4　they have the first right to it
그들이 그 시간을 쓸 첫 번째 권한[권리]을 갖고 있다
• it = his time

내용　한쪽이 유명해질 경우의 친구 관계

cope with ~과 대항하다, 대처하다
in due course 결국, 마침내는(= finally, in the long run)
subside [səbsáid] 가라앉다, 멎다, 꺼지다
subsist [səbsíst] 존속하다, 살아가다
eminence [émənəns] 고위, 명성(= renown, fame)
awkward [ɔ́:kwərd] 서투른, 어색한(= embarrassing, annoying, uncomfortable)
inexorable [inéksərəbl] 불변의, 굽힐 수 없는(= unchangeable, relentless)

Composition

당신이 유명해지면, 당신을 좀 만나자는 요구가 수없이 많이 들어올 것이다.

Key　유명해지다 **become famous** ｜ 만나자는 요구 **claims on one's time**

232 History proves that dictatorships do not grow out of strong and successful governments, but out of weak and helpless ones. If by democratic methods people get a government strong enough to protect them from fear and starvation, their democracy succeeds; but if they do not, they grow impatient. Therefore, the only sure bulwark of continuing liberty is a government strong enough to protect the interests of the people, and a people strong enough and well enough informed to maintain its sovereign control over its government.

Key Structure ▶

1 **out of weak and helpless** ones
   약하고 무기력한 정부들로부터
   • ones = governments

2 **the only sure bulwark of continuing liberty**
   자유를 유지하는 단 하나의 확실한 보루

내용 독재는 강력한 국민이 있을 때에는 나타날 수 없다.

dictatorship [diktéitərʃip] 독재 (정부)(= despotism, tyranny, autocracy)
starvation [stɑːrvéiʃən] 굶주림, 아사
bulwark [búlwərk] 보루, 방파제(= defence, protection, rampart)
sovereign [sávərin] 주권자로서의, 최대한의(= dominant, supreme)

Composition ◀

국민이 그 정부에 대하여 주권자로서의 통제를 행사할 때 그들의 민주주의가 성공한다는 것을 역사는 입증하고 있다.

Key 국민 **a people** │ 주권자로서의 통제 **sovereign control** │ 행사하다 **exercise** │ 입증하다 **prove**

233 As well as studying the processes which go to make mountains and change the distribution of land and sea, geology is also concerned with the wearing away of the rocks and the deposition of sediments in the sea, since these processes affect the weight of the crust and its pressure on the sub-crust. These matters are also the concern of geographers; and thus the study of the action of air, wind, rain, rivers, frost, and ice upon the earth's surface is common ground to both sciences, and is sometimes known as 'physiography.'

Key Structure •

1 **As well as studying the processes which ~ , geology...**
~한 과정들을 연구할 뿐만 아니라 지질학은 …과도 관련되어 있다
• geology 이하가 주절.
• go to make ~을 형성하는 데 도움이 되다

2 **be common ground to** ~에 공통의 기초가 되다

내용 지질학과 지리학은 공기, 바람, 비, 강, 서리, 얼음 등을 그 연구 대상으로 한다.

distribution [dìstrəbjúːʃən] 배열, 배분, 분포
geology [ʤiɑ́ləʤi] 지질학 *cf.* geography 지리학, geometry 기하학
wear away 닳아 없어지다
deposition [dèpəzíʃən] 침전(물), 퇴적(물)
sediment [sédəmənt] 침전물, 앙금
crust [krʌst] 지각, 지구표면
sub-crust [sʌ̀bkrʌ́st] 최상단 지각의 아래층
physiography [fìziɑ́grəfi] 지형학, 지문학

Composition «

지질학과 지리학은 얼핏 차이가 나 보이지만, 그 연구 대상은 근본적으로 같다.

Key 지질학 **geology** │ 지리학 **geography** │ 얼핏 **at a glance** │ 근본적으로 **fundamentally**

234 The history of life on earth has been a history of interaction between living things and their surroundings. To a large extent, the physical form and the habits of the earth's vegetation and its animal life have been molded by the environment. Considering the whole span of earthly time, the opposite effect, in which life actually modifies its surroundings, has been relatively slight. Only within the moment of time represented by the present century has one species—man—acquired significant power to alter the nature of his world.

Key Structure

Only within ~ has one species—man—acquired significant power ~
금세기로 대변되는 짧은 시기 내에서만 인류라는 하나의 종(種)만이 자기 세계의 본질을 바꾸어 놓을 중요한 힘을 얻어내었다
• 부사구 Only within ~을 강조하기 위해 도치된 구문.

내용 지구상의 생명체의 역사는 살아 있는 생물체와 그 환경 간의 상호 작용의 역사이다.

interaction [ìntərǽkʃən] 상호 작용
to a large extent 상당히, 대부분은
vegetation [vèdʒitéiʃən] (집합적) 초목, 식물
mold [mould] 주조하다, 형성하다
span [spæn] (한 뼘의) 길이, 전장(全長)
modify [mádəfài] 수정하다, 한정하다(= amend, change)
relatively [rélətivli] 상대적으로, 비교적(= comparatively)

Composition

네가 마음을 열 경우에만 그녀는 너를 결혼 상대자로 받아들일 것이다.

Key ~할 경우에만 only when │ 마음을 열다 open one's mind │ 결혼 상대자 an object of marriage

235 The effort to create a new manifestation of life—be it a new species of mollusc or a new species of human society—seldom or never succeeds at the first attempt. Creation is not so easy an enterprise as that. It wins its ultimate successes through a process of trial and error; and accordingly the failure of previous experiments, so far from dooming subsequent experiments to fail in their turn in the same way, actually offers them their opportunity of achieving success through the wisdom that can be gained from suffering.

Key Structure ▸

1 **be it a new species of mollusc or ~**
= whether it (may) be a new species of ~
그것이 새로운 종의 연체동물이든지 아니면 새로운 인간 사회이든지

2 **so far from dooming A to fail in ~** A에게 ~의 실패를 운명 지우기는커녕
• far from -ing ~이기는커녕

내용 새로운 생명체의 창조는 첫 시도에 성공하는 법이 거의 없다.

manifestation [mæ̀nəfestéiʃən] 표현, 명시
mollusc [máləsk] 연체동물(= mollusk)
ultimate [ʌ́ltəmit] 최후의, 궁극적인(= final, fundamental)
trial and error 시행착오
doom [duːm] ~에게 …의 운명을 지우다
in their turn 그들 차례가 되어

Composition

새로운 생명체의 창조는 일련의 시행착오의 과정을 통해 성공을 거두어야 할 만큼 어려운 일이다.

Key 새로운 생명체 **a new manifestation of life** │ 시행착오 **trial and error**

236 In any matter of which the public has imperfect knowledge, public opinion is as likely to be erroneous as is the opinion of an individual equally uninformed. To hold otherwise is to hold that wisdom can be got by combining many ignorances. A man who knows nothing of algebra cannot be assisted in the solution of an algebraic problem by calling in a neighbor who knows no more than himself, and the solution approved by the unanimous vote of a million such men would count for nothing against that of a competent mathematician.

Key Structure

1 public opinion is as likely to be ~ as is the opinion of ~
여론은 ~의 견해만큼 잘못될 가능성이 있다
- as ~ as ~ 동등비교 구문으로 뒤의 as 이하는 도치된 구조임.

2 To hold otherwise
달리 생각하는 것은
- otherwise = in other way

3 against that of a competent mathematician
유능한 수학자의 그것에 비하여
- that = the solution

내용 대중이 부정확한 지식을 가지고 있는 문제에서 여론은 잘못된 것일 수도 있다.

public opinion 여론
erroneous [iróniəs] 잘못된, 틀린(= wrong)
uninformed [ʌninfɔ́ːrmd] 무학의, 지식이 없는(= ignorant)
algebra [ǽldʒəbrə] 대수학
call in 불러들이다
unanimous [juːnǽnəməs] 만장일치의, 이의 없는
count for nothing 전혀 중요하지 않다
competent [kámpətənt] 유능한, 자격이 있는(= capable)

Composition

무식을 많이 합한다고 지혜가 되지 않는 것처럼 수학 문제의 해법도 만장일치의 투표로 얻어질 수는 없다.

Key 무식 ignorance | 합치다 combine | 해법 solution | 만장일치의 투표 unanimous vote
- no more ~ than을 이용한다.

237 Education is the instruction of the intellect in the laws of Nature, under which name I include not merely things and their forces, but men and their ways; and the fashioning of the affections and of the will into an earnest and loving desire to move in harmony with those laws. For me, education means neither more nor less than this. Anything which professes to call itself education must be tried by this standard, and if it fails to stand the test, I will not call it education, whatever may be the force of authority, or of numbers, upon the other side.

Key Structure •

1 **under which name ~**
   교육이라는 이름 아래에 ~
   • which는 education을 받는 관계대명사.

2 **the** fashioning **of the affections ~** into **an earnest and loving desire**
   애정과 의지를 진지하고 사랑스러운 욕구로 변화시키는 것
   • fashion A into B = change A into B

3 **whatever may be ~ upon the other side**
   반대편에 선 자들의 권위가 아무리 세고 숫자가 아무리 많아도

   내용 교육은 자연법칙에 따라 지혜를 가르치는 것이다.

instruction [instrʌ́kʃən] 가르침(= teaching)
not merely A but B A뿐만 아니라 B도(= B as well as A)
harmony [háːrməni] 조화, 융화(= euphony, concord | ≒ cacophony, discord)
profess [prəfés] 공언하다, 확언하다(= declare, assert, vow)
stand the test 시험에 견디다, 합격하다
authority [əθɔ́ːrəti] 권위, 권력 *cf.* authorities 당국

Composition ⟨⟨

교육은 인간에게 다른 인간들과 조화롭게 살아가는 법을 자연법칙에 따라 가르친다고 단언할 때 그 이름값을 한다.

··

Key 조화롭게 살아가다 **live in harmony with** | 자연법칙 **laws of Nature** | 단언하다 **profess to** | 이름값을 하다
     be worth the name

238   Much is being done nowadays to produce better newspapers, but much more is yet to be done to produce better newspaper readers. The newspaper is controlled by its readers. They raise it up or pull it down. It can hardly be better than the reading public wants it to be or allows it to be. No newspaper can be the pillar of free democracy unless readers have a good understanding of it. Thus, a keen consciousness on the part of the general public as to the role of the newspaper is a prerequisite to the successful maintenance of a democratic society.

Key Structure

1   much more is yet to be done
   = much more should yet be done 아직 더욱 많은 일이 이루어져야 한다
   • be+to부정사 (의무)

2   It can hardly be better than the reading public wants it to be ~
   신문은 독자 대중이 원하고 허용하는 이상의 수준이 거의 될 수 없다

3   a keen consciousness ~ newspaper
   신문의 역할에 관하여 일반 대중편에서 보여 주는 날카로운 의식
   • on the part of ~의 편에서 갖고 있는[보여 주는]
   • as to ~에 대하여(= concerning)

내용   보다 좋은 신문을 만들기 위해 많은 일이 이루어지고 있지만, 보다 나은 독자를 만들기 위해 해야 할 일이 더 많다.

raise ~ up 끌어올리다(≒ pull ~ down)
the reading public 독자 대중
pillar [pílər] 기둥, 대들보(= prop, shaft, baluster)
prerequisite [prì(:)rékwizit] 선행조건(의), 기초 필수과목
maintenance [méintənəns] 유지, 지속, 생계(= conservation, upkeep) ⓥ maintain

Composition

대학의 역할에 대하여 학생들 편에서 진정한 토론이 없었다는 것은 대단히 가슴 아픈 일이다.

Key 대학의 역할 **the role of the university** │ 학생들 편에서 **on the part of the students** │ 진정한 토론 **genuine discussion** │ 가슴 아픈 **disheartening**

239 Truth as ultimate reality, if such there is, must be eternal, imperishable, unchanging. But that infinite, eternal, and unchanging truth cannot be apprehended in its fullness by the finite mind of man which can only grasp, at most, some small aspect of it limited by time and space, and by the state of development of that mind and the prevailing ideology of the period. As the mind develops and enlarges its scope, as ideologies change and new symbols are used to express that truth, new aspects of it come to light, though the core of it may yet be the same.

Key Structure •

1 if such there is
   = if there is such a thing
   만약에 그러한 것이 있다면

2 can**not** be apprehended in its fullness
   완벽하게 이해될 수는 없다
   • not ~ in its fullness = not ~ fully (부분부정)

내용 진리는 영원하고 불멸하며 불변해야 한다.

imperishable [impériʃəbl] 사라지지 않을(= unchanging, unending)
apprehend [æprihénd] 이해하다, 감상하다(= understand, appraise)
grasp [græsp] 움켜쥐다, 이해하다
prevailing [privéiliŋ] 유행하는, 힘을 발휘하고 있는
enlarge [inlάːrdʒ] 확대하다(= expand)
scope [skoup] 범위, 영역(= range)
come to light 빛을 보다(= be brought to light)
core [kɔːr] 핵심, 속(= essence)

Composition 《

반짝이는 것이 모두 다 금은 아니다.

Key 반짝이다 **glitter** | 모두 다 ~은 아니다 **all ~ not**

240 What is liberalism? It is not easy to describe, much less to define, for it is hardly less a mood than a doctrine. As the latter, no doubt, it is directly related to freedom; for it came as the foe of privilege conferred upon any class in the community by virtue of birth. But the freedom it sought had no title to universality, since its practice was limited to men who had property to defend. As the former, it tends to be subjective and anarchist. It has always preferred to bless individual action rather than to approve the uniformities sought for by political power.

Key Structure •

1 It is not easy to describe, much less to define
그것은 설명하기가 쉽지 않고, 정의 내리기는 더욱 그렇다

2 it is hardly less a mood than a doctrine
= it is no less a mood than a doctrine = it is a mood as well a doctrine
그것은 주의(主義)일 뿐만 아니라 또한 풍조이다

3 have no title to universality
보편성이라는 이름을 얻을 자격이 없다

4 prefer to V1 rather than to V2
V2 하는 것보다 V1 하는 것을 선호하다

내용 자유주의는 기술하기도 어렵고 정의 내리기도 어렵다. 그것은 하나의 주의[원칙]이며 풍조이기 때문이다.

liberalism [líbərəlìzəm] 자유주의
latter [lǽtər] 후자(≒ former 전자)
privilege [prívəlidʒ] 특권, 특전, 명예
by virtue of ~을 통하여(= by means[dint] of)
anarchist [ǽnərkist] 무정부주의재(의)
approve [əprúːv] 인정하다
uniformity [jùːnəfɔ́ːrməti] 획일(성), 일률(성)

Composition 《

그는 영어를 말할 줄 모른다. 하물며 프랑스어는 두말할 필요도 없다.

Key • not ~, much less를 이용한다.
(much less = still less = let alone = not to mention = not to speak of)

270

241 The more carefully nature has been studied, the more widely has order been found to prevail, while what seemed disorder has proved to be nothing but complexity, until at present, no one is so foolish as to believe that anything happens by chance, or that there are any real accidents, in the sense of events which have no cause. And if we say that a thing happens by chance, everybody admits that all we really mean is that we do not know its cause or the reason why that particular thing happens. Chance and accidents are only aliases of ignorance.

Key Structure ▸

1　The more **carefully** ~, the more **widely** ~ **prevail**
　자연을 좀 더 조심스럽게 관찰해 볼수록 질서가 더 널리 자리 잡고 있음이 밝혀졌다

2　**has proved to be** nothing but **complexity**
　= **has turned out to be** only **complexity**
　단지 복잡성 이외의 다른 것이 아닌 것으로 판명되었다

3　**no one is** so **foolish** as **to believe** ~
　누구도 ~이라고 믿을 만큼 어리석지는 않다

　내용　자연에서 발생하는 모든 일에는 원인이 있다.

prevail [privéil] 우세하다, 이기다
complexity [kəmpléksəti] 복잡함
by chance 우연히(= by accident | ≒ on purpose, by design, intentionally)
alias [éiliəs] 일명, 별명

Composition ◂

우주에는 무질서만 존재한다고 믿을 만큼 어리석은 사람은 없다.

Key　우주 **the universe** | 무질서 **disorder** | ~라고 믿을 만큼 어리석다 **so[as] foolish as to believe**

242 So, in one way or another, life forces man apart and breaks up the goodly fellowships for ever. The very flexibility and ease which make men's friendships so agreeable while they endure make them the easier to destroy and forget. And a man who has a few friends, or one who has a dozen (if there be any one so wealthy on this earth), cannot forget on how precarious a base his happiness reposes; and how by a stroke or two of fate—a death, a few light words, a piece of stamped paper, a woman's bright eyes—he may be left, in a month, destitute of all.

Key Structure ▸

1 **life forces man apart**
삶은 사람을 강제로 갈라놓는다

2 **make them** the easier **to destroy and forget**
그것들을 파괴하고 잊게 하는 것을 그만큼 더 쉽게 만든다
• the는 지시부사로 쉬움의 '정도'를 나타냄.

3 **by a stroke or two of fate**
한두 가지 운명의 장난에 의해

내용 인생은 사람을 강제로 갈라놓고 좋은 우정을 영원히 깨뜨려 버리기도 한다.

in one way or another 이모저모로, 어떻게 해서든지
goodly [ɡúdli] 아름다운, 고급의
flexibility [flèksəbíləti] 유연성, 융통성(= elasticity, pliability)
precarious [prikέ(:)əriəs] 불안정한, 위험한(= unstable, dangerous, insecure)
repose on ∼에 입각하다, ∼에 머무르다
stroke [strouk] 한 번 치기, 일격
light words 가볍게 던지는 몇 마디 말
stamped paper 우표 붙은 편지
be destitute of ∼이 없다(= be lacking in, be void of)

Composition ≪
한두 가지 운명의 장난에 의해 사람들이 강제로 갈라지고, 좋은 우정도 깨어지는 경우가 있다.

Key 한두 가지 운명의 장난 **a stroke or two of fate** │ 강제로 갈라지다 **be forced apart** │ 깨어지다 **be broken up**

243 It is commonly urged that, in a war between liberals and fanatics, the fanatics are sure to win, owing to their more unshakable belief in the righteousness of their cause. This belief dies hard, although all history, including that of the last few years, is against it. Fanatics have failed, over and over again, because they have attempted the impossible, or because, even when what they aimed at was possible, they were too unscientific to adopt the right means; they have failed also because they roused the hostility of those whom they wished to coerce.

Key Structure

1 the fanatics are sure to win
   = the fanatics will surely win

2 although all history is against it
   모든 역사가 그렇지 않음을 보여 줌에도 불구하고
   • it = this belief

3 what they aimed at
   그들이 목표를 두었던 것

내용 자유주의자와 광신자 사이의 싸움에서 광신자가 필히 이긴다고 흔히 주장되지만 역사는 그렇지 않음을 보여 준다.

urge [əːrdʒ] 주장하다, 강조하다(= claim, assert)
liberals [líbərəlz] 자유주의자
fanatic [fənǽtik] 열광자, 광신자
unshakable [ʌnʃéikəbl] 확고한, 흔들리지 않는
righteousness [ráitʃəsnis] 올바름, 공정(성)
cause [kɔːz] 대의명분, 주장
die hard 좀처럼 죽지 않다
rouse [rauz] 불러일으키다, 고무하다(= stimulate)
coerce [kouə́ːrs] 강요하다(= bludgeon, compel, force)

Composition

한국이 수년 내에 경제 위기에서 벗어날 것이라는 믿음은 국민들 사이에서 좀처럼 죽지 않고 있다.

Key 경제 위기 economic crisis | 좀처럼 죽지 않다 die hard

244 The hypothesis of natural selection may not be a complete explanation, but it led to a greater thing than itself—an acceptance of the theory of organic evolution, which the years have but confirmed. Yet at first some naturalists joined the opposition, and the famous anatomist Sir Richard Owen wrote an adverse review. To the many, who were unable to judge the biological evidence, the effect of the theory of evolution seemed incredible as well as devastating, to run counter to common sense and to overwhelm all philosophic and religious landmarks.

Key Structure ▸

1 **To the many = To many people**
많은 사람들에게는

2 **run counter to common sense**
상식에 역행하다

> 내용 자연도태의 가설은 완벽한 설명이 될 수는 없지만 생물은 진화한다는 이론을 우리가 받아들이게끔 한 결과를 가져왔다.

hypothesis [haipάθisis] 가설, 가정
natural selection 자연도태 *cf.* Darwinism
organic evolution 생물 진화
anatomist [ənǽtəmist] 해부학자
adverse [ædvə́ːrs] 반대의, 불리한(= opposed)
theory of evolution 진화론
devastating [dévəstèitiŋ] 파괴적인, 황폐화시키는(= destructive)
overwhelm [òuvərhwélm] 압도하다, 억누르다
landmark [lǽndmàːrk] 표지물, 경계 표지

Composition ◀

다윈의 진화론은 당시 사람들의 철학적, 종교적인 생각들에 심대한 영향을 미쳤다.

Key 다윈의 진화론 **Darwin's theory of evolution** | 심대한 영향 **a serious effect**

245 Modern history begins when history becomes concerned with the future as well as with the past. Modern man peers eagerly back into the twilight out of which he has come, in the hope that its faint beams will illuminate the obscurity into which he is going; conversely his aspirations and anxieties about the path which lies before him sharpen his insight into what lies behind. No consciousness of the future, no history. Between past and future, action and interaction are constant. Past, present and future are woven together in an endless chain.

Key Structure •

1   the twilight out of which he has come
    그[인간]가 빠져나온 여명(즉 과거)

2   the obscurity into which he is going
    그[인간]가 지금 들어가고 있는 어둠의 세계(즉 미래)

3   conversely = conversely speaking   바꾸어 말하면

4   the path which lies before him   그 앞에 놓인 길(즉 미래)

5   what lies behind   뒤에 놓인 세계(즉 과거)

6   No consciousness of the future, no history.
    미래에 대한 의식이 없으면, 역사도 없다.

내용   역사의 과거, 현재, 미래는 끊임없는 고리로 함께 짜여져 있다.

peer back into ~을 눈여겨 되돌아보다
faint [feint] 희미한
beam [biːm] 빛, 열
illuminate [iljúːmənèit] 밝히다
obscurity [əbskjú(ː)ərəti] 어둠, 불명료함
aspiration [æ̀spəréiʃən] 열망, 야심(= desire)
sharpen [ʃáːrpən] 날카롭게 하다(= strop, whet | ↔ blunt)
consciousness [kánʃəsnis] 의식, 지각, 자각
weave [wiv] 짜다, 엮다   cf. weave-wove-woven

Composition ◀

과거는 인간이 빠져나온 어스름이고, 미래는 인간이 들어가는 어둠이다.

Key   어스름 the twilight | 빠져나오다 come out of | 어둠 the obscurity

246　Law, in its true notion, is not so much the limitation as the direction of a free and intelligent man to his proper interest, and prescribes no farther than is for the general good of those under that law. Could they be happier without it the law, as a useless thing, would of itself vanish; and that hardly deserves the name of confinement which hedges us in only from deep streams and precipices. So that the end of law is not to abolish or restrain but to preserve and enlarge freedom. For in all states of rational beings, where there is no law there is no freedom.

Key Structure •

1　not so much **the limitation** as **the direction ~ interest**
제약을 가하는 것이라기보다는 자유로운 지성인이 자신의 마땅한 이득을 얻도록 인도해 주는 것[지침]
• not so much A as B A라기보다는 오히려 B이다

2　than is **for the general good of those ~**
그 법의 지배를 받는 사람들의 일반적인 이득을 위하는 것(보다)
• than은 유사관계대명사(주격).

3　Could they be happier without it = **If** they could be happier without it
그들이 그것(법)이 없이도 행복할 수 있다면

4　that hardly ~ which hedges ~
깊은 강이나 낭떠러지로부터 우리를 보호하기 위해서만 존재하는 법률은 제한이라는 이름에 어울리지도 않는다
• that은 the law를 받음.
• which는 that으로 연결되는 관계대명사.

내용　법의 목적은 자유의 말살이나 제약이 아니라 자유를 보존하고 확장하는 것이다.

prescribe [priskráib] 규정하다, 처방하다, 명령하다
deserve [dizə́:rv] 값어치가 있다, ~할 자격이 있다
confinement [kənfáinmənt] 제한, 감금
hedge [hedʒ] 구속하다, 가두다
precipice [présəpis] 낭떠러지, 절벽(= cliff)
abolish [əbáliʃ] 폐지하다(= do away with)
restrain [ristréin] 억제하다(= check, hold back, limit, regulate)

Composition 《

그는 너의 설명에 화가 났다기보다는 오히려 그것에 실망하였다.

Key　설명 explanation ｜ 화가 나다 be angry at ｜ ~라기보다는 오히려… not so much ~ as... ｜ ~에 실망하다
be disappointed with

247 He has experienced poverty, and he is deeply thankful for his poverty. He has known what it is to be poor; he has seen others dear to him suffer to the bare necessities; there is, in fact, not a single step on that road that he has not travelled. He can, therefore, sympathize with the fullest understanding with those similarly situated, can help as one who knows from practice and not from theory. He realizes what a marvellous blessing poverty can be; but as a condition to experience, to derive from it poignant lessons, and then to get out of, not as a condition to stay in.

Key Structure •

1 what it is to be poor
가난이 어떠한 것인가를
• it(가주어) ~ to be poor(진주어) 구문. what은 의문대명사로 주격보어.

2 he has seen others ~ suffer to ~ necessities
그는 다른 사람들이 삶의 최저한의 필수품조차 갖지 못해 고통 받는 것을 보았다

3 sympathize with those (who are) similarly situated
비슷한 상황에 처한 사람의 입장에 공감하다

내용 그는 가난이 어떠한 것인가를 경험하였으며, 그래서 비슷한 상황에 처한 사람의 처지에 공감할 수 있다.

necessity [nəsésəti] 필수품 *cf.* bare necessities 최저한의 생활필수품
sympathize [símpəθàiz] 동정하다, 공감하다
marvellous [máːrvələs] 놀라운, 신기한(= amazing, exceptional, magnificent)
poignant [póinjənt] 매서운, 통쾌한(= painful, stirring, touching, heartening)

Composition 《

가난이 축복이 될 수 있음을 그는 이론이 아닌 실제를 통해 알게 되었다.

Key 축복 **a blessing** | 이론을 통해 **from theory** | 실제를 통해 **from practice**

248 Our speech is not confined to the communication of facts and thoughts; we also talk to express our feelings, to arouse feelings in others, and to influence their behavior. Clarity and precision are essential on the rational plane, but the emotive side of language will benefit by the suggestiveness of vague words with blurred outlines and rich overtones. At the same time, the very limitations of language are a challenge and a means of self-discipline: our thoughts become more articulate and more elegant by being forced into the molds of a plastic and yet resistant medium.

Key Structure

1 **on the rational plane**
합리적인[이성적인] 측면에서는

2 **by being forced into ~ medium**
유연하기는 하지만 저항적인 매체의 형태로 표현되는 과정을 통하여
• medium은 language를 의미함.

내용 언어는 의사소통을 위한 수단일 뿐만 아니라 감정을 표현하고 다른 사람의 감정을 불러일으키며 그들의 행위에 영향을 미치는 매개체이다.

arouse [əráuz] 일으키다, 깨우다(= awaken, provoke)
clarity [klǽrəti] 명쾌, 명석 ⓐ clear
suggestiveness [səgdʒéstivnes] 암시, 시사
vague [veig] 희미한, 모호한(= ambiguous)
blurred [bləːrd] 흐릿한, 어렴풋한(= bleary, clouded, dim, hazy, nebulous)
overtone [óuvərtòun] 함축, 뉘앙스(= implication)
self-discipline [selfdísəplin] 자기 수양(= self-control)
articulate [ɑːrtíkjəlit] 분명한, 명확한
resistant [rizístənt] 저항하는

Composition

인간의 삶은 이 세상에서 그가 존재한 것에 국한되는 것이 아니라, 죽은 후에 유성처럼 무엇을 남기느냐에 국한된다.

Key 그의 존재 **his existence** | ~에 국한되다 **be confined to** | 유성 **a shooting star**

249 The acquisition of learning is much more dangerous than that of any other food or drink. For with other things, we carry home what we have bought in some vessel; and there we have leisure to examine its value and decide how much of it we shall use, and when, but learning we cannot at the beginning put in any other vessel but our minds; we swallow it as we buy it, and by the time we leave the market we are already either infected or improved. There is some that only obstructs and burdens us instead of nourishing us; and some too that, while pretending to cure us, gives poison.

Key Structure

1 than that of ~
   • that = the acquisition

2 For with other things, we carry home ~
   왜냐하면 다른 물건들의 경우에는 집으로 가져오기 때문이다 (for는 이유를 나타내는 접속사)

3 and when = and when we shall use it

4 but learning we cannot ~ put in any other vessel ~
   • learning은 put의 목적어로서, 강조하기 위해 앞으로 나갔음.

5 by the time (when) ~
   ~하게 될 때에는

내용 학문을 습득하는 것은 음식물의 섭취보다 훨씬 더 위험하다.

acquisition [æ̀kwizíʃən] 획득, 습득 ⓥ acquire
vessel [vésəl] 그릇, 배(= container, boat)
swallow [swálou] 들이키다, 삼키다 ⓝ 제비
infect [infékt] (악풍에) 물들게 하다, 나쁜 영향을 주다, 감염시키다
obstruct [əbstrʌ́kt] 가로막다, 방해하다(= hinder)
burden [bə́:rdən] 괴롭히다, 부담을 주다(= bother, encumber)
nourish [nə́:riʃ] 기르다, 양분을 주다(= nurture)
pretend to ~인 체하다

Composition

그녀가 여기 도착할 때쯤이면 그는 이미 떠나고 없을 것이다.

Key ~할 때쯤이면 **by the time (when)** | 떠나고 없다 **will have left**

250　Advice, as it always gives a temporary appearance of superiority, can never be very grateful, even when it is most necessary or most judicious. Vanity is so frequently the apparent motive of advice that we, for the most part, summon our powers to oppose it without any very accurate inquiry whether it is right. It is sufficient that another is growing great in his own eyes, at our expense, and assumes authority over us without our permission; for many would contentedly suffer the consequences of their own mistakes rather than the insolence of him who triumphs as their deliverer.

Key Structure ▸

1　**Advice can never be very grateful**
　　충고란 (받는 사람 쪽에서) 그다지 고맙게 느껴질 수 없다
　　• cannot ~ too(아무리 ~해도 지나치지 않다)와 혼동하지 말 것.

2　**oppose it**
　　• it는 advice를 가리킴.

3　**for many would contentedly suffer ~**
　　왜냐하면 많은 사람들이 기꺼이 참으려 할 것이기 때문이다
　　• many = many people

　내용　충고는 충고하는 사람의 우월감이 들어 있으므로 충고를 듣는 사람들에게는 그다지 고맙게 느껴지지 않는다.

temporary [témpərèri] 일시적인(= brief, transient, short)
judicious [ʤu:díʃəs] 현명한, 사려분별이 있는(= astute, prudent, thoughtful)
vanity [vǽnəti] 자만심, 허영심(= arrogance, conceit)
summon [sʌ́mən] 소환하다, 호출하다(= call, convene)
at our expense 우리를 희생하여
insolence [ínsələns] 무례함, 오만(= arrogance, boldness, impertinence, impudence, presumptuousness)
deliverer [dilívərər] 구원자, 구조자(= rescuer)

Composition ◀

충고는 일반적으로 그다지 고마운 것이 아니라는 것은 아무리 빨리 알아도 지나치지 않다.

Key　그다지 고맙지 않다 **can never be very grateful** ｜ 아무리 ~해도 지나치지 않다 **cannot ~ too**

251 Life is the only property which is peculiar to living beings. All of them, however, present two further characteristics which are found also in some other objects, though only in such as owe their existence to living beings. One of these characteristics is the presence in them of the substance known as *Protoplasm*. This they share with things that have been alive and are now dead. The other is the existence in them of *Organization*. This they share not only with dead things but with some others, such as machines and human societies, that have been made by living beings.

Key Structure

1 though only in such as owe ~ beings
살아 있는 생물체에 그 존재를 힘입고 있는 그러한 물체들에게서만 (발견되지만)
• such = such objects
• as는 준관계대명사로 주어 역할을 하고 있음.

2 the presence in them of the substance ~
그들 속에 ~라는 물질이 존재하는 것

3 This they share with ~
= They share this with ~
• share의 목적어 this가 문두로 도치된 구문.

내용 생명은 생물에게 독특한 유일한 속성이다.

property [prɑ́pərti] 속성, 특성
peculiar (to) 특유한, 독특한
substance [sʌ́bstəns] 물질, 재료
protoplasm [próutəplæzəm] 원형질, 세포질(= cytoplasm)
organization [ɔ̀ːrgənizéiʃən] 유기체, 생물
share A with B A를 B와 나누어 갖다[공유하다]

Composition

오늘의 그가 있게 된 것은 그의 어머님의 희생과 사랑이 있었기 때문이다.

Key 오늘의 그 what he is (today) | 희생 sacrifice
• owe A to B를 이용한다.

252 One of the most alarming aspects of the chemical pollution of water is the fact that here—in river or lake or reservoir, or for that matter in the glass of water served at your dinner table— are mingled chemicals that no responsible chemist would think of combining in his laboratory. The possible interactions between these freely mixed chemicals are deeply disturbing to officials of the United States Public Health Service, who have expressed the fear that the production of harmful substances from comparatively innocuous chemicals may be taking place on quite a wide scale.

Key Structure

here ~ are mingled chemicals that ~ chemist would think of ~ laboratory
책임 있는 화학자는 누구도 실험실에서 결합하려고 결코 생각하지도 않을 화학 물질이 여기에 뒤섞여 있다
• 위 구문에서 주어는 chemicals (that ~).

내용 화학 물질에 의한 물의 오염이 주는 가장 놀라운 점의 하나는 강, 호수, 저수지, 심지어 우리가 식사 때 마시는 물에까지도 화학 물질이 섞여 있다는 것이다.

alarming [əláːrmiŋ] 놀라운(= astonishing, astounding, surprising)
chemical [kémikəl] 화학(제품)의
reservoir [rèzərvwáːr] 저수지, 저수장
for that matter 그 이유로, 실제로(= indeed)
mingled [míŋgld] 혼합된, 뒤섞인
disturbing [distớːrbiŋ] 불안하게 하는, 우려할 만한
innocuous [inákjuəs] 무해한(= harmless)

Composition

우리가 마시는 물 속에 화학 물질이 뒤섞여 있다는 사실은 대단히 놀라운 일이다.

Key 화학 물질 chemical | 놀라운 alarming

Misfortunes never come singly. (= One misfortune rides upon another's back.)
불행은 혼자 오는 법이 없다. (엎친 데 덮친다.)

253   Education is one of the key words of our time. A man without an education, many of us believe, is an unfortunate victim of adverse circumstances deprived of one of the greatest twentieth-century opportunities. Convinced of the importance of education, modern states 'invest' in institutions of learning to get back 'interest' in the form of a large group of enlightened young men and women who are potential leaders. Education, with its cycles of instruction so carefully worked out, punctuated by textbooks—those purchasable wells of wisdom—what would civilization be like without its benefits?

Key Structure •

1   an unfortunate victim of adverse circumstances deprived of ~
20세기가 제공하는 커다란 기회 중의 하나를 빼앗겨 버린 불리한 환경의 불행한 희생자
• deprived 앞에 who is가 생략됨.

2   Convinced of ~ = As they are convinced of ~
그들이 ~을 확신하고 있기 때문에
• 이유를 나타내는 분사구문.

내용   교육은 20세기가 주는 가장 위대한 기회들 중 하나이다.

victim [víktim] 희생자, 희생물(=prey, sacrifice)
adverse [ædvə́:rs] 거꾸로의, 불리한 *cf.* adverse circumstances 역경
deprive A of B A에게서 B를 빼앗다
institutions of learning 교육 기관
interest [íntərəst] 이자, 이득
potential [pəténʃəl] 가능한, 잠재력이 있는
work out (계획 등을) 잘 세우다
punctuate [pʌ́ŋktʃuèit] 강조하다, 구두점을 찍다
purchasable [pə́:rtʃəsəbl] 살 수 있는(= can be bought)

Composition ◀

고등 교육을 받지 못하는 것은 20세기가 주는 기회의 하나를 빼앗긴 것이나 다름이 없음을 확신하였기 때문에 그는 더욱 열심히 공부하였다.

Key   고등 교육 **a higher education** | 빼앗기다 **be deprived of** | 다름이 없다 **be as good as** | 확신하다 **be convinced of[that]**

254　Language is one of man's precious possessions. Without it he would be unable to exchange ideas with his fellow men. In the modern world, however, it is not enough to speak only the language of one's own country. It is said that the man who speaks two languages has two minds, for in learning a foreign language, we acquire, to a certain extent, the mentality of a foreign people. Language study, accordingly, is one of the best means of enabling us to understand our fellow men. It is difficult, to be sure, but rich in rewards. It makes us better citizens of the international world in which we live.

Key Structure •

Without **it**

= But for **it** = If it were not for **it** = Were it not for **it**

그것이 없다면

• it = language

내용　언어는 인간이 지닌 고귀한 소유물 중 하나이고, 모국어뿐만 아니라 외국어도 할 줄 아는 것은 국제 사회의 보다 훌륭한 시민이 되게끔 한다.

precious [préʃəs] 고귀한, 값비싼(= invaluable, priceless)
acquire [əkwáiər] 획득하다, 배우다(= come by, obtain, procure)
mentality [mentǽləti] 사고방식, 정신(활동)
accordingly [əkɔ́ːrdiŋli] 따라서(= therefore)
rewards [riwɔ́ːrdz] 보상, 보수

Composition 〈〈

동시에 두 개의 외국어를 배우는 것은 분명히 어렵지만, 나중에 그 보상이 큰 것으로 판명될 것이다.

Key　동시에 **at the same time** ｜ 분명히 **to be sure** ｜ 보상이 크다 **be rich in rewards** ｜ 판명되다 **turn out**

284

255 There are men who cannot be friends except when they are under an illusion that their friends are perfect, and when the illusion passes there is an end of their friendship. But true friendship has no illusions, for it reaches to that part of a man's nature that is beyond his imperfections, and in doing so it takes all of them for granted. It does not even assume that he is better than other men, for there is egotism in assuming that. A man is your friend, not because of his superiorities, but because there is something open from your nature to his, a way that is closed between you and most men.

Key Structure

1 except when ~
  ~하는 경우를 제외하고

2 it reaches to that part of a man's nature that is ~ imperfections
  그것[우정]은 그의 불완전함을 넘어서는 인간 본성의 한 부분에 미친다
  • that 이하는 관계대명사절로 선행사는 that part임.

3 not because of A, but because B
  A의 이유가 아니라 B의 이유로
  • not A but B의 구문. (A는 명사(구), B는 절)

내용 진정한 우정에는 환상이 없다.

illusion [ilʃúːʒən] 환상, 착각
reach to ~에 뻗다, 미치다
imperfection [ìmpərfékʃən] 결점, 결함(= defect, flaw, infirmity)
egotism [íːgətìzəm] 자기중심적 성향

Composition

내가 그를 높이 생각하는 것은 그가 영리해서가 아니라 맡겨진 모든 일에 언제나 최선을 다하기 때문이다.

Key 높이 생각하다 think highly of | 영리하다 clever | 맡겨진 모든 일 everything entrusted to him | 최선을 다하다 do one's best

256   Thus, one reason why we read is to get beyond our own lives and understand those of others. But this is not the only reason for the pleasure we derive from books. In everyday life we are too involved in what is happening to see events clearly, too much under the sway of our emotions to savor them properly. The lives of many of us would make a novel worthy of Dickens or Balzac, but we get no pleasure from the experience—quite the contrary. The writer's task is to give us a faithful picture of life, but to keep it far enough away for us to be able to appreciate it without fear or entanglement.

Key Structure

1   we are too involved in ~ to see...
    = We are so involved in ~ that we cannot see...

2   we are too much under ~ to savor...
    = We are so much under ~ that we cannot savor...

3   to keep it far enough away
    그것을 충분히 거리를 두어 유지하다

내용   독서를 하는 이유의 하나는 자신의 삶을 뛰어넘어 다른 사람의 삶을 이해하기 위해서이다.

get beyond ~을 넘어서다
be under the sway of ~의 지배하에 놓이다
savor [séivər] 음미하다, 맛보다
contrary [kántreri] 반대의
entanglement [intǽŋglmənt] 얽힘, 연루
cf. Dickens, Charles 찰스 디킨스 (1812~1870, 영국의 소설가. *David Copperfield, Christmas Carol, Hard Times* 등의 작품이 있음.)
      Balzac, Honoré de 오노레 드 발자크 (1799~1850, 프랑스의 사실주의 작가. *Le Lys dans la vallée*(골짜기의 백합꽃), *Les Chouans*(올빼미 당원) 등의 작품이 있음.)

Composition

우리는 삶의 사소한 일들에 너무 신경을 쓴 나머지 정말로 중요한 일이 무엇인지를 잘 깨닫지 못한다.

Key   사소한 일들 **trivialities** | ~에 대해 신경 쓰다 **be concerned about** | 정말로 중요한 일 **what is really important**

257 No man can shave every morning for twenty or thirty years without learning something. Even if he is too lazy or too incompetent to shave himself, and submits himself to barbers, he can hardly escape learning something about human nature by the time he is middle-aged. For barbers contain in their ranks every variety of human nature. I have known barbers who were angels; I have known barbers who were devils. Some of them have a touch as light as a falling feather; others wield a razor like a weapon of the stone age, and are not content unless they are allowed to flay as well as to shave you.

Key Structure •

1   No man can shave ~ without learning something.
누구든 20~30년 동안 매일 아침 면도를 하게 되면 무엇인가를 배우게 된다.
• not ~ without… ~하면 반드시 …한다

2   submit himself to barbers
자신을 이발사에게 맡기다

3   by the time (when) he is middle-aged
그가 중년이 될 때쯤에는

내용   누구든 오랫동안 면도를 하게 되면 무엇인가 배우게 된다.

incompetent [inkǽmpitənt] 무능한, 서투른(= incapable, unskilled, inexpert)
wield [wi:ld] (검을) 휘두르다
flay [flei] 껍질을 벗기다
cf. the stone age 석기 시대, the Paleolithic era 구석기 시대, the Neolithic era 신석기 시대, the Mesolithic era 중석기 시대

Composition ◀

네가 중년의 나이가 될 때쯤에는 왜 내가 이러한 이야기를 하는지를 깨닫게 될 것이다.

Key ~때쯤에는 **by the time (when)** | 중년의 **middle-aged** | 깨닫다 **realize**

258   In the past decade, it has become the conventional wisdom in the academic establishment that moral education is illegitimate because it constitutes 'indoctrination.' As a result, teachers have approached the subject in a diffident manner. And our children are growing up with very confused and sometimes dangerous notions of what it means to act morally and responsibly in today's society. The problems of alcoholism, drug abuse, vandalism, promiscuity, and simple lack of common decency which pervade our schools are clearly related to the terrible state of moral education in the American classroom.

Key Structure ▸

1   it has become ~ that moral...
- it은 가주어, that 이하는 명사절로 진주어.

2   what it means to act ~ society
요즈음의 사회에서 도덕적으로 책임 있게 행동하는 것이 무엇을 뜻하는지를
- it은 가주어, to act~ 는 진주어, what은 means의 목적어로 쓰인 의문대명사.

내용   알코올 중독, 약물 남용 등의 문제에서 오늘날 미국의 도덕 교육은 위기에 처해 있다.

decade [dékeid] 10년간
conventional [kənvénʃənəl] 전통에 따른, 틀에 박힌(= traditional)
illegitimate [ìlidʒítəmit] 불법의, 비합법적인(= improper, spurious)
constitute [kánstitjùːt] 형성하다, 구성하다
indoctrination [indáktrənèiʃən] 주입, 교화
diffident [dífidənt] 자신 없는, 조심성 있는(= shy, timid | ≒ confident)
drug abuse 마약 남용, 약물 남용
vandalism [vǽndəlìzm] (예술문화, 공공물의) 파괴, 오손
promiscuity [prɑ̀məskjúːəti] 혼란, 난잡, 난교(亂交)
pervade [pəːrvéid] 배어들다, 고루 미치다

Composition ≪

오늘날 젊은이들에게 침투해 들어오는 알코올 중독, 약물 남용의 문제는 우리나라 도덕 교육의 현주소를 잘 보여 주고 있다.

Key   침투해 들어오다 **pervade** | 알코올 중독 **alcoholism** | 약물 남용 **drug abuse** | 도덕 교육 **moral education** | 현주소 **present status**

259 Why does the idea of progress loom so large in the modern world? Surely because progress of a particular kind is actually taking place around us and is becoming more and more manifest. Although mankind has undergone no general improvement in intelligence or morality, it has made extraordinary progress in the accumulation of knowledge. Knowledge began to increase as soon as the thoughts of one individual could be communicated to another by means of speech. With the invention of writing, a great advance was made, for knowledge could then be not only communicated but also stored.

Key Structure ·

1 Surely because ~
   = It is surely because ~

2 undergo no general improvement in ~ morality
   지성과 도덕의 면에서 결코 전체적인[보편적인] 진보를 겪지 않다

3 it has made ~ knowledge
   그것은 지식의 축적에서 특출한 진보를 이루었다
   • it = mankind

내용 말과 글을 통한 인간 지식의 발전.

loom [lu:m] 어렴풋이 나타나다(= emerge)
manifest [mǽnəfèst] 분명한, 명백한(= evident, clear)
undergo [ʌ̀ndərgóu] 겪다, 경험하다
extraordinary [ikstrɔ́:rdənèri] 특출한, 비범한
accumulation [əkjù:mjəléiʃən] 축적, 쌓기
communicate [kəmjú:nəkèit] 전달하다, 통신하다
store [stɔ:r] 축적하다

Composition ◀

컴퓨터의 발명과 함께, 인간의 지식과 정보의 분야에서 전에는 도저히 상상할 수 없던 발전이 있었다.

Key ~의 발명과 함께 **with the invention of** │ 도저히 상상할 수 없던 **could hardly be imagined**

260 Man differs from the lower animals because he preserves his past experiences. What happened in the past is lived again in memory. About what goes on today hangs a cloud of thoughts concerning similar things undergone in bygone days. With the animals, an experience perishes as it happens, and each new doing or suffering stands alone. But man lives in a world where each occurrence is charged with echoes and reminiscences of what has gone before, where each event is a reminder of other things. Hence he lives not like the beasts of the field, in a world of merely physical things but in a world of signs and symbols.

Key Structure

1 About what goes on today hangs a cloud of thoughts concerning ~
   = A cloud of thoughts hangs about what goes on today concerning ~
   • 도치 구문으로 주어는 A cloud of thoughts.
   • concerning은 주어를 꾸미는 전치사구.

2 a world where each occurrence is ~ before
   매번 일어나는 일이 전에 있었던 일의 메아리와 회상으로 채워진 세계
   • where 이하는 a world를 수식하는 관계부사절.
   • be charged with ~으로 장전되다, 채워지다

3 where each event is ~ things 사건 하나하나가 다른 일들을 생각나게 하는 (세계)
   • where는 앞의 a world로 연결됨.

내용 인간과 하등 동물의 차이는, 인간은 과거의 경험을 기억 속에 보존한다는 점이다.

preserve [prizə́:rv] 보존하다(= conserve)
concerning [kənsə́:rniŋ] ~과 관련하여(= as to)
bygone [báigò:n] 과거의, 지나가 버린
perish [périʃ] 사라지다(= disappear)
reminiscence [rèmənísəns] 회상, 추억(= remembrance, memory)
reminder [rimáindər] 생각나게 하는 것[사람], 독촉장
beast [bi:st] 짐승

Composition

그가 너와 다른 것은 지나간 날에 있던 일들을 꼼꼼히 기록하고 있기 때문이다.

Key 지나간 날들 bygone days │ 꼼꼼히 기록하다 make a meticulous record of
   • A differs from B because를 이용한다.

261 Liberty, of the sort that communists despise, is important not only to intellectuals or to the more fortunate sections of society. Owing to its absence in Russia, the Russian Government has been able to establish a greater degree of economic inequality than exists in Great Britain, or even in America. An oligarchy which controls all the means of publicity can perpetrate injustices and cruelties which would be scarcely possible if they were widely known. Only democracy and free publicity can prevent the holders of power from establishing a servile state, with luxury for the few and overworked poverty for the many.

Key Structure ▸

1 **of the sort that communists despise**
공산주의자들이 경멸하는 그런 종류의
• of는 '성질'을 나타내는 전치사.

2 **not only to A or to B**
A 또는 B에게만이 아니라
• not only A but also B 구문이 아님에 유의.

3 **a greater degree of economic inequality than exists in Great Britain**
영국에 존재하는 것보다 더 큰 경제 불평등
• than은 유사관계대명사로 주어 역할을 하고 있음.

4 **the few**
소수의 사람들
• ≒ the many 다수의 사람들

내용 민주주의와 자유로운 선전[정책]만이 권력을 쥔 자가 노예 국가를 만드는 것을 막을 수 있다.

despise [dispáiz] 경멸하다, 얕보다(= look down upon)
oligarchy [áləgà:rki] 소수독재 정치, 과두 정치
publicity [pʌblísəti] 선전, 홍보, 광고
perpetrate [pə́:rpitrèit] 범하다, 저지르다(= commit)
servile [sə́:rvil] 노예(상태)의, 비굴한(= subservient)

Composition ◀

민주주의는 자유로운 선전을 허용하고 다수에게 행복을 준다는 점에서 독재 정치와 차이가 난다.

Key 자유로운 선전 **free publicity** | 다수 **the many** | 독재 정치 **dictatorship**

262 Human nature does not change, or, at any rate, history is too short for any changes to be perceptible. The earliest known specimens of art and literature are still comprehensible. The fact that we can understand them all and can recognize in some of them an unsurpassed artistic excellence is proof enough that not only men's feelings and instincts, but also their intellectual and imaginative powers, were in the remotest times precisely what they are now. In the fine arts it is only the convention, the form, the incidentals that change: the fundamentals of passion, of intellect and imagination remain unaltered.

Key Structure

1 history is too short for ~ to be perceptible
   = history is so short that no changes can be perceptible
   역사는 너무 짧아서 어떤 변화도 감지하기가 어렵다

2 The fact that we can ~ is proof enough that...
   우리가 ~을 이해할 수 있다는 사실은 …에 대한 틀림없는 증거이다
   • The fact가 주어. 동사는 is.

3 precisely what they are now 정확하게 오늘날의 모습대로

4 it is only the convention, ~ , that change
   변화하는 것은 단지 인습, 형식, 그리고 부수적인 것들이다
   • it is ~ that 강조 구문으로 only the convention ~ 부분이 강조됨.

내용 인간 본성은 변화하지 않는다.

perceptible [pərséptəbl] 지각할 수 있는
specimen [spésəmən] 견본, 실례(= example)
unsurpassed [ʌ̀nsərpǽst] 탁월한, 유례없는(= unprecedented, unparalleled)
fine arts 시각(조형) 예술(그림, 조각, 건축 등)
convention [kənvénʃən] 인습, 관행, 전통(= tradition)
fundamental [fʌ̀ndəméntəl] 기본, 원칙 ⓐ 기본적인
unaltered [ʌnɔ́:ltərd] 변하지 않는, 불변의(= unchanged)

Composition

그의 그러한 행동은 그가 외모는 많이 바뀌었으나, 본성은 바뀌지 않았음을 보여 준다.

Key 외모 appearance(s) | 본성 his nature | 보여 주다 reveal

263 Of course a series of previous failures does not guarantee success to the next comer, any more than it condemns him to be a failure in his turn. There is nothing to prevent our Western civilization from following historical precedent, if it chooses, by committing social suicide. But we are not doomed to make history repeat itself; it is open to us, through our own efforts, to give history, in our case, some new and unprecedented turn. As human beings, we are endowed with this freedom of choice, and we cannot shuffle off our responsibility upon the shoulders of God or nature. We must shoulder it ourselves. It is up to us.

Key Structure ▸

1 **does** not **guarantee** ~ any more than...
~을 보장하지 못하는 것은 …을 하지 못하는 것과 같다 (양자 부정)

2 **shuffle off our responsibility upon ~ nature**
우리의 책임을 하느님이나 자연의 어깨로 전가하다

3 **It is up to us.**
그것은 우리에게 맡겨진 일이다.

내용 문명이 퇴보하지 않도록 우리가 스스로 책임지는 마음가짐을 가져야 한다.

a series of 일련의(= a train of, a succession of)
guarantee [gὰrəntíː] 보증하다(= assure, certify)
condemn [kəndém] ~에게 …을 선고하다
precedent [prisíːdnt] 전례, 선례
be doomed to ~할 운명에 처하다
unprecedented [ʌnprésidèntid] 전례가 없는, 미증유의(= unparalleled)
be endowed with ~을 부여받다, ~이 주어지다
shuffle off 전가하다
shoulder [ʃóuldər] 어깨에 메다[지다]

Composition ◀

역사가 과거의 실수를 되풀이하지 않도록 우리의 노력을 통하여 막아 내는 것은 우리에게 맡겨진 일이다.

....

Key 과거의 실수를 되풀이하다 **repeat previous failures** | 우리의 노력을 통하여 **through our efforts** | 우리에게 맡겨지다 **it is up to us**

264 Language alone is not, of course, enough to explain the rise of modern nationalism. Even language is a shorthand for the sense of belonging together, of sharing the same memories, the same historical experience, the same cultural and imaginative heritage. When in the 18th century nationalism began to take form as a modern movement, its forerunners in many parts of Europe were not soldiers and statesmen but scholars and poets who sought to find in ancient legends and half forgotten folksongs the 'soul' of the nation. But it was language that enshrined the memories, the common experience and the historical record.

Key Structure

1 **not enough to explain ~**
~을 설명하기에 충분하지가 않다

2 **scholars and poets who ~ nation**
오래된 전설과 반쯤 잊혀진 민요에서 민족의 정수를 찾으려 한 학자와 시인들
• find in A B = find B in A A에서 B를 찾다
A = ancient legends and half forgotten folksongs
B = the 'soul' of the nation

3 **it was language** that **enshrined ~**
~을 소중히 간직한 것은 언어였다
• it ~ that 강조 구문임에 유의.

내용 언어만으로는 현대 민족주의의 등장을 설명하기에 충분하지 않지만, 국민의 기억과 공통의 경험과 역사적 기록을 고이 간직하고 있는 것은 언어이다.

shorthand [ʃɔ́:rthæ̀nd] 속기(법)(= stenography)
heritage [héritidʒ] 세습[상속] 재산, 유산
forerunner [fɔ́:rrʌ̀nər] 선구자, 선조(= predecessor)
statesman [stéitsmən] 정치가 cf. politician 정객, 정상배
legend [lédʒənd] 전설, 구전, 일화집
enshrine [inʃráin] 소중히 모시다, (사당에) 안치하다

Composition

언어는 한 민족의 오래된 전설과 민요, 국민의 공통 경험과 역사적 기록을 나타내는 민족 정신의 정수라고 말할 수 있다.

Key 전설 legend │ 민요 folksong │ 공통의 경험 common experience │ 민족 정신 soul of the nation

265 What hunger is in relation to food, zest is in relation to life. The man who enjoys watching football is to that extent superior to the man who does not. The man who enjoys reading is still more superior to the man who does not, since opportunities for reading are more frequent than opportunities for watching football. The more things a man is interested in, the more opportunities of happiness he has, and the less he is at the mercy of fate, since if he loses one thing he can fall back upon another. Life is too short to be interested in everything, but it is good to be interested in as many things as are necessary to fill our days.

Key Structure •

1 What hunger is in relation to food, zest is in relation to life.
   열정이 인생에 대해서 갖는 관계는 배고픔이 음식에 대해 갖는 관계와 마찬가지이다.
   • A is to B what C is to D에서 'A is to B'가 뒤로 옮겨간 형태.

2 still more superior to ~ ~보다 더욱더 우월하다
   • still more는 비교급 superior를 꾸미는 부사

3 The more things ~, the more ~ he has, and the less he is ~ fate
   사람이 더 많은 일에 관심을 가지면 가질수록 그는 행복의 기회를 더 많이 갖게 되고, 운명에 덜 좌우된다

4 Life is too short to be ~ everything
   = Life is so short that we cannot be ~ everything
   인생은 너무 짧아서 모든 일에 관심을 가질 수는 없다

5 as many things as are ~ days 우리의 시간을 채우는 데 필요한 만큼의 많은 일들
   • as ~ as 비교구문으로 뒤의 as는 유사관계대명사.

   내용 인생에서 열정은 필요한 것이고, 많으면 많을수록 좋다.

zest [zest] 풍미, 열의
to that extent 그 정도만큼
frequent [frí:kwənt] 자주 일어나는 ⓥ [frikwént] 자주 가다
be at the mercy of ~에 좌우되다(= be under the power of)
fall back upon ~에 의지하다(= rely on, depend on, count on)

Composition ❮

너에게 이득이 될 그런 사람들을 친구로 사귀려고 노력하여라.

Key 이득이 되다 benefit | ~와 친구로 사귀다 keep company with

Part 2 Reading & Composition

266 It is a great nuisance that knowledge cannot be acquired without trouble. It can only be acquired by hard work. It would be fine if we could swallow the powder of profitable information made palatable by the jam of fiction. But the truth is that, so made palatable, we can't be sure that the powder will be profitable. I suggest to you that the knowledge the novelist imparts is biased and thus unreliable, and it is better not to know a thing at all than to know it in a distorted fashion. If readers wish to inform themselves of the pressing problems of the day, they will do better to read, not novels but the books that specifically deal with them.

Key Structure

1 It would be fine if we could swallow ~
   우리가 ~을 삼킬 수 있다면 좋을 것이다
   • 가정법 과거 구문

2 the powder of profitable information made palatable
   입맛에 맞게 만들어진 이득이 되는 정보의 분말

3 so made palatable = even if it is made palatable
   • it = the powder

4 they will do better to read
   = they had better read = it will be better for them to read
   읽어 보는 것이 나을 것이다

내용 지식은 수고 없이는 얻을 수 없고, 오늘날의 중대사에 관한 내용을 알기 위해서는 소설보다는 그 문제를 다루는 서적을 읽는 것이 낫다.

nuisance [njúːsəns] 불쾌한 일, 귀찮은 존재
swallow [swálou] 삼키다, 들이켜다 ⓝ 제비
palatable [pǽlətəbl] 입에 맞는, 맛있는
impart [impáːrt] 알리다, 나누어 주다
distorted [distɔ́ːrtid] 찌그러진, 뒤틀린(= deformed, twisted, warped)
pressing problem 긴급한 문제

Composition

그러한 시련의 시기에는 과도한 소비를 억제하는 것이 더 나을 것이다.

Key 시련의 **trying** | 과도한 소비 **excessive consumption** | 억제하다 **refrain from** | 더 낫다 **do better to**

267 No man can work long at any trade without being brought to consider much whether that which he is daily doing tends to evil or to good. I have written many novels and have known many writers of novels, and I can assert that such thoughts have been strong with them and with myself. But in acknowledging that these writers have received from the public a full measure of credit for such genius, ingenuity, or perseverance as each may have displayed, I feel that there is still wanting to them a just appreciation of the excellence of their calling, and a general understanding of the high nature of the work which they perform.

Key Structure •

1 No man can work long ~ without...
   누구든 한 직업에 오래 종사하면 꼭 …하게 된다
   • no[not] ~ without... ~하면 반드시 …한다

2 such genius, ingenuity, ~ displayed
   각자가 보여 주었을지 모르는 천재성, 창의력, 혹은 참을성

3 there is still wanting to them ~
   = a just appreciation is still wanting to them ~
   그들에게는 아직도 〜이 부족하다

내용 누구든 한 가지 직업에 오랫동안 종사하게 되면 반드시 자기가 하는 일이 좋은 결과를 가져오는지 나쁜 결과를 가져오는지 많이 생각하게 된다.

trade [treid] 직업(= job, occupation)
tend to 〜을 향하여 가다, 〜하는 경향이 있다, 〜이 되다
assert [əsə́ːrt] 단언하다, 주장하다(= claim, contend, proclaim, asseverate)
acknowledge [əknálidʒ] 인정하다, 승인하다(= admit, concede, acquiesce)
a full measure of credit 충분한 명예, 신용
ingenuity [ìndʒənjúːəti] 창의력, 정교
wanting [wántiŋ] 결핍된, 부족한
calling [kɔ́ːliŋ] 직업, 천직(= occupation)

Composition 《

요사이는 비가 왔다 하면 억수처럼 쏟아진다.

Key 요사이 **these days** │ (비가) 억수처럼 쏟아지다 **pour**
     • never ~ without 구문을 이용한다.

268 It is not by prayer and humility that you can cause things to go as you wish, but by acquiring knowledge of natural laws. The power you acquire in this way is much greater and much more reliable than that formerly supposed to be acquired by prayer, because you never could tell whether your prayer would be favorably heard in heaven. The power of prayer, moreover, had recognized limits: it would have been impious to ask too much. But the power of science has no known limits. We were told that faith could remove mountains, but no one believed it; we are now told that the atomic bomb can remove mountains, and everyone believes it.

Key Structure ▸

1 It is not by A that ~, but by B
~하는 것은 A에 의해서가 아니라 B에 의해서이다
• It is ~ that 강조 구문에서 not A but B를 강조하되 but B를 뒤로 빼낸 외치(外置) 구문.

2 much more reliable than that formerly ~
• that는 지시대명사로 the power를 받음.

3 it would have been impious to ask too much
= it would have been impious if you had asked too much
너무 많은 것을 요구했더라면 불경한 일이 되었을지도 모른다

내용 기도나 믿음보다는 과학을 아는 것이 현대에 있어서는 더 중요하다.

prayer [prɛər] 기도 *cf.* [préiər] 기도하는 사람
humility [hju:mílǝti] 겸손, 겸양
natural law 자연법칙
favorably [féivərəbli] 유리하게, 호의적으로
recognized [rèkəgnáizd] 인식된, 알려진(= known)
impious [ímpiəs] 불경한, 사악한(= profane, wicked, unreligious)

Composition ≪

과학이 산을 움직일 수 있는 것은 사실이지만, 기도의 힘도 그에 못지않다는 것을 아는 사람들은 많지 않다.

Key 산을 움직이다 **remove mountains** │ 그에 못지않다 **no smaller than that**

269 Knowledge, according to Aristotle, is of three main kinds— theoretical, practical, or productive, according as it is pursued for its own sake, as a means to conduct, or as a means to making something that is useful or beautiful. The supreme practical science—that to which all others are subordinate and ministerial— is politics, or, as we, with our fuller consciousness of man's membership of communities other than the state, might be more inclined to call it, social science. Of this science ethics is but a part, and accordingly Aristotle never speaks of 'ethics' as a separate science, but only of 'the study of character' or 'our discussions of character.'

Key Structure •

1 **is of three main kinds** 세 가지 중요한 종류로 구성되어 있다
 • of는 '구성'을 나타냄.

2 **according as**+주어+동사 ~에 따라서
 cf. according to+명사(구)

3 **that to which ~ ministerial** 다른 모든 학문이 그것에 종속되고 그것의 도구가 되는 그러한 학문
 • which의 선행사는 that. / be subordinate to ~에 종속되다
 • be ministerial to(= be instrumental to) ~에 도구가 되다

4 **as we, with our ~ , might be ~**
 • with 이하는 삽입구로, as we might be ~가 절을 이룸에 유의할 것.

5 **with our fuller ~ state** = because we are fully conscious of ~ state

6 **Of this science ethics is but a part** = Ethics is but a part of this science
 • but = only

내용 아리스토텔레스에 의하면 지식은 이론적 지식, 실용적 지식, 생산적 지식의 세 가지로 분류된다.

theoretical [θì(:)ərétikəl] 이론(상)의, 학리적인(≒ practical)
supreme [sju prí:m] 최고의, 절대의(= best, choicest, first-rate, superlative)
other than ~이 아닌, ~을 제외한
be inclined to ~하기 쉽다, ~하는 경향이 있다

Composition 《

우리는 인문과학을 자연과학이나 사회과학보다 더 못한 것으로 간주하는 경향이 있다.

Key 인문과학 **liberal science** | ~보다 더 못한 **inferior to** | ~하는 경향이 있다 **be inclined to**

270 An earthquake comes like a thief in the night, without warning. It was necessary, therefore, to invent instruments that neither slumbered nor slept. Some devices were quite simple. One, for instance, consisted of rods of various lengths and thicknesses which would stand up on end like ninepins. When a shock came it shook the rigid table upon which these stood. If it were gentle, only the more unstable rods fell. If it were severe, they all fell. Thus the rods by falling, and by the direction in which they fell, recorded for the slumbering scientist the strength of a shock that was too weak to waken him and the direction from which it came.

Key Structure ▸

1 the rods by falling, and ~ fell, recorded...
막대는 넘어지고, 또 넘어지는 방향을 통하여 …을 기록하였다
• the rods가 주어이고 recorded가 동사.

2 recorded ~ the strength
• recorded의 목적어는 the strength 이하.

내용 지진은 경고 없이 찾아온다. 따라서 이 지진을 기록하는 기구를 만들어 낼 필요가 있고, 그중 한 방법은 막대기를 이용하는 방법이다.

slumber [slʌ́mbər] 잠시 졸다, 선잠 자다
device [diváis] 장치, 고안물 *cf.* devise [diváiz] ⓥ 고안하다, 궁리하다
stand up on end 곧추서다, 똑바로 서다
ninepins [náinpìnz] 구주희(볼링의 일종)
rigid [rídʒid] 고정된, 딱딱한
unstable [ʌnstéibl] 불안정한(= inconsistent, shifting, unsteady)

Composition ⟪

지진은 밤중의 도둑처럼 찾아오기 때문에, 꾸벅꾸벅 조는 과학자는 미미한 충격파일 경우 그 힘을 거의 느끼지 못한다.

Key 도둑 thief │ 꾸벅꾸벅 졸다 slumber │ 미미한 충격파 weak shock

271 Custom has not been commonly regarded as a subject of any great moment. The inner workings of our own brains we feel to be uniquely worthy of investigation, but custom, we have a way of thinking, is behavior at its most commonplace. As a matter of fact, it is the other way around. Traditional custom is a mass of detailed behavior more astonishing than what any one person can ever evolve in individual actions, no matter how aberrant. Yet that is a rather trivial aspect of the matter. The fact of first-rate importance is the predominant role that custom plays in experience and in belief, and the very great varieties it may manifest.

Key Structure •

1 The inner workings of our own brains we feel ~
   = **We feel** the inner workings of our own brains **to be** ~
   • The inner ~ brains는 feel의 목적어로 도치 구문.

2 it is the other way around
   상황은 그 반대이다

3 no matter how aberrant (it may be)
   그것이 아무리 비정상적인 것이라 하더라도
   • it = detailed behavior

4 the very great varieties (that) it may manifest
   그것이 분명히 나타내는 매우 큰 바로 그 다양성들
   • it = custom

내용 습관은 우리의 경험과 믿음에 압도적인 역할을 행사한다.

of moment 중요한(= momentous) *cf.* of the moment 순간의
evolve [ivάlv] 발전시키다, 이끌어 내다
aberrant [æbérənt] 비정상인, 변종인(= deviant)
trivial [tríviəl] 사소한(= unimportant)
predominant [pridάmənənt] 우월한, 영향력 있는(= preponderant, prevailing)

Composition《

모두가 그가 그녀의 유혹에 넘어가 결혼한 것으로 생각하는데, 사실은 그 반대이다.

Key 유혹에 넘어가 결혼하다 **A is seduced by B into marrying** | 그 반대이다 **it is the other way around**

272 The problem for democracy is to be right with regard to its ends—its ultimate goals and objectives in the state—as well as with regard to the methods and the means by which it seeks to accomplish its ends. What is sought in a democracy is not only an external objective order which is based upon justice, but also an internal or subjective one; that is, an ordered society understood by the people, and whose government acts with the support of the people—with their knowledge and also with their will. This tremendous challenge involves two things: it involves justice with freedom, and order with individual responsibility.

Key Structure

1 What is sought in a democracy
   민주 국가에서 추구되는 것

2 not only an ~ order ~ , but also an ~ one
   • one = order

내용 민주주의에 있어서 해결해야 할 문제는 국가의 궁극적 목표뿐만 아니라 그 목표를 추구하는 수단과 방법도 정당해야 한다는 점이다.

with regard to ~과 관련하여(= with respect to)
ultimate [ʌ́ltəmit] 최후의, 궁극적인
objective [əbdʒéktiv] 목적, 목표(= aim)
external [ikstə́ːrnəl] 밖의, 외부의(≒ internal)
tremendous [triméndəs] 무서운, 소름 끼치는(= alarming, awful, frightening)
involve [inválv] 수반하다(= include, contain)

Composition

민주 국가의 정부는 국민의 지지와 의지를 기초로 그 목표를 달성하려고 추구해야 한다.

Key 국민의 지지 **the support of the people** | 국민의 의지 **the will of the people** | 그 목표를 달성하다 **accomplish its ends**

273 The instinctive foundation of the intellectual life is curiosity, which is found among animals in its elementary form. Intelligence demands an alert curiosity, but it must be of a certain kind. The sort that leads village neighbors to try to peer through curtains after dark has no very high value. The widespread interest in gossip is inspired, not by love of knowledge, but by malice: no one gossips about other people's secret virtues, but only about their secret vices. Accordingly most gossip is untrue, but care is taken not to verify it. Our neighbor's sins, like the consolations of religion, are so agreeable that we do not stop to scrutinize the evidence closely.

Key Structure

1 it must be of a certain kind
그것은 특정한 종류이어야 한다

2 care is taken not to verify it
= people take care not to verify it
그것을 입증하지 않으려 주의한다

내용 지적인 삶의 기초는 호기심이지만, 그것은 동물적인 호기심과는 종류가 달라야 한다.

instinctive [instíŋktiv] 본능의, 직관적인
alert [ələ́ːrt] 방심하지 않는, 민첩한(= awake, heedful | ≒ absent-minded)
peer through ~을 통해 들여다보다
gossip [gásəp] 험담, 쑥덕공론 ⓥ ~에 관하여 뒷공론을 하다
malice [mǽlis] 악의, 원한(= animosity, ill-will, malevolence, vindictiveness | ≒ good-will, benevolence)
verify [vérəfài] 진실임을 입증하다(= prove)
consolation [kànsəléiʃən] 위안, 평안(= comfort, encouragement, relief, solace)
scrutinize [skrúːtənàiz] 자세히 조사하다(= analyze, examine, sift, investigate)

Composition

남의 실수와 비밀스러운 악덕에 대한 호기심은 높은 가치를 지닌 진정한 종류의 호기심이라고 말할 수 없다.

Key 실수 **error** | 비밀스러운 악덕 **secret vices** | 높은 가치를 지니다 **have high value** | 진정한 종류의 **(of) a real kind**

274 It is scarcely an exaggeration to say that at present mankind as a species is demented and that nothing is so urgent upon us as the recovery of mental self-control. We call an individual insane if his ruling ideas are so much out of adjustment to his circumstances that he is a danger to himself and others. This definition of insanity seems to cover the entire human species at the present time, and it is no figure of speech but a plain statement of fact, that man has to "pull his mind together" or perish. To perish or to enter upon a phase of maturer power and effort. No middle way seems open to him. He has to go up or down. He cannot stay at what he is.

Key Structure •

1 It is scarcely an exaggeration to say ~
   ~라고 말한다고 해서 거의 과장은 아니다

2 nothing is so urgent upon us as ~
   ~만큼 우리에게 긴급한 일은 없다
   • 부정어+so ~ as… …만큼 ~한 것은 없다

내용 현재 인간은 미친 상태에 있고 정신적 자제의 회복이 대단히 중대한 문제로 등장하였다.

species [spí:ʃiːz] 종, 종류
demented [diméntid] 발광한, 정신 착란의(= mad, crazy, insane)
insane [inséin] 미친, 광기의, 어리석은(= mad)
out of adjustment to ~에 대한 적응력에서 벗어난
figure of speech 과장법, 비유법
pull one's mind together 정신을 바짝 차리다
phase [feiz] 단계, 국면(= stage, step)

Composition 《

오늘처럼 복잡하고 다양한 특징들을 가진 사회에서는 정신을 바짝 차리는 일만큼 긴급한 일도 없다는 말은 거의 과장이 아니다.

Key 복잡한 complex | 다양한 multitudinous | 특징 characteristic | 정신을 바짝 차리다 pull one's mind together | 긴급한 urgent | 과장 exaggeration

275
The happy man is the man who lives objectively, who has free affections and wide interests, who secures his happiness through these interests and affections and through the fact that they, in turn, make him an object of interest and affection to many others. To be the recipient of affection is a potent cause of happiness, but the man who demands affection is not the man upon whom it is bestowed. The man who receives affection is, speaking broadly, the man who gives it. But it is useless to attempt to give it as a calculation, in the way in which one might lend money at interest, for a calculated affection is not genuine and is not felt to be so by the recipient.

Key Structure •

1 the man upon whom it is bestowed
그것이 주어지는 사람

2 in the way in which ~ interest
돈을 빌려주고 이자를 받는 방식으로

3 a calculated affection ~ is not felt to ~ recipient
계산된 애정은 애정을 받는 자한테 진정한 것으로 느껴지지 않는다

내용 행복한 사람은 객관적인 삶을 살고, 자유로운 애정과 폭넓은 흥미를 가진 사람이다.

affection [əfékʃ∂n] 애정, 연정
secure [sikjúər] 지키다, 확보하다
in turn 이번에는 자기가
recipient [risípiənt] 수령인, 수취인
potent [póutənt] 강력한, 세력 있는
bestow A on[upon] B B에게 A를 수여하다[주다]
at interest 이자를 받고

Composition ◀

애정은 요구한다고 주어지는 것이 아니다. 애정을 주는 것은 받는 것이나 다름없다.

Key 애정 **affection** │ 요구하다 **demand** │ 주어지다 **be given** │ ~이나 다름없다 **be as good as**

276

When anyone opens a current account at a bank, he is lending the bank money, repayment of which he may demand at any time, either in cash or by drawing a check in favor of another person. Primarily, the banker-customer relationship is that of debtor and creditor—who is which depending on whether the customer's account is in credit or is overdrawn. But in addition to that basically simple concept, the bank and its customer owe a large number of obligations to one another. Many of these obligations can give rise to problems and complications but a bank customer, unlike, say, a buyer of goods, cannot complain that the law is loaded against him.

Key Structure

1 repayment of which he may ~
= he may demand its repayment at any time
그는 그것의 상환을 언제나 요구할 수 있다

2 who is which depending on whether ~ overdrawn
은행 고객의 구좌에 예금이 아직 남아 있느냐 아니면 잔고 이상으로 찾아냈느냐에 따라 채권자도 되고 채무자도 되는데

3 the law is loaded against him
법이 자신에게 부담이 되고 있다

내용 은행과 고객의 관계는 기본적으로 채무자·채권자의 관계이지만, 상황이 반전될 수도 있으며, 둘은 상호 간에 여러 가지 의무를 진다.

current account 당좌 계정
repayment [riːpéimənt] 상환, 변제
debtor [détər] 빚진 사람, 채무자(≒ creditor)
be in credit 은행 구좌에 잔액이 남아 있다 *cf.* on credit 외상으로
be overdrawn (어음 수표를) 초과 발행하다, 잔액이 부족하다
give rise to ~을 야기하다, 일으키다(= bring about)
unlike [ʌnláik] ~과는 달리
say [sei] (명령법에서) 이를테면(= as it were, let us say)

Composition

미국에서는 고객의 은행 계좌가 저축 계좌와 수표 발행 계좌로 나누어져 있다.

Key 은행 계좌 **bank account** | 저축 계좌 **savings account** | 수표 발행 계좌 **checking account**

277 Some old people are oppressed by the fear of death. In the young there is a justification for this feeling. Young men who have reason to fear that they will be killed in battle may justifiably feel bitter in the thought that they have been cheated of the best things that life has to offer. But in an old man who has known human joys and sorrows, and has achieved whatever work it was in him to do, the fear of death is somewhat abject and ignoble. The best way to overcome it—so at least it seems to me—is to make your interests gradually wider and more impersonal, until bit by bit the walls of the ego recede, and your life becomes increasingly merged in the universal life.

Key Structure ▸

1 the thought that they have been cheated of ~ offer
인생이 줄 수 있는 최고의 것들을 자신들은 속아서 빼앗겼다는 생각
• cheat A of B A를 속여서 B를 빼앗다

2 whatever work it was in him to do
자신의 힘이 닿는 한 할 수 있는 모든 일
cf. It was in him to do the work. 그 일을 하는 것은 그의 능력 안에 있었다.

> 내용 노인네들에게 있어서 죽음에 대한 두려움은 약간은 비굴한 것이며, 이것을 극복하는 최선의 길은 관심사를 넓히고 개인적인 생각을 덜 하는 것이다.

be oppressed by 〜에 짓눌리다
abject [ǽbdʒekt] 비참한, 상스러운(= ignoble)
bit by bit 조금씩, 차차(= by bits)
recede [risíːd] 후퇴하다, 퇴각하다(= retreat, go back)
(become) merged in 〜에 합병되다

Composition ◁

나는 나의 힘이 닿는 한 모든 힘을 들여 그 일을 끝냈다.

Key 나의 힘이 닿는 한 모든 힘을 들여 **with all the strength I have in me**

278 　It is unlikely that many of us will be famous, or even remembered. But no less important than the brilliant few that lead a nation or a literature to fresh achievements, are the unknown many whose patient efforts keep the world from running backward; who guard and maintain the ancient values, even if they do not conquer new; whose inconspicuous triumph it is to pass on what they inherited from their fathers, unimpaired and undiminished, to their sons. Enough, for almost all of us, if we can hand on the torch, and not let it down; content to win the affection, if possible, of a few who know us, and to be forgotten when they in their turn have vanished.

Key Structure •

1　But no less important than ~ , are the unknown many
　특출 난 소수 못지않게 중요한 자들은 ~ 알려지지 않은 다수이다
　• 주어는 the unknown many

2　even if they do not conquer new　그들이 새로운 가치를 정복하지 못한다고 해도
　• new = new values

3　whose inconspicuous triumph it is to pass on ~
　~을 전해 주는 것이 그들의 보이지 않는 승리인
　• it가 가주어, to pass on ~이 진주어, whose inconspicuous triumph는 be동사의 보어.
　　cf. it is their inconspicuous triumph to pass on ~.

내용　유명한 사람들 못지않게 중요한 사람들은 과거의 가치들을 보존하여 줄어들지 않은 상태로 후손에게 물려주는, 알려지지 않은 다수의 사람들이다.

brilliant [bríljənt] 찬란하게 빛나는, 훌륭한
conquer [káŋkər] 정복하다, 극복하다(= overcome, win, defeat)
inconspicuous [ìnkənspíkjuəs] 두드러지지 않는(= hidden, invisible)
unimpaired [ʌ̀nimpɛ́ərd] 손상되지 않은
undiminished [ʌ̀ndimíniʃt] 줄지 않은, 쇠퇴하지 않은
let ~ down 꺼지게 하다, 떨어뜨리다

Composition 《

그의 드러나지 않는 업적들 중의 하나는 조국이 외국 세력에 의해 지배되지 않도록 모든 노력을 기울였다는 것이다.

Key　드러나지 않는 **inconspicuous** ｜ 업적 **achievement** ｜ 외국 세력 **foreign powers** ｜ 노력을 기울이다 **make an effort**

279 Purely physical fatigue, provided it is not excessive, tends if anything to be a cause of happiness; it leads to sound sleep and a good appetite, and gives zest to the pleasures that are possible on holidays. But when it is excessive it becomes a grave evil. In the most advanced parts of the modern world, however, physical fatigue has been much minimized through the improvement of industrial conditions. The kind of fatigue that is most serious in the present day in advanced communities is nervous fatigue. This kind, oddly enough, is most pronounced among the well-to-do, and tends to be much less among wage-earners than it is among businessmen and brainworkers.

Key Structure •

1 provided it is not excessive ~
   = if it is not excessive ~
   그것이 지나치지만 않다면

2 oddly enough
   참 이상하게도

내용 육체적 피로와 오늘날 문제가 되는 신경의 피로.

physical fatigue 육체적 피로
excessive [iksésiv] 지나친, 과도한(= extreme, immoderate, intemperate)
if anything 어느 편이냐 하면
sound [saund] 건실한, 충분한 ⓝ 소리 ⓥ 울리다, 측량하다
zest [zest] 열정, 욕구(= desire, appetite, exuberance, thirst, zeal)
minimize [mínəmàiz] 최소화하다(≒ maximize)
nervous fatigue 신경의 피로
pronounced [prənáunst] 특출 난, 두드러진(= distinct, recognizable, striking)
the well-to-do 부유한 사람들
wage-earner 임금 노동자

Composition 《

돈에 대한 추구는 만약 지나치지만 않다면 그렇게 개탄할 만한 일은 아니다. 그러나 그것이 지나칠 때에는 많은 악의 근원이 된다.

Key 추구 **quest for** │ 개탄할 만한 **deplorable** │ 근원 **source** │ 악 **evil**

280 Criticism must always profess an end in view, which, roughly speaking, appears to be the elucidation of works of art and the correction of taste. The critic's task, therefore, appears to be quite clearly cut out for him; and it ought to be comparatively easy to decide whether he performs it satisfactorily, and, in general, what kinds of criticism are useful and what are otiose. But on giving the matter a little attention, we perceive that criticism, far from being a simple and orderly field of activity, from which impostors can be readily ejected, is no better than a Sunday park of contending and contentious orators, who have not even arrived at the articulation of their differences.

Key Structure ▸

1 on giving the matter a little attention
   = as soon as (when) we give the matter a little attention
   그 문제를 조금 주의해 보기만 하면

2 far from being ~ activity 소박하고 질서 잡힌 활동의 장이기는커녕
   • far from -ing ~이기는커녕

3 no better than = as good as ～이나 다름없는

내용 비평은 예술 작품의 해설과 취미의 교정이라는 목표를 항상 분명히 밝혀야 하는데, 그렇지 못한 경우가 많다.

profess [prəfés] 분명히 말하다, 공언하다
end [end] 목표(= purpose, object)
in view 시야에 들어온, 고려하고 있는
elucidation [ilù:sidéiʃən] 설명, 해명
be cut out for ～에게 어울리는, 적합한
otiose [óuʃiòus] 쓸모없는, 나태한(= useless, idle, indolent)
impostor [impástər] 협잡꾼, (신분) 사칭자
eject [i(:)dʒékt] 축출하다
contend [kənténd] 말다툼하다, 주장하다
contentious [kənténʃəs] 논쟁을 좋아하는
orator [ɔ́(:)rətər] 연사, 변사, 웅변가
articulation [ɑːrtìkjəléiʃən] 명확한 표현[발언]

Composition ‹‹

어린아이들을 가르치는 직업은 그에게 매우 잘 어울리는 것 같다.

Key 매우 잘 어울리다 be clearly cut out for

310

281 The problem of creative writing is essentially one of concentration, and the supposed eccentricities of poets are usually due to mechanical habits or rituals developed in order to concentrate. Concentration, of course, for the purpose of writing poetry, is different from the kind of concentration required for working out a sum. It is a focusing of the attention in a special way, so that the poet is aware of all the implications and possible developments of his idea, just as one might say that a plant was not concentrating on developing mechanically in one direction, but in many directions, towards the warmth and light with its leaves, and towards the water with its roots, all at the same time.

Key Structure •

1 **one of concentration** 집중력의 문제
   • one = a problem

2 **mechanical habits or rituals** (which have been) **developed in order to concentrate**
   집중하기 위하여 개발된 기계적인 습관이나 의식들

3 **just as one might say that ~**
   마치 우리가 ~라고 말할 수 있는 것처럼

4 **towards the warmth ~ its roots**
   잎사귀로는 온기와 빛을 향하고, 뿌리로는 물을 향하여

5 **all at the same time** 모든 일을 동시에 (행하다)

내용 창작은 근본적으로 집중력의 문제이고, 시인의 괴벽은 집중에 따른 기계적인 습관의 결과이다.

concentration [kànsəntréiʃən] 집중
eccentricity [èksentrísəti] 기행, 괴팍함, 비정상(= anomaly, singularity)
be due to ~에 기인하다(= be brought about by, be caused by)
ritual [rítʃuəl] 의식, 예절
implication [ìmpləkéiʃən] 포함, 함축(된 뜻)

Composition 《

작가의 기행은 작품을 쓰는 과정에서 집중하려는 노력의 결과에서 나온 것이다.

Key 기행 **eccentricity** | ~에서 나오다 **be due to**

282 When in the eighteenth century offences against the law that today would not earn a month in prison were punished with the death penalty, the severity of the penal code had no serious effect on the prevalence of crime. When it made no difference to the fate of a highwayman whether he had killed his victim or merely robbed him of a few pieces of silver, there were no more murders then than there were when men like Sir Francis Burdett succeeded in lightening the excessive severity of the penal laws. In those days the sacredness of life on earth was not greatly regarded because a life in the world to come was taken for granted except by a comparatively small minority of philosophers.

Key Structure •

1 there were no more murders then than ~
   그때에는 ~보다 더 많은 살인 사건이 있지도 않았다

2 a life in the world to come
   내세(來世)의 삶

내용 18세기에는 형법이 너무 잔인하여 오늘날 한 달간의 감옥 생활에 해당하는 범죄가 그 당시에는 사형을 받게끔 되어 있었다.

offence [əféns] (법률 규범 등의) 위반, 반칙
death penalty 사형
severity [sivérəti] 가혹, 엄함
penal code 형법(전)(= penal law)
prevalence [prévələns] 보급, 유행, 횡행 ⓥ prevail
make no difference to ~에 영향을 미치지 않다
highwayman [háiwèimən] 노상강도
rob A of B A에게서 B를 강탈하다
sacredness [séikridnes] 신성함

Composition ◀

그 노상강도는 동전 몇 닢을 강탈한 죄로 5년의 감옥 생활이라는 형을 받았다.

Key 노상강도 highwayman | 동전 몇 닢 a few pieces of coin | 5년의 감옥 생활 five years of imprisonment |
     형을 선고 받다 be sentenced to

283 The study of one's mother tongue has an importance different in kind from that which attaches to other branches of study. One can do with or without other subjects, but one's own language is inescapable. It can be studied for its own sake, as all subjects can, but it has the added importance that it is the medium through which knowledge of any other subject is normally acquired. It does not follow that a detailed knowledge of the nature and history of one's own language is indispensable, or that the historical approach is the only one possible, but such knowledge has some importance for everyone and not merely for professed students of the history of the English language.

Key Structure ▸

1 different in kind from that which attaches to ~ study
다른 분야의 학문에 부수되는 중요성과는 다른
• that = the importance

2 One can do with or without other subjects
우리는 다른 과목들이 있어도 되고 없어도 된다
• do without ~없이 지내다

3 as all subjects can
= as all subjects can be studied for their own sake
모든 과목들이 그 자체를 위해 연구될 수 있듯이

4 It does not follow that ~
반드시 ~라는 이야기가 뒤따르는 것은 아니다

내용 모국어 연구는 다른 학문 연구와는 본질적으로 다른 중요성을 지닌다.

mother tongue 모국어(= mother language)
inescapable [ìneskéipəbl] 회피할 수 없는
medium [míːdiəm] 매개체 *pl.* media
indispensable [ìndispénsəbl] 없어서는 안 되는
professed student 전문 연구생

Composition ◀◀

외국어의 공부가 중요하다고 해서 모국어 공부를 소홀히 해도 된다는 말은 아니다.

Key 외국어 foreign language │ 모국어 mother tongue │ 소홀히 하다 neglect │ ~라는 말은 아니다 it does not follow that ~

284 It is commonplace to say that the fear of nuclear energy, nuclear weapons, and nuclear war is widespread and abiding among the peoples of the world. The question is whether such fear is and will remain politically efficacious, so that the power of the atom can be used for beneficent, rather than destructive, purposes. Granted that the assessments of the precise dangers confronting us may differ widely, to what extent do the fears (both rational and irrational) of policy-making elites and political masses produce actual effects upon the behavior of governments which are, after all, the only entities in control of nuclear weapons or capable of acquiring them—thus far?

Key Structure

1 The question is whether such fear is and will remain ~ efficacious
   문제는 그러한 두려움이 효과적인가 또한 앞으로 효과적일 것인가 아닌가 하는 점이다

2 Granted that ~
   = Though it is granted that ~

3 to what extent do the fears ~ produce actual effects
   그 두려움은 어느 정도까지 실제적인 효과를 발휘하는가?

내용 핵무기, 핵전쟁에 대한 두려움은 어느 정도까지 원자의 유용한 이용에 영향을 미칠 수 있을까?

abiding [əbáidiŋ] 지속적인, 불변의(= enduring)
efficacious [èfəkéiʃəs] 효과가 있는(= effective)
beneficent [bənéfisənt] 친절한, 인정 많은, 이익이 되는(= beneficial)
assessment [əsésmənt] 사정, 평가(= evaluation)
precise [prisáis] 정확한, 딱 들어맞는
confront [kənfrʌ́nt] 직면하다, 마주 보다
irrational [iráʃənəl] 이성이 없는, 불합리한
entity [éntəti] 실재하는 것

Composition

핵전쟁에 대한 너의 두려움이 근거가 있는 것이라고 인정하여도, 매우 가까운 미래에 핵전쟁이 일어날 것이라는 너의 주장은 인정하기 어렵다.

Key 핵전쟁 nuclear war │ 두려움 fear │ 근거가 있다 be well-grounded │ 가까운 미래 the near future │ 주장 assertion │ 인정하다 approve

285 A large part of your work in college consists of digesting the contents of books and essays and being able to explain what you have read. When material is complex... as it often is in essays on economics, history, literary criticism, and philosophy... the practice of reducing it to an outline provides two advantages: it forces you to watch carefully what the author is doing and how he is doing it, and it gives you in a form convenient for review, a digest of the basic content. In both these respects the outline is to the essay what a map is to a city you do not know very well. It is an efficient and streamlined device for understanding the total structure and the relations between its parts.

Key Structure ▸

1 as it often is in ~
   ~에서 종종 그러하듯

2 the practice of reducing it to an outline
   그것을 줄거리로 요약하는 연습

3 the outline is to the essay what a map is to a city
   요약된 내용과 수필의 관계는 지도와 도시의 관계와 같다.
   • A is to B what C is to D A 대 B의 관계는 C 대 D의 관계와 같다

내용 대학 공부는 많은 부분이 읽은 책의 내용을 소화하고 설명하는 것으로 구성되어 있다.

consist of (~으로) 구성되다
digest [didʒést] 소화하다, 읽고 이해하다 *cf.* [dáidʒest] ⓝ 요약, 다이제스트
complex [kámpleks] 복잡한(= complicated | ≒ simple, simplex)
literary criticism 문학 비평
reduce A to B A를 B로 축소하다
outline [áutlàin] 개요, 요약(= digest, summary)
streamlined [stríːmlàind] 간소화된, 능률화된, 현대적인(= efficient, smooth)

Composition ◀

지력과 정신의 관계는 시력과 신체의 관계와 같다.

Key 지력 **intellect** | 시력 **sight**
   • A is to B what C is to D를 이용한다.

286   I find young people exciting. They have an air of freedom, and they have not a dreary commitment to mean ambitions or love of comfort. They are not anxious social climbers, and they have no devotion to material things. All this seems to me to link them with life, and the origins of things. It's as if they were in some sense cosmic beings in violent and lovely contrast with us suburban creatures. All that is in my mind when I meet a young person. He may be conceited, ill-mannered, presumptuous or fatuous, but I do not turn for protection to dreary clichés about respect for elders— as if mere age were a reason for respect. I accept that we are equals, and I will argue with him, as an equal, if I think he is wrong.

Key Structure

1   cosmic beings in violent ~ creatures
    우리처럼 교외에 살고 있는 자들과 극단적으로 그러나 잘 대조가 되는 범우주적 존재들

2   I do not turn for protection to ~ elders
    자신의 보호를 위하여 나이 많은 사람들을 존경해야 한다는 진부한 생각에 의존하지 않는다

3   as if mere age were a reason for respect
    단순히 나이 먹는 것이 존경을 받아야 할 이유인 것인 양

내용   젊은이는 흥미 있는 존재들이고 나이 든 자들과 대조가 되는 자들이다.

dreary [drí(:)əri] 지루한, 지겨운(= dull)
commitment [kəmítmənt] 몰두, 전념
mean [miːn] 열등한, 천한(= ignoble, churlish, shabby)
social climber 사회적으로 출세를 바라는 사람
cosmic [kázmik] 우주의, 무한한
conceited [kənsíːtid] 우쭐대는, 젠체하는(= arrogant, supercilious)
presumptuous [prizʌ́mptʃuəs] 건방진, 뻔뻔스러운(= bold, insolent, impudent)
fatuous [fǽtʃuəs] 어리석은, 어수룩한(= silly, foolish)
cliché [kliːʃéi] 진부한 상투어

Composition

그녀의 친절한 말씨는 그에 대한 쌀쌀한 대접과 몹시 대조가 되었다.

Key   친절한 말씨 kind words | 쌀쌀한 대접 cold treatment | ~과 몹시 대조가 되다 be in striking contrast with

287   When reduced to its simplest terms a migration is caused by an expulsion and an attraction, the former nearly always resulting from dearth of food or from over-population, which practically comes to the same thing. Sooner or later, a time comes when the increase of the population of a country exceeds its normal food-supply. Among hunting communities the game may be so reduced by overhunting or by disease that it cannot support even a stationary or decreasing population. The chief danger to be feared by pastoral peoples is lack of water; a succession of small droughts can make pasturing unprofitable, but when a whole country definitely becomes more arid, migrations on a large scale are inevitable.

Key Structure •

1   When (it is) reduced to ~ terms
   간단한 말로 줄여서 이야기하면

2   the former nearly always resulting ~
   = and the former nearly always results ~
   • 주어가 다른 분사구문. / 주절은 a migration is caused by 이하임.

3   which practically comes to the same thing
   실제로는 같은 이야기인데

내용   이민은 추방에 의한 경우와 유인에 의한 경우, 두 가지가 있다.

expulsion [ikspʌ́lʃən] 추방, 배제 ⓥ expel
attraction [ətrǽkʃən] 유인, 견인
dearth [dəːrθ] 부족, 결핍(= lack, shortage)
game [ɡeim] 사냥감
stationary [stéiʃənèri] 정지된, 움직이지 않는   cf. stationery 문방구, 편지지
pastoral [pǽstərəl] 양치기인, 전원의, 시골의
drought [draut] 가뭄, 한발   cf. draught [dræft] 퍼내기, (물약) 1회분
arid [ǽrid] 메마른(= dry, parched)

Composition ◀

간단히 줄여서 이야기하면, 식량 생산이 인구 폭발을 따라잡지 못할 날이 곧 올 것이다.

Key 간단히 줄여서 이야기하면 **when (it is) reduced to the simplest terms** | 인구 폭발 **population explosion** | ~을 따라잡다 **catch up with** | ~할 날이 오다 **there will come a time when**

288 Do not let us be deceived by the argument that culture is the same for all time—that art is a unity and beauty an absolute value. If you are going to talk about abstract conceptions like beauty, then we can freely admit that they are absolute and eternal. But abstract conceptions are not works of art. Works of art are things of use—houses and their furniture, for example; and if, like sculpture and poetry, they are not things of immediate use, then, they should be things agreeing with the things we use—that is to say, part of our daily life, adapted to our daily habits, accessible to our daily needs. It is not until art expresses the immediate hopes and aspirations of mankind that it requires its social adaptability.

Key Structure ▸

1   that art is a unity and beauty (is) an absolute value
　　예술은 통일성이고 아름다움은 절대가치라는 주장
　　• that은 앞의 argument의 내용을 설명하는 동격접속사.

2   It is not until art ~ that ~
　　= Not until art ~ mankind does it require ~
　　예술이 인간이 갖는 당장의 희망이나 열망을 표현하게 될 때에야 비로소 ~하다
　　• it is ~ that 강조 구문임에 유의.

　　내용 미(美)와 같은 추상적 개념은 예술 작품이 아니다. 예술 작품은 사용할 수 있는 물건들이다.

eternal [i(:)tə́:rnəl] 영원한, 무한한(= permanent, perpetual | ≒ temporary)
sculpture [skʌ́lptʃər] 조각(술)
immediate [imíːdiət] 즉시의, 즉석의, 당면한(= direct, instant, prompt)
accessible (to) 접근하기 쉬운
aspiration [æ̀spəréiʃən] 갈망, 동경, 야심(= craving, longing, yearning)
adaptability [ədæ̀ptəbíləti] 적응력, 융통성

Composition ⟪

부모님이 돌아가시기 전까지 우리는 부모님의 진정한 사랑을 깨닫지 못한다.

Key 돌아가시다 **pass away** | 진정한 사랑 **real love** | 깨닫다 **realize**

289 It is fairly clear that the sleeping period must have some function, and because there is so much of it the function would seem to be important. Speculations about its nature have been going on for literally thousands of years, and one odd finding that makes the problem puzzling is that it looks very much as if sleeping is not simply a matter of giving the body a rest. 'Rest,' in terms of muscle relaxation and so on, can be achieved by a brief period lying, or even sitting down. The body's tissues are self-repairing and self-restoring to a degree, and function best when more or less continuously active. In fact a basic amount of movement occurs during sleep which is specifically concerned with preventing muscle inactivity.

Key Structure •

1 **when** (they are) **more or less continuously active**
(근육 조직이) 다소간 지속적으로 활동하고 있을 때
 • they = the body's tissues

2 **which is specifically ~**
 • which 이하는 movement를 수식하는 관계대명사절.

내용 잠자는 시간 동안에도 근육 운동은 일어나고 그 기능은 중요하다. 또한 육체의 근육 조직은 어느 정도 지속적으로 활동 상태에 있을 때 최고의 기능을 발휘한다.

speculation [spèkjəléiʃən] 사색, 심사숙고(= meditation, rumination)
literally [lítərəli] 문자[말] 그대로(≒ figuratively)
odd [ɑd / ɔd] 이상한, 여분의(= strange, curious, unusual)
puzzling [pʌ́zliŋ] 당황하게 하는, 영문 모를(= perplexing, bewildering, baffling)
muscle relaxation 근육의 이완
self-repairing 스스로를 수정하는
to a degree 어느 정도는(= to a certain extent)

Composition 《

우리가 대학 생활을 어떻게 보낼 것인지에 대한 숙고는 졸업 후 우리의 삶의 질을 높이는 데 상당한 정도에 이르기까지 중요하다.

Key 어떻게 보내는가 **how to spend** | 숙고 **speculations** | 졸업 후 **after graduation** | 삶의 질 **quality of life** |
높이다 **enhance** | 상당한 정도에 이르기까지 **to a considerable degree**

290 Wise men beget fools, and honest men knaves; but these instances, although they may be frequent, are not general. If there is often a likeness in feature and figure, there is generally more in mind and heart because education contributes to the formation of these as well as nature. The influence of example is very great and almost universal, especially that of parents over their children. In all countries it has been observed that vices as well as virtues very often run down in families from age to age. Any man may go over in his thoughts the circle of his acquaintance, and he will probably recollect instances of a disposition to mischief, malice, and revenge, descending in certain breeds from grandfather and son.

Key Structure •

1 there is generally more (likeness) in mind and heart
보통은 정신과 마음에 닮은 점이 더 많다

2 especially that of parents over their children
특히 부모가 자식에게 미치는 영향력
• that = the influence

내용 예외는 있지만 현명하고 정직한 혈통에 좋은 결과가 나타난다.

beget [biɡét] 낳다(= bear, produce, give birth to)
knave [neiv] 악한, 깡패, 머슴
likeness [láiknis] 닮음(= similarity)
feature [fíːtʃər] 이목구비, 용모, 특징 cf. figure 모양, 형상, 인물
contribute [kəntríbjuːt] 기여하다, 제공하다
run down (전해) 내려오다(= descend)
acquaintance [əkwéintəns] 아는 사람, 친지
disposition [dìspəzíʃən] 기질, 성미, 경향
breed [briːd] 혈통, 품종

Composition 《

부모가 자식에게 미치는 영향력은 대단한 것이므로, 우리는 어린이들이 우리를 본받도록 처신을 잘 하여야 한다.

Key A가 B에 미치는 영향력 **the influence of A over B** │ 본받다 **imitate** │ 처신을 잘 하다 **behave well**

291 There are at least four things which are more or less under our own control and which are essential to happiness. The first is some moral standard by which to guide our actions. The second is some satisfactory home life in the form of good relations with family or friends. The third is some form of work which justifies our existence to our own country and makes us good citizens. The fourth thing is some degree of leisure and the use of it in some way that makes us happy. To succeed in making a good use of our leisure will not compensate for failure in any one of the other three things to which I have referred, but a reasonable amount of leisure and a good use of it is an important contribution to a happy life.

Key Structure •

1 some moral standard by which to guide our actions
  = some moral standard by which we may[can] guide our actions
  우리가 지침으로 삼아 우리의 행동을 안내해 갈 도덕 기준

2 the other three things to which I have referred
  내가 언급한 다른 세 가지 일들

내용 행복에 필수적인 것으로 도덕적 기준, 만족스러운 가정생활, 훌륭한 시민이 되게 하는 노동, 그리고 여가의 선용 등이 있다.

moral standard 도덕(적) 기준
justify [dʒʌstəfài] 정당화하다
make a good use of 잘 이용하다
compensate for 보상하다, 보충하다(= make up for, atone for)
refer to 언급하다, 조회시키다
contribution [kàntrəbjúːʃən] 기여(도)

Composition ◀

여가가 아무리 많다고 해도 그것을 잘 이용하지 못하면 행복에 기여할 수 없다.

Key 여가 leisure │ 잘 이용하다 make a good use of │ 기여하다 contribute to

292   Parents are often upset when their children praise the homes of their friends and regard it as a slur on their own cooking, or cleaning, or furniture, and often are foolish enough to let the adolescents see that they are annoyed. They may even accuse them of disloyalty, or make some spiteful remark about the friends' parents. Such a loss of dignity and descent into childish behavior on the part of the adults deeply shocks the adolescents, and makes them resolve that in future they will not talk to their parents about the places or people they visit. Before very long the parents will be complaining that the child is so secretive and never tells them anything, but they seldom realize that they have brought this on themselves.

Key Structure

1 They may even accuse them of disloyalty
    부모들은 자식들이 효성이 없다고 비난한다
    • they = parents, them = children

2 Such a loss of dignity and descent into ~ adults
    어른들이 보여 주는 유치한 행위로의 하강(어린이처럼 유치한 행위를 하는 것)

3 they have brought this on themselves
    그들이 스스로에게 이 일을 가져왔다(자업자득이다)

   내용 자식들이 친구 집을 칭찬하고 자기 집을 비난할 때 부모는 화를 내는데, 이것은 잘못된 것이다.

be upset 기분이 상하다
slur [sləːr] 중상, 비방(= insult, libel)
adolescent [ӕdəlésənt] 청년(13~16세)
be annoyed 괴롭힘을 당하다, 불쾌하다
accuse A of B A를 B의 죄로 고발(비난)하다
spiteful [spáitfəl] 악의적인, 심술궂은(= acid, acrimonious, ill-natured)
dignity [dígnəti] 위엄, 품위
resolve [rizálv] 결심하다, 작정하다(= make up one's mind, determine)
secretive [síːkrətiv] 숨기는, 터놓지 않는

Composition

아이들이 엄마의 요리가 형편없다고 불평한다고 해서, 그것을 효성이 없다고 비난하는 것은 유치한 행위이다.

Key 형편없는 quite unsatisfactory | 효성이 없음 disloyalty | 유치한 childish

293 No refining of one's taste in matters of art or literature, no sharpening of one's powers of insight in matters of science and psychology, can ever take the place of one's sensitiveness to the life of the earth. This is the beginning and the end of a person's true education. Art and literature have been shamefully abused, have been perverted from their true purpose, if they do not conduce to it. The cultivation in one's inmost being of a thrilling sensitiveness to Nature is a slow and very gradual process. The first conscious beginnings of it in early childhood are precious beyond words as the origin of dominant memories; but the more deliberately we discipline our sensitive grasp of these things, the deeper our pleasure in them grows.

Part 2 Reading & Composition

Key Structure

1 No refining of ~, no sharpening of ~ psychology
아무리 ~을 세련시키고, 아무리 ~에서 자신의 통찰력을 날카롭게 한다 해도, 그것은
• 이 부분 전체가 주부, can ever take the place of~가 술부.

2 The cultivation in one's inmost being of a thrilling sensitiveness to Nature
자신의 깊숙한 곳에 자연에 대한 떨리는 감수성을 개발하는 것
• cultivation in B of A ⇐ cultivate A in B A를 B 속에 개발하다[개발해 넣다]

3 the more deliberately ~, the deeper ~
우리가 이것들에 대한 민감한 이해를 더욱 신중히 하면 할수록 그것들에 대한 우리의 즐거움은 더욱 깊어진다
• the 비교급 ~, the 비교급 ~ 구문.

내용 어린 시절에 자연에 대한 감수성을 날카롭게 하는 것은 말로 표현할 수 없을 정도로 고귀하다.

refine [rifáin] 순화하다, 세련되게 하다
sharpen [ʃɑ́ːrpən] 날카롭게 하다, 갈다
powers of insight 통찰력
shamefully [ʃéimfəli] 부끄럽게도
pervert [pə́ːrvərt] 오해하다, 곡해하다, 왜곡하다
conduce to ~을 가져오다, ~에 도움이 되다
beyond words 말을 할 수 없을 정도로
dominant [dámənənt] 지배적인, 유력한(= influential, ruling, reigning)
deliberately [dilíbəritli] 일부러, 신중히(= carefully, intentionally)
discipline [dísəplin] 훈련하다, 단련하다(= drill)

Composition

우리가 자연에 대한 감수성을 이른 나이에 기르면 기를수록 문학과 예술에 대한 취미도 그만큼 더 커진다.

Key 감수성 sensitiveness | 취미 taste | 더욱더 커지다 grow the bigger

294

A young man sees a sunset and, unable to understand or to express the emotion that it rouses in him, concludes that it must be the gateway to a world that lies beyond. It is difficult for any of us in moments of intense aesthetic experience to resist the suggestion that we are catching a glimpse of a light that shines down to us from a different realm of existence, different and, because the experience is intensely moving, in some way higher. And, though the gleams blind and dazzle, yet do they convey a hint of beauty and serenity greater than we have known or imagined. Greater too than we can describe; for language, which was invented to convey the meanings of this world, cannot readily be fitted to the uses of another.

Key Structure

1   yet do they convey ~ = yet they do convey ~
    그러나 그것들은 ~을 지니고 있다
    • 도치 구문임에 유의.

2   Greater too than we can describe = It is greater too than we can describe
    우리가 묘사할 수 없을 만큼 위대한

3   the uses of another = the uses of another world
    다른 세상에서 이루어지는 용법(의미 내용)

내용   마음속에서 벌어지는, 표현할 수 없는 심미적인 경험.

rouse [rauz] 깨우다, 자극하다(= wake up, agitate, excite, galvanize)
gateway [géitwèi] 통로, 입구(= passage, entrance)
aesthetic / esthetic [esθétik] 미의, 미학의, 심미안이 있는(= artistic)
catch a glimpse of ~을 언뜻 보다, 포착하다
realm [relm] 영역, 왕국(= field, domain, kingdom)
gleam [gli:m] 빛, 미광
dazzle [dǽzl] 눈이 부시다, 반짝이다
serenity [sərénəti] 평정, 고요
readily [rédəli] 쉽사리, 곧, 즉시(= easily, soon)

Composition

미적 감흥이 강력하게 나타나는 순간에 인간은 저 멀리 놓여 있는 또 다른 미지의 세계로 가는 통로를 보게 된다고들 한다.

Key 미적 감흥 **aesthetic emotion** | 저 멀리 놓여 있다 **lie beyond** | 미지의 세계 **an unknown world** | 통로 **gateway** | ~라고들 한다 **it is said that ~**

295 The lover of literature has a medicine for grief that no doctor can furnish; he can always transmute his pain into something precious and lasting. None of us in this world can expect to be very happy; the proportion of happiness to unhappiness in the average human life has been estimated as something less than one-third. No matter how healthy or strong or fortunate you may be, every one of you must expect to endure a great deal of pain; and it is worth while for you to ask yourselves whether you cannot put it to good use. For pain has a very great value to the mind that knows how to utilize it. Nay, more than this must be said; nothing great ever was written, or ever will be written, by a man who does not know pain.

Part 2 Reading & Composition

Key Structure •

1 **a medicine for grief ~ furnish** 어떠한 의사도 제공할 수 없는 고통을 덜어주는 약

2 **the proportion of happiness to unhappiness**
불행에 대한 행복의 비율

3 **less than one-third** 1/3이 채 안 되는

4 No matter how **healthy ~** = However **healthy ~**
아무리 건강하다고 해도

5 **it is worth while for you to ask yourselves**
스스로에게 물어보는 것이 가치 있는 일이다

6 **nothing great ever was written**
위대한 것은 어느 것도 쓰인 적이 없다

내용 문학은 우리에게 고통을 고귀한 무엇으로 변화시키는 힘을 준다.

furnish [fə́ːrniʃ] 공급하다(= supply)
transmute [trænsmjúːt] 바꾸다(= change, mold)
put ~ to use ~을 이용하다(= make use of)
nay [nei] 아니(= no), 사실은(= indeed)

Composition

아무리 건강한 사람이라고 해도 문학 작품을 읽지 않으면 마음의 건강을 유지할 수 없다.

Key 아무리 건강하여도 **no matter how healthy a man may be** | 문학 작품 **literary works** | 마음의 건강 **the health of the mind**

296 Earlier religions and belief-systems were largely adaptations to cope with man's ignorance and fears, with the result that they came to concern themselves primarily with stability of attitude. But the need today is for a belief-system adapted to cope with his knowledge and his creative possibilities; and this implies the capacity to meet and to inspire change. In other words, the primary function of earlier systems was of necessity to maintain social and spiritual morale in face of the unknown; and this they accomplished with a considerable measure of success. But the primary function of any system today must be to utilize all available knowledge in giving guidance and encouragement for the continuing adventure of human development.

Key Structure

1 **with the result that ~** 그 결과로 (~하게 되었다)
  • 앞에서부터 '결과'로 해석.

2 **for a belief-system adapted to ~** ~할 수 있게끔 적응력을 갖춘 신앙 체계
  • for a ~ adapted(의미상의 주어)+to부정사(to cope with ~)
  • adapted는 belief-system을 수식하는 형용사.

3 **this they accomplished = they accomplished this** 그들은 이것을 성취하였다

내용 과거의 종교나 신앙 체계는 인간의 무지나 두려움을 극복하기 위한 적응의 방편이었지만, 오늘날에 있어서는 인간의 지식과 창의적 가능성을 발휘하기 위한 것이다.

adaptation [æ̀dəptéiʃ*ə*n] 적응, 적용
cope with 대항하다, 대처하다
concern oneself with 관심을 갖다(= be concerned with)
imply [implái] 의미하다(= mean)
inspire [inspáiər] (영감을) 불어넣다
morale [mərǽl] 사기, 풍기
in face of ~에 직면하여
the unknown 미지의 것[세계]
utilize [jú:təlàiz] 이용하다(= make use of)

Composition

오늘날 우리가 필요로 하는 것은 미지의 것에 직면하여서도 모험을 지속할 용기를 북돋아 줄 신앙 체계이다.

Key 미지의 것 the unknown | 모험을 지속할 용기 the encouragement for continuing adventure

297 Each civilization is born, it culminates, and it decays. There is a widespread testimony that this ominous fact is due to inherent biological defects in the crowded life of cities. Now, slowly and at first faintly, an opposite tendency is showing itself. Better roads and better vehicles at first induced the wealthier classes to live on the outskirts of the cities. The urgent need for defence had also vanished. This tendency is now spreading rapidly downwards. But a new set of conditions is just showing itself. Up to the present time, throughout the eighteenth and nineteenth centuries, this new tendency placed the home in the immediate suburbs, but concentrated manufacturing activity, business relations, government, and pleasure in the centers of the cities.

Key Structure •

1 an opposite tendency is showing itself
   반대의 성향이 모습을 드러내고 있다

2 concentrated manufacturing ~ in the centers of the cities
   제조 활동 분야, 기업체, 정부[관공서], 오락업체 등을 도시 중심부에 집중시켰다
   • concentrated ~의 주어는 this new tendency.

내용 문명이 태어나고 성장하고 사라지는 것은 복잡한 도시 생활이 지니는 생물학적인 약점에 기인한다.

culminate [kʌ́lmənèit] 최고조에 달하다(= climax, rise to a peak)
testimony [téstəmòuni] 증거, 증명(= evidence, affidavit)
ominous [ámənəs] 심상치 않은, 불길한(= baleful, dire, sinister) ⓝ omen 흉조
inherent [inhí(:)ərənt] 타고난, 고유의(= built-in, congenital, inborn, intrinsic)
induce ~ to... ～에게 …하도록 작용하다[유발하다]
outskirts [áutskə̀ːrts] (도시의) 변두리, 교외(= borders, suburbs, fringe)
manufacturing activity 제조업(체)

Composition

방어에 대한 긴급한 필요가 사라짐에 따라, 제조업체들, 기업체들, 정부 기관들이 도시의 외곽에 위치하게 되었다.

Key 방어 **defence** | 긴급한 필요 **urgent need** | 제조업체 **manufacturing activities** | 기업체 **business relations** | 정부 기관 **government agency** | 외곽 지대 **suburbs**

298 Education is necessarily concerned with ends and purposes which vary from age to age and from one community to another. The conception of the function of education is dependent upon the nature of the society in which it plays its part, and is determined by the philosophy, implicit or explicit, which governs relations between the individual and the community. There is thus no 'theory of education' which may be regarded as carrying absolute authority. A consideration of certain values will appear in any statement of educational principles, but in so far as education is a matter of action as well as thought, each community is faced with the problem of interpreting those values in relation to the 'here and now' of political, economic and social life.

Key Structure

1 in so far as education ~ thought
교육이 생각의 문제일 뿐만 아니라 행동의 문제인 한

2 the 'here and now' of ~ life
지금 이곳에서 문제가 되는 정치, 경제, 사회생활의 일들

내용 교육은 시대와 지역에 따라서 그 목표가 달라지고, 그 기능은 교육이 행하여지는 사회의 본질 및 교육 철학에 의존하게 된다.

necessarily [nèsəsérəli] 필연적으로
end [end] (궁극적인) 목적(= aim)
purpose [pə́ːrpəs] 의도, 목표
function [fʌ́ŋkʃən] 기능, 직무
implicit [implísit] 무언의, 함축된
explicit [iksplísit] 터놓은, 솔직한
absolute authority 절대 권위
interpret [intə́ːrprit] 해석하다, 이해하다

Composition

교육은 그것이 행해지는 사회의 이상과 철학, 그리고 그 사회가 안고 있는 문제에 관심을 가질 때에 진정한 교육이라고 할 수 있다.

Key 이상 **ideal** | ~에 관심을 갖다 **be concerned with**

299 Language both spoken and written is, after all, only a way of communicating or expressing thought. But thought itself is a marvelously quick, wayward and complicated thing; and the translation of thought into language is never an easy process. True, in speech we can often use gestures and facial expressions to help when language fails us; indeed, a frown, the raising of an eyebrow, a wave of the hand are really units, or 'words,' in the spoken language. But in writing we have to search for the exact word, phrase, idiom, turn of expression that will represent our thought. To see how hard this is even to the great writers—the novelist, the critic and the poet—we have only to study the manuscript of a great work in the British Museum.

Part **2** Reading & Composition

Key Structure •

1 when language fails us
   = when we fail to express ourselves
   말로 의사 표현이 되지 않을 때

2 **To see how hard this is even to the great writers**
   이것이 위대한 작가들에게도 얼마나 힘든 일인가를 알기 위하여

내용 사고는 빠르고 자꾸 변하는 복잡한 것으로, 이것을 언어로 바꾸는 것은 결코 쉬운 일이 아니다.

marvelously [mὰːrvələsli] 이상하게, 훌륭하게
wayward [wéiwərd] 불법의, 제멋대로의
complicated [kámpləkèitid] 복잡한, 혼잡한
frown [fraun] 언짢은 얼굴, 찡그림
eyebrow [áibràu] 눈썹
search for 찾다(= look for)
turn of expression 표현법
critic [krítik] 비평가 ⓥ criticize ⓝ criticism 비평 ⓐ critical
manuscript [mǽnjəskrìpt] 사본, 필사본, 원고
the British Museum 대영 박물관(London에 위치)

Composition 《

우리의 생각을 글로 바꾸는 것은 결코 쉽지 않다. 왜냐하면 글을 쓸 때 우리는 말할 때와는 달리 정확한 어휘를 찾아야 하기 때문이다.

Key 생각을 글로 바꾸다 **translate thought into written language** | 정확한 어휘 **exact words**

300   We can assert with some confidence that our own period is one of decline; that the standards of culture are lower than they were fifty years ago; and that the evidences of this decline are visible in every department of human activity. I see no reason why the decay of culture should not proceed much further, and why we may not even anticipate a period, of some duration, of which it is possible to say that it will have no culture. Then culture will have to grow again from the soil; and when I say it must grow again from the soil, I do not mean that it will be brought into existence by any activity of political demagogues. The question asked by this essay is whether there are any permanent conditions, in the absence of which no higher culture can be expected.

Key Structure

1   We can assert ~ that...; that...; and that...
우리는 ~을 주장할 수 있다
- assert의 목적절인 that절이 세 개 나오고 있음.

2   I see no reason why ~ not ~하지 못할 이유가 없다고 본다

3   a period, of some duration ~ 약간의 지속 기간이 있는 시기

4   a period of which it is ~ no culture 그것에 대해 문화가 없을 것이라고 말할 수 있는 시기

5   in the absence of which ~ expected 그것이 없는 경우 결코 높은 문화를 기대할 수 없다

내용   우리 시대가 문명이 쇠퇴하는 시대라는 게 모든 분야에서 역력히 나타나고 있다.

assert [əsə́ːrt] 단언하다, 주장하다
confidence [kánfidəns] 확신, 믿음 ⓥ confide
decline [dikláin] 퇴보, 쇠퇴(≒ progress)
decay [dikéi] 부패, 붕괴(= corruption, corrosion)
from the soil 밑바탕에서부터
bring ~ into existence 생겨나게 하다
demagogue [déməgàg] 선동자, 선동 연설가

Composition

나는 네가 그렇게 사치스러운 여자와 결혼을 해야 하는 이유를 모르겠다.

Key   사치스러운 luxurious │ ~할 이유를 모른다 I see no reason why

PART
3

Advanced Reading
장문 독해를 통해 독해력을 강화하자!

301 World-wide co-operation with our present scientific technique could abolish poverty and war, and could bring to all mankind a level of happiness and well-being such as has never hitherto existed. But although this is obvious, men still prefer to confine
5 co-operation to their own groups, and indulge towards other groups a fierce hostility which fills daily life with terrifying visions of disaster. The reasons for this absurd and tragic inability to behave as everybody's interests would dictate lie not in anything external but in our own emotional nature. If we could feel in our
10 moments of vision as impersonally as a man of science can think, we should see the folly of our divisions and contests, and we should soon perceive that our own interests are compatible with those of others but are not compatible with the desire to bring others to ruin.

Key Structure •

3 such as **has never ~ existed**
지금까지 결코 존재한 적이 없는 그러한 것
• such as 구문. as는 유사관계대명사 주격.

5 indulge towards ~ a fierce hostility
= indulge a fierce hostility towards other groups
다른 집단에게 심한 적개심을 표하다

7 **The reasons for ~ lie** not in A but in B
~에 대한 이유는 A에 있는 것이 아니라 B에 있다 (not A but B 구문)

8 behave as everybody's interests would dictate
개개인의 이득이 명령하는 대로 처신하다(개개인의 이득이 되도록 행동하다)

9 feel ~ as impersonally as ~ think
과학자가 생각하는 만큼 비개인적인 감정을 느끼다(개인의 입장을 초월하여 느끼다)

12 our own interests are compatible with A but are not compatible with B
우리 자신의 이해는 A와는 양립하여도 B와는 양립할 수 없다
• those of others = the interests of others

내용 과학 기술의 세계적인 협력을 통해 가난과 전쟁을 없앨 수 있지만, 인간은 아직도 다른 집단에 대하여 적개심을
표하고 있다.

abolish 제거하다, 말살하다(= get rid of) **hitherto** 지금까지(= until now) **obvious** 분명한 **confine A to B**
A를 B에 국한하다 **folly** 어리석음 **compatible** 양립하는

302 Man's chief purpose is the creation and preservation of values: that is what gives meaning to our civilization, and the participation in this is what gives significance, ultimately, to the individual human life. Only in so far as values are fostered—through art and religion
5 and science and love and domestic life—can men effectively use the machines and powers that have enabled them to tame nature and secure human existence from the worst outrages and accidents that forever threaten it. Civilization, our very capacity to be human, rests on that perpetual effort. If any nation or group thinks
10 that the job is finished, or if man puts his confidence solely in the instruments and forgets the ends and ideals and metaphysical purposes—then the structure crumbles away: then man himself is finished.

Key Structure ▸

4   Only in so far as values are fostered
가치가 창조될 때에만
• 뒤에 도치 구문이 옴에 유의할 것. (can man effectively use ~)

8   Civilization, our very capacity to be human
우리가 인간일 수 있는 바로 그 능력인 문명은
• civilization과 our ~ human은 동격 관계.

내용 인간의 문명에 의미를 부여하는 것은 가치의 창조와 보존이다.

preservation 보존   **significance** 의미, 중요성   **ultimately** 궁극적으로   **foster** 기르다(= cultivate, nurture)
domestic life 가정생활   **tame** 길들이다   **secure** 지키다, 확보하다   **outrage** 난폭한 일   **threaten** 위협하다
rest on ~에 달려 있다(= rely on)   **perpetual** 영속적인   **metaphysical** 형이상학적인   **crumble away**
망하다

No pains, no gains.
수고하는 것이 없으면 얻는 것이 없다.

303 What light does the study of past history cast on the meaning of human experience and, in particular, to what extent does it sustain the belief in the progress of civilization? Leaving on one side the pessimistic theories widely prevalent in antiquity but alien to modern thought, we reached the conclusion that, while the last four centuries have witnessed a steady advance in the fields of pure, and even more clearly applied, science, any wide generalization as to the onward march of civilization can hardly be supported. In particular, it remains highly questionable whether man's intellectual progress has been attended by any corresponding growth in his moral achievement. This doubt has inevitably been intensified by the catastrophic events that have menaced the very foundations of our culture within our own life-time.

Key Structure

3 Leaving on one side ~
　～을 한쪽으로 밀어 놓고[제쳐 놓고]

5 the last four centuries have witnessed ~
　= in the last four centuries we have witnessed ~
　우리는 지난 4세기 동안 ～을 목격해 왔다
　• 무생물 주어 구문

7 any wide generalization as to ~ civilization
　문명은 앞으로 전진한다고 하는 어떤 폭넓은 일반화

내용 순수 · 응용과학 분야의 꾸준한 진보가 있었지만, 문명이 반드시 진보했느냐 하는 점은 의문이다.

cast 던지다(cast-cast-cast)　sustain 지탱하다, 유지하다　pessimistic 비관적인(≒ optimistic)　prevalent 득세하는, 퍼져 있는 ⓥ prevail　antiquity 고대, 상고(上古)　witness 목격하다　pure science 순수 과학 applied science 응용과학　as to ～에 관하여(=concerning)　onward 앞으로, 전진하여　corresponding 상응하는　inevitably 연적으로　intensify 강화하다　catastrophic 대참사의, 큰 재앙의 ⓝ catastrophe menace 위협하다(= threaten)　life-time 생애

304 History, like the drama and the novel, grew out of mythology, a primitive form of apprehension and expression in which—as in fairy tales listened to by children or in dreams dreamt by sophisticated adults—the line between fact and fiction is left undrawn. It has, for example, been said of the *Iliad* that anyone who starts reading it as history will find that it is full of fiction but, equally, anyone who starts reading it as fiction will find that it is full of history. All histories resemble the *Iliad* to this extent, that they cannot entirely dispense with the fictional element. The mere selection, arrangement and presentation of facts is a technique belonging to the field of fiction, and popular opinion is right in its insistence that no historian can be 'great' if he is not also a great artist.

Key Structure

2   **in which ~ the line between fact and fiction is left undrawn**
그 속에서는 사실과 허구의 선이 분명하게 그어져 있지 않은

2   **as in fairy tales ~ or in dreams**
동화나 꿈에서처럼
  • fairy tales (which are) listened to by children 어린이들이 듣는 동화
  • dreams (which are) dreamt by sophisticated adults 세상 물정에 닳고 닳은 어른들이 꾸는 꿈

8   **to this extent, that ~**
~에 이르기까지, ~라는 점에서

11   **popular opinion is right in its insistence that ~**
~라고 주장함에 있어서 대중의 의견은 옳다

내용   역사는 신화에서 나왔고, 따라서 사실과 허구의 구별이 쉽지 않다.

mythology 신화   **primitive** 원시의   **apprehension and expression** 해석과 표현   **sophisticated** 세상 물정에 닳고 닳은, 학식이 많은, 궤변의   *Iliad* 일리아드(호메로스가 쓴 트로이의 서사시)   **dispense with** ~없이 지내다   **arrangement** 배열   **presentation** 제시   **insistence** 주장, 고집

305   It is remarkable that after a century of incessant change the paths of change have not become smooth and easy. On the contrary, our world seems to be getting less and less suitable for people who undergo change. Never before has the passage from boyhood
5 to manhood been so painful and so beset with explosions. The passage from backwardness to modernity which in the nineteenth century seemed a natural process is now straining a large part of the world to the breaking point. The hoped-for changes from poverty to affluence, from subjection to freedom, from work to leisure
10 do not enhance social stability but threaten social dissolution. However noble the intention and wholehearted the efforts of those who initiate change, the results are often the opposite of that which was reasonable to expect.

Key Structure ▸

4 Never **before** has the passage ~ **been so**...
   ~의 길이 그렇게 …한 적은 예전에 없었다
   • 부정어(never)의 문두 강조로 주어, 동사가 도치된 구문.

8 **The hoped-for changes ~**
   = The changes which have been hoped for ~
   희망해 왔던 변화들

11 **However noble the intention ~ of those...**
   변화를 일으키는 사람들의 의도가 아무리 고상하고, 그들의 노력이 아무리 전력투구한 것이라고 해도
   • however noble the intention (may be) and (however) whole-hearted the efforts of those ~ change (may be)의 구조에 유의할 것.

12 **the opposite of** that which ~ expect
   기대하기에 합리적인 것의 반대
   • that which = what

내용 역사상 인간의 삶에 꾸준한 변화가 있었지만, 가난을 벗어나고 자유를 얻고 여가를 얻으려는 인간의 희망은 아직 완전히 실현되지 못하고 있다.

incessant 끊임없는(= ceaseless)   on the contrary 그와는 반대로   undergo 겪다, 경험하다   be beset with ~으로 포위되다[막히다]   explosions 폭발적인 일들   backwardness 후진성, 미개함   strain 긴장시키다   breaking point 파열점   affluence 풍요, 부유함   subjection 복종   enhance 높이다, 끌어올리다   threaten 위협하다(= menace)   dissolution 분열, 파괴   initiate 시작하다

306 Religions have helped greatly in the development of humanity. They have laid down values and standards and have pointed out principles for the guidance of human life. But with all the good they have done, they have also tried to imprison truth in set forms and dogmas, and encouraged ceremonials and practices which soon lose all their original meaning and become mere routine. While impressing upon man the awe and mystery of the unknown that surrounds him on all sides, they have discouraged him from trying to understand not only the unknown but what might come in the way of social effort. Instead of encouraging curiosity and thought, they have preached a philosophy of submission to nature, to the established church, to the prevailing social order, and to everything that is.

Key Structure ▸

3   with all the good ~
    = for all the good ~ = in spite of the good ~
    이로운 일들에도 불구하고

7   While impressing upon man the awe ~ sides (분사 구문)
    = While they impress upon man the awe ~ sides
    사방에서 인간을 둘러싸고 있는 미지의 존재에 대한 외경과 신비감을 인간에게 새겨 넣어 주면서도
    • impress A upon B = impress upon B A의 구조로, 목적어인 A가 뒤로 간 형태.

9   what might come in the way of social effort
    사회적 노력에 방해가 될지도 모르는 것

13 everything that is
    존재하는 모든 것
    • is = exists

내용 종교는 인간성의 발전에 기여한 바가 크지만, 진리를 고정된 교리로 나타내는 등 잘못도 많다.

lay down 세우다, 제정하다(= set up)   **the good** 선, 이득, 이로운 일   **imprison** 가두다, 수감하다(= shut up)
set 고정된, 틀에 박힌(= fixed)   **dogma** 독단, 교리, 신조   **ceremonials and practices** 의식적이고 상투적인
일들(예배 의식 등)   **routine** 틀에 박힌 (일)   **impress** 새겨 넣다   **awe** 두려움, 외경심   **come in the way of**
~의 방해가 되다   **preach** 설교하다   **submission** 복종   **the established church** 기성 교회   **prevailing**
널리 퍼진

307 The students of human nature can find endless matter for observation in the behavior of his fellow card-players. Meanness and generosity, prudence and audacity, courage and timidity, weakness and strength; all these men show at the card-table according to their natures, and because they are intent upon the game they drop the mask they wear in the ordinary affairs of life. Few are so deep that you do not know the essential facts about them after a few rubbers of bridge. The card-table is a very good school for the study of mankind. The unhappy persons who have no card sense say that playing cards is a waste of time, but it is never a waste of time to amuse oneself; besides, the day has twenty-four hours and the week seven days, there is always a certain time to be wasted.

Key Structure ▸

4 all these men show ~
= men show all these ~
이 모든 것들을 사람들은 보여 준다
• 목적어가 도치된 구문.

6 Few are so deep that ~
심중이 너무 깊어 당신이 ~하지 못할 사람은 거의 없다

11 the week (has) seven days

내용 카드놀이는 인간성 연구에 많은 관찰 자료를 제공한다.

meanness 인색, 비열, 야비   **prudence** 신중함, 사려   **audacity** 뻔뻔스러움, 대담성   **timidity** 수줍음, 소심함
be intent upon ~에 열중하다   **drop the mask** 가면을 벗다   **deep** 자기 마음을 숨기는   **rubbers of bridge**
카드놀이의 일종(3회 승부 게임)

308 External events and their consequences affect us powerfully, and yet the greatest shocks come to our minds through inner fears and conflicts. While we advance on the external plane, as we must if we are to survive, we have also to win peace with ourselves and between ourselves and our environment, a peace which brings satisfaction not only to our physical and material needs but also to those inner imaginative urges and adventurous spirits that have distinguished man ever since he started on his troubled journey in the realms of thought and action. Whether that journey has any ultimate purpose or not we do not know, but it has its compensations and it points to many a nearer objective which appears attainable and which may again become the starting point for a fresh advance.

Key Structure ▸

3 **as we must if we are to survive**
우리가 살아남기 위해서는 그래야 하는 것처럼
  • if we are to survive = if we wish to survive

4 **win peace with ourselves ~ environment**
우리 자신의 평화와 함께 자신과 환경 사이에도 평화를 얻다[화해하다]

5 **a peace which brings ~**
  • 바로 앞의 peace의 내용을 다시 설명하는 동격 명사구.

9 **Whether that journey ~ know**
= We do not know whether ~ or not
  • know의 목적어인 whether ~ or not절이 문두로 강조되어 나간 것.

> 내용 외적인 사건들이 우리에게 강력한 영향력을 행사하지만, 가장 큰 충격은 내적 두려움과 갈등으로부터 온다.

consequence 영향(력) **conflict** 투쟁, 갈등 **external plane** 외적인 면 **win peace with** ~와 화해하다 **adventurous** 모험심이 많은 **ever since** ~ 이래로 줄곧 **realm** 영역(= field, sphere) **compensation** 배상, 보상 **point to** 가리키다

309 A new civilization is always being made: the state of affairs that we enjoy today illustrates what happens to the aspirations of each age for a better one. The most important question that we can ask is whether there is any permanent standard by which we can compare one civilization with another, and by which we can make some guess at the improvement or decline of our own. We have to admit, in comparing one civilization with another, and in comparing the different stages of our own, that no society and no one age of it realizes all the values of civilization. Not all of these values may be compatible with each other: what is at least as certain is that in realizing some we lose the appreciation of others. Nevertheless, we can distinguish between higher and lower cultures; we can distinguish between advance and retrogression.

Key Structure

2 the aspirations of each age for a better one
더 나은 세대가 되고자 하는 각 세대의 갈망들
• one = age

8 no one age of it
그 사회의 어떤 세대도 (~하지 못하다)
• it = the society

9 Not all of these ~ other
이 모든 가치가 서로 조화를 이루는 것은 아니다 (부분 부정)

10 what is at least as certain
적어도 확실한 것은

내용 어느 사회, 어느 시대도 문명의 모든 가치를 다 인식하지는 못한다.

aspiration 열정(= ardent desire) make some guess at ~에 대해 약간의 추측을 하다 decline 쇠퇴, 하락
be compatible with ~과 조화를 이루다(= be in harmony with) distinguish between A and B A와 B를
구별하다 retrogression 후퇴

310   A great book owes its greatness in the first instance to the greatness of the personality which gave it life; for what we call genius is only another name for freshness and originality of nature, with its resulting freshness and originality of outlook upon the world, of insight, and of thought. The mark of a really great book is that it has something fresh and original to say, and that it says this in a fresh and independent way. It is the utterance of one who has himself been close to those aspects of life of which he speaks, who has looked at them with his own eyes, who by the keenness of his vision has seen more deeply into things, and by the strength of his genius has apprehended their meaning more powerfully than the common race of men; and who in addition has the artist's wonderful faculty of making us see and feel with him.

Part 3 Advanced Reading

Key Structure ▸

1   the greatness of the personality which gave it life
    책에 생명을 넣어준 위대한 개성
     • it = a great book

3   with its resulting ~ 그 결과 ~이 나타난다

9   by the keenness of his vision
    = by his keen vision
    그의 날카로운 통찰력에 의해

10 by the strength of his genius
    = by his strong genius
    그의 강한 천재성에 의해

내용   위대한 책은 작가의 위대한 개성에 힘입어 나온다.

owe A to B A를 B에 힘입다   outlook upon the world 세상을 보는 안목   insight 통찰력   utterance 발언
keenness 날카로움   see into 조사하다, 검사하다   apprehend 이해하다(= comprehend)   the common
race of men 보통 사람들   faculty 능력, 기능

311   The simplest cases of migration by attraction are those of a people living on poor steppes or plateaus adjoining cultivated land or rich valleys. Agricultural peoples are, as a rule, averse to and ill-prepared for war, and the more prosperous their circumstances, the
5 more they are likely to be enervated by their very civilization. They are thus liable at all times to be attacked by neighboring brigands, who in some cases retire to their barren homes with their booty, but in others remain among the conquered people, and, becoming assimilated with them, in due course become more civilized, and in
10 their turn are subject to invasions from their barbarian kinsmen of the borders. Thus is set up an automatic social mechanism which at the same time civilizes the barbarians and energizes those who have become softened by easy circumstances.

Key Structure

1   those **of a people**
- those = the cases of migration

4   the more **prosperous their circumstances,** the more **they are ~ civilization**
그들이 처한 환경이 순조로우면 순조로울수록, 그들은 자신들의 바로 그 문명에 의해 약화될 가능성이 더더욱 많아진다
- the+비교급, the+비교급 구문.

5   **They are thus liable ~ to be attacked**
따라서 그들은 언제나 공격을 받기 쉽다

8   **but in others** = but in other cases

8   **becoming assimilated with them**
그들과 동화되었다가

10 **(they) are subject to invasions from ~**
～로부터 침략을 당하다

11 **Thus is set up an automatic social mechanism**
이렇게 해서 자동적인 사회 구조가 형성이 된다
- 주어 an automatic social mechanism이 동사 뒤로 옮겨간 도치 구문.

내용 유혹에 의한 이주의 가장 간단한 경우는 초원이나 고원 지대에 사는 자들이 이웃하는 비옥한 땅으로 옮겨가는 경우이다.

attraction 유인   steppe 스텝 지대, 대초원(지대)   plateau 고원, 대지   adjoining 이웃하는(= neighboring) averse to ~을 싫어하는[반대하는]   enervate 기력을 약화시키다(= weaken)   brigand 산적(= bandit), 약탈자 barren 불모의(= desolate, infertile, sterile)   booty 전리품, 노획물   assimilated 동화된   in due course 결국, 마침내는   in their turn 이번에는 그들이   kinsman 일가, 동족   energize 활기를 불어넣다

312 No political form has hitherto been discovered which is equally favorable to the prosperity and the development of all the classes into which society is divided. These classes continue to form, as it were, so many distinct communities in the same nation; and experience has shown that it is no less dangerous to place the fate of these classes exclusively in the hands of any one of them, than it is to make one people the determiner of the destiny of another. When the rich alone govern, the interest of the poor is always endangered; and when the poor make the laws, that of the rich is subject to very serious risks. The advantage of democracy does not consist, therefore, as has sometimes been asserted, in favoring the prosperity of all, but simply in contributing to the well-being of the greatest number.

Key Structure •

2 **all the classes into which society is divided**
사회를 구성하는 모든 계층들

5 **it is no less dangerous to place ~ than it is to make ~ another**
이 계층들의 운명을 한 계층의 손에 전적으로 맡기는 것은, 한 민족을 다른 민족의 운명의 결정자로 만드는 만큼이나 위험한 일이다
• no less A than B B하는 것과 마찬가지로 A하다 (양자 긍정의 의미)

9 **that of the rich is subject to ~ risks**
부자들의 권익은 매우 심각한 위험에 처한다
• that = the interest

10 **does not consist in A, but simply in B**
A에 있는 것이 아니라 단지 B에 있다

11 **as has sometimes been asserted**
가끔 주장되어 왔듯이
• as는 주어로 쓰인 준관계대명사.

11 **favor the prosperity of all**
모든 사람의 번영에 조력[찬성]하다

내용 한 사회를 구성하는 모든 계층의 번영과 발전에 똑같은 혜택을 주는 정치 제도는 없었다.

favorable 이익[혜택]을 주는   **prosperity** 번영, 번성   **as it were** 말하자면(= so to speak)   **exclusively** 배타적으로, 오로지   **the rich** 부자들(≒ the poor)   **endanger** 위태롭게 하다   **be subject to** ~에 처하다   **consist in** ~에 놓여 있다(= lie in)   **favor** 찬성하다, 노력하다   **well-being** 복지

313　That the offspring of rabbits were rabbits, of monkeys, monkeys, of men, men, and so on, was taken for granted until comparatively recent times. Charles Darwin and his forerunners directed attention to the variability of species and postulated an evolutionary scheme in which, to the general horror, the offspring of worms were insects, of reptiles, birds, and of monkeys, men. More exactly, they pictured each species as a transitional stage in the formation of one or more new species; one frame in a cinematograph film of biological history. The offspring of rabbits, they said, are rabbits, but not quite the same rabbits, and in the course of evolution this discrepancy may accumulate, so that the rabbits of today differ considerably from the rabbits of a hundred thousand years ago.

Key Structure

1　That the offspring ~ , and so on
　 = That the offspring of rabbits were rabbits, the offspring of monkeys were monkeys, (and) the offspring of men were men, and so on

5　the offspring of worms were insects, (the offspring) of reptiles, (were) birds, and (the offspring) of monkeys, (were) men

내용　다윈의 진화론이 나타난 후 소름 끼치게도 인간은 원숭이의 후예라는 이야기가 나왔다.

offspring 후손, 자손　**forerunner** 선구자, 이론의 전파자　**variability** 변이성, 가변성　**postulate** 가정하다, 기초적인 원리로서 요구하다　**to the general horror** 모두가 소름 끼치게도　**reptile** 파충류　**transitional stage** 과도기적인 단계　**cinematograph** 영화 촬영　**discrepancy** 불일치, 차이(= inconsistency)　**accumulate** 쌓이다

314 Strange is our situation here upon earth. Each of us comes for a short visit, not knowing why, yet sometimes seeming to divine a purpose. From the standpoint of daily life, however, there is one thing we do know: that man is here for the sake of other men—above all for
5 those upon whose smile and well-being our own happiness depends, and also for the countless unknown souls with whose fate we are connected by a bond of sympathy. Many times a day I realize how much my own outer and inner life is built upon the labors of my fellow-men, both living and dead, and how earnestly I must exert
10 myself in order to give in return as much as I have received. My peace of mind is often troubled by the depressing sense that I have borrowed too heavily from the work of other men.

Key Structure •

3 **there is one thing (that) we do know:**
우리가 정말로 아는 것이 하나 있다
• 콜론(:) 이하의 that절은 one thing의 내용을 설명하는 동격 명사절. / do는 강조어.

4 **above all for those ~**
무엇보다도 ~하는 사람들을 위하여

5 **those upon whose smile ~ depends**
그들의 미소와 행복에 우리의 행복이 달려 있는 그러한 사람들

6 **the countless unknown souls ~ sympathy**
그들의 운명에 우리가 공감대라는 고리에 의해 연결되어 있는 수많은 알려지지 않은 사람들

10 **in order to give in return** as much as **I have received**
내가 받은 만큼 그 대가로 돌려주기 위하여
• as much as 구문. 뒤의 as는 관계대명사로서 received의 목적어.

내용 우리가 왜 태어나게 되는지 모르지만, 인간은 다른 사람을 위해 존재한다는 것은 틀림없는 사실이라고 생각한다.

divine 간파하다, 예언하다 *cf.* divine ⓐ 신의, 성스러운   **countless** 무한한   **bond** 끈, 유대   **exert oneself** (스스로) 노력하다, 분투하다   **depressing** 우울한, 억압적인

315 Science may be defined as the reduction of multiplicity to unity. It seeks to explain the endlessly diverse phenomena of nature by ignoring the uniqueness of particular events, concentrating on what they have in common and finally abstracting some kind of 'law,' in terms of which they make sense and can be effectively dealt with. For example, apples fall from the tree and the moon moves across the sky. People had been observing these facts from time immemorial. They were convinced that an apple is an apple is an apple whereas the moon is the moon is the moon. It remained for Isaac Newton to perceive what these very dissimilar phenomena had in common, and to formulate a theory of gravitation in terms of which certain aspects of the behavior of apples, of the heavenly bodies and indeed of everything else in the physical universe could be explained and dealt with.

Key Structure

5 **in terms of which they ~ with**
그것[법]을 통하여 그것들은 의미를 갖고 효과적으로 설명될 수 있다
• which의 선행사는 law.
• they = particular events

8 **an apple is an apple is an apple**
사과는 어디까지나 사과이며 다른 것이 아니다
• 매우 특이한 표현으로 Gertrude Stein의 "A rose is a rose is a rose."를 모방한 표현.

9 **It remained for Isaac Newton to perceive ~**
~을 인식하는 것은 뉴턴의 몫으로 남아 있었다(뉴턴이 나타나서 ~을 인식하였다)
• It(가주어)+for+목적어(의미상의 주어)+to부정사(진주어) 구문.

내용 과학은 다양성을 단일성으로 축소하는 것이고, 사물들이 갖는 공통점을 통하여 법칙을 만들어 내는 것이다.

reduction 축소, 환원   **multiplicity** 다양성   **unity** 단일성   **diverse** 다양한   **phenomenon** 현상
pl. phenomena   **uniqueness** 특이성   **abstract** 추상화하다, 이끌어내다   **from time immemorial** 태곳적부터
dissimilar 상이한   **gravitation** 인력(引力)   **heavenly bodies** 천체(天體)들   **physical universe** 물질세계,
자연계

316 This, we often say, is the age of the Common Man. But we are not quite sure what we mean by that. In so far as we mean only the age of universal opportunity, nothing but good could seem to come of it. But many people do, sometimes without being entirely aware of it, mean something more. When we make ourselves the champion of any particular group we almost inevitably begin to idealize that group. From defending the common man we pass on to exalting him, and we find ourselves beginning to imply, not merely that he is as good as anybody else, but he is actually better. Instead of demanding only that the common man be given an opportunity to become as uncommon as possible, we make this commonness a virtue and, even in the case of candidates for high office, we sometimes praise them for being nearly indistinguishable from the average man in the street.

Key Structure ▸

1 This **is the age of** ~
   • This는 독립된 소유격 형태로 명사 표현까지를 나타내며 그 명사는 보어에서 찾을 수 있음.
   • This = This age

2 **what we** mean by **that**
   그 말이 무엇을 뜻하는지
   • mean A by B   B로서 A를 의미하다

10 **demanding only that the common man be given** ~
   • be는 가정법 현재의 원형임. / 요구(demand), 제안(suggest) 등의 동사에 따라오는 that절에는 동사의 원형이 쓰이지만, should가 앞에 오기도 함.

내용 이 시대를 흔히 보통 사람의 시대라고 말하지만, 보통 사람이라는 의미가 정확히 정의되어 있지 않고, 많은 사람들은 자기가 속한 집단을 이상화하여 보통 사람이 아닌 집단으로 미화한다.

the Common Man 보통 사람(= the Ordinary Man)   **inevitably** 필연적으로(= unavoidably)   **exalt** 칭찬하다, 찬양하다(= praise, uplift)   **imply** 내포하다, 의미하다, 암시하다(= mean, suggest)   **candidate** 후보자, 지망자 **indistinguishable** 구별되지 않는   **the man in[on] the street** 보통 사람, 아마추어 *cf.* a woman of the streets 매춘부

317   Patriotism, however much it may be debased, is still patriotism; and although it might be exaggeration to contend that the more debased patriotism becomes, the more patriotic it is reputed to be, it is on the other hand certainly true that a pure and rational patriotism is generally condemned as a kind of treason. As usual, irreconcilable meanings lurk behind the convenient word. Many of the feelings sanctified by it are wholly brutish, and one can think of many modern instances of Dr. Johnson's famous saying that patriotism is the last refuge of a scoundrel. But apart from these contemptible hypocrisies there is plenty of sincere and honest patriotism which, though turned to base uses, is potentially an inexhaustible source of strength to the general good of the country and the world.

Key Structure ▸

1   however **much it may be debased**
     아무리 그것의 품위가 떨어진다고 해도
     • however = no matter how

11 **though (it is) turned to base uses** 천한 용도로 쓰이기는 하지만

내용   애국심은 그 값이 아무리 떨어져도 애국심이며, 국가와 세계의 일반적인 이득을 위해 힘의 원천이 되는 애국심
     또한 많이 있다.

exaggeration 과장   **contend** 주장하다   **condemn A as B** A를 B라고 비난하다   **treason** 반역, 배신
(= betrayal, treachery)   **irreconcilable** 양립할 수 없는, 모순되는   **lurk** 잠복하다, 숨어 있다   **sanctify** 옳다고
인정하다, 정당화하다(= justify)   **brutish** 야비한 ⓷ brute   **refuge** 피난처   **scoundrel** 악당   **contemptible**
비열한   **hypocrisy** 위선, 가장   **be turned to base use** 비천한 용도로 쓰이다   **inexhaustible** 고갈되지 않는

318 When I was very young and the urge to be someplace else was on me, I was assured by mature people that maturity would cure this itch. When years described me as mature, the remedy prescribed was middle age. In middle age I was assured that greater age would calm my fever and now that I am fifty-eight perhaps senility will do the job. Nothing has worked. Four hoarse blasts of a ship's whistle still raise the hair on my neck and set my feet to tapping. The sound of a jet, an engine warming up, even the clopping of shod hooves on pavement brings on the ancient shudder, the dry mouth and vacant eye, the hot palms and the churn of stomach high up under the rib cage. In other words, I don't improve; in further words, once a bum always a bum. I fear the disease is incurable.

Key Structure

4 greater age would calm my fever
   나이가 더 들면 나의 열병이 식을 것이다

7 raise the hair on my neck
   내 목덜미의 머리카락을 쭈뼛 세우다

7 set my feet to tapping
   내가 똑똑 소리를 내며 달려가게 하다

9 brings on ... the churn of ~ cage
   흉곽 아래의 가슴은 크게 요동친다

11 once a bum (is) always a bum
   한때의 방랑자는 영원한 방랑자이다

   내용 한때의 방랑자는 영원한 방랑자이다.

urge 충동   **mature** 성숙한, 어른의   **itch** 욕망, 가려움   **remedy prescribed** 처방된 해결책   **senility** 고령
ⓐ **senile**   **hoarse** 요란한   **blast** (피리 · 고동) 소리   **tap** 똑똑 소리내다   **clop** (말발굽이) 딸가닥거리다   **shod hooves** 편자 박은 말발굽   **churn** 요동   **rib cage** 흉곽   **bum** 방랑자, 부랑자(= tramp)   **incurable** 치료될 수 없는

319　It matters little whether a poet had a large audience in his own time. What matters is that there should always be at least a small audience for him in every generation; there should always be a small vanguard of people, appreciative of poetry, who are
5　independent, and somewhat in advance of their time or ready to assimilate novelty more quickly. The development of culture does not mean bringing everybody up to the front, which amounts to no more than making everybody keep step; it means the maintenance of such an elite, with the main, more passive body of readers not
10　lagging more than a generation or so behind. The changes and developments of sensibility which appear first in a few will work themselves into the language gradually, through their influence on other, more readily popular authors; and by the time they have become well established, a new advance will be called for.

Key Structure •

1　It matters little whether ~
　～이냐 아니냐는 별로 중요하지가 않다
　• whether 이하가 진주어.

2　What matters is ~　중요한 것은 ～이다

6　assimilate novelty more quickly　새로운 것을 보다 빨리 자기 것으로 만들다

7　bring everybody up to the front
　모든 사람을 전면에 나서게 하다

11　work themselves into the language
　언어 속으로 파고들다

13　by the time (when) they have become ~
　그들이 ～되었을 때쯤에는
　• they have become의 현재완료는 미래완료를 나타냄. (때나 조건의 부사절에서 현재(완료)가 미래(완료)를 대신함)

내용　시인에게는 자신의 시대에 몇몇 독자가 있느냐보다는 매 세대마다 그의 작품을 읽고 선봉에 서서 그것을 퍼뜨릴 수 있는 소수의 독자가 더 필요하다.

audience 독자, 청중　vanguard 전위 부대, 선봉장　appreciative 감상할 줄 아는　in advance of ～보다 앞서가는　assimilate 동화시키다, 제것으로 받아들이다　novelty 새로운 것, 신제품　front 최전방, 전면　keep step 보조를 맞추다　maintenance 유지, 보존 ⓥ maintain　lag 뒤떨어지다　call for 요구하다

320   We are so accustomed to the conventions of our own world that we lose sight of the fact that such conventions are learned, and that without them our perceptions would not be the same. An American who showed an African village woman a picture postcard of the Empire State Building was startled when the woman exclaimed, "What a beautiful garden!" Not until then did the American become conscious of the basis of his own perception of the picture as that of a tall building. The photograph was not only an interpretation of a three dimensional terms, but the observer accustomed to photographs had mentally stood on end the picture lying on the table. The African woman had never seen a building higher than the low huts of her native village, and she had never seen a picture or a photograph of any kind. What she saw was an array of rectangles, which she perceived as a well laid-out garden.

Key Structure ▸

3   without **them**
    = if it were not for **them**
     • them = such conventions

6   Not until then did the American become ~
    = It was not until then that the Americans became ~
    그때까지 그 미국인은 ~을 전혀 깨닫지 못하였다

6   become conscious of the basis of his ~ building
    그 그림(엽서)을 높은 건물로 보는 그 자신의 지각의 바탕을 의식하다

10   had mentally stood on end the picture lying on the table
    책상 위의 그림을 정신적으로[머릿속에서] 세워 놓았다
     • stand ~ on end ~을 세우다
     • stood의 목적어는 the picture lying on the table

내용   자신이 사는 세계의 인습에 익숙해지면 다른 세계의 모습을 보지 못하게 된다.

convention 인습, 관행   lose sight of 모습을 놓치다[잊다]   perception 지각   be startled 놀라다 (= be surprised)   conscious of ~을 의식하는   interpretation 해석, 설명   three dimensional 3차원의(가로 · 세로 · 높이)   stand 곧추세우다   hut 오두막   array 배열, 죽 늘어선 것   rectangle 사각형   lay out 설계하다

321

Meetings of primitive and civilized cultures are events of extreme significance, with consequences of the deepest and subtlest import for both. Neither of them can be the same afterwards. The European, arrogantly aware of his differences from the primitive, tends to believe that the consequences are only for the primitive and that he in conscious superiority is free from them. But actually there is no one-way traffic on these eventful occasions. The meeting with the primitive in the world without stimulates the primitive within the civilized. The civilized may reject it with the most stubborn determination, but the process goes on regardless of it. What happens is that, because of his rejection, the primitive enters his life secretly by some back door of his spirit. Instead of it becoming a positive factor, it becomes a negative, vengeful and destructive one, because he denies it the welcome of his heart and the service of his mind.

Key Structure

2 **with consequences of ~** 그 결과 ~이 나타난다

3 **Neither of them can be ~ afterwards.** 둘 중 어느 것도 그 후에 똑같은 모습일 수가 없다.

4 **(as he is) arrogantly aware of ~** 거만하게 의식하고 있는[있어서]

6 **he in conscious superiority is ~** 의식적으로 우월성을 느끼는 그는 ~
   • in conscious superiority는 주어 he를 수식함.

6 **he ~ is free from them** 그는 그것들을 벗어나 있다(그는 그것들과는 관계없다)
   • them = the consequences

8 **the world without = the outside world** 외부에 있는 세계
   • 전치사 without이 world를 꾸미는 역할을 하여 형용사처럼 쓰임.

12 **Instead of it becoming ~** 그것이 ~이 되기는커녕
   • 동명사 구문. instead of 다음의 it이 동명사 becoming의 의미상의 주어.

14 **he denies it the welcome ~ mind**
   그는 가슴에서 나오는 환영과, 마음에서 나오는 봉사를 그것에 주기를 거부한다
   • deny는 4형식 동사(V+I.O.+D.O.)로 refuse의 뜻. / it = the meeting (with the primitive)

내용 원시문화와 개화된 문화의 만남은 양자에게 심오하고 섬세한 의미를 부여하는 사건이나, 유럽인은 그 만남을
진심으로 맞이할 준비가 되어 있지 않다.

subtle 미묘한, 섬세한 **import** 의미, 취지, 중요(성) **arrogantly** 거만하게, 무례하게 **superiority** 우월감 **one-way traffic** 일방통행 **stimulate** 자극하다 **regardless of** ~에 상관없이 **vengeful** 보복적인, 앙심 깊은

322 Science and technology have come to pervade every aspect of our lives and, as a result, society is changing at a speed which is quite unprecedented. There is a great technological explosion around us, generated by science. This explosion is already freeing vast numbers of people from their traditional bondage to nature, and now at last we have it in our power to free mankind once and for all from the fear which is based on want. Now, for the first time, man can reasonably begin to think that life can be something more than a grim struggle for survival. But even today, in spite of the high standard of living which has become general in the more fortunate West, the majority of people in the world still spend nearly all their time and energy in a never-ending struggle with nature to secure the food and shelter they need. Even in this elementary effort millions of human beings each year die unnecessarily and wastefully from hunger, disease, or flood.

Key Structure •

6　we have it in our power to free ~
　우리는 ~을 해방할 힘을 가지고 있다
　• it는 to free 이하를 가리키는 가목적어.

13　the food and shelter (that) they need
　그들이 필요로 하는 식량과 주택

> **내용** 과학과 기술의 발전이 우리 삶의 모든 면에 파고들어 사회가 전례 없는 속도로 변화하고 있다.

pervade 침투하다, 스며들다　**unprecedented** 선례가 없는　*cf.* **precede** 앞서 가다　**technological explosion** 기술의 폭발　**free A from B** A를 B에서 해방시키다　**bondage** 속박, 예속　**once (and) for all** 처음이자 마지막으로　**want** 부족, 결핍　**a grim struggle** 격투　**never-ending** 끊임없는　**secure** 확보하다　**unnecessarily** 불필요하게

323 In a society devoted wholly to labor, leisure would be thought of as merely rest or spare time; if there is continuous leisure, it becomes idleness or distraction. Idleness and distraction are reactions against the unpleasantness of labor: they make up for the time wasted on work by wasting time in other ways. A life divided only between dull work and distracted play is not life but essentially a mere waiting for death, and war comes to such a society as deliverance, because it relieves the strain of waiting. It is generally realized that idleness and distraction are very close to the kind of boredom that expresses itself in smashing things, and hence there is a widespread feeling, which is at least a century old, that mass education is needed simply to keep people out of mischief. This is not a very inspiring philosophy of education, nor one at all likely to effect its purposes.

Key Structure •

1　a society devoted wholly to labor
　　= a society that is wholly devoted to labor
　　전적으로 노동에 몰두하고 있는 사회

3　reactions against ~
　　~에 대한 반응

5　A life divided only between A and B
　　= A life composed only of A and B
　　A와 B로만 나뉘어진 삶. 즉 A와 B로만 구성된 삶

9　the kind of boredom that expresses itself in smashing things
　　= the kind of boredom that is expressed in smashing things
　　물건은 때려 부수는 것으로 표현되는 권태의 종류

10　there is a widespread feeling, ~, that...
　　~라는 널리 퍼진 정서가 있다(~라는 정서가 널리 퍼져 있다)

13　This is not ~ , nor one (that is) at all likely to...
　　~도 아니며 전혀 …할 것 같지도 않은 것 (one = a philosophy of education)

내용　비행을 저지르는 것을 막기 위해 대중 교육이 필요하다는 좋지 않은 교육 철학.

distraction 주의 산만, 기분 전환　　**make up for** ~을 보상하다(= atone for, compensate for)　　**dull** 재미없는 (= uninteresting)　　**deliverance** 해방, 구출　　**relieve** 경감하다　　**strain** 긴장　　**keep ~ out of mischief** ~을 비행에서 벗어나게 하다　　**inspiring** 고무적인, 영감을 불어넣는　　**effect** (목적을) 성취하다, 완수하다

324 The history of civilization shows how man always has to choose between making the right and wrong use of the discoveries of science. This has never been more true than in our own age. In a brief period amazing discoveries have been made and applied to
5 practical purposes. It has become common knowledge to say we are living in an age of revolution. It would be ungrateful not to recognize how great are the blessings which science has given to mankind. It has brought within the reach of multitudes benefits and advantages which only a short time ago were the privilege of
10 the few. It has shown how malnutrition, hunger and disease can be overcome. It has not only lengthened life but it has deepened its quality. Through the work of science the ordinary man today has been given the opportunity of a longer and fuller life than was ever possible to his grandparents.

Key Structure •

1   choose between making the right and wrong ~ science
    과학이 발견한 일들을 잘 이용하거나 잘못 이용하는 것 중 하나를 선택하다
    • make the right use of ~을 잘 이용하다
      make the wrong use of ~을 잘못 이용하다

3   This has never been ~ age.
    이것이 우리 시대보다 더 진실된 때는 없었다.

6   It would be ungrateful not to recognize ~
    ~을 인식하지 못한다면 배은망덕한 일이 될 것이다
    • not to recognize = if we did not recognize ~

8   It has brought within ~ multitudes
    그것은 다수의 사람들이 이용할 수 있게 하였다
    • brought의 목적어는 benefits 이하임.

13 a longer and fuller life than was ~ grandparents
    그의 조부모들에게 조금이라도 가능했던 것보다 더 길고 더 완벽한 삶
    • than은 주어로 쓰인 유사관계대명사.

내용   과학이 이룩한 발견을 잘 이용함으로써 인간의 삶이 더욱 나아지게 되었다.

blessing 축복   **multitudes** 다중(多衆)   **privilege** 특권, 특전   **the few** 소수의 사람들   **malnutrition** 영양실조
overcome 극복하다(= get over (from))   **lengthen** 늘이다   **deepen** 깊이 있게 하다

325 The wonderful material changes that have been wrought in modern life by science and the scientific method are liable to blind us to other great achievements of science, which if less material are none the less real and valuable. First among all the intellectual contributions of science to civilization stands the emancipation of man from various forms of bondage and superstition. Science has largely freed civilized man from slavery to environment. It has wellnigh annihilated time and space and has brought all nations into one neighborhood. It has levied tribute upon practically the whole earth to supply his wants. It has taught him how to utilize the great resources of nature, and to a large extent it has given into his hands the control of his destiny on this planet. It has made it possible to live in and exploit the whole earth. It is responsible for enormous increases of population and the size of social units.

Key Structure •

3 which ~ are none the less real and valuable
(그렇다고) 결코 덜 실질적이고 덜 가치가 있는 것은 아닌(마찬가지로 실질적이고 가치가 있는)

3 (even) if (they are) less material
덜 물질적이기는 하지만 (삽입구 역할)

4 First among ~ stands the emancipation of...
~ 중에서 …의 해방이 첫 번째로 꼽힌다
• 부사구가 문두로 도치된 구문으로 the emancipation ~가 주어, stands가 동사.

5 the emancipation of man from ~ superstition
인간을 여러 형태의 속박과 미신들로부터 해방시키는 것

11 it has given into ~ planet
그것은 이 지구상에서 인간이 갖는 운명을 제어하는 힘을 그의 손에 쥐어 주었다

12 It is responsible for ~
그것은 ~에도 책임이 있다(그것은 ~을 야기했다)

내용 과학이 우리의 현대 생활에 가져온 물질적인 변화 이외에도, 인간을 여러 가지 구속과 미신, 환경의 노예 상태에서 해방시킨 점을 간과해서는 안 된다.

be wrought(= be made) *cf.* (古) work-wrought-wrought   blind ~ to... ~가 …을 알지 못하게 하다
emancipation 해방(= liberation)   well-nigh 거의(= almost)   annihilate 말살하다   levy tribute on ~에게
조공을 부과하다   to a large extent 상당한 범위에 이르기까지   exploit 개발하다

326 The movements of peoples which are sufficiently dramatic for the ordinary historian to record, are often of less importance than the quiet, steady drift of a population from one area into another, as, for example, in the emigration from Europe to America in modern times. Movements of this kind may result in a noticeable or even fatal depletion of a country, and the parent country may long remain desolate, or may be filled up in the course of time by an alien people, as in the case of eastern Germany and the Slavs. Although immigrant peoples may bring a culture and language permanently affecting the conquered peoples, yet the aboriginal population, if allowed to survive in sufficient numbers, will eventually impair the racial purity of the new comers, and there is a tendency for the indigenous racial type to reassert itself and become predominant once more.

Key Structure •

1 The movements ~ are often of less importance than…
    ~한 이주는 …보다 종종 덜 중요하다
    • of less importance = less important

8 as in the case of eastern Germany and the Slavs
    동부 독일과 슬라브 국가들의 경우처럼

11 if allowed to survive = if it is allowed to survive

내용 한 지역에서 다른 지역으로 소리 없이 계속되는 이민이 더 중대한 결과를 가져오기도 한다.

drift 유입   **depletion** 고갈, 소모 ⓥ deplete 고갈시키다   **desolate** 황폐한, 버려진   **alien** 외국의, 외계의 **aboriginal** 토착의   **impair** 해치다(= damage)   **indigenous** 토착의, 고유의(= aboriginal)   **reassert oneself** 자신을 다시 내세우다   **predominant** 지배적인, 득세하는

327
We must conclude from the work of those who have studied the origin of life, that given a planet only approximately like our own, life is almost certain to start. Of all the planets in our own solar system we are now pretty certain the Earth is the only one on which
5 life can survive. Mars is too dry and poor in oxygen, Venus far too hot, and so is Mercury, and the outer planets have temperatures near absolute zero and hydrogen-dominated atmospheres. But other suns, stars as the astronomers call them, are bound to have planets like our own, and as the number of stars in the universe
10 is so vast, this possibility becomes virtual certainty. There are one hundred thousand million stars in our own Milky Way alone, and then there are three thousand million other Milky Ways, or Galaxies, in the universe. So the number of stars that we know exist is now estimated at about 300 million million million.

Key Structure

2 given a planet ~
= if a planet ~ is given
우리의 행성[지구]과 대략적으로만이라도 닮은 행성이 있다면

5 Venus (is) far too hot
금성은 너무나 뜨겁다

7 hydrogen-dominated atmospheres
수소가 가득한 공기

8 other suns, stars as ~ them
천문학자들이 별들이라고 부르는 다른 태양들
• stars는 other suns와 동격 명사.

내용 모든 행성 중에서 지구만이 생명체가 살 수 있는 곳이지만, 태양계에는 다른 별들도 많고 그 별들은 또 지구와 같은 행성을 가지고 있을 것이다.

approximately 대략   **solar system** 태양계   **pretty** 꽤, 상당히; 예쁜   **Mars** 화성 *cf.* Venus 금성, Mercury 수성   **absolute zero** 절대영도   **astronomer** 천문학자 *cf.* astrologer 점성가, astronaut 우주비행사   **be bound to** 틀림없이 ~하다(= be sure to)   **virtual certainty** 실질적인 필연성[확실성]   **Milky Way** 은하계 (= Galaxy)   **300 million million million** 3만 경(京)

328 To other Europeans the best known quality of the English is 'reserve.' A reserved person is one who does not talk very much to strangers, does not show much emotion and seldom gets excited. It is difficult to get to know a reserved person: he never tells you
5 anything about himself, and you may work with him for years without ever knowing where he lives, how many children he has, and what his interests are. English people tend to be like that. If they are making a journey by bus, they will do their best to find an empty seat. If they have to share the seat with a stranger, they may
10 travel many miles without starting a conversation. This reluctance to talk with others is an unfortunate quality in some ways, since it tends to give the impression of coldness, and it is true that the English are not noted for their generosity and hospitality. On the other hand, they are perfectly human behind their barrier
15 of reserve, and may be quite pleased when a friendly stranger or foreigner succeeds for a time in breaking the barrier down.

Key Structure •

5 you may work ~ lives
   수년간 그와 같이 일하면서도 그가 어디에 사는지 모르는 경우도 있다

10 This reluctance to talk with others
   다른 사람과 이야기하기를 꺼리는 이 경향

12 the English are not noted for ~ hospitality
   영국인은 관대함과 후한 대접으로 잘 알려져 있지는 않다

내용 영국인의 과묵한 성격과 그것이 남에게 주는 인상.

reserve 과묵, 침묵 *cf.* reserved 말이 없는, 내성적인 reluctance 꺼림 coldness 차가움, 냉정 noted for
~로 알려진 generosity 관대함 hospitality 후대, 환대 barrier 장벽 for a time 잠시나마 break down
부수다, 깨뜨리다

329 Civilization in America has been the result of three factors: the original introduction of Western European customs and institutions, the effect of the New World on the ways brought from the Old, the continuing influence of the Old World. Historians have given
5 considerable attention to the first of these factors, somewhat less to the second and very little to the third. Europe's continuing influence has generally been disposed of with an account of governmental relations or the foreign-born additions to the population. These subjects, however, leave out the most essential fact—that America
10 has shared all along in the principal changes of thought and accomplishment abroad. There can be no doubt that the presence of immigrants aided this; yet, had they stayed at home, United States history still would have been closely tied to world history. No people bound to Western culture could have escaped, if it had wished, the
15 current flowing in the older civilization.

Key Structure ▸

3 **the effect of ~ on the ways** (which were) **brought from the Old**
신세계가 구세계에서 가져온 삶의 방식에 끼친 영향 (the Old = the Old World)

5 (they have given) **somewhat less** (considerable attention) **to the second**
그들은 둘째 요소에 약간 덜한 주의를 기울여 왔다

6 **and** (they have given) **very little** (attention) **to the third**
그리고 셋째 요소에는 거의 주의를 기울이지 않았다

8 **the foreign-born additions to the population**
외국에서 태어난 사람들이 이민하여 인구가 늘어나는 것

9 **America has shared ~ abroad**
미국은 외국에서 이루어진 사상이나 업적의 주요한 변화를 줄곧 같이 해 왔다

12 had they stayed **at home** = (even) if they had stayed **at home**
그들이 모국에 머물러 있었다고 하더라도
 • home = the home country

14 if they had wished (to escape) 설령 그들이 (피하기를) 희망하였다고 하더라도

내용 미국의 문명을 형성한 것은 세 가지 요소인데, 흔히 가장 무시되고 있는 구세계의 영향력의 문제를 너무 도외시해서는 안 된다.

give attention to ~에 주의를 기울이다 **dispose of** 처리하다 **leave out** 제외하다, 무시하다(= rule out, omit) **share in** ~에 함께하다 **all along** 줄곧, 계속하여 **bound to** ~과 관련된 **the current flowing** 현재의 흐름

330 The solar system is not unique. It is unreasonable and unscientific to say that throughout the numberless celestial systems there are no other planets which support life in advanced form. The human mind, however, has found it difficult enough to get used to the idea
5 that we are not at the center of all things. Even after Copernicus discovered that the earth was not the center of the cosmos, we persisted in believing that the main purpose of the universe is to serve human life. Now we must make our peace with the fact that, though we may be superbly endowed as a species, we are not
10 unique. In a relative sense, life is still rare enough to console the most inflated earth-minded ego. But what is important about life is not that it may or may not be rare or unique. Life is precious because we can do things for the first time. We can create in ways we have never created before. Nothing about human life is more
15 precious than that we can define our own purpose and shape our own destiny.

Part **3** Advanced Reading

Key Structure ▸

3 **The human mind has found** it **difficult enough** to get **used ~**
인간 정신은 ~에 익숙해지는 것이 무척이나 어렵다는 것을 알아내었다
• it는 가목적어, to get 이하가 진목적어, difficult enough는 목적격보어임.

8 **we must make our peace with the fact that, ~**
우리는 ~라는 사실과 화해하여야 한다(~라는 사실을 인정하여야 한다)

13 **in ways** (that) **we have ~ before**
우리가 그 전에 창조해 보지 못한 방식으로
• that는 관계부사로, how를 대신 쓸 수는 없음.

내용 지구상의 생명체가 희귀한 존재이기는 하지만 우주에서 유일한 존재는 아니다. 인류는 지구만이 유일하다는 자기중심적인 자기도취에서 벗어나야 한다.

solar system 태양계   **celestial system** 천계, 하늘의 별자리계   **cosmos** 우주   **persist in** ~을 고집하다, 주장하다   **be endowed** (재능, 자질 등을) 부여받다   **superbly** 최고로, 웅장하게, 당당하게   **console** 위로하다, 달래다   **inflated** 부풀려진, 우쭐대는   **precious** 고귀한

331 With the Space Age, a new phrase came into use—space science, meaning basic scientific research in or directly related to space. In broad perspective, space science includes two major areas of research—exploration of the solar system and investigation of the universe. The first category includes the scientific investigation of our earth and its atmosphere, the moon and planets, and the interplanetary medium. The nature and behavior of the sun and its influence on the solar system, especially on the earth, are of prime importance. With the availability of space techniques, we are no longer limited, in direct observations, to a single body of the solar system; we may now send our instruments and men to explore and investigate other objects in the solar system. The possibility of comparing in detail the properties of the planets adds greatly to our power to investigate our own planet. Potentially far-reaching in its philosophical implications is the search for life on other planets.

Key Structure •

2 basic scientific research in or directly related to space
우주 안에서 이루어지거나 또는 우주와 직접 관련된 기초적인 과학적 탐구
• space는 전치사 in과 (related) to의 공통 목적어. (in space or directly related to space)

8 are of **prime** importance
더할 나위 없이 중요하다
• of importance = important (be+of+추상명사 = be+형용사)

9 With the availability of **space techniques**
= As **space techniques** are available

15 the search for life on other planets
다른 행성에 있을 수 있는 생명체에 대한 조사

내용 우주 시대의 도래와 더불어 태양계의 다른 행성에도 생명체가 있느냐에 대한 조사가 가능하게 되었고, 이것은 철학적 의미가 대단히 큰 일이다.

the Space Age 우주 시대   space science 우주 과학   perspective 관점, 조망   exploration 탐사
investigation 연구   category 범주, 영역   interplanetary 행성 간의   medium 매개체   availability 이용
가능성   be limited to ~에 국한되다   in detail 자세히   add to ~에 도움이 되다, 증가시키다   potentially
잠재적으로, 아마도   far-reaching 멀리 미치는   implication (함축된) 의미   life 생명체

Science is empirical, rational, general, and cumulative; and it is all four at once. Science is empirical in that all its conclusions are subject to test by sense experience. Observation is the base on which science rests, but scientific observation is more than keeping one's eyes open. It is observation, made by qualified observers under controlled conditions, of those things which confirm or disconfirm, verify or refute a theory. Sherlock Holmes could tell by the stains on a coat what a man had eaten for breakfast. From a number of such observations he arrived at a theory about why and how a particular crime was committed. This procedure is excellent for detection but insufficient for science, because it yields only knowledge of particular events. Science would go on to ask why and how crime, not a particular crime, is committed. Science uses facts to test general theories and general theories to make predictions about particular facts.

Key Structure

1 it is all four at once
그것은 4가지 속성을 한꺼번에 지닌다

2 in that all its conclusions are subject to test ~
그것[과학]의 모든 결론이 ~에 의해 시험 받아야 한다는 점에서
• in that ~ ~라는 점에서
• be subject to ~ ~의 적용을 받다, ~을 필요로 하다

14 and general theories to ~
= and science uses general theories to ~
그리고 과학은 특수한 사실에 대해 예측을 하기 위해 일반화된 이론들을 이용한다

내용 과학에는 관찰이 중요하고, 관찰은 하나의 이론이 옳은가 그른가를 확인해 주는 사실들에 대해 과학자들이 내리는 관찰이어야 한다.

empirical 경험적인   rational 합리적인   cumulative 누적하는, 축적되는   rest on ~에 기초하다, 놓여 있다
confirm 확인해 주다   verify 입증하다   refute 반박하다   stain 얼룩, 흠   crime 범죄   insufficient 불충분한
yield 산출하다(=produce)   prediction 예언, 예측

333   The debate about how to revive U.S. industry and its global competitiveness has been lively, centering around two related concepts: (1) free trade versus protectionism and (2) industrial policy. Protectionism consists of tariffs and import-export
5 restrictions favoring domestic industries over foreign competitors. Laissez-faire suggests that such restrictions are counterproductive, that the unrestricted market will encourage the most efficient production of goods and services. Support for the North American Free Trade Zone, encompassing Canada, the United States, and
10 Mexico, is grounded in this assertion. By contrast, proponents of protectionist policies contend that certain national interests (maintaining domestic production and control of vital industries, for example, or favoring the welfare of domestic workers over that of foreign workers) outweigh the benefits of a free market. Besides,
15 they contend, because of protectionist policies in other nations, no genuinely free market exists; to act as if it did is to leave one's own interests prey to others' manipulations.

Key Structure ▸

5   favoring domestic industries over foreign competitors
외국 경쟁자들보다 자국 산업체에게 혜택을 주는

13   favoring the welfare of ~ foreign workers
외국인 노동자와 자국 노동자의 복지에 혜택을 주는 것
• over that of foreign workers의 that = the welfare

16   to act as if it did = to act as if a genuinely free market existed
마치 그것이 존재하는 것처럼 행동하는 것은

16   leave one's own interests prey to ~
자기 자신의 이익을 ~의 희생물이 되게 하다
• 'leave(동사)+one's own interests(목적어)+prey(목적격보어)'의 5형식 구문.

내용   미국의 산업과 세계 경쟁력을 되살리기 위한 방편으로 활발히 토론이 된 자유무역과 보호무역의 내용과 그 지지자들의 주장.

revive 되살리다, 회생시키다   **center around** ~ 주위로 모이다   **free trade** 자유 무역   **versus** (경기, 소송의) 대(對)   **protectionism** 보호무역(주의)   **tariff** 관세   **favor** 편애하다, 편들다   **competitor** 경쟁자   **laissez-faire** (Fr.) 자유방임주의   **counterproductive** 반생산적인, 생산을 저하시키는   **encompass** 포괄하다   **assertion** 주장, 단언   **by contrast** 대조적으로   **proponent** 지지자   **contend** 주장하다   **outweigh** ~보다 더 중대하다   **genuinely** 진정으로(= really)   **prey** 희생물   **manipulation** 농간, 속임수

Rockets and artificial satellites can go far above the ionosphere, and even escape from the Earth. Yet they are complex and expensive, and in their present stage of development they cannot lift massive telescopes, keep them steady while the observations are being carried out, and then return them safely. Balloons are much easier to handle, and are also vastly cheaper. Their main limitation is that they are incapable of rising to the ionosphere. A height of between 80,000 and 90,000 feet is as much as can reasonably be expected, and so balloon-borne instruments can contribute little to either ultra-violet astronomy or X-ray astronomy. All the same, the balloon has much to be said in its favor, since it can at least carry heavy equipment above most of the atmospheric mass—thus eliminating blurring and unsteadiness of the images. Moreover, water-vapor and carbon dioxide in the lower air absorb most of the infra-red radiations sent to us from the planets. Balloon ascents overcome this hazard with ease.

Part 3 Advanced Reading

Key Structure ▸

8 is as much as can reasonably be expected
합당하게 기대할 수 있는 만큼이다

9 balloon-borne instruments
= instruments borne by balloons
풍선으로 운반되는 기구들

9 contribute little to either A or B
A나 B에 거의 기여하지 못하다

11 the balloon has much to be said in its favor
풍선에 관한 많은 호의적인 이야기를 할 수 있다(풍선은 좋은 점이 많다)

내용 우주 탐사에서 로켓, 인공위성과 풍선의 강·약점 비교.

artificial satellite 인공위성   **ionosphere** 이온층, 전리층   **ultra-violet** 자외선   **all the same** 그럼에도 불구하고   **equipment** 장비   **eliminate** 제거하다   **blurring** 희미해짐   **unsteadiness** 불안정한 상태   **water-vapor** 수증기   **carbon dioxide** 이산화탄소 *cf.* carbon monoxide 일산화탄소   **absorb** 흡수하다   **infra-red** 적외부(선)의   **hazard** 위험, 장애

335   How it came about that snakes manufactured poison is a mystery. Over the periods their saliva, a mild, digestive juice like our own, was converted into a poison that defies analysis even today. It was not forced upon them by the survival competition; they could have caught and lived on prey without using poison just as the thousands of non-poisonous snakes still do. Poison to a snake is merely a luxury; it enables it to get its food with very little effort, no more effort than one bite. And why only snakes? Cats, for instance, would be greatly helped; no running fights with large, fierce rats or tussles with grown rabbits—just a bite and no more effort needed. In fact, it would be an assistance to all the carnivorae—though it would be a two-edged weapon when they fought each other. But, of the vertebrates, unpredictable Nature selected only snakes (and one lizard). One wonders also why Nature with some snakes concocted poison of such extreme potency.

Key Structure

1   How it came about that ~ poison
뱀이 독을 만들어내는 것이 어떻게 가능한 일인가
• it은 가주어, that ~은 진주어.

3   It was not forced ~ competition
그것은 생존 경쟁에 의해 그들에게 강요된 것이 아니다

4   they could have caught and lived on prey
그들은 먹이를 잡아서 그것을 먹고살 수 있었을 것이다

8   Cats, for instance, would be greatly helped
예를 들어 고양이가 (독을 가지고 있다면) 크게 도움을 얻을 수 있을 것이다

14 why Nature ~ potency
= why Nature concocted poison of such extreme potency with some snakes

내용 뱀이 독을 어떻게 해서 갖게 되었는가 하는 것은 미스터리이다.

saliva 침, 타액   convert 변화시키다   defy 거부하다, 불허하다   live on ~을 먹고살다   running fights 연속되는 싸움   tussle with ~과 맞잡고 싸우기   carnivora 육식 동물 *pl.* carnivorae *cf.* herbivore 초식 동물   two-edged weapon 양날(= double-edged)의 무기   vertebrate 척추동물   concoct 꾸미다, (음모를) 꾀하다   potency 힘, 능력

336 Given two countries with equal natural resources, one a dictatorship and the other allowing individual liberty, the one allowing liberty is almost certain to become superior to the other in war technique in no very long time. As we have seen in Germany and Russia, freedom in scientific research is incompatible with dictatorship. Germany might well have won the war if Hitler could have endured Jewish physicists. Russia will have less grain than if Stalin had not insisted upon the adoption of Lysenko's theories. It is highly probable that there will soon be, in Russia, a similar governmental incursion into the domain of nuclear physics. I do not doubt that, if there is no war during the next fifteen years, Russian scientific war technique will, at the end of that time, be very markedly inferior to that of the West, and that the inferiority will be directly traceable to dictatorship. I think, therefore, that, so long as powerful democracies exist, democracy will in the long run be victorious.

Part

3

Advanced Reading

Key Structure •

1 Given two countries ~
   = If there are given two countries ~
   = If two countries ~ resources are given
   똑같은 천연자원을 가진 두 나라가 있을 때

6 Germany might well have won the war
   독일은 전쟁에 당연히 이겼을지도 모른다 (might well 당연히 ~하다)

7 Russia will have less grain than if ~ theories.
   스탈린이 리센코의 학설을 채택하도록 강요하지 않았더라면 얻었을 수도 있는 식량의 양보다도 덜 식량을 얻게 될 것이다.
   • than과 if 사이에 Russia would have had를 넣어 생각할 것.

12 be very markedly inferior to that of the West
   서구의 그것(과학을 이용한 전쟁 수행 기술)에 비해 현저하게 열등하다
   • that = scientific war technique

내용 독재 정권과 민주 정권 중 민주 정권이 훨씬(특히 전쟁 수행 기술에서) 우월하다.

natural resources 천연자원   dictatorship 독재 국가   be superior to ~보다 우월하다(≒ be inferior to)   in no very long time 얼마 못 가서   be incompatible with ~과 양립하지 못하다(= be not in harmony with) incursion 침입(= invasion)   markedly 현저하게   traceable 더듬어 찾을 수 있는, ~에 기인하는
cf. Lysenko 리센코 (1898~1976, 러시아(구 소련)의 유전학자. '체세포의 변화는 유전 인자를 변화시킨다'는 이론을 체계화함)

367

337   Until recently, many archaeologists took the view that civilized communities first arose in Egypt, though only a very short time before a similar development in Mesopotamia; a more recent opinion is now that the earliest advances may have taken place in Mesopotamia. Whichever view is followed, it is necessary to bear in mind that geographical conditions in both regions were not identical, and it can in fact be stated that in Mesopotamia environmental factors were not as wholly favorable as in the valley of the Nile. The Nile is a single stream, without tributaries in its lower course; but the Tigris and Euphrates are both braided streams, and the former receives important affluents which bring down immense masses of silt that block the lower courses of both rivers, giving rise to swamps, lagoons, shifting banks and coastlines. Moreover, the floods of Mesopotamia are more variable, since they depend on rainfall that occurs within the Middle East area, and this tends to be capricious and unreliable.

Key Structure ▸

2 though (it is) only a very short time before ~
그것이 ~보다 바로 전이기는 하지만

5 Whichever view is followed
= Whichever view we follow
어떤 견해를 따르든

7 in Mesopotamia environmental factors were not as wholly ~
메소포타미아 지역의 환경 요소들은 나일 강 계곡만큼 전적으로 호의적인 것은 아니었다 (부분 부정)

12 giving rise to ~
= and gives rise to ~
그래서 ~을 만들어 낸다

내용 세계 문명의 발상지인 이집트와 메소포타미아 지방의 환경은 달랐다.

archaeologist 고고학자   bear in mind 명심하다   identical 동일한   favorable 호의적인   tributary 지류(支流)   lower course 하류   braided stream 여러 갈래의 지류가 얽힌 강   affluent 지류(= tributary) silt 미사(微砂)(물에 운반되어 침적된 모래 등)   swamp 습지, 늪지대   lagoon 작은 늪   shifting 변화하는 capricious 변덕스러운   unreliable 믿지 못할

338 A person who is called upon to act is more likely to act fortunately if he has previously meditated upon actions of a similar kind. If we wish to play an effective part as members of a community, we must avoid two opposed dangers. On the one hand there is the danger of rushing into action without thinking about what we are doing, or—which in practice comes to the same thing—by taking it for granted that it is 'all right' to do as others do, although we don't in the least know why they act thus. On the other hand, there is the danger of indulging in an academic detachment from life. This is the peculiar temptation of those who are inclined to see both sides of a question and are content to enjoy an argument for its own sake. But thinking is primarily for the sake of action. No one can avoid the responsibility of acting in accordance with his mode of thinking. No one can act wisely who has never paused to think about how he is going to act and why he decides to act as he does.

Key Structure

1 **A person who is called upon to act**
행동하도록 요청을 받은 사람은
• call upon ~ to... ~에게 …하도록 요청하다

6 **which in practice comes to the same thing**
실제로는 같은 이야기가 되지만
• which는 by taking 이하를 가리키는 관계대명사.

6 **by taking it for granted that ~**
~를 당연한 일로 받아들임으로써

7 **we don't in the least know**
우리는 전혀 모른다 (전체 부정)

9 **indulging in an academic detachment from life**
생활과 동떨어져 학문에 몰입하는 것

13 **No one can act wisely who ~**
~해 보지 않은 사람은 누구도 현명하게 행동할 수 없다
• who 이하는 No one을 선행사로 하는 관계대명사절.

내용 누구든 자신의 행동의 결과에 대한 책임을 벗어날 수 없으므로 심사숙고한 후에 행동을 해야 한다.

meditate upon 숙고하다   **indulge in** ~에 빠지다[몰입하다]   **detachment** 초연, 무관심   **temptation** 유혹
be inclined to ~하는 성향이 있다   **for the sake of** ~를 위하여   **in accordance with** ~에 따라서

339

Does history give us any information about our own prospects? And, if it does, what is the burden of it? Does it spell out for us an inexorable doom, which we can merely await with folded hands— resigning ourselves, as best we may, to a fate that we cannot avert or even modify by our own efforts? Or does it inform us, not of certainties, but of probabilities, or bare possibilities, in our own future? The practical difference is vast, for, on this second alternative, so far from being stunned into passivity, we should be roused to action. On this second alternative, the lesson of history would not be like an astrologer's horoscope; it would be like a navigator's chart, which affords the seafarer who has the intelligence to use it a much greater hope of avoiding shipwreck than when he was sailing blind, because it gives him the means, if he has the skill and courage to use them, of steering a course between charted rocks and reefs.

Key Structure ●

2 **if it does** = if it gives us information about our own prospects
만약에 그렇다면 (do(es)는 대동사)

4 **resign ourselves to a fate** ~ 우리 자신을 ~ 운명에 맡기다

4 **as best we may** 될 수 있는 한, 그럭저럭

5 **inform us, not of A, but of B** 우리에게 A가 아닌 B를 알려 주다

8 **be stunned into passivity** 정신이 멍해져서 수동적이 되다

9 **be roused to action** 행동에 나서다

9 **On this second alternative**
• On this second alternative는 Or does it inform us ~ future?의 내용을 가리킴.
첫째의 alternative는 Does it spell out ~ efforts?를 받음.

11 **which affords A B** A에게 B를 제공하다
• 여기에서 A는 the seafarer ~ it, B는 a much greater ~ shipwreck임.

내용 역사가 우리의 길을 알려 준다면 그 부담에는 두 가지 방도가 있을 수 있는데, 두 번째 방도에서 역사의 교훈은 우리가 해도를 갖고서 항해하는 능숙한 항해자가 되어야 한다는 점이다.

spell out 한 자 한 자 쓰다, 자세하게 설명하다   **inexorable** 냉혹한, 가차 없는(= relentless)   **await** 기다리다(= wait for)   **with folded hands** 깍지 낀 손으로   **avert** 피하다, 막다(= prevent)   **modify** 수정하다, 개조하다   **alternative** 방도, 대안(= choice)   **stun** 쳐서 기절시키다, 얼이 빠지게 하다   **astrologer** 점성가   **horoscope** (점성용) 천궁도, 12궁도   **navigator** 항해자   **chart** 해도(海圖)   **seafarer** 항해자(= sailor, navigator)   **shipwreck** 난파   **sail blind** 맹목적으로 (해도(海圖) 없이) 항해하다   **steer** 키를 잡다, 조종하다

340 This question of ends and means is of great ethical importance. The difference between a civilized man and a savage, between an adult and a child, between a man and an animal, consists largely in a difference as to the weight attached to ends and means in conduct. A civilized man insures his life, a savage does not; an adult brushes his teeth to prevent decay, a child does not except under compulsion; men labor in the fields to provide food for the winter, animals do not. Forethought, which involves doing unpleasant things now for the sake of pleasant things in the future, is one of the most essential marks of mental development. Since forethought is difficult and requires control of impulse, moralists stress its necessity, and lay more emphasis on the virtue of present sacrifice than on the pleasantness of the subsequent reward. You must do right because it is right, and not because it is the way to get to heaven. You must save because all sensible people do, and not because you will ultimately secure an income that will enable you to enjoy life.

Key Structure

1 This question of ~ importance.
목적과 수단의 이 문제는 윤리적으로 매우 중요하다.
• be of great importance = be greatly important

4 a difference as to ~
~에 관한 차이
• as to = concerning ~에 관한

4 the weight (which is) attached to ~ conduct
행동의 목적과 수단에 가해진 무게[중요도]

6 except under compulsion
강요를 받는 경우가 아니라면(강요를 받지 않으면)

12 lay more emphasis on A than on B
B보다는 A를 더 강조하다

내용 문명인은 미래의 기쁨을 위해서 현재의 고통을 감내한다.

ethical 윤리적인 consist largely in 주로 ~에 달려 있다 insure 보험에 들다 compulsion 강요 ⓥ compel
forethought 선견, (장래에 대한) 깊은 생각 impulse 충동(심) lay emphasis on 강조하다(= emphasize)
subsequent 뒤이은 reward 보상 heaven 천국 ultimately 궁극적으로

341 The atom bomb, and still more the hydrogen bomb, have caused new fears, involving new doubts as to the effects of science on human life. Some eminent authorities, including Einstein, have pointed out that there is a danger of the extinction of all life on this planet. I do not myself think that this will happen in the next war, but I think it may well happen in the next but one, if that is allowed to occur. If this expectation is correct, we have to choose, within the next fifty years or so, between two alternatives. Either we must allow the human race to exterminate itself, or we must forgo certain liberties which are very dear to us, more especially the liberty to kill foreigners whenever we feel so disposed. I think it probable that mankind will choose its own extermination as the preferable alternative. The choice will be made, of course, by persuading ourselves that it is not being made, since (so militarists on both sides will say) the victory of the right is certain without risk of universal disaster. We are perhaps living in the last age of man, and, if so, it is to science that he will owe his extinction.

Key Structure

1   still more the hydrogen bomb
    더더욱 수소 폭탄은

6   it may well happen in the next but one
    그것은 다다음 전쟁에서 당연히 일어날 것이다 (but = except)

11 whenever we feel so disposed
    우리에게 그러한 마음이 내키면 언제나

15 the victory of the right
    정의의 승리

17 it is to science that he will owe his extinction
    인류가 망한다면 그것은 과학 때문이다
    • it is ~ that 강조 구문, to science를 강조.
    • owe A to B A를 B에 힘입다, A는 B 때문이다

내용 원자 폭탄, 수소 폭탄 등 과학의 발전이 인간의 생존에 위협을 가하게 되었다.

the atom bomb 원자 폭탄   the hydrogen bomb 수소 폭탄   authority 권위자   extinction 말살
ⓥ extinguish ⓐ extinct   may well ~하는 것도 당연하다   alternative 선택의 방도(= choice), 대안
exterminate 전멸시키다, 몰살하다   forgo 삼가다, 그만두다(= do without)   universal disaster 인류 전체의 재앙

342 At first Man is hardly conscious of the wonders of nature, for he is absorbed in getting the means of existence, in procuring food for himself and his children. In primitive painting you will find a tree represented merely by a bough on which an animal is feeding. Man
5 hunts the animal, and does not notice the tree, except as a sort of accessory to the animal which absorbs his interest. And even now, in civilized countries, how few people look at the beautiful things which surround them for their own sake! The farmer looks at the bare fields and sees the crops which he has sown already rising
10 and bringing him his harvest. The builder looks at the fields and sees the houses he wants to build there. The climber looks at the mountains and thinks of the way by which he will ascend and conquer them. The miner looks at the mountains and thinks of the riches they hide in their rocks and how he will extract them. It is
15 only the artist who sees the fields and the trees and the mountains as they are, for their own sake.

Key Structure

4 a bough on which an animal is feeding
동물이 먹이를 따먹고 있는 나뭇가지

5 except as ~
〜으로서가 아니면

5 a sort of accessory to ~ interest
자신의 흥미를 끄는 동물의 한 부속품

13 the riches (which) they hide in their rocks
산들이 그 바위 속에 숨기고 있는 부[재산]
• they = the mountains

14 It is only the artist who ~
단지 예술가만이 〜한다
• It is ~ who(= that) 강조 구문.

16 ~ as they are, for their own sake
〜을 그 자체만을 위하여 있는 모습 그대로

내용 자연의 사물들을 사물 그대로 보는 사람은 극히 적고, 단지 예술가만이 있는 그대로 볼 뿐이다.

be conscious of 〜을 의식하다(= be aware of)   **be absorbed in** 〜에 열중하다   **procure** 확보하다, 획득하다
bough 나뭇가지   **feed on** 〜을 먹고 살다   **accessory to** 〜에 대한 부속품   **crop** 작물, 수확   **sow** (씨를)
뿌리다(sow-sowed-sown)   **harvest** 수확(물)   **extract** 캐내다, 추출하다

343   The belief in a supernatural agency which ordains everything has led to a certain irresponsibility on the social plane, and emotion and sentimentality have taken the place of reasoned thought and inquiry. Religion, though it has undoubtedly brought comfort to innumerable human beings and stabilized society by its values, has checked the tendency to change and progress inherent in human society. As knowledge advances, the domain of religion, in the narrow sense of the word, shrinks. The more we understand life and nature, the less we look for supernatural causes. Whatever we can understand and control ceases to be a mystery. The processes of agriculture, the food we eat, the clothes we wear, our social relations, were all at one time under the dominion of religion and its high priests. Gradually they have passed out of its control and become subjects for scientific study.

Key Structure •

4   Religion, ~ , has checked the tendency to ~
종교는 ~할 경향을 저지해 왔다

7   in the narrow sense of the word
그 단어가 갖는 좁은 의미에서
• the word는 knowledge를 지칭.

9   Whatever we can ~ mystery.
우리가 이해하고 통제하는 모든 것은 더 이상 신비스러운 것이 되지 못한다.
• cease to ~하는 것을 중단하다, ~이 되지 못하다

13 Gradually they have passed ~ scientific study.
서서히 그것들은 종교의 통제에서 벗어나 과학적 연구의 대상이 되었다.

내용   인간의 지식이 발달될수록 종교의 영역은 축소된다.

supernatural agency 초자연적인 힘   ordain 운명을 정하다   sentimentality 감상벽, 감상적인 태도   take the place of ~를 대신하다(=replace)   innumerable 무수한   stabilize 안정시키다   check 저지하다   inherent in ~에 내재하는[본질적인]   domain 영역   shrink 줄어들다   dominion 지배권, 영토   pass out of its control (~의) 통제에서 벗어나다   subject for ~의 대상[주제]

344 The subject of education is one of the most difficult that any reformer has to consider. It might seem at first sight as though education afforded the key to social improvement, since undoubtedly better education would make all other reforms easy. But in fact most of the evils of existing education are direct consequences of the other evils from which industrial civilization is suffering, and cannot be radically cured until our economic system has been changed. Nevertheless something can be done, through public opinion among teachers, and to a lesser extent among parents, to make education less harmful in the meantime. There is not any one key position to be captured by those who aim at a less competitive and unjust organization of society; there are a number of connected positions to be attacked simultaneously, since any advance in one place brings with it correlated advances in all the others. In this chapter, we are concerned, not with education in Utopia, but with what can be done here and now to prevent the grosser evils of education as it is at present. I propose to confine myself in the main to elementary education, since that alone can be considered as one of those mass phenomena with which this book is concerned.

Key Structure •

1 one of the most difficult (subjects)

2 It might seem at first sight as though education afforded ~
언뜻 보기에는 마치 ~일지 모른다
• as though[if] ~의 가정법 구문이므로, 과거형 afforded가 온 것임.

8 something can be done, ~, to make... …로 만들기 위해 무엇인가를 할 수 있다

8 though public opinion among A, and to a lesser extent among B
A 사이의 여론, 그리고 조금 적게는 B의 여론을 통하여

10 capture[attack] the position ~ ~한 입장을 취하다

13 any advance in one place brings with it correlated advances in all the others
한 분야의 진보는 그것[진보]과 더불어 다른 분야들의 관련된 진보를 가져온다

16 education as it is at present 현재 모습으로서의 교육

내용 교육은 개혁가가 고려해야 할 가장 어려운 문제 중의 하나이며 현 교육의 폐해는 다른 사회적 폐해의 결과이다.

reformer 개혁가   at first sight 언뜻 보기에   nevertheless 그럼에도 불구하고   to a lesser extent 조금 적게는
in the meantime 그 사이에   correlated 상호 연관된   gross 커다란   phenomenon 현상 *pl.* phenomena

345 Universities have by tradition aimed at providing a liberal education in depth. Specialized study is thought necessary in order that graduates may know enough on leaving the university to take up posts in the professions, in the public services, and in industry and
5 commerce. They need to be experts, and the vastness of modern knowledge prevents them from being experts in more than one or two subjects. Again, the intensive study of a limited field is believed to be the best way, some would say the only way, of training the mind. But specialization should come only after some acquaintance
10 with what a philosopher has called 'the system of vital ideas which every age possesses and by which it lives,' a sense at least of the whole range of human achievement. The greater the need of specialization, the greater the need to give it a solid basis of general culture. And only with experience of different subjects can anyone
15 make an intelligent choice of specialization in the first place, let alone be able to see his subjects in any kind of perspective.

Key Structure •

3 **on leaving the university** = when they leave the university
그들이 대학을 졸업할 때

5 **the vastness of modern knowledge ~ two subjects**
요사이 알아야 할 것이 너무 많아서 그들은 한 두 과목 이상에서 전문가가 되기 어렵다

8 **some would say the only way, ~**
어떤 사람들은 유일한 방법이라고 말하기도 한다
• the best way와 the only way가 of training the mind에 공통으로 연결됨.

11 **a sense at least ~**
• sense는 앞의 acquaintance를 지칭한다고 볼 수 있음.

12 **The greater the need ~, the greater the need to give ~ culture.**
전문화의 필요성이 크면 클수록 그것에다 일반교양의 견고한 기초를 줄 필요성은 더욱 더 커진다.

15 **let alone be able to ~**
~할 수 있는 점은 두말할 필요도 없다

내용 대학 교육은 일반교양 교육과 전공 교육으로 구성되어 있으나, 전공 교육은 일반교양 교육을 튼튼히 하고 난 후에 이루어져야 한다.

liberal education (일반)교양 교육   **in depth** 깊이 있게   **specialized study** 전공, 전문적인 연구(= specialization)   **public service** 공공 업무, 공직, 관공서의 직   **vastness** 광대함   **vital** 중요한, 필수적인   **range** 범위   **solid** 튼튼한, 굳건한(= sound)   **general culture** 일반교양   **perspective** 관점, 균형 감각

346

A conflict between the generations—between youth and age—seems the most stupid of all conflicts, for it is one between oneself as one is and oneself as one will be, or between oneself as one was and oneself as one is. Everyone in the course of life is young, and everyone who survives long enough becomes old. And it is the same person who is both—the same soul, the same mind and the same heart. So if any kind of conflict can properly be described as suicidal, it is this. Persisted in, it would make the continuance of human society impossible. The old must place their wisdom and experience at the service of the young, yet allow the vitality, energy and enthusiasm of youth freedom of scope, while the young must respect and honor the achievements and practical sense of their elders and place their physical strength and vigor, while they still possess them, at the service of the continuing community. Both, for their mutual benefit, must be tolerant of one another and of the frailties that are common to all.

Key Structure

2 it is one between ~
• one = a conflict

2 oneself as one is / will be / was 현재 / 미래 / 과거 모습으로서의 자신

5 it is the same person who is both
젊기도 하고 늙기도 한 동일한 인물이다 (both = young and old)

8 Persisted in
= If it were persisted in 그것을 고집한다면

9 place A at the service of B B를 위하여 A를 사용하다

10 allow the vitality, ~ youth freedom of scope
젊은이의 활력, 정력, 열정이 잘 발휘되도록 자유롭게 해 주다
• 'allow+간접목적어+직접목적어' 구문: 간접목적어는 the vitality ~ youth, 직접목적어는 freedom of scope.

14 Both, ~, must be tolerant ~
• Both = the young and the old

내용 젊은이와 늙은이 사이의 갈등은 자살행위이고, 상호 간의 이득을 위해 서로 참아야 한다.

conflict 갈등   survive 살아남다   suicidal 자살행위의   vitality 활력   cf. vigor 활기   enthusiasm 열정
mutual 상호 간의, 공통의   be tolerant of ~을 참아 내다   frailty 약함, 결점

377

347

Those who aim at any radical reform of our social system are faced by the difficulty that the existing system is advantageous to the holders of power, and is therefore difficult to change. It is not easy to see how power is to be wrested from those who now possess it, unless by a struggle so terrible as to destroy our whole civilization. The apparent hopelessness of this problem causes many to acquiesce in present evils in spite of keen consciousness of their magnitude, while it leads others to a recklessly revolutionary attitude which estranges those who have a sense of social responsibility. I believe that the problem is by no means as insoluble as it is thought to be. Power, even the most monarchical, requires a popular basis, either in the general opinion of some large group or in its traditions and habits. Traditions and habits, strong as they are, are diminishing forces in our kaleidoscopic world. Thus opinion becomes the decisive factor in determining who is to hold power in the future.

Key Structure

5 unless (it is) by a struggle ~ 그것이 ~한 투쟁에 의한 것이 아니라면

5 a struggle so terrible as to destroy ~ civilization
우리의 전 문명을 파괴할 만큼 무서운 투쟁

6 causes many (people) to acquiesce in ~ 많은 사람들로 하여금 ~을 묵인하게끔 만든다

10 be by no means as ~ as... …만큼 결코 ~은 아니다

13 Traditions and habits, strong as they are, ~
= Traditions and habits, though they are strong, ~
전통과 습관은 그것들이 강력한 것이라고 해도

16 Who is to hold power in the future
누가 장래에 권력을 쥐어야 하느냐
• is to = should

내용 사회 제도는 권력을 지닌 자에게 유리하기 때문에 그것을 개혁하는 것이 매우 어렵지만 생각처럼 불가능한 것은
아니다.

radical 급진적인   be faced by ~에 직면하다   holders of power 권력을 쥔 자들   wrest 억지로 얻어내다
hopelessness 절망적인 상태   acquiesce in ~를 묵인하다   magnitude 방대함   recklessly 무모하게
estrange 떼어놓다. 소원하게 하다   insoluble 해결할 수 없는   monarchical 군주(제)의   kaleidoscopic
변화무상한   decisive 결정적인

348 However unjustly society is organized, certain technological advances are bound to benefit the whole community, because certain kinds of goods are necessarily held in common. A millionaire cannot, for example, light the streets for himself while darkening them for other people. Nearly all citizens of civilized countries now enjoy the use of good roads, germ-free water, police protection, free libraries and probably free education of a kind. Public education in England has been meanly starved of money, but it has nevertheless improved, largely owing to the devoted efforts of the teachers, and the habit of reading has become enormously more widespread. To an increasing extent the rich and the poor read the same books, and they also see the same films and listen to the same radio programes. And the differences in their way of life have been diminished by the mass production of cheap clothes and improvements in housing. So far as the outward appearance goes, the clothes of rich and poor, especially in the case of women, differ far less than they did thirty or even fifteen years ago.

Key Structure •

1 certain technological advances are bound to benefit the whole community
몇몇 기술적인 진보는 전 지역 사회(의 구성원)에 이득을 줄 수밖에 없다

15 So far as the outward appearance goes
외적 모습[외모]에 관해 말하자면

16 the clothes of rich and poor
부자나 가난한 자들의 의복
• rich and poor = the rich and the poor 대구를 이룬 말의 경우 관사(the)가 생략되기도 함.

17 far less than they did ~
30년 전 혹은 15년 전에 그랬던 것보다 차이가 훨씬 덜하다
• they = the clothes of rich and poor
  did = differed

내용 기술의 진보는 부자나 가난한 자들에게 똑같이 혜택을 준다.

unjustly 부당하게 be bound to 틀림없이 ~하다(= be sure to) be held in common 공통으로 소유되다, 모두 가지고 있다 germ-free 세균이 없는 free education 무상 교육 be starved of ~에 굶주리다 diminish 줄이다, 축소하다 mass production 대량 생산 outward appearance 외모, 외적 모습

349 Democracy is, among other things, the ability to say 'no' to the boss. But a man cannot say 'no' to the boss, unless he is sure of being able to eat when the boss's favor has been withdrawn. And he cannot be certain of his next meal unless he owns the means of producing enough wealth for his family to live on, or has been able to accumulate a surplus out of past wages, or has a chance of moving to virgin territories, where he can make a fresh start. In an overcrowded country, very few people own enough to make them financially independent; very few are in a position to accumulate purchasing power; and there is no free land. Moreover, in any country where population presses hard upon natural resources, the general economic situation is apt to be so precarious that government control of capital and labor, production and consumption, becomes inevitable. It is no accident that the twentieth century should be the century of highly centralized governments and totalitarian dictatorships; it had to be so for the simple reason that the twentieth century is the century of planetary overcrowding.

Key Structure •

2 unless he is sure of ~ = if he is not sure of ~
   만약 ~에 대한 확신이 없다면

4 unless he owns ~ = if he does not own ~
   만약에 그가 ~을 가지고 있지 않다면

8 very few people own enough to ~
   ~할 만큼 충분히 소유한 사람들은 거의 없다
   • enough는 own의 목적어로 쓰인 명사로서 enough money로 보면 됨.

11 country where population ~ resources
   인구가 천연자원에 심한 압박을 가하는 국가(천연자원보다 인구가 훨씬 많은 국가)

14 It is no accident that ~   ~이 우연은 아니다

내용 민주주의란 직장 상사에게 '아니오'라는 말을 할 수 있는 능력인데, 자신의 생계에 자신이 없는 경우 그것은 불가능한 일이다.

among other things 무엇보다도, 우선   **surplus** 잉여   **virgin territory** 새로운 영역   **purchasing power** 구매력   **press hard upon** ~에 심히 압박을 가하다   **precarious** 불확실한(= uncertain)   **centralized government** 중앙집권화된 국가   **totalitarian dictatorship** 전체주의 독재 국가   **planetary overcrowding** 지구 전체의 인구 과잉

350 The Freudian psychology is the only systematic account of the human mind which, in point of subtlety and complexity, of interest and tragic power, deserves to stand beside the chaotic mass of psychological insights which literature has accumulated
5 through the centuries. To pass from the reading of a great literary work to a treatise of academic psychology is to pass from one order of perception to another, but the human nature of the Freudian psychology is exactly the stuff upon which the poet has always exercised his art. It is therefore not surprising that the
10 psychoanalytical theory has had a great effect upon literature. Yet the relationship is reciprocal, and the effect of Freud upon literature has been no greater than the effect of literature upon Freud. When, on the occasion of the celebration of his seventieth birthday, Freud was greeted as the 'discoverer of the unconscious,' he corrected the
15 speaker and disclaimed the title. "The poets and philosophers before me discovered the unconscious," he said. "What I discovered was the scientific method by which the unconscious can be studied."

Key Structure •

3 **deserves to stand beside ~**
~과 견줄 만하다

3 **the chaotic mass ~ the centuries**
문학이 수세기 동안 축적해 온 혼란스러운 대부분의 심리 통찰

5 **To pass from A to B**
A를 읽다가 B로 넘어가는 것

8 **the stuff upon which the poet has always ~ art**
시인이 늘 자신의 예술성을 훈련하던 재료

11 **the effect of Freud ~ no greater than ~**
프로이트가 문학에 끼친 영향력은 문학이 프로이트에 끼친 영향력과 거의 같다

13 **Freud was greeted as the 'discoverer of the unconscious'**
프로이트는 무의식 세계의 발견자로 환영받았다

내용 프로이트 심리학은 인간 정신을 체계 있게 설명한 유일한 이론으로 문학에 많은 영향을 미쳤으며 또한 많은 영향을 받았다.

account 설명   **subtlety** 섬세함, 예리한 인식   **deserve** ~할 자격이 있다   **chaotic** 혼돈의   **treatise** 논문
on the occasion of ~에 즈음하여   **correct** 정정하다   **disclaim** 부인하다, 포기하다
cf. Freud, Sigmund 지그문트 프로이트 (1856-1939, 정신분석학의 대가인 오스트리아의 의학자)

351

Analysts of the political attitudes and knowledge of Americans sometimes characterize the public as consisting of four groups: chronic know-nothings, the general public, the attentive public, and the opinion leaders and policymakers. Estimates of the sizes of these groups vary. For example, one analyst estimates the chronic know-nothings at 20 percent of the public, whereas another pegs them at only 4 percent. The size of the general public is also hard to gauge; it seems to vary according to the issue involved. Unlike the know-nothings, who never become informed or involved, the general public has some information and can sometimes be stirred to political action. At the next highest level of political involvement is the attentive public, estimated at 15 to 20 percent of the population. The attentive public seeks information, develops opinions, and can have a significant impact on policymaking. The size of the attentive public grows as a particular issue develops and becomes dramatized. Beyond the attentive public are the people who shape opinions and policies the most. This group consists primarily of leaders in politics and the media.

Key Structure ▶

1 Analysts ~ characterize the public as... 정세 분석가들은 대중을 …로 특징짓는다

4 Estimates of the sizes ~ vary. 이 그룹들의 크기에 대한 추정치는 차이가 난다.

6 another (analyst) pegs them at only 4 percent
다른 정세 분석가는 그들을 단지 4%로 못박는대[추정한다]

10 be stirred to political action (자극되어) 정치 활동에 나서다

16 Beyond the attentive public are the people ~
이 주의력 깊은 대중 너머에[위에] ~한 사람들이 있다 (the people ~이 주어)

16 the people who shape ~ the most
여론과 정책들을 가장 크게 형성하는 사람들

내용 정치적 태도와 지식에 따라 분류되는 미국 국민의 네 가지 부류.

analyst 분석가, 평론가 characterize 특징짓다 chronic 만성적인 cf. chronic disease 만성병, acute disease 급성병 know-nothing 아무것도 모르는 자, 문맹자 opinion leader 여론지도층 policymaker 정책결정자 vary 다르다, 변화하다 peg 못을 박다, 평가하다 gauge 측정하다, 재다 stir 휘젓다 impact 영향(력) dramatize 극화하다, 생생하게 하다 the media 언론 매체

352 The comparatively sudden change from foetal into human existence and the cutting off of the umbilical cord mark the independence of the infant from the mother's body. But this independence is only real in the crude sense of the separation of the two bodies. In a functional sense, the infant remains part of the mother. It is fed, carried, and taken care of in every vital respect by the mother. Slowly the child comes to regard the mother and other objects as entities apart from itself. One factor in this process is the neurological and the general physical development of the child, its ability to grasp objects—physically and mentally—and to master them. Through its own activity it experiences a world outside of itself. The process of individuation is furthered by that of education. This process entails a number of frustrations and prohibitions, which change the role of the mother into that of a person with different aims which conflict with the child's wishes, and often into that of a hostile and dangerous person. This antagonism, which is one part of the educational process though by no means the whole, is an important factor in sharpening the distinction between the "I" and the "thou."

Key Structure ▸

2 **the cutting off of the umbilical cord**
신생아의 몸에서 탯줄을 자르는 것

12 **is furthered by that of education**
교육 과정에 의해 촉진된
• that = the process

17 **though (it is) by no means the whole**
결코 전체는 아니라고 해도
• the whole = the whole of the educational process

내용 출생은 육체적으로는 엄마에게서 독립하는 것이지만 기능적으로는 아직 엄마의 일부이다.

foetal 태아(상태)의(= fetal) **umbilical cord** 탯줄 **crude** 개략적인, 조잡한 **entity** 실재물 **neurological** 신경(학)의 **grasp** 움켜쥐다, 이해하다 **individuation** 사람되기 **further** 조성하다, 촉진하다 **entail** (필연적으로) 수반하다 **frustration** 욕구 불만 **prohibition** 금지 **conflict with** ~과 갈등을 겪다 **hostile** 적대감을 지닌 **antagonism** 적대감, 적대 관계 **sharpen** 분명히 하다 **thou** 당신(= you)

353 The reasons for desiring international government are two: first, the prevention of war, secondly the securing of economic justice as between different nations and different populations. Of these the prevention of war is the more important, both because war (especially as it will become) is more harmful than injustice, and because the grosser forms of injustice will not often be inflicted upon civilized nations except as the result of war. It would not be common, for example, in a time of profound peace to deprive a nation of its means of livelihood and at the same time prevent its population from emigrating, as we have done in Austria. If peace can be preserved, it is probable that some degree of justice will ultimately result. Even if a considerable measure of injustice were to remain, it is probable that the least fortunate populations in a time of secure peace would be better off than the most fortunate in a period of frequent wars. We have therefore to consider internationalism primarily from the point of view of preventing war, and only secondarily from the point of view of justice between nations. This is important because, as we shall see, some of the most probable approaches to international government involve considerable injustice for long periods of time.

Key Structure

2 **economic justice as between ~** ~ 사이에 존재하는 것 같은 경제적 정의
   • as는 원래 접속사이지만 여기에서는 동사가 없어져서 전치사처럼 쓰이고 있음.
   economic justice as is seen between ~

7 **except as the result of war** 전쟁의 결과로서가 아니면

8 **deprive a nation of its means of livelihood** 한 나라로부터 생계 수단을 빼앗다
   • deprive A of B A에게서 B를 빼앗다

13 **the least fortunate populations ~ frequent wars**
   안전한 평화 시에 가장 불행한 민족이라도 빈번한 전쟁 시에 가장 행복한 민족보다 더 잘 지낼 것이다

내용 국제[세계] 정부의 설립을 바라는 이유는 두 가지로, 그 하나는 전쟁의 억제를 위한 것이고, 또 하나는 국가나 민족들간의 경제적 정의를 확보하기 위한 것이다.

international government 세계 정부(= world government) **secure** 확보하다 **injustice** 부당, 불공평 **be inflicted upon** ~에 부과되다, 가해지다 **profound** 심오한, 깊은(= deep) **livelihood** 생계 **emigrate** 이민 (나)가다 *cf.* immigrate 이민 오다 **preserve** 보존하다 **be better off** 더 잘 살다 **involve** 수반하다, 포함하다

354 A philosophical principle at least as ancient as Aristotle says that fairness demands that one treat equals equally *and unequals unequally*. Now the question becomes, as citizens, in what ways are we equal and in what ways are we naturally and properly unequal? Let's go back to
⁵ the Declaration of Independence. "We hold these truths to be self-evident, that all men are created equal, and that they are endowed by their Creator with certain unalienable rights, that among these are Life, Liberty and the pursuit of Happiness." No matter how complete an original state of equality, give people the liberty to pursue their own
¹⁰ happiness and before long, *inevitably*, significant inequality will arise. Is this wrong? Not necessarily. But it does point to another core value in the American political culture: achievement. To be free to achieve and to be *rewarded* for achievement is as important to Americans as equality is. In everything from cheerleader tryouts to astute stock
¹⁵ portfolio management, we believe that achievement deserves to be recognized and rewarded. The freedom to achieve and to be rewarded *unequally* for achievement is a contradictory, competing value to equality. How do we choose between conflicting values?

Key Structure •

2 **fairness demands that one treat ~**
  • demands라는 동사 때문에 treat라는 가정법 현재형의 원형동사가 온 것.

5 **We hold these truths to be self-evident, that ~**
  우리는 ~라는 진리가 자명한 것으로 받아들인다
  • that 이하는 these truths를 받는 동격명사절.

8 **No matter how complete an ~ equality (may be)**
  평등의 원래 상태가 제아무리 완벽하다고 해도
  • no matter how = however

9 **give people ~ and...** 사람들에게 ~을 주어 보라, 그러면 …하게 될 것이다

13 **~ is as important... as equality is** ~은 평등만큼 중요하다

내용 평등의 진정한 의미는 무엇인가? 평등과 더불어 또 하나 중요한 미국의 가치인 성취는 사람들을 불평등하게 취급하게 하는데, 이것은 평등에 대한 모순이다. 어느 것을 택해야 할 것인가?

fairness 공평성 **equals** 평등한 사람들 **unequals** 불평등한 사람들 **self-evident** 자명한 **be endowed with** ~을 부여받다 **Creator** 조물주, 창조주 **unalienable** 양도할 수 없는(= inalienable) **before long** 얼마 가지 않아(= soon) **inevitably** 필연적으로, 반드시(= unavoidably) **tryout** 예비 시험, 적격 시험 **astute** 민첩한, 교활한 **portfolio** 유가증권 증서 **deserve** 자격이 있다 **contradictory** 모순된, 정반대의 **conflicting** 충돌하는, 일치하지 않는

Part **3**

Advanced Reading

355 What characterizes almost all Hollywood pictures is their inner emptiness. This is compensated for by an outer impressiveness. Such impressiveness usually takes the form of a truly grandiose realism. Nothing is spared to make the setting, the costumes, all of the surface details correct. These efforts help to mask the essential emptiness of the characterization, and the absurdities and trivialities of the plots. The houses look like houses; the streets look like streets; the people look and talk like people; but they are empty of humanity, credibility, and motivation. Needless to say, the disgraceful censorship code is an important factor in predetermining the content of these pictures. But the code does not disturb the profits, nor the entertainment value of the films; it merely helps to prevent them from being credible. It isn't too heavy a burden for the industry to bear. In addition to the impressiveness of the settings, there is a use of the camera which at times seems magical. But of what human import is all this skill, all this effort, all this energy in the production of effects, when the story, the representation of life is hollow, stupid, banal, childish?

Key Structure ▶

1　What characterizes ~ pictures
　거의 모든 할리우드 영화의 특징이 되는 것
　• pictures 다음의 is가 위의 관계대명사절의 동사임.

4　Nothing is spared ~
　어느 것도 아끼지 않는다

13　It isn't too heavy a burden for the industry to bear.
　그것은 영화 산업이 견디기에 그다지 무거운 짐은 아니다.
　• too ~ to 구문

15　But of what human import is all this ~?
　그러나 이 모든 ~이 인간적으로 무슨 의미가 있는가?

내용　오늘날 할리우드에서 제작되는 영화의 특징은 내적으로 공허하다는 점이다.

be compensated for by ~에 의해 보상되다　grandiose 웅장한, 장엄한　spare (비용·노력 등을) 아끼다
mask 감추다　absurdity 불합리, 모순　triviality 하찮은 일[점]　censorship code (영화, 연극 등의) 검열 규정
entertainment value 오락적 가치　credible 믿을 만한　hollow 속이 빈, 공허한　banal 진부한

356 The good teacher consciously or unconsciously recognizes the dramatic possibilities in his profession as the average or second-rate teacher never does. He does not count it beneath his dignity to put on a show for his students; indeed he cannot help doing this if he would, so inseparably is he one with what he is teaching. Thus his show is not of himself, else he becomes ridiculous and his teaching empty and useless. All good teachers know the experience of interesting themselves as well as their students, a proof of the fact that they are playing the part of someone vastly bigger than themselves, the part of Euclid, or of Shakespeare, or of Plato, or of whoever else has given them power and life. In the classroom of the poor or the average teacher there are always three distinct and distinguishable elements: the teacher, the subject or material which he is endeavoring to teach, and the students. In the classroom of the good teacher there is no such division. The students are caught up with the teacher in a common ownership of that which he is at once interpreting and recreating both for them and for himself, just as in a good play the audience becomes for two hours the actors and the playwright.

Key Structure

3 He does not count it beneath his dignity to put on ~
그는 학생들을 위해 쇼를 하는 것을 권위를 깎아내리는 것으로 생각하지 않는다
• it은 가목적어, to put on ~이 진목적어임.

5 so inseparably is he one with ~ = so he is inseparably one with ~
그래서 그는 분리할 수 없을 만큼 ~과 하나가 되다
• be one with ~ ~과 하나가 되다

6 else = if not ~ 그렇지 않다면

8 a proof of the fact that ~
• 앞에 나온 'All good ~ students'와 동격의 명사구. which is를 a proof 앞에 넣어 볼 것.

10 or of whoever else ~ = or of anyone else who ~
자신에게 힘과 생명을 제공해 준 그 밖의 다른 모든 사람의
• of 앞에 the part를 넣어 생각할 것.

15 The students are caught up with the teacher 학생들은 선생님과 하나가 된다

내용 훌륭한 선생은 이류의 선생이 하지 못하는 일을 의식적이든 무의식적이든 행하게 된다.

unconsciously 무의식적으로 *cf.* subconsciously 잠재의식적으로   **beneath one's dignity** 위신을 추락시키는
endeavor 노력하다   **playwright** 극작가
cf. Euclid 유클리드 (기원전 300년경 알렉산드리아의 수학자, 기하학의 대가)

357 This is a skeptical age, but although our faith in many of the things in which our forefathers fervently believed has weakened, our confidence in the curative properties of the bottle of medicine remains the same as theirs. This modern faith in medicines is proved by the fact that the annual drug bill of the Health Services is mounting to astronomical figures and shows no signs at present of ceasing to rise. The majority of the patients attending the medical out-patients departments of our hospitals feel that they have not received adequate treatment unless they are able to carry home with them some tangible remedy in the shape of a bottle of medicine, a box of pills, or a small jar of ointment, and the doctor in charge of the department is only too ready to provide them with these requirements. There is no quicker method of disposing of patients than by giving them what they are asking for, and since most medical men in the Health Services are overworked and have little time for offering time-consuming and little-appreciated advice on such subjects as diet, right living, and the need for abandoning bad habits, etc., the bottle, the box, and the jar are almost always granted them.

Key Structure •

1 **This is a skeptical age** = This age is a skeptical age
이 시대는 회의적인 시대이다

6 **shows no signs ~ rise** 현재로서는 상승이 멈출 기미가 보이지 않는다

9 **unless they are able to ~** = if they are not able to ~
• carry의 목적어는 some tangible ~ ointment임.

11 **the doctor ~ is only too ready to…** 의사는 …할 준비가 너무나도 많이 되어 있다

13 **There is no quicker method of disposing of patients than ~**
환자들을 떨쳐 보내는 방법으로 ~보다 더 빠른 방법은 없다

내용 오늘날 공공 의료 기관에 찾아오는 환자들은 약에 대한 믿음이 너무 강하다.

skeptical 회의적인(= skeptical)   **fervently** 열렬히(= fervidly)   **curative** 치료력이 있는   **Health Services** (미국) 공공 의료 서비스, 건강보험   **mount to** ~에 이르다   **astronomical figures** 천문학적인 숫자   **out-patient** 외래 환자   *cf.* in-patient   **tangible** 만질 수 있는, 실재하는   **dispose of** 처리하다, 치우다   **be overworked** 과로하다   **little-appreciated advice** 별로 달가워하지 않는 충고

358 Democracy is, historically speaking, something very recent. It is first of all the belief that individual human beings are what matters most—more than the State, or the total of national wealth, or anything else whatsoever. Then it is the belief in equality, not in the
₅ sense that everybody is alike or equally gifted, which is obviously untrue, but in the sense that everyone should have certain basic opportunities. The European political theorists of the eighteenth century thought in terms of 'natural rights'; the American Constitution speaks of 'life, liberty, and the pursuit of happiness.'
₁₀ Today we are more inclined to use phrases like 'privileges and opportunities.' What each age has meant is that everyone should have an equal chance to a reasonable development as individual human beings, irrespective of accidents of birth or fortune. The democratic ideal is also the belief that governments should exist
₁₅ not only to benefit but to represent the people as a whole. So democracy, since it thus presupposes government by consent, implies tolerance; since it presupposes equality, implies equal opportunities; since it presupposes the ultimate value of individual men and women, implies freedom.

Key Structure ▸

2 **what matters most** = what is most important 가장 중요한 것

4 **not in the sense that A, but in the sense that B**
   A라는 의미에서가 아니라 B라는 의미에서

12 **an equal chance to a ~ human beings**
   인간 개개인으로서 합리적으로 성장할 수 있는 동등한 기회

13 **irrespective of accidents of birth or fortune**
   출생이나 행운이라는 우연에 의해 이루어지는 팔자에 상관없이

17 **implies tolerance / implies equal opportunities / implies freedom**
   • 세 표현의 주어는 모두 democracy.

내용 민주주의는 평등에 대한 믿음이다.

matter 중요하다(= be important)   **gifted** 재능을 타고난   **natural right** 천부 인권   **privilege** 특권
irrespective of ~에 관계없이(= regardless of)   **accidents of birth or fortune** 출생이나 행운 등의 팔자
presuppose 전제로 삼다

359 At the close of the middle ages, Western man seemed to be headed for the final fulfillment of his keenest dreams and visions. He freed himself from the authority of a totalitarian church, the weight of traditional thought, the geographical limitations of our but half-discovered globe. He built a new science which eventually has led to the release of hitherto unheard-of productive powers, and to the complete transformation of the material world. He created political systems which seemed to guarantee the free and productive development of the individual; he reduced the time of work to such a level that man was free to enjoy hours of leisure to an extent his forefathers had hardly dreamed of.

Yet Where Are We Today?

The danger of an all-destructive war hangs over the head of humanity, a danger which is by no means overcome by the spirit of Geneva prevalent at the time of this writing. But even if man's political representatives have enough sanity left to avoid a war, man's condition is far from the fulfillment of the hopes of the sixteenth, seventeenth, and eighteenth centuries.

Key Structure

5 has led to the release of ~ powers
이때까지 들어 본 적이 없는 생산력의 표출을 가져왔다

9 to such a level that ~
~할 그런 정도로

10 to an extent (that) ~
~할 정도로

16 have enough sanity left
충분한 제정신이 남아 있다

내용 중세가 끝날 때쯤에는 인간은 자신의 꿈과 이상을 실현하고 있었지만, 오늘날에는 전쟁의 위협 등으로 인해 꿈을 전혀 실현하지 못하고 있다.

be headed for ~으로 향하다   totalitarian 전체주의의, 1당 독재의   hitherto 그때까지   unheard-of 전례가 없는   an all-destructive war 모든 것을 파괴하는 전쟁   hang over 걸쳐 있다   prevalent 널리 퍼진, 유행하는, 풍미하는   sanity 제정신, 건전한 정신   be far from ~에서 거리가 멀다, ~을 결코 이룩하지 못하다

360 Television is a method of communication. It is about as revolutionary as the invention of printing. Neither printing nor television is in itself an idea, or power, or good or bad. They are simply methods by which ideas and experiences can be communicated faster to more people. It is perhaps because the characteristics of television, which determine what it can best communicate, are so different from those of printing, that professional educationists were reluctant for so long to interest themselves in the newer method.

Printing and television are certainly alike in that both are costly to the producers of the communication and relatively cheap to the receiver. They are both, therefore, mass media which depend upon reaching great numbers. But whereas the printed word, being relatively permanent, can communicate to numbers of like minds over centuries, television is relatively ephemeral and communicates, using both pictures and words, to millions of unlike minds at the same moment in time. Moreover television appeals not only to those who can read but to those who can't.

Key Structure ▶

1 It is about as revolutionary as ~ printing.
그것은 인쇄술의 발명만큼이나 거의 혁명적이다.

5 It is perhaps because ~ that professional...
• It ~ that 강조 구문. because절이 강조된 것.

8 to interest themselves in = to become interested in

9 the newer method = television

10 Printing and television ~ in that...
인쇄술과 TV는 …라는 점에서 분명히 유사하다

14 being relatively permanent = as it is relatively permanent

내용 텔레비전은 의사소통의 한 수단으로서, 생각이 서로 다른 많은 사람들에게 정보를 전달한다.

be reluctant to 마음 내키지 않다, 마지못해 하다(= be unwilling to) **costly** 값비싼(= expensive) **mass media** 대중 전달 매체 **like minds** 같은 생각을 가진 자들 **ephemeral** 단명한, 하루살이의 **unlike minds** 생각이 다른 사람들

361 Poetry is worth discovering if only because to hear and understand poetry is to know beauty. And if you have not yourselves begun to find out already what beauty means to life, and what life is like without beauty, there is no wise man of the present who is not ready to tell you. Without the love of beauty your life would be poor in spite of riches. As the soul thrives on virtue and the body on health, so the mind lives and grows by the knowledge of beauty. And poetry is not only a form of beauty, but for many the means by which they find the way to all beauty in life and art. You are living in an age when ugliness seems to be steadily increasing, when people seem to be more and more content to have ugly things all around them. This makes it all the more necessary that you should aim at knowing and loving beauty wherever it is yet to be found. If you can learn to know beauty as expressed by the poet, you will have trained your mind to see and know beauty everywhere. And only thus can your life be full and your happiness complete.

Key Structure

1 **if only because ~** ~라는 이유만으로도

3 **what life is like without beauty** 미가 없다면 삶은 어떠한 모습일까

4 **there is no wise ~ you** 현대의 현명한 사람치고 너에게 이야기할 준비가 안 된 사람은 없다

6 **As the soul ~, so the mind ~**
영혼이 미덕 위에 번성하고 육체는 건강 위에 번성하는 것처럼, 정신은 아름다움을 앎으로써 살고 성장한다
• the body on health = the body thrives on health

11 **This makes it all the more necessary that ~** 이것 때문에 ~는 더더욱 필요하다

13 **wherever it is yet to be found**
그것이 아직 발견될 수 있는 곳에서는 어디에서나(그것이 아직 발견되지 않은 곳은 어디에서나)

14 **as expressed by the poet** 시인에 의해 표현된 모습으로서

15 **only thus can your life be full** 이렇게 할 경우에만 너의 인생은 완벽해질 수 있다 (도치 구문)

16 **and your happiness complete** = and can your happiness be complete

내용 아름다움은 인생에 큰 의미가 있고 시(詩)는 인생과 예술에서 아름다움을 아는 길이다.

in spite of riches 부가 아무리 많아도   **thrive** 번영하다   **for many** 많은 사람들에게는(= for many people)
means 수단   **ugliness** 추함

362 Why is it that only fewer than half of those entering college ever get their degrees? From the number of students who fail, it might be assumed that they lack either proper study skills or mental ability. But this is true in only a small number of cases, for students who are admitted to college on the basis of their high school achievement must have some scholarly abilities. From the number of those who drop out voluntarily, it might be assumed that more exciting outside attractions are too great to resist. But this, too, is only a partial answer, for most students are able to see the advantages and long-range rewards of a college education. The real answer lies in the difference between the students' goals and the goals that the institution has set for them. Admittedly or not, most students want their degrees as quickly as possible, in order to get the financial, professional, and social rewards that are supposed to come with a college degree. The college, on the other hand, sees education as an end in itself, and not merely as a means to an end. The majority of students, therefore, who are interested in knowledge not for its own sake but only for the material rewards it may bring, become discouraged and impatient with an institution that makes them fulfill requirements that are both difficult and apparently irrelevant to their career choices.

Key Structure ▸

1 **Why is it that ~?** ~은 어찌된 영문인가?
   • 의문사 why가 강조된 구문: It is why that ~ ⇒ Why is it that ~

3 **it might be assumed that ~** ~라고 가정해 볼 수 있을 것이다
   • might이 쓰인 것을 보면 그 가정이 옳지 않음을 암시하고 있음.

8 **more exciting outside ~ resist** 학교 밖의 더 매력적인 일들이 거역하기에는 힘이 너무 크다

12 **Admittedly or not = Whether it is admitted or not** 우리가 그것을 인정하든 안 하든

18 **the material rewards (which) it may bring** 그것이 가져올 수 있는 물질적인 보상들

> **내용** 대학에 입학하는 학생의 절반이 채 안 되는 수만이 학위를 따고 졸업하는 것은 대학이 설정한 교육 목표와 학생들의 직업 선택의 욕구 사이에 존재하는 괴리 때문이다.

assume 가정하다, 추측하다 **high school achievement** 고등학교 성적 **attraction** 매력적인 일 **long-range rewards** 장기적인 면에서의 보상 **institution** 공공기관(학교, 병원 등) *여기에서는 대학 **in itself** 그 자체로서 **for its own sake** 그 자체를 위하여 **be impatient with** ~을 참지 못하다 **irrelevant to** ~에 관련이 없는

363　For a majority of people in the West, purposeless reading, purposeless listening-in, purposeless looking at films have become addictions, psychological equivalents of alcoholism and morphinism. Things have come to such a pitch that there are many millions of men and women who suffer real distress if they are cut off for a few days or even a few hours from newspapers, radio music, moving pictures. Like the addict to a drug, they have to indulge their vice, not because the indulgence gives them any active pleasure, but because, unless they indulge they feel painfully subnormal and incomplete. Without papers, films and wireless they live a diminished existence; they are fully themselves only when bathing in sports news and murder trials, in radio music and talk, in the vicarious terrors, triumphs and eroticisms of the films. Even by intelligent people, it is now taken for granted that such psychological addictions are inevitable and even desirable, that there is nothing to be alarmed at in the fact that the majority of civilized men and women are now incapable of living on their own spiritual resources, but have become abjectly dependent on incessant stimulation from without.

Key Structure •

4 Things have come to such a pitch that ~ 상황이 ~한 정도에 이르렀다

7 they have to indulge their vice 그들은 그들의 악습을 충족시켜야 한다

9 unless they indulge ~ = if they do not indulge ~ 그들이 ~에 빠지지 않으면

11 only when bathing in ~ = only when they bathe in ~

14 it is now taken for granted that such ~ , that there is ~
　　~은 이제 당연하게 받아들여지고 있다 (granted 다음에 두 개의 that절이 나옴)

17 live on their own spiritual resources 자신의 정신적인 자원[수단]을 기초로 살아가다

> 내용 많은 서구인들이 목적 없는 독서, 목적 없는 남의 이야기 엿듣기, 목적 없는 영화 감상 등에 빠져 있는데, 이것은 심리적으로 알코올 중독, 마약 중독에 걸린 것이나 마찬가지이다.

purposeless 목적 없는, 무의미한　**listen in** (전화나 남의 말을) 엿듣다　**addiction** 중독, 상용　*cf.* addict 중독자, 탐닉자　**equivalent** 상당물, 등가물　**morphinism** 모르핀 중독, 마약 중독　**pitch** 위치, 정도　**indulge** 만족시키다(= satisfy) ⓝ indulgence 탐닉　**subnormal** 정상 이하의　**wireless** 라디오, 무선 전화　**murder trials** 살인 사건 이야기　**vicarious** 대리의, 대신의　**be alarmed at** ~을 걱정하다, ~에 놀라다　**abjectly** 굴욕적으로, 비열하게　**incessant** 끝없는(= unceasing)　**stimulation** 자극　**without** ⓝ 외부

364 At the age of twelve years, the human body is at its most vigorous. It has yet to reach its full size and strength and its owner his or her full intelligence; but at this age the likelihood of death is least. Earlier, we were infants and young children, and consequently more vulnerable; later, we shall undergo a progressive loss of our vigor and resistance which, though imperceptible at first, will finally become so steep that we can live no longer, however well we look after ourselves, and however well society, and our doctors, look after us. This decline in vigor with the passing of time is called ageing. It is one of the most unpleasant discoveries which we all make that we must decline in this way, that if we escape wars, accidents and diseases we shall eventually 'die of old age,' and that this happens at a rate which differs little from person to person, so that there are heavy odds in favor of our dying between the ages of sixty-five and eighty. Some of us will die sooner, a few will live longer—on into a ninth or tenth decade. But the chances are against it, and there is a virtual limit on how long we can hope to remain alive, however lucky and robust we are.

Key Structure

2 **its owner** (has to reach) **his ~ intelligence**
신체의 주인은 자신의 두뇌를 충분히 개발해야 한다

6 **though** (it is) **imperceptible at first**
처음에는 잘 지각할 수 없지만

13 **there are heavy odds in favor of ~** ~할 가망이 많이 있다

15 **a few will live longer—on into ~** 몇 명만이 오래 살아 90~100세까지 될 것이다

15 **on into a ninth or tenth decade** 90세 또는 100세가 되도록

16 **the chances are against it** 그러할 가망은 없다

내용 인간은 12세에 그 신체가 가장 정력적이고, 그 후로 체격, 힘, 지능이 서서히 쇠퇴한다.

vigorous 정력적인 **vulnerable** 상하기 쉬운, 공격받기 쉬운 **imperceptible** 지각할 수 없는 **steep** 경사가 급한 **ageing** 나이 먹음, 노화 **odds** 승산, 가능성 **a ninth or tenth decade** 90~100세 **virtual** 사실상의, 실질적인 **robust** 강건한, 튼튼한(= strong)

365 What may be happening elsewhere we do not know, but it is improbable that the universe contains nothing better than ourselves. With increase of wisdom our thoughts acquire a wider scope both in space and in time. The child lives in the minute, the boy in the day, the instinctive man in the year. The man imbued with history lives in the epoch. Spinoza would have us live not in the minute, the day, the year or the epoch, but in eternity. Those who learn to do this will find that it takes away the frantic quality of misfortune and prevents the trend towards madness that comes with overwhelming disaster. Spinoza spent the last day of his life telling cheerful anecdotes to his host. He had written: 'A free man thinks of death least of all things, and his wisdom is a meditation not of death but of life.' And he carried out this precept when it came to his own death. I do not mean that the man who is freed from the tyranny of unwisdom will be destitute of emotion—on the contrary, he will feel friendship, benevolence and compassion in a higher degree than the man who has not emancipated himself from personal anxieties.

Key Structure •

3 With increase of wisdom = As wisdom increases
지식이 늘어나면서

4 the boy (lives) in the day, the instinctive man (lives) in the year
소년은 하루 단위로 살고, 본능적인 성인은 일 년 단위로 산다

5 The man (who is) imbued with history
역사 의식에 젖은[고취된] 사람

6 Spinoza would have us live ~
= Spinoza wished to make us live ~
스피노자는 우리가 ～ 속에서 살게 하고 싶었다

내용 지혜와 사려가 있는 사람은 현재에 살지 말고 앞을 내다보는 영원 속에서 살아야 한다.

scope 시야, 영역   imbue A with B A에게 B를 불어넣다   eternity 영원, 영겁   frantic 미친 듯이 날뛰는, 세속적인   overwhelming 압도하는   anecdote 일화   least of all things 가장 ～이 아니다, 거의 ～하지 않다   meditation 숙고, 명상   precept 가르침, 교훈   tyranny 독재   unwisdom 무지, 우둔   be destitute of ～을 결여하다   benevolence 자비심, 선행   compassion 연민, 동정심   emancipate 해방시키다(= liberate)
cf. Spinoza, Baruch 바뤼흐 스피노자 (1632～1677, 네덜란드의 철학자)

366 It is impossible to be happy without activity, but it is also impossible to be happy if the activity is excessive or of a repulsive kind. Activity is agreeable when it is directed very obviously to a desired end and is not in itself contrary to impulse. A dog will pursue rabbits to the point of complete exhaustion and be happy all the time, but if you put the dog on a treadmill and gave him a good dinner after half an hour he would not be happy till he got the dinner, because he would not have been engaged in a natural activity meanwhile. One of the difficulties of our time is that, in a complex modern society, few of the things that have to be done have the naturalness of hunting. The consequence is that most people, in a technically advanced community, have to find their happiness outside the work by which they make their living. And if their work is exhausting their pleasures will tend to be passive. Watching a football match or going to the cinema leaves little satisfaction afterwards, and in no degree gratifies creative impulses. The satisfaction of the players, who are active, is of quite a different order.

Key Structure •

2   be of a repulsive kind
반감을 사는[불쾌한] 종류이다

5   if you put ~ and gave him ~ after half an hour
개 한 마리를 답차 위에 올려놓고 반 시간 후에 맛있는 음식을 준다면
• put, gave가 과거형인 것은 가정법 과거 구문이기 때문.

10 have the naturalness of hunting
사냥에서 보는 자연스러움을 갖다

12 the work by which ~ living   그들이 생계를 꾸려가는 일

15 in no degree ~   결코 ~하지 못하다

17 is of quite a different order
전혀 다른 종류의 것이다
• order = kind

내용 인생의 행복은 인간의 활동에 따르는 것이지만, 그 활동은 욕구에 반하지 않아야 하며 지나치거나 불쾌한 것이어서는 안 된다.

excessive 지나친   **repulsive** 불쾌한, 반감을 사는   **be contrary to** ~에 반대되다   **impulse** 충동, 욕구
exhaustion 기진맥진   **treadmill** 쳇바퀴, 답차   **be engaged in** ~에 종사하다   **gratify** 만족시키다(= satisfy)

367 Mankind, ever since there have been civilized communities, has been confronted with problems of two different kinds. On the one hand there has been the problem of mastering natural forces, of acquiring the knowledge and the skill required to produce tools
5 and weapons and to encourage Nature in the production of useful animals and plants. This problem, in the modern world, is dealt with by science and scientific technique, and experience has shown that in order to deal with it adequately it is necessary to train a large number of rather narrow specialists. But there is a second problem,
10 less precise, and by some mistakenly regarded as unimportant— I mean the problem of how best to utilize our command over the forces of nature. This includes such burning issues as democracy versus dictatorship, capitalism versus socialism, international government versus international anarchy, free speculation versus
15 authoritarian dogma. On such issues the laboratory can give no decisive guidance. The kind of knowledge that gives most help in solving such problems is a wide survey of human life, in the past as well as in the present, and an appreciation of the sources of misery or contentment as they appear in history.

Key Structure ▶

5 **encourage Nature in ~** 자연을 장려하여 ~하도록 하다

10 **less precise** = though it is less precise (than the first)
(첫째 문제보다) 덜 명확한 것이기는 하지만

10 **by some mistakenly ~ unimportant**
어떤 사람들에게는 중요하지 않은 것으로 잘못 여겨지고 있는 것이지만

12 **democracy** versus **dictatorship** 민주주의 대 독재 정권 (A versus B A 대 B)

19 **as they appear in history** 그것들이 역사에 나타난 모습대로

내용 문명 사회가 생겨난 이래로 인류는 자연력을 장악하는 문제와 그것을 어떻게 가장 잘 이용하느냐 하는 두 문제에 직면해 왔다.

be confronted with ~에 직면하다(= be faced with)   **natural forces** 자연력   **narrow specialist**
좁은 범위의 전문가   **precise** 정확한, 명확한   **command** 운용력, 억제력   **burning issue** 중대한 문제
dictatorship 독재   **speculation** 사색, 사유   **authoritarian** 권위주의의, 권력주의의   **dogma** 독단, 교리
survey 조사, 탐사   **appreciation** 감상   **misery** 불행

368 In the organization of industrial life the influence of the factory upon the physiological and mental state of the workers has been completely neglected. Modern industry is based on the conception of the maximum production at lowest cost, in order that an
5 individual or a group of individuals may earn as much money as possible. It has expanded without any idea of the true nature of the human beings who run the machines, and without giving any consideration to the effects produced on the individuals and on their descendants by the artificial mode of existence imposed by
10 the factory. The great cities have been built with no regard for us. The shape and dimensions of the skyscrapers depend entirely on the necessity of obtaining the maximum income per square foot of ground, and of offering to the tenants offices and apartments that please them. This caused the construction of gigantic buildings
15 where too large masses of human beings are crowded together. Civilized men like such a way of living. While they enjoy the comfort and banal luxury of their dwelling, they do not realize that they are deprived of the necessities of life. The modern city consists of monstrous edifices and of dark, narrow streets full of petrol
20 fumes, coal dust, and toxic gases, torn by the noise of the taxi-cabs, lorries and buses, and thronged ceaselessly by great crowds. Obviously, it has not been planned for the good of its inhabitants.

Key Structure •

1 **the influence of A upon B** A가 B에 끼친 영향
  • A = the factory, B = the physiological ~ workers

4 **the maximum production at lowest cost** 최소 비용으로 최대 생산을 얻어내는 것

9 **the artificial mode of existence** (which is) **imposed by the factory**
  공장에 의해 부과된 인위적인 생활 양식

18 **they are deprived of the necessities of life** 그들은 생활필수품을 빼앗겼다
  • deprive A of B ⇒ A is deprived of B A에게서 B를 빼앗다

내용 현대의 산업 도시는 전혀 인간에 대한 고려 없이 팽창하고 성장해 왔다.

physiological 생리적인   **the artificial mode of existence** 인위적인 생활 양식   **skyscraper** 마천루   **per square foot** 1평방피트당   **tenant** 차용자, 임차인   **banal** 진부한   **monstrous** 괴물 같은 ⓝ monster   **edifice** 건축물   **petrol fumes** 가솔린[석유] 연기   **toxic gases** 유독성 가스   **torn by** ~에 찢겨진 (tear-tore-torn)   **lorry** 화물 자동차(= truck)

369

I am always amazed when I hear people saying that sport creates goodwill between the nations, and that if only the common peoples of the world could meet one another at football or cricket, they would have no inclination to meet on the battlefield. Even if one didn't know from concrete examples (the 1936 Olympic Games, for instance) that international sporting contests lead to orgies of hatred, one could deduce it from general principles.

Nearly all the sports practiced nowadays are competitive. You play to win, and the game has little meaning unless you do your utmost to win. On the village green, where you pick up sides and no feeling of local patriotism is involved, it is possible to play simply for the fun and exercise, but as soon as the question of prestige arises, as soon as you feel that you and some larger unit will be disgraced if you lose, the most savage combative instincts are aroused. Anyone who has played even in a school football match knows this. At the international level sport is frankly mimic warfare. But the significant thing is not the behavior of the players but the attitude of the spectators, and, behind the spectators, of the nations that work themselves into furies over these absurd contests, and seriously believe—at any rate for short periods—that running, jumping and kicking a ball are tests of national virtue.

Key Structure

2 **if only ~** ～하기만 한다면

13 **you and some larger unit will be ~ lose** 당신과 더 큰 편이 지면 굴욕적이다

18 **of the nations that ~ contests**
이 불합리한 시합에 분노를 터뜨리는 국가들의 (태도)
• of는 앞의 attitude로 연결할 것.

18 **work themselves into furies ~**
차츰차츰 흥분하여 ～에 대한 분노를 터뜨리다

내용 스포츠가 선린 관계를 만들어 낸다는 말은 맞지 않는 말이다.

goodwill 선린 **orgies of hatred** 증오의 난장판 **deduce** 추론하다. 연역하다 **competitive** 경쟁의 **the village green** 동네의 잔디밭 **pick up sides** 편을 가르다 **combative** 투쟁적인 ⑪ combat **mimic warfare** 모의 전투

370 It is a well-known fact that one of the most widespread and dangerous elements absorbed by us is strontium-90. It is stored in the bones and emits from there its rays into cells of red bone marrow, where the red and white corpuscles are made. If the radiation is too great, blood diseases—fatal in most cases—are the result. The cells of the reproductive organs are particularly sensitive. Even relatively weak radiation may lead to fatal consequences. The most sinister aspect of internal as well as external radiation is that years may pass before the evil consequences appear. Indeed, they make themselves felt, not in the first or second generation, but in the following ones. Generation after generation, for centuries to come, will witness the birth of an ever-increasing number of children with mental and physical defects. We must not disregard our responsibility to guard against the possibility that thousands of children may be born with the most serious mental and physical defects. It will be no excuse for us to say later that we were unaware of that possibility. Only those who have never been present at the birth of deformed baby, never witnessed the whimpering cries of its mother, should dare to maintain that the risk of nuclear testing is a small one. The well-known French biologist and geneticist Jean Rostand calls the continuation of nuclear tests "a crime into the future" (le crime dans l'avenir). It is the particular duty of women to prevent this sin against the future. It is for them to raise their voices against it in such a way that they will be heard.

Key Structure

8 **years may pass before ~** ~하려면 수년의 세월이 흘러야 한다(수년의 세월이 지나서야 ~된다)

9 **they make themselves felt ~** = they are felt ~ 그들이 느껴지게 된다

18 **the risk of nuclear ~ one** 핵 실험의 위험은 작은 위험이다 (one = risk)

22 **raise their voices against it** 그것에 반대하는 목소리를 높이다

23 **in such a way that ~** ~하는 방식으로

내용 핵 실험의 결과는 매우 심각하다. 특히 여성들은 기형아를 출산할 위험이 높다.

strontium-90 스트론티움 90(방사성 강하물 속에 포함되어 있고 인체에 가장 위험한 반감기가 28년이나 되는 핵분열 물질)
emit 분출하다　**bone marrow** 골수　**red corpuscle** 적혈구　**white corpuscle** 백혈구　**radiation** 방사선
sinister 불길한(= unfortunate)　**guard against** (위험에) 대비하다　**deformed** 불구의　**whimper** 처량하게
울다　**geneticist** 유전학자　**le crime dans l'avenir** 미래에 대한 범죄(a crime into the future의 프랑스어 표현)

371 We can read of things that happened 5,000 years ago in the Near East, where people first learned to write. But there are some parts of the world where even now people cannot write. The only way that they can preserve their history is to recount it as sagas—legends handed down from one generation of story-tellers to another. These legends are useful because they can tell us something about migrations of people who lived long ago, but none could write down what they did. Anthropologists wondered where the remote ancestors of the Polynesian peoples now living in the Pacific Islands came from. The sagas of these people explain that some of them came from Indonesia about 2,000 years ago. But the first people who were like ourselves lived so long ago that even their sagas, if they had any, are forgotten. So archaeologists have neither history nor legends to help them to find out where the first 'modern men' came from. Fortunately, however, ancient men made tools of stone, especially flint, because this is easier to shape than other kinds. They may also have used wood and skins, but these have rotted away. Stone does not decay, and so the tools of long ago have remained when even the bones of the men who made them have disappeared without trace.

Key Structure

5 **legends handed down ~ another**
한 세대의 이야기꾼들에게서 또 다른 세대의 이야기꾼들로 전해 내려오는 전설들
• another = another generation of story-tellers

13 **if they had any** (sagas)
설령 그러한 무용담이 있었다 하더라도

내용 글자가 없는 지역에서는 인간의 역사는 무용담[역사 이야기]에 의해 전해진다.

the Near East 근동 지방 *cf.* the Far East 극동 지방, the Middle East 중동 지방 **saga** 무용담, 역사 이야기 **migration** 이민, 이주 **anthropologist** 인류학자 **archaeologist** 고고학자 **flint** 부싯돌, 석기 **without trace** 흔적도 없이

372 I believe the intellectual life of the whole of western society is increasingly being split into two polar groups. When I say the intellectual life, I mean to include also a large part of our practical life, because I should be the last person to suggest the two can at
5 the deepest level be distinguished. Two polar groups: at one pole we have the literary intellectuals—at the other scientists, and as the most representative, the physical scientists. Between the two a gulf of mutual incomprehension—sometimes (particularly among the young) hostility and dislike, but most of all lack of understanding.
10 They have a curious distorted image of each other. Their attitudes are so different that, even on the level of emotion, they cannot find much common ground. Non-scientists tend to think of scientists as brash and boastful. They have a rooted impression that the scientists are shallowly optimistic, unaware of man's condition. On the other
15 hand, the scientists believe that the literary intellectuals are totally lacking in foresight, peculiarly unconcerned with their brother men, in a deep sense anti-intellectual, anxious to restrict both art and thought to the existential moment. On each side there is something which is not entirely baseless. It is all destructive. Much of it rests on
20 misinterpretations which are dangerous.

Key Structure ▸

4 **I should be the last person to ~**
나는 ~할 사람이 결코 아니다

6 **at the other** (pole we have) **scientists**
다른 끝머리에 우리는 과학자를 가지고 있다

9 **most of all** (there exists) **lack of understanding**
무엇보다도 이해의 부족이 존재한다

> **내용** 서구 사회 지식인의 삶은 그 양극에 문학가와 과학자가 있는데, 양자는 서로를 적대시하고 혐오하며, 서로 이해력을 갖지 못하고 있다고 비난하고 있다.

split 나누다, 쪼개다   **polar** 양극의, 정반대의   **representative** 대표자(의)   **physical scientist** 자연과학자
gulf 심해, 넘을 수 없는 한계   **incomprehension** 이해하지 못함   **hostility** 적대감   **distorted** 왜곡된, 비뚤어진
common ground 공통의 장, 일치점   **brash** 건방진, 성미 급한(= saucy)   **boastful** 허풍이 센   **shallowly**
천박하게   **be lacking in** ~을 결여하다   **foresight** 선견(지명)   **anti-intellectual** 반지성적인   **existential**
moment 실존의 면, 순간   **baseless** 근거 없는

373 One of the most important effects of industrialism is the break-up of the family resulting from the employment of women. The employment of women has two effects: on the one hand it makes them economically independent of men, so that they cease to be
5 subject to husbands; on the other hand it makes it difficult for them to bring up their children themselves. The tradition of the monogamic family is so strong in all the chief industrial countries that the effect of industrialism on the family has taken a long time to show itself. Even now, it has hardly begun in America, where Christianity is still
10 not uncommon; but throughout Europe the process of disintegration, which had already begun, has been enormously accelerated by the war, owing to the ease with which women found employment, in Government offices, in munition works, or on the land. Experience has shown that the average woman will not submit to the restraints
15 of the old-fashioned marriage, or remain faithful to one man, when she can be economically independent. For the moment, the restraints and concealments imposed by the upholders of traditional morality have somewhat obscured the extent of the change thus brought about. But the change will grow greater with time, since it belongs to the
20 inherent tendencies of industrialism. In a pre-industrial community rich men held their wives as property, while poor men made them co-operators in their work. Peasant women do much of the hard work of agriculture, and working-class women have hitherto had their time fully taken up with household work and the rearing of children. In this
25 way, whether in town or country, the family formed an economic unit.

Key Structure ▸

8 ~ has taken a long time to… ~이 …하는 데 많은 시간이 걸렸다

23 have hitherto had their time fully taken up with ~ 지금까지 자신들의 시간을 ~에 다 바쳤다

내용 산업화는 여성 고용으로 가정의 붕괴를 가져왔으며 여성 고용은 여성을 남성에 대한 예속 상태에서 벗어나게 했고, 또 한편으로는 아이들의 양육을 어렵게 만들었다.

break-up 붕괴, 와해   be subject to ~에 종속되다   monogamic 일부일처제의   disintegration (가정의) 분열, 붕괴   munition works 군수품 공장   submit to ~에 굴복하다   faithful 충실한   for the moment 우선은, 당장은   concealment 은폐, 숨김   inherent 고유의, 본래의   peasant 농부   working-class 근로 계층 hitherto 지금까지   economic unit 경제 단위

374 Parents have to do much less for their children today than they used to do, and home has become much less of a workshop. Clothes can be bought ready made, washing can go to the laundry, food can be bought cooked, canned or preserved, bread is baked and delivered by the baker, milk arrives on the doorstep, meals can be had at the restaurant, the works' canteen, and the school dining-room.

It is unusual now for father to pursue his trade or other employment at home, and his children rarely, if ever, see him at his place of work. Boys are therefore seldom trained to follow their father's occupation, and in many towns they have a fairly wide choice of employment and so do girls. The young wage-earner often earns good money, and soon acquires a feeling of economic independence. In textile areas it has long been customary for mothers to go out to work, but this practice has become so widespread that the working mother is now a not unusual factor in a child's home life, the number of married women in employment having more than doubled in the last twenty-five years. With mother earning and his older children drawing substantial wages father is seldom the dominant figure that he still was at the beginning of the century. When mother works economic advantages accrue, but children lose something of great value if mother's employment prevents her from being home to greet them when they return from school.

Key Structure ▸

8 rarely, if ever, ~ 있다손 치더라도 거의 ~하지 않는다

15 a not unusual factor = a usual factor 흔히 있는 일[요소]

15 the number of ~ having… = and the number of ~ has **more than doubled**
~의 숫자는 두 배 이상이 되었다

18 **the dominant figure that he still was ~** 20세기 초만 해도 (그가 보여 주었던) 영향력 있는 존재
 • that는 관계대명사로 was의 보어 역할.

내용 어머니가 직장을 갖게 되고 아이들이 일자리를 갖게 되면서 가정에서 아버지의 존재는 점점 약해지고 있으며,
아이들은 그만큼 가치 있는 무엇을 잃고 있다.

workshop 작업장, 연구 집회   **ready made** 기성품으로   **laundry** 세탁실   **canned** 통조림 상태로(= preserved)
canteen 매점   **textile** 직물의, 방직의   **draw substantial wages** 상당한 수입을 올리다   **accrue** 생기다

375

It seems almost inevitable that, when a country is in the early stages of industrialism, the economic organization should be oligarchic, and the bulk of the population should be very poor unless it is possible to borrow extensively from more advanced countries. To take first the question of poverty: when a country has not yet become industrial its methods of production are not highly efficient, and do not, in general, produce any very great surplus above what is needed for subsistence. The first effect of a movement towards the development of industry in such a country is to take a number of workers away from work which is immediately productive, and to cause them instead to build railways or construct machines or export their produce to other countries where machines can be bought or such things as steel rails manufactured. The result is that, at first, there is a diminution in the amount of consumable commodities to be distributed. As there was already not much to spare (owing to the country having been hitherto unindustrial), the result of a diminution is apt to be serious poverty for the ordinary worker. The only way to avoid this is to industrialize very slowly, or to borrow heavily from economically more advanced countries. The latter is the expedient usually adopted when the relations with advanced countries are friendly. But when, as in Russia, borrowing is impossible owing to hostility, there remains only the alternative of great poverty or very slow industrialization.

Key Structure

3 unless it is possible to ~ = if it is not possible to ~

5 To take first the question of poverty 가난의 문제를 우선 예로 들어 보자

12 other countries where ... such things as steel rails (can be) manufactured
강철레일 같은 제품들을 만들 수 있는 다른 국가들

15 As there was already not much to spare 나눌 것이 이미 많지 않기 때문에

내용 산업화의 초기 단계에서는 경제 개발이 소수 독재에 의존하게 되고, 선진국으로부터 물자 조달이 없을 경우 대다수 국민은 가난을 면치 못하게 된다.

oligarchic 소수 독재 정치의   bulk 대부분   efficient 효율적인   subsistence 생존(= existence)
immediately productive 즉각 생산성이 입증되는   diminution 축소   consumable commodities 소비재
distribute 분배하다   expedient 방편, 수단   alternative 선택(권), 대안

376 According to eighteenth-century proponents of capitalism, the ideal capitalist society would be made up of many small enterprises competing for a portion of the market. Government would play a minor role in this society, handling various public functions, such as building and maintaining roads; conducting foreign policy and providing for the national defense; and enforcing the law. In this liberal-capitalist concept of minimum government, espoused by many early leaders of the United States, government was seen as the chief threat to freedom. In this view, freedom to do business as one pleased was linked with freedom of conscience and freedom of speech. The ideal government functioned as a "night watchman"—a guardian of the existing distribution of property.

In the early nineteenth century it was widely believed that laissez-faire (unregulated) capitalism would liberate society from the tyrannies of political oppression, bureaucratic control, and stifling traditions. Capitalism, many theorists held, would create a new world of immense wealth, a far more efficient and productive economy—without any conscious direction from government. In attempting to profit as much as possible, each person would create wealth, and this would benefit the whole society. Selfishness, in other words, would serve social ends. In this ideal capitalistic world, individuals would be judged on their merits—the value of their skills in the marketplace—not on such noneconomic criteria as social status, color, gender, or religion.

On its own terms, capitalism succeeded almost immediately. The new economic system revolutionized the production and distribution of goods, stimulated worldwide trade, and broke down ancient and often oppressive traditions and social barriers. The economic freedom of capitalism and the political freedom of democracy formed a perfect partnership for great numbers of people.

Key Structure ▸

6 In this liberal-capitalist concept of minimum government
정부의 권한이 최소한으로 축소된 이 자유주의–자본주의의 개념에 비추어 보면

24 On its own terms 그 자체의 용어로 보면[나름대로는]

28 formed a perfect partnership 완벽한 한 동아리를 이루었다

내용 18세기에 나타난 자본주의는 정부의 권한을 축소하고 개인의 자유로운 경제 활동을 보장하는 이상적인 경제 제도였다.

proponent 제창자, 지지자   enterprise 기업, 사업   compete for ~을 얻기 위해 경쟁하다   enforce law 법을 시행하다   minimum government 권한이 최소화된 정부   espoused by ~에 의해 지지되다   freedom of conscience 양심의 자유   freedom of speech 언론의 자유   night watchman 밤의 파수꾼   guardian 감시자, 보호자   laissez-faire 자유방임(주의)의   tyranny 독재   bureaucratic 관료체제·정치의   stifling 숨막힐 듯한   immense 엄청난   criteria 기준들 sg. criterion   revolutionize 혁신하다, 혁명화하다   break down 무너뜨리다

377   Not only the economic, but also the personal relations between men have this character of alienation; instead of relations between human beings, they assume the character of relations between things. But perhaps the most important and the most devastating instance of this spirit of instrumentality and alienation is the individual's relationship to his own self. Man does not only sell commodities, he sells himself and feels himself to be a commodity. The manual laborer sells his physical energy; the businessman, the physician, the clerical employee, sell their "personality." They have to have a "personality" if they are to sell their products or services. This personality should be pleasing, but besides that its possessor should meet a number of other requirements: he should have energy, initiative, this, that, or the other, as his particular position may require. As with any other commodity it is the market which decides the value of these human qualities, yes, even their very existence. If there is no use for the qualities a person offers he has none; just as an unsalable commodity is valueless though it might have its use value. Thus, the self-confidence, the "feeling of self," is merely an indication of what others think of the person. It is not he who is convinced of his value regardless of popularity and his success on the market. If he is sought after, he is somebody; if he is not popular, he is simply nobody. This dependence of self-esteem on the success of the "personality" is the reason why for modern man popularity has this tremendous importance. On it depends not only whether or not one goes ahead in practical matters, but also whether one can keep up one's self-esteem or whether one falls into the abyss of inferiority feelings.

Key Structure •

10 **if they are to sell ~** = if they wish to sell ~

11 **besides that** = in addition to that 그것 외에도

12 **meet a number of other requirements** 그 밖의 여러 요구 조건을 충족시키다

13 **as his particular position may require** 그가 처한 특수한 상황에 따라서

14 **As with any other commodity** 다른 어떤 상품의 경우에서처럼

14 it is **the market** which **decides ~**
   • it is ~ that 강조 구문에서 that 대신 which가 쓰인 것.

16 **he has none** = he has no use

17 **though it might have its use value** 그것이 사용 가치는 있을지 몰라도

21 **he is somebody(↔ nobody)** 그는 상당한 존재(↔ 별 볼 일 없는) 존재이다

24 **On it depends** not only A, but also B ~ A뿐만 아니라 B도 그것에 달려 있다

내용 상품으로 가치가 있으면 그 사람은 높이 평가되고, 그렇지 못할 때는 별볼일 없는 존재가 된다.

alienation 소외, 이간   **devastating** 황폐화시키는   **instrumentality** 수단, 도구   **manual laborer** 육체노동자
initiative 솔선수범   **unsalable** 잘 팔리지 않는(= unsellable)   **regardless of** ~과는 상관없이(= irrespective of)
self-esteem 자기존중, 자부심(= self-respect)   **abyss** 심연   **inferiority feeling** 열등의식

---

378 The concept of liberal democracy first came into political thought about three hundred years ago, when a great debate raged in Europe over the powers of kings and the rights of citizens. The monarchs of the seventeenth and eighteenth centuries claimed they ruled by "divine right," but the early liberal democrats envisioned a different kind of political society. Besides arguing for a society based on the consent of those governed, they also began to talk about basic human rights, equality among citizens, and the right to protest and rebel against oppressive governments.

These critics of monarchy were in no sense egalitarians, however. Many of them wanted a government based only on the consent of a small, prosperous middle class; very few were willing to advocate a society based on the consent of all. The notion that every person should have a voice in shaping the destiny of political life was so radical that it was barely conceivable. Many of the struggles over

Part **3** Advanced Reading

409

democracy in the past two centuries have focused directly on this issue: Whose consent is to be sought by a government based on the consent of the governed?

These modern democratic ideas developed in concert with a new socioeconomic system known as capitalism. The rising middle classes of the seventeenth and eighteenth centuries wanted to gain full freedom to buy and sell, to accumulate wealth, and generally to conduct business without government interference. Many observers have argued that democracy became possible only because of the rise of capitalism, which emphasized individual rights and individual potential. Capitalists struggled to limit government power, defending the individual's rights to carve out a sphere of private life exempt from government interference. It must be noted, however, that though these efforts contributed to an atmosphere in which democratic ideas could take hold, the simultaneous development of a capitalist economic system and a democratic political system also created problems and tensions that persist to this day.

Key Structure

2　a great debate raged ~ over…
　…에 관하여 커다란 논쟁이 한창이었다

6　Besides arguing for ~ = In addition to arguing for ~
　~을 옹호하는 주장 외에도

7　the consent of those (who are) governed 피통치자들의 동의

27　carve out a sphere of ~ interference
　정부의 간섭이 배제된 개인적 삶의 한 부분을 (잘라내어) 개척하다

내용　초기 자유민주주의자들은 신권을 기초로 한 왕권에 도전하여 기본적 인권, 평등권, 압제 정부에 대한 반항권에 기초를 둔 사회를 염두에 두고 싸웠다.

rage 한창이다, 고조에 달하다　monarch 군주　divine right 신권(神權)　envision 마음에 그리다, 상상하다(= envisage, visualize)　basic human rights 기본적 인권　protest 항의하다　rebel against ~에 반대하다　oppressive 압제적인, 억누르는　egalitarian 평등주의자　advocate 옹호하다　conceivable 생각해 볼 수 있는　in concert with ~와 제휴하여　socioeconomic 사회·경제의　accumulate 축적하다　interference 간섭　potential 잠재력　carve out 베어내다, 개척하다　exempt from ~에서 면제된[자유로운](= free from)　take hold 굳건히 자리잡다　simultaneous 동시의　persist 지속하다, 살아남다

Ironically, causes with almost universal appeal—such as drives to promote clean air and safe consumer goods—are often the most difficult to organize. Some observers argue that broadly shared interests rarely capture the imagination of prospective supporters, and organizational success therefore eludes them. For potential members of groups dedicated to such causes, it may be hard to see how joining the group will make much difference; that is, the payoffs for joining an interest group dealing with diffuse public issues are usually exceeded by the costs of joining and acquiring information. Nonetheless, such groups do exist and often prosper.

Narrowly focused interest groups, in contrast, can count on staunch support because the people directly affected by a specific public policy have a strong incentive to organize. Suppose, for example, that regulations allowing competition in the sale of eyeglasses were proposed. Consumers might benefit from such regulations, but most of them would have only a vague idea of how those regulations would affect them. Opticians, however, surely would organize to lobby against regulations that would, in effect, force them to lower prices. Here we see a chronic problem of interest group politics: widely shared interests that affect many people slightly are less likely to prompt an organized response than narrowly shared interests that affect a few people more deeply.

A related problem stems from the subtlety of most interest group activity: the process of influence seeking is often hidden from public scrutiny. Interest group lobbying frequently resembles subtle osmosis much more than pressurized arm-twisting. Critics decry this cozy arrangement, charging that it circumvents the open, public debate so crucial to the exercise of democracy.

Key Structure ▸

7 the payoffs for ~ are usually exceeded by the costs…
~에 대한 보상이 …에 들어가는 비용보다 보통은 적다

11 Narrowly focused interest groups
작은 문제에 관심을 갖는 이익 단체들

21 are less likely to prompt an organized response
조직적인 반응을 촉진시킬 가능성이 더 적다

내용 많은 사람의 이해관심사가 걸린 문제를 다루기 위한 운동을 결성하는 것은 소수의 이익 단체가 자신들의 이익을
보호하기 위한 운동을 결성하기보다 더 어렵다.

cause 운동(= drive, movement), 명분 **appeal** 호소(력) **prospective** 예상되는, 장래가 있는 **elude** ~의 눈을
피하다 **payoff** 보수, 보상, 결말 **interest group** 이익 집단 **diffuse** 널리 퍼진[알려진] **prosper** 번영하다,
성공하다 **staunch** 단단한, 충실한(= loyal, faithful) **incentive** 동기(= motive), 자극 **vague** 흐릿한, 모호한
optician 안경 판매업자 **lobby against** ~에 반대하는 로비를 하다 **chronic** 고질적인, 만성의 **subtlety** 정교함,
미묘함 **scrutiny** 면밀한 조사 **osmosis** 삼투(성) **decry** 비난하다, 헐뜯다(= find fault with) **cozy** 아늑한
charge 책망하다 **circumvent** 방해하다 **crucial** 중대한, 결정적인

380 The most basic and straightforward notion of democracy is that of
simple majority rule. This means that a majority of the people give
their consent to specific policies or leaders. They can do so either
directly or through representatives selected to rule in the name of the
people. But does majoritarian democracy give rise to a reasonably
workable, equitable, and fair political system? Will a majority, for
example, decide to outlaw certain religions or political factions? Will
it take away the property of the few who hold great wealth? Will it be
able to run the government in a coherent and sensible fashion? These
are questions that a simple definition cannot answer. Yet they are the
very questions that have been asked about majoritarian democracy
since its beginnings in ancient Greece.

It was in Athens that the issues associated with majority rule first
became highly charged. Democracy in ancient Athens took the form
of a legislative assembly selected by lot, which meant that any citizen
might be called on to serve. In addition, there were popular courts,
whose members were also selected by lot. Basic issues of public policy
were debated in the assembly, with the citizens listening, participating,
and finally voting to decide the issues. Defenders of majority rule in
Athens saw this system as a device for allowing the populace to have
a voice in political decision making. Any other arrangement, they
argued, would tend to place power exclusively in the hands of the
rich or the well-born—as had often been the case in Athens before
the democratic reforms. For democrats the Athenian political system
demonstrated that a random selection of the people could assemble

and attend to the public's business in a reasonable fashion. Some also argued that the Athenian experience showed that people who participate in making and enforcing the laws are likely to be more law-abiding. Democracy made for a more committed citizenry.

Key Structure •

10 **they are the very questions that ~**
그것들은 ~한 바로 그 문제들이다

13 **It was in Athens that ~**
~한 것은 바로 아테네에서였다

16 **be called on to serve**
(국가에) 봉사하도록 요구받다

18 **with the citizens listening**
시민들은 경청하고
• 부대상황을 나타내는 독립분사구문.

29 **Democracy made for a more committed citizenry.**
민주주의는 보다 헌신적인 시민을 만드는 데 기여하였다.

내용 민주주의의 가장 기초적이고 명백한 개념은 다수에 의한 지배인데, 이것은 아테네의 민주정치에서 잘 실현되었다.

straightforward 솔직한, 명백한   **majority rule** 다수(에 의한) 지배   **consent** 동의   **majoritarian democracy** 다수 지배에 의한 민주주의   **give rise to** ~을 야기하다(= bring about), 가져오다   **workable** 실현 가능한   **equitable** 공정한   **outlaw** 금하다, 불법화하다   **political faction** 정당, 정치 파벌   **become charged** 부각되다, 쟁점화되다, 비난받다   **legislative assembly** 입법부   **by lot** 제비뽑기로   **device** 방편, 고안품   **populace** 민중, 대중   **random** 무작위의   **enforce the laws** 법을 집행하다   **law-abiding** 법을 준수하는   **make for** ~에 기여하다   **committed** 헌신적인   **citizenry** (집합적) 시민

PART

4

Sentence Completion

문장완성 문제로 독해력을 평가해보자!

381 The quarterback raised his arm and hurled the football. The fullback grabbed the ball, _____ the tackle, and raced toward the goal line. It was truly a beautiful run as he avoided all the downfield defensive players.

(고려대 편입)

(A) eluded   (B) distilled
(C) impaired   (D) reduced

382 The essence of liberty is not its existence as a theoretical right; rather, it consists in the possibility of exercising this right. When one's subsistence is so meager as to require him to seize any course of action that presents itself, he is denied any opportunity for choice or indecision. His freedom then _____.

(고려대 편입)

(A) is inalienable   (B) is an important one
(C) permits bargaining   (D) really does not exist

383 A million people have died in earthquakes this century, experts say. The next century might see 10 times as many deaths, with a million lost in a single blow, they add, unless major steps are taken to _____ dozens of sprawling cities expected to teem with billions of added residents.

(고려대 편입)

(A) adorn   (B) fortify
(C) outshine   (D) uncover

384 The evidence was so strong against his client that the lawyer thought the jury would certainly find him guilty. He therefore advised the client to plead guilty, to have a trial by a judge, and to hope for _____.

(고려대 편입)

(A) appeal
(B) mercy
(C) conviction
(D) acquittal

385 There are those who say that the Industrial Revolution left a world that is hopelessly unattractive and uninspiring. According to them, the modern artist is faced with a difficult choice: either he must retreat into a world of fantasy or he must face the real world and allow his art to reflect its _____.

(고려대 편입)

(A) ugliness
(B) splendor
(C) strength
(D) possibilities

386 The governments of ancient Asia had been absolute monarchies; obedience to authority was thus the ruling principle of life, political and social. The ancient Greeks, however, formed a republican city-state in which people had a voice in their government and had some liberties. They were not subjects but citizens. Their duty was to obey the law, not to be _____.

(고려대 편입)

(A) students of government
(B) free and thinking citizens
(C) subservient to authority
(D) different from ancient people

387 There are three main ways that vitamins are lost from foods. First, some vitamins dissolve in water. When vegetables are cooked in water, the vitamins go into the water. If the water is thrown away, the vitamins are lost. _____, heat, light, and oxygen change some vitamins. If vegetables are cooked, the heat changes some of the vitamins. Then these vitamins are no longer healthful. For instance, boiling grapefruit destroys some of its vitamin C. Finally, people sometimes throw away part of a plant which has the most vitamins. For example, when flour is processed, the wheat germ, which is very rich in vitamins, is lost.   (고려대 편입)

(A) Not only   (B) In addition
(C) Therefore   (D) Nevertheless

388 Each human culture sees itself as a world of permanence and stability. Each of the items that we find in a museum tells us this story. The individuals whose craftsmanship created these items knew that they themselves would perish, but it was inconceivable to them that their culture should _____.   (고려대 편입)

(A) disappear   (B) be permanent
(C) be renowned   (D) influence other people

389 Every society has its own notion of time that determines its social customs about punctuality. In some cultures, being early and on time for appointments is expected. If one comes late, it is considered disrespectable and a personal _____ to the waiting party.   (고려대 편입)

(A) affront   (B) adoration
(C) laudation   (D) deference

390 The best counseling is not that which confines itself to the solution of specific problems but rather that which teaches the person counseled those habits of thinking and acting that give him the ability to solve his own problems as they arise. The aim of counseling is to give to the individual _____. (고려대 편입)

(A) the answer to the present problems
(B) a new attitude toward his problems
(C) the ability to foresee future difficulties
(D) insight into the techniques of counseling

391 Like the much-doubted tales of clone babies, the idea of species-crossing stem cells sparks _____ among some researchers that policy-makers will go beyond a ban on reproductive cloning, to rule out therapeutic cloning as well. (고려대 편입)

(A) dreams   (B) ecstasies
(C) worries   (D) fantasies

392 Hundreds of thousands of people marched through Florence on Saturday in a protest against globalization and US policy on Iraq, and _____ the high turnout there was none of the violence that marred last year's Group of Eight summit in Genoa. (고려대 편입)

(A) despite   (B) due to
(C) based on   (D) stemmed from

393 As every child knows, lop the tail off a lizard and, astonishingly, it grows back. Unfortunately, the ability to _____ missing or damaged organs and body parts is largely lost in human beings. (한국외대 편입)

(A) furnish   (B) produce

(C) regenerate   (D) compensate

394 Young discoverers need not despair. Though there are few blanks left on today's map of the world, there are still _____ realms to be charted in the depths of the ocean, the remote recesses of the rain forests and the furthest reaches of outer space. (한국외대 편입)

(A) cultivated   (B) inevitable

(C) inhabited   (D) unexplored

395 The man's house sat on four acres, and his life's goal was to make it a forest. He came from the "no pains, no gains" school of horticulture, but he never watered a new tree. When I asked why, he said that watering plants made them grow _____. Trees that weren't watered, he said, had to grow deep roots in search of moisture. (한국외대 편입)

(A) weak branches   (B) shallow roots

(C) strong trunks   (D) broad leaves

396   The natural world and the human environment do not stand in diametric opposition, but are instead inexorably _____. Consequently, the distinction between the natural and the cultural is often a _____ one.   (한국외대 편입)

(A) separated – futile   (B) separated – fruitful
(C) intertwined – futile   (D) intertwined – fruitful

397   The decline of civility has increasingly become the subject of lament both in the popular media and in daily conversation. Civility _____ potential unpleasantness in social relationships. Without it, daily social exchanges can turn nasty and sometimes hazardous. Civility thus seems to be a(n) _____ virtue of social life.   (한국외대 편입)

(A) encourages – momentous   (B) encourages – unnecessary
(C) inspires – momentous   (D) forestalls – basic

398   Strange things are easier to understand than those we know too well. The nearer, the more everyday and familiar an event is, the greater the difficulty we find in comprehending it or realizing it is an event that actually takes place. _____ causes us to react automatically to the things which surround us.   (한양대 편입)

(A) Habit   (B) Necessity
(C) A rule   (D) An event

399 Clothes protect us from extremes of weather, and provide a degree of modesty. What is also important is the way clothing transmits messages about the wearer's personality, attitudes, and social status. Some professionals are more sensitive to dress signals than others, but there are very few who _____ clothes into account at all when forming first impressions. (한양대 편입)

(A) fail to take
(B) try putting
(C) consider to put
(D) succeed in taking

400 Do you know how the female mosquito decides whom to bite? She's quite selective, and she chooses her victims carefully. First, she uses sensors to find her victim. With these sensors, she tests your body moisture, body warmth, and chemical substances in your sweat. If she likes what she finds, she bites. But if you don't appeal to her, she'll reject you. The next time a mosquito bites you, just remember that you _____. (한양대 편입)

(A) are in big trouble
(B) were chosen
(C) need an insecticide
(D) should sleep in a mosquito net

401 We all go through life wearing spectacles colored by our own taste, our own calling, and our own prejudices. We see _____, what we are capable of seeing, not what there is to be seen. It is not wonderful that we make so many bad guesses at the prismatic thing, the truth. (한양대 편입)

(A) objectively, not subjectively
(B) subjectively, not objectively
(C) both objectively and subjectively
(D) neither subjectively nor objectively

402 Men are born with two eyes, but with one tongue, in order that they should see twice as much as they say; but from their conduct one would suppose that they were born with two tongues, and one eye; for those who observe the least talk the most, and those who have seen into nothing _____. (한양대 편입)

(A) have only one eye
(B) try to see everything
(C) do not want to talk much
(D) express their opinion about everything

403 No one could foresee in the Middle Ages that English, not Latin, would be the language of learning and knowledge. No one could foresee in the eighteenth century, and even in the 1950s, that English, not French, would be the first language of international diplomacy. The future of a language is _____. (한양대 편입)

(A) difficult to learn   (B) certain to change
(C) impossible to predict   (D) easy to describe

404 The project was in trouble. It was costing more than planned and was taking too long to finish. The design team members decided they must _____ a new plan, otherwise the project would be canceled. (한양대 편입)

(A) go back on   (B) put up with
(C) do away with   (D) come up with

405 Life is full of choices. We often choose between doing something the easy way and doing something the hard way. Unfortunately, we almost always choose the easy way because it's just easier. For example, we almost always choose to do the easiest assignment, to take the easiest job, or to find the easiest people to talk to at a party. However, these choices are not always the best choices. Sometimes by choosing the hardest way, there is more to gain. By choosing the hardest assignment, we might learn more. By choosing to talk to someone who seems unapproachable at a party, we might end up making a new friend. In short, _____.

(A) the easy way isn't always the best way
(B) we do not know what is the best choice
(C) the best way is to make correct choices
(D) it's not always easy to make right choices

406 No hero of ancient or modern times can surpass the American Indian with his lofty contempt of death and the _____ with which he sustained the cruelest affliction.

(성균관대 편입)

(A) concern   (B) condemnation
(C) fortitude   (D) disaster

407 Farmers use chemicals to artificially ripen fruits and vegetables. But some farmers now grow produce by the old-fashioned way—without chemicals. We call this kind of produce _____.

(성균관대 편입)

(A) pure   (B) organic
(C) environmental   (D) uncontaminated

408   How could high-school girls understand their place in American history if their textbooks told them that from _____ America to the present, women have had equal opportunity for upward mobility and political participation? (성균관대 편입)

(A) colonial

(B) savage

(C) ancient

(D) prehistoric

409   Utility industry leaders, in determining which of the various types of energy sources to develop, make their decision, in the privacy of their room, on the basis of profitability, but publicly they _____ their choice on the basis of lowered rates and increased safety. (성균관대 편입)

(A) deny

(B) justify

(C) replicate

(D) underwrite

410   As the official investigation of the plane crash revealed, the ground crew work schedule was so crowded that they could not have conducted more than the most _____ of preflight inspections of the ill-fated aircraft prior to takeoff. (성균관대 편입)

(A) cursory

(B) preemptory

(C) repetitive

(D) thoroughgoing

411 Although he had but a _____ knowledge of horticulture, Wills persisted in offering advice on the care of orchids to the eminent botanist, to the great embarrassment of their host. (성균관대 편입)

(A) genuine   (B) profound
(C) superficial   (D) professional

412 Everybody by now is aware that the cost of the American way is enormous, that air conditioning is an energy glutton. It uses some 9 percent of all the electricity produced. Such an extravagance merely to provide comfort is peculiarly American and strikingly _____ all the recent rhetoric about national sacrifice in a period of menacing energy shortages. (중앙대 편입)

(A) in conformity with   (B) familiar with
(C) compatible with   (D) at odds with

413 If there are more than two people in a conversation, then it is like doubles in tennis, or like volleyball. There's no waiting in line. Whoever is nearest and quickest hits the ball, and if you step back, someone else will hit it. No one stops the game to give you a turn. You're responsible for _____. (중앙대 편입)

(A) keeping your position
(B) taking your own turn
(C) returning the ball to me
(D) what might happen in the future

414   Time is a core system of cultural, social, and personal life. In fact, nothing occurs except in some kind of time frame. A complicating factor in _____ relations is that each culture has its own time frames in which the patterns are unique.   (중앙대 편입)

(A) personal
(B) indigenous
(C) intercultural
(D) deterministic

415   With the availability and affordability of the personal computer, more and more households are wired to the World Wide Web on the Internet. This puts the individual in instantaneous contact with other computer users anywhere in the world. Information on the World Wide Web has _____ to the point where much of what once was in libraries and archives can now be found on the Internet.   (중앙대 편입)

(A) proliferated
(B) relinquished
(C) traversed
(D) undermined

416   Hinduism has no founder and no prophet. It has no specific church structure, nor does it have a set of system of beliefs defined by one authority. The emphasis is on the way of living rather than on a way of thought. Radhakrishnan, a former president of India, once remarked: "Hinduism is more culture than a _____."   (중앙대 편입)

(A) tradition
(B) property
(C) legend
(D) creed

417 For a newly graduated college student, the "real world" can be a scary place to be when he or she is faced with such issues as handling credit, planning a budget, or knowing what to look for when making a purchase and whom to purchase it from. Entering this "real world" could be made _____ if persons were educated in dealing with these areas of daily life. What better place to accomplish this than in college?

(중앙대 편입)

(A) less promising   (B) less traumatic
(C) more dynamic   (D) more overwhelmed

418 As a newborn, you quickly developed a relationship with your parents and later, while you were growing, you formed relationships with your siblings. According to psychologists, your birth order affected how your parents and your brothers and sisters reacted to you and treated you. That is, you and they behaved in certain ways depending on your _____ in the family.

(중앙대 편입)

(A) position   (B) power
(C) significance   (D) identity

419 After our ancestors had learned to communicate with each other, a long series of amazing developments began. Creativity _____ among such peoples as the ancient Egyptians, Minoans, Greeks, Mayans, and the Benin of Africa. Long before the modern age of machines, our ancestors had already developed sophisticated techniques and systems in mathematics, engineering, art, and literature.

(중앙대 편입)

(A) changed   (B) diminished
(C) dominated   (D) flourished

420   After Leonardo had painted his most famous works, he began to spend more time on his other dreams. As a military engineer, Leonardo had drawn plans for primitive tanks and airplanes long before they were ever dreamed possible. He is also _____ with having designed the first parachute and having constructed the first elevator. (중앙대 편입)

(A) described   (B) credited
(C) evidenced   (D) acknowledged

421   A learning team, also called a study group, is a group of students that meets on a regular basis to talk about class readings, study for exams, and do other things to improve the students' grades. Research has shown that students who study together outside of class often do better than students who _____. (중앙대 편입)

(A) are introverted   (B) read a lot of books
(C) only study on their own   (D) are less attentive in class

422   When one considers the countless number of schools of modern art, the multiplicity of artists, and the various types of media through which art is expressed, one can sympathize with those who claim that it reflects _____. (건국대 편입)

(A) uniformity   (B) inertia
(C) cornerstones   (D) diversity

423 Although compact discs are more expensive than cassette tapes, many music lovers prefer to buy them. First of all, the sound quality of compact discs is considered to be superior to that of cassette tapes, due to advanced recording technology. _____, compact discs have a longer life span than cassette tapes—twenty-five years compared to about ten years. (건국대 편입)

(A) Nevertheless
(B) In addition
(C) In conclusion
(D) On the contrary

424 Most people see a college degree as a guarantee of a decent job. And in the economic boom of the late nineties, most college grads had multiple job offers after getting their diplomas. But members of the class of 2002 are learning that eager companies who embraced their older classmates just a few years ago are giving this year's grads _____. What is causing this job shortage and what are grads doing about it? (동국대 편입)

(A) the cold shoulder
(B) a comfortable berth
(C) the blank check
(D) the thumbs up

425 Credit-card numbers obtained by theft or from anarchist websites on the Internet are used to access pornographic net pages, and _____ people are charged. This huge fraud probably results from negligence by banks, and raises the possibility that credit-cards as currently operated are unsuitable for electronic commerce. (동국대 편입)

(A) suspicious
(B) guilty
(C) innocent
(D) persecuted

426 For years, caffeine was linked to hypertension. However, new research shows that although this stimulant may initially cause a sharp rise in blood pressure, _____ to caffeine usually develops rapidly and coffee has little effect. (숭실대 편입)

(A) tolerance
(B) antagonism
(C) addiction
(D) vulnerability

427 The great majority of city streets are safe, as long as you don't go into _____ areas and travel alone too late at night. For extra safety and comfort, you might follow the mapped-out walking routes some tourist bureaus supply. (숭실대 편입)

(A) noisy
(B) deserted
(C) redeveloped
(D) underdeveloped

428 Some anthropologists claim that a few apes have been taught a rudimentary sign language, but skeptics argue that the apes are only _____ trainers. (단국대 편입)

(A) imitating
(B) condoning
(C) instructing
(D) acknowledging

429   You can wreck your liver and die on a bottle of Tylenol. Too much aspirin causes gastrointestinal bleeding. Too much lithium damages your thyroid and kidney. The point is that it matters how much you take of a drug. There's a saying in medicine: the difference between a poison and a cure is the _____.   (인하대 편입)

(A) time   (B) effects
(C) dose   (D) contents

430   Most of us recognize the danger of trusting too much. But we often underestimate the danger of trusting too little. A parent who helps a child do everything perfectly, or tries to protect a child from any risk, decreases the child's responsibility and diminishes the likelihood that the child will become worthy of trust. Why should the child look both ways before crossing a street if someone else always does it? The same is true of an employer who supervises an employee too closely. In some factories, the addition of quality control inspectors has caused production workers to _____.   (인하대 편입)

(A) pay less attention to quality
(B) compete more with each other
(C) make products of better quality
(D) spend more time helping each other

431   Language, like sleep, is not a substance but a process; in practice it is known to everyone, yet its theory _____ defies formulation.   (행정고시)

(A) anything but   (B) all but
(C) all nothing   (D) but nothing

432 At the budget hearing, both the _____ and the opponents of the tax increase will be able to present their views. (서울대 대학원)

(A) auditor
(B) cons
(C) proponents
(D) subscribers

433 Mountain-climbing involves many risks, and the climber must be alert all times. Reckless climbers soon meet with an accident. The job is really one for a man who is _____. (서울대 대학원)

(A) bold
(B) strong
(C) frightened
(D) prudent

434 Contemporary composers have been showing a strong reaction to this kind of realism. In fact, _____ began as far back as the beginning of our century. (서울대 대학원)

(A) the revolt
(B) the show
(C) the ideal
(D) the realism

435 The new knowledge and the new techniques developed in biological research over recent decades have slowly begun to provide understanding of human disease and the hope of definitive therapeutic and _____ measures. (서울대 대학원)

(A) drastic   (B) preventive
(C) repressive   (D) rigorous

436 Fears of massive unemployment have greeted technological changes ever since the Industrial Revolution. Far from destroying jobs, however, rapid technological advance has generally been accompanied by high rates of job _____. (서울대 대학원)

(A) deprivation   (B) creation
(C) derision   (D) loss

437 The present upsurge of the Negro people of the United States grows out of a deep and passionate determination to make freedom and equality a _____ 'here' and 'now.' (서울대 대학원)

(A) reality   (B) revolution
(C) possibility   (D) significance

438   The forces of socialization that lead the individual to accept social
       institutions in their present form are not easily broken and _____.

(서울대 대학원)

       (A) valued   (B) emphasized
       (C) transformed   (D) mended

439   His success in converting the people to his way of thinking was largely
       a result of his _____ criticisms of the existing order.

(행정고시)

       (A) persuasive   (B) substantial
       (C) indiscreet   (D) emotional

440   Human cognitive systems, when seriously investigated, prove to be no
       less marvelous and _____ than the physical structures that develop
       in the life of the organism.

(서울대 대학원)

       (A) simple   (B) intricate
       (C) broad   (D) responsible

Part 4 Sentence Completion

441 From the beginning of recorded history, those men who have success-fully maintained control of government have come eventually to use that control selfishly. Hence, in a government operated by political and economic specialists, _____.

(A) one would expect efficient democracy to be the result
(B) the layman should be relieved of political concern
(C) agreement in vital governmental matters would be expected
(D) the common man is likely to suffer in the long run

442 One of the first messages to be sent over the new transatlantic cable was one between the President of the United States and the Queen of England. Both of the rulers were happy that the cable now had _____.

(A) enabled them to declare war on each other
(B) made the diplomatic corps unnecessary
(C) aided communications between their countries
(D) been laid by an American

443 The geographers of the Roman Empire were engaged primarily in the compilation of information about particular areas of the world. Their lack of interest in theorizing about the dimensions of the earth and about its relations to the rest of the solar system was a reflection of the Roman emphasis on _____.

(A) astronomy   (B) practical information
(C) theoretical geography   (D) metaphysical speculation

444   The American Indian, wandering the plains of this continent, utilized only sparingly the natural resources available to him. It seems that he anticipated that during some years he would be compelled to live on what he had previously conserved, for he was not _____.

(A) worried   (B) wasteful
(C) agricultural   (D) thrifty

445   Provision was made by the government for the maintenance of armies and navies whose duty it is to protect this nation from enemy aggression. This provision permits a citizen to enjoy a measure of security even though he does not give of his own time to _____.

(A) defense   (B) business
(C) politics   (D) progress

446   Throughout many centuries, forests were able to maintain their balance with nature, even though fires or other disturbances sometimes temporarily upset this balance. However, when man came into the picture with plows and axes and cattle, the forests _____.

(A) were no longer useful to man
(B) could no longer maintain their equilibrium
(C) provided raw materials for civilization
(D) competed with man by producing more seeds

447 Every citizen in a democracy, it is said, must have equality, and the will of the majority is supreme; thus the poor have more power than the rich because _____.

(A) it is their turn to rule
(B) there are more of them
(C) their needs are greater
(D) the rich are ever wicked

448 Until relatively recent times, commerce was geographically restricted because of transportation inadequacies. Only luxury goods and rare articles were exchanged over long distances. Man depended on his immediate environment, so that crop failure in a particular area resulted in _____.

(A) famine and starvation
(B) the importation of food
(C) little misfortune for anyone
(D) an increase in commerce

449 You cannot judge by appearances. Because of their clumsy appearance and slow ponderous movements, bears have earned a reputation of stupidity. However, among zoo keepers it is agreed that, of all the animals they handle, bears are among the most _____.

(A) dangerous
(B) intelligent
(C) peaceful
(D) stupid

450   Hypotheses must be understood through their history, for they are the result of progressive evolution rather than the products of sudden creation. If we follow the course of some concept, we will see slow and gradual transformations, but we will not find _____.

(A) a sudden and arbitrary creation of new hypotheses
(B) the causes for these changes
(C) much information concerning the beliefs of the ancients
(D) the predecessors of present-day theories

451   If a man disagrees with the majority decision, he may be justified in keeping silent, for it is quite understandable that he may not wish to take the role of a martyr. However, it is inexcusable for him to voice assent that he does not feel. There can be no justification of _____.

(A) investigation   (B) dissent
(C) doubt   (D) insincerity

452   It is silly to burden yourself with all sorts of things for which you have no particular desire simply to keep pace with your neighbors. You would find greater enjoyment in spending your money according to your personal whims, buying only _____.

(A) what suits your station   (B) unusual bargains
(C) the necessities of life   (D) what you want

453   Before superstition was replaced by understanding, the fates of nations
       were indeed sometimes changed by the eclipse of the sun. History is
       one area in which the movement of celestial bodies has _____.

       (A) caused little disturbance   (B) been left to astronomers
       (C) occurred with regularity   (D) played an astonishing part

454   The opponents of democracy contend that the present complexity
       of civilization calls for specialized knowledge on the part of those
       in control of government. They say that only a favored few have the
       qualifications required and that since democracy places control in the
       hands of the electorate, it precludes _____.

       (A) deference to the specialists   (B) equal rights for all
       (C) governmental control   (D) special knowledge

455   Science may be regarded either from a static or from a dynamic
       point of view. Considered statically, science is a body of knowledge,
       descriptive of the universe and regarded as explanatory, whereas to
       anyone with a dynamic orientation science implies continuous activity
       with today's state of knowledge as _____.

       (A) a basis for further operations
       (B) valueless
       (C) not incorporated in textbooks
       (D) an adequate description of life

456　The drama critic claimed that the play would not be popular, not because it dealt with love, but because it dealt with the love of two characters for each other, and, according to the critic, the people of his country had lost interest in _____.

(A) reviews by critics   (B) individual problems
(C) going to the theater   (D) love as an emotion

457　Robin's family had no clock. Robin wished that his father would buy one, because he was often late for school. He wasn't late for school intentionally, but because, upon leaving home each morning, he never knew exactly _____.

(A) if the clock were correct   (B) what time it was
(C) what time school started   (D) how far it was to school

458　Over sixty-three percent of the families in Iowa own their homes and live in private homes rather than in apartments. There is plenty of room for gardens and parks. In fact, one of the notable things about Iowa is _____.

(A) its variety of beautiful flowers
(B) the lack of traffic congestion
(C) its housing problem
(D) the high degree of industrialization

459 It is not only the human species which is engaged in the turmoil of political strife. In almost every ant community, there are communist malcontents who, resentful of the hoards of honey which their provident neighbors accumulate, attack these neighbors for being _____.

(A) capitalists   (B) petty thieves
(C) manufacturers   (D) unionists

460 One explanation that has been offered for the sparsity of theories of aesthetics is that the creator of such a theory must possess a passion for art and at the same time must be willing to assume an attitude of objective curiosity toward it. We have few theories of aesthetics because these qualities are seldom _____.

(A) recognized in others   (B) considered desirable
(C) productive of theory   (D) found in combination

461 It is the rule in a barbarian society that the upper classes never engage in industrial occupations but instead devote their lives to occupations to which a high degree of honor is attached. Whether they hold the positions of priests or warriors, their distinctive employment is the social expression of their _____.

(A) concern with war and religion
(B) patriotism
(C) superior status
(D) general laziness

462   In classical times the Mediterranean Sea and its surroundings comprised the only well-known part of the globe. However, the boundaries between the familiar and the unknown were vague and indefinite. When historians in the eleventh century approached the outer edges of their contemporary knowledge of world geography, facts faded into _____.

(A) mythology and legend   (B) new discoveries
(C) scientific investigation   (D) extensive migrations

463   We are most moved by what we read when we can think of the narrated events as occurring in our own lives. It is easiest to draw parallels between our lives and what we read when the material read deals with events in the life of a specific person. It is for this reason that I would seek to encourage the writing of _____.

(A) description   (B) history
(C) narration   (D) biography

464   The attitude is common that there is danger in flooding the world with too much knowledge. The story of Faust, which permeates literature, is evidence of the wide-spread, age-long belief in the bond between the man of knowledge and the powers of darkness. The belief will persist as long as _____.

(A) the alliance continues   (B) men seek knowledge
(C) superstition persists   (D) literature persists

465   The king, displeased because his newborn child was a girl, ordered one of his men to take baby into the forest and leave her there. The child was all alone in the forest. She cried, but only the birds heard her. After some time the baby became very weak. Indeed, had she not been rescued by hunters, she would have _____.

(A) befriended animals   (B) become civilized
(C) perished   (D) survived

466   There are two general ways in which to pay a worker: one, by the piece, so that his wages depend upon his skill; and, two, by the hour or week. In this age of mechanization, when so often the machine sets the limit of production, there would be no incentive value in paying a worker _____.

(A) by the piece   (B) by the hour
(C) for new ideas   (D) for his overtime

467   There are only two alternatives: space must be either finite or infinite. It seems incredible that space should be never-ending, but it is equally difficult to imagine boundaries of space. One of these alternatives must be true, and yet it seems that neither of them can be true. Our conception of space is plagued by a _____.

(A) legend   (B) contradiction
(C) fallacy   (D) boundary

468   We welcome new explanatory ideas, for they free us from the
       despotism of older ideas. But perhaps we now have a surplus of
       explanatory possibilities from which to choose. If only one of these can
       be correct, this large selection may be disconcerting to the theorist, for
       his chances of being wrong are _____.

       (A) increased   (B) eliminated
       (C) theoretical   (D) insignificant

469   Even though early farmers knew nothing about the laws of heredity,
       they did improve their crops by selecting seeds from their finest fruits
       and sowing them. Although results varied, continued selection of
       such seeds caused the crops to become differentiated from their wild
       ancestors. Selection of seeds by observation is still used as a method of
       _____.

       (A) fertilization   (B) plant study
       (C) agriculture   (D) improving crops

470   The early Americans lived in a rapidly changing world. Almost daily,
       everything seemed to move along the road of progress. Life was still
       uncomplicated enough, though, that these people could prosper
       gloriously throughout successive alterations. They were immersed in
       life but not overwhelmed by it. History was moving fast, but it seemed
       _____.

       (A) manageable   (B) stagnant
       (C) incomprehensible   (D) dynamic

471   Many university professors leave the classroom to become deans and department heads. These new positions usually are more rewarding financially, but money is not their only reason for changing jobs. The modern educational system is organized in such a way that a major portion of academic recognition goes to the _____.

(A) administrators
(B) older teachers
(C) faculty members
(D) trustees

472   Tropical vegetables are much less palatable than vegetables grown in temperate countries. In the tropics there has been no selective cultivation of the best native varieties, and the tasty varieties developed in temperate countries do not bear good seed in the tropics. The tropical gardener who would raise good vegetables must _____.

(A) ignore modern horticulture
(B) grow native plants
(C) import seed from temperate zones
(D) buy them from foreign dealers

473   The boiling point of water is not constant for all altitudes. One hundred degrees centigrade is the temperature at which water boils at sea level. At a height of 18,000 feet water boils at eighty-three degrees centigrade. Thus, it is possible for mountain climbers to make an approximation of their altitude by boiling water and _____.

(A) quickly cooling it
(B) varying the air pressure
(C) taking its temperature
(D) collecting the vapor

474   One mistake of the classical economists was the assumption of universal validity for economic laws extracted from their own particular economy. The historical school opposed this and tried to show that each society developed its own economy which operated with regularities _____.

(A) peculiar to that economy
(B) like those of neighboring societies
(C) demonstrating universal principles
(D) much like those of history

475   One of management's greater problems is finding skilled workers. The pay differential between skilled and unskilled workers is becoming less and less even though skilled workers require a much longer training period. It is thus quite natural that _____.

(A) skilled workers are taking more pride in their jobs
(B) management should want to decrease the pay differential
(C) the number of skilled workers is decreasing
(D) the pay differential should continue to decrease

476   When a pan of water is placed on the stove, the water gets hotter and hotter until it begins to boil. Once it has boiled, however, its temperature remains at the fixed boiling point for water. If the pan is left on the stove, the additional heat from the stove functions to boil away the steam, but it does not _____.

(A) help to heat the water in the first place
(B) raise the temperature of the water
(C) do any work
(D) leave the water temperature unchanged

477 Of the three hundred former students who were sent questionnaires, two hundred responded, of whom 175 reported that they had become successful, monetarily speaking. This rosy picture might have been different had all three hundred filled out the questionnaires, for there is a good probability that the one hundred who did not reply _____.

(A) were living at different addresses
(B) were not making large salaries
(C) felt no desire to give private information
(D) would not have affected the overall results

478 It is collegiate duty for the nonparticipants at an athletic event to keep up the morale of their team by cheering for it. Parallel to the athletic contest is the cheering contest. Yale may make more touchdowns than Harvard, but if Harvard supporters yell louder and longer than Yale's, the victory is Harvard's and _____.

(A) to the rooters belongs the praise
(B) to the victors belong the spoils
(C) the best team has won at last
(D) her team will be better next time

479 The standard of human life in any society is determined by the beliefs which human beings have about life. The quality of life at anytime is determined by the scale of values by which a society measures and compares the ways in which human beings live. When the standard of living of a society is altered, we may infer that the members of the society have altered their _____.

(A) productive efficiency   (B) educational standards
(C) ideas about life   (D) basic social structure

480　Constructive reading involves reacting and adjusting to what you are reading. Do not accept everything you read blindly, but do not be so critical as to reject the author's ideas just because they are different from your own. Weigh what you read in terms of logic and evidence supporting it. Base your acceptance or rejection of the author's ideas on the _____.

(A) rationality of the ideas　　(B) author's training

(C) critic's reviews　　(D) author's reputation

481　Although ancient Egyptian writing has been preserved for thousands of years, we were not able to read it until about a hundred and fifty years ago. The French under Napoleon invaded Egypt in 1798. While building some military works at Rosetta, they uncovered a stone on which the same message was inscribed both in hieroglyphics and in Greek. By the use of Greek as a key, after many hours of tedious effort, the hieroglyphics were _____.

(A) deciphered　　(B) reburied

(C) destroyed　　(D) copied

482　Those who studied heredity before the time of Mendel were unsuccessful because they included in their investigations entire generations, or even entire species, of plants or animals. They were able to study such a large number of individuals only summarily. Mendel confined his investigations to the study of particular characteristics as found in single plants. He was successful where his predecessors had failed because he was content to study _____.

(A) successive generations　　(B) individual plants

(C) many kinds of plants　　(D) the vertebrates

483   It is not difficult to explain the failure of France to take an active part in overseas enterprises during the sixteenth century. She was remote from and uninterested in the New World in the first half of the century; during the latter part she was involved in the Wars of Religion. Only after settlement of these religious difficulties did the French people direct their energies to _____.

(A) an improved social system   (B) religious reformation
(C) a new revolution   (D) lands across the ocean

484   The universities have added another to their already many functions—that of public entertainment in the form of athletics. Public interest in this particular aspect of university life is greater than in any of its educational activities. Less attention is given to a university's appointment of a president than to its _____.

(A) physical education program   (B) educational policy
(C) freshman enrollment   (D) new football coach

485   The majority of fatalities in fires have been caused by asphyxiation by smoke. The carbon monoxide in smoke causes dizziness and eventual collapse. To protect yourself, always act on the assumption that poisonous gases are present at the scene of a fire. Since an increase in breathing activity would lead to an increase in the amount of poison gas inhaled, it is important not to stimulate breathing, and it is safest to _____.

(A) walk away from the fire   (B) hurry to put out the fire
(C) run out of the danger zone   (D) stay where you are

486   Inventions may be viewed from several angles: one, as the result of
inspiration on the part of the inventor and, two, as the result of the
recombining of previously existing techniques and instruments. One
of the amazing features of a new technique or instrument is that so
often the same technique is discovered independently by two persons
at about the same time. This situation can be understood best by
considering inventions from the aspect of _____.

(A) inspiration   (B) independent work
(C) combining known techniques   (D) simultaneous action

487   Men are more likely to view the community in terms of production,
whereas women see it, not only as a place where people can earn
their livelihood, but also as a place where all can attain and enjoy the
good life. That is why women must be counted on to take an interest
in education, child and family life, public health, and so on, and to
participate in work to achieve the best conditions under which all
these can function for the welfare of _____.

(A) their own sex   (B) the whole population
(C) underprivileged groups   (D) delinquent children

488   Advertising frequently seeks to establish desire for a product by trying
to convince us that possessing the product will make us the center of
attention and the envy of our fellows. This is an adolescent appeal,
for maturity is based on the ability to live with one's equals. Much
advertising makes us want things _____.

(A) so that we can be like everybody else   (B) because we need them
(C) because of their educational value   (D) for immature reasons

489   Gestures are meaningful movements of the body, particularly of the face. Gestures are utilized to express feelings and moods over and above those transmitted by words. Although lovers may talk much, more is conveyed by their gestures than their words. In like manner, parents may threaten a child, but a knowing child will compare the threat with _____.

(A) what his parents have done in the past
(B) the expressions on his parents' faces
(C) the consequences of his action
(D) their love for him

490   Not too long ago, schoolteachers were expected to be strict disciplinarians. There was a set punishment for violation of each of the many rules of the classroom. Of course, the teacher still must have well-behaved class in order to teach effectively, but she is coming to adopt more positive means of fostering good conduct. She tries to understand why her pupils misbehave and to maintain an orderly classroom by emphasizing _____.

(A) new standards of good conduct
(B) learning by doing
(C) the unimportance of obedience
(D) the rewards of good conduct

491 Words are like mirrors in that they reflect exactly the feeling of the person who used them. They reflect the tears of a sorrowful writer and the smiles of the happy writer. The basis for this reflection is not in the mechanics or style of writing, as such, for the written words will reveal neither tears, smiles, nor any other feelings unless _____.

(A) the subject matter is quite emotion-laden
(B) they are very strong adjectives or verb phrases
(C) the words came from the man who wrote them
(D) the person who reads them has had the same experience

492 Increasing emphasis on the irrational and unconscious motivations of man has led some pessimists to strip rationality of all value, indeed, to deny its existence. The new findings, of course, must be recognized in any adequate theory of human behavior, but the discovery that the flowers of human life are rooted in dark soil in no way refutes the _____.

(A) importance of sunlight
(B) notion of unconscious motivation
(C) need to prevent erosion
(D) irrationality of their blossoms

493 We experience no particular feeling of satisfaction when we are allowed to breathe freely, but when breathing is restrained, we experience definite unpleasantness. It is the same with thought. We have no reaction to thoughts that flow freely to a logical conclusion, but when our thinking is beset by difficulties, we _____.

(A) breathe shallowly   (B) experience anguish
(C) are but slightly disturbed (D) finally feel pleasure

494   Magazines, like books, are designed to be read in the order, front cover to back cover. A large segment of the magazine-reading population, however, has formed the pernicious habit of thumbing backward through periodicals. Such individuals are frequently observed absent-mindedly reading a four-page story _____.

    (A) by skimming topic sentences
    (B) with noticeable lack of interest
    (C) as if it were a full-length novel
    (D) from the last paragraph to the introduction

495   As a result of some maneuver, a particular group of men, a race or nation, may come to occupy a strategic position in the world. They may strengthen this position until they dominate some region of the earth's surface. But their dominance is only temporary; they are superseded by a new race or nation. The center of the stage of human history has been occupied by _____.

    (A) many races and nations concurrently
    (B) a succession of races or nations
    (C) one group through all the ages
    (D) the wise rather than the strong

496   It is frequently said that America has no indigenous culture, that for
       her forms of art and literature she is deeply in debt to Europe. But
       even in Europe, assimilation over time is mistakenly called native
       originality. To go back even further, the culture of the Romans was
       inevitably derived from that of the Greeks. In accordance with an
       unchanging historical pattern, _____.

       (A) critics are notoriously unperceptive
       (B) each culture borrows from a preceding one
       (C) Europe must fall from her pinnacle of greatness
       (D) the best of one age is absorbed into the next

497   During the last century Western scholars have done much to under-
       stand and explain the structures of other present civilizations, as well
       as to illuminate the histories of civilizations no longer extant. In all
       cases, the scholars have found that each civilization at the time of its
       meeting with the Western world had reached a state of decay, in some
       instances approaching _____.

       (A) dissolution   (B) rejuvenation
       (C) westernization   (D) communism

498   From early childhood, man develops deep-rooted attitudes about
       his rights to material possessions and about the social and religious
       practices of his culture. In this realm, he thinks emotionally rather
       than rationally. Many men who would be quite willing to admit that
       the present railway system could be improved by changes would think
       that anyone who suggested changes in the present economic system or
       in the customs of our society was _____.

       (A) obviously enlightened   (B) supporting popular views
       (C) old-fashioned in his views   (D) either a madman or a criminal

499   Before the refinement of microscopic techniques, scientists could study matter only in relatively large units, each of which contained many individual molecules. No prediction could be made about the behavior of these smaller structures which composed the larger observable units, for there was no assurance that they followed the same laws. Similarly, it is at present impossible to predict individual human behavior from crowd behavior, since the rules which govern the two levels of action seem to be _____.

(A) easily observable   (B) virtually identical
(C) vastly different   (D) internally consistent

500   It is virtually impossible for a person effectively to oppose the climate of opinion and to resist the intrusion into his own thinking of opinions contrary to his own. If these contrary opinions are greatly publicized, they unavoidably become stimuli for every individual, who must ask of himself whether the opinions are just. The character of the answer is determined by the character of the question. The individual will soon find himself thinking along the lines represented in his opponent's opinions, in order to oppose them. Before long the individual discovers that he now holds the opinions held a short time before by the opponent, while still opposing his latest statements. Thus it is that _____.

(A) uniformity of opinion is developed
(B) political adversaries are defeated
(C) differences of opinion are developed
(D) alternative opinions are considered

501 After Jack Roseman hired his two-man company's first employee—an urgently needed computer programmer—the man dropped by Roseman's office and said, "Incidentally, Jack, what's my title?" Roseman told him, "I'll tell you what. I'm chairman. You can be assistant to the chairman."

Within about a week, the new employee had business cards with "Assistant to the Chairman" printed on them and was handing them out to visitors.

Roseman, who was astonished by the move, said the episode has influenced his business habits. He now believes that although a rose by any other name would smell as sweet, people care deeply about their titles. Business academics agree.

"Your self-concept depends on what you do and _____, and even if you simply change the title it affects your ego. It affects your personality," said Patrick Lennahan, director of the Career Center at Roger Williams University in Bristol, Rhode Island. He, who has studied ego involvement in careers, found that many people would rather have a prestigious title than money, probably because a title boosts job satisfaction.

(A) what your academic backgrounds are
(B) how well you get along with your colleagues
(C) how well your job performance is
(D) what you're called

Reading Comprehension

독해 문제를 통해 실전 감각을 기른다!

[502-511] 밑줄 친 부분 중에서, 어법에 어긋나는 것을 고르시오.

502   (A) On most of us the effect of our general education has been (B) such that we have tended to believe rather (C) uncritical, first that liberty is a good thing, and secondly that the possession of it is likely to increase our happiness. It may well be said, however, that at all times (D) a moment's consideration should have been sufficient to have shown us that neither of these propositions (E) is self-evident.

503   In the past men were often (A) bound together for survival by bonds of mutual fear. Our survival now requires that our common bond (B) is shared knowledge. Improved understanding will (C) not necessarily bury old antagonisms, but misunderstanding (D) is certain to contribute to them. It is therefore important that we increase communication, understanding and cooperation among people, (E) as among nations.

504   The temperature of the body becomes lower during the hours when a person is usually (A) asleep. A lowered body temperature makes a person (B) feel chilly. That is why a person who is sleeping must be covered. People who are accustomed to (C) be up during the day and sleeping at night will have a drop in body temperature at night, even when they stay up (D) all night. People who work at night and sleep during the day will have a drop in body temperature during the day, (E) whether they go to bed or not.

505   (A) We are impossible to draw up a balance-sheet of the goods and ills of industrialism. There (B) would be no agreement (C) as to whether its ills or goods are increasing or decreasing. Some enthusiasts would identify industrialization and civilization. But most people would allow that its results are (D) both good and bad. In most parts of the world industrialism has meant (E) an advance in material civilization, a rise in the standards of living, and greater political power for the humbler classes.

506   One of the most important factors in connection with the diffusion of cultural elements (A) is that they transfer from one society to (B) another almost exclusively in terms of their form. In other words, the borrowing society copies particular patterns of behavior (C) as it apprehends them, usually without understanding their original culture context. The new element (D) is thus transferred at the objective level and comes into the receiving culture (E) to be stripped of most of the meanings and associations which it carried in its original context.

507   People (A) all over the world have begun to realize the countless possibilities of a new freedom: Leisure. This (B) is especially true in countries with a highly-developed technology. Modern technology, shorter (C) working days, longer weekends, earlier retirement, and better health have given people much more free time than they have ever had before. But only students have not gained leisure time in this day and age. They have to study (D) longer and harder than ever before in order to keep up with our (E) rapid-changing world and prepare for the future. The life of a student has always been, and probably always will be, one of much effort and little free time.

508   I am closing my fifty-two years of military service. When I joined the army, even before the turn of the century, it was the fulfillment of all of my boyish hopes and dreams. The world (A) turned over many times since I took the oath on the plain at West Point, and the dreams (B) have long since vanished, but I still remember the refrain of one of the most popular barrack ballads of that day which proclaimed (C) most proudly that old soldiers never die; they just fade away. And (D) like the soldier of that ballad, I now close my military career and just fade away, an old soldier who tried to do his duty as God gave him the light (E) to see that duty. Good-by.

509   Modern literatures show innumerable debts (A) to classical writings, and the models are Latin authors (B) much more often than Greeks. It is obvious that this applies not only to modern literatures but also to the modern languages. These contain huge numbers of words from the classical languages, and the greater part of them come from Latin. This indebtedness of our modern languages and literatures is (C) so profound that very large parts of them are impossible (D) of understanding and appreciating without a knowledge of Latin. We owe to the Romans (E) scarcely less than the Romans owed to the Greeks.

510   Many people in our society feel that the best way to (A) <u>get people to work</u> harder is to increase their profits or their wages. They feel that it is just 'human nature' to want to increase one's material possessions. This sort of dogma might well go (B) <u>unchallenging</u>, if we had no knowledge of other countries. In certain societies, however, (C) <u>it has been found</u> that the profit motive is not an effective incentive. After contact with whites the Trobriand Islanders in Melanesia (D) <u>could have become</u> fabulously rich from pearl diving. They would, however, work only (E) <u>long enough</u> to satisfy their immediate wants.

511   One of the earliest observations (A) <u>that impressed me</u>, at the age of about fifteen, is something which seems to happen to all strata of society, perhaps particularly to the upper class. It struck me that pain and suffering among men (B) <u>are caused more often</u> by basically avoidable evils than by unavoidable ones such as the loss of a loved one, serious illness, extreme poverty, or catastrophes (C) <u>occurring in nature</u>. Most cases of unhappiness seem to (D) <u>be resulted from</u> petty feuding with one's fellow man or from inner conflicts. This unhappiness derives to a large extent from frustrated desires and vain ambitions or, speaking generally, from a false sense of values. Many people feel miserable without being either poor or physically ill; others feel (E) <u>badly injured</u> though nothing but their vanity has been hurt.

[512- 521] 밑줄 친 부분 중에서, 글의 내용상 어울리지 <u>않는</u> 것을 고르시오.

512 Something like half the entries into houses are made (A) <u>by way of</u> doors and windows which have been left open or unfastened, and (B) <u>due to</u> our repeated warnings, housewives still continue to advertize (C) <u>their absence</u> when they go away (D) <u>by leaving</u> newspapers and milk bottles to accumulate on the doorstep or by putting notices on the door saying, (E) "<u>Away until Monday.</u>"

513 The truly wise will recognize that there is no attitude of mind (A) <u>so fitting as</u> that of humility. The greatest thinkers have always been most deeply conscious of their own (B) <u>ignorance</u>. (C) <u>Beholding</u> a wider circle of light than other men, they have also beheld a (D) <u>wider circle of surrounding darkness</u>. What they have known has only convinced them of the (E) <u>smallness</u> of what remained unknown.

514 Through memory man (A) <u>keeps alive</u> the knowledge and experience that have been gained (B) <u>in past times</u>. He (C) <u>preserves records</u> of the steps in his progress, so that he can learn from those who have lived in earlier days and (D) <u>who will live in the future</u>. Thus whatever advance toward human comfort has been achieved by one generation becomes the foundation on which (E) <u>a new generation</u> may build.

515 We are often tempted to do the thing which gives us (A) <u>immediate pleasure</u> even though that may prevent us from achieving a future good (B) <u>of much greater importance</u>. Overeating and overdrinking are obvious examples of (C) <u>intemperance</u> which often result in our subsequent inability to discharge our obligations or do a good job. Temperance can, (D) <u>however</u>, be defined as a habitual ability to resist the temptation of immediate pleasures which would (E) <u>interfere with</u> our accomplishing greater, though more remote, goods.

516 History has no end, and I do not pretend to be able to predict the future. But I do think it worth while to reiterate my general disbelief in the doctrine that history is just one continuous line of (A) <u>progress onward and upward</u>, or even in the more ancient view of Aristotle, Vico, and Nietzche, that history is (B) <u>a series of repeatable cycles</u>. I accept (C) <u>either</u> of these views because I do not believe history is (D) <u>as simple as that</u>. In fact, I do not believe that if we take the whole complex of history we can form any adequate symbol for it. What we can do is to (E) <u>consider certain phases of it</u>.

517 Fairy tales interest us because they give us pictures of a world in which men do marvellous things (A) <u>with ease</u>, and are helped or hindered by all kinds of small and great creatures who lurk and hide in forests and underground; and magic delights us because it accomplishes (B) <u>so much with means so few</u> and materials so apparently inadequate. In the same way and (C) <u>for the same reason</u> men are always (D) <u>reluctant to hear</u> the stories of heroes, those who have overcome great difficulties, got over great obstacles, and won the race in spite of all kinds of (E) <u>discouragement</u>.

518   The importance of the fast-moving stream of events in our modern world makes it imperative that we (A) be well informed. Significant social, economic, and political issues, all demanding (B) serious and open-minded investigation, require more than ever before (C) a higher level of reader enlightenment. To advance in knowledge one must forever learn more, study more, reason more. (D) Reading helps accomplish this; in college about eighty-five percent of all study involves reading. If, as it certainly does, progress comes through study, then reading is perhaps the student's (E) easiest means to academic progress.

519   The growth of circulating libraries aided (A) the expansion of literature. At a time when the prices of books were very high in relation to the purchasing power of the great majority of the population, circulating libraries were (B) an important social invention. They furnished those who had acquired a taste for reading (C) with access to books otherwise out of their reach. They helped to (D) reduce the gap between interest in reading and purchasing power. The first circulating library was opened in London in 1740. Rivals quickly sprang up in London and in the provincials as well. By the end of the century, about 1,000 libraries dotted the country. Their rapid success testifies to (E) the declining interest in reading.

520   Art is a mirror of the artist's mind and its relationship to the world around him. The world, as we know it now, has become a very (A) <u>complex</u> experience. In its political and social development it has seen in the past forty years more far-reaching changes and has been shaken by (B) <u>less</u> disasters than at almost any other period in recorded history. It would be strange indeed (C) <u>not to find</u> some trace of these changes in the literature of our time. The writer of today no longer dwells in an ivory tower. He is a part of the world in which he lives, and in conveying (D) <u>his heightened impression</u> of it he is always seeking new forms of expression, and adequate techniques. It is his central purpose not to make confusion more confused, but to win imaginative unity, (E) <u>order and harmony</u> out of apparent chaos.

521   Up to the middle of the last century the chief interest of the historian and of the public alike lay in political and constitutional history, in political events, wars, dynasties, and in political institutions and their developments. Substantially, therefore, history concerned itself with (A) <u>the lower classes</u>. 'Let us now praise famous men,' was the historian's motto. He did (B) <u>not care to examine</u> the obscure lives and activities of (C) <u>the great mass of humanity</u>, upon whose slow toil was built up the prosperity of the world and who were the (D) <u>hidden foundation</u> of the political and constitutional edifice reared by the famous men he praised. To speak of the ordinary people would have been (E) <u>beneath the dignity of history.</u>

[522- 532] 아래 글들을 읽고 물음에 가장 알맞은 답을 고르시오.

522 　If you want to get a sense of ⓐ_____, just take a tour of your neighborhood school. Enter the cafeteria and you'll probably find wrappers from Taco Bell, Arby's, and Subway, fast food chains that provide school lunches. The third grade class may be learning math by counting Tootsie Rolls. Science curricula might well come from Dow Chemical, Dupont, or Exxon. It doesn't end there. Education in the U.S. has become big business. The 'education industry,' a term coined by EduVentures, an investment banking firm, is estimated to be worth between $630 and $680 billion in the U.S. The stock value of publicly traded educational companies is growing twice as fast as the Dow Jones Average. Brokerage firms like Lehman Brothers and Montgomery Securities have specialists seeking out venture capital for the education industry.

　Analysts at the conservative think tanks, like the Heritage Foundation, Hudson and Pioneer Institutes, tell us that the problems in education stem from inefficient, bloated school bureaucracies. Conservatives talk about "school choice," referring to vouchers and other public/private schemes. Free marketeers strike a chord with many parents when they point out that families do not have the choices they deserve, especially in urban school districts. ⓑ_____, according to progressive school activists, the problems in education have their roots in decades of unequal school funding. They say that as long as school districts are financed through property taxes, kids in poor, urban districts will never receive an equal education with suburban school kids. Wide disparities in school resources open the door for corporations to fill the gap (and their pockets), especially in inner city schools.

(경희대 편입)

A bird in the hand is worth two in the bush.
손 안의 새 한 마리가 숲 속의 두 마리보다 낫다. (남의 돈 천 냥이 내 돈 한 푼만 하랴.)

1 윗글의 제목으로 가장 적절한 것은?

(A) The Problem of the Education Industry in the U.S.
(B) How Companies Can Help School
(C) The Clash between Two Parties on Property Taxes
(D) Privatization Is not Necessarily Bad

2 윗글의 내용과 일치하지 <u>않는</u> 것은?

(A) 많은 도시 지역 학부모들은 자신들이 합당한 선택권을 갖고 있지 못하다고 생각한다.
(B) 보수주의자들은 비효율과 과도한 팽창이 현재 미국 교육문제의 근원이라고 생각한다.
(C) 진보주의자들은 재산세를 통한 학교재정 지원이 교육 상업화의 원인이라고 생각한다.
(D) 필자는 학부모들과 보수주의자들의 견해에 동의하며 '교육산업'의 필요성을 강조한다.

3 빈칸 ⓐ_____ 에 들어갈 표현으로 어법상 가장 적절한 것은?

(A) how pervasive influence in U.S. education is corporate
(B) how pervasive corporate influence in U.S. education is
(C) how corporate influence in U.S. education pervasive is
(D) how influence in U.S. education is pervasive corporate

4 빈칸 ⓑ_____ 에 들어갈 가장 적절한 단어는?

(A) Therefore   (B) And
(C) However   (D) Since

New brooms sweep clean.
새 빗자루가 깨끗이 쓴다. (신임자는 구악 일소에 여념이 없다.)

523 As mobile increasingly takes center stage in telecommunications, we expect a major consolidation effect spreading from operators to system vendors. Globalization will lead to fewer, bigger multinational operators of fixed and mobile services. The incumbent telecommunications operators are preparing for new entrants in the telecommunications arena. They anticipate that these new entrants will compete to gain market share with a broad range of services. Cable companies may pose a direct threat to incumbent telecoms operations. The obstacle for cable companies, however, is that they tend to be much smaller, highly geared businesses that may not attract the investment needed to develop a substantial telecoms operation. Their balance sheets tend to be unattractive to investors because they show high growth, but with high investment, and their management skills tend to be thin. To be credible, long-term competitors to telephone companies, cable companies will have to be astute in how they upgrade or engineer their cable networks to accommodate two-way interactive services. Telecommunications companies, on the other hand, have high benefits but slow growth, and they must prepare for the inevitable erosion of their profits with competition. They are often hindered by bureaucratic cultures that are ill-equipped to respond nimbly to competition or to pursue emerging opportunities effectively. (고려대 편입)

Heaven helps those who help themselves.
하늘은 스스로 돕는 자를 돕는다.

1 What is the best title for the passage?

(A) The Rise and Fall of the Telecommunications Boom

(B) Escalating Competition in the Telecommunications Market

(C) Risk-Taking in Telecommunications Innovation

(D) Setting Standards for the Telecommunications Industry

2 Which of the following can be inferred from the passage?

(A) Telecommunication companies may have to reform their bureaucratic structure to meet new challenges.

(B) New entrants into the telecommunications market are more likely to succeed than incumbents.

(C) Competition will slow down the globalization of telecommunications companies.

(D) Well-established cable companies should take the lead in acquiring smaller ones.

3 According to the passage, which aspect is NOT associated with cable companies?

(A) They are relatively small in terms of capacity.

(B) They are multinational and globalized.

(C) They do not attract much investment.

(D) They want to enter the telecoms market.

524 Style is one part identity: self-awareness and self-knowledge. You cannot have style until you have articulated a self. And style requires security—feeling at home in one's body, physically and mentally. Of course, like all knowledge, self-knowledge must be updated as you grow and evolve; style takes ongoing self-assessment.

Style is also one part personality: spirit, verve, attitude, wit, inventiveness. It demands the desire and confidence to express whatever mood one wishes. Such variability is not only necessary but a reflection of a person's unique complexity as a human being. People want to be themselves and to be seen as themselves. In order to work, style must reflect the real self, the character and personality of the individual; anything less appears to be _____.

Lastly, style is one part fashion. It is possible to have lots of clothes and not an ounce of style. But it is also possible to have very few clothes and lots of style. Fashion is the means through which we express style, but it takes less in the way of clothes to be stylish than you might imagine. That is why generations of women have coveted the little black dress, a garment so unassuming in line and perfect in proportion that it is the finest foil for excursions into self-expression.

(고려대 편입)

---

1 Choose the one that best fills in the blank.

(A) a costume (B) a reality

(C) a snare (D) a homage

2 Which of the following can be inferred about "style"?

(A) It rarely changes over time after a certain age.
(B) It should not make you uncomfortable.
(C) It is dictated by what others think of you.
(D) It is dependent on current fashion trends.

3 According to the passage, style is associated with the _____ of clothes.

(A) pretentiousness (B) extravagance

(C) conveyance (D) alteration

525 Every culture feels the call of conscience—the voice of internal self-criticism. ⓐ But Western Christian culture has conscience on steroids, so to speak. Our sense of guilt is comparatively extreme, and, with our culture of original sin and fallen status, we feel guilty about our very existence. In the belly of Western culture is the feeling that we're not worthy. Why is this feeling there?

All this internalized self-loathing is the cost we pay for being civilized. In a very well-organized society that protects the interests of many, we have to refrain daily from our natural instincts. We have to repress our own selfish, aggressive urges all the time, and we are so accustomed to it as adults that we don't always notices it. But if I was in the habit of acting on my impulses, I would regularly kill people in front of me at coffee shop who order elaborate whipped-cream mocha ⓑ concoctions. In fact, I wouldn't bother to line up in a queue, but would just storm the counter and muscle people out of my way. But there is a small wrestling match that happens inside my psyche that keeps me from such natural aggression. And that's just morning coffee—think about how many times you'd like to strangle somebody on public transportation.

(서강대 편입)

1 Which of the following expressions refers to the concept of conscience?

   (A) natural instinct   (B) selfish, aggression urges
   (C) internalized self-loathing   (D) impulses

2 What does the underlined sentence ⓐ suggest?

   (A) We repress our conscience at all times.
   (B) Western culture overemphasizes a sense of guilt.
   (C) Humans often have no conscience in their daily thoughts.
   (D) Humans naturally have criminal instincts.

3 What does the underlined word ⓑ mean?

   (A) blends   (B) glades
   (C) convolutions   (D) droves

526   On this ground, actions in conformity with virtue must be intrinsically pleasant. And certainly they are good as well as noble, and both in the highest degree, if the judgment of the good man is any criterion; for he will judge them as we have said. It follows, therefore, that happiness is at once the best and noblest and pleasantest of things. For our best activities possess all of these attributes; and it is in our best activities, or in the best one of them, that we say happiness consists. ⓐ _____, happiness plainly requires external goods as well; for it is impossible, or at least not easy, to act nobly without the proper equipment. There are many actions that can only be performed through such instruments as friends, wealth, or political influence; and there are some things, again, the lack of which must ⓑ _____ felicity, such as good birth, fine children, and personal comeliness: for the man who is repulsive in appearance, or ill-born, or solitary and childless does not meet the requirements of a happy man, and still less does one who has worthless children and friends, or who has lost good ones by death. As we have said, then, happiness seems to require the addition of external prosperity, and this has led some to identify it with "good fortune," just as others have made the opposite mistake of identifying it with virtue.

(이화여대 편입)

It is dark at the foot of a candle.
등잔 밑이 어둡다.

1 Which of the following may NOT precede the above passage?

(A) Pleasure is something that intrinsically belongs to the soul of each man.

(B) A man who does not enjoy doing noble actions is not a good man.

(C) Most men should take pleasure in their relationship with family or friends.

(D) We are in agreement with those who identify happiness with virtue.

2 Which of the following does NOT correspond with the author's main point?

(A) External goods should also be considered important for happiness.

(B) "Good fortune" should not be regarded as part of external prosperity.

(C) The important of appearance or family should not be overlooked for happiness.

(D) Virtuous actions should be considered joyful and exalted.

3 Which of the following may fit in ⓐ and ⓑ best?

(A) Consequently – redefine   (B) Unsurprising – encourage

(C) Nevertheless – mar   (D) Accordingly – spoil

4 According to the author, which of the following is NOT included as one of "good fortune"?

(A) love for social relations   (B) desire for a good family

(C) love for justice   (D) desire for physical attraction

No rose without a thorn.
가시 없는 장미는 없다. (세상에 완전한 행복은 없다.)

527   One of the most important discoveries the researchers have made from their hundreds of interviews with people involved in fires is the problems recognizing that there is a fire at all. A fire is such an unusual experience that people will accept almost any other explanation of the early signs of a fire first. In one hotel fire, for example, the residents, hearing cracking and popping noises, put it down to vandals at work, made sure their doors were locked, and went back to the television. Similarly, the research has shown that fire alarms are usually interpreted as drills, tests or malfunctions. In fact, faced with evidence of a possible fire nearly everyone _____. "There is a strong social stigma attached to getting it wrong," says one researcher. So people are reluctant to make fools of themselves by rushing out into the street or calling the fire brigade at what may be a false alarm. Even when a fire is definitely identified there is no immediate rush for the doors. Under the stress of a fire many people do things they afterwards see to have been inappropriate.

(성균관대 편입)

1 The above passage is _____.

    (A) emotional   (B) informative   (C) mythical

    (D) critical   (E) romantic

2 Which of the following is most appropriate for the blank?

    (A) tries to reach his family members

    (B) telephones the fire brigade

    (C) tries to leave the building immediately

    (D) seeks further information

    (E) chooses a safe escape route

3 According to the passage, people are often slow to respond when they think there is a fire because _____.

    (A) they are afraid of making a mistake

    (B) they fail to find out emergency stairs

    (C) they want to watch through televisions programs

    (D) they tend to lock themselves in the rooms out of fear

    (E) they act more effectively under extreme stress

528 In starting, a definition of science may be advisable. ① <u>For the present</u>, we can take it to mean the conscious effort man has made to understand and control his environment. This clearly lays a very wide net, and nobody would be surprised to find the multifarious divisions which have to be made according to the different aspects of Nature. Most people think of science in terms of such subjects as astronomy, physics, chemistry, and biology. These certainly are the best developed branches, and when we come to consider them in depth we find that they in turn are divided into many sections. Physics naturally ② <u>divides itself into</u> such aspects as the study of motion, of heat, light, sound, magnetism, electricity, and the general properties of matter. ③ <u>Despite of all such divisions</u>, however, a close consistency is found within each subject; and there are many connections and applications of one subject to another. In other words, the whole range of the usually accepted scientific studies "hangs together," and what is well established in one division is confidently carried over into all the others.

(중앙대 편입)

1 밑줄 친 ①~③ 중에서 어법상 잘못된 것을 고르시오.

  (A) ①   (B) ②   (C) ③   (D) No error.

2 Which of the following is the best title of the passage?

  (A) An Advisable Definition of Science
  (B) Human Efforts to Control Environment
  (C) The Best Developed Branches of Science
  (D) Close Connections between Scientific Divisions

529 The development of all kinds of techniques has been so rapid and so drastic that mankind has had no time of adjusting itself to it. The result is the chaos which we are witnessing today and which is upsetting our spiritual as well as our material world. To consider the latter first, the growth of industrial, commercial and financial methods and machines has been so reckless and merciless that large communities have been ruined by the very activities which should have made them ① _____ . The excessive mechanization of life has poisoned the wells of individual and social happiness. The greatest problem which the statesmen of our time have to solve is the humanization of industry and labor, but it will not be easy to undo the evils of a century of technical ruthlessness and unrestrained greed, and in any case the problem is exceedingly difficult, for it is not enough to find a theoretical solution; one must be able to overcome prejudices, to undo wrong purposes and uncover false ideals. ② _____ , economic questions have become largely international, and social ills cannot be cured completely except on an international basis. (한국외대 편입)

1 Which of the following best fits into ① and ②?

(A) happy – However

(B) dejected – Likewise

(C) resolute – Moreover

(D) privileged – Therefore

(E) prosperous – Moreover

2 Which of the following is most likely to solve the problems coming from technical developments?

(A) Ensuring international cooperation

(B) Reducing the rate of mechanization of life

(C) Purifying poisoned wells of human happiness

(D) Finding a way of humanizing industry and labor

(E) Adjusting our lives to the pace of industrialization

3 Which of the following is most likely to be discussed in the next paragraph?

(A) Spiritual chaos and its solution

(B) History of technical development

(C) Evils of excessive mechanization of life

(D) Harmonization of life with its mechanization

(E) Ways of getting rid of false purpose and ideals

530   In 1859 the biologist Charles Darwin published his *Origin of Species*, a book that was to produce a revolution in thought as radical and ① far-reached as that brought about in the seventeenth century by the scientific discoveries of Galileo and Newton. Most people in mid-nineteenth century accepted literally the account of Creation given in the Bible, ② according to which all forms of life appeared on earth about six thousand years ago in the space of a single week. Darwin went beyond his predecessors. After years of studying the work of earlier scientists and of collecting and analyzing his own biological data, he not only agreed with earlier conclusion about the age of the earth ③ but concluded that instead of all forms of life ④ appearing at once complex forms had evolved from simpler ones during a great struggle for existence in which only ⑤ the fittest survived. Although many people eventually came to see that there was no real conflict between the teachings of religion and the findings of the new biology, Darwin's work had the initial effect of throwing many individuals into doubts about their religious beliefs. Some people remained in a state of doubt. Others passed from doubt to despair. Still others reacted by renouncing science in favor of faith or giving up faith in favor of science.

(한국외대 편입)

One mischief comes on the neck of another.
하나의 불행은 다른 불행의 목에 매달려 온다. (엎친 데 덮친다. 설상가상.)

480

1 Which of the underlined parts is grammatically INCORRECT?
   (A) ①   (B) ②   (C) ③   (D) ④   (E) ⑤

2 What is the major topic of the passage?
   (A) Struggle for life of the forms of life
   (B) Effects of Darwin's biological findings
   (C) Evolution and the survival of the fittest
   (D) Trends in the nineteenth-century science
   (E) Victory of Evolution Theory over Creation Theory

3 Which of the following is true of the passage?
   (A) All forms of life living on earth now are aged six thousand.
   (B) It took a week for God to change simple forms of life into complex ones.
   (C) Darwin's biological work forced all Europeans to abandon their religious beliefs.
   (D) Darwin's biological findings were in effect not in real conflict with religious teachings.
   (E) The scientific discoveries of Galileo and Newton were not so radical as those of Darwin.

Out of sight, out of mind.
눈에서 멀어지면 마음에서 멀어진다.

531 It has long been known that the air and water encountered by people in their daily lives are filled with all sorts of micro-organisms. ___①___, most of these are benign and even the unsavory ones can usually be washed down the drain without causing any harm. Not always, though. A team of researchers reports that taking showers can pose a danger to some people. They took samples of the biofilm that builds up inside showerheads from 45 sites in nine American cities and analysed the genetic material which it contained. ___②___, in some of the samples they found high concentrations of a microbe which can cause respiratory illnesses. This is found in tap water, but remains harmless unless turned into an aerosol and inhaled—precisely what happens when bug-laden water is forced through a showerhead at high pressure. As the tiny particles are inhaled, they get into the lungs and can start an infection. Is this cause for alarm? Not for healthy people, but those with a compromised immune system or who are at risk of pulmonary diseases such as the elderly may want to take precautions. Cleaning showerheads with bleach will not do since the microbes will simply return with a fresh flow of water. Replacing bug-prone plastic showerheads with metal ones is a better idea.

(한양대 편입)

1 Which of the following best fits into the blanks ① and ②?

(A) Thankfully – Strikingly

(B) Strikingly – Thankfully

(C) Happily – Especially

(D) Especially – Happily

2 According to the passage, which of the following is true?

(A) Elderly people should not take showers too often.

(B) A microbe in tap water causes cardiovascular illnesses.

(C) Healthy people should use metal showerheads instead of plastic ones.

(D) Forcing out microbes from a showerhead at high pressure can make them harmful.

532 Since 1960, worldwide production of meat has quadrupled to more than 280 million tons a year. Even if everyone in the rich nations swore off meat today, consumption would continue to soar. (ⓐ) For this reason, serious environmental planners have recently focused not on eliminating the meat industry but on turning it green. Making beef, pork, or chicken can be an environmentally devastating process. (ⓑ) And among animal proteins, to make a kilogram of beef takes seven times more farmland than is needed to produce a kilo of chicken, and 15 times the area needed for a kilo of pork. Yet scientists, herders, and green groups are convinced they can curb the damage by making adjustments all along the supply chain, changing the way we farm and feed livestock and building a cleaner cow through modern genetics. (ⓒ) When a cow eats, its stomach produces methane as a byproduct. Cows are pretty efficient at eating grass, but the soybeans and corn that most industrial livestock farms feed them make the bovine stomach rumble with excess gas. (ⓓ) To fight this, some farms found they could improve health and boost milk production in the herds, and reduce methane emissions, by eliminating soybean and corn-based feed. Instead, they give their cows old-fashioned alfalfa, which is packed with nutrients and benign fatty acids.

(한양대 편입)

1 According to the passage, which of the following is true?

(A) People in the rich nations are trying to stop consuming meat today.

(B) Methane produced by cows is not environmentally harmful.

(C) Cows' stomachs are efficient in digesting soybeans and corn.

(D) To produce a kilo of meat, pork needs less farming area than beef or chicken.

2 Where does the following sentence fit best in the passage?

> The effort starts with the animals themselves.

(A) ⓐ   (B) ⓑ   (C) ⓒ   (D) ⓓ

[533- 540] 아래 글들을 읽고, 질문에 알맞은 답을 고르거나 쓰시오.

533   Most American folk songs are importations. Brought over by the settlers, influenced by new living conditions, changed to reflect another scene and setting, they still show their origins. Under different titles, and celebrating another set of characters, the story songs of Vermont and the mountain tunes of the Appalachians are largely adaptations of such English and Scottish ballads as "Barbara Allen," "The Hangman's Song," "The Two Sisters," and "Lord Randal." But a few, and perhaps the best, of the American ballads are <u>genuinely</u> native, as original in subject as they are lively in expression. Beginning as reports of local events or current beliefs or merely as play songs, they have become part of the national life. The five most vivid are also the most popular: "Dixie," "My Old Kentucky Home," "Frankie and Johnny," "Casey Jones," and "John Henry." Unlike most folk songs, the authors of at least two of them are known.

Penny-wise and pound-foolish.
푼돈 아끼다가 천 냥을 잃는다. (싼 것이 비지떡.)

484

1 The underlined word "genuinely" is closest in meaning to '_____.'

   (A) truly   (B) probably

   (C) genetically   (D) genially

2 Which of the following can rightly be inferred from the passage?

   (A) The authors of American folk songs did not publicly announce their names.

   (B) American folk songs are found only in the state of Vermont and mountain areas.

   (C) American folk songs mostly sang of the lives of the celebrated people like Frankie, Johnny, Jones, etc.

   (D) Some of the American folk songs may be a clue to getting a glimpse of how people lived at the time they were written.

3 The central idea of this passage is _____.

   (A) Although the authors of most American folk songs are unknown, a few can definitely be identified.

   (B) American folk songs are unlike those of other countries because of the difference in living conditions, settings, and local events.

   (C) Most American folk songs are variations of older ballads imported from abroad, though a few of the best and most popular are American originals.

   (D) Such vivid and popular folk songs as "Frankie and Johnny" and "John Henry" are actually only adaptations of much older English and Scottish ballads.

Riches have wings.
돈에는 날개가 달렸다.

534   Some of the notebooks that George Washington kept as a young man are still in existence, and they show that he learned a little Latin, that he acquired some of the basic elements of good conduct, and that he read a little English literature. At school he seems to have cared only for mathematics. His was a brief and most incomplete education for a gentleman, and it was all the formal education he was to have, since, unlike some of the other young Virginia gentlemen of his time, he did not go on to the College of William and Mary in the Virginian capital of Williamsburg. In terms of intellectual preparation and power, then, Washington is in sharp contrast with some other early American presidents, such as John Adams, Thomas Jefferson, and James Madison. In later years, Washington probably regretted his lack of intellectual training. He never felt comfortable in formal debate, or in discussions that were not concerned with everyday, practical matters. And inasmuch as he never learned to speak French, he refused to visit France because he felt he would be <u>embarrassed</u> at not being able to speak directly to the statesmen of that country. Thus, unlike Jefferson and Adams, he never reached Europe.

Rome was not built in a day.
로마는 하루아침에 이루어지지 않았다.

1 The underlined word "embarrassed" is closest in meaning to '_____.'

(A) dejected

(B) annoyed

(C) perplexed

(D) inhibited

2 Which of the following can rightly be inferred from the passage?

(A) Presidents Thomas Jefferson and John Adams could speak French.

(B) George Washington had a problem of stammering in the debate of formal issues.

(C) The notebooks Thomas Jefferson and James Madison kept as president do not exist now.

(D) John Adams and James Madison were proud that they had received much intellectual training.

3 The central idea of this passage is _____.

(A) Washington's education was probably equal to that of other Virginia gentlemen of his age.

(B) Washington's limited education did not prevent him from executing his duties as President.

(C) Washington's education was very limited and put him at a definite disadvantage in later life.

(D) Washington showed unusual talents in solving mathematical problems and in writing essays in Latin.

Silks and satins put out the fire in the kitchen.
치레(사치)가 심하면 끼니를 굶는다.

535 We observe that poetry differs from every other art in having a value for the people of the poet's race and language, which it can have for no other. It is true that even music and painting have a local and racial character, but certainly the difficulties of appreciation in these arts, for a foreigner, are much less. It is true on the other hand that prose writings have significance in their own language, ① which is lost in translation. But we all feel that we lose much ② (more / less) in reading a novel in translation than in reading a poem, and in a translation of some kinds of scientific work the loss may be virtually ③ nil. That poetry is much more local than prose can be seen in the history of European languages. Through the Middle Ages to within a few hundred years ago Latin remained the language for philosophy, theology, and science. The impulse towards the literary use of the languages of the peoples began with poetry. And this appears perfectly natural when we realize that poetry has primarily to do with the expression of feeling and emotion, and that feeling and emotion are particular, whereas thought is general. It is easier to think in a foreign language than it is to feel in it. Therefore no art is more stubbornly national than poetry.

1 What does ① <u>which</u> refer to? (Write one word.)

_____

2 In ②, which word is proper in the context of the passage?

_____

3 Which is closest in meaning to ③ <u>nil</u>?
   (A) nothing
   (B) common
   (C) practical
   (D) the largest

4 Which of the following correctly describes the content of the passage?
   (A) It is easier to read poetry in translation than to read it in original text.
   (B) Many of European languages are not good enough to express the people's feeling and emotion in poetry.
   (C) Poetry is more individual than any other art, since it purports to express feeling and emotion of a people.
   (D) Latin still enjoys its position as a commonly-used medium of delivering philosophical, scientific, and religious thoughts.

Spare the rod and spoil the child.
매를 아끼면 자식을 망친다.

536   Mass-production in America, the use of advertising to standardize the desires and taste of the public and so standardize production, the consequent (①) of production costs and the increase in wages, have all created an immense rise in the scale of American living from the purely material standpoint. With a population of over a hundred millions, undivided by tariff barriers, with most of the raw materials produced at home, with a people singularly lacking in individuality, more than willing to live and have everything exactly like everyone else, the leaders of industry have been able to achieve their ideal of standardized production. But the achievement of this result has brought about the (②) of certain values that the Europeans still think of vital importance. What the cultured European desires above all else is to be an individual, to be able to express his own unique personality in work and play. The dreary (③) of American life throughout an entire and vast continent appalls him. Of what use to travel three thousand miles from New York to San Francisco if for the most part one sees only the same sort of people, reads the same comic strips and syndicated news column, ④talks the same "shop", and sees the same city architecture?

1 Which is the correct set of words for the blanks?

	①	②	③
(A)	increase	abandoning	slowness
(B)	soaring	corrosion	monotony
(C)	lowering	surrender	sameness
(D)	standardization	creation	variety

2 Which best defines the meaning of the underlined phrase ④?

(A) always goes to the same coffee-shop

(B) always shops at the same department store

(C) talks about one's store in a proud way

(D) talks about one's same work in a boring way

3 According to the passage, which of the following is correct?

(A) Americans did not mind the dreariness of their life.

(B) Europeans find American style of living very unchallenging.

(C) Americans placed mass-production before everything else in evaluating their life.

(D) The standardization of the desires of people and in production has made the life of Americans very individual.

Strike while the iron is hot.
쇠가 달았을 때 두들겨라. (호기를 잃지 마라.)

537   When the first white men came to America, they found vast amounts of natural resources of tremendous value. Forests covered a large part of the land. Later, gas, oil, and minerals were found in unbelievable amounts. There was a great abundance of very fertile soil. Forests, prairies, streams, and rivers ① (abounded / were abounded) with wild life. So vast were the resources that it seemed that they could never be used up. So forests were destroyed to make way for farmland. Grasslands and prairies were plowed and harrowed. Minerals and oil were used in great quantities to supply a young industrial nation. Almost every river became the scene of factories, mills, and power companies. Animals and birds were killed for food and sport.

Within a short time, the results were obvious. Floods caused millions of dollars' worth of damage yearly. The very fertile soil was washed away or blown up in great clouds. The seemingly inexhaustible oil and minerals showed signs of ② (exhaust). Rivers were filled with dirt and waste from factories and homes. Many of the rivers were made unfit for fish. Several species of birds disappeared, and some animals were on the verge of disappearing. Future timber shortages were predicted. Some sort of preservation programs therefore began to be set up, since Americans came to realize the importance of them. They seriously believed that they were (③), if future, as well as present, Americans were to share in the resources that are the heritage of the American nation.

1 Which of the two expressions in parenthesis ① is grammatically correct?

_____

2 Change the word in parenthesis ② into a proper form.

_____

3 Which of the following words best fills in blank ③?
   (A) natural
               (B) hopeful
   (C) costly
               (D) indispensable
   (E) endangered

4 According to the passage, which of the following does NOT count among the results of the overuse of the natural resources by Americans?
   (A) Washing away of the fertile soil
   (B) Shortage of mills and power companies
   (C) Contamination of rivers by dirt and waste
   (D) Development of nature-preservation programs
   (E) Disappearance of several species of birds and animals

538　When a man finds himself ⓐ plunged back into the conditions of an earlier age, he inevitably discovers many things. He rediscovers ⓑ forgotten uses of his tools, and learns ⓒ to think about them in the cruder categories of a primitive age. The sharp stone which early man used for killing was hardly different from the one he used for cutting, but in more ⓓ developed cultures there arose a distinction between "weapon" and "tool" as each of them became a more ⓔ specializing implement. Thus, in 18th-century Europe, the firearm became primarily a weapon; but for the colonial American backwoodsman, who had to protect himself and his family from raiding savages and who often shot meat for his table, the distinction between "weapon" and "tool" once again had ① little meaning. ⒜ What was true of implements was also true of occupations. Under primitive conditions, there seem to have been ② few distinctions among those who practiced the different modes of healing and curing—between the man who muttered the prayer, the man who inserted the knife, and the man who mixed the medicine. But in 18th-century England all these tasks were ③ distinguished: each had become the private preserve of a different group. In America such distinctions would have been ④ easy to preserve; the healer (sometimes a lawyer or a governor or a clergyman) once again performed ⑤ all these different tasks.

1 Which of the underlined parts from ⓐ to ⓔ is grammatically INCORRECT?
   (A) ⓐ   (B) ⓑ   (C) ⓒ   (D) ⓓ   (E) ⓔ

2 Which of the underlined parts from ① to ⑤ is semantically UNACCEPTABLE?
   (A) ①   (B) ②   (C) ③   (D) ④   (E) ⑤

3 Put the underlined sentence Ⓐ into Korean.

_____

4 According to the passage, which of the following is true?
   (A) Changing jobs was difficult in eighteenth-century America.
   (B) The eighteenth-century Europe had more specified jobs than
       America.
   (C) In a primitive age the systems of healing and curing were the
       same.
   (D) Early man in a primitive age used the sharp stone mainly for
       killing animals.
   (E) The American colony of the eighteenth century had no tools to
       use as weapons.

There is no smoke without fire.
아니 땐 굴뚝에 연기 날까.

539   Hunger continues to be an ever-present companion of a large part of the world's population. Millions of people do not have enough food, and every year more than sixty-five million persons seek a share of the world's food. Although farmers have grown more food, they have not grown enough more to correct the serious under-nutrition which has long existed in many countries. Food production has been increasing more rapidly in the richer, (①) countries, while the poorer countries have lagged behind. In fact, the balance between food supplies and population growth in many countries is a very <u>narrow</u> one. Failure of normal rainfall or other climatic irregularities in a single year may lead to crises in food supplies, and shipments from the countries with more adequate food supplies are necessary to maintain even the low levels of nutrition which prevail. A favorable weather may lead to a temporary increase in the available food in many countries. (②), rapid growth of population continually requires an increase in production, if current levels of nutrition are to be maintained. In many countries, the size of the population is so great, and the rate of growth so high, that very large numbers of people are added every year, and the problem of increasing food supplies is correspondingly great. If nutrition is to be brought up to generally accepted levels of adequacy for health and normal physical activity, food production in the developing countries must increase more rapidly than population, or nonfood production must increase sufficiently to secure the required food through international trade. Reduction of the rates of population growth is (③) primary importance in improving the levels of nutrition of the population of those countries.

1 Which of the following best fills in blank ①?
    (A) better-feed   (B) better-feeding
    (C) better-fed   (D) better-to-feed
    (E) feeding-better

2 Which of the following best fills in blank ②?
    (A) However   (B) Therefore
    (C) Otherwise   (D) Notwithstanding
    (E) To the contrary

3 Insert an appropriate preposition into blank ③.

_____

4 The underlined word "narrow" is closest in meaning to '_____.'
    (A) straight   (B) reliable
    (C) dangerous   (D) difficult
    (E) short-lived

5 The theme of the passage can be summarized as follows. Fill in the blanks with a proper word.

> Unless the rates of population growth is (r   ), the increase in food production will not be (   ) much help to overcoming the hunger problem facing the current world.

540 The single business of Henry Thoreau, during his forty-odd years of eager activity, was to discover an economy calculated to provide a satisfying life. His one concern that gave to his ramblings in Concord fields a value of high adventure was to explore the true meaning of wealth. As he understood the problem of economics, there were three possible solutions open to him: to exploit himself, to exploit his fellows, or to reduce the problem to its lowest denominator. The first was quite impossible—to imprison oneself in a treadmill when the morning called to great adventure. To exploit one's fellows seemed to Thoreau's sensitive social conscience an even greater <u>infidelity</u>. Freedom with abstinence seemed to him better than serfdom with material well-being, and he was content to move to Walden Pond and so set about the high business of living, "to front only the essential facts of life and to see what it had to teach." He did not advocate that other men should build cabins and live isolated. He had no wish to dogmatize concerning the best mode of living—each must settle that for himself. But that a satisfying life should be lived, he was vitally concerned. The story of his emancipation from the lower economics is the one romance of his life, and *Walden* is his great book. It is a book in praise of life rather than of Nature, a record of two years of his life at Walden Pond. But it is a book of social criticism as well, in spite of its explicit denial of such a purpose. In considering the true nature of economy he concluded, with Ruskin, that the cost of a thing is the amount of life which is required in exchange for it, immediately or in the long run. In *Walden* Thoreau elaborated the text: "The only wealth is life."

1 The main idea of this passage is best expressed as _____.

   (A) Problems of economics
   (B) Life at Walden Pond
   (C) How Thoreau saved money
   (D) Thoreau's philosophy of life
   (E) *Walden*, Thoreau's great book

2 Thoreau's chief aim in life was to _____.

   (A) live in isolation
   (B) write about Nature
   (C) discover a satisfactory economy
   (D) do as little work as possible
   (E) convert others to his way of living

3 According to the passage, Thoreau was _____.

   (A) very stingy   (B) very active
   (C) very gluttonous   (D) somewhat unsociable
   (E) pretty pessimistic

4 Thoreau's solution to the problem of living was to _____.

   (A) work in a mill   (B) write for a living
   (C) study nature minutely (D) live in a simple way
   (E) make other men work for him

5 In Thoreau's opinion, the price of a thing should be measured in terms of

   _____.

   (A) life   (B) business   (C) abstinence
   (D) money   (E) romance

6 Which is closest in meaning to <u>infidelity</u>?

   (A) theft   (B) unhappiness   (C) adventure
   (D) indulgence   (E) unfaithfulness

독해 · 문법 · 작문을 한 번에 완성하는

NEXUS
영문
독해연습

저자 해설 강의 www.brownstudy.co.kr

김일곤 지음

501 +
플러스

ENGLISH READING PRACTICE

4th Edition

모범 답안 & 우리말 번역과 해설

수능 · 편입 · 공무원시험 · 교원임용고사
TOEFL · TOEIC · TEPS 대비
영문 독해 필독서!

넥서스

독해·문법·작문을 한 번에 완성하는

NEXUS
영문
독해연습

김일곤 지음

501
플러스 +

ENGLISH READING PRACTICE

4th
Edition

모범 답안 & 우리말 번역과 해설

넥서스

PART 1
Grammar & Reading

001 지도를 한 번만 들여다보면 어떻게 하여 그리스가 다른 유럽의 국가들보다 먼저 문명화되었는가 하는 점을 충분히 알 수 있다. 그리스는 문명이 처음 발생한 국가들과 가장 가까운 곳에 위치하고 있으며, 동양과 서양의 경계선임을 알 수 있다.

002 행운이나 하늘의 은총이 인생의 여러 가지 일에 연루되는 것처럼 보일진 모르지만, 우리가 그 일들이 일어나는 원인들을 조금 더 깊숙이 살펴보면, 대부분의 사람들이 상상하는 것 이상으로 우리 자신의 노력이 그 일들이 발생하는 데 더 많은 책임이 있었음을 알게 된다.

003 그 시계는 결코 싼 값은 아니었고, 나같이 옹색한 생활을 하는 사람에게는 너무 비싼 물건이었다. 그러나 성능으로 보면 다른 것에 비교될 수 없을 정도여서, 부른 값으로 보면 그래도 싼 편이었다.

004 사실 읽을 가치가 있는 모든 책은 즐거움만을 위해서가 아닌 과학 서적을 읽는 것과 똑같은 방식으로 읽혀야 한다. 그리고 그 가치가 전혀 다른 종류라고 하더라도 읽을 가치가 있는 책은 과학 서적이 가지고 있는 것과 같은 양의 가치를 지녀야 한다.

005 워싱턴은 말은 하는 데 있어서 대단히 신중하였으며, 상대방을 이용한다거나 논쟁에서 일시적인 승리를 노린다거나 하는 일은 결코 하지 않았다.

006 내가 어린 소년이었을 때, 안주인의 등 뒤에서는 정말 형편없는 험담을 하다가도 그녀가 방에 들어오자마자 만면에 미소를 짓고 정중해지는 한 늙은 신사를 알고 있었다.

007 평탄한 인생길을 걷고 있는 동안에는 약하디 약하고 의지할 줄밖에 모르며 조금만 함부로 대해도 일일이 신경을 쓰던 연약하고 눈물 헤픈 여성이, 갑자기 정신력을 가다듬고 불행에 짓눌린 남편의 위안자, 부조자가 되어 주며 굽힐 줄 모르는 단호한 태도로 역경의 쓰라린 돌풍을 견디어 나가는 모습을 보는 것보다 더 감동적인 일은 있을 수 없다.

008 가능하면 언제나 당신 자신보다 나은 사람을 친구로 사귀도록 하고, 유감스럽게도 자신보다 못한 사람들과 어울리게 되는 경우, 그들을 당신 수준으로 끌어올리는―여기에는 사랑과 지혜가 필요하지만―적절한 기회를 움켜쥐지 못하면, 그들이 오히려 당신을 그들 수준으로 끌어내리는 데 분명히 주저하지 않을 것이라는 점을 진지하게 명심하라.

009 사생활은 인간 생활에 있어서 필수불가결한 것 중의 하나이며, 자신의 사생활을 잃게 되면 삶은 참기 어려운 것이 된다. 이것이 바로 불행하게도 왕족으로 태어난 사람들이 자신들의 생활 방식을 깨뜨리고 사적인 삶을 얻으려고 가끔 미치광이 같은 짓을 하는 이유이다. 왕족으로 태어난다는 것은 자신의 삶을 공적으로 영위해야 한다고 미리 선고를 받는 것과 마찬가지이며, 이것은 거의 참을 수 없는 노예 상태인 것이다.

010 인간이 다른 어떤 정복을 이룩한다 하더라도 자기 자신을 다스리지 못한다면 그 사람은 패배자로 남게 된다. 알렉산더의 경우만큼 이 사실을 더 비극적으로 보여 주는 경우는 없다. 그는 32세의 나이에 지중해 지역 세계를 지배한 정복자이면서도 자신의 정복이라는 최대의 것의 정복에 실패하였다.

011 사회과학의 방법론은 자연과학의 그것과 필연적으로 차이가 난다. 그것은 하나의 기본적인 이유에서 차이가 나고, 또 차이가 있어야 하는데, 이는 사회과학의 연구자가 다루는 자료는 외부가 아닌 내부에 존재한다는 점이다. 인간은 외적 자연을 연구하는 것과 똑같은 방법으로 인간을 연구할 수는 없다.

012 외국어가 사용되는 환경 속에 놓인 어린이는 그 새로운 외국어를 만족스럽게 사용하는 능력을 놀라운 속도로 얻게 되는데, 그것은 그가 언어 사용에 있어서 보다 유연성이 있고 제약과 자의식이 없다는 이유뿐만 아니라 언어를 사용해야 할 필요성이 교육받은 성인의 경우에 비하여 훨씬 적다는 이유 때문이기도 하다. 모국어에 대한 경험과 어휘가 상당히 제한되어 있고, 이 점은 그 아이로 하여금 새로운 언어의 동량(同量) 어휘를 획득하는 데 비교적 시간이 들지 않게 한다.

013 육체와 마찬가지로 당신의 정신력은 노력에 의해서 길러지는 것이다. 그것이 바로 학문에서 열심히 노력하게 되는 주된 이유이다. 신체를 단련하지 않으면 운동선수가 될 수 없으며, 정신을 단련하지 않으면 학자로서 상당한 위치에 오를 수가 없다. 뱃사공이 전속력으로 노를 저어 가는 4마일은 그 자체로서는 이득을 가져오는 것이 아니지만, 그 과정을 견디어 내는 육체적인 능력은 상당한 가치가 있는 것으로 여겨진다.

014 내가 지난번에 만났을 때 애머벨은 야심으로 가득 차 있었는데 그 이유인즉, 그녀와 같이 학교를 다니고 평범한 소녀에 불과하며 사실은 약간 다른 사람의 웃음거리에 지나지 않던 한 소녀가, 극장에서 우연히 만났을 때 자신은 잡지에 단편소설을 기고함으로써 상당한 수입을 올리고 있다고 말했기 때문이었다. "그녀도 그런 일을 하는데, 왜 내가 못해?"라고 잘못된 논리로 가득 차 애머벨은 이야기하였다.

015 이론과 실제에 관련하여 두 개의 견해가 있다. 어떤

2

사람들은 이론과 실제는 전혀 별개의 것이어서 그것들이 반드시 어울리는 것은 아니라고 이야기한다. 또 어떤 사람들은 양자가 일치하지[어울리지] 않는 것은 이론이 부정확하기 때문이라는 견해를 피력한다.

016 한편으로는 아들이 안전하고 건강하게 되돌아온 것을 보고, 또 한편으로는 운도 좋아서, 그 소년의 어머니는 며칠 지나자 몸이 나았다. 그녀는 아들을 대단히 자랑하기 시작하였고, 그가 한 모험들을 방문객들에게 이야기하는 일에 지칠 줄 몰랐다.

017 과학의 목표는 예견하는 것이지 흔히 이야기되어 오듯 이해하는 것이 아니다. 과학은 사실과 사물과 현상들을 자세하게 기술하고 미래의 사건들을 예측하기 위해서 소위 법칙이라고 부르는 것들로 그들을 통합하려 시도한다.

018 우리들 중 우주가 어떻게 생겨났을까 하고 생각해 보지 않은 사람은 아무도 없다. 꽃, 강, 길, 하늘, 별, 태양 그리고 달이 있는 이 세계가 우연히 생겨난 것은 아니라고 우리는 생각한다. 우리 주위에서 보는 모든 것과 우리가 알고 있는 모든 것은 어떠한 과정에 의해서 오늘날의 모습이 되었음에 틀림없다. 우리가 그 과정을 이해할 수만 있다면 우주의 본성도 이해할 수 있을 텐데.

019 사회는 건물과 같아서 기초가 튼튼하고 목재가 온전할 때 굳건히 서게 된다. 믿을 수 없는 사람이 사회에 대하여 갖는 관계는 일단의 썩은 목재가 집에 대하여 갖는 관계와 마찬가지이다.

020 나쁜 예절에 전염성이 있다면 좋은 예절 또한 마찬가지이다. 명랑한 사람들에게 기분 나빠할 사람은 아무도 없다. 날씨의 경우도 예절의 경우와 마찬가지이다. "활짝 갠 날처럼 나의 기분을 맑게 해 주는 것은 없다"라고 키츠가 말하였지만, 쾌활한 사람은 우리들 중 가장 우울한 사람에게도 마치 맑게 갠 날이 주는 축복을 가지고 오듯 다가온다.

021 어린이들은 가끔은 조금 엄한 어른이 자신들에게 가장 좋은 사람이라는 것을 쉽사리 알아차린다. 그들은 본능적으로 자신들이 사랑을 받고 있는지 아닌지를 알게 되며, 자신들을 사랑해 주는 사람이라고 느끼는 사람들로부터는 자신들의 올바른 발전을 위한 진지한 갈망에서 우러나오는 엄격함은 어떠한 것이라도 참아 내려 한다. 따라서 이론상으로는 해결책은 간단하다. 교육자들에게 현명한 사랑을 갖도록 하라. 그러면 그들은 올바른 일을 하게 될 것이다.

022 몹시 힘든 상황에서도 당신은 있을 수 있는 모든 해학의 요소를 찾아볼 수 있다. 어떤 일을 웃어넘길 수 있는 능력은 교실과 사회생활에서 부딪치는 많은

거북한 상황들에서 벗어나게 해 준다. 세상(사람들)은 웃음을 만들어 내는 사람에게 감사하게 된다. 웃음에는 걱정, 시기심, 심지어 혐오증까지도 쓸어가 버리는 무엇인가가 있다. 웃음은 상호 자극적이다. 당신이 웃게 되면 다른 사람도 웃게 되고, 그의 웃음은 이어서 당신으로 하여금 보다 마음껏 웃게 할 것이다.

023 죽은 다음에도 사람들의 기억 속에 남을 만한 작품을 남겨 놓은 작가들 중에는 자신의 동시대 사람들뿐만 아니라 후세에게도 마찬가지로 자신의 개성을 새겨 넣는 독특한 힘을 가진 작가가 드물게 몇 명씩은 있으며, 따라서 후세 사람들은 보통은 살아 있는 작가들에게만 느끼는 그러한 유의 관심을 가지고 그 작가를 생각한다. 그의 이름을 보거나 듣기만 해도 일련의 즐거운 연상이 떠오르고, 옛 친구가 뜻밖에 또 찾아왔을 때 느끼는 것과 똑같은 즐거움이 솟아난다.

024 인간성은 어리석은 의견이 그러하다고 계속 주장하듯 그렇게 물질적인 것은 결코 아니다. 내가 인간에 대하여 배운 점으로 판단해 보건대, 인간에게는 세상의 겉 표면에 드러나는 것보다 훨씬 많은 이상적인 힘이 있다고 확신한다.

025 만약에 교육의 상당 부분이 분명히 낭비되고 있다면, 농부가 밭에 뿌리는 무 씨앗의 많은 양도 낭비되고 있는 것이다. 농부가 1급의 수확을 얻고자 한다면 필요 이상의 씨앗을 뿌릴 필요가 있다고, 우리는 말할 수 있을지 모른다.

026 인간의 모든 우정에 있어서 당신이 자신의 마음 깊숙한 곳까지 파고들어 가 그 속에 있는 것을 친구에게 적나라하게 드러내 보이고, 친구의 대답을 두려워하면서 기다려야만 할 때가 온다는 것을 여러분 모두 알게 될 것이다. 그렇게 하는 데에는 아주 짧은 시간이면 충분하며, 아마 그러한 일은 일생에 한 번밖에는 하지 못할지 모른다. 그러나 우정이 우정이라는 이름값이 있으려면 아무래도 그 일을 해야만 한다. 서로의 가슴 깊숙이 있는 것을 찾아내야만 하는 것이다.

027 문법 지식은 우리에게 상당한 도움이 될 수 있다. 왜냐하면 문법 지식을 통하여 왜 어떤 표현 방식이 올바른 것이고 다른 방식은 잘못되었는지를 알 수 있고, 우리가 저질렀을지도 모르는 실수를 정정할 수 있기 때문이다. 나아가 문법 규칙을 확실히 알아 두면 위대한 작가들이 쓴 글의 의미를 그렇지 않은 경우에 가능한 정도보다 훨씬 더 잘 이해하고, 따라서 그들의 작품을 더 완벽하게 감상할 수 있다.

028 평범한 모습에 재미를 끌지 못하는 대화를 하는 남자나 여자를 접하게 될 때 우리는 "안녕하십니까?"라는 인사를 던지고 얼굴을 돌려 버린다. 그러나 바로 그

PART 1
Grammar & Reading

사람이 소설을 쓴 작가라는 사실을 알게 되면 우리는 이내 관심을 갖고 대단히 계시적인 이야기가 나올 것이라는 기대감으로 그 사람에게 다시 시선을 돌린다. 경험도 우리에게서 그러한 망상적인 희망을 떨쳐 버리게 하지 못하는 것 같다.

029 마음을 결정하기 가장 어려운 일들 중의 하나는 자유가 어디에 있느냐 하는 점이다. 나는 자신이 유산을 물려받게 되었을 때 그 유산을 다 처분할 때까지는 결코 자유를 느끼지 못할 것이라고 이야기한 여성을 한 번 만난 적이 있다. 그녀는 재산은 우리를 노예로 만들고, 사람은 재산의 주인이 되는 것이 아니라 종이 된다고 주장한다. 그래서 자신의 자유를 회복하는 유일한 희망은 어떻게 해서든 재산을 처분하고 소로나 인도의 현자(賢者)처럼 재산 없는 삶을 살아가는 것이라 한다.

030 평범한 인간 본성의 모든 특징 중에서 가장 불행한 것은 시기심이다. 시기심이 있는 사람은 타인에게 불행을 입히기를 희망하고, 또 벌 받지 않고 할 수 있을 때는 언제나 그렇게 하기를 바랄 뿐만 아니라, 시기심에 의해서 그 자신도 불행해진다. 자신이 가진 것으로부터 즐거움을 이끌어 내는 대신에 타인이 가진 것으로부터 고통을 받는다. 그는 만약 그럴 수 있다면 다른 사람들로부터 이점을 빼앗는데, 이것은 똑같은 이점을 그 스스로 확보하는 것만큼 바람직한 것으로 여긴다.

031 약물[마약]에 중독된 사람이 그 약물을 투여 받지 못할 때 느끼는 그러한 유의 권태는, 시간 말고는 치료책으로 어느 것도 제안할 수 없는 그런 것이다. 그래서 약물에 적용되는 이야기는 어느 정도 한계는 있지만 모든 종류의 쾌락에도 적용된다. 흥분으로 가득 찬 삶은 심신을 지치게 하는 소모적인 삶이고, 그 삶에서는 쾌락의 필수적인 부분으로 간주되는 쾌감[전율]을 얻기 위하여 계속적으로 더 강력한 자극제가 필요한 것이다.

032 비가 오지 않는 것은 모든 기후 조건 중에서 아마도 가장 해로운 조건일 것이다. 왜냐하면 비가 오지 않음으로 해서 현 세대뿐만 아니라 미래의 세대들도 엄청난 양의 식량을 잃게 되고, 넓은 지역의 좋은 농토가 사막으로 변할 가능성이 있기 때문이다. 인공 비를 만들어 내는 과제는, 따라서 중대한 문제이다.

033 우리 자신이 앞으로 어떻게 될 것인지의 전망에 대하여 역사는 우리에게 어떠한 정보라도 제공해 주는가? 그리고 만약 그렇다면, 그것이 우리에게 주는 짐은 무엇인가? 역사는, 우리가 우리 자신의 노력에 의해 돌이키거나 수정을 가할 수 없는 운명에 우리가 할 수 있는 한 능력껏, 우리를 단념한 채 팔짱을 끼고 기다릴 수밖에 없는 냉혹한 운명을 우리에게 한 자

한 자씩 분명하게 설명해 주는가? 아니면 확실성이 아니라 우리의 미래에서 나타날 수 있는 가능성들, 단순한 가능성들만을 우리에게 알려 주는 것인가?

034 사치와 예의범절의 무시, 그리고 누구나가 자신이 살고 있는 시대에 대하여 비난하는 다른 악덕들이 특히 우리 시대의 특징이라고 여러분이 생각한다면 그것은 잘못된 것이다. 역사상의 어느 시기도 (이러한) 비난을 면한 시기는 결코 없었다.

035 오늘 참석하신 여러분 중 누구도 제가 사회주의를 (민주주의에 대한) 대안으로 제안하기 위하여 서구 제도를 개인적으로 비난하고 있다고 생각하지 않으시기를 바랍니다. 아니, 사회주의가 실현된 국가에서 살아 본 경험을 지니고 있는 저는 분명히 그러한 대안(민주주의 대신 사회주의를 채택해야 한다는 대안)을 결코 좋게 이야기할 수 없습니다.

036 3년 동안 그는 일을 하면서 학교를 다녔다. 그리고 1890년 그는 아이오와 주립대학에 등록하였다. 4년 후에 그는 농업 분야의 학위를 받았는데, 그 동안 들어간 비용은 모두 벌어서 댔다. 그의 학업 성적이 너무 뛰어나서 대학 당국은 그에게 선생으로 남아 줄 것을 요청하였다.

037 그는 조용히 앉아서 말을 건넬 때만 매우 간략히 대답하였다. 그는 단둘이 있게 되면 로즈와 결판을 내리라고 마음먹고 있었다.

038 인간은 여러 가지 결론에 불가사의하게 서둘러 도달하면서도, 다른 사람들을 설득해 똑같은 결론을 내릴 수 있다는 희망을 결코 잃지 않는 존재이다.

039 그곳은 뱀과 다른 무서운 동물들로 가득 차 있었고, 정글은 너무 빽빽하여 칼로 온종일 나무를 베면서 매우 느린 속도로 나아갈 수밖에 없었다.

040 만약 우리의 문명이 영속화되려면, 문명이 그 눈을 고정시킬 (우리가 주시해야 할) 별, 즉 멀리 있지만 문명을 이끌어 내는 자력이 있으며 순간의 변화하는 욕구나 열정 그리고 편견을 뛰어넘어 우리가 추구해 볼 그 무엇을 가져야 한다. 인간의 삶의 위엄을 높이고자 하는 사람들은 문명에 그 별을 제공하려 노력해야 하고, 악의(惡意)와 그 악의로 나아가는 미친 경쟁으로부터 세상을 구할 수 있는 유일한 이상을 이 세상에 제공하려고 노력해야 할 것이다.

041 어린이들을 위한 가장 좋은 책을 찾으려 한다면 그 책들을 판단하는 기준이 있어야 한다. 우리는 두 가지 사실을 계속해서 염두에 두어야 하는데, 그것은 어린이들에게 좋은 책은 그들이 그 책을 즐기는 경우에만 좋은 책이 되고, 어른들이 그 책을 고전으로 평가해도 어린이들이 그 책을 읽지 못하거나 그

4

내용에 지루함을 느끼게 되는 경우에는 그 책은 어린이들에게는 보잘것없는 책이 된다는 점이다. 간단히 이야기해서 우리는 다방면에 걸친 수많은 책과, 그 책의 가치나 약점을 알아야 하지만, 또한 그 책이 대상으로 하고 있는 어린이들, 즉 그들의 관심과 요구 사항도 알아야 한다.

042 좋은 음식을 혼자 먹기 위해 앉아 있는 것에는 탐욕스러운 점이 있다. 사람은 그럴 바에야 차라리 단지 살기 위해 먹는 동물이 되는 것이 낫다. 다른 사람들과 같이 어울려 먹게 되면 우리 식욕의 야비함을 숨기는 데 도움이 된다.

043 이 자유정신이 없다면 사회의 진보는 느린 속도로 진행될지도 모른다. 아마도 그 속도가 너무 느려서 기술적 능력들이 무서운 속도로 가속화되어 가고 있는 세계의 급속도로 팽창하는 욕구에 부응하지 못할지도 모른다. 내가 느끼기에는, 이 자유정신을 통한 접근 방식은 우리가 믿는 자유롭고 민주적인 사회를 보존하는 데 있어서 유일한 희망이 아닌가 한다. 아마도 그것은 인간 사회의 어떠한 형태라도 보존하는 유일한 희망일지도 모른다.

044 오늘날의 상황에서 볼 때, 많은 교사들이 자신들이 할 수 있는 최선을 다할 수가 없다. 여기에는 많은 이유가 있는데, 어떤 이유들은 다소 비본질적인 것들이고 또 어떤 이유들은 대단히 뿌리 깊은 이유들이다. 전자의 경우를 들어 이야기를 시작하자면, 대부분의 교사들이 과로하고 있고 학생들에게 자유로운 교육을 한다기보다는 오히려 그들에게 시험 준비만 시키도록 강요를 받고 있다는 점이다.

045 'Please'와 'Thank you'라는 말은 우리가 사회적 존재로서 빚지지 않고 살아 나가는 잔돈이라 할 수 있다. 그것들은 우리가 인생이라는 기계에 기름을 쳐서 부드럽게 작동해 나가도록 하는 조그마한 예절이다. 그것들은 윗사람이 아랫사람에게 명령을 하는 기초가 아니라 서로 양보해서 공평하게 주고받는 친근미가 넘치는 협력의 기초 위에 우리의 교제를 올려놓는다. 부탁을 함으로써 봉사를 받을 수 있고, 그것도 분개하는 마음 대신에 기꺼이 좋은 기분으로 대접받을 수 있는데도 명령을 하고자 하는 사람은 매우 천한 마음의 소유자이다.

046 랑케는 다음의 의견을 강력히 소유하고 있었다. "야심에 불타고 호전적이며 국민적 자부심에 자극받은 프랑스 국민은, 억압받는 민족은 종종 해방시키고 또 더욱 빈번하게는 자유로운 민족은 억압하면서 이웃 국가들을 끊임없이 괴롭혀 왔다."

047 건강은 값을 매길 수 없을 만큼 귀중한 보물이지만 그 가치는 건강을 잃을 때까지는 거의 인식이 되지 않는다. 개인적 경험을 토대로 해서 토머스 칼라일은 "건강한 사람들은 자신의 건강에 대해 모르며, 병든 사람들만이 안다."고 말하였다. 젊은이들은 특히 건강을 당연한 것으로 받아들이고 장래의 성공과 행복, 심지어는 삶 그 자체가 사람의 성장기 시절에 얻어진 생활 습관에 의해 많은 영향을 받고, 또 많은 경우 실제로 결정이 된다는 사실을 거의 인식하지 못한 채 젊음을 낭비하는 경향이 있다.

048 나는 여행에 관하여 분석적인 방법보다는 종합적인 방법을 찬성한다. 나는 그때 생각들을 저장하고 나중에 그것을 검토하고 분해하기를 좋아한다. 나는 나의 어렴풋한 생각들이 산들바람에 날리는 엉겅퀴의 솜털처럼 둥둥 떠다니는 것을 보고 싶어하지, 논란의 가시 속에 엉키게 하고 싶지는 않다. 한 번만이라도 나는 그것을 내 마음대로 하고 싶은 것이다. 그러나 이것은, 당신이 홀로 있지 않거나 원하지 않는 사람과 같이 있으면 불가능하다.

049 현대 문명이 직면하고 있는 많은 문제 가운데서 노인의 운명이라고 하는 문제는, 이 문제에 관해서 신문, 잡지에 실린 기사의 수로 판단해 볼 때 확실히 일반 사람들의 마음속에 제일 먼저 떠오르는 것 중의 하나이다. 지난 세기에 걸쳐서 사실상 산업화된 국가들의 평균 수명은 비약적으로 연장되어, 마침내 오늘날에는 73세까지 달하게 되었다.

050 우리나라의 현대 대중교육 제도는 사실 필수불가결한 것이었고 또한 이 나라에 많은 이익을 갖다 주었으나, 또 한편으로는 몇 가지 중요한 면에 있어서 실망을 주어 왔다. 일반적으로 이야기한다면 이 제도는 글을 읽을 수 있지만 선풍을 일으키고 값싼 마음에 호소하는 작품들에 이용당해 읽을 만한 가치가 있는 책을 구별하지 못하는 많은 사람들을 만들어 내었다. 그 결과로 문학과 신문은 1896년 이래 크게 저속화되어 왔다. 왜냐하면 그것들이 오늘날 수많은 반 인텔리와 1/4 인텔리들을 즐겁게 해 주기 때문이다.

051 영국 사람들이 대화에 관하여 좀 더 이론을 많이 가졌으면 하고 바랄 수밖에 없는 때가 가끔 있다. 진정으로 훌륭한 대화는 있을 수 있는 최고의 쾌락 중의 하나이다. 그럼에도 그러한 훌륭한 대화를 접할 기회가 얼마나 적은가!

052 중국이 일본보다 훨씬 오래되고 더 위대한 국가로서 극동 지방에서 문명의 요람이었다는 사실, 그리고 일본이 조그마한 그리고 오랜 기간 동안 중국 문명의 뒤떨어진 하나의 지류에 불과하였다는 사실을 부인할 수는 없었다.

053 인생길에는 돌아오는 법이 없다. 우리가 걸어가는

시간이라는 연약한 다리는 우리가 내딛는 발걸음마다 영원 속으로 가라앉는다. 과거는 우리에게서 영원히 사라져 버리는 것이다. 그것은 모아져서 축적이 되고 더 이상 우리의 것이 되지 않는다.

054 젊은 시절에 우리는 우리와 다른 취미를 가진 사람들을 참아 내지 못한다. 내가 소년이었을 때, 정치와 문학에서 내가 정열을 쏟아붓던 일들에 대해 무관심한 사람에게 적대감을 느끼지 않을 수 없었다.

055 가끔 우리 자신의 원기를 북돋우기 위해 이런저런 오락에 눈을 돌려 볼 필요가 있다는 것은 두말할 필요가 없다. 그러나 동시에 우리는, 우리가 인생에서 차지하는 위치를 곰곰이 생각해 볼 필요가 있는데, 그것은 하나의 즐거움이나 쾌락이 그 자체로서는 해가 없다고 하더라도 우리의 수단이나 능력을 고려하지 않고 그것을 받아들이게 되면 우리에게 하나의 불행한 일로 나타날 수도 있기 때문이다.

056 영국의 유명한 화가인 터너는 이렇다 할 전통적인 교육을 받지 못하고 평생 동안 문맹의 상태로 지냈는데, 이것이 그의 시각적인 감각을 날카롭게 했을지도 모른다.

057 우리가 일상적으로 사용하는 언어는 그것에 대해 깊이 생각해 보지도 않고 당연한 것으로 받아들이는 경향이 있는 대상이다. 그러나 우리가 언어에 대하여 실제로 생각해 보기 시작하면, 우리는 그것이 평범한 것이기는커녕 하나의 신비스러운 일—그 기원이 신비하고 그 무한한 잠재 능력이 신비한—이라는 것을 곧 깨닫게 된다.

058 여러분은 매일 수많은 어리석은 사람들이 마치 자유가 명예스러운 일이거나 한 것처럼 이야기하는 것을 듣는다. 자유는 명예스러운 일이기는커녕 대체로, 그리고 광범위한 의미에서 볼 때, 불명예스럽고 또한 하등 동물의 속성이다.

059 오늘날 우리 모두는 무시무시한 공포의 상태에 놓여 있다. 우리는 미래에 대한 공포에 휩싸여 있는데, 그렇지 않은 체해 봐야 쓸모없는 일이다. 우리가 두려워하는 것은 우리 자신이나 우리의 친구들에게 다가오는 거침없는 파괴의 위험이라기보다는, 우리들 중에서 정말로 뛰어난 사람들이 의지하며 살아 온 이상에 다가오는 위험과 죽음이다.

060 교육은 그것이 목적 그 자체로 여겨질 때 무익한 것이 되고 또한 이기적 감정이나 한 집단의 이해에 종속될 때 위험한 것이 된다. 그것이 아무리 대단한 것이라고 하더라도 만약 인간이 그것을 단지 외적으로만 이용하고 책임 있는 한 구성원으로서 큰 발전을 이룩하지 않은 채 인생의 종말에 다다른다고 하면 지식의 축적은 인간에게 아무런 우월성도 주지 못한다.

061 우리의 현대 세계는 여러 가지 점에서 그리스와 로마 세계의 연속이라 할 수 있다. 다른 영향력[요소]들이 같이 합쳐져서 오늘의 우리를 만들어 냈지만 그리스, 로마적 요소는 가장 강력하고 풍부한 요소들 중의 하나이다. 그 그리스, 로마적 요소가 없다면 우리의 문명은 오늘의 모습과 다를 뿐만 아니라 문명이라고 부르기에는 좀 가치가 덜한 상태가 될지도 모른다. 왜냐하면 그 정신적 업적이 (오늘의 그것보다) 덜 위대할 것이기 때문이다.

062 우리가 가지고 있는 지식과 믿음의 대부분은 다른 사람들이 창조해 낸 언어라는 매체를 통해서 타인들에 의해 우리들에게 전달되어 왔다. 언어가 없다면 우리의 정신 능력은 정말 보잘것없고, 소위 고등 동물의 정신 능력에 비교될 수 있을지도 모른다. 따라서 우리는, 우리가 짐승보다 낫다는 주요한 이점을 인간 사회에 살고 있다는 사실에 힘입고 있다는 것을 인정할 수밖에 없는 것이다.

063 습관은 유용하기도 하고 동시에 필요하기도 하다. 삶은 우리의 시간과 주의력을 많이 요구하고 있어서, 결정을 내리고 그것을 실천하는 데 따르는 정신적, 정서적 긴장으로부터 우리를 해방시키는 습관이 없다면 고통스러우리만치 어려울 것이다.

064 누구든 언제나 심각한 것은 좋지 않다. 그러한 사람에게는 인생이 주는 긴장이 가끔은 너무 힘들다. 링컨 대통령은 우스운 이야기를 대단히 좋아했다. 그는 전쟁이 가져오는 긴장과 부담을 너무 강하게 느껴서, 이와 같은 (긴장을 풀어 주는) 구제책이 없었더라면 전쟁이 끝나기 훨씬 전에 무너지고 말았을 것이다.

065 인생에서 우리가 가는 길과 우리의 마지막 운명에 실제로 영향을 미치는 일들에 대해서도 우리는 부분적으로밖에 모른다. 그것을 사건이라고 부를 수가 있다면 우리에게 가까이 왔다가 실제적인 결과도 남기지 않은 채, 또는 우리의 마음에 어떤 빛을 드리우거나 그림자를 남김으로써 그들이 가까이 접근해 왔다는 것을 나타내지도 않은 채 지나가 버리는 사건들이 있다. 우리가 우리에게 지워진 운명의 모든 변천을 알 수 있다면 인생은 희망과 두려움으로 너무나 가득 차서 우리에게 일순간의 진정한 평정도 제공하지 못할 것이다.

066 어떤 나라든 문명국은 법이 대단히 많고 또 아주 복잡해서 어느 누구도 그 모든 법을 완전히 알 수는 없다. 그러나 모든 사람은 법을 아는 것으로 여겨지고, 그가 만약 법을 어기면 그 법을 몰랐다고 해서 처벌을

면할 수는 없다. 물론 이것은 당연한 상식에 지나지는다. 왜냐하면 어떤 사람이 자신이 법을 어기고 있다는 점을 몰랐다고 주장을 함으로써 자신의 범법 행위에 대한 결과를 면할 수가 있다면 전 정치 조직(국가 조직)은 무너질 것이기 때문이다.

067 시를 읽음으로써 우리는 시인 자신이나 시인의 상상력에 의해 창조된 인물의 감정에 공감을 느낄 수가 있다. 우리는 그들의 고생과 승리와 실패를 목격한다. 우리는 그들의 사랑과 증오, 즐거움과 슬픔, 희망과 두려움을 마치 그것들이 우리의 것인 양 느낀다. 그럼에도 우리가 그들의 번민과 슬픔에 같이 고민하게 된다면 우리는 (시를 읽는) 그 경험으로부터 즐거움을 얻게 된다.

068 여러분이 지닌 기회를 잘 개발하는 것이 얼마나 중요한가 하는 점을, 또한 그 기회를 소홀히 한 경우 나중에 아무리 쓸모없이 후회해 보아도 쓰라림만 남는다는 점을 여러분 마음속에 새겨 넣어 주고 싶은 마음이며, 이제는 기회가 지나가고 사라져 버린 지 오래된 우리들 몇몇이 나중에 그러한 기회를 사려고 할 때 얼마나 많은 비용이 드는가 하는 점을 여러분에게 알려 주고 싶은 마음이다.

069 오늘날 기억력 훈련 코스가 대단한 유행을 타고 있다. 그리고 우리가 더 많은 일들을 기억하면 기억할수록 우리는 더욱더 행복해진다는 점이 당연시되고 있는 것 같다. 기억이 주는 쾌락은 높이 평가되어야 하지만, 나는 망각도 인간을 행복하게 하는 데 일익을 담당하고 있다고 확신한다. 맥베드 부부는 던칸을 죽인 것을 잊을 수 있었더라면 더 많은 것을 내놓으려고 했을 것이고, 또한 많은 정치가들은 자신의 선거 공약을 잊어버리고 싶어하였다.

070 아리스토텔레스가 아내의 입을 벌리게 하여 이의 수를 세어 보는 간단한 일만 해 보았던들 여성이 남성보다 이의 수가 더 적다고 생각하는 실수를 면할 수 있었을 것이다. 그는 자신이 그 점을 안다고 생각했기 때문에 그렇게 하지 않았다. 실제로는 모르면서도 안다고 생각하는 것은 우리 모두가 저지르기 쉬운 치명적인 실수이다.

071 천재는 단지 끊임없는 노력을 하는 힘이다. 실패와 성공의 경계선은 너무 가늘어서 우리는 그 경계선을 지날 때 그것을 거의 모른다. 또한 그 경계선은 너무 가늘어 그 선 위에 있으면서도 그 점을 모른다. 조금만 더 노력하고 조금만 더 참았더라면 성공을 이룩했을 시기에 얼마나 많은 사람이 손을 털고 일어났던가! 바닷물은 뚜렷이 빠져나가는 때가 있는 것처럼 또 뚜렷이 들어오는 때도 있는 것이다.

072 어느 방향에서 자연에 접근해 가든지 자연을

명료하게 보는 것을 막는 장애물은 나타난다. 그리고 (진보를 위한) 동기가 순수하게 자연에 대한 지식의 추구이든 또는 유리한 이점이든, 강력한 욕망뿐만 아니라 끊임없는 노력은 진보의 모든 단계에서 필요한 것이다.

073 대부분의 사치품과 소위 인생의 안락이라는 것들은 많은 경우 필수불가결한 것이 아니기도 하고 또한 인간성의 고양에 명확한 장애물이기도 하다. 사치품과 안락한 물건들과 관련하여, 가장 현명한 사람들은 가난한 사람들보다 더 소박하고 빈약한 삶을 살았다.

074 스포츠 정신이란, 인생 전체가 규칙에 입각하여, 그러나 전체를 너무 심각하게 받아들임 없이 열심히 행해야 하는 경기라는 사실을 우리가 결코 잊어서는 안 됨을 의미한다. 또한 그것은 경기 감각뿐만 아니라 경기장의 스포츠 정신을 가지고 인생의 가장 중요한 순간을 살아야 함도 의미한다.

075 문학이 종교의 대용물이 결코 될 수 없는 것은 우리가 종교를 필요로 한다는 이유에서뿐만 아니라 우리에게 종교와 마찬가지로 문학도 필요하다는 이유에서이다. 그리고 종교가 드라마의 대용물이 아닌 것에게서만큼은 드라마가 종교의 대용물이 아닌 것과 마찬가지이다.

076 우리 모두는 어느 정도는 시인이다. 왜냐하면 우리 모두는 감정을 가지고 있고 또 우리가 느끼는 바를 다른 사람들에게 전달할 힘을 지니고 있기 때문이다. 그러나 우리가 시인이라고 부르는 사람들은 보다 넓은 감정의 영역을 지니고 있어서 감수성이 더욱 예민할 뿐만 아니라 동시에 자신들이 느끼는 바를 표현하여 다른 사람들로 하여금 그 감정을 나누어 갖도록 감동을 주는 능력이 더 강하다.

077 과학적인 태도는 사고의 한 방식이며 처신의 한 방식이고 또한 삶의 한 방식이기도 하다. 그것은 건설적인 과학의 진보에 필수적인 것으로 밝혀져 온 태도이며, 만약 그것이 보다 널리 퍼지고 받아들여지고 진가가 인식되고 또 이용된다면, 인류로 하여금 지금 직면하고 있는 많은 문제점들을 해결하는 데 상당한 도움을 주게 될 것이다. 과학적인 태도는 많은 구성분자를 갖고 있는데, 그중 가장 중요한 부분은 분명하고 이해하기에도 쉽다.

078 그러나 얼마 되지 않아 나는 호감이 가는 이 젊은 청년이 목수일이나 기계 분야의 일에 있어서 실제로 어떠한 일이든 할 수 있다는 점을 알게 되었다. 물건을 고치거나 무엇을 짓는 일에 있어서 그는 말보다 행동을 앞세웠다.

079 올해는 오랜 기간 동안 햇볕이 쪼는 해였다. 몇 달이고

하늘은 친절함을 베풀어 주었고, 7월이 가고 8월이 되는가 했더니 어느새 9월에 접어들어 있었다. 가을 꽃으로 인해 노란색으로 순화된 오솔길을 보게 되는 일이 없다면, 나는 아직도 계절이 여름인가 하고 생각할 정도이다.

080 한때는 소로를 무척이나 좋아했지만, 나는 결코 돈을 (인간) 노예화의 원인으로 보아 오지 않았음을 밝혀 둔다. 호주머니에 1실링밖에 없을 때보다는 1파운드를 가지고 있을 때 나는 언제나 더 많은 자유로움을 느꼈다. 누군가를 식사에 초대하고 그에게 들도록 권한 요리와 음료 값을 지불할 돈이 호주머니에 충분히 있는지 없는지를 걱정하지 않는 것은 많은 가난한 사람들이 종종 갈망해 왔음에 틀림없는 자유 중 하나이다.

081 인간의 젊음은 놀랄 만한 것이다. 그것은 번민과 마력으로 가득 차 있고, 그것이 인간으로부터 영원히 사라지게 될 때까지 인간은 젊음을 있는 그대로 깨닫지 못한다. 젊음은 인간이 그것을 상실하게 됨을 도저히 참지 못하는 것이고, 그것이 사라져 감을 무한한 슬픔과 회한으로 바라다보는 것이고, 그것을 상실하면 영원히 비탄해 함에 틀림없는 것이며, 한편으로는 상실됨을 슬프고 비밀에 찬 기쁨으로 정말로 환영하는 것이고, 자신에게 그것이 다시 되돌려진다고 해도 기꺼이 다시 살고 싶지는 않을 그러한 것이다.

082 인류의 역사 및 선사 시대를 연구해 보면 윤리와 종교의 놀라운 발전이 있어 왔음을 알게 된다. 이것들(윤리와 종교)이 완벽한 형태로 하늘로부터 전수되었다고 하는 만족할 만한 증거는 없지만, 이것들이 다른 것들과 더불어 진화해 왔고 이 진화의 과정이 아직 끝나지 않았다는 증거는 충분히 있다. 오늘날 행해지고 있는 윤리규범과 종교의식 중 몇몇은 앞으로 다가올 시대에는 아마 야만적인 것으로 간주될지도 모른다.

083 분명히 모든 사람은 전기(傳記) 작가의 연구 대상이 될 자격이 있다. 평범한 사람들에게서도 비범한 사람들에게서만큼 많은 것을, 또는 그 이상을 배울 수 있다. 만약에 의사가 자신의 관심을 예외적인 사람에게만 국한시키게 된다면, 그는 인간 본성에 관해 배우는 바가 거의 없을지도 모른다.

084 시는 눈으로 읽어야 할 뿐만 아니라 귀로도 들어야 한다. 만약에 우리가 시를 소리 내어 읽지 않으면 시어(詩語)의 리듬과 음악성을 감상할 수 없다. 이것들(리듬과 음악성)은 시어 자체의 의미만큼 시의 완전한 이해를 위해서 중요하다.

085 그가 스스로 가난에서 벗어나 43세의 나이로 죽기

전에 위대한 위치를 차지하게 된 원인은, 대부분의 가난한 소년들이 후년에 성공을 얻게 되는 그런 야망 때문은 아니라고 나는 생각한다. 내가 판단하기로는, 그는 이 세상에 산 그 누구보다도 야망이라는 단어가 지니는 일반적인 의미에서 가장 거리가 멀었다.

086 천재성이 정확성을 요하는 (정밀)과학 분야에서 창조적인 업적으로 인류의 지식을 살찌게 하고 깊이 있게 한 사람들 중에서, 주된 활동 분야가 대다수의 사람들에게 낯설고 노력의 결과가 이해하는 데 어려움이 있다는 사실에도 불구하고 케플러만큼 많은 사람의 공감을 누리는 자도 거의 없다.

087 우리가 인생은 마땅히 재미있어야 한다고 생각하는 만큼 그렇게 재미있는 경우는 드물다. 모험으로 가득 차 보이는 것은 다른 사람의 삶이다. 당신의 직업이 무엇이든지 간에, 혹은 그 직업에서 당신이 아무리 행복하다 해도, 다른 직업을 택했더라면 하고 바라는 순간들이 있는 것이다.

088 때로 남에게 좋은 충고도 하지 못할 만큼 어리석은 사람도 없고, 자기 자신의 지혜 외에는 남의 지혜를 빌리지 않고도 쉽게 실수를 저지르지 않을 만큼 현명한 사람도 없다.(즉 바보도 충고할 수 있고 현명한 사람도 실수할 수 있다.) 그러나 자기 자신만의 지혜로 현명해지는 사람도 드물고, 자기 자신만의 학업으로 박식해지는 사람도 드물다. 왜냐하면 혼자서 공부한 사람은 바보를 자신의 스승으로 삼았기 때문이다.

089 자신의 생계 수단에 관하여 끊임없이 걱정하는 것처럼 불명예스러운 일은 없다. 돈을 멸시하는 사람들에게 나는 멸시밖에 보낼 게 없다. 그들은 위선자들이거나 바보들이다. 돈이란 그것이 없다면 다른 오감을 완벽하게 사용할 수 없는 육감과 같은 것이다. 적절한 수입이 없이는 삶의 가능성은 절반이 차단된 것이나 다름없다.

090 문학도로서 여러분이 해야 할 가장 중요한 일은 스스로가 정직한 학생이 되리라고 다짐하는 것이다. 왜냐하면 이지(理智)의 세계에서는 어쨌든 정직이 최고의 방책이기 때문이다. 만약에 여러분이 셰익스피어의 시보다 삼류 시인의 시를 더 좋아한다면 그것은 대단히 개탄스러운 일이다. 그러나 삼류 시인의 시를 좋아하면서 반대로(즉 셰익스피어의 시를 좋아한다고) 말하는 것만큼 개탄스럽지는 않다.

091 다른 사람이 당신과 다른 의견을 가지고 있다는 이유로 그 사람에게 화를 내는 것만큼 부당하고 우스꽝스러운 일도 없다. 이해관계, 교육 그리고 사람이 지식을 획득하는 방편은 대단히 달라서 그

사람들이 모두 똑같이 생각한다는 것은 불가능한 일이다. 그리고 당신이 그에게 화를 내는 만큼 그도 당신에게 화를 낼 만한 충분한 이유를 지니고 있는 것이다.

092 인간이 지닌 이상을 향한 모든 의지 중에서 단지 일부분만이 행동으로 나타날 수 있다. 나머지는 보이지 않는 결과로 나타날 운명에 처해 있다. 그러나 이 보이지 않는 결과[효과]는 세상의 이목을 끄는 활동보다 천 배, 또는 그 이상의 가치를 나타낸다. 그것이 후자에 대해서 갖는 관계는, 깊은 바다가 바다 표면을 휘젓는 파도에 대해 지니는 관계와 같다.

093 한 외국어를 습득하는 일에 착수하는 방법에는 여러 가지가 있다. 그중 한 가지 방법은 그 언어를 사용하는 사람을 구해 같이 공부하면서 그를 모방하고 그에게서 그 언어를 배우는 것이다. 물론 그 사람이 모국어 화자에 가까우면 가까울수록 더 좋다. 다른 한 가지 방법은 책을 한 권 구해서 혼자서, 또는 여러 사람이 같이 앉아서 그 책을 읽어 가는 것이다. 그 외국어를 다소간 말해 봄으로써 습득하며, 하지만 말보다는 주로 (눈으로) 읽으면서 외국어를 습득하려 노력하면서.

094 언어는 다리를 놓는 만큼 장벽도 만든다. 우리 자신의 언어와 다른 언어를 사용하는 개인들이나 집단들을 싫어하고 불신하고 또 우리보다 열등한 것으로 간주하는 뿌리 깊은 추세가 존재한다. 마치 언어를 지니지 않았다는 이유로 원숭이를 보다 하등한 동물로 여기듯. 오늘날 문화는 주로 언어에 의해 전해지고 있으며, 언어 차이가 크면 클수록 문화적인 거리감도 그만큼 커진다.

095 대부분의 사람들에게는 자신들이 궁극적으로 죽게 된다는 사실을 인식하는 것이 현재 살아 있다는 것에 대한 즐거움을 약화시키지는 않는다. 시인에게는 시들어 버릴 운명에 처한 꽃들을, 그리고 너무 일찍 끝나 버리는 봄철을 바라다볼 때 세상이 더욱더 아름답게 보인다. 모든 생명체가 죽게 된다는 생각이 그에게 즐거움을 주어서가 아니라 그 쾌락이 영원히 자기의 것이 될 수 없다는 사실을 알기 때문에 그만큼 더 소중하게 그 쾌락을 포용하는 이유에서이다.

096 어떤 한 사람이 평범하면 평범할수록 그 사람이 사용하는 말[언어]은 살고 있는 사회의 특색을 더 많이 띠게 될 것이고, 그 사람의 본성이 독특하면 독특할수록 사용하는 언어의 색채는 더욱더 독특하게 자신의 것이 될 것이다. 그 사람은 목소리에 의해 쉽게 인식될 뿐만 아니라 그 사람의 특수한 개성은 그가 사용하는 말과 어구, 심지어 글이라는 매체를 통해서도 인식될 것이다.

097 나에게 커다란 의미를 준 책들이 당신에게도 커다란 의미를 주게 될 바로 그 책들이라고 생각한다면 그것은 비합리적인 생각이다. 그러나 그 책들은 내가 그것들을 읽었기 때문에 그만큼 풍요로움을 느끼는 책들이며, 만약 그 책들을 읽지 않았더라면 오늘날의 내가 되지는 못했을 것이라고 생각한다.

098 시골의 몰락은 영국 역사의 비극적인 현상들 중의 하나이며, 그 비극이 널리 인식되지 않고 있다는 이유로 결코 덜 비참한 것은 아니다. 이제 이 몰락도 그치고 시골을 다시 복구하려는 전망도 있고 하니, 새로운 상황을 이해하고 현대적인 환경과 추세에 합치하는 면으로 시골을 복구하는 것이 필수적이다.

099 그들은 패배를 몰랐고 더군다나 점령된다는 것은 꿈에도 생각지 않았다. 그래서 전례가 없는 상황에 처해 어떻게 처신해야 할지에 관하여 그 국민들은 진정으로 어찌할 바를 몰랐다.

100 미래를 현재와 관련시켜 생각해 보는 것은 문명에 필수적인 일이다. 문명화된 국가에서는 아무리 평범한 일꾼이라도 그렇게 한다. 벌어들이는 즉시 모든 돈을 써 버리는 것이 아니라, 그가 만약 현명한 사람이라면, 수입의 상당 부분을 미래에 필요할 때 쓰기 위해 저축할 것이다.

101 여행의 정수는 자신이 바라는 대로 생각하고 느끼고 행동하는 자유—완벽한 자유—를 얻는 것이다. 우리가 여행을 가는 것은 주로 모든 장애물과 불편한 일들로부터 벗어나기 위한 것이요, 우리 자신을 뒤에 남겨 두기 위한 것이며, 하물며 다른 사람들을 따돌리기 위한 것이라는 것은 두말할 필요도 없다.

102 숲속을 통과하고 있을 때 숲의 전체 모습을 볼 수 없듯이, 우리 시대가 어떠한 모습인가를 우리가 본다는 것은 정말 불가능한 일이다. 숲을 빠져나와 전체로서 보게 될 때까지 우리는 어떤 나무들이 숲의 전체 모습[윤곽]에 필수적인 부분이 되는지를 판단할 수 없다.

103 야망은 그것이 취하는 목적에 따라 대단히 훌륭한 것일 수도 있고 대단히 나쁜 것일 수도 있다. 좋은 목적이든 나쁜 목적이든, 탄환을 펑 하는 소리와 함께 나아가게 하는 것이 화약인 것처럼, 삶에 힘과 동기를 부여하는 것은 야망이다. 장전한 총을 올바른 쪽으로 향하게 하는 것이 중요한 것처럼, 야망도 올바른 쪽으로 방향을 잡는 것이 중요하다. 그러나 야망이 없는 삶은 화약이 없는 총보다 나을 게 없다.

104 나는 논쟁을 할 마음이 되어 있지 않은 사람들, 또 돌을 버터로 바꿀 수 없는 것처럼 논쟁에 의해 마음을 변화시킬 수 없음을 내가 아는 사람들과 맹렬히 말다툼을 하는 경우가 자주 있다.

105 우리의 정신 속을 흘러가는 사악한 생각들에 대해서 우리가 책임이 없는 것은, 허수아비가 자신이 지켜야 하는 묘상 위에 날아오는 새들에 대해서 책임이 없는 것과 마찬가지이다. 그 어느 경우에 있어서나 져야 할 하나의 책임은 그것들(즉 사악한 생각들, 또는 새들)이 자리 잡지 못하게 하는 일이다.

106 만약 어떤 사람이 자신 외에는 누구도 결코 보지 못할 것이라고 확신하는 일기를 쓰게 되는 경우, 아마 그는 완전히 진실된 마음으로 그 일기를 쓰게 될 것이다. 다르게 행동해야 할 동기는 있을 수 없다. 그가 목욕을 하면서 자신의 벌거벗은 모습을 보고 부끄러워하지 않는 것처럼 그는 좋기도 하고 나쁘기도 한 자신의 행동을 일어난 모습 그대로 기록하는 데 부끄러움을 느끼지 않는다.

107 생각을 하는 일은 자연스러운 일이고 숨을 쉬거나 영양을 섭취하는 것만큼 자연스럽다. 이 말은 우리가 숨을 쉬고 음식을 섭취하는 것을 배우지 않는 것처럼, 생각하는 것을 배우지 않는다는 것을 의미한다. 누구도 사는 것을 배울 수는 없는 것이고, 단지 잘 사는 것만을 배울 뿐이다. 생각도 마찬가지이다. 여러분은 생각하는 것을 배우는 것이 아니라 여러분의 사고를 개선하는 것을 배우는 것이다.

108 그러나 단념도 역시 행복을 정복하는 데 있어서 담당하는 역할이 있으며, 이 역할은 노력이 담당하는 것 못지않게 필수적인 것이다. 현명한 사람은 그가 막아 낼 수 있는 불행 아래에 그냥 앉아 있지도 않을 것이지만, 피할 수 없는 불행에 시간과 감정을 낭비하지도 않을 것이다.

109 두 다리로 걷는 것이 원숭이들에게 부자연스럽고 힘든 일인 것처럼, 생각하는 일은 인간에게 있어서 마찬가지로 부자연스럽고 힘든 일이다. 우리는 해야 할 생각 이상을 하는 경우가 드물고, 생각을 하지 않으려는 우리의 성향은 우리가 가장 편안하다고 느낄 때 일반적으로 가장 크다. 사고의 노동을 싫어하는 인간의 반감이 사적인 일에서처럼 공적인 삶에서도 마찬가지로 분명하기 때문에, 인류는 편하고 번영하는 시대에는 역사에 남을 만한 생각을 별로 할 수 없었다.

110 나의 관심을 끈 첫 번째 과목은 종교였다. 왜냐하면 내가 살고 있는 이 세계가 생각해 볼 유일한 세계인지, 아니면 내가 이 세계를 앞으로 다가올 삶에 대해서 준비를 시켜 주는 단지 시련의 장소로 여겨야 하는지를 결정하는 일이 나에게는 가장 중요한 일로 보였기 때문이었다.

111 우정은 이성을 초월한다. 왜냐하면 당신이 한 친구에게서 미덕을 찾아낸다 해도 당신이 그 미덕을 찾아내기 이전에 그는 이미 당신의 친구이기 때문이다. 우정은 우리가 주어야 하기 때문에 주는 선물이며, 우정을 미덕의 보상으로 주게 된다면 그것은 우정에 값을 매기는 일이 될 것이고 그러한 일을 하는 사람들은 (자신들이) 줄 우정을 갖고 있지 않은 것이다. 당신에게 미덕이 있고 그래서 미덕이 있는 사람들을 친구로 원한다는 이유를 내세워 친구를 택하게 된다면, 당신이 금전적인 이유로 그들을 택하는 경우만큼 진정한 우정과는 멀어지게 되는 것이다.

112 단지 자기 자신만으로 만족하고, 따라서 자기 이하가 되는 사람은 감옥 속에 있는 것과 같다. 문학 서적을 읽는 경험은 개성의 특권을 손상시키지 않고 개성의 상처를 고쳐 준다. 위대한 문학 서적을 읽음으로써 나는 천 명의 다른 사람이 될 수 있지만, 그러나 나 자신인 것에는 변함이 없다. 여기에서 (위대한 문학 서적을 읽을 때) 신앙, 사랑, 도덕적인 행위 그리고 지식을 추구할 때와 마찬가지로 나는 나 자신을 초월하며, 이렇게 할 때보다 더 나 자신이 되는 경우도 결코 없다.

113 옛날에 야생 동물과 거의 다름없던 인간은 동굴과 숲속에서 자연과 다른 인간들, 동물들과 자신의 생존을 위해 싸우면서 홀로 살았다. 그들이 필요로 했던 것은 별로 많지 않았는데, 그날그날 먹을 양식과 밤에 잠을 잘 수 있는 안전한 장소뿐이었다.

114 진정으로 부유한 사회는 경제적 부를 목표 그 자체로 계속 축적해 가는 사회가 아니라 그 부를 풍요롭고 다양한 문화를 건설할 수 있는 토대로 사용하는 사회이다. 이러한 관점에서 볼 때 거의 모두가 충분한 음식을 하루에 겨우 한 번밖에 먹지 못한 고대 그리스 같은 국가가 번영의 정점에 선 미국보다 더 부유한 사회였다.

115 만약 당신이 박식한 사람들이 중요하고 읽을 만하다고 여기는 책에 지루함을 느끼게 되면, 자신에게 정직해져서 어려움이 아마도 책에 있는 것이 아니라 당신에게 있는 듯하다고 솔직히 인정하라. 지금은 재미없거나 어려워 보이는 책이 당신이 지적으로 보다 성숙해졌을 때에는 이해하기에 쉽고 읽기에 흥미진진한 것으로 종종 드러날 것이다.

116 이즈음에는 유일한 소식이래야 입에서 입으로 전해지는 것뿐이었다. 종이도 부족하고 잉크도 딸리고 일손도 모자라다 보니, 포위 공격이 시작된 후로 신문들이 휴간을 해 왔고, 그래서 아주 엉뚱한 뜬소문들이 난데없이 나타나 온 시내를 휩쓸고 다녔다.

117 어느 책도 글을 어떻게 쓰는지를 가르쳐 주지 않는다.

아무리 책을 많이 읽어도 글을 어떻게 쓰는지를 가르쳐 주지 않는다. 독서는 필수적이고, 실질적인 책이 도움을 줄 수 있다. 그러나 작가가 될 수 있는 맹아[싹]를 가지고 있지 않는 한, 다시 말하여 글을 쓰고자 하는 꺾을 수 없는 의지가 없는 한, 성공할 수 없는 법이다. 더군다나 글로 성공을 거두고자 한다면 열심히 노력을 해야 한다.

118 여행은 항상 모든 사람에게 커다란 기쁨이다. 교외를 걷는다든가 기차를 타고 시골로 여행을 한다든가 배나 비행기를 타고 먼 나라로 여행해 보는 것은 우리 인간에게 나름의 특이한 즐거움을 가져다준다. 그러나 우리 모두는 다른 나라들을 방문해 볼 수 있을 만큼 다 행운이 있는 것은 아니다. 어떤 사람들에게는 시간이 없고 어떤 사람들에게는 돈이 없다.

119 우리에게 일어날 수 있는 모든 특이한 재난을 생각해 봄으로써 우리가 재난을 견디어 내도록 스스로를 훈련시킬 수는 없다. 그렇게 하게 되면 준비하는 습관이 아니라 허둥대는 (공포의) 습관만 만들어질 뿐이다. 그리고 일어날 수 있는 모든 재난에 대하여 자세히 준비할 수도 없다. 또한 우리는 실제의 즐거움을 어느 것이라도 누리는 것을 거부함으로써 있을 수 있는 슬픔에 대비하여 우리 자신을 견고하게 대비시킬 수도 없다. 왜냐하면 즐거움은 정신 건강을 증진시키고 슬픔이 다가왔을 때 마음을 든든하게 해주기 때문이다.

120 모든 사람이 얻고자 바라는 것이 하나 있다면 그것은 성공이다. 성공한다는 것은 반드시 부와 명예와 권력을 얻는 것만을 의미하지는 않는다. 최고의 부를 지닌 자, 가장 많은 명예를 가진 자, 또 권력을 쥔 자들 중에서 어떤 자들은 가장 형편없는 실패자인 경우도 있는데, 그것은 그들이 깨끗한 양심을 팔아서 원하는 것을 얻었기 때문이다.

121 좋은 행운이 반드시 모든 이득을 의미하지는 않는 것처럼, 불운이 반드시 모든 상실을 의미하는 것은 아니다. 로마가 그리스를 정복하였지만 그리스 문명은 로마 문명을 압도하였고, 한 위대한 작가가 말한 바 있듯이 "오늘날 유럽에서 움직여 다니는 것치고 그리스에 기원을 두지 않은 것은 없다."

122 생각들 사이에도 생존 경쟁이 있고, 인간의 변화하는 조건에 일치하는 생각들만이 이기게 된다고 하는 믿음을 뒷받침해 주는 것들이 많다. 그렇다고 해서 우세한 생각들이 경쟁에 지는 생각들에 비해 도덕적으로 더 우수하고, 또한 자연의 법칙을 더 충실히 반영한다는 이야기가 반드시 성립되는 것은 아니다.

123 소설을 읽는 최선의 방법은 과거의 작품을 희생 시키면서 현대의 작품을 편애하지도 않고, 현대의 작품을 희생시키면서 과거의 작품을 편애하지도 않고, 현대와 과거의 소설을 섞어서 읽는 것이다. 그리고 이 방법을 취하면 현대의 작품이 과거의 대작에 비하여 얄팍하고 시시하게 보일 것이라고 생각하지 말아라. 상황이 반드시 그러한 것도 아니다.

124 언어는 결코 가만히 서 있지 않는다. 모든 언어는 그것이 죽게 될 때까지, 다시 말하여 더 이상 사용되지 않게 될 때까지 끊임없는 변화의 상태에 있게 된다. 우리가 말하고 글로 표현하는 영어는 우리의 할아버지대(代)에서 말하고 쓰던 영어가 아니고, 또한 할아버지대의 영어는 엘리자베스 여왕 시대의 영어와도 똑같지 않다. 우리가 과거로 거슬러 올라갈수록 우리는 우리 선조들이 사용한 언어가 더욱 낯선 것임을 알게 되고 마침내 우리는, 마치 그것이 외국어나 되는 것처럼, 우리에게 매우 낯선 영어에 접하게 된다.

125 우리는 매우 강력하고 영속적인 우정이 국적이 다른 사람들 사이에서도 존재하고, 이러한 우정을 형성하는 데 있어서 주된 장애물은 국적이라기보다는 오히려 언어의 차이라는 점을 종종 깨닫는다.

126 만약 당신이 진정한 행복이 있는 곳을 알고자 한다면 궁핍한 상황에 처해 있는 사람들의 삶을 눈여겨 보고 위안을 찾기만 하면 된다. 행복은 환경에 달려 있기보다는 우리가 자신의 운명을 바라다보는 방법에 달려 있다.

127 만약 인간이 태어날 때부터 홀로 남겨지게 된다면, 그 사람은 생각과 느낌에 있어서 우리가 거의 상상할 수 없을 정도로 원시적이고 짐승과 같은 상태에 있게 될지도 모른다. 인간이 현재의 모습을 지니고 현재의 중요성을 지니게 되는 것은 그 사람의 개성 덕택이라기보다는, 태어나서 죽을 때까지 그 사람이 물질적, 정신적 존재를 지배하는 커다란 인간 사회의 한 구성원으로 존재하기 때문이다.

128 인생사 또는 사업상의 일에 있어서 효력이 있는 것은 지력이라기보다는 오히려 성격이고, 두뇌라기보다는 오히려 마음이며, 천재성이라기보다는 오히려 판단력에 의해 인도되는 자제심과 인내심이다.

129 훌륭한 아내가 되는 것, 훌륭한 어머니가 되는 것, 간단히 말해서 훌륭한 가정주부가 되는 것은 이 세상의 모든 직업 중에서 가장 중요한 직업이다. 인간을 길러 내는 것은 다른 어느 것을 만들어 내는 일보다 훨씬 더 중요한 직업이고, 어린아이의 삶의 형성기 시절에 어머니는 아이가 나중에 의지할 수 있는 굳건한 기초를 제공해 줄 준비가 가장 잘 되어 있어야 함은 아무리 자주 지적해도 오히려 부족하다.

130 큰 사업이든 작은 사업이든 장사에 종사하는 사람은 고객의 습관, 태도, 요구사항에 대해 아무리 많이 알아도 지나치지 않다고 종종 이야기되어 왔는데, 그 말은 현명한 말이다.

131 우리가 일상생활에서 쓰고 있는 언어에 관하여 아무리 많이 알아도 지나침이 없다. 사실 우리들 대부분은 우리의 언어에 관해 그다지 많은 것을 알지 않고서도, 또한 「옥스포드 영어사전」을 한 번이라도 펼쳐 보는 수고를 들이지 않고도 잘 살아나갈 수 있다. 그러나 지식은 힘이다. 잘 선택된 단어의 힘은, 그 단어들이 정보를 제공하고 즐거움을 주고 또 우리를 감동시키는 어떠한 의도를 지니고 있든지 간에, 대단히 크다.

132 모든 사람을 위한 식량의 확보는 몇 가지 이유로 해서 중대한 세계 문제가 되고 있다. 가난한 세계는 결코 평화로운 세계가 될 수 없다. 세계 여러 곳에서 일어나는 불안은 대단히 자주 일어나는 식량과 관련된 생활수준에 관한 불만에 그 원인이 있다고 해도 지나친 말은 아니다. 클라크가 말한 것처럼 안정된 문명은 농사를 잘 짓고 맛있는 음식을 만드는 기초 위에서만 건설될 것이다.

133 나와 내 주위의 세계에 관한 과학적이거나 그렇지 않은 어떠한 설명에도 나는 만족을 느낄 수가 없어서 우주의 신비 앞에서 경탄을 하지 않고 보내는 날이 하루도 없다. 인간 지식의 승리를 알리고 돌아다니는 것은 유치함만 못한 것 같고, 이제 옛날과 마찬가지로, 우리는 단 하나의 사실만을 알고 있다. 우리가 아무것도 아는 것이 없다는 것을.

134 사랑하는 어머님, 당신께서 어머니로서 보여 주신 친절함뿐만 아니라, 당신께서 저의 어린 정신에 미덕의 원칙들을 집어넣어 주시고자 노력하신 그 끊임없는 보살핌에 대해 아무리 감사드려도 오히려 부족함을 저는 알고 있습니다.

135 문학이 없다면 우리의 삶은 사막처럼 무미건조한 것이 될지도 모른다. 우리가 우리의 정신을 계발하는 매체로서 문학의 가치를 아무리 높이 평가해도 지나치지 않다. 그러나 문학 작품은 너무나 많고, 그것들을 읽을 우리의 시간은 너무나 제약되어 있다. 재미없는 문학을 읽을 때에는 우리의 실망은 더욱 쓰리게 된다. 따라서 고전을 읽는 것이 가장 안전한 방법이다. 왜냐하면 고전은 시대의 시련을 견디어 냈기 때문이다.

136 상당한 가치가 없는 책은 전혀 책으로서 가치가 없다. 또한 그 책은 읽고 또 읽고, 사랑받고 또 사랑받고, 그래서 그 속에 들어 있는 구절을 나중에 참조할 수 있도록 표식[주석]을 해 놓을 때까지는 책으로서

가치가 없다.

137 현재의 대학을 해체하여 세 개의 특수 학교로 대치해야 한다는 제안까지 있었다. 즉 전문기술 훈련학교, 일반교육기관 그리고 연구기관으로. 그러나 대학의 이상 속에는 이 세 가지가 분해할 수 없게끔 통합이 되어 있다. 나머지 두 개로부터 하나를 분리시키면 반드시 대학의 지적 본질을 파괴하게 되고, 동시에 대학을 불구로 만들게 된다. 이 세 가지는 모두가 하나의 살아 있는 생명체 전체를 구성하는 요소들이다. 이것들을 따로 분리함으로써 대학의 정신은 사라지게 된다.

138 사람들은 마치 악과 덕이 서로 다른 별개의 것들인 양, 또 양자의 어느 것도 다른 어느 하나의 요소는 전혀 갖고 있지 않은 것인 양 악과 덕을 구분한다. 그러나 상황은 반드시 그러한 것만은 아니다. 유익한 덕치고 어느 정도 악의 혼합물을 갖지 않은 것은 없으며, 약간의 덕을 지니지 않은 악은, 있다고 해도 거의 없다.

139 형이상학이 토론하는 또 하나의 문제는 우주의 목적에 관한 문제이다. 전체로서의 우주는 목적을 갖고 있다고 이야기될 수 있는가? 만약에 그렇다면(목적이 있다면) 그 목적을 진흥시키는 데 우리가 할 수 있는 역할이 있다면 무엇일까? 더 나아가 그 목적을 어떠한 용어로 생각해 볼 수가 있을까? 보다 커다란 도덕적 완벽을 기하는 것이라고 볼까? 보다 높은 의식의 수준이라고 볼까? 아니면 하나님과 보다 친숙한 영적 교섭으로 볼 수 있을까? 이러한 문제들, 또 비슷한 유의 문제들에 대해 우리가 제공하는 해답이 우리의 윤리관에 심오한 영향을 끼치리라는 것은 분명하다.

140 대부분의 사람들은 아니라고 하더라도 많은 사람들이 문학 취미를 볼 때, 그것을 획득함으로써 자신들을 완벽하게 하고 궁극적으로는 올바른 사회의 구성원으로 어울리게끔 만들어 내는 우아한 교양으로 보고 있다.

141 우리가 오늘날 미국에서 보고 알고 있는 모습으로서 여가는 새로운 현상이다. 그렇게 많은 사람들이 그렇게 많은 자유 시간을 갖게 되고, 그 자유 시간을 즐길 수 있는 그렇게 많은 돈을 가진 적은 예전에 없었다.

142 왜 책을 쓰는 사람이 자신을 버터를 만드는 사람보다 더 나은 사람으로 보아야 하는지 나는 그 이유를 모르겠다. 버터를 만드는 사람이 자신은 책을 만드는 사람보다 덜 가치가 있다고 믿는 것에 왜 동의를 해야 하는지는 더더욱 모르겠다. 그러나 분명히 그러한 미신이 우리 대부분의 마음속에 도사리고 있다.

143 이제 그 동물이 정말로 죽어서 누구에게도 더 이상 상처를 입히지 못할 것이라고 우리가 그녀를 확신시킬 때까지 케이트는 자신에게 그렇게 무서운 충격을 준 이 방문객[동물]을 잠시나마도 처다볼 생각을 감히 하지 못했다.

144 세계인권선언이 교육을 강조하고 있는 또 하나의 이유는 최근의 역사가 보여 주듯 교육이 이 시대에는 비난을 받을 가능성이 너무 많고 교육의 자유가 특히 침해받기 쉽기 때문이다. 더욱이 인권선언이 교육에 관심을 갖는 것은 그 이유가 교사도 또한 시민이고, 다른 시민들처럼 확인받아야 할 권리와 책임을 지니고 있기 때문이다.

145 오늘 우리가 누리는 정치적 자유는 보존하기가 그렇게 쉬운 것은 아니다. 그것은 투쟁을 통해 얻은 것이고 아직도 투쟁을 요구하고 있다. 그것은 지혜와 인내심을 통해 얻은 것이다. 우리는 현재 우리 스스로가 그들이 처했던 위험과 그들의 용기를 이해할 수 있는 위기의 시점에 살고 있어서 독립선언의 기초자들을 더욱더 높이 평가할 수 있을 것이다.

146 교육을 받은 육체노동자에게는 육체노동보다 더 나은 어떤 일이 더 어울린다고 하는 믿음을 우리는 결코 인정해서는 안 된다. 인간의 품위를 떨어뜨리는 것은 그가 어떠한 일을 해야 하느냐기보다는 습관이나 교제의 면에서 그가 어떠한 인간이냐 하는 점이다.

147 어떤 개인에 대한 날카롭고 교묘한 비판은 종종 나중에 후회의 원인이 된다. 우리들은 꽤 재미있기는 하지만 좀 불친절한 것도 같은 말을 하기 쉽다. 그리고 그러한 말은 고통을 주게 된다. 그러한 말이 입에서 떨어지기가 무섭게 우리는 그렇게 말하지 않았더라면 하고 마음속으로 바란다.

148 어린이의 예절은 그의 인생에서 위치에 따라 다소간 중요성을 달리할 수 있다. (그러나) 어린이의 도덕은 그의 위치가 어떠한 것이든 간에 아무리 일찍 주의를 기울여도 지나치지 않다.

149 어느 인간에게 있어서든 가장 중요한 사실은 그가 어떠한 신을 숭배하느냐—즉 그가 무엇을 위해 진정으로 사느냐—하는 점이다. 그것을 보면 그가 지닌 인격의 숨겨진 샘을 알아낼 수 있다. 그것이야말로 그의 존재인 내적 심장부에 존재하는 현재의 인간 됨됨이를 진정으로 측정하는 방법이다. 사람들은 자신에게는 종교가 없다고 주장하지만, 사실은 모든 사람은 무엇인가를 숭배한다. 그 숭배의 대상이 자신이든 돈이든 아니면 개를 경주시키는 일이든.

150 아프리카가 진실의 면에서 또는 신화의 면에서 지금까지 어떤 존재가 되어 왔든지 간에, 이제는 더 이상 옛 모습을 유지할 수는 없을 것이다. 민족주의라고 부르든 반식민주의라고 부르든, 그것을 무엇이라 부르든지 간에 아프리카는 변혁을 겪고 있다.

151 자식의 모든 비행(非行)에도 불구하고 불쌍한 늙은이인 어머니는 자식을 사랑하였다. 그가 더 형편없이 행동하면 행동할수록 그녀는 자식을 더욱 사랑하는 것 같았고, 그가 세상의 눈 밖에 나면 날수록 그녀는 그 자식을 더욱더 마음에 두었다.

152 예술 작품 하나를 만들어 내는 것은 기적의 산물은 아니다. 그것에는 준비가 필요하다. 토양은 그것이 아무리 비옥하다 해도 비료를 주어야 한다. 생각을 하고 의도적인 노력을 통해 예술가는 자신의 개성을 확장하고 깊이 있게 하며 다양하게 해야 한다. 그리고 토양은 (경작하지 않고) 묵혀 두어야 한다. 그리스도의 신부처럼(즉 교회에 성령이 임하듯) 예술가는 새로운 영적 삶을 가져올 계시를 기다린다.

153 아마도 행동의 면에서 새들과 인간이 차이가 나는 가장 분명한 방식은, 새들은 몇몇 상당히 복잡한 일을 포함하여 자신들이 해야 하는 일들을 전혀 배우지 않고도 할 수 있다는 점이다. 우선 나는 일은, 균형을 유지하고 비행상의 조절을 해야 하는 놀라운 복잡성에도 불구하고, 새들은 배우지 않고도 행할 수 있다.

154 링컨의 '국민의, 국민에 의한, 국민을 위한 정치'는, 그것이 고상하기도 하고 또한 그 스스로가 그것을 당당하게 믿기는 하였지만, 이 세상 사람들에게 대단히 유리한 모습으로 제시된 수려하고 추상적인 개념에 불과하며 정치적인 운영에 관한 한 실제로 정확하게 실현하기는 어려운 것이다.

155 배우지 못하고 세련된 맛은 없었지만 그는 몇 가지 대단히 중요한 면에서 아직은 신사라고 할 만하였다. 그는 당당하고 세력 있는 귀족사회의 일원이었으며, 귀족들이 지니고 있는 좋은 자질뿐만 아니라 나쁜 자질 때문에도 사람들에게 잘 알려졌다.

156 우리가 경험할 수 있는 가장 아름다운 것은 신비이다. 그것은 모든 진실한 예술과 과학의 원천이다. 이 감정이 낯설게 느껴지는 사람, 하던 일을 멈추고 경이로움에 싸여 외경심에 넋을 잃지 못하는 사람은 죽은 것이나 다름없다. 그의 눈은 닫혀 있는 것이나 마찬가지다. 인생의 신비를 내다보는 이 통찰력은, 그것이 두려움과 결부되어 생각되기는 하지만, 또한 종교를 만들어 내게 되었다.

157 한 언어의 역사는 그 언어를 사용하는 국민의 역사를 많이 반영한다. 프랑스어를 아주 피상적으로만

연구해 보더라도 프랑스어가 거의 전적으로 라틴어에서 유래했음을 알게 되고, 그래서 이 점으로부터 프랑스가 오랜 기간 동안 로마 제국의 한 부분이었음을 알 수 있다.

158 인간은 실제의 역사를 지니는 유일한 존재이므로 얼굴을 지닌 유일한 피조물이다. 모든 얼굴은 그 소유주가 어쩌면 지금의 모습이 아니었을 과거를 소유하고 있고, 또한 어떤 가능성들이 다른 가능성들보다는 현실적으로 더 있을 수 있는 미래를 자기 앞에 지니고 있다는 사실에 대한 현재의 목격자인 셈이다. 한 사람의 얼굴을 '뜯어보는' 것은 과거에 어떠한 일이 가능했을 것인지, 또 앞으로 어떠한 일이 가능할 것인지에 대하여 추측을 해 보는 것이다. 아무리 고상한 얼굴도 (뜯어보면) 잠재적인 악이 극복되어 있음을 보여 주고, 아무리 사악한 얼굴도 (뜯어보면) 잠재적인 선이 억압되어 있음을 보여 준다.

159 금기라는 개념은 원시 부족들의 삶에서 커다란 역할을 한다. 금기는 불행이나 죽음이 뒤따르기 때문에 무엇인가를 금해야 한다는 것을 의미한다. 이러한 금기의 생각들이 어떻게 유래하였는지는 불명확하다.

160 만약에 당신의 견해와 다른 견해로 인해 화가 난다면, 그것은 당신이 지금 생각하듯이 생각할 하등의 이유가 없음을 의식하고 있다는 표시이다. 그러니 견해의 차이로 인해 화가 날 때마다 조심하시라. 검토해 보면 당신의 믿음이 증거의 한계를 넘어서고 있다는 것을 아마도 알게 될 것이다.

161 새들은 때때로 자기들을 보호하는 자들과 괴롭히는 자들을 구별할 수 있지만, 좀처럼 썩 잘 구별하지는 못한다고 나는 생각한다. 새들은 얼굴만 보는 것이 아니라 전체 모양을 보기 때문이다. 그래서 우리가 옷을 자주 갈아입으면 새들이 알고 있고 신뢰하는 사람들을 낯선 사람들과 구별하기가 어려워지게 된다. 심지어 개도 지난번에는 검정 옷을 입었던 주인이 밀짚모자를 쓰고 하얀 옷을 입고 다시 나타나면 가끔은 잘못 알아보는 실수를 한다.

162 예술과 종교의 관계는 우리가 직면하여야 하는 가장 어려운 문제 중의 하나이다. 과거를 되돌아 들여다보면 선사 시대의 희미한 구석진 곳에서 예술과 종교가 손을 맞잡고 나오는 것을 보게 된다. 수세기 동안 양자는 불가분의 상태의 (단단하게) 연결된 모습으로 있다가 약 600년 전쯤 유럽에서 서로가 단절되는 증표가 처음으로 나타났다. 그리고 마침내 문예부흥과 더불어 우리는 그 기원이 독창적이고, 예술가 자신의 개성을 넘어서는 것은 어느 것도 표현하려 하지 않는 데에 목표를 둔,

근본적으로 자유롭고 독립적인 예술을 갖게 되었다.

163 동맹파업과 노동전쟁은 노동자, 고용주나 일반 대중에게 값비싼 것이다. 그래서 정부는 조정과 중재, 또 어떤 경우에는 동맹파업의 금지를 통하여 여러 가지 방법으로 산업평화를 유지하도록 도우려고 노력을 해 왔다. 조정의 과정에서, 조정자 또는 공정한 의장으로 알려진 어느 쪽에도 치우치지 않는 제3자가 불러들여진다. 그는 고용주와 노동자 대표들과 우호적이며 허물없이 만나 협의하고 그들을 하나로 모으려고 요령 있게 노력한다. 만약에 그가 그렇게 할 수 없는 경우에는 노동분쟁에서 그는 어떠한 결론도 내리지 말아야 한다.

164 산들바람이 언덕 너머에서 향기로운 내음으로 내 방 안으로 불어오고 있었다. 갑자기 초원으로 나가고 싶었다. 초원에 나오자 태양은 내 머리 위에서 밝게 빛나고 있었고, 발밑의 땅은 담요를 덮고 잘 수 있을 만큼 따뜻하였다. 야생 해바라기 한 송이를 꺾어 들고 그 금빛 심장을 들여다보다가 갑자기 향수가 밀려와서 거의 울먹일 뻔하였다. 상냥한 목소리에 조용하면서도 단호하시던 어머니가 보고 싶었고, 아버지의 즐거운 노랫소리를 듣고 그의 반짝거리는 파란 눈이 보고 싶었다. 해가 지평선 너머로 질 때까지 데이지와 야생 해바라기를 꺾으며 초원에서 같이 놀던 누이가 없어서 허전한 마음이었다.

165 날씨가 맑고 고운 날 오후에 당번이 아닐 때, 그는 부근의 들판과 오솔길을 혼자서 얼마간 걷기를 좋아하였다. 그에게는 홀로 있는 것이 결코 지루하게 느껴지지 않았다. 오후의 이 산책 중에 그를 만났더라면, 아마도 당신은 그가 걷는 동안 그의 얼굴에서 잔잔한 미소를 볼 수 있었을 것이다. 분명히 그는 기분을 좋게 하는 것들만 생각하였다. 햇볕과 시골의 고요함과, 무엇보다도 찰나의 독립감이나마 느낄 수 있음을 좋아하였다.

166 중세에는 건축과 회화(繪畵)와 조각이 거의 전적으로 교회를 위해서만 쓰였다. 교회 건물은 그 당시의 중심 예술이었고 다른 예술은 교회 건물을 장식하고 아름답게 꾸미는 데에 쓰였다. 교회 하나를 짓고 아름답게 꾸미는 일은 중세에는 공동체가 같이 참여해서 이루어야 할 프로젝트였다. 중세 사람들은 교회에다 자신들의 종교적 감정과 지역의 자존심을 표현하였다.

167 1773년 9월에 동인도회사는 (아메리카 대륙의) 대서양에 연해 있는 항구에 있던 미국의 대행업자들에게 50만 파운드의 차(茶)를 선적해 보내려는 계획을 세웠다. 식민지 이주자들이 동인도회사의 계획에 대한 이야기를 알게 되었을 때, 사우스캐롤라이나 주에서 메인 주에 이르기까지

연안 항구의 지역 차 상인들은 그들을 폐업으로 몰고 가려는 이 시도에 맞서서 조처들을 취하였다. 보스턴 차 사건은 이러한 조처들 중에서 가장 격렬한 조처였다. 이 반란 사건이 있은 후에 주지사 허친슨은 이 행위를 "아메리카 대륙에 지금까지 있었던 타격 중에서 가장 대담한 타격"이라고 불렀다.

168 말하자면, 어린아이 시절의 걱정거리들은 우리 어른들을 괴롭히는 걱정거리들보다 지속되는 기간이 더 짧다. 그러나 이 걱정거리들은 근본적으로 우리의 것과 성질이 유사하고, 특히 이것들이 대개 상상에서 나온 것이며 또 이것들이 매우 자주 남몰래 겪는 걱정거리라는 점에서 우리의 걱정거리들과 닮았다.

169 평범한 서양인에게 동양은 언제나 신비의 땅이었다. 현대의 통신 수단과 정보 전달 방식들, 특히 카메라와 영화와 인터넷과 스마트폰 등등이 서양인을 동양 문명의 외적인 특성들과 친숙하게 만들고는 있지만, 동양 문명의 내적인 정신은 아직도 낯설고 먼 곳에 머무르고 있다.

170 바벨탑 이야기는 구약 성경에 나온다. 하나님의 신비를 알기 위하여 인간은 하늘나라에 닿을 수 있는 탑을 건설하려고 하였다. 인간의 자만심에 대한 처벌로 탑은 무너졌고 일꾼들의 언어는 혼돈에 빠졌다. 이것은 세계에서 사용되고 있는 다양한 언어들의 기원에 대한 하나의 우화적인 설명이다. 오늘날 전 세계적으로 3,000개 이상의 언어가 사용되고 있는데 그중 많은 언어들이 공통의 기원을 가지고 있다. 프랑스어, 스페인어, 이탈리아어 등의 로망스어군의 언어들은 모두 라틴어에서 기원한다. 한편, 영어는 게르만어군에 속하나, 많은 요소들이 그리스어, 라틴어, 프랑스어 등으로부터 여러 가지 이유로 차용되었다.

171 정규 학교 교육의 과정에 있을 때에는, 호기심을 갖고 수업에 들어오는 것은 매우 중요한 일이다. 배우고자 하는 욕망은 공부하고 배워가는 행위를 하나의 기쁨으로 만들어 준다. 여러분들 중 너무나 많은 학생들이 선생님들과 학교교육체제에 대해 너무 많은 불평을 하여서 공부에 전념하지 못하고 있다. 결국 공부가 학교에 다니는 주된 이유인데도 말이다. 내가 대학을 나온 후 30년 동안 학교교육체제는 그다지 변화하지 않았고, 향후 30년 동안 그다지 큰 변화는 없을 것이다. 그러니 그것에 대해 불평을 하지 말고 차라리 그것과 싸워 이기려고 해 보는 것은 어떤가?

172 학교에서 시를 암기하도록 강요를 받는 것은 나쁜 일이라고 생각하지 않는지 소년 소녀들이 종종 내게 묻는다. 그 답은 '좋기도 하고 나쁘기도 하다'이다. 만약에 당신이 시는 어리석은 물건이고 쓸모가 없거나 권위에 어울리지 않는 것이라는 생각을 이미

해 오고 있다면 시를 암기하는 것에서 분명히 많은 것을 얻을 수 없을 것이다. 그러나 기억을 훈련시키는 것은 좋은 일이라는 것을 기억하라. 그러면 시를 배우는 일은 적어도 예를 들어 전화번호부에서 20개의 번호를 외우는 일보다는 훨씬 재미있는 기억 훈련의 방식이 될 것이다. 더욱 중요한 것은 시를 배우는 일은 단어들에 대한 존경심을 배우는 일이고, 단어들에 대한 이러한 존경심이 없다면 당신은 명확하게 생각하거나 자신의 견해를 분명하게 표현하는 일을 결코 잘 하지 못할 것이다.

173 철의 장막 뒤에서 나온 한 이야기는 어느 날 아침 영화관에서 상영된 몇 편의 영화에 관해서 알려 준다. 그 영화관은 동독의 조그마한 마을에 있었다. 그 영화들은 (정치적) 선전의 성격을 띠고 있었고 몇몇 러시아 군인들이 러시아 강(江) 배로부터 한 독일 항구 도시의 부두에다 식량 공급분을 내리는 모습을 보여 주고 있었다.

174 영어 성경이 셰익스피어(가 쓴 작품들) 다음으로 영문학에서 가장 위대한 작품이며, 영국 민족의 문어나 구어에 심지어 셰익스피어보다 더 큰 영향을 미칠 것이라고 말해도 결코 과장은 아니다. 이 이유 때문에 영어 성경과 영문학의 관계에 대한 약간의 전체적인 지식 없이 영문학을 공부한다는 것은 자신의 문학 교육을 매우 불완전한 모습으로 남겨놓는 셈이 될 것이다.

175 과학을 중단시키면 해결책들보다는 문제들을 더 많이 만들어 낼 것이다. 군사적인 고려 사항들을 제외해 놓고라도 현재 정점에 도달해 있는 문화를 (그 상태에서) 얼린다는 것은 재앙을 초래하는 일이 될 것이다. 20세기 후반과 21세기 초의 고도화된 기술 문명은 비행 중인 항공기와 같아서 앞으로 나아가려는 움직임에 의해 지탱된다. 그것을 멈추면 반드시 추락하게 되어 있다. 예를 들어, 만약에 온 세계 사람들이 천연자원을 현재 미국인들이 사용하는 만큼 빠른 속도로 사용하기를 배우면 많은 필수 자원들이 고갈될 것이다. 과학자들은 대체자원을 충분히 제공하기 위하여 자신감 있게 핵에너지를 포함한 개선책에 의존해야 하는데, 현재의 (과학)기술로는 아직 그 일을 할 수가 없다.

176 아주 작은 원자 깊숙한 곳에 무시무시한 힘이 숨겨져 있다. 이 힘은 우리 현대 세계에 매우 무서운 파괴의 힘으로 등장하였다.

177 배가 항구를 벗어나자마자 바람이 불기 시작하였고, 파도가 몹시 무시무시한 기세로 일기 시작하였다. 그리고 나는 전에 해상에 나가 본 적이 없었으므로 거의 표현할 수 없을 만큼 몸이 뒤틀리고 정신적인 공포를 느꼈다.

178 그는 어린아이였지만 체격이 크고 잘생긴 젊은 아빠가 더 이상 돌아오시지 못할 것이라는 점을 눈치챘고, 또한 어떤 이상한 상황이 이런 슬픔을 초래하였는지는 정확하게 이해하지는 못했지만 다른 사람들이 말하는 것을 들었었기 때문에 아빠가 이 세상 사람이 아니라는 것을 알았다.

179 나는 내가 가진 어떤 지식도 남에게 전하고 싶은 욕심이 없고, 또한 그들이 잘못된 생각을 가졌다고 해서 그들을 고쳐 줄 필요성도 느끼지 않는다. 지루한 사람들에게서도 잘 듣고 있으면 상당한 양의 즐거움을 얻을 수 있다. 기억하기로는 언젠가 외국에서 나를 이리저리 구경시켜 주고 싶은 한 여성이 나를 차에 태워서 안내한 적이 있었다. 그녀의 말은 전부 뻔히 아는 이야기였고 그 문장도 매우 진부한[평범한] 어구들이 많았지만, 그것들 속에는 기억할 가치가 있는 것도 있었다.

180 우리 시대는 인간이 마침내 자신의 정당한 권리를 얻는 것처럼 보이는 시대로 시작하였다. 문명의 역사 그 어느 시기에도 인간의 자유, 존엄, 행복, 심지어 우리가 "번영"이라 부르는 것들이 중요하게 여겨지는 유일한 일들이라는 점이 널리 당연하게 받아들여진 적은 없었다. 그전에는 어느 때에도 정치가들과 철학자들이 사람은 어떤 사람이든 그리고 누구든 모두가 중요한 존재라는 점을 그렇게 강조한 적이 없었다.

181 언어는 의사소통의 한 수단이다. 언어는 주로 (기본적으로) 말로 표현되는 무엇이다. 그리고 글로서의 언어는 말로서의 언어에 대한 유용하고, 또 오늘날에 와서는 필수불가결한 대체물이기는 하지만, 어디까지나 대체물에 불과하다. 언어가 없다면 진정한 의미에서의 공동체나 사회는 없을 것이다. 왜냐하면 누구도, 가장 낮은 지적 수준에서조차도, 다른 사람과 접촉을 할 수 없을 것이기 때문이다.

182 계곡은 이제 점점 넓어지고 벌거벗은 바위산들은 소나무로 덮인 언덕들로 바뀌고 있었다. 그러다가 이 소나무 언덕들은 포도원과 농장과 익어가는 옥수수밭이 있는 평지에 자리를 내주고 있었다. 나를 매우 놀라게 한 것은 조그마한 넓이의 목초지였는데 그것은 거의 전역이 경작이 되고 있었다.

183 장기간에 걸쳐서 특별한 책임을 떠맡고, 맡은 바 할 일을 대규모로 해내야 하는 사람들에 의해서 지닌 걱정과 정신적인 과도한 긴장을 피하도록 하는 많은 치료법이 제안되고 있다. 어떤 사람들은 운동을 권하고, 어떤 사람들은 휴식을 권한다. 또 어떤 사람들은 여행을 조언하고, 다른 사람들은 쾌활해지도록 조언한다. 개개인의 기질에 따라 이 모든 조언들이 그 역할을 할 것이라는 것은 의심의 여지없이 분명하다. 그러나 이 모든 조언들에 늘 공통으로 들어 있는 요소는 기분 전환이다.

184 모든 시대를 통틀어 보면, 괴짜인 사람은 그가 (당시 존재하던 사회 상황들에) '순응하지 못했다는 사실에도 불구하고'가 아니라 아마도 그 '불순응성 때문에' 과학 발전을 촉진하였고, 대 제국을 건설하였으며, 공공복지를 향상시켰고, 또한 기억될 만큼 특출 난 예술 작품들을 만들어 왔다. 자신들이 살던 시대에 칸트, 소로, 파가니니, 파스칼, 디즈레일리, 포, 휘트먼, 그리고 하이네와 같은 사람들은 괴짜라고 여겨졌다. 역사에는 셀 수 없이 많은 희한한 다른 괴짜들의 이름들이 기록되어 있는데, 시인 샤를 보들레르와 백만장자 사업가 러셀 세이지도 그들 중의 하나이다.

185 가까이에서는 저 깊고 사람을 해칠 것 같은 황금색 강, 즉 양쯔강이 굽이굽이 흐르고 있었다. 그리고 그 아이는 자신의 삶에서 가장 즐겁고 재미있는 순간들이면서도 가장 무섭고 불길한 순간들을 그 강가에서 보냈다.

186 땅거미가 가져온 달콤한 정적 속에서 그 신혼부부는 해변에서 신혼여행을 즐기고 있었다. "여보." 신부는 떨리는 목소리로 입안에서 말을 우물우물하였다. "이제 우리가 결혼한 사이니까 말인데요, 당신한테 한 가지 비밀을 이야기할 게 있어요." "그래, 뭔데, 여보?" 신랑이 부드럽게 받았다. "실은… 제 왼쪽 눈은 유리로 만들어 넣은 거예요!" 남편이 은근한 목소리로 속삭이며 말했다. "신경 쓰지 말아요, 여보. 당신의 약혼반지에 들어간 다이아몬드들도 마찬가지인데, 뭘 그래!"

187 이 모든 세월이 지나고 난 이제 와서 옛날을 회고해 보고, 글을 써서 살아간다는 것이 얼마나 어려운지, 또 있을 수 있는 성공의 가능성이 얼마나 적은지를 실인즉 알고 나서야, 내가 무서울 정도의 큰 위험을 무릅쓰고 있었다는 것을 깨닫는다. 그때는 그런 생각이 전혀 들지 않았었다.

188 마침내 어셔 가(家)의 모습이 시야에 들어오는 곳에 다다랐다. 어찌된 영문인지는 모르겠으나, 그 집을 보는 순간 침울함이 가슴을 움켜쥐었다. 그 느낌은 참을 수 없는 것이었다. 가장 황폐하고 처참한 자연의 모습조차도 우리로 하여금 직면하여 이겨 내게 하는 시적(詩的) 기분이 설령 들었다손 치더라도, 나는 그 모습을 도저히 참아 낼 수가 없었을 것이다. 나는 내 앞에 펼쳐진 광경을 바라보았다. 집과 주변의 모습, 황량한 벽, 멍한 눈초리 모습의 창문, 무성하게 자란 몇몇 사초(莎草), 쇠하여 말라 버린 나무들의 몇몇 하얀 줄기에 눈길이 머물렀다. 그것들을 바라다보고 있노라니, 아직도 사라지지 않고 있는

아편 효과—아편을 먹고 난 후 꿈꾸는 듯 몽롱하던 상태에서 깨어나면서 느끼는 쓰라린 느낌—에서 벗어나지 못하는 것처럼 절망 속으로 주저앉았다. 그것은 망상의 베일이 벗겨지면서 나타나는 소름 끼치는 느낌이었다.

189 마음 상하고 화가 난 것이 어떠한 기분인지, 또 아무도 우리를 사랑하지 않는다고 느끼는 것이 어떠한 것인지 우리 모두는 알고 있다. 그러한 때에는 아마 우리를 사랑하지 않는 자들이 미안한 기분을 갖도록 죽고 싶어할 것이다. 그러나 이러한 감정들은 자주 나타나는 것이 아니고 또 이내 사라져 버린다. 아마 울다가 잠이 들겠지만 눈을 뜨면 나쁜 생각들이 사라져 버렸음을 알게 된다.

190 어떤 커다란 시도가 물론 실패로, 비참한 실패로, 끝난다고 하여도 결국에는 열매를 맺고 결과를 남긴다는 것도 가끔은 있는 일이다. 그 결과가 바라던 결과가 아닌 것은 사실이지만, 그러한 시도가 없었더라면 결코 얻어질 수 없었을 것이다. 한 젊은이가 불가능한 일을 이룩하고자 추구하는 경우, 그는 그것을 손대어 보지도 못한 이유로 가슴 아파할 수도 있지만, 그럼에도 그의 전 생애는 그 추구를 했다는 이유로 그만큼 더 달콤한 인생이 되는 것이다.

191 훌륭한 작가들의 작품을 알고 좋아하고자 하는 사람은 신문 판매대에 가득히 채워져 있는 값싼 잡지나 신문들에 만족하지 않을 것이다. 만약 어떤 사람이 모차르트와 브람스의 음악을 수고스럽게 감상하고자 한다면, 아마 그는 오늘날의 통속적인 음악에 대해서는 그렇게 열광적이지 않을 것이다.

192 어떤 다과가 상에 오르게 되는 경우 주인이 당신에게 들라고 권하자마자, 또는 주인이 그것을 먹기 시작하자마자 망설이지 말고 들어라. 만약 그 음식물을 손대지 않고 너무 오랫동안 식탁 위에 그대로 놓아두면 그때그때 상황에 맞게 음식을 뜨겁게 또는 차갑게 내놓는 주인의 노력을 당신이 고맙게 여기지 않는 것처럼 보이게 되는 것이다.

193 독서를 하는 데 있어서 자유는 훌륭한 일이라는 점을 우선 인정해야 한다. 그러나 독서할 준비가 되어 있지 않다면 기쁨보다는 무관심과 혼돈으로 더 이끌어질 수 있다. (따라서) 마치 건강과 의복과 예절에 관련된 문제에 대한 책임을 받아들이듯이 부모들이 이 분야에 있어서 책임을 받아들이는 것이 의무이다.

194 마치 언덕의 아래로 흘러내리는 것이 물의 본질인 것처럼 창작을 하는 것은 예술가의 본성이다. 예술가들이 자신들의 작품을 자기들 두뇌의 자식들이라고 말하고 창작의 고생을 출산의 고통에 비겨 온 것은 일리가 없는 것이 아니다.

195 여러분이 지금 직면하는 것이 좋은 사실이 하나 있는데, 그것은 가장 손쉬운 일이 여러분에게 가장 좋은 일이 되는 경우는 드물다는 점이다. 고통은 인류에게 가장 커다란 축복 중의 하나가 되어 왔다. 질병, 기아, 가난 그리고 다른 불행을 극복하기 위하여 인류는 치료법[해결법]을 그것들 때문에 실제로 생각해 내지 않으면 안 되었던 것이다.

196 어떤 경우라도 소음을 제거할 수는 없고, 그러니 그것을 즐기는 것을 배우는 것이 낫다. 사실 소음에 대해 좋은 생각을 갖기 위해서는, 만약에 모든 소리가 완전히 없어진다면 현대의 도시가 어떠한 모습이 될지를 상상해 보기만 하면 된다. 일주일쯤 지나서 만약 모든 개들이 갑자기 다시 짖기 시작하고, 부둣가와 공장의 고동 소리가 지긋지긋한 뿌우뿌우 소리를 다시 내기 시작하면 우리는 기뻐서 눈물을 흘리게 될지도 모른다.

197 5피트 폭의 강가에 와서 점프를 하여 4피트 반밖에 뛰지 못했다면 물에 빠져 익사하게 된다. 그럴 바에야 차라리 강의 맞은편에서 물에 뛰어들어 점프하는 수고를 더는 게 나았을지도 모른다.

198 우리 시대에 와서 책이 너무 많아져서, 책을 선택하는 데 있어서 책을 이용하는 데 쓰는 만큼의 시간을 쓰지 않기 위해서는 그 많은 책들 중에서 즉시 그리고 현명하게 어떻게 책을 선택하느냐 하는 문제가 더욱 중요하게 되었다.

199 동서의 긴장을 야기하는 문제들 중 어느 하나라도 그 해결에 진전이 있으려면, 협상자들은 상대를 혼란스럽게 하려는 희망에서가 아니라 합의점에 반드시 도달할 수 있다는 절대적인 결심을 가지고 만나야 한다.

200 오늘날 이 세상에 알려진 지식의 근본적인 원천은 우리들의 도서관에 있는 책이다. 미국의 도서관 제도에 진보가 있어 왔지만, 박식한 미국을 만드는 데 필요한 기준을 유지하고자 할 때 요구되는 것에는 아직 미치지 못하고 있다.

201 언론의 자유는, 말로서든 글로서든 사상의 자유로부터 독립된 것이고 어떠한 경우에도 후자(사상의 자유)를 빼앗을 수는 없다고 종종 생각해 왔다. 왜냐하면 사상의 자유는 그것에 도달할 수 없는 정신의 내부에서 진행된다는 이유 때문이다. 이 생각보다 더 잘못된 생각은 없을 것이다. 만약 (정신 속에) 생겨난 생각들을 전달할 수가 없다면 그 생각들은 사라져 버리거나 혹은 비뚤어지고 병적인 것이 될 것이다.

> **영작** A wife can have property independently of her husband.

202 어린이 교육은 한 사회가 감당해야 할 가장 중요한 임무라고 말로는 떠들어대면서도, 어린이 교육에 관계된 사람—교사들, 탁아소의 보모들, 집에서 보살피는 어머니들—모두가 그 교육을 올바르게 수행할 위신과 보상을 부인당하고 있다. 이혼의 증가, 재혼, 양부모 관계는 어린이 교육에 있어서 혼란을 증가시키고 보다 복잡한 상황을 만들어 내고 있다.

> **영작** He is a man of lip-service, not a man of action.

203 나의 정치적 이념은 민주주의이다. 모든 사람은 한 인간으로 존중을 받아야 하고 누구도 우상화되어서는 안 된다. 나에게 내가 바라지도 않은, 분에 넘치는 칭찬과 존경이 쏟아지게 된 것은 운명의 아이러니가 아닐 수 없다. 아마 이 아첨은, 내가 비록 빈약하나마 나의 힘으로 개진한 몇몇 생각들을 이해하고자 하는 대중들의 성취되지 않은 욕구에서 우러나온 것이 아닌가 한다.

> **영작** It is very surprising that he should have failed in the examination.

204 삶이 해내야 하는 가장 중요한 과업은 문명에서 남아 있는 것을 보존하고, 그것으로부터 우리 가슴에 들어 있는 욕망에 더 가까운 무언가를 만들어 내는 일이다. 교육은 (이와 같은) 가장 중요한 과업에서 우리에게 도움을 주지 못한다면 별로 가치가 없다. 우리가 교육의 목표를 수많은 정의로서 진술할 수 있다고 해도, 교육이 최고의 목표를 지니고 있으며 다른 모든 정의는 이것에 의존할 수밖에 없다는 사실을 바꾸어 놓지는 못한다.

> **영작** Education is of great value when it contributes to the development of a society where it is done.

205 책은 우리를 우리 자신 밖으로 끌어낼 수 있다. 우리들 중 누구도 다른 사람들, 아니 사실 자기 자신도 철저히 알 수 있는 개인적 기회를 충분히 갖지 못했다. 우리 모두는 이 광활하고 반응이 없는 세상에서 외로움을 느낀다. 우리는 그 점 때문에 괴로워하고 세상의 부당함과 삶의 어려움에 충격을 받는다. 그러나 책을 통해 우리는 우리보다 더 위대한 다른 사람들도 우리처럼 고통을 받고 무언가를 추구해 왔음을 배우게 된다.

> **영작** Travel takes us out of the world which we have been familiar with.

206 우리가 먹는 음식물에 화학적 찌꺼기가 남아 있다는 점은 열띤 논란이 되는 문제이다. 그러한 찌꺼기가 존재한다는 점이 산업체에 의해서는 중요하지 않은 문제로 경시되고 혹은 단호히 부인되기도 한다. 동시에, 자신들이 먹는 음식물에서 살충제를 제거해 달라고 요구할 정도로 고집이 센 사람들 모두를 광신자니 열광자니 하여 오명을 씌우려는 강한 경향도 있다. 이 모든 엄청난 논란 속에서, 정말로 사실은 무엇일까?

> **영작** He flatly denied the possibility that there might be chemical residues on the food we eat every day.

207 우리의 원래 가정이 옳고, 그래서 인간의 본성이 전 역사를 통하여 사실상 근본적으로 변화되지 않은 채 머물러 왔다면, 우리는 현대 세계가 과거의 세계만큼 미신으로 가득 차 있음을 알게 되리라고 기대해 볼 수 있겠다. 왜냐하면 미신적인 믿음이나 의식은 일정한 인간 정신의 표현이며, 그리고 만약 그러한 정신 상태가 존재한다면 의식과 믿음도 존재해야 하기 때문이다.

> **영작** The assumption that the contemporary world is a world full of superstitions is fundamentally wrong.

208 문학을 공부하는 목적은 여가 시간을 즐기는 것이 아니라 자신을 잠에서 깨우고, 활기가 있고, 쾌락을 느끼고, 공감을 하고, 이해할 줄 아는 자신의 능력을 강화하는 것이다. 그것은 한 시간 정도에 영향을 미치는 것이 아니라 24시간 하루 종일 영향을 미치는 것이다. 그것은 한 개인이 세상과 맺고 있는 관계를 완전히 변화시키는 것이다. 문학을 이해하며 감상한다는 것은 세상을 이해하며 느낀다는 뜻이며 다른 어떤 의미도 아니다.

> **영작** The main purpose of literary study is to have a right understanding of the world through an understanding appreciation of literary works.

209 사회조직 전체의 변화는 상황이 변화한다는 이유에서뿐만 아니라—물론 부분적으로는 그 이유

때문이기도 하지만—사람들 자체가 변화한다는 이유에서도 피할 수 없는 일이다. 당신과 나, 우리는 변화하고, 세월이 감에 따라 우리는 참으로 많이 변한다. 새로운 느낌이 우리에게 나타나고 오래된 가치가 사라지고 새로운 가치가 생겨난다. 정말로 강력히 원하는 것으로 생각했던 일들을 우리는 더 이상 안중에도 두지 않게 된다. 우리의 삶을 (그 위에) 세웠던 것들이 허물어져 사라져 간다.

영작 ▶ I like her not merely because she is beautiful but (also) because she is talented.

210 따라서 핵전쟁에 의해 인류가 멸종할 것이라는 가능성과 더불어 우리 시대의 중심적인 문제가 된 것은 인간의 환경 전체가 엄청난 폐해의 잠재력을 지닌 물질로 오염이 된다는 점이다. 이 물질들은 식물과 동물의 조직 속에 축적되고, 심지어는 생식 세포에까지 침투해 들어가서 미래의 형성을 좌우하는 유전의 바로 그 형질까지도 파괴하거나 변형시켜 놓는 물질들이다.

영작 ▶ Our future depends upon how we may protect our environment against the substances of incredible potential for harm.

211 어떤 사람이 당신이 사용하는 기술적인 언어를 이해하지 못한다고 해서 바보가 아닌 것은 미국인이 페르시아어를 알지 못한다고 해서 바보가 되는 것이 아님과 같다. 전문가와 비전문가가 섞여 있는 청중을 상대로 이야기할 때에, 물론 연사는 우선 어떤 집단을 대상으로 이야기해야 할지를 결정해야 한다. 여기에서 확립된 원칙은 없고, 자신에게 이야기할 것이 아니라 자신이 이야기를 전달하고 있는 대상을 위해 이야기하라는 일반적인 타이름만 있을 뿐이다.

영작 ▶ I do not marry her because I really love her.

212 만약 어떤 국가가 근본적으로 통합이 되지 못하고 있다면, 국가를 단합시키는 일은 정부에게 맡겨진 일이다. 이렇게 되면 정부의 지출을 늘리고, 국가를 개발하는 데 이용될 수 있는 경제 자원의 양을 그에 따라 줄이게 된다. 그리고 그러한 자원들이 가난하고 뒤진 후진국에서는 얼마나 미미한가를 잊어서는 안 된다. 정부의 비용이 높은 곳에서는 개발의 자원은 그에 따라 낮아지는 것이다.

영작 ▶ Where there is a will, there is a way.

213 언어는 우리 삶의 너무 많은 부분이 되어서 우리는 언어에 대하여 생각해 보는 경우가 드물다. 우리는 우리가 사용하는 말들이 자신을 표현하고 의사소통을 하는 단순한 피동적인 수단, 도구임을 당연시 여긴다.

그러나 언어를 보는 방법에는 또 다른 것도 있다. 말은 분명히 우리의 생각을 전달하는 수단이지만, 그 이상의 것일 수도 있다. 말은 우리의 사고 과정과 우리의 전체적인 관점을 형성하고, 미리 결정짓는 그들 자신의 영향력을 얻을 수도 있는 것이다.

영작 ▶ Don't take it for granted that the rich are happier than the poor.

214 과거에는 경제 발전이 혼란스러운 인플레이션에 의해 호되게 상쇄되기는 하였지만, 서구 세계가 모든 세계에 성공적인 경제 발전의 길을 보여 주고 있다고 거의 보편적으로 인식되고 있다. 그러나 서구에 살고 있는 많은 사람들은 자신들의 사회에 대하여 불만을 가지고 있다. 그들은 그들 사회가 인류가 이룩한 성숙의 수준에 더 이상 이르지 못하고 있다 하여 사회를 무시하고 비난하고 있다. 그리고 이 점은 많은 사람들로 하여금 사회주의 쪽으로 방향을 바꾸도록 하는데, 이것은 잘못되고 위험한 풍조이다.

영작 ▶ My children accuse me of not being up to the thoughts and needs of their generation.

215 부당함에 직면하고서도 매번 침묵을 지키게 되면 자유의 상실을 묵과하는 것이 된다. 그것이 우리가 상관할 바 아니라고 주장하면 할수록 우리는 선동 정치가의 일을 더욱더 쉽게 해 주는 것이 된다. 왜냐하면 자유가 자신을 유지해 나가려면 겸허한 사람들의 마음속에 일으키는 존경에 의존해야 한다는 것은 자유의 본질이기 때문이다. 겸허한 사람들의 자유를 유지하는 힘은 자유를 유지하기 위하여 자신들을 조직화하려는 의지에 놓여 있다. 자신의 무관심이나 무기력을 보이는 것보다 더 교활한 적은 자유에게는 없다.

영작 ▶ The more things we are interested in, the happier we become.

216 개성은 한때 어떤 사람들은 갖고 있지만 다른 사람들은 갖고 있지 않은, 정의 내릴 수 없는 그 무엇으로 여겨졌다. 정신이 그러한 것처럼 개성도 훈련에 의해서 개발될 수 있음을 이제 심리학자들은 알아내었다. 개성의 발달은 다른 사람들과 함께, 또 그들을 위해서 계속해서 늘어나는 많은 일들을 해나가는 법을 배우는 데 달려 있다. 개성이라 말할 때 우리가 뜻하는 바는 개인이 다른 사람들에게 흥미를 주고, 또 봉사도 하는 능력의 범위를 말한다. 이 능력은 습관과 연습을 통해 얻어진 기술로 이루어져 있다.

영작 ▶ By happiness we mean the extent to which we can control ourselves.

217 아무리 원시적이라 하더라도 종교와 마술을 지니지 은 종족은 없다. 즉시 덧붙여 이야기할 수 있는 것은 어떠한 야만족도 과학적인 태도나 과학(그 자체)을 결여하고 있지는 않다는 점이다. 물론 이 결핍이 빈번히 그것들(종교와 마술) 탓으로 돌려져 왔지만. 믿을 만하고 유능한 관찰자들의 연구에 의하면 모든 원시부락[사회]에서 두 개의 확연히 구분되는 영역—신성한 영역과 세속적인 영역—이 있음이 알려졌고, 이 두 영역은 다른 말로는 마술과 종교의 영역, 그리고 과학의 영역이다.

> 영작 ▸ You must not give up your life however tough and displeasing (it may be).

218 대부분의 사람들이 해야만 하는 일의 상당량은 그 자체로서는 재미가 없지만, 그러한 일도 어느 정도 커다란 이점을 지니고 있다. 우선 첫 번째로 들 수 있는 것은, 그 일은 무엇을 해야 할까를 결정할 필요 없이 하루의 많은 시간을 채워 준다는 점이다. 자신의 선택에 따라서 시간을 메우도록 자유를 허락받은 때 많은 사람들이 할 만한 가치가 있을 정도로 충분히 즐거운 일을 생각해 내는 데에도 쩔쩔매게 된다. 그리고 그들이 무엇을 결정하든지 간에 그들은 다른 일을 했더라면 더 즐거웠을 텐데라는 생각으로 괴로움을 느끼게 된다.

> 영작 ▸ Most students, when they are left free to do as they please, don't devote themselves to studying.

219 용감성, 정직성, 그리고 강한 인품은 영웅 숭배의 요소이다. 소년의 수준에서 보면 이 영웅 숭배는 훌륭한 행동을 한 사람 쪽으로 기울고, 보통 성인의 수준에서 보면 권력을 휘두르는 사람 쪽으로 기울며, 보다 더 비판적인 판단력을 지닌 자의 눈으로 보면 이상주의와 도덕적 자질 쪽으로 기운다. 모두의 숭배를 받는 영웅은 이 모든 특질을 만족시킬 수 있는 자이다. 용기와 성실성과 강력한 인품을 여러 형태로 형성함으로써 워싱턴, 링컨, 리 장군은 이것을 이룩할 수 있었다.

> 영작 ▸ Children are liable to respect a person as a hero at the sight of his spectacular deeds.

220 인간 정신, 특히 교육받은 인간 정신의 가장 특출 난 특색 중의 하나는 우유부단이다. 기묘한 속담에 이르기를, 사람은 아는 것이 많을수록 결정을 내리기가 더욱 어려워진다고 한다. 일생 동안 우유부단함으로 고생하는 사람이 많고 엘리자베스 여왕이 그랬다고 하듯 우유부단(미결정)을 확정된 정책으로 채택하면서 일을 끝내는 사람도 많다.

재빠르고 적극적인 결론에 이르는 능력을 소유하고 개발할 수 있는 사람은 극히 소수에 불과하다.

> 영작 ▸ Indecision is the inability to come to quick and positive conclusions in doing a great task.

221 역사가 단지 과거에 대한 연대기적 기록 이상이 되기 위해서는 과거 사건들의 순서를 정하고 해석하는 데 있어서 약간의 주관적인 판단은 필수적인 것이다. 따라서 편견이 없는 역사는 있을 수 없다는 고전적인 진술이 가능하다. 한 학문의 역사에 있어서, 그리고 언어학의 역사라는 현재의 경우에 있어서, 과거의 언어학자들이 취한 행동과 목표의 어느 것이 언어학의 범주에 들어오고 또 그 역사에 속하게 되는가를 결정하는 데 따르는 부가적인 주관적 요소가 존재하게 된다.

> 영작 ▸ If a university is to be more than just a place for getting an academic degree, some sincere consideration on the part of the students is inevitable as to what and how to study.

222 실용적인 정신의 소유자인 미국인(들)이 프랭클린이 만들어 놓은 본보기를 의식적으로 따랐다고 말하는 것은 지나친 이야기이다. 모든 미국인들 중에서 예민하고 사려 깊은 프랭클린이 나중에 전 미국인들이 가야 할 운명에 처한 길을 처음으로 밟고 갔다고 말하는 것이 진실에 더 가까운 이야기이다. 그는 실용적인 기계와 발명에 관심을 갖고 있었고, 진보와 대중의 발전을 중시했으며 이웃들과 잘 지내려는 욕망을 지니고 있었다. 프랭클린은 자신이 건설에 도움을 준 모든 미국민들의 선구자였다.

> 영작 ▸ It is not too much to say that he is the author of the economic crisis of our country.

223 한 인간이 진정으로 위대한 인간인가를 시험하는 수단은 그가 겸손한가를 알아보는 것이라고 나는 믿는다. 겸손이라는 말로서 내가 의미하는 바는, 그가 자신의 능력을 의심한다거나 자신의 견해를 피력하는 데 망설이느냐 하는 점이 아니라, 그가 행동하고 말할 수 있는 것과 나머지 세상 사람들이 말하고 행동하는 것들 사이의 관계를 올바르게 이해하느냐 하는 점이다. 모든 위대한 사람들은 그들이 하는 일을 알 뿐만 아니라 그들이 그 점을 알고 있다는 점을 또한 보통은 알고 있으며, 자기들의 주된 의견을 펴는 데 있어서 정당할 뿐만 아니라, 그들의 의견이 정당하다는 점을 또한 보통은 알고 있다. 단지 그들은 그 이유로 자신들을 높이 생각하지는 않는 것이다.

영작 He thinks much of himself; it is because he lacks humility.

224 과거의 기록과 유적들을 교육의 주된 자료로 삼는 것이 갖는 잘못은, 그렇게 함으로써 현재와 과거의 중요한 관계를 잘라내고, 과거를 현재의 경쟁자로, 또한 현재를 다소간 쓸모없는 과거의 모방으로 만드는 경향이 있다는 점이다. 그러한 환경 하에서는 문화는 장식물과 위안물이 되고 도피처와 은신처가 된다. 사람은 과거가 제공해 주는 것을 이 조잡한 것들을 익히는[성숙하게 하는] 하나의 대리물로 이용하지 못하고, 현재의 조잡한 상태를 피하여 상상된 세련미 속에 안주하여 살게 되는 것이다.

영작 The mistake of making money the only aim of life is that it leads us to be blind to other good facets of life.

225 위대한 소설이나 전기를 읽는 사람은 마음의 평화를 방해받지 않고서 커다란 모험을 하게 된다. 산타야나의 말을 빌리면 예술은 우리의 눈앞에 우리가 행동에서 찾을 수 없는 것, 즉 삶과 평화의 결합을 가져다준다고 한다. 역사를 읽게 되면 정신 건강에 좋다. 역사는 우리에게 중용과 견인 정신을 가르쳐 주고, 한때는 내란과 세계대전을 야기한 무서운 논쟁거리가 지금에 와서 보면 죽어 없어지거나 묻혀 버린 단지 입씨름에 불과하다는 것도 보여 준다. 그리고 그것은 지혜를 일깨우는 교훈이고 가치관의 상대성을 일깨우는 교훈이다.

영작 A person reading a classical literary work gets the peace of mind which we cannot find in action.

226 말은 일상생활의 아주 친숙한 일부분이어서 우리는 한순간이라도 멈춰 서서 말이 무엇인지 정의 내리는 법이 거의 없다. 말은 인간에게는 걷는 것만큼 자연스러운 것이고, 숨 쉬는 것에 비하면 단지 조금 덜 자연스러울 뿐이다. 그러나 말의 이 자연스러움이 단지 현혹적인 감정에 지나지 않는다는 점을 우리가 확신하는 데에는 한순간의 생각이면 족하다. 언어를 습득하는 과정은, 냉정한 입장에서 보면, 걷는 것을 배우는 과정과는 완전히 다른 종류의 일이다. 후자적인 기능의 경우에 있어서 문화—다른 말로 하여 사회적 용례의 전통적인 체계는 (그것을 습득하는 데) 그다지 심각하게 이용되지 못하고 있다.

영작 A moment's reflection is sure enough to convince us that speech is not so natural to man as walking.

227 풍부한 지식과 다양한 취미를 지닌 사람은 재미있는 대화를 나눌 기초를 갖고 있는 셈이다. 재기가 빛나는 문장들이 머리가 빈 사람에게서 나올 수 없는 것은 빈 주전자에서 우유가 나올 수 없는 것과 마찬가지이다. 책을 읽고 사람의 이야기들을 들어 그것을 자기 것으로 만들어 낸 사람의 말은 존경심으로 경청된다. 연구와 독서 그리고 날카로운 관찰에서 나온 내적인 풍요로움은 조용한 자신감을 길러 낸다. 그리고 자신감은 개성과 웅변의 씨앗이다.

영작 A whale is no more a fish than a horse is.

228 삶을 살아가는 대부분의 시간 동안 우리는 어떠한 의식을 하거나 의견을 개진하거나 의문을 제기함이 없이 모국어를 사용하며 또 이해하고 있다고 여긴다. 옛 어린 시절의 기억과 어린이들을 기르면서 느낀 경험은 모든 정상적인 사람의 언어 능력이 얼마나 복잡한가 하는 점을 우리로 하여금 잠시나마 생각하게 하고, 자신의 모국어에 숙달된 다음에 한두 개의 외국어를 배우는 과정을 생각해 보면 인간이 언어를 통해 의사전달의 능력을 얻어내는 데 얼마나 많은 노력이 들어가는지를 알게 된다.

영작 To master a foreign language in a short period of time is not so easy as we (may) think.

229 나폴레옹은 프랑스에서 권위에 대한 존경심을 복구시켰다. 그는 혼돈을 발견하고서 (그곳에) 질서를 남겨 놓았으며, 반란을 물려받았지만 규율을 창조해 내었다. 사회 조직을 갈기갈기 찢어 놓은 열정은 10년 동안이나 제지받지 않고 날뛰었고, 반면에 사회 조직을 강화하는 데 도움이 되는 도덕력은 비참한 소멸의 과정을 겪어야만 했었다. 존경이라는 감정은 비웃음의 대상이 되어 왔었다. 종교, 고대의 제도, 오랫동안 전해 내려온 프랑스의 전통들, 심지어 삶의 평범한 예절[품위]조차도 독재적인 과거에서부터 사라지지 않고 남아 있는 모순되고 비합리적인 잔재들로 보이도록 만들어져 있었다.

영작 The efforts of Napoleon to calm down the passions which had rent the social fabric and to create discipline were laughed away by the (French) people.

230 국가 개발 계획을 짜는 데 있어서 이용될 수 있는 천연자원 중에서 아마 가장 중요한 것은 인력일 것이다. 남성과 여성으로 구성된 집단을 묘사하는 능력에 있어서 영어는 약점을 소유하고 있기 때문에 보통 manpower로 기술된다. 효율적인 지도력과 현명한 중간 경영진을 포함하는 생산적인 노동력이 없다면, 아무리 외국의 원조가 많고 천연자원이 풍부하다 해도 성공적인 개발이나 근대화는 확보될 수 없다.

영작 ▸ No amount of wealth could soothe his sorrow and loneliness coming from the loss of his wife and two children in a car accident.

231 사람이 인생을 살아가면서 대처해야만 하는 어려움 중의 하나는 자신이 한때는 친근한 관계를 유지했으나 시간이 경과되어 관심이 줄어든 사람들을 어떻게 할까 하는 점이다. 양편이 모두 수수한 위치에 있게 되면 연이 끊기는 것은 자연스럽게 다가오고 별로 나쁜 감정이 개입되지는 않는다. 그러나 두 사람 중의 하나가 유명해지면 처지는 난처해진다. 그는 수많은 친구를 새로 사귀게 되지만 옛 친구들은 움직일 수 없는 존재이며, 여기저기서 시간을 내달라는 요청을 받지만 옛 친구들은 그의 시간을 맨 먼저 요구할 권리가 있다고 느낀다.

영작 ▸ When you become famous, you will have a thousand claims on your time.

232 독재는 강력하고 성공을 거둔 정부에서 생겨나지 않고 약하고 무기력한 정부에서 생겨난다는 점을 역사는 입증하고 있다. 만약에 민주적인 방식에 의해서 국민들이 스스로를 공포와 굶주림으로부터 보호할 수 있을 만큼 강력한 정부를 얻게 된다면 그들의 민주주의는 성공을 거둔다. 그러나 그렇지 못한 경우, 그들은 인내심이 없어지게 된다. 따라서 자유를 지속시키는 유일하고 확실한 방파제는 국민들의 이익을 지켜 줄 정도로 강력한 정부와, 정부에 대하여 자주적인 통제를 가할 수 있을 정도로 강력하고 충분히 견문이 넓은 국민이다.

영작 ▸ History proves that democracy succeeds when a people exercises its sovereign control over its government.

233 지질학은 산을 형성하고 땅과 바다의 분포 상태를 바꾸어 놓는 데 기여하는 과정을 연구하는 것 외에도 바위들이 닳고, 바다에 침전물이 축적되는 것에도 관련이 있다. 왜냐하면 이러한 과정들은 지각의 무게와 그 무게가 아래쪽 지층에 미치는 압력에 영향을 행사하기 때문이다. 이 문제들은 또한 지리학자들의 관심거리인데, 따라서 공기, 바람, 비, 강, 서리, 얼음 등이 지구 표면에 미치는 행위에 관한 연구는 두 가지 학문(지질학과 지리학)의 공통 분야이고, 이 연구는 가끔은 'physiography'(지형학)라고 일컬어진다.

영작 ▸ At a glance geology seems to be different from geography, but their objects of study are fundamentally the same.

234 지구상에서 삶의 역사는 생명체와 그 환경 사이의 상호 작용의 역사가 되어 왔다. 지구상에 존재하는 초목과 동물의 형체와 습관은 대부분 환경에 의해 형성되어 왔다. 지구 역사의 전 길이를 고려해 볼 때 생명체가 자신의 환경을 수정하는 것에 대한 역효과는 비교적 약했다. 단지 금세기로 대변되는 짧은 시기에서만 인류라는 종(種)만이 자기가 살고 있는 세계의 본질을 바꾸어 놓을 중요한 힘을 얻게 되었다.

영작 ▸ Only when you open your mind to her will she accept you as an object of marriage.

235 하나의 새로운 모습의 생명체를 창조해 내려는 노력은—그것이 새로운 유의 연체동물이든 또는 새로운 인간 사회이든—첫 번째 시도에서는 거의 또는 전혀 성공을 거두지 못한다. 창조란 그렇게 쉬운 작업이 아니다. 창조는 시행과 착오라는 일련의 과정을 통해서 궁극적으로 성공을 얻게 되고, 따라서 지난번 실험에서 나타난 실수는 그 다음의 실험이 마찬가지로 실패로 끝나게끔 운명 지우기는커녕, 고통을 통해 얻어질 수 있는 지혜를 통해 성공을 얻어내는 기회를 실제로 제공한다.

영작 ▸ The creation of a new manifestation of life is so difficult as to win its successes through a series of process of trial and error.

236 대중이 불완전한 지식을 가지고 있는 문제 어느 것에 있어서나, 이와 마찬가지로 견식이 없는 개인의 의견처럼 여론도 잘못될 가능성이 있다. 그렇지 않다고 생각하는 것은 많은 무지를 합쳐서 지혜를 얻어낼 수 있다고 생각하는 것과 같다. 대수를 전혀 알지 못하는 사람은 자신과 마찬가지로 대수를 전혀 알지 못하는 이웃 사람을 불러들여서 의논을 해 보아도 대수 문제를 푸는 데에는 도움을 얻을 수가 없다. 그리고 그와 같은 사람 백만 명이 만장일치의 투표로 찬성한다 해도 그 해답은 유능한 수학자의 해답과 비교해 보면 전혀 아무것도 아닐 것이다.

영작 ▸ A solution to a mathematical problem can no more be obtained by the unanimous vote than wisdom can by combining many ignorances.

237 교육은 자연법칙 속에 나타난 지혜를 가르치는 것인데, 나는 그 이름 아래에 사물과 사물의 힘뿐만 아니라 인간과 인간의 방식까지도 포함시키고, 애정과 의지를 그 자연법칙과 조화를 이루면서 활동하는 진지하고 사랑스러운 욕망으로 변화시키는 것까지 포함시킨다. 나에게 있어서 교육은 이 이상도 이 이하도 의미하지 않는다. 스스로를 교육이라고

부르기를 단언하는 것은 어느 것이나 이 기준에 의해 평가되어야 하고, 만약에 이 테스트에 합격하지 못하면, 다른 주장을 펴는 쪽의 권위가 아무리 세고 그 숫자가 아무리 많아도 나는 그것을 교육이라고 부르지 않을 것이다.

영작 ▶ Education is worth the name when it professes to teach man in the laws of Nature how to live in harmony with others.

238 보다 나은 신문을 만들어 내려고 오늘날 많은 노력이 경주되고 있지만, 보다 원숙한 구독자를 만들어 내기 위해서는 아직은 더욱 많은 일이 이루어져야 한다. 신문은 독자에 의해서 감독을 받는다. 독자들은 신문을 높은 수준으로 끌어올리기도 하고 낮은 수준으로 끌어내리기도 한다. 신문은 대중이 원하거나 허락하는 그 이상으로 나아질 수가 거의 없다. 독자가 신문에 대한 좋은 이해력을 갖지 못할 때에는 어떠한 신문도 자유 민주주의의 기둥이 될 수 없다. 따라서 신문의 역할에 관하여 일반 대중이 보여 주는 날카로운 의식은 민주사회를 성공적으로 유지해 가는 데 있어서 필수 조건이다.

영작 ▶ It is very disheartening that there has been no genuine discussion on the part of the students as to the role of the university.

239 궁극적인 현실로서의 진리는, 만약에 그러한 것이 존재한다면, 영원하고 사라지지 않고 변화되지 않아야 한다. 그러나 그 무한하고 영원하고 변화하지 않는 진리는 시간과 공간에 의해서 제약을 받고, 인간 정신이 발달해 가는 상태와 또한 한 시기에 풍미하는 이데올로기[관념]에 제약을 받아서, 고작해야 진리의 매우 작은 부분만을 포착할 수 있는 유한한 인간 정신에 의해서 완벽하게 이해될 수는 없다. 정신이 발달하고 그 영역을 확장해 감에 따라, 또 관념이 변화하고 그래서 그 진리를 표현하기 위해 새로운 상징들이 사용됨에 따라, 그 진수는 아직 똑같은 것일지라도 진리의 새로운 면면들이 드러나 빛을 보게 된다.

영작 ▶ All that glitters is not gold. / All is not gold that glitters.

240 자유주의란 무엇인가? 그것은 기술하기 쉽지 않으며 정의 내리기는 더더욱 쉽지 않다. 왜냐하면 그것은 하나의 주의[원칙]이며 또한 풍조이기 때문이다. 후자로서(즉, 주의로서) 자유주의는 분명히 자유와 직접적으로 관련되어 있다. 왜냐하면 그것은 사회의 어떤 계층에게 출생이라는 과정을 통하여 부여된 특권에 대한 적으로 나타났기 때문이다. 그러나

자유주의가 추구한 자유는 보편성이라는 이름을 얻을 자격은 없었다. 왜냐하면 자유를 누리는 것은 그것을 방어할 재산이 있는 사람들에게만 국한되어 있었기 때문이다. 전자로서의(즉, 풍조로서의) 자유주의는 주관적이고 무정부주의적인 경향을 띤다. 그것은 언제나 정치권력에 의해서 추구되는 획일성들을 인정하기보다는 개인의 행동을 축복하려고 해 왔다.

영작 ▶ He cannot speak English, much less French.

241 자연을 더욱 주의 깊게 관찰해 보면 할수록 질서가 더욱 널리 자리 잡고 있음이 밝혀지게 되었고, 그래서 과거에 무질서로 보이던 것이 다름 아닌 복잡성에 불과함이 입증이 되고, 마침내 오늘날에는 어떤 일이 우연히 생겨난다거나 원인 없는 사건이 실제로 존재한다고 믿을 만큼 어리석은 사람은 없다. 그리하여 만약 우리가 어떠한 일이 우연히 발생하였다고 말을 하게 된다면, 그때 우리가 실제로 의미하는 바는 우리가 그 일이 발생하게 된 원인이나 왜 그 특별한 일이 일어나게 되는지를 모르는 것이라고 모두가 인정할 것이다. 우연과 뜻하지 않은 일은 단지 무식함의 다른 이름에 불과하다.

영작 ▶ No one is so foolish as to believe that nothing but disorder exists in the universe.

242 그래서 이러저러한 방식으로 인생은 사람을 강제로 떼어 놓고 훌륭한 우정 관계를 영원히 깨뜨려 버린다. 우정이 지속되는 동안에는 그것을 그렇게 즐거운 것으로 만드는 (우정의) 유연성과 용이함, 바로 그 점이 나중에는 우정을 깨뜨리고 망각하는 것을 그만큼 쉽게 하는 요인이 된다. 그리고 친구를 몇몇 가지고 있는 사람, 또는 열두 명 정도 가진 사람(이 세상에 그렇게 많은 친구를 가진 사람이 있다면)도 자신의 행복이 얼마나 불확실한 기초 위에 자리 잡고 있는가 하는 점을, 그리고 (한 친구의) 죽음, 가볍게 던진 몇 마디 말, 한 통의 편지, 그리고 한 여성의 빛나는 두 눈 등, 한두 가지 운명의 장난에 의해 한 달 후에는 그 모든 것을 잃어버린 상태에 있게 될 수도 있다는 점을 잊을 수는 없을 것이다.

영작 ▶ There are cases[moments] when men are forced apart and the goodly friendship is broken up by a stroke or two of fate.

243 자유주의자들과 광신자들 사이의 싸움에서는 광신자들이 틀림없이 이긴다고 흔히 주장하는데, 그것은 그들이 내세우는 명분의 정당성에 대한 믿음이 더 흔들리지 않고 있다는 이유 때문이다. 지난 수년간의 역사를 포함하여 모든 역사가 그렇지

않음을 보여 주고는 있지만, 이러한 믿음은 좀처럼 죽지 않고 살아 있다. 광신자들은 계속하여 실패를 거듭해 왔는데, 그것은 그들이 불가능한 일을 하려고 시도하였거나 또는 그들이 목표한 바가 가능한 일인 경우에도 그들이 너무 비과학적이어서 올바른 방법을 채택하지 못했기 때문이었다. 그들이 실패한 이유의 또 하나는 그들이 강요하고자 하였던 사람들의 적개심을 불러일으켰기 때문이었다.

영작 ▶ The belief dies hard among the Korean people that their country will get out of its economic crisis within a few years.

244 자연도태라는 가설이 완벽한 설명이 되지는 못하지만 그 가설은 그 자체보다 더 커다란 것을 이끌어 내었는데, 그것은 우리로 하여금 생물은 진화한다는 이론을 받아들이게 한 것이었고, 이것은 세월이 흐름에 따라 확인이 되었다. 그러나 처음에는 몇몇 자연주의자들이 반대의 입장을 취하였고, 리처드 오언 경 같은 유명한 해부학자는 반대의 견해를 글로 나타내기도 하였다. 생물학적인 증거를 판단할 능력이 없던 많은 사람들에게 진화론이 갖는 효과는 파괴적일 뿐만 아니라 믿기 어려운 것이었고, 상식과 반대되기도 하였고, 또한 철학적·종교적인 모든 이정표를 압도하는 것으로 보였다.

영작 ▶ Darwin's theory of evolution had a serious effect on the prevalent philosophic and religious thoughts of the people of that time.

245 역사가 과거에 대해서뿐만 아니라 미래에 대해서도 관심을 갖게 될 때 현대 역사는 시작된다. 현대인은 자신이 빠져나온 여명을, 그 여명의 희미한 불빛이 자신이 지금 향하여 가고 있는 어둠의 세계를 밝혀 줄 것이라는 희망을 가지고 진지한 눈으로 되돌아본다. 거꾸로 말하면 자신의 앞에 놓여 있는 길(미래)에 대해 현대인이 갖는 열망과 걱정은 자신의 뒤에 놓여 있는 것(과거)에 대한 통찰력을 날카롭게 해 준다. 미래에 대한 의식이 없이는 역사도 없다. 과거와 미래 사이에서 작용과 반작용은 꾸준히 존재한다. 과거, 현재 그리고 미래는 끊임없는 고리로 함께 짜여져 있다.

영작 ▶ The past is the twilight out of which man has come, and the future is the obscurity into which he is going.

246 진정한 의미에 있어서 법률이란, 제약이라기보다는 자유로운 지성인에게 제시되는 지침이며, 따라서 자신의 마땅한 이득을 얻도록 이끌어 가는 것이며 그 법률의 지배하에 있는 사람들의 일반적인

이득을 위한 것 이상으로 특별한 규정을 내세우지 않는다. 만약 그 법률이 없어져서 사람들이 더 행복할 수 있다면 그 법률은 가치가 없는 것으로, 저절로 사라지게 될 것이다. 그리고 깊은 강이나 낭떠러지로부터 우리를 보호하기 위해서만 존재하는 법률은 제한이라는 이름에 어울리지도 않는다. 그래서 법률의 목적은 자유를 폐지하거나 제약을 가하는 것이 아니라 자유를 보존하고 확대하는 것이다. 왜냐하면 이성적인 인간의 모든 상태에서 법이 없는 곳에서는 자유도 없기 때문이다.

영작 ▶ He is not so much angry at your explanation as disappointed with it.

247 그는 가난을 경험하였고 가난에 대해 깊이 감사하고 있다. 그는 가난하다는 것이 어떠한 것인지를 알았고, 자신에게 소중한 사람들이 목숨을 부지할 만한 최저한의 필수품도 없어 고통을 겪는 것을 보아 왔다. 사실 그 길에서 그가 발걸음을 내디뎌 보지 않은 곳은 한 군데도 없었다. 그래서 그는 비슷한 상황에 처한 사람들을 완벽하게 이해하며 동정할 수 있고, 이론이 아닌 실제를 통해서 깨달아 아는 사람으로서 그들을 도울 수가 있다. 그는 가난이 얼마나 커다란 축복이 될 수 있는지를 깨닫고 있으며 그 깨달음은 가난을 그 속에 계속 머물러 있는 조건으로서가 아니라, 경험을 해 보고 거기에서 통렬한 교훈을 이끌어 내고 그리고 마침내 그곳에서 빠져나올 수 있는 하나의 조건으로서 깨달은 것이었다.

영작 ▶ He has known from practice, not from theory, that poverty can be a blessing.

248 언어의 기능은 사실과 생각을 전달하는 데에만 국한되지는 않는다. 우리의 감정을 표현하고 다른 사람들의 감정을 불러일으키고 그들의 행동에 영향을 행사하는 데에도 역시 우리는 말을 사용한다. 이성적인(합리성이 요구되는) 단계에서는 명료함과 정확성이 필수적이지만, 감정을 나타내는 언어의 측면은 흐릿한 개요와 풍부한 함축미를 담은 모호한 어휘가 던지는 암시에 의해서 이득을 볼 수가 있다. 동시에 언어가 갖는 제약성이야말로 자기 수양에 대한 도전이며 또한 그 한 방법이다. 유연하기는 하지만 저항적인 매체의 형태로 표현되는 과정을 통해서 우리의 사고들은 보다 명확해지고 보다 우아해진다.

영작 ▶ Man's life is not confined to his existence on this earth, but to what he leaves behind after death like a shooting star.

249 학문의 습득은 다른 어떤 음식물을 습득하는 것보다 훨씬 위험하다. 왜냐하면 다른 물건들로 말하자면,

우리는 우리가 산 것을 그릇에 담아 집에 가져와서 그 가치를 검토하고 얼마만큼을 언제 사용할 것인지를 결정할 여유가 있기 때문이다. 그러나 학문이란 처음에는 우리의 정신을 제외한 어떠한 그릇에도 담을 수 없는 것이며, 그것을 사는 순간 삼키게 되고, 우리가 시장을 나서게 될 때에는 우리는 이미 나쁜 영향을 입었든지 좋은 이득을 얻었든지 둘 중의 하나이다. 학문에는 우리에게 자양분을 제공하는 것이 아니라 우리를 방해하고 짐이 되는 것이 있으며, 또 우리를 치료해 주는 체하면서 독약을 주는 것도 있다.

영작 ▸ By the time (when) she arrives here, he will have already left.

250 충고는 그것이 항상 우월감의 모습을 일시적으로 보여 주기 때문에, 매우 필요하고 아주 슬기로운 경우에도 그다지 고마운 것이 되지 못한다. 또한 허영심이 꽤 자주 충고의 명백한 동기가 되고 있어서, 우리는 어떠한 충고가 정당한 것인지 아닌지를 정확하게 알아보지도 않고서 힘을 발휘하여 그 충고를 받아들이기를 거부한다. 어떤 사람이 우리를 희생의 대가로 하여 나름대로 위대해지고, 우리의 허락도 없이 우리에게 권위를 행사하게 될 때 그것은 그런 대로 있을 수 있는 일이다. 왜냐하면 많은 사람들이 자신들을 구원하는 사도인 양 기뻐 날뛰는 사람의 오만불손을 참느니보다는 차라리 자신들의 실수로 인해 나타나는 결과들을 기꺼이 참으려 하기 때문이다.

영작 ▸ We cannot realize too early that advice in general can never be very grateful.

251 삶은 살아 있는 생물체들에게 유일하게 있는 독특한 속성이다. 그러나 이 살아 있는 생물체들 모두는 몇몇 다른 물체들—물론 자신들의 존재를 살아 있는 물체에 의존하는 물체들이기는 하지만—에서도 역시 발견되는 두 개의 속성을 더 갖고 있다. 이 속성들 중의 하나는 그 물체들 속에 원형질이라고 알려진 물질이 존재한다는 점이다. 이 물체들은 원형질을, 지금까지 생존해 왔으나 지금은 죽은 상태가 된 물체들과도 공유한다. 또 다른 속성은 이 물체들 속에 유기체가 존재한다는 점이다. 이 유기체는 죽고 없는 물체들과 공유될 뿐만 아니라 살아 있는 생물체들에 의해서 만들어진 다른 물체들, 가령 기계와 인간 사회 같은 것들과도 공유된다.

영작 ▸ He owes what he is (today) to his mother's sacrifice and love.

252 화학 물질에 의한 수질 오염이 갖는 가장 경악스러운 면 중의 하나는, 여기에—강, 호수, 또는 저수지, 그리고 그 이유로 해서 식탁에 올려져 마시게 되는 유리잔 속의 물속에—책임 있는 화학자라면 누구도 자기 실험실에서 합성을 도저히 생각해 볼 수 없는 화학 물질이 뒤섞여 있다는 점이다. 이 자유롭게 뒤섞이는 화학 물질 사이에 나타날 수 있는 가능한 상호 작용은 미국 공공의료서비스의 관리들에게는 심히 심각한 것으로 받아들여지고 있는데, 그 관리들은 비교적 해가 없는 화학 물질에서 해가 되는 물질의 생산이 광범위하게 나타날지도 모른다는 두려움을 줄곧 피력해 왔다.

영작 ▸ The fact that chemicals are mingled in the water we drink is very alarming.

253 교육이라는 말은 우리 시대의 중요한 어휘들 중의 하나이다. 교육을 받지 못한 사람은 20세기가 주는 가장 위대한 기회들 중의 하나를 빼앗긴, 역경의 불행한 희생자라고 많은 사람들은 생각한다. 교육의 중요성을 확신하고 있기 때문에, 현대 국가들은 교육 기관에 투자를 하고 그 이자를 앞으로 지도자가 될 잠재 능력을 지닌 개화된 젊은 남녀라는 커다란 집단의 형태로 되돌려 받기를 바란다. 가르침의 주기가 매우 주의 깊게 계획되고 구매 가능한 지식의 샘인 교과서에 의해 강조되는 교육, 그 교육이 가져다주는 이득이 없다면 문명은 어떠한 모습으로 나타나 보일까?

영작 ▸ He studied the harder because he was convinced that not receiving a higher education was as good as being deprived of one of the twentieth-century opportunities.

254 언어는 인간의 고귀한 소유물 중 하나이다. 언어가 없다면 인간은 동료와 의사를 교환할 수 없을 것이다. 그러나 현대 세계에 있어서는 자신의 모국어 하나만을 말하는 것으로는 충분하지가 않다. 두 개의 언어를 말하는 사람은 두 개의 정신을 소유하고 있다고 한다. 왜냐하면 외국어를 배우는 과정에서 우리는 어느 정도까지는 외국인의 사고방식을 획득하기 때문이다. 따라서 언어 공부는 우리로 하여금 우리의 동료들을 이해할 수 있게 하는 가장 훌륭한 수단 중의 하나이다. 그것이 어려운 것은 분명하지만 보상은 크다. 언어 공부는 우리가 살고 있는 국제 사회의 보다 나은 시민이 되게끔 한다.

영작 ▸ To learn two languages at the same time is difficult, to be sure, but it will later turn out to be rich in rewards.

255 자신이 사귀는 친구가 완벽하다는 환상에 취해 있는 경우를 제외하고는 친구가 될 수 없는 사람들이 있는데, 이러한 환상이 지나가면 그들의 우정은 끝장이 난다. 그러나 진정한 우정에는 환상이 결코

없다. 왜냐하면 우정은 친구의 불완전한 면을 뛰어넘은 인간의 본성에 이르는 것이고, 이 과정에서 우정은 친구의 불완전한 면을 당연한 것으로 받아들이기 때문이다. 진정한 우정은 친구가 다른 사람들보다 더 낫다고 생각하지도 않는다. 왜냐하면 그렇게 생각하는 데에는 자기중심적 사고가 들어 있기 때문이다. 한 사람이 당신의 친구인 것은 그가 우월한 점을 지니고 있어서가 아니라, 당신과 대부분의 사람들 사이에서는 닫혀 있는 하나의 길이, 당신의 본성과 그의 본성 사이에는 열려 있는 그 무엇으로 존재하기 때문이다.

> **영작▶** I think highly of him not because he is clever but because he does his best in everything (which is) entrusted to him.

256 따라서 우리가 책을 읽는 하나의 이유는 우리 자신의 삶을 뛰어넘어 다른 사람들의 삶을 이해하는 것이다. 그러나 이것만이 우리가 책으로부터 즐거움을 이끌어 내는 유일한 이유는 아니다. 매일매일의 삶에서 우리는 일어나고 있는 일에 너무 많이 개입되어 그 일들을 분명히 보지 못하고 있고, 또한 우리의 감정에 너무 많이 좌우되어 그것들을 적절히 감상하지 못하고 있다. 우리들 중 많은 사람들의 삶은 디킨스나 발자크 같은 작가가 쓸 만한 가치가 있는 소설의 자료가 되지만, 그와 정반대로, 우리는 경험으로부터 즐거움을 결코 얻지 못하고 있다. 작가의 일은 삶의 충실한 모습을 우리에게 보여 주는 것이지만, 우리가 두려움이나 휘말림 없이 잘 이해할 수 있도록 충분히 거리를 두고 그것을 보여 주어야 한다.

> **영작▶** We are too much concerned about trivialities of life to realize what is really important in life.

257 누구든 20~30년 동안 매일 아침 면도질을 해 본 사람이면 무엇인가를 꼭 배우게 된다. 너무 게으르거나 면도 솜씨가 너무 서툴러서 이발소의 면도사에게 면도를 부탁하는 사람이라고 해도, 그가 중년의 나이가 될 때쯤이면 인간의 본성에 관하여 무엇인가를 꼭 깨닫게 되는 것이다. 왜냐하면 이발사들은 그 부류 내에 인간 본성의 모든 종류를 수용하고 있기 때문이다(즉, 이발사에는 이런 사람, 저런 사람 별별 다른 본성의 소유자가 많기 때문이다). 나는 천사 같은 이발사들도 알았고, 악마 같은 이발사들도 알았다. 어떤 이발사들은 살랑거리는 가벼운 깃털처럼 부드러운 손길을 지니고 있는가 하면, 또 다른 이발사들은 면도를 구석기 시대의 무기인 양 휘두르고, 당신의 수염을 깎을 뿐만 아니라 얼굴 가죽을 벗기도록 용인될 때까지는 결코 만족을 하지 않는다.

> **영작▶** By the time (when) you are middle-aged, you will realize why I am telling you like this.

258 지난 10년 동안, 도덕 교육이 교화(教化)를 형성한다는 이유로 해서 불법적이라는 생각이 학계에서는 전통적인 생각이 되어 왔다. 그 결과 교사들은 도덕 교육을 자신 없는 태도로 접근해 왔다. 그리고 우리의 어린이들은, 오늘의 사회에서 도덕적으로 책임 있게 행동한다는 것이 무엇을 의미하는지에 관하여 대단히 혼란스러워하고 가끔은 위험천만한 생각을 지닌 채 성장해 가고 있다. 우리 학교에 침투하고 있는 알코올 중독, 마약 남용, 파괴 행위, 혼잡, 그리고 평범한 품위도 유지하지 못하는 등의 문제는 미국의 학교 교실에서 이루어지는 도덕 교육의 무시무시한 상태와 분명한 연관을 맺고 있다.

> **영작▶** The problems of alcoholism and drug abuse which pervade the young today vividly reveal the present status of the moral education in our country.

259 진보라는 생각이 현대 세계에서는 왜 그렇게 크게 나타나 보이는 것일까? 그것은 분명히, 특별한 한 종류의 진보가 실제로 우리 주위에서 이루어지고 있고, 또한 더욱더 명백해지고 있다는 이유 때문이다. 인류가 지성이나 도덕성에 있어서 전체적인 진보를 결코 이룩한 것은 아니라고 하더라도 인류는 지식의 축적에 있어서는 놀라운 진보를 이룩해 왔다. 말을 통해서 한 개인의 생각이 다른 사람에게 전달될 수 있게 되자마자 지식은 증가하기 시작했다. 글자의 발명과 더불어 엄청난 진보가 이루어졌는데 그 이유는, 지식이 이제는 (말로서) 전달될 수 있을 뿐만 아니라 또한 축적될 수도 있기 때문이었다.

> **영작▶** With the invention of the computer, a great advance was made in man's knowledge and information, which could hardly be imagined in the past.

260 인간은 과거의 경험들을 보존하기 때문에 하등 동물과 차이가 난다. 과거에 발생한 일이 기억 속에 다시 살아남는 것이다. 오늘 발생하는 일 주위에는 과거에 이루어진 비슷한 일들에 관한 구름 같은 생각들이 나타난다. 동물들의 경우에는 경험은 발생하면서 사라지게 되고 새로운 행위와 고통은 매번 홀로 남게 된다. 그러나 인간은 생겨나는 일 각각이 과거에 행해진 일의 메아리와 회상으로 채워지는 세계, 매 사건이 다른 일을 상기시키는 촉진제가 되는 세계에 살고 있다. 따라서 인간은 단순히 물질적인 일들로만 구성된 세계에서 들판의 짐승들처럼 살아가는 것이 아니라 신호와 상징의

세계에서 살아가고 있는 것이다.

> 영작 ▶ He differs from you because he makes a meticulous record of everything undergone in bygone days.

261 공산주의자들이 멸시하는 그러한 유의 자유는 지식인들이나 혹은 사회에서 보다 행운이 많은 부류의 사람들에게만 중요한 것은 아니다. 러시아에 자유가 존재하지 않음으로 해서 러시아 정부는 영국이나 심지어 미국에서 존재하는 것보다 훨씬 더 큰 경제적 불균형을 만들어 낼 수 있었다. 선전의 모든 수단을 통제하는 소수에 의한 독재 정치는, 만일 널리 알려진다면 거의 불가능하게 될 부정과 잔인한 행위들을 저지를 수가 있다. 단지 민주주의와 자유로운 선전만이 권력을 쥔 자들이 소수에게 사치를 허용하고 다수 대중에게는 가난을 가져오는 노예 국가를 세우는 것을 막아 낼 수가 있다.

> 영작 ▶ Democracy differs from dictatorship in that it allows free publicity and gives happiness to the many.

262 인간의 본성은 변화하지 않는다. 아니 적어도 역사는 어떠한 변화를 감지하기에는 너무나 짧다. 아주 오래된 옛날에 만들어진 예술과 문학의 견본들은 아직도 이해될 수 있다. 우리가 그 본보기들을 모두 이해하고 또 몇몇 견본 속에서 지금까지 능가한 적이 없는 예술적 우수성을 인식할 수 있다는 사실은, 인간의 감정이나 본능뿐만 아니라 지적인 힘과 상상력이 옛날에도 오늘날의 모습 그대로였다는 것을 충분히 입증하는 것이다. 미술 부문에 있어서 변화되는 것은 단지 관례와 형태, 부수적인 내용들뿐이고, 정열과 지성, 상상력의 기본 내용은 변화되지 않고 그대로 남아 있다.

> 영작 ▶ Such a behavior of his reveals that he has (been) changed in appearances, but not in his nature.

263 물론 과거에 발생한 일련의 실패가 그 다음 사람의 차례가 되었을 때 실패자가 되도록 운명을 지우지 않는 것처럼 그에게 성공을 보장하지도 않는다. 우리의 서구 문명만큼, 원하기만 한다면 사회적 자살 행위를 함으로써 역사적 선례를 따라가지 않도록 막는 것도 없다. 그러나 우리는 역사가 스스로를 반복하도록 강제하는 운명에 처해 있는 것은 아니며, 우리 자신의 노력으로 역사에 새롭고 전례가 없는 약간의 성향을 제공하는 것은 열려 있는 일이다. 인간으로서 우리는 이 선택의 자유를 받았고, 우리의 책임을 신이나 자연의 어깨 위로 전가시킬 수는 없다. 우리는 그 책임을 우리 스스로가 져야 한다. 즉,

그것은 우리에게 맡겨진 일이다.

> 영작 ▶ It is up to us to prevent history from repeating its previous failures through our own efforts.

264 물론 언어만으로는 근대 민족주의의 생성을 설명하는 데 충분하지가 않다. 언어라고 하는 것도 실은 같이 소속되어 있다는 인식, 또한 똑같은 기억들, 똑같은 역사적 경험, 똑같은 문화적 유산과 상상의 유산을 공유하고 있다는 감각의 속기술에 지나지 않는다. 18세기에 들어와 민족주의가 현대적인 (사회) 운동의 하나로 형성되기 시작했을 때 유럽의 여러 지역에서 민족주의를 먼저 주도하던 선구자들은 군인이나 정치가가 아니라, 고대의 전설과 반쯤은 잊힌 민요에서 국가의 '영혼'을 찾고자 한 학자와 시인들이었다. 그러나 여러 가지 (공통의) 기억과 공통의 경험과 역사적 기록을 고이 간직하고 있는 것은 언어였다.

> 영작 ▶ Language may be said to be the 'soul' of the nation which represents the ancient legends, folk songs, the common experience of the people, and the historical record.

265 열정이 인생에 대해서 갖는 관계는 배고픔이 음식에 대해 갖는 관계와 마찬가지이다. 축구 보는 것을 즐기는 사람은 그렇지 않는 사람에 비해 그만큼 우월하다. 독서를 즐기는 사람은 그렇지 않는 사람에 비해 더욱더 우월하다. 왜냐하면 독서의 기회는 축구를 보는 기회보다 더 많기 때문이다. 사람이 많은 일에 관심을 가질수록 그는 더 많은 행복의 기회를 갖게 되고, 운명에 좌우될 기회는 더욱더 줄어든다. 왜냐하면 그가 만약 한 가지 일을 놓치게 되더라도 다른 일에 의존할 수 있기 때문이다. 인생은 모든 일에 관심을 갖기에는 너무 짧지만, 우리의 매일을 채우는 데 필요한 만큼의 일에 흥미를 갖는 것은 좋은 일이다.

> 영작 ▶ Try to keep company with such (people) as will benefit you.

266 지식이 고통 없이는 얻어질 수 없다는 점은 매우 불쾌한 일이다. 지식은 힘든 노력을 통해서만 얻어지는 것이다. 소설이라는 잼에 의해 입맛에 맞게 만들어진 유익한 지식의 가루를 삼킬 수만 있다면 좋은 일일 것이다. 그러나 사실은, 그렇게 입맛에 맞게 만들어진 경우라 해도 그 가루가 우리에게 유익한 것이 될지는 확신할 수 없다. 그래서 여러분에게 말씀드리는 점은 소설가가 전해 주는 지식은 편견에 차 있고 믿을 수 없다는 점이며, 왜곡된 모습으로 어떠한 일을 아느니 차라리 전혀 모르는 것이 낫다는

점이다. 만약 독자가 그날의 긴급한 문제들을 알고 싶으면 소설보다는 그 문제들을 전문적으로 다루는 책들을 읽는 것이 나을 것이다.

> **영작▶** In such a trying period we will do better to refrain from excessive consumption.

267 누구든 어떠한 직업에 오랫동안 종사하게 되면, 그가 매일매일 하고 있는 일이 세상 사람들에게 손해가 되는지 혹은 이득이 되는지를 반드시 많이 생각하게 된다. 나는 많은 소설을 써 왔고, 또 많은 소설가를 알아 왔지만, 그러한 생각이 그들에게나 나 자신에게나 강하게 존재해 왔다고 단언할 수 있다. 그러나 이 작가들이 각자가 보여 주었을 것이라고 생각되는 천재성이나 창의성, 인내심에 대하여 대중으로부터 충분한 명예를 받아 왔다고 인정하는 과정에서, 그들에게는 자기 직업의 우월성을 올바르게 평가하고 자기들이 하는 일이 갖는 고상한 본질을 전반적으로 이해하는 힘이 아직은 부족하다고 나는 생각한다.

> **영작▶** These days it never rains without pouring.
> (These days it rains cats and dogs.)

268 일의 상황이 당신이 원하는 방향으로 진행되어 나가게끔 하는 것은 기도를 올리거나 겸손을 보여서가 아니라, 자연법칙에 대한 지식을 획득함으로써 가능한 것이다. 이렇게 언게 되는 힘은 과거에는 기도를 올림으로써 얻어진다고 생각되어진 힘보다 더 크고 더욱더 믿을 만하다. 왜냐하면 당신은 당신이 올리는 기도가 하늘나라에서 호의적으로 받아들여지는지 아닌지를 결코 말할 수 없기 때문이다. 더군다나 기도의 힘에는 인식된 한계가 있었다. 너무 많은 것을 요구한다는 것은 불경한 짓이 되는 것이었으니까. 그러나 과학의 힘에는 알려진 한계는 없다. 과거에 신앙이 깊으면 산도 움직일 수 있다는 말을 들었으나 누구도 그 말을 믿지 않았다. 오늘날에는 원자폭탄이 산을 없애 버릴 수 있다는 이야기를 듣고 있으며 모든 사람이 그 점을 믿고 있다.

> **영작▶** It is true that science can remove mountains, but not many (people) know that the power of prayer is no smaller than that.

269 아리스토텔레스에 의하면, 지식은 세 가지 커다란 종류로 구성이 되어 있는데, 그것은 지식 그 자체를 위해 추구되느냐, 행위를 수단으로 추구되느냐, 혹은 유용하거나 아름다운 무엇을 만들어 내는 수단으로 추구되느냐에 따라 이론적, 실용적, 혹은 생산적 지식 세 가지로 나뉜다. 다른 모든 학문이 그것에 종속되고 도구가 되는 최고의 실용적 학문은 정치학이다. 아니, 인간이 국가와는 다른 공동체의 구성원임을

보다 잘 의식하고 있는 우리로서는 그 학문을 오히려 사회과학이라 부를 수도 있겠다. 윤리학은 이 학문의 일부분에 지나지 않으며, 따라서 아리스토텔레스는 윤리학을 하나의 독립된 학문으로 부르지 않고 단지 '인격을 연구하는 분야' 내지 '인격에 대한 토론' 정도로 이야기하고 있다.

> **영작▶** We are inclined to consider liberal science as inferior to natural science or social science.

270 지진은 밤중의 도둑처럼 경고 없이 찾아온다. 따라서 졸지도 않고 잠들지도 않는 기구를 고안해 내야 할 필요가 생겨났다. 어떤 고안물은 매우 간단하였다. 예를 들어 어떤 기구는 구주희처럼 곧추설 수 있는 다양한 길이와 두께를 지닌 막대로 구성되어 있었다. 지진의 충격파가 나타나면 이 막대기가 서 있는 탄탄한 탁자가 흔들리게 된다. 충격파가 미미하면 좀 더 불안정한 막대기들이 쓰러진다. 만약 충격파가 세면 모든 막대기들이 쓰러진다. 그래서 막대기들은 쓰러짐에 의해서, 또는 쓰러진 방향에 의해서, 너무 미미해서 그를 깨울 수 없을 정도의 충격파의 강도와 또 그 지진이 어느 방향에서 생겨났는가 하는 점을 졸고 있는 과학자를 위해 기록을 하게 되는 것이다.

> **영작▶** As an earthquake comes like a thief in the night, the slumbering scientist cannot feel the strength of a shock when it is weak.

271 습관은 흔히 어떤 대단한 중요성을 지니는 주제로 간주되지 못해 왔다. 우리의 두뇌 속에서 이루어지는 내부 활동을 조사해 볼 만한 독특한 가치가 있는 것으로 느끼면서도, 우리는 습관은 가장 평범한 행위일 따름이라고 생각하는 버릇이 있다. 사실 상황은 그 반대이다. 전통적인 습관은 그것(행동)이 아무리 비정상적인 것이라고 하더라도 어떤 한 사람이 개인의 행위들로부터 이끌어 낼 수 있는 이상으로 더욱 놀라운 세세한 행동의 집합체이다. 그러나 이것은 오히려 그 문제의 사소한 일면에 지나지 않는다. 가장 중요한 사실은 습관이 경험과 믿음 속에서 담당하는 압도적인 역할과, 그것이 분명히 보여 주는 매우 여러 가지의 다양성, 바로 그것들이다.

> **영작▶** Everyone thinks that he was seduced by her into marrying her, but as a matter of fact, it is the other way around.

272 민주주의의 문제는 민주주의가 그 목적을 성취하고자 추구하는 수단과 방법뿐만 아니라 국가가 지니는 궁극적인 목표와 대상인 그 목적에 있어서 정당해야 한다는 점이다. 민주주의 국가에서 추구되는 것은 정의에 입각한 외적인 객관적 질서뿐만 아니라 내적

또는 주관적인 질서이다. 다시 말하여 국민에 의해 이해되고, 그 정부가 국민의 지지—국민의 인식과 국민의 의지—를 받고 행동하는 질서 잡힌 사회를 추구해야 한다. 이 엄청난 도전에는 두 가지 일이 수반되는데, 그것은 자유와 관련하여 정의를 이룩하는 것이고 또 하나는 개인의 책임과 관련하여 질서를 이룩하는 것이다.

> **영작▶** The government of a democracy must seek to accomplish its ends with the support and will of the people.

273 지적인 삶의 근간을 이루는 본능적인 기초는 호기심이며, 이 호기심은 그 기본적인 형태를 동물들 속에서 찾아볼 수 있다. 지성은 기민한 호기심을 요구하지만, 그것은 일정한 종류의 것이어야 한다. 마을의 이웃 사람들로 하여금 어둠이 진 뒤에 다른 집의 커튼 속을 들여다보게끔 하는 그러한 유의 호기심은 그다지 높은 가치를 지니지 못한다. 가십[부질없는 세상 이야기]에 사람들이 널리 관심을 갖는 것은 지식을 사랑해서가 아니라 악의에 의해서 고무되는 것이고, 누구도 다른 사람들의 비밀스러운 미덕에 대해서는 수군거리지 않으면서도, 그들의 악덕에 대해서는 이러쿵저러쿵 입방아를 찧는다. 따라서 대부분의 가십은 사실이 아니며, 또한 그것을 입증하지 않으려고 주의를 기울인다. 우리 이웃의 죄악은, 종교의 위안처럼 우리의 마음에 꼭 들어 우리는 그 증거를 면밀하게 조사하려고 하지도 않는다.

> **영작▶** Curiosity about other people's errors and secret vices cannot be said to be a real kind of curiosity having high value.

274 오늘날 인류 전체가 미쳐 있고, 그래서 정신적 자아통제의 회복만큼 우리에게 절실하게 부과된 일도 없다고 이야기한다 해도 그것은 결코 과장이 아니다. 우리는, 어떤 사람의 지배적인 생각이 그 자신의 환경에 대한 적응력에서 많이 벗어나 자기 자신과 다른 사람들에게 위험한 존재로 나타나게 될 때, 그를 미쳤다고 부른다. 이와 같은 미친 상태에 대한 정의는 현재 모든 사람들에게 들어맞는 것처럼 보이고, 인간은 "정신을 바짝 차려야지" 그렇지 않으면 곧 멸망하게 된다는 점은 비유법이 아니라 엄연한 사실의 진술이다. 사라지든지 아니면 보다 성숙된 힘과 노력의 장으로 들어가든지 해야 한다. 인류에게는 중간 단계는 열려 있지 않다. 인류는 오르든지 아니면 내려가든지 해야 한다. 그는 현재의 위치에 머물러 있을 수는 없다.

> **영작▶** It is scarcely an exaggeration to say that nothing is so urgent as to pull our mind

together in a society with complex and multitudinous characteristics.

275 행복한 사람이란 객관적으로 삶을 영위하고, 자유로운 애정과 광범위한 흥미를 소유하며, 이러한 흥미와 애정을 통해서, 또한 이러한 것들이 이제는 자신을 다른 많은 사람들에게 흥미와 애정의 대상이 되게끔 한다는 사실을 통해서 자신의 행복을 도모하는 사람이다. 애정을 받는 수혜자가 된다는 것은 행복을 얻는 강력한 원인이지만, 애정을 요구하는 사람은 우리가 애정을 쏟아 넣을 만한 사람이 아니다. 광범위하게 말해서, 애정을 받는 사람은 애정을 주는 사람이다. 그러나 돈을 빌려주고 이자를 받듯이 하나의 계산된 행위로서 애정을 주려 하는 것은 쓸모없는 일이다. 왜냐하면 계산된 애정은 진실된 것이 아니고 그것은 받는 자의 입장에서도 그렇게(진실된 것으로) 느껴지지 않기 때문이다.

> **영작▶** Affection is not such a thing as is given when we demand it. To give affection is as good as to receive it.

276 어떤 사람이 은행에 현재 구좌를 트고 있을 때 그는 은행에 돈을 빌려주고 있는 것이며, 그 돈을 현금으로 또는 다른 사람 앞으로 수표를 끊음으로써 자기가 맡긴 돈을 언제든지 돌려 달라고 요청할 수 있다. 기본적으로 은행과 고객의 관계는 채무자와 채권자의 관계이고, 채무자냐 채권자냐의 문제는 고객의 구좌에 예금이 아직 있느냐 아니면 잔고 이상으로 돈을 찾아냈느냐에 따라 결정이 된다. 그러나 그와 같은 기본적인 개념 외에 은행과 고객은 서로 간에 많은 의무를 지게 된다. 이 의무 중 많은 부분이 여러 가지 문제와 복잡한 상황을 야기할 수 있지만, 은행의 고객은 말하자면 상품 구매자와는 달리 법이 자신에게 불리하게 부담을 지우고 있다고 불평할 수는 없다.

> **영작▶** A customer's bank account in America is divided into savings account and checking account.

277 어떤 노인네들은 죽음의 공포로 고통을 받고 있다. 젊은이들이 이 감정을 느끼게 된다면 그럴 만한 정당성이 있다. 전투에서 죽게 될 것이라는 두려움을 느낄 만한 이유가 있는 젊은이들은 자신들이 인생이 제공해 주는 가장 좋은 것들을 속아서 빼앗겨 버렸다고 생각하는 경우 씁쓸한 기분이 들 것이고 그것은 정당한 것이다. 그러나 인생의 쓴맛 단맛을 다 알고 자신의 힘이 닿는 한 모든 일을 다 성취한 노인에게 있어서는, 죽음에 대한 공포를 느끼는 것은 어느 정도는 비굴하고 천한 짓이 된다. 적어도 내가 보기에는 그것을 극복하는 가장 좋은 방법은

관심거리의 영역을 서서히 넓히고 자기 자신에 대한 생각을 덜 하여 마침내 자아의 벽이 조금씩 허물어지고, 당신의 삶이 계속해서 보편적인 삶 속에 합병이 되도록 하는 것이다.

영작▶ I finished the work with all the strength (that) I had in me.

278 우리들 중 많은 사람이 유명하게 되거나 남에게 기억될 가능성은 없다. 그러나 한 국가나 문학 세계가 새로운 업적을 쌓도록 이끌어 가는 재기에 넘친 소수의 사람들 못지않게 중요한 사람들은, 자신들의 끊임없는 노력으로 세계가 퇴보하는 것을 막아주고, 새로운 가치를 인도하고 유지하며, 자신들이 선조로부터 물려받은 것을 자식들에게 손상되지 않고 줄어들지 않은 상태로 물려주는 것이 자신들의 드러나지 않는 승리가 되는 이름 없는 다수의 사람들이다. 우리들 대부분에게 있어서는 (물려받은) 햇불을 꺼뜨리지 않고 후손에게 전해 줄 수만 있다면 족한 것이다. 또한 가능하다면 우리를 알고 있는 소수의 사람들의 애정을 얻고, 그들이 자기 차례가 되어 사라졌을 때 그들의 뇌리 속에서 잊히는 데 만족하는 것만으로도 족하다.

영작▶ One of his inconspicuous achievements is that he made every effort to keep his fatherland from being ruled by foreign powers.

279 순전한 육체의 피로는 그것이 지나치지 않는다면, 어느 편이냐 하면 행복을 가져오는 원인이 될 수 있다. 그것은 곤한 잠과 좋은 식욕을 가져오고 휴일에 가능한 즐거움에 강한 욕구를 제공하기 때문이다. 그러나 피로가 지나치면 그것은 중대한 해악이 된다. 그러나 현대 세계의 선진화된 곳에서는 산업 환경의 개선을 통하여 육체의 피로는 많이 줄어들었다. 오늘날 선진화된 사회에서 대단히 심각한 피로는 신경의 피로이다. 이상하게도 이 피로는 부유한 사람들 사이에서 제일 특출 나고, 사업가나 정신노동자들에게 있어서보다는 임금 노동자들 사이에서 훨씬 덜 두드러지는 경향이 있다.

영작▶ Quest for money, provided it is not excessive, is not so deplorable, but when it is excessive, it becomes the source of many evils.

280 비평은 (무엇을 어떻게 비평할까 하고) 고려 중인 목표를 항상 분명히 밝혀야 하는데, 대충 이야기하여 그 목표는 예술 작품을 해설하고 취미를 수정하는 것을 뜻하는 것으로 보인다. 따라서 비평가의 임무는 그만이 할 수 있도록 되어 있는 것처럼

보이며, 그가 자신의 임무를 성공적으로 수행하는지 아닌지를 결정하는 일은 비교적 쉬워야 하며, 또한 일반적으로 어떤 종류의 비평이 유용하고 어떤 종류가 쓸모없는지를 결정하는 것도 비교적 쉬워야 한다. 그러나 이 문제에 조금만 주의를 기울여 보면 비평이라는 것이 협잡꾼들을 쉽사리 축출해 낼 수 있는 간단하고 질서 잡힌 행위의 장(場)이기는커녕, 자신들의 의견 차이를 분명히 나타내지도 못하면서도 논쟁을 하고 또 논쟁하기 좋아하는 말꾼들이 모인 일요일의 한 공원에 불과하다는 것을 우리는 깨닫게 된다.

영작▶ The job of teaching young children seems to be clearly cut out for him.

281 창작이라는 문제는 본질적으로 집중의 문제이고, 시인들이 가지고 있다고 생각되는 괴벽들은 일반적으로 집중을 목적으로 하여 개발된 기계적인 습관이나 의식에 기인한다. 물론 시를 쓰기 위한 목적으로 이루어지는 집중력은 숫자 계산을 하는 데 요구되는 집중력과는 그 종류가 다르다. 그것은 시선을 특수한 방식으로 집중하는 것인데, 그렇게 하여 시인은 자신의 생각이 갖는 모든 의미와, 생각의 가능한 전개 과정을 의식하게 된다. 이는 마치 하나의 식물이 한 방향으로만 기계적으로 성장하는 데 집중하지 않고 온기와 빛을 위해서는 잎으로, 물을 얻기 위해서는 뿌리로, 모든 행동을 동시에 행하면서 여러 방향으로 성장을 꾀한다고 말할 수 있는 것과 같다.

영작▶ The eccentricities of a writer are due to the efforts of concentration in the course of writing.

282 오늘날에는 징역 1개월이 채 안 되는 선고를 받을 범법 행위가 사형이라는 처벌을 받았던 18세기에는, 형법의 엄한 내용도 범죄 행위의 팽배에 결코 심각한 영향을 미치지 못하였다. 노상강도가 사람을 죽였든 단지 은화 몇 닢을 강탈하였던 그것이 그의 운명에 별 차이를 나타내지 않던 그 시절에는, 프랜시스 버뎃 경 같은 사람들이 형법의 엄청난 가혹성을 가볍게 하는 데 성공하게 된 때에 비해 더 많은 살인 행위가 있는 것도 결코 아니었다. 그 당시에는 지구상에서 생명의 신성함은 그다지 높이 여겨지지 않았는데, 그것은 앞으로 다가올 내세의 삶이 비교적 적은 숫자의 철학자들을 제외하고는 모두에게 당연한 것으로 받아들여졌기 때문이었다.

영작▶ The highwayman was sentenced to five years of imprisonment for having robbed his victim of a few pieces of coin.

283 모국어 공부는 다른 학문 분야에 따르는 중요성과는 그 종류가 다른 중요성을 지니고 있다. 우리는 다른 공부거리는 있어도 좋고 없어도 좋지만, 자신의 언어는 피할 수 없다. 다른 모든 공부 분야처럼 언어는 그 자체로서 연구될 수가 있지만, 다른 분야에 대한 지식을 습득하게 하는 매체라는 덧붙여진 중요성이 있다. 그렇다고 해서 자신의 모국어의 본질과 역사에 관한 자세한 지식이 필수불가결하다거나 역사적인 접근 방식이 유일한 접근 방식이라는 의미는 아니고, 그러한 지식이 영어의 역사를 전문적으로 연구하는 사람들뿐만 아니라 모든 사람들에게도 어느 정도의 중요성은 지닌다는 의미이다.

> 영작 ▸ The study of foreign languages is important, but it does not follow that we may neglect the study of our mother tongue.

284 핵에너지, 핵무기, 핵전쟁에 대한 공포가 세계 여러 민족들 사이에 널리 퍼져 있고, 계속 나타나고 있다고 말하는 것은 흔한 일이다. 문제는 그러한 두려움이 현재 그리고 미래에 정치적으로 효과가 있어서 원자의 힘이 파괴적인 목적이 아닌 이익이 되는 목적에 사용될 수 있느냐 하는 점이다. 현재 우리가 직면하고 있는 정확한 위험에 대한 평가들이 상당히 차이가 나고 있음을 인정해도, 정책을 만드는 엘리트층과 정치 대중이 갖고 있는 (합리적이거나 비합리적인) 두려움은, 결국 핵무기를 통제하거나 확보할 능력이 있는 유일한 실체인 정부의 행동에 어느 정도까지 실질적인 영향력을 미칠 수 있을 것인가 하는 것이다.

> 영작 ▸ Granting that your fear of a nuclear war is well-grounded, I cannot approve your assertion that it will break out in the very near future.

285 대학에서 공부는 많은 부분이 책과 평론의 내용을 소화하고 여러분이 읽은 내용을 설명할 수 있는 것으로 구성되어 있다. 읽는 내용이 복잡한 경우—경제학, 역사, 문학 비평 그리고 철학 등의 내용이 종종 그러하지만—그 내용을 개요로 요약하는 연습은 두 가지 이점을 가져다준다. 즉 그렇게 함으로써 여러분은 글쓴이가 무엇을 행하고 있고 그것을 어떻게 행하는지를 주의 깊게 관찰하게 된다는 점과, 나중에 복습[검토]하기에 편리한 형태로 기본적인 내용의 개요를 얻을 수 있다는 점이다. 이 두 가지 점에 있어서 요약된 내용이 평론에 대하여 갖는 관계는 지도가 잘 알지 못하는 도시에 대해 갖는 관계와 같다. 그것은 전체의 구조와 또 각 부분 간의 관계를 이해하는 효과적이고 능률화된 방편이다.

> 영작 ▸ Intellect is to the mind what sight is to the body.

286 젊은이들은 신나는 존재들이라고 나는 생각한다. 그들에게는 자유의 분위기가 있고 천한 야망에 전념하거나 혹은 편안함을 애호하는 일에 전념하거나 하지 않는다. 그들은 사회적으로 출세하기를 안달하는 자들도 아니고 물질적인 것들을 얻고자 헌신하지도 않는다. 나에게는 이 모든 것이 그들을 생명력이나 사물의 기원에 관련시키는 것처럼 보인다. 그들은 마치 어떤 의미에서 우리들 변두리에 살고 있는 존재들과 극단적으로 그러나 잘 대조가 되는 우주적인 존재들인 것 같다. 내가 한 젊은이를 대하게 되면 이 모든 생각으로 내 마음은 가득 찬다. 젊은이가 자만심이 강하고 버릇이 없으며 뻔뻔스럽고 얼빠졌다 해도 나는 나이 먹은 것이 마치 존경받을 이유나 되는 것인 양, 나이 든 사람을 존경해야 한다는 지겨운 진부한 표현을 빌려 나 자신을 보호하려 하지는 않는다. 나는 우리가 동등한 존재임을 인정하며, 만약 젊은이가 잘못되었다고 생각이 드는 경우에는 동등한 존재로서 그와 토론을 벌이리라.

> 영작 ▸ Her kind words were in striking contrast with her cold treatment of him.

287 가장 간단한 용어로 줄여서 말하자면 이민은 추방과 유인에 의해 야기되는데, 전자, 즉 추방은 거의 언제나 식량의 결핍에 의해서, 혹은 실제로는 거의 같은 이야기가 되지만, 인구 과잉에 의해 초래된다. 한 국가에 있어서 인구의 증가가 정상적인 식량 공급을 초과하는 때가 얼마 안 가서[조만간] 나타난다. 사냥을 하는 공동체 내에서 보면 사냥감이 과잉 사냥이나 질병에 의해서 줄어들어, 증감이 없는 혹은 숫자가 줄어드는 인구도 먹여 살리지 못할 수도 있다. 유목 민족들이 두려워하는 주요한 위험은 물 부족이다. 조그마한 가뭄이 계속되면 목축업은 이득이 없게 되며, 그래서 전국토가 완전히 메마르게 되면 광범위한 수준의 이민은 필연적이 된다.

> 영작 ▸ When reduced to the simplest terms, there will come a time when the food production may not catch up with population explosion.

288 문화는 어느 시대이건 똑같다는 주장, 예술은 통일성이고 아름다움은 절대가치라는 주장에 속지 말자. 만약 당신이 아름다움과 같은 추상적인 개념에 관하여 이야기하고자 한다면, 그 개념들이 절대적이고 영원하다는 점을 우리는 자유롭게 인정할 수가 있다. 그러나 추상적인 개념들은 예술 작품이 아니다. 예술 작품은 예를 들어 가옥, 가옥 속의 가구 등 쓸모 있는 물건들이다. 그리고 만약 조각품이나 시처럼 그것들이 당장에 쓸모가 있는 물건들이 아니라면,

31

PART 2
Reading & Composition

적어도 그것들은 우리가 사용하는 물건들과 어울리는 것들이 되어야 한다. 다시 말하여 우리들 일상 생활의 일부가 되어야 하며 우리의 일상적인 습관에 어울리는 것이어야 하고 우리가 매일매일 필요로 하는 것들에 접근할 수가 있어야 한다. 예술이 인간이 갖는 당장의 희망이나 열망을 표현하게 될 때에야 비로소 예술은 그 사회적 적응력을 요구할 수 있다.

영작 ▶ It is not until our parents pass away that we realize their real love.

289 잠자는 시간이 어떤 기능을 발휘하고 있음에 틀림없다는 것은 꽤 분명한 사실이며, 잠자는 시간이 많기 때문에 그 기능은 중요한 문제가 되는 것 같다. 그 기능의 본질이 무엇이냐에 관한 사색은 문자 그대로 수천 년 동안 지속되어 왔고, 이 문제를 수수께끼화하는 하나의 이상한 발견 내용은, 잠을 자는 것이 단지 육체에 휴식을 제공하는 문제만은 아닌 것으로 많이 생각되어진다는 점이다. 근육 이완 등의 관점에서 휴식은 잠시 동안 드러눕거나, 심지어 앉아 있는 것으로도 이루어질 수 있다. 육체의 근육 조직은 어느 정도까지는 스스로 복구하는 능력이 있고, 어느 정도 지속적으로 활동 상태에 있을 때 최고의 기능을 발휘한다. 사실 잠을 자고 있는 동안에도 기본량의 움직임은 이루어지고, 이 움직임은 근육이 활동을 중지하지 않도록 하는 점에 특히 연관되어 있다.

영작 ▶ Speculations about how to spend our university life is important to a considerable degree to enhancing the quality of our life after graduation.

290 현명한 사람들이 바보를 낳고, 정직한 사람들이 악한을 낳는다. 그러나 이러한 경우가 빈번히 나타난다고 해도 그것들이 일반적인 상황은 아니다. 이목구비와 전체적인 체격이 종종 닮은 경우가 있다고 해도, 보통은 정신과 마음이 닮은 경우가 더 많다. 왜냐하면 교육은 본성뿐만 아니라 이것들을 형성하는 데에 기여하기 때문이다. 본보기가 주는 영향력, 특히 부모가 자식들에게 미치는 영향력은 매우 크고 또한 거의 보편적이다. 모든 나라의 경우에서 보면 미덕뿐만 아니라 악덕도 세대에서 세대로 가족의 혈통에 전해져 내려온다는 것이 관찰되어 왔다. 누구든 자기가 알고 있는 친구들을 생각해 보면, 몇몇 혈통에서 할아버지 대에서 자식 대로 이어지는 비행과 악의와 복수를 향한 기질을 아마 기억해 낼 수 있을 것이다.

영작 ▶ The influence of parents over their children is so great that we must behave well for our children to imitate us.

291 다소간 우리가 통제할 수 있고 또 행복에 필수적인 일로 적어도 다음 네 가지가 있다. 첫째는 우리가 우리 행동의 지침으로 삼을 약간의 도덕적 기준이다. 둘째는 가족이나 친구들과 선린 관계를 유지하는 형태로서 만족스러운 가정생활이다. 셋째는 우리 자신의 국가에 대해서 우리의 존재를 정당화시키고 우리를 훌륭한 시민으로 만드는 작업이다. 넷째 것은 약간의 여가와 우리를 행복하게 하는 방향으로 그 여가의 이용이다. 우리의 여가를 잘 이용하는 데 성공한다고 해서 그것이 내가 지금 언급한 다른 세 가지 것 중의 어느 하나에서 벌어진 실패를 보상하지는 못하는 것이고, 적정량의 여가와 그것의 훌륭한 이용은 행복한 삶을 누리는 데 중요하게 기여하는 것이다.

영작 ▶ However much leisure we have, it may not contribute to happiness unless we make a good use of it.

292 자식들이 친구들의 가정을 칭찬할 때 부모들은 종종 당황하고, 그 칭찬을 자신들이 하는 요리나 청소, 또는 가구 관리에 대한 비난으로 여기며, 가끔은 어리석게도 자식들에게 자신들이 화를 내고 있는 모습을 보여 준다. 부모들은 심지어 자식들을 불효하다고 비난하며, 자식들의 친구의 부모에 대해 악의에 찬 욕설까지 퍼붓는다. 어른들이 이렇게 위엄을 상실하고 유치한 행동으로 빠져들게 되면 자식들은 심히 충격을 받게 되고, 자신들이 찾아가는 곳이나 사람들에 관해서 나중에는 부모들에게 이야기하지 않겠다고 결심을 하게 된다. 얼마 가지 않아 부모들은 자식이 비밀 감추기를 좋아하고 자신들에게 아무 이야기도 하지 않으려 한다고 불평을 터뜨리게 되나, 그들은 이러한 상황을 자신들이 야기했다는 점을 거의 깨닫지 못하고 있다.

영작 ▶ It is a childish behavior if parents accuse their children of disloyalty when they complain that their mother's cooking is quite unsatisfactory.

293 예술과 문학 문제에 대한 우리들의 취미를 아무리 세련화하고 과학과 심리학 문제에 있어서 우리의 통찰력을 아무리 날카롭게 하더라도 그것이 지구상의 생명체에 대한 우리의 감수성을 대신할 수는 없다. 이것은 개인을 진정으로 교육시키는 시작이며 끝이다. 예술과 문학은 수치스럽게 오용되어 왔으며 그 진정한 목표에 공헌하기는커녕 왜곡되어 왔다. 인간의 가장 심오한 내부에 자연에 대한 강렬한 감수성을 일깨우는 것은 느리고 매우 점진적으로 진행되는 과정이다. 어린 시절에 이 감수성을 의식적으로 처음 일깨우기 시작한다는 것은 우리의 뇌리에서

사라지지 않는 기억들을 가져다주는 원천으로서, 말로 표현할 수 없을 정도로 고귀한 것이다. 그리고 우리가 이러한 일들을 민감하게 포착하는 힘을 의식적으로 훈련시키면 시킬수록 그것들에 대한 우리의 즐거움은 더욱더 늘어난다.

영작 ▶ The earlier we cultivate our sensitiveness to Nature, the bigger our taste in literature and arts grows.

294 한 젊은이가 일몰 광경을 보고 마음속에 일어나는 감정을 이해하거나 표현할 수가 없어서 그것이 저 멀리 놓여 있는 세계로 들어가는 출입구임에 틀림없다는 결론을 내린다고 하자. 강렬한 미적 경험을 하게 되는 순간에 우리들 중 누구도 우리가 살고 있는 곳과는 다른—다르기도 하고 또한 경험이 강렬하게 감동적이어서 어떻게 보면 더 고상하기도 한—존재의 영역으로부터 우리에게 내리비치는 하나의 불빛의 모습을 어렴풋이 보고 있다고 하는 암시를 거역하기란 어려운 일이다. 그리고 그 불빛에서 발해지는 광채가 눈을 멀게 하고 눈을 부시게 하지만, 그 광채는 우리가 지금까지 알아 오거나 상상해 본 것보다 훨씬 더 커다란 아름다움과 진지함의 모습을 지니고 있다고 하는 점을 거역하기란 힘들다. 또 그 아름다움과 진지함은 우리가 묘사할 수 없을 정도로 위대한데, 그 이유는 이 세상의 의미들을 전달하기 위해 만들어진 언어가 다른 세상에서 이루어지는 의미 내용에 쉽게 어울릴 수 없기 때문이다.

영작 ▶ It is said that man, in moments of intense aesthetic emotion, sees the gateway to an unknown world that lies beyond.

295 문학을 애호하는 사람은 어느 의사도 줄 수 없는 고통에 대한 치료약을 가진 셈이다. 그는 언제나 자신의 고통을 고귀하고 영속적인 무엇으로 변화시킬 수 있다. 이 세상의 우리들 누구도 대단히 행복해지기를 기대할 수는 없다. 평균적인 인간의 삶에 있어서 행복과 불행의 비율은 1:3이 채 되지 못하는 것으로 평가되어 왔다. 당신이 아무리 건강하고 힘이 세고 행운이 있다고 해도, 여러분 누구나가 상당한 고통을 견디어 내야 한다는 것쯤은 내다보아야 하고, 그래서 그 고통을 좋은 용도에 사용할 수 없을까 하고 스스로에게 물어보는 것은 가치 있는 일이다. 왜냐하면 고통은 그것을 이용하는 법을 아는 사람에게는 대단히 큰 가치를 지니기 때문이다. 아니, 그것 말고 또 이런 말을 할 수도 있겠다. 고통을 모르는 사람에 의해서는 위대한 것은 어느 것도 전혀 쓰인 적이 없고, 앞으로도 결코 쓰이지 않을 거라고.

영작 ▶ No matter how healthy a man may be, he cannot keep up the health of the mind unless he reads literary works.

296 옛날의 종교와 신앙 체계는 주로 인간의 무지와 두려움을 타개하기 위한 적응의 방편이었는데, 그 결과 종교와 신앙 체계는 태도의 안정성에 관심을 갖게 되었다. 그러나 오늘날에는 인간의 지식과 창조적 가능성에 대적하는 데 적응하는 신앙 체계가 필요하다. 그리고 이것은 변화에 부응하고 변화를 부추기는 능력을 말한다. 다른 말로 하자면 옛날의 신앙 체계의 기본적인 기능은 필연적으로 미지의 존재에 직면하여 사회적, 정신적 사기를 유지하는 것이었고, 이것은 상당한 성공을 거두었다. 그러나 오늘날의 신앙 체계는 어떠한 것이든지 간에 그 기능은 인간의 발달을 위한 끊임없는 모험이 지속되도록 안내하고 용기를 북돋아 주는 데에 있어서 이용 가능한 모든 지식을 이용하는 것이 되어야 한다.

영작 ▶ What we need today is the belief systems which give us the encouragement for continuing adventure even in the face of the unknown.

297 모든 문명은 태어났다가 절정에 달하고 그러다가 쇠퇴해 간다. 이와 같은 불길한 사실이 도시의 혼잡한 삶에 본질적으로 존재하는 생물학적인 결점에 기인한다고 하는 증거[이야기]가 널리 퍼져 있다. 이제 느릿느릿 그리고 처음에는 미미하게 그 반대의 경향이 모습을 드러내고 있다. 더 나은 도로와 더 나은 교통수단이 처음에는 보다 부유한 계층을 도시의 외곽지대에서 살 수 있도록 하였다. 방어에 대한 긴급한 필요성도 또한 사라졌다. 이러한 추세는 지금 급속도로 하향화의 방향으로 퍼져 나가고 있다. 그러나 여기에는 일련의 새로운 조건들이 나타나고 있다. 18, 19세기 전체를 통하여 오늘에 이르기까지 이 새로운 추세는 가정을 도심에서 곧장 닿을 수 있는 가까운 외곽 지대에 자리 잡게 했지만 제조업 분야, 기업체, 정부(관공서) 그리고 오락 업체를 도시의 중심부에 집중시키게 되었다.

영작 ▶ As the urgent need for defence vanished, manufacturing activities, business relations and government agencies were placed in the suburbs of the cities.

298 교육은 시대에 따라 또한 공동체에 따라 달라지는 목적과 의도에 필연적으로 관련이 되어 있다. 교육의 기능이 어떠한 것인지에 대한 개념은 교육이 그 역할을 하는 사회의 성질에 의존하고, 개인과 공동체 사이의 관계를 지배하는 철학—그것이 함축적인

것이든 분명한 것이든—에 의해서 결정된다. 따라서 절대 권위를 행사하는 것으로 간주될 수 있는 '교육 이론'은 없다. 몇몇 가치관에 대한 고려가 교육 원칙을 천명하는 성명서 어느 것에든 등장하지만, 교육이 사고의 문제일 뿐만 아니라 행동의 문제인 한 개의 공동체는 그 가치관들을 정치적, 경제적, 사회적 삶의 '지금 이 자리에서 문제되는 것'과 관련해 해석해야 하는 문제에 직면하고 있다.

> **영작** ▶ Education can be genuine only when it is concerned with the ideals, philosophies, and problems of a society it is carried on.

299 말로서의 언어든 글로서의 언어든 언어는 결국 생각을 전달하고 표현하는 하나의 방법에 지나지 않는다. 그러나 생각 자체는 놀라울 정도로 재빠르고 변덕스럽고 복잡한 것이고, 생각을 언어로 바꾸는 일은 결코 쉬운 과정이 아니다. 말을 할 때 언어로 표현이 힘든 경우 손짓, 발짓, 얼굴 표정을 이용할 수 있는 것이 사실이고, 실제로 얼굴을 찡그리거나 눈썹을 추켜올리거나 손을 흔드는 행위는 구어(口語)에서 표현의 단위 혹은 '어휘'가 된다. 그러나 글을 쓸 때 우리는 우리의 사고를 나타낼 정확한 단어, 구절, 숙어 그리고 표현법을 찾아내야만 한다. 소설가, 비평가, 시인 등 위대한 작가들에게도 이것이 얼마나 힘든 작업인지 알기 위해서는 영국 박물관에 소장된 위대한 작품의 원고본을 연구해 보기만 하면 된다.

> **영작** ▶ To translate our thoughts into written language is never easy, because in writing, unlike in speaking, we have to search for exact words.

300 우리가 살고 있는 시기가 퇴보의 시기라는 점을 우리는 어느 정도 확신을 가지고 주장할 수 있다. 또한 문화 수준이 50년 전보다 더 낮아졌으며, 이 퇴보의 흔적들이 인간 활동의 모든 분야에서 눈에 띄고 있다는 점도 주장할 수 있다. 그래서 나는 문화의 부패가 더욱더 많이 진척되지 못할 이유는 없다고 보며, 문화란 전혀 존재하지 않았다고 말할 수 있는—어느 정도 지속되는—그러한 시기가 나타나리라고 기대하지 못할 이유 또한 없다고 본다. 그렇게 되면 문화는 다시 토양으로부터 성장해야 하며, 내가 그것이 토양으로부터 성장해야 한다고 말할 때 그 의미는 문화가 어떠한 정치적 선전 활동에 의해 생겨나야 한다는 뜻은 아니다. 이 이야기가 던지는 질문은, 그것들이 존재하지 않는 경우에는 높은 수준의 문화를 전혀 기대할 수 없는 그러한 영원불멸의 조건들이 존재하느냐 하는 점이다.

> **영작** ▶ I see no reason why you should marry such a luxurious woman.

301 현재 우리가 소유하고 있는 과학 기술을 범세계적으로 협력하여 사용하면 가난과 전쟁을 제거할 수 있고, 지금까지 전혀 존재하지 않던 행복과 복지의 수준을 모든 인류에게 가져다줄 수 있을지도 모른다. 그러나 이것이 분명히 가능한 일임에도 불구하고 인간은 아직도 자신들의 집단에게만 협력을 국한시키기를 좋아하고 다른 집단에게는 무시무시한 재난의 모습으로 일상생활을 가득 채우고 있는 사나운 적개심을 보여 준다. 모든 사람에게 이득이 되게끔 행동을 하지 못하는 이 모순되고 비극에 찬 무능력에 대한 이유는 외부적인 그 무엇에서 찾아볼 수 있는 것이 아니라 우리 자신의 감성적 본성에서 찾아볼 수 있다. 섬광이 비치는 순간에 과학자가 생각하듯 개인의 입장만 생각하는 상황을 초월하여 느낄 수만 있다면 우리가 이렇게 여러 갈래로 나뉘어 경쟁을 벌이는 어리석음을 볼 수 있을 것이고, 우리 자신의 이해가 다른 사람들의 그것과 양립할 수는 있어도, 다른 사람들을 파멸의 구렁텅이로 몰아넣으려는 욕구와는 양립할 수 없다는 점을 곧 깨달을 수 있을 텐데……

302 인간의 주된 목표는 가치의 창조와 보존이다. 그것이야말로 우리 문명을 뜻깊게 하는 것이고, 그것에 참여하는 것은 궁극적으로 개인의 삶에 의미를 부여하게 된다. 예술, 종교, 과학, 사랑, 가정생활을 통해 가치가 창조될 때에야 비로소 인간은, 자신으로 하여금 자연을 길들이고, 인간 존재를 끊임없이 위협하는 가장 형편없는 무도한 일과 사건들로부터 그 존재를 안전하게 보호할 수 있게끔 해준 기계와 힘을 효과적으로 사용할 수 있다. 인간이 인간일 수 있는 바로 그 능력이라고 부를 수 있는 문명은 그와 같은 영원한 노력 위에 자리 잡고 있다. 만약 어떤 국가나 집단이 이 일을 끝낸 것이라고 생각하거나 인간이 도구적인 것에만 신임을 주고 목적과 이상과 형이상학적인 목표를 망각하게 된다면, 그때는 문명은 무너지고 인간 자신도 끝장이 난다.

303 과거 역사에 대한 연구는 인간 경험의 의미에 어떤 빛을 던져 주는가? 그리고 특히 문명은 발전한다는 믿음을 어느 정도까지 유지해 주는가? 고대에는 널리 퍼져 있었으나 현대인의 생각에는 낯선 비관적인 이론들을 한쪽으로 밀어 놓고, 우리는 지난 4세기 동안 순수 과학의 분야에서, 더욱 분명하게는 응용과학의 분야에서 꾸준한 발전이 있어 왔음을 목격해 왔지만, 문명이 전진해 왔다고 폭넓게 일반화하는 것은 어떠한 것도 지지할 수 없다는 결론에 도달하였다. 특히 인간의 지적 성장에 상응하는 도덕적 성취의 성장이 조금이라도 있었느냐 하는 점은 대단히 의심스러운 일로 남아 있다. 이러한 의구심은 우리 생애에 우리 문화의 바로

그 기초마저도 위협해 온 대참사의 사건들에 의해 필연적으로 더 깊어졌다.

304 연극이나 소설처럼 역사는 해석과 표현의 원시적인 형태인 신화로부터 유래되었는데, 그 원시적인 표현 형태에서는 어린이들이 듣는 동화나 세상 물정에 닳고 닳은 어른들이 꾸는 꿈처럼, 사실과 허구의 선이 분명하게 그어지지 않은 채로 남아 있다. 예를 들어 「일리아드」에 대하여는, 그것을 한 권의 역사로 읽기 시작하는 사람은 누구나 그것이 허구로 가득 차 있다는 것을 알게 되고, 그것을 허구로 읽기 시작하는 사람은 누구나 그것이 역사로 가득 차 있음을 알게 된다고 이야기되어 왔다. 모든 역사[책]는 그것들에게서 허구적인 요소를 전적으로 없앨 수는 없다는 점에서 「일리아드」를 닮았다. 단순히 사실을 선택하고 배열하여 제시하는 것은 허구[소설]의 영역에 속하는 기술이며, 역사가가 동시에 위대한 예술가가 될 수 없다면 결코 위대할 수 없다고 주장하는 대중의 의견은 옳다.

305 끊임없는 변화의 한 세기가 지난 후에도 변화의 길이 부드럽고 쉬워지지 않았다는 것은 특기할 만한 일이다. 그와는 반대로 우리의 세상은 변화를 겪는 사람들에게 점점 더 적합하지 않은 곳이 되어 가고 있는 것처럼 보인다. 소년 시절을 지나 성년으로 가는 길이 그렇게 고통스럽고 폭발적인 일들로 둘러싸인 적은 그전 어느 때에도 없었다. 19세기에는 자연스러운 과정으로 보였던 후진 상태에서 근대화로 가는 길이 지금은 세상의 많은 지역을 한계점에 이르기까지 긴장시키고 있다. 가난에서 풍요로, 복종에서 자유로, 노동에서 여가로, 희망했던 변화들은 사회를 안정으로 끌어올리지 못하고 사회의 분열을 예고하며 협박하고 있다. 변화를 일으키는 사람들의 의도가 아무리 고상하고 그들의 노력이 아무리 진심 어린 것이라고 하더라도, 나타나는 결과는 종종 합리적으로 기대할 수 있는 것과는 정반대가 된다.

306 종교는 인간성의 발달에 커다란 도움을 주었다. 종교는 여러 가지 가치와 기준을 설정하고, 인간의 삶을 안내하는 원칙을 지적하였다. 그러나 종교가 행한 이로운 일들에도 불구하고, 종교는 또한 진리를 일정한 틀과 교리 속에 가두어 놓으려 하였으며, 원래의 의미를 곧장 다 잃고 단지 일상적인 일에 지나지 않게 될 의식적이고 상투적인 예배 의식만을 조장해 왔다. 사방에서 인간을 둘러싸고 있는 미지의 존재에 대한 두려움과 신비감을 인간에게 새겨 넣어 주었으면서도, 종교는 인간이 그 미지의 존재뿐만 아니라 사회적 노력에 방해가 될 수 있는 일들을 알려고 노력하는 것도 하지 못하게 하였다. 호기심과 사고를 북돋아 주기는커녕 종교는 자연과 기성 교회,

현존하는 사회 질서와 존재하는 모든 것에 복종해야 한다는 철학을 설교하였다.

307 인간의 본성을 연구하는 사람들은 카드놀이 하는 동료들의 행동을 보고 그 속에서 인간 본성에 대한 지속적인 관찰 자료들을 찾아낼 수 있다. 야비한 짓과 관대한 행위, 신중한 태도와 대담성, 용기 있는 태도와 소심함, 연약함과 강함, 이 모든 점들을 사람들은 본성에 따라 카드판에서 보여 준다. 그리고 사람들은 카드놀이에 열중해 있어서 평상시 쓰고 있던 가면을 떨어뜨린다. 브리지 게임 몇 번 해 보고서도 그들의 본질적인 모습을 여러분이 깨닫지 못할 정도로 자기 마음을 숨기는 사람은 드물다. 따라서 카드판은 인간의 본성을 연구하는 대단히 좋은 학교인 셈이다. 카드놀이에 대한 센스가 없는 불행한 사람들은 카드놀이가 시간을 낭비하는 짓이라고 말하지만, 자신을 즐긴다는 점에서 결코 시간 낭비는 아니며, 더군다나 하루는 24시간, 일주일은 7일이나 되니 낭비할 시간쯤은 어느 정도는 꼭 있게 마련이다.

308 외적인 사건들과 그 사건들의 결과는 우리에게 강력한 영향력을 행사하지만, 가장 커다란 충격은 내적인 두려움과 갈등을 통해 우리의 마음속에 찾아온다. 우리가 살아남기 위해서는 그러하지 않을 수 없듯이, 우리가 외부적으로는 진보를 해 나가는 중에도 우리는 우리 자신의 평화, 또 자신과 환경 사이의 평화—즉 우리의 육체적이고 물질적인 욕구뿐만 아니라 사상과 행동의 영역에서 인간이 그 고통에 찬 여행을 시작한 이래로 인간을 다른 동물과 구별되게끔 한 그 내면적인 상상의 충동과 모험심에도 만족을 가져다주는 평화—를 우리는 또한 얻어내야 한다. 그 여행이 어떠한 궁극적인 목표를 가지고 있는지 우리는 모른다. 그러나 그 여행에는 (여행에 따른) 보상이 뒤따르고, 획득이 가능한 것처럼 보이는, 새로운 진보를 위한 시발점이 될 수도 있는 보다 접근된 목표를 많은 사람들에게 지적해 주기도 한다.

309 새로운 문명은 언제나 만들어지고 있다. 오늘날 우리가 누리고 있는 여러 가지 인간사의 상태는 매 세대가 가지고 있는 보다 나은 세대를 향한 갈망에 어떠한 일이 발생하는지를 예증한다. 우리가 던질 수 있는 가장 중요한 질문은 한 문명과 다른 문명을 비교하고, 우리 시대의 문명이 진보해 나가는지 아니면 쇠퇴해 나가는지 약간이나마 헤아려 볼 수 있는 영원한 가치 판단의 기준이 조금이라도 존재하느냐 하는 점이다. 한 문명을 다른 문명과 비교하고 우리 자신의 문명의 여러 가지 다른 단계를 비교함에 있어서, 어떠한 한 사회도, 또한 그 사회의 어떠한 한 세대도 문명의 모든 가치를 전부 인식할 수는 없다는 점을 우리는 인정해야 한다. 또 이 가치들

모두가 서로서로 조화를 이루는 것도 아니다. 적어도 확실한 점은 몇몇 가치를 인식하는 과정에서 우리는 다른 가치를 인식하지 못하기도 한다는 점이다. 그럼에도 불구하고 우리는 높은 수준의 문화와 낮은 수준의 문화를 구별할 수 있고, (문화의) 진보와 퇴보를 구별할 수 있다.

310 훌륭한 책은 우선 그 훌륭함을 책에 생명을 불어넣어 준 개성의 위대함에 힘입고 있다. 왜냐하면 우리가 천재라고 부르는 것은 본성의 신선미와 독창성, 그리고 그 결과 나타나는 세상을 보는 안목, 통찰력, 그리고 사고의 신선함과 창조성을 나타내는 또 다른 이름에 다름 아니기 때문이다. 진정으로 훌륭한 책이라는 표시는 그 책이 무언가 신선하고 독창적인 할 이야기를 가지고 있다는 것이며, 그 이야기를 신선하고 독창적인 방법으로 전달한다는 것이다. 그 이야기는, 지금 이야기하고 있는 삶의 모습에 자신이 가까이 접근해 보았고, 그것들을 자신의 눈으로 바라다보았고, 날카로운 시각을 통해 보통 사람들보다 더 강력하게 그 의미를 이해하였고, 또한 거기에 덧붙여 우리 독자에게 자신과 함께 보고 느끼도록 하는 예술가로서의 훌륭한 능력을 가진 사람이 털어놓는 속마음의 진술한 이야기이다.

311 다른 지역의 좋은 조건에 이끌려 이주를 하게 되는 이민의 가장 간단한 경우는 경작된 땅이나 풍요로운 계곡에 이웃한 형편없는 초원이나 고원 지대에 살고 있는 민족이 보여 주는 이민의 경우이다. 농경 민족은 일반적으로 전쟁을 싫어하고 전쟁에 대한 준비가 서투르며, 자신들이 살고 있는 환경이 태평스러우면 태평스러울수록 그들 자신의 문명 바로 그것에 의해 기력이 약화될 가능성이 더욱 많다. 그래서 그들은 언제나 이웃하는 약탈자들의 공격을 받기 쉽고, 그 약탈자들은 어떤 경우에는 전리품을 챙겨 불모의 고향땅으로 돌아가지만, 또 어떤 경우에는 피지배 국민들 속에 남아 그들과 동화된 다음 마침내는 보다 개화되고, 그러다가 이번에는 국경에 살고 있는 자신들과 동족인 민족들로부터 침략을 당한다. 한편으로는 야만들을 개화시키고 또 동시에 태평스러운 환경에 의해 연약해진 종족들에게 활기를 불어넣는 사회구조가 이렇게 자동적으로 형성이 된다.

312 사회를 구성하는 모든 계층의 번성과 발전에 똑같이 혜택을 베푸는 정치 형태는 지금까지 어느 것도 발견된 것이 없다. 말하자면 이 계층들은 한 국가 내에서 그렇게 상이한 여러 공동체 집단을 계속해서 형성하고 있으며, 지금까지의 경험으로 미루어 이 계층들의 운명을 어느 한 계층의 손아귀에 놓아두는 것은 한 국민이 다른 국민의 운명을 결정하는 결정자가 되는 것만큼이나 위험스러운 일이다. 부자들만이 지배하게 되면 가난한 자들의 권익은

항상 위협을 받게 되고, 가난한 자들이 법을 만들면 부자들의 권익은 매우 심각한 위험에 처하게 된다. 따라서 민주주의의 이점은, 흔히 주장되어 오듯 모든 사람이 번영하도록 노력하는 데에 있는 것이 아니라 단지 최대 다수가 복지를 누리도록 기여하는 데 놓여 있는 것이다.

313 토끼의 후손은 토끼이고, 원숭이의 후손은 원숭이이고, 사람의 후손은 사람이라는 것은 비교적 최근까지 당연한 것으로 받아들여졌다. 찰스 다윈과 (그의 이론을 전파하는) 선구자들은 종(種)의 변이성에 시선을 집중시키고, 모두에게 소름이 끼치게끔 벌레의 후손이 곤충이 되고, 파충류의 후손이 새가 되며, 원숭이의 후손이 사람이 되는 진화의 구조를 가설로 내세웠다. 보다 정확히 이야기하면, 그들은 개개의 종을 한두 개의 새로운 종을 만들어 내는 과정에서 과도기적인 단계로 보았다. 즉, 생물학적 역사를 내용으로 다루는 영화의 한 장면으로 보았다. 그들의 이야기에 의하면 토끼의 후손은 토끼이지만 똑같은 토끼는 아니며, 진화의 과정에서 이 차이점이 축적되어 그 결과 오늘날의 토끼는 수십만 년 전의 토끼와 상당한 차이가 난다는 것이다.

314 여기 지구상에서 우리의 위치는 이상하다. 우리들 각자는 짧은 방문을 위해 오지만, 그 이유는 모른다. 그러면서도 가끔은 어떤 목표를 간파하는 것처럼 보인다. 그러나 일상생활의 관점에서 보면 우리가 정말로 알고 있는 일이 하나 있는데, 그것은 인간은 다른 사람들을 위해 이 세상에 존재한다는 점이다. 특히 우리 자신의 행복이 그들이 짓는 미소와 누리는 복지에 달려 있는 그 사람들을 위해서, 또한 우리가 그들의 운명과 공감대라는 고리에 의해서 연관된 셀 수 없을 만큼 많은 알려지지 않은 사람들을 위해서. 나의 외적, 내적 삶이 현재 살아 있기도 하고 죽어 있기도 한 나의 동료들의 노고 위에 세워져 있다는 점과 내가 받은 만큼을 그 대가로 돌려주기 위해서 얼마나 진지하게 노력해야 하는지를 하루에도 여러 번 깨닫는다. 내 마음의 평화는 내가 다른 사람들의 노고로부터 너무 많은 것을 빌어 왔다는 가슴을 짓누르는 감정으로 가끔은 깨어진다.

315 과학은 다양성을 단일성으로 축소하는 것으로 정의될 수 있다. 과학은 특수상황의 특이성을 무시하고 이러한 상황이 공통적으로 가지고 있는 점에 주의를 기울이며, 궁극에 가서는 어떤 종류의 '법칙'을 추상화함[이끌어 냄]으로써 자연계의 끝없이 다양한 현상을 설명하고자 한다. 그리고 그 법칙을 통해 특수 상황들이 의미를 갖고 유효하게 설명될 수 있다. 예를 들어, 사과는 나무에서 떨어지고 달은 하늘을 돈다. 사람들은 태곳적부터 이러한 사실들을 관찰해 왔다.

그들은 사과는 어디까지나 사과이며, 달은 어디까지나 달이라고 믿고 있었다. 아이작 뉴턴이 나타나서 이와 같은 매우 상이한 현상들이 가지고 있는 공통점을 인식하고 만유인력 이론을 체계 있게 설명하였으며, 이 이론을 통하여 사과나 천체뿐만 아니라 사실상 자연계의 모든 물체들의 어떤 양상들이 설명되고 (자세히) 다루어질 수 있었다.

316 이 시대를 보통 사람의 시대라고 우리는 흔히 말한다. 그러나 그 말이 무엇을 의미하는지 우리는 확실히 알지 못하고 있다. 그것이 어디까지나 보편적 기회의 시대를 뜻한다면 좋은 점만이 결과로 나올 수 있을 것처럼 보인다. 그러나 많은 사람들이 뜻하는 바는 그 이상인데, 가끔은 그 사실을 전혀 의식하지 못한 채 말이다. 우리가 어떠한 특별한 집단의 우두머리가 될 때 우리는 거의 필연적으로 그 집단을 이상화하기 시작한다. 우리는 보통 사람을 옹호하는 입장에서 벗어나 그를 찬양하는 쪽으로 넘어가고, 그 보통 사람이 그 밖의 다른 사람과 매양 마찬가지라는 점을 넘어서 그가 실제로는 더 나은 사람이라는 점을 이제 암시하기 시작한다. 가능한 한 그 보통 사람에게 보통이 아닌 사람이 될 기회가 주어져야 한다는 점을 단지 요구하는 대신에 우리는 이 보통의 자질을 미덕으로 만들고, 심지어 가끔씩은 높은 직책의 후보자들의 경우에 있어서도 그들이 길거리의 보통 사람과 거의 구분이 안 된다[별로 다를 바 없다]는 이유를 내세워 가끔씩은 그들을 칭찬한다.

317 애국심은 그것이 아무리 가치가 떨어진다 하더라도 역시 애국심이다. 애국심의 가치가 떨어질수록 더욱더 애국적인 것으로 평판이 난다고 주장하는 것은 과장일지 몰라도, 또 한편으로는 순수하고 이성적인 애국심이 일반적으로 일종의 반역으로 비난받는다는 점은 분명한 사실이다. 흔히 모순된 의미들이 이 편리한 단어[애국심] 뒤에 숨어 있다. 애국심이라는 단어에 의해서 올바른 것으로 인정된 많은 감정은 대단히 야비하고, 현대적인 예를 찾기 위해서는 애국심은 악당들의 마지막 피난처라는 존슨 박사의 이야기를 떠올리면 될 것이다. 그러나 비열한 위선적인 행위 외에도 천하게 이용되기는 하지만 국가와 세계의 전체적인 이득에 어쩌면 고갈되지 않는 힘의 원천이 되는 진지하고 정직한 애국심도 많이 있다.

318 내 나이가 매우 어려 어디론가 떠나고 싶은 충동이 나를 가득 싸고 있던 시절에, 나이 드신 어른들은 나이가 들면 그 욕망이 가라앉을 것이라고 말씀하셨다. 세월이 흘러 내가 성인이 되었을 때 처방된 치료약은 '중년'이라는 약이었다. 중년의 나이가 되었을 때, 또다시 좀 더 나이가 들면 (어디론가 떠나고 싶은) 나의 열병이 수그러들

것이라고 말들을 하였는데, 지금 내 나이가 58세이므로 아마 고령이 되어야 치료가 될지 모르겠다. 효과를 본 것은 아무것도 없었다. 네 번씩 요란하게 불어대는 뱃고동 소리는 아직도 목의 머리카락을 쭈뼛 세우고, 내 발은 벌써 타닥타닥 부둣가로 달려간다. 제트기 소리, 엔진 달구는 소리, 심지어 포장도로 위로 지나가는 편자 박은 말발굽 딸가닥거리는 소리는 옛날의 전율을 다시 가져다주고, 입이 타고, 눈은 멍해지고, 손바닥에는 땀이 어리고, 가슴은 크게 요동친다. 다시 말해 나는 나아지는 것이 없다. 덧붙여 말하자면 한때의 방랑자는 영원히 방랑자인 셈이다. 이 병이 불치병일까 봐 두렵다.

319 한 시인이 그 자신의 시대에 많은 독자를 가졌느냐 아니냐 하는 점은 별로 중요하지 않다. 정말로 중요한 것은 그의 시를 읽는 독자가 매 세대마다 약간씩은 있어야 한다는 점이다. 즉, 독립심이 있고 자신들이 사는 시대를 약간은 앞서 가고 새로운 것을 더욱 빨리 자기 것으로 받아들이는, 시를 이해하는 몇몇의 전위부대(선봉장)들이 언제나 있어야 한다. 문화의 발달이란 모든 사람을 최전방으로 데려오는 것을 뜻하는 것이 아니라 단지 모든 사람에게 보조를 맞추도록 만드는 것에 지나지 않는 것이다. 문화의 발달이란 그러한 엘리트층을 유지하면서, 보다 수동적인 대다수의 독자들이 한두 세대 이상 뒤떨어지지 않도록 하는 것이다. 몇몇 작가(시인)에게 처음으로 나타나는 감수성의 변화와 발달은, 더 쉽게 인기를 끄는 다른 작가들에게 소수의 작가들이 영향을 끼침으로써 서서히 언어 속으로 파고들게 되고, 그 변화와 발달의 내용들이 제대로 자리 잡게 될 때쯤에는 새로운 진보가 요구될 것이다.

320 우리는 우리가 사는 세계의 인습에 매우 익숙해져 있어서, 그러한 인습은 학습된 것이고 또한 그것들이 없다면 우리의 지각 작용도 똑같지 않을 것이라는 사실을 잊어버린다. 한 아프리카 시골 여성에게 엠파이어 스테이트 빌딩의 그림엽서를 보여 준 한 미국인은 그 여성이 "참 아름다운 정원이네요!"라고 말하는 것을 듣고는 놀랐다. 그때까지 그 미국인은 그 그림을 높은 건물로 보는 그의 지각 작용의 기초를 전혀 인식하지 못하고 있었다. 그는 그 사진을 3차원 용어로 해석했을 뿐만 아니라, 사진에 익숙해진 덕분에 책상 위에 놓인 그림을 두뇌 속에 곧추세워 놓고 있었던 것이다. 그 아프리카 여성은 지금까지 자신이 사는 시골 마을의 낮은 오두막보다 더 높은 건물을 본 적이 없었고 어떤 종류의 그림이나 사진도 본 적이 없었다. 그런 그녀가 본 것은 줄지어 선 사각형들이었고, 이 사각형들을 그녀는 잘 설계된 정원으로 보았던 것이다.

321 원시문화와 개화된 문화의 만남은 엄청난 중요성을 갖는 사건으로, 양 문화에 대단히 심오하고 미묘한 의미가 주어지는 결과가 나타난다. 각각의 문화는 만남 이후에 결코 예전과 같을 수 없기 때문이다. 원시인과 자신이 차이가 난다는 점을 거만하게 의식하고 있는 유럽 사람은 만남의 결과가 원시인에게만 의미가 있고 의식적으로 우월성을 느끼는 자신들은 그 결과와 관계가 없다고 믿는 경향이 있다. 그러나 실제로 이 중대한 사건에서 일방통행은 없다. 외부 세계에 있는 원시인과의 만남은 문명인의 원시성을 자극한다. 문명인은 대단히 완고한 결심을 가지고 그 만남을 거부할지 모르지만, 그래도 그 과정은 그것과는 상관없이 계속된다. 실제로 나타나는 상황은, 그가 거부를 하기 때문에 원시인이 개화된 삶에 그 영혼의 뒷문을 통해 몰래 들어온다는 점이다. 그것은 긍정적인 요소가 되기는커녕 부정적이고 보복적이며 파괴적인 요소가 되는데, 그것은 개화인이 그 만남을 가슴으로 환영하고 마음으로 봉사하지 못하기 때문이다.

322 과학과 기술이 우리 삶의 모든 면에 침투하게 되었고, 그 결과 사회는 예전에 없던 속도로 변화하고 있다. 우리들 주변에는 과학에 의해서 생성된 엄청난 기술의 폭발이 존재하고 있다. 이 폭발은 이미 수많은 사람들을 자연에 대한 전통적인 속박의 상태에서 벗어나게 했으며, 마침내 우리는 이제 인류를 궁핍에 기인하는 두려움에서 결정적으로 해방시킬 힘을 갖게 되었다. 그리하여 비로소 처음으로 인간은 삶이라는 것이 생존을 위한 격투 이상의 무엇이 될 수도 있다고 합리적으로 생각하기 시작했다. 그러나 오늘날에도 보다 행운이 많은 서구에서 높은 생활수준이 일반화되었음에도 불구하고, 세계의 거의 대부분의 사람들은 자신들에게 필요한 식량과 주택을 확보하기 위해 자연과 끝없는 싸움에 자신들의 시간과 정력을 거의 다 소모하고 있다. 심지어 이 기본적인 노력의 과정에서도 매년 수백만의 사람들이 굶주림과 질병 혹은 홍수에 의해 불필요하게 죽어가면서 아까운 인명만 낭비되고 있다.

323 전적으로 노동에 몰두하고 있는 사회에서는 여가는 단지 휴식이나 여분의 시간으로 생각될지 모른다. 여가가 계속되면 그것은 게으름이나 주의산만이 된다. 게으름과 주의 산만은 즐겁지 않은 노동에 대한 반응이고, 이것들은 다른 방식으로 시간을 낭비케 함으로써 노동에 낭비된 시간을 보상한다. 재미없는 노동과 주의 산만한 놀이로만 나뉜 삶은 삶이 아니라 단지 죽음을 기다리는 것이고, 그러한 사회에서는 전쟁이 구출의 방편으로 등장한다. 왜냐하면 전쟁은 기다림의 긴장을 덜어 주기 때문이다. 게으름과 주의 산만은 물건을 깨부수는 것으로 표현되는 권태와 그 종류가 매우 닮았다고 널리 인정되고 있으며, 따라서

적어도 한 세기쯤 된, '대중 교육은 단지 사람들이 비행을 저지르지 않도록 막기 위해서 필요하다'고 하는 널리 퍼진 정서가 있게 된다. 이것은 그다지 고무적인 교육 철학이 아니며, 그 목적을 전혀 달성할 것 같지도 않은 교육 철학이다.

324 문명의 역사는 인간이 항상 과학이 이룩한 여러 가지 발견들을 올바르게 이용하느냐 아니면 잘못 이용하느냐의 둘 중에서 어떻게 하나를 선택해야만 하는가를 보여 주고 있다. 그것이 우리 시대보다 더 진실된 때도 없었다. 짧은 기간 동안에 놀라운 발견들이 이루어지고 실질적인 목적에 이용되어 왔다. 우리가 혁명의 시대에 살고 있다고 이야기하는 것은 상식이 되었다. 과학이 인류에게 베풀어 준 은혜가 얼마나 큰지를 인식하지 못한다면 그것은 배은망덕한 짓이 될 것이다. 과학은 얼마 전까지만 해도 소수의 특권이었던 이득과 이점을 다수의 사람들이 이용할 수 있는 범위 내로 가져다주었다. 과학은 영양실조와 기아와 질병이 어떻게 극복될 수 있는가 하는 점을 보여 주었다. 과학은 수명을 연장시켰을 뿐만 아니라 또한 생명의 질을 높여 주었다. 과학의 작용을 통하여 오늘날의 보통 사람은 그의 조부모들에게 가능하던 것보다 더 길고 더 충실한 삶을 누릴 기회를 갖게 되었다.

325 현대의 생활에 있어서 과학과 과학적인 방법이 가져다준 놀라운 물질적 변화는, 덜 물질적이기는 하지만 마찬가지로 진실되고 가치 있는, 과학이 이룩한 또 다른 커다란 성과들을 우리로 하여금 보지 못하게 할 수도 있다. 우선 과학이 문명에 끼친 지적인 공헌들 중에는 인간을 여러 가지 형태의 속박과 미신들로부터 해방시켰다는 점이 있다. 과학은 문명화된 인간을 환경의 노예 상태에서 거의 벗어나게 하였다. 과학은 시간과 공간 개념을 거의 무너뜨렸고 모든 국가들을 하나의 이웃으로 만들었다. 과학은 실질적으로 전 지구에게 자신이 필요로 하는 조공을 바치도록 의무를 부과하였다. 과학은 인간에게 자연이 갖고 있는 엄청난 자원을 이용하는 방법을 가르쳐 주었고, 지구상에서 인간의 운명을 제어하는 힘을 인간의 손에 상당 부분 쥐어 주었다. 또한 과학은 전 지구에서 살아가고 그것을 개발하는 점도 가능하게 하였다. 또한 엄청난 인구 증가와 커다란 사회집단을 야기했다.

326 보통의 역사가가 기록하기에 매우 극적인 민족의 이동은, 예를 들어 현대에 들어와 나타난 유럽에서 미국으로의 이주처럼 한 지역에서 다른 지역으로 인구가 조용히 그러나 꾸준히 유입되는 이동보다 가끔은 중요성이 덜하다. 이러한 종류의 이동은 한 국가를 눈에 띄게 할 정도로 또는 치명적으로 고갈시키는 결과가 될 수 있고, 그래서 그 국가는

오랫동안 황폐해진 상태로 존재하거나, 시간이 경과함에 따라 동부 독일과 여러 슬라브 계통 나라들의 경우에서 보듯 다른 외국 민족에 의해 채워지기도 한다. 이민해 오는 민족들이 피정복 민족에게 영속적으로 영향을 미치는 문화와 언어를 가지고 옴에도 불구하고 토착 민족이 충분한 숫자로 살아남게 되는 경우 새로 들어온 이주민들의 종족적 순수성을 해하게 되고, 토착 민족이 자기의 권리를 펴고 다시 한 번 득세하는 경향이 나타난다.

327 생명의 기원을 연구해 온 사람들의 연구를 통하여, 우리가 살고 있는 지구라는 행성과 대략적으로라도 닮은 행성이 주어져 있다면 생명체가 거의 틀림없이 생겨나기 시작한다고 결론을 내려야 한다. 태양계에 존재하는 모든 행성들 중에서 지구만이 생명이 살아남을 수 있는 유일한 행성임을 우리는 지금 상당히 확신하고 있다. 화성은 너무 메말라 있고 산소가 부족하며, 금성은 너무 뜨겁고, 수성도 또한 마찬가지이다. 그리고 더 외곽 쪽에 있는 행성들은 거의 절대영도에 가까운 기온과 수소가 지배하는 공기를 지니고 있다. 그러나 천문학자들이 별들이라고 부르는 다른 태양들은 우리들의 행성과 비슷한 행성들을 틀림없이 가지고 있을 것이며, 우주에 존재하는 별들의 숫자는 엄청나게 많아서 이 가능성은 실질적인 필연성이 된다. 우리의 은하계만 하더라도 수천억 개의 별들이 존재하고, 우주에는 3백억 개의 은하계가 있다. 그래서 우리가 존재하는 것으로 알고 있는 별들의 수는 3만 경(京)이 되리라고 본다.

328 다른 유럽인들에게 가장 잘 알려진 영국인의 특질은 과묵함이다. 과묵한 사람은 낯선 사람들에게 많은 말을 하지 않고 많은 감정도 보이지 않고 거의 흥분도 하지 않는다. 과묵한 사람을 사귀는 것은 어렵다. 그는 당신에게 자신에 관하여 아무 이야기도 하지 않으며, 당신이 그와 몇 년간을 일하고서도 그가 어디에서 살고 있는지, 자식이 몇 명이나 되는지, 그리고 그의 흥밋거리가 무엇인지 전혀 알지 못하기 때문이다. 영국 사람들은 그런 식이다. 버스를 타고 여행을 할 때 그들은 빈자리를 찾기 위해 최선을 다할 것이다. 낯선 사람과 옆에 앉아 가야 할 때 그들은 대화 한 마디도 나누지 않고 몇 마일씩 가기도 한다. 다른 사람과 이야기하기를 꺼려하는 이 점은 어떤 면에서는 불행한 특질이다. 왜냐하면 다른 사람에게 냉정하다는 인상을 주는 경향이 있고 영국인이 관대함과 친절한 접대로 잘 알려져 있지 않은 것도 사실이기 때문이다. 그러나 한편으로 그 과묵함의 장벽 뒤에 들어가 보면 완벽하게 인간적이고, 친근한 이방인이나 외국인이 잠시나마 장벽을 깨뜨리게 되면 매우 기뻐하기도 한다.

PART ③
Advanced Reading

329 미국의 문명은 세 가지 요소의 결과이다. 그 세 가지란 첫째로 서구의 관습과 제도를 원상태로 받아들인 것, 둘째로 신세계가 구세계에서 가져온 (삶의) 방식에 미친 영향, 그리고 셋째로 구세계의 지속적인 영향력이다. 역사가들은 이 세 가지 요소 중 첫 번째 것에 상당한 관심을 기울여 왔고, 두 번째 것에는 그보다 덜한 관심을, 그리고 마지막 것에는 거의 관심을 기울이지 않았다. 유럽이 갖는 지속적인 영향력은 보통 정부 간의 관계 또는 외국에서 태어난 사람[이민자]들이 인구를 늘린 것 등의 설명을 깃들여 처리[무시]되어 왔다. 그러나 이러한 문제는 가장 필수적인 사실, 즉 외국에서 이루어진 사상이나 업적의 주요한 변화에 미국이 줄곧 함께 해 왔다는 점을 간과하고 있다. 이민자들이 있다는 사실이 이 점에 도움을 주었다는 것에는 의심의 여지가 없지만, 그들이 모국에 머물러 있었다 하더라도 미국의 역사는 여전히 세계 역사와 밀접한 관련을 가졌을 것이다. 서구 문화와 밀접하게 관련된 어떠한 민족도, 설령 그러기를 바랐다고 하더라도, 구세계 문명에서 나타나는 당대의 흐름을 피할 수는 없었을 것이다.

330 태양계는 유일하지 않다. 수많은 천계(天界)를 통틀어 진화된 형태의 생명체를 지탱하고[갖고] 있는 다른 행성은 없다고 말하는 것은 비합리적이고 비과학적이다. 그러나 인간 정신은 우리가 모든 물체의 중심에 있지 않다는 생각에 익숙해지는 것이 매우 어려운 것을 알아냈다. 코페르니쿠스가 지구가 우주의 중심이 아니라는 것을 밝혀낸 후에도 우리는 우주의 주된 목표는 인간의 삶에 봉사하는 것이라고 계속 믿었다. 이제 우리는, 우리가 하나의 종으로 당당하게 재능을 가지고 태어났지만 유일한 존재는 아니라는 사실을 받아들여야 한다. 상대적인 의미에서, 생명체는 몹시 부풀려진 지구 중심적인 자기도취를 위로해 줄 만큼 아직은 희귀하다. 그러나 생명체에 대해 중요한 것은 그것이 희귀하거나 유일한 것일 수도 있고 그렇지 않을 수도 있다는 점이 아니다. 생명체는 우리가 어떤 일들을 비로소 처음으로 할 수 있다는 점 때문에 아직은 고귀하다. 우리는 그전에는 전혀 창조해 보지 못한 방식으로 창조를 할 수 있다. 인간의 삶의 어떠한 것도 우리가 스스로의 목표를 정의하고 스스로의 운명을 결정할 수 있다는 점보다 더 고귀하지는 않다.

331 우주 시대의 도래와 더불어 새로운 표현이 사용되게 되었는데 그것은 '우주 과학'이라는 말로서, 우주 안에서 이루어지거나 또는 우주와 직접 관련된 기본적인 과학적 탐구[조사]를 뜻한다. 넓은 관점에서 보면 우주 과학은 두 개의 주요한 탐구 분야를 갖는데, 하나는 태양계의 탐사, 또 하나는 우주의 탐구이다. 첫 번째 범주에는 지구와 그 대기, 달과 행성, 그리고 행성 간의 매체에 대한 탐구가 포함된다. 태양의 본질과 움직임, 태양이 태양계, 특히 지구에 미치는 영향력은 가장 큰 중요성을 지닌다. 우주 탐구 기술을 이용할 수 있음으로 해서 우리는 직접 관찰을 함에 있어서 태양계의 하나의 별에만 제한되지 않는다. 이제 우리는 태양계의 다른 별들을 탐사하고 연구하기 위해 우리의 탐사 기구와 인간을 보낼 수가 있다. 행성들의 속성을 자세하게 비교할 수 있음으로 해서 우리의 행성[지구]을 조사할 능력이 크게 증가되었다. 다른 행성에 존재할 수도 있는 생명체에 대한 조사는 그 철학적 의미가 잠재적으로 대단히 멀리 미친다.

332 과학은 경험적이고 합리적이며 일반적이고 또한 누적적이다. 그리고 이 4가지 속성을 동시에 지닌다. 과학은 그 모든 결론이 감각 경험에 의해 시험 받는다는 점에서 경험적이다. 관찰은 과학이 그 위에서는 기초가 되지만, 과학적 관찰은 우리가 눈을 뜨고 있는 것 이상이다. 그것은 자격 있는 관찰자들(즉, 과학자들)이 통제된 조건 하에서 만들어 내는 것으로, 하나의 이론을 그렇거나 그렇지 않은 것으로 확인하거나 입증하거나 반박해 주는 사물들에 대한 관찰이다. 셜록 홈즈는 외투에 묻은 얼룩을 보고 어떤 사람이 아침에 무엇을 먹었는지를 알아낼 수 있었다. 그러한 관찰을 여러 번 한 후에 그는 왜, 어떻게 하나의 특수한 범죄가 저질러졌는지에 대한 가설에 도달했다. 이 과정은 탐정로는 훌륭한 것이지만 과학으로는 불충분하다. 왜냐하면 그것은 단지 특별한 사건에 대한 지식만을 산출해 내기 때문이다. 과학은 계속해서 왜, 어떻게 범죄—하나의 특수한 범죄가 아닌—가 저질러지는지를 질문한다. 과학은 사실을 이용하여 일반적인 이론을 시험하고, 일반적인 이론을 이용하여 특수한 사실에 대한 예측을 해낸다.

333 미국의 산업과 그 세계 경쟁력을 어떻게 하면 되살릴 수 있는지에 대한 논의는 다음 두 개의 서로 관련된 개념을 중심으로 활발히 진행되어 왔다. 그 개념 중 하나는 자유무역 대 보호무역이고, 또 하나는 산업 정책이다. 보호무역은 외국의 경쟁자들보다 국내 산업에 혜택을 주는 관세와 수출입 규제들로 구성된다. 자유방임주의는 그러한 규제들이 반생산적이며, 규제[제약]받지 않는 시장은 재화와 용역을 가장 능률적으로 생산하도록 힘을 부여할 것이라고 암시한다. 캐나다, 미국, 멕시코를 포함하는 북미자유무역지대에 대한 지지는 이 주장에 근거하고 있다. 그와는 대조적으로 보호무역정책 지지자들은 일정한 국가 이익들(예를 들어 국내 생산을 유지하고 주요 산업을 통제하는 것, 또는 외국의 노동자보다 자국 노동자들의 복지에 우선 혜택을 주는 것 등)이

자유 시장의 이득보다 더 중대하다고 주장한다. 이 외에도, 다른 나라들이 취하는 보호무역 정책들 때문에 진정한 자유(무역) 시장은 존재하지 않는다고 그들은 주장하며, 마치 자유 시장이 진정으로 존재하는 것처럼 행동하는 것은 자기 자신의 이익을 다른 사람들의 농간의 희생물이 되게 하는 것이라고 말한다.

334 로켓과 인공위성은 전리층을 뛰어넘어 멀리 날아갈 수 있고 심지어 지구로부터 벗어날 수도 있다. 그러나 이 물체들은 복잡한 구조를 지니고 있고 만드는 데 돈이 많이 들며, 현재의 발전 추세로 보아 거대한 망원경을 실어 나르거나 관찰이 수행되는 동안 그 망원경들을 움직이지 않게 고정시키거나 일을 마치고 안전하게 그것들을 다시 가져오는 등의 일은 할 수 없다. 풍선은 다루기가 훨씬 용이하고, 또한 값도 훨씬 싸다. 풍선의 주된 약점은 전리층에까지 다다를 수 없다는 점이다. 8만 내지 9만 피트가 풍선이 무리 없이 다다를 수 있을 것으로 예상되는 높이이며, 따라서 풍선에 의해 운반되는 기구들은 자외선 천문학이나 X 레이 천문학에는 별로 기여할 수가 없다. 그럼에도 불구하고 풍선에 대해서는 많은 호의적인 이야기가 가능한데 그 이유는 풍선이 대기권의 질량을 넘어서는 무거운 장비를 운반할 수 있으며, 그렇게 함으로써 영상이 흐려지거나 불안정한 상태를 제거할 수 있기 때문이다. 게다가 아래쪽 공기층 속에 존재하는 수증기나 이산화탄소는 행성들이 쏟아내서 우리에게 전달되는 적외선의 대부분을 흡수한다. 풍선을 띄워 올림으로써 이 장애는 쉽게 극복이 된다.

335 뱀들이 독을 만들어 내는 것이 어떻게 가능한 일인가 하는 점은 하나의 불가사의이다. 오랜 기간에 걸쳐 인간의 침처럼 순하고 소화력을 지닌 액인 뱀의 타액이 오늘날에도 그 분석이 불가능한 독으로 변화되었을 것이다. 생존을 위한 경쟁 때문에 뱀이 독을 갖지 않으면 안 되는 상황은 아니었을 것이다. 뱀들은, 아직도 수천의 독성을 품지 않은 뱀들이 그러하듯, (그렇게 하려고만 한다면) 독을 사용하지 않고도 먹이를 잡아 그것을 먹고살 수 있었을 것이다. 뱀이 가지고 있는 독은 하나의 사치품이다. 독이 있음으로 해서 뱀은 별반의 노력 없이 먹을 것을 얻을 수 있다. 즉 한 번만 물면 되는 것이다. 그러면 왜 뱀들만이 독을 갖고 있는 것일까? 예를 들어 고양이가 독을 가지고 있다면 커다란 도움을 얻을 수 있을 텐데. 크고 사나운 쥐와 쫓고 쫓기는 싸움도 필요 없고, 다 큰 토끼들과 맞잡고 싸울 필요도 없고 단지 한 번만 먹이를 물면 더 이상의 수고가 필요 없을 테니까. 사실상 독을 지니고 있다면 그것은 모든 육식 동물에게는 하나의 보조 수단이 될 것이다.

물론 서로가 싸우는 경우에는 양날을 지닌 무기가 되기는 하겠지만. 그러나 예측할 수 없는 자연은 모든 척추동물 중에서 단지 뱀들만을(그리고 한 종류의 도마뱀만을) 선택하여 독을 선사하였다. 우리는 왜 자연이 그렇게 무시무시한 힘을 지닌 독을 몇몇 뱀에게만 음모를 꾸미듯 부여하였는지 또한 의아하게 생각한다.

336 똑같은 천연자원을 소유하고 있는 두 국가—한 나라는 독재 국가이고 다른 한 나라는 개인의 자유를 허용하는 국가—가 있을 때, 자유를 허용하는 국가가 전쟁을 수행하는 기술면에서 다른 국가에 비해 곧 우월해질 것이라는 점은 확실하다. 독일과 러시아에서 보았듯이 과학 탐구에 있어서 자유는 독재와 양립할 수 없다. 히틀러가 유태인 물리학자들을 죽이거나 추방하지 않고 참아 낼 수만 있었더라면 독일이 전쟁에서 이겼을지도 모른다. 스탈린이 리센코의 이론을 받아들이기를 고집하지만 않았더라면 얻을 수도 있었던 식량의 양보다 더 적은 양의 식량을 러시아는 얻게 될 것이다. 러시아에서 핵물리학 분야에 과거처럼 정부가 간섭을 해 들어오는 일이 나타날 것이라는 점은 대단히 가능성이 많은 일이다. 앞으로 15년 동안에 전쟁이 발발하지 않는다면 러시아의 전쟁 수행 기술은 서구의 그것에 비해 현저하게 열세를 면치 못할 것이며, 이 열세는 직접적으로 독재 정권 때문에 나타난다는 점을 나는 의심치 않는다. 따라서 강력한 민주 정부가 존재하는 한 민주주의는 결국 승리하게 된다고 나는 생각한다.

337 최근에 이르기까지 많은 고고학자들이 문명사회가—메소포타미아 지역에서 이와 유사한 문명의 발전이 있기 바로 조금 전이기는 하지만—이집트에서 처음으로 생겨났다는 견해를 견지하고 있었다. 그러나 보다 최근에는 최초의 문명이 메소포타미아 지역에서 일어났을 것이라는 견해가 나타난다. 어느 견해를 따르든 두 지역의 지리적 조건이 동일하지 않았다는 점을 명심할 필요가 있으며, 사실상 메소포타미아 지역에서는 환경적 요소들이 나일 강 계곡만큼 전적으로 좋은 것은 아니었다고 이야기할 수 있다. 나일 강은 그 하류에 지류를 갖지 않은 하나의 커다란 물줄기이지만 티그리스 강과 유프라테스 강은 여러 갈래의 지류가 얽힌 강들로서, 전자(티그리스 강)는 두 강의 하류 쪽을 막아 버리는 엄청난 양의 침적토를 실어내리는 중요한 지류를 받아들이고 있으며, 이 침적토로 인해 늪지대, 작은 늪, 변화가 심한 강둑과 해안선이 생겨난다. 더군다나 메소포타미아 지역의 홍수는 보다 변화가 심하다. 그 이유는 홍수가 중동 지방 내에서 오는 강수량에 의존하고, 이 강수량은 변덕스럽고 믿을 만한 것이 못 되기 때문이다.

338 어떤 행동을 해 주도록 요청을 받은 사람이 그와

비슷한 종류의 행동들에 대하여 미리 생각해 보았다면 운 좋게 그 일을 행할 가능성은 더 커진다. 우리가 한 공동체의 구성원으로서 효과적인 역할을 하고자 바란다면 우리는 두 개의 상반된 위험을 피해야 한다. 우선은, 우리가 무슨 일을 하고 있는지 생각하지도 않고 행동으로 돌진하는 위험이다. 다른 말로 해서, 결국은 같은 이야기가 되지만, 다른 사람들이 왜 그렇게 행동하는지에 대하여 전혀 알지도 못한 채 다른 사람들이 하는 대로 하면 옳다고 하는 점을 당연시하면서 행동으로 돌진하는 위험이다. 또 한편으로는, 생활과 동떨어져 학문적으로 초연함에 빠지는 위험이다. 이것은 한 문제의 양면을 보고서 논쟁 그 자체를 즐기는 데 만족하는 경향이 있는 사람들이 특히 빠지기 쉬운 유혹이다. 그러나 생각은 주로 행동을 위해 있는 것이다. 누구도 자신의 생각의 형태에 따라 행동해야 하는 책임을 면할 수는 없다. 어떻게 행동을 할 것인가 또한 왜 그렇게 하기로 결심하게 되는가를 잠시라도 멈추어 생각하지 않는 사람은 결코 현명하게 행동할 수 없다.

339 역사는 우리 자신의 장래의 전망에 대하여 어떠한 정보를 제공해 주는가? 그리고 실제로 그렇다면 그 부담은 무엇인가? 역사가 우리에게 냉혹한 운명을 자세히 설명해 주어서, 우리가 우리 자신의 노력으로는 피할 수도 없고 수정할 수도 없는 운명에, 될 수 있는 한 우리 자신을 맡기고, 깍지 낀 손을 한 채로 그 운명을 단지 기다려야만 하는가? 아니면, 역사는 우리에게 우리 자신의 미래에 있어서 확실성이 아닌 가능성, 단지 가능성만을 알려 주는 것인가? 실질적인 차이는 엄청나다. 왜냐하면 이 두 번째 갈림길[방도]에서 우리는 멍하니 수동적으로 되기는커녕 행동에 나서야 하기 때문이다. 이 두 번째 방도에서 역사의 교훈은 점성가의 천궁도와 같을 수는 없고, 항해자의 해도(海圖)와 같은 것이다. 이 해도는 그것을 사용할 수 있는 머리가 있는 항해자에게, 맹목적으로 (해도도 없이) 항해했을 때보다, 난파를 피할 수 있는 훨씬 더 큰 희망을 줄 것이다. 왜냐하면 그가 그 수단을 이용할 기술과 용기를 가지고 있다면 해도에 표시된 암석과 암초 사이의 길을 키를 잡고 잘 헤쳐 나갈 수 있는 수단을 제공하기 때문이다.

340 이와 같은 목적과 수단의 문제는 윤리적으로 대단히 중요하다. 문명인과 야만인, 어른과 아이, 인간과 동물 사이의 차이점은 주로 행동의 목적과 수단에 덧붙여지는 무게와 관련된 차이점에 놓여 있다. 문명인은 자신의 생명을 보험에 들지만 야만인은 그렇게 하지 않는다. 어른은 치아의 부식을 막기 위해 이를 닦지만 어린이는 강제에 의하는 경우가 아니고서는 이를 닦지 않는다. 인간은 겨울에 먹을

식량을 얻기 위해 들판에서 일하지만 동물들은 그렇지 않다. 미래에 즐거운 일을 얻기 위해 현재 달갑지 않은 일을 행하는 선견은 정신적 발달의 가장 필수적인 표시 중의 하나이다. 선견을 갖는 것은 어려운 일이고 충동의 억제를 요구하기 때문에 도덕론자들은 선견의 필요성을 강조하고, 앞으로 있게 될 보상의 즐거움에 대해서보다는 현재의 희생정신의 미덕을 더 강조한다. 여러분은 올바른 행위를, 그것이 천국에 이르는 길이기 때문이 아니라 올바른 일이기 때문에 행해야 한다. 여러분이 절약을 해야 되는 것은, 당신으로 하여금 인생을 즐기게끔 해 줄 수입을 궁극적으로 확보할 것이라는 이유에서가 아니라, 모든 지각 있는 사람들이 그렇게 하기 때문에 그래야 하는 것이다.

341 원자 폭탄, 그리고 더더욱 수소 폭탄은, 과학이 인간의 생명에 미치는 효과와 관련하여 새로운 의구심을 필연적으로 포함하여 새로운 공포심을 야기하였다. 아인슈타인을 포함한 몇몇 유명한 권위자들은 이 지구상에 존재하는 모든 생명체가 멸망할 위험이 있다고 지적해 왔다. 나 자신은 이러한 현상이 다음 번 전쟁에서 일어나리라고 생각하지는 않지만, 만약에 일어나도록 놓아둔다면 다음다음 전쟁에서는 당연히 일어날 수도 있을 것이라고 생각한다. 이 예상이 맞는다면, 우리는 향후 50여 년 내에 두 개의 방안 중에서 하나를 선택해야만 한다. 즉 인류가 자신을 말살시키게끔 하든지 아니면 우리에게 대단히 귀중한 몇몇 자유들, 특히 우리가 그러한 마음이 내킬 때는 언제나 외국인을 살해하는 자유를 삼가든지 해야 한다. 나는 인간이 보다 나은 방편으로 자신의 말살을 택할 가능성이 있다고 본다. 물론 그 선택은 우리 자신에게 그러한 일이 이루어지지 않고 있다고 설득함으로써 이루어질 것이다. 왜냐하면 (양 진영의 군사주의자들은 그렇게 말할 것이다) 정의의 승리는 모두가 죽는 재난의 위기 없이도 확실한 것이기 때문이다. 우리는 아마 인간의 마지막 세대에 살고 있는지도 모른다. 만약에 그렇다면 인간이 소멸되는 것은 과학 때문이다.

342 처음에 인간은 자연의 경이로움을 깨닫지 못한다. 왜냐하면 생존 수단을 얻거나 자신 또는 아이들을 위한 먹을 것을 확보하는 데 몰두해 있기 때문이다. 원시 시대의 그림을 보면 동물이 먹이[열매]를 따먹고 있는 가지 하나로만 나무가 그려진 것을 보게 된다. 인간은 동물을 사냥하면서도, 나무에 대해서는 자신의 관심을 끄는 동물에 대한 일종의 부수물로서가 아니면 시선을 기울이지 않았다. 그리고 오늘날에도 문명화된 나라에서 자신들의 주위에 있는 아름다운 사물들을 그 자체로 보는 사람들이 얼마나 적은가? 농부는 빈 들판을 보고서 그가 뿌린

씨앗이 자라 그에게 수확을 가져다주는 농작물을 생각한다. 건축가는 들판을 보고서 그가 그곳에 짓고 싶은 집들을 생각한다. 등산가는 산을 보고 그가 올라가서 등정하는 등산로를 생각한다. 광산업자는 산을 보고 산들이 바위 속에 숨기고 있는 부와, 어떻게 하면 그 부를 추출할까를 생각한다. 단지 예술가만이 들판과 나무와 산들을 있는 모습 그대로, 그 자체로 볼 뿐이다.

343 모든 것의 운명을 결정하는 초자연적인 힘이 존재한다고 하는 믿음은 사회적 국면에 일정한 무책임성을 가져다주었고, 감정과 감상적인 태도가 숙고된 사고와 탐구를 대신하게 되었다. 종교는, 물론 그것이 분명히 수많은 인간들에게 위안을 주고 그 가치를 통해 사회를 안정화하기는 하였지만, 인간 사회에 본래부터 존재하는 변화와 발전을 저해하였다. 지식이 증가함에 따라 좁은 의미로 본 종교의 영역은 축소된다. 우리가 삶과 자연을 더 많이 알면 알수록 우리는 초자연적 원인들을 덜 찾게 된다. 우리가 이해할 수 있고 통제할 수 있는 것은 무엇이나 신비의 대상이 되지 못한다. 영농의 과정들, 우리들이 먹는 음식, 우리가 입는 의복, 우리의 사회적 유대 관계들은 모두가 한때는 종교와 그 고귀한 사제들의 지배 하에 있었다. 이것들이 서서히 종교의 지배 영역 밖으로 빠져나와 과학적 탐구의 대상이 되었다.

344 교육이라는 주제는 어떠한 개혁가라도 숙고해 보아야 할 문제 중 가장 어려운 문제 중의 하나이다. 언뜻 보아서는 마치 교육이 사회 개선에 열쇠를 제공하는 것처럼 보일지 모른다. 왜냐하면 더 나은 교육은 다른 모든 개혁을 쉽게 해 줄 수 있기 때문이다. 그러나 사실상 현존하는 교육이 갖는 대부분의 폐해는 현재 산업 문명이 고통을 받고 있는 다른 폐해들의 직접적인 결과들이며, 우리의 경제 제도가 변화될 때까지는 철저하게 치료될 수는 없다. 그럼에도 불구하고 교육을 당분간은 덜 해롭게 만들기 위해 무엇인가가 이룩될 수 있는데, 그것은 교사들, 조금 적게는 부모들 사이에 나타나는 여론을 통해서이다. 사회를 덜 경쟁적이고 덜 부당한 조직으로 만들려는 목표를 가진 사람들이 취할 어떤 주된 입장은 없다. 단지 동시에 취해야 할 서로 연관된 수많은 입장들만이 있는데, 그 이유는 한 분야에서의 진보는 다른 분야에서 그와 상관된 진보를 가져오기 때문이다. 이 장(章)에서 우리가 관심을 갖는 것은 유토피아 세계의 교육이 아니라 현재 모습 그대로의 교육이 갖는 더 큰 폐해를 막기 위해 지금 이곳에서 어떤 일을 할 수 있느냐이다. 나는 나의 관심을 주로 초등학교 교육에 국한시키고자 하는데, 그 이유는 그것만이 이 책에서 내가 관심을 갖는 저 큰 문제들 중의 하나로 여겨질 수 있기 때문이다.

345 대학은 전통적으로 (일반)교양 교육을 깊이 있게 제공하는 것을 목표로 삼아 왔다. 전문적인 연구는 대학 졸업생이 졸업을 하면서 전문직, 공직, 산업과 상업 분야에서 직업을 갖는 데 있어서 충분한 지식을 갖기 위하여 필요한 것으로 생각되고 있다. 졸업생들은 전문가가 될 필요가 있지만, 현대 지식의 범위가 너무나도 광범위하여 그들이 한두 가지 이상의 분야에서 전문가가 되기는 어렵다. 또한 한정된 분야에 대한 집중적인 연구가 머리를 훈련시키는 데 최선의 방법이고, 어떤 사람들의 이야기로는 유일한 방법이라고 믿어지고 있다. 그러나 전문화는 어떤 철학가가 '모든 시대가 소유하고 있고 또한 그것에 의해 살아가는 필수적인 생각의 체계'라고 부른 것, 즉 인류가 이룩한 업적의 전 분야에 대하여 적어도 조금은 안 후에야, 비로소 이루어져야 한다. 전문화의 필요성이 크면 클수록 그것에 일반교양의 튼튼한 기초를 제공할 필요가 더욱더 커진다. 그리고 여러 가지 다른 과목을 경험하고 난 후에야 비로소 누구든 전공 분야를 현명하게 선택할 수 있고, 자신이 배운 여러 가지 과목을 올바른 균형 감각으로 볼 수 있다는 점은 더 말할 필요도 없다.

346 세대 간—젊은이와 늙은이 간—의 갈등은 모든 갈등 중에서 가장 어리석은 것으로 보인다. 왜냐하면 그것은 현재 모습의 자신과 앞으로의 자신 사이의 갈등이며, 또는 과거 모습의 자신과 현재 모습의 자신 사이의 갈등이기 때문이다. 누구나 살아가는 동안 젊었던 때가 있고, 살아남은 사람은 누구나 나이가 든다. 그리고 젊기도 하고 나이가 들기도 한 자는 같은 영혼, 같은 정신, 같은 가슴을 지닌 동일 인물이다. 그래서 어떤 갈등을 자살행위로 기술한다면 바로 위와 같은 갈등이다. 그것을 고집한다면 인간 사회의 지속은 불가능하게 될지도 모른다. 나이 든 사람들은 자신의 지혜와 경험을 젊은이들을 위해 쓰면서도 젊은이들이 지닌 활력, 정력, 열정 등이 잘 발휘될 수 있도록 자유롭게 놓아두어야 한다. 한편 젊은이들은 나이 든 사람들이 이룩한 업적과 실질적인 감각을 존경하고 경의를 표하고, 그들의 신체적 힘과 활기를, 그들이 그것을 아직 가지고 있는 동안, 지속되는 사회를 위해 봉사할 수 있도록 해야 한다. 젊은이와 늙은이는 서로의 이익을 위하여 서로를 참고, 모두에게 공통으로 나타나는 결점들을 참아야 한다.

347 우리의 사회 제도를 급진적으로 개혁하려는 목표를 가진 사람들은 현존하는 제도가 권력을 가진 자들에게 유리하고 따라서 변화시키기가 어렵다는 문제에 직면하게 된다. 권력이라는 것이, 우리의 전체 문명을 파괴할 만큼 무시무시한 투쟁에 의한 경우가 아니라면, 그것을 쥐고 있는 자에게서 어떻게

빼앗을 수 있는가 하는 것은 알기가 쉽지 않다. 이 문제가 분명히 가망이 없어 보임으로 해서 결국 많은 사람들로 하여금 현재의 폐해들이 엄청나다는 사실을 날카롭게 의식하고 있으면서도 그것들을 묵인하게끔 만들고, 한편으로는 다른 사람들로 하여금 사회적 책임 의식을 지니고 있는 사람들을 소원하게 만드는 무모한 혁명적인 태도를 취하게 한다. 나는 그 문제가 흔히 생각되듯이 결코 풀 수 없는 것이 아니라고 믿는다. 권력은, 심지어 가장 군주적인 권력도, 어떤 큰 집단의 사람들이 내어놓는 의견이나 그 전통과 관습에서 대중적인 기초가 필요하다. 전통과 관습은, 설령 그것들이 강력한 것들이라고 해도, 우리의 변화무쌍한 세계에서 그 힘을 잃어 가고 있다. 따라서 누가 장래에 권력을 쥐어야 하느냐를 결정함에 있어서 (사람들의) 의견이 결정적인 요소가 된다.

348 사회 조직이 아무리 부당하게 되어 있다고 하더라도, 몇몇 기술적인 진보는 전 사회에 이득을 줄 수밖에 없다. 왜냐하면 몇몇 종류의 재화는 누구나 반드시 공통으로 소유하기 때문이다. 예들 들어 백만장자라고 해도 다른 사람들을 위한 거리를 어둡게 해놓고 자신만을 위해서 거리를 밝힐 수는 없다. 문명국들의 거의 모든 시민들은 지금 훌륭하게 닦은 도로를 이용하고, 무균질의 물을 마시고, 경찰의 보호를 받고, 무료 도서관을 이용하고, 그리고 일종의 무상 교육을 누리고 있다. 영국의 공교육은 돈이 대단히 부족하였으나 교사들의 헌신적인 노력에 주로 힘입어 개선되어 왔고, 독서의 습관은 엄청나게 퍼지게 되었다. 부자나 가난한 사람들이나 점점 상당한 수준에 이르기까지 똑같은 책을 읽고 있고, 똑같은 영화도 보고, 똑같은 라디오 프로그램도 듣고 있다. 삶의 방식의 차이들도 값싼 의복의 대량 생산과 가옥의 개선으로 인해 많이 줄어들었다. 외적 모습에 관한 한 부자나 가난한 사람들의 의복은, 특히 여성의 경우에 있어서, 30년 전 아니 15년 전에 비해 훨씬 차이가 덜 나고 있다.

349 민주주의는 무엇보다도 사장[우두머리]에게 '아니오'라고 말할 수 있는 능력이다. 그러나 사장의 호의가 없어졌을 때에 벌어먹을 능력에 대한 확신이 서지 않는 경우 그 사람은 사장에게 '아니오'라는 대답을 할 수가 없다. 또한 그가 가족이 먹고살 충분한 부를 만들어 낼 방편을 가지고 있지 못하거나, 과거에 벌어들인 임금에서 여분을 축적할 수 없었거나, 새로이 출발할 수 있는 새로운 영역으로 옮겨갈 기회가 없는 경우에 그는 다음 끼니도 확신할 수가 없다. 인구 과잉이 된 국가에서는 재정적으로 독립할 수 있을 만큼 충분한 부를 소유한 사람도, 구매력을 축적할 위치에 있는 사람도 거의 없다. 그리고 자유롭게 움직일 수도 없다. 게다가 인구가

천연자원에 심한 압박을 가하는 국가에서는 전체적인 경제 상황이 대단히 불안할 가능성이 많아 자본과 노동, 생산과 소비를 정부가 통제하는 것은 피할 수 없는 상황이 된다. 그래서 20세기가 고도로 중앙집권화된 국가들이 나타나고 전제적인 독재 정권이 나타나는 세기가 된다는 것이 우연한 일은 아니며, 20세기가 지구 전체가 인구 과잉이 되는 세기라는 단순한 이유만으로도 그렇게 될 수밖에 없다.

350 프로이트 심리학은 인간 정신을 조직적으로 설명한 유일한 것인데, 이것은 미묘함과 복잡성, 흥미와 비극적인 힘의 관점에서 보면, 지금까지 수세기 동안 문학이 축적해 온 혼란스러운 다수의 심리 통찰에 견줄 만하다. 하나의 위대한 문학 작품으로부터 심리학에 관한 학문적 연구 논문에 이르기까지 그것을 읽다 보면 한 가지 종류의 인지 상태를 경험하다가 다른 종류의 인지 상태를 경험하게 되는 것이나 마찬가지인데, 프로이트 심리학이 다룬 인간의 본성은 시인이 언제나 자신의 예술성을 행사한 바로 그 재료이다. 따라서 심리 분석 이론이 문학에 커다란 영향을 행사해 왔다는 것은 놀라운 일이 아니다. 그렇지만 양자 간의 관계는 상호적이고, 프로이트가 문학에 끼친 영향은 문학이 프로이트에게 끼친 영향과 거의 같았다. 70세 생일 축하에 즈음하여 '무의식의 발견자'로 소개받게 되었을 때 프로이트는 그 말이 잘못되었다고 수정하고 그 직함으로 불리길 거부하였다. "나보다 앞서 간 시인들과 철학자들이 무의식을 이미 발견하였고, 내가 발견한 것은 무의식의 세계를 연구할 수 있는 과학적인 방법이었습니다"라고 프로이트는 말하였다.

351 미국인들의 정치적 태도와 지식을 분석하는 정세 분석가들은 때때로 대중들이 네 그룹으로 구성된 것으로 특징짓는다. 그 네 그룹은 만성적인 무식자, 일반 대중, 주의력이 깊은 대중, 그리고 여론 지도층과 정책 결정자들이다. 이 그룹들의 크기에 대한 추정치는 차이가 있다. 예를 들어 한 분석가는 만성적인 무식자를 대중의 약 20%로 평가하나, 다른 분석가는 그들이 단지 4% 정도에 불과하다고 못을 박는다. 일반 대중의 크기도 측정하기가 역시 어렵다. 관련된 이슈에 따라 측정의 크기가 달라지는 것 같다. 결코 교육되지도 않고 문제에 말려들지도 않는 무식자들과는 달리, 일반 대중은 약간의 정보를 가지고 있고 가끔은 정치 활동에 나서기도 한다. 정치와 관련된 그 다음 높은 층에는 주의력이 깊은 대중이 있는데, 인구의 약 15~20% 정도 되는 것으로 측정된다. 이 주의력 깊은 대중들은 정보를 찾고, 여론을 만들고, 정책 결정에 중요한 영향을 미칠 수 있다. 특수한 이슈가 만들어져 극적으로 변하면

주의력 깊은 대중의 크기는 늘어난다. 이 주의력 깊은 대중 위에는 여론과 정책을 가장 많이 형성하는 사람들이 있다. 이 그룹은 주로 정치나 언론 매체의 지도층으로 구성되어 있다.

352 태아 상태의 존재에서 인간의 존재로 비교적 갑작스럽게 변화되고 (신생아의) 몸에서 탯줄을 잘라냄으로써 유아는 엄마의 몸에서 독립이 된다. 그러나 이 독립은 두 몸이 분리된다는 개략적인 의미에서만 그렇다. 기능인인 의미에서 유아는 엄마의 일부로 남아 있다. 모든 중요한 점[단계]에서 엄마는 아이에게 먹을 것을 주고, 안고 다니고, 보살핀다. 아이는 서서히 엄마와 다른 물체를 자신과는 다른 존재라고 여기게 된다. 이 과정의 한 요소는 아이가 신경의 면에서, 또 전체적인 신체의 면에서 성장하고, 또 신체적으로 정신적으로 물체를 움켜쥐며[이해하며], 그것들을 장악하는 능력이다. 자신의 행동을 통하여 아이는 자신의 외부 세계를 경험한다. 사람이 되는 과정은 교육 과정에 의해서 더욱 촉진된다. 이 과정에는 수많은 욕구 불만과 금지 사항들이 필연적으로 뒤따르게 되고, 이렇게 됨으로써 엄마의 역할은 아이의 욕구와 갈등을 겪는 상이한 목표를 지닌 사람의 역할, 또는 종종 적의를 품고 위험한 인간의 역할로 변화한다. 전체는 결코 아니지만 교육 과정의 일부인 이 적대 관계는 "나"와 "당신" 사이의 차이점을 분명히 하는 데 있어서 중요한 요소이다.

353 국제 정부[세계 정부]를 바라는 이유는 두 가지이다. 첫째는 전쟁의 예방이고, 둘째 이유는 서로 다른 국가들 사이에서와 서로 다른 민족들 사이에서처럼 경제 정의를 확보하는 것이다. 이 두 이유 중에서 전쟁의 예방이 더 중요한데, 그것은 전쟁이 (특히 앞으로 발생한다면) 불공평보다 더 해롭기 때문이며, 또한 더 큰 불공평의 형태들이 전쟁의 결과로서가 아니면 문명국들에게는 종종 가해지지 않을 것이라는 이유 때문이다. 예를 들어 평화가 깊게 자리 잡은 시대에는 한 나라에게서 그 생계 수단을 빼앗고 동시에, 오스트리아의 경우에서처럼, 그 인구가 이민 나가는 것을 막는 것이 흔하지 않을 것이다. 만약에 평화가 유지될 수 있으면, 어느 정도의 정의는 궁극적으로 나타날 가능성이 많다. 상당량의 불공평이 남게 된다 하더라도 안전한 평화 시에 가장 불행한 민족도 빈번한 전쟁 시에 가장 행복한 민족보다는 더 나을 가능성이 많다. 따라서 우리는 국제 정부 설립을 전쟁 억제의 관점에서 주로 고려하고, 단지 이차적으로만 국가 간의 공정성의 입장에서 고려해야 한다. 앞으로 보게 되겠지만 국제 정부에 대한 가장 그럴듯한 접근 방식 중 어떠한 것들은 긴 세월 동안 상당한 불공평[부당함]을 수반할 것이기 때문에 이

점은 중요하다.

354 적어도 아리스토텔레스만큼 오래된 하나의 철학 원리는, 공평성은 우리가 평등한 자들은 평등하게, 불평등한 자들은 불평등하게 취급함을 요구한다고 이야기한다. 그렇다면 문제는 다음처럼 귀결되는데, 그것은 시민으로서 우리가 어느 면에서 평등하고, 또 어느 면에서 당연히 올바르게 불평등한가이다. 독립선언문으로 돌아가 보자. "우리는 모든 사람이 평등하게 태어났고, 누구나 조물주에게서 일정한 양도할 수 없는 권리를 부여받았으며, 이 권리에는 생존권과 자유를 누릴 권리와 행복추구권이 포함된다는 진리를 자명한 것으로 받아들인다." 평등의 원래 상태가 아무리 완벽하다고 해도, 사람들에게 자신의 행복을 추구할 권리를 주어 보라. 그러면 얼마 가지 않아 필연적으로 중대한 불평등이 나타날 것이다. 이것이 잘못된 일인가? 반드시 그렇지는 않다. 그러나 그것은 성취라는 미국 정치 문화의 또 다른 중심적인 가치를 지적한다. 성취할 자유가 있고 성취에 대해 보상을 받는 것은 미국인들에게 평등만큼 중요하다. 응원단장 적격 시험에서부터 민첩한 주식 포트폴리오 관리에 이르기까지 성취는 인정받고 보상 받을 자격이 있다고 우리는 믿는다. 성취를 이루고 성취에 대해 부당하게 보상 받는 자유는 평등에 모순되고 경쟁적인 가치. 이 충돌하는 가치들 중에서 우리는 어느 것을 선택해야 하는가?

355 할리우드에서 제작되는 거의 모든 영화의 특징은 내적으로 공허하다는 점이다. 이 공허함은 외적인 번지르르함에 의해서 보상이 되고 있다. 그러한 외적으로 번지르르한 인상은 정말로 웅장한 사실적인 모습의 형태를 보통 띠고 있다. 세팅과 의상, 모든 표면적인 세부 항목을 올바르게 하는 데에는 아무것도 아끼지 않는다. 이러한 노력은 인물 묘사의 필연적인 공허함과 플롯의 모순점과 사소한 점들을 가리는 데 도움이 된다. 집들은 정말 집들처럼 보이고, 거리는 정말 거리처럼 보이며, 사람들은 사람들처럼 보이고 또 그렇게 대화를 나누지만, 그것들은 인간성과 믿음성과 동기가 결여되어 있다. 두말할 필요도 없이 수치스러운 검열 규정이 이 영화들의 내용을 미리 정해 주는 중요한 요소들이다. 그러나 이 법규는 영화가 노리는 이득이나 오락적인 가치를 방해하지는 않는다. 단지 이 영화들이 믿을 만한 영화가 되지 못하게끔 하는 데 도움을 줄 뿐이다. 그것은 영화 산업이 참아 내기에 그렇게 힘든 짐이 아니다. 세팅의 화려한 모습 외에도 가끔은 마술적인 것처럼 보이는 카메라의 이용도 있다. 그러나 전달하고자 하는 이야기, 삶의 모습이 공허하고 어리석고 진부하고 유치하다면 효과를

PART ❸
Advanced Reading

내려는 이 모든 기술, 이 모든 노력, 이 모든 에너지가 인간적으로 무슨 의미가 있는가?

356 훌륭한 교사는 평범한 교사 혹은 이류의 교사가 전혀 느끼지 못하는, 자신의 직업 속에 내재하는 극적 가능성을 의식적으로든 무의식적으로든 인식한다. 그는 학생들을 위해서 쇼를 벌이는 것을 위신이 깎이는 일이라고 생각하지 않는다. 사실 그가 그렇게 하고자만 한다면 그렇게 하지 않을 수가 없고, 그래서 그와 그가 가르치는 것은 분리할 수 없을 정도로 혼연일체가 된다. 따라서 그가 벌이는 쇼는 자기 자신에 대한 것이 아니다. 그렇지 않다면 그는 우스꽝스러워지고 그가 가르치는 것은 공허하고 쓸모없는 것이 된다. 모든 훌륭한 교사들은 학생들뿐만 아니라 자신도 즐겁게 할 수 있는 경험을 잘 알고 있는데, 이것은 그들이 자신들보다 훨씬 위대한 사람—유클리드나 셰익스피어나 플라톤이나 또는 자신들에게 힘과 삶을 제공해 준 그 밖의 누구든—의 역할을 하고 있다는 사실을 보여 주는 증거이다. 형편없거나 평범한 교사가 가르치는 학급에서는 언제나 세 가지 뚜렷이 구별되는 요소가 존재한다. 즉 교사, 그가 가르치려고 애쓰는 과목이나 자료, 그리고 학생들이다. 훌륭한 교사가 가르치는 학급에서는 그러한 구별이 없다. 마치 훌륭한 연극을 볼 때 관객이 두 시간 동안 배우도 되고 극작가도 되는 것처럼, 선생님이 학생들과 자신을 위해서 설명해 주고 재창조해 내기도 하는 것을 공통으로 소유한다는 점에서 학생들은 선생님과 한마음이 된다.

357 현대는 회의적인 시대이다. 그러나 우리의 조상들이 열렬히 신봉하였던 많은 것들에 대한 우리의 믿음이 약화되기는 하였지만, 약병 하나가 갖는 치료적인 속성에 대한 우리의 신임은 아버지 대의 믿음과 마찬가지로 변하지 않고 있다. 의약에 대한 오늘날의 이러한 신임은 의료기관에 집계된 1년 동안의 총 의약품 값 청구서가 천문학적인 숫자에 이르고 현재로서는 이것의 상승이 멈출 기미가 없다는 사실에 의해 입증이 된다. 병원의 외래환자 진료소에 다니는 대부분의 환자들은 물약 한 병, 한 통의 정제약, 조그마한 연고제라는 형태로 나타나는 어느 정도의 실체적인 치료약을 받아들고서 집에 돌아오지 못하면 적절한 치료를 받지 못했다고 느끼며, 각 과(科)를 담당하고 있는 의사는 환자들이 요구하는 이 요구품을 제공할 준비가 너무 많이 되어 있다. 환자들이 요구하는 약을 주는 것 말고는 환자들을 떨쳐 버리는 보다 빠른 방법은 없으며, 의료기관에 근무하는 대부분의 의사들은 과로하고 있고, 다이어트를 한다든지, 바른 생활 태도를 갖는다든지, 나쁜 습관을 떨쳐 버리는 필요 등의 주제에 관하여 시간이 걸리고 별로 인정받지도 못하는 충고를 해 줄

시간이 거의 없어서, 물약 한 병, 정제약 한 통, 연고제 등이 거의 언제나 환자들에게 투여되고 있는 것이다.

358 역사적으로 이야기하여 민주주의는 매우 최근의 일이다. 우선 민주주의는 개개의 인간이 국가나 국가 전체의 부, 그 밖의 다른 어떠한 것보다 더 중요하다고 하는 믿음이다. 그렇게 되면 민주주의는, 모든 사람이 똑같다거나 똑같이 재능을 부여받았다는 분명히 잘못된 의미에서가 아니라, 모든 사람이 일정한 기본적인 기회를 지녀야 한다는 의미에서 평등에 대한 믿음인 것이다. 18세기 유럽의 정치이론가들은 이것을 '천부인권'의 관점에서 생각하였고, 미국의 헌법은 이것을 '삶을 누릴 권리, 자유, 행복의 추구'로 이야기하고 있다. 오늘날에는 '특권과 기회'라는 표현을 더 사용하는 경향이 있다. 각 시대가 (18세기 유럽이든, 미국의 헌법이든, 오늘날이든) 의미했던 바는, 모든 사람이 출생이나 행운 등의 우연한 팔자에 관계없이 개개인이 인간으로서 잘 발전할 수 있는 똑같은 기회를 지녀야 한다는 것이다. 민주주의 이상은 또한 정부는 국민에게 이득을 줄 뿐만 아니라 국민 전체를 대변하기 위해 존재해야 한다는 믿음이다. 따라서 민주주의는, (국민의) 동의에 의한 정치를 전제로 하기 때문에 인내심을 가져야 함을 의미하며, 평등을 전제로 하기 때문에 동등한 기회의 부여를 의미하여, 개인으로서 남녀의 궁극적인 가치를 전제로 하기 때문에 자유를 의미한다.

359 중세가 끝나던 시기에 서양 사람들은 자신의 가장 예리한 꿈과 이상들을 마지막으로 달성하는 방향으로 나아가고 있는 것 같았다. 사람들은 전체주의적인 교회의 권위로부터, 전통적인 사고의 중압감으로부터, 또한 단지 지구의 절반밖에는 발견되지 않은 지리상의 제약으로부터 자신들을 해방시켰다. 그들은 결국 이때까지 들어 본 적이 없는 생산적인 힘을 궁극적으로 풀어 주고, 물질세계를 완전히 변형시킨 새로운 과학을 건설하였다. 그들은 개인의 자유롭고 생산적인 발전을 보장해 주는 것처럼 보이는 정치 제도를 만들어 냈다. 또한 선조들은 거의 꿈꾸어 보지도 못했을 정도로 여가 시간을 자유롭게 누릴 만큼 노동 시간도 단축하였다.

그렇다면 오늘날 우리는 어떠한 위치에 있는가?

모든 것을 파괴해 버리는 전쟁의 위협은 인류의 머리 위에 떠 있고, 이 위협은 이 글을 쓰고 있는 이 시간에도 널리 퍼져 있는 제네바 회담의 정신에 의해서도 결코 극복되지 않는 위협이다. 정치 대표자들이 전쟁을 피할 수 있을 만큼 충분한 제정신이 남아 있다고 해도, 인간이 현재 처한 상황은 16세기, 17세기, 18세기에 지녔던 희망을 전혀 성취할 수 없게끔 되어 버렸다.

360 텔레비전은 의사소통의 한 방편이다. 그것은 인쇄술의

46

발명만큼이나 혁명적이다. 인쇄술도 텔레비전도 그 자체로서는 아이디어라거나 힘이라거나 좋은 것이라거나 또는 나쁜 것이라거나 한 것은 아니다. 그것들은 단지 생각과 경험을 보다 많은 사람들에게 보다 빨리 전달하는 방법일 뿐이다. 전문적인 교육학자들이 이 새로운 방편(즉 텔레비전)에 그렇게 오랫동안 관심을 두기를 꺼려한 것은 아마도, 무엇이 가장 잘 전달될 수 있는 내용인지를 결정하는 텔레비전의 성격이 인쇄술의 성격과 매우 차이가 나기 때문이다.

인쇄술과 텔레비전은 제작자들에게는 비용이 많이 들고, 그것을 수용하는 사람에게는 비교적 값이 싸다는 점에서 분명히 닮은 점이 있다. 따라서 양자는 둘 다 수많은 사람들과 접촉하는 것에 의존하는 대중 매체이다. 인쇄된 글이 비교적 오래 가기 때문에 수세기에 걸쳐 같은 생각을 가진 많은 사람에게 전달될 수 있는 반면에, 텔레비전은 비교적 수명이 짧아서 그림과 글자를 사용하여 생각이 다른 수많은 사람들에게 같은 순간에 전달된다. 더구나 텔레비전은 글을 읽을 수 있는 사람들뿐만 아니라 글을 읽지 못하는 사람들에게도 호소력을 지닌다.

361 시를 듣고 이해하는 게 아름다움을 아는 거라는 이유만으로도 시는 알아볼 가치가 있다. 그리고 아직 당신이, 아름다움이 인생에 의미하는 것이 무엇이고, 아름다움이 없다면 인생이 어떠한 모습일까 하는 점을 알아내려고 하지 않았다면, 현명한 사람치고 그 점을 당신에게 이야기해 줄 준비가 되지 않은 사람은 현재로선 없을 것이다. 아름다움에 대한 사랑이 없다면 당신의 삶은 부가 있다 해도 보잘것없을 것이다. 영혼이 미덕을 기초로 해 번성하고 육체는 건강을 기초로 해 번성하듯, 마음은 아름다움을 앎으로써 살고 성장한다. 그리고 시는 아름다움의 한 형태일 뿐 아니라 많은 사람들에게는 인생과 예술 속에 존재하는 모든 아름다움으로 향하는 길을 찾아내는 수단이다. 여러분은 추한 것이 계속해서 증가하는 것처럼 보이고, 사람들이 자기 주변에 추악한 모습의 물건들을 갖는 것에 더욱더 만족해하는 것처럼 보이는 시대에 살고 있다. 따라서 여러분이 아직 찾아낼 수 있는 곳에서는 어디서나 아름다움을 알고 사랑하는 데 목표를 두는 것이 더욱 필요한 것이다. 시인이 표현한 바의 모습처럼 아름다움을 아는 것을 배울 수만 있다면, 여러분은 아름다움을 어디서나 보고 알도록 여러분의 마음을 훈련한 셈이 된다. 그렇게 해야만 여러분의 인생은 완벽해지고, 행복은 더할 나위 없는 것이 된다.

362 대학에 입학하는 자들의 절반이 안 되는 학생들만이 학위를 취득하는 것은 어찌된 영문인가? 학위 취득에 실패하는 학생들의 숫자를 보고 그들이 적절한 공부 기술이나 지적 능력이 부족하다고 가정해 볼 수 있을 것이다. 그러나 이 점은 몇몇 경우에만 들어맞는 이야기인데, 그것은 고등학교 때의 학업 성취도를 근거로 대학에 입학 허가를 받는 학생들은 어느 정도의 학문을 할 능력을 가지고 있음에 틀림없기 때문이다. 자발적으로 학교를 그만두는 숫자를 보고 학교 외부의 더 흥미로운 일들이 거역하기에 그 매력이 너무 크다고 가정해 볼 수도 있을 것이다. 그러나 이것도 단편적인 해답에 불과하다. 왜냐하면 대부분의 학생들은 대학 교육이 주는 이점과 장기적인 보상을 알 수 있기 때문이다. 진정한 해답은 학생들이 세우는 목표와 대학이 학생들을 위해 설정해 놓은 목표 사이의 차이점에 놓여 있다. 인정하든 안 하든 대부분의 학생들은 학위를 취득함으로써 얻게 된다고 생각되는 재정적인, 전문적인 사회적 보상을 얻기 위하여 가능한 한 빨리 학위를 얻기를 원한다. 그와는 반대로 대학은 교육을 단지 목적을 위한 수단으로서가 아니라 목적 그 자체로 본다. 따라서 지식을 그 자체를 위해서가 아니라 단지 그것이 가져올 물질적인 보상으로서 관심을 갖는 대다수의 학생들은 낙심을 하고, 어렵기도 하고, 또한 그들의 직업 선택에 분명한 관련이 없는 요구 조건(학과목의 이수 등등)을 완수하도록 강제하는 대학을 참아 내지 못하는 것이다.

363 서구의 대다수 사람들은 목적 없는(무의미한) 독서, 목적 없는 엿듣기, 목적 없는 영화 감상 등에 푹 빠져 있는데, 이것들은 알코올 중독과 모르핀 중독의 심리적 등가물이라고 할 수 있다. 오늘의 상황은, 만약에 며칠 또는 몇 시간 동안 신문, 라디오 음악, 영화 등을 보거나 듣지 못하게 되면 정말로 고통을 겪게 되는 남녀의 수가 수백만에 달하는 지경에 이르렀다. 마약 중독자처럼 그들은 그들의 악습을 충족시켜야 하는데, 그러한 충족이 실제적인 어떤 즐거움을 주어서가 아니라 그러한 일들을 하지 않으면 고통스러우리만치 비정상적이 되고 불충분함(불안)을 느끼기 때문이다. 신문, 영화, 라디오가 없을 때 그들은 축소된 삶을 산다. 스포츠 뉴스를 듣고 살인 추리극을 보며, 라디오 음악이나 토크쇼를 듣고, 대리 공포와 승리, 그리고 에로티즘을 느끼게 하는 영화 속에 파묻혀 있을 때에만 그들은 완벽하게 자신이 된다. 심지어 현명한 사람들조차도 그런 심리적인 중독이 피할 수 없는 것이거나 심지어 바람직한 것이라고 당연히 받아들이고 있으며, 대다수의 문명화된 남녀들이 지금 자신들의 정신적 수단을 기초로 살아갈 수 없고 외부에서 오는 끝없는 자극에 굴욕적으로 의존하게 되어 버린 사실에도 걱정할 만한 일이 없다고 당연히 받아들이고 있다.

364 인간의 신체는 12세의 나이에 가장 활기 있는 수준에

달한다. 아직은 전체의 몸집 크기와 힘이 더 뻗어 나가야 하고, 신체의 주인은 자신의 두뇌를 충분히 개발시켜야 하지만, 이 나이에 죽음의 가능성은 가장 희박하다. 12세 이전에 우리는 유아와 어린 소년, 소녀였고, 결과적으로 보다 상처 입기 쉬웠다. 12세 이후에는 정력과 저항력의 지속적인 상실을 겪게 되는데, 이 상실은 처음에는 잘 느껴지지 않지만 결국에는 매우 급격한 하향 추세를 이루어 우리가 자신을 아무리 잘 돌보고, 사회와 의사들이 우리를 아무리 잘 돌보아 주어도 우리는 더 살지 못한다. 시간이 경과함에 따라 나타나는 이와 같은 정력의 상실은 노화라고 불린다. 우리가 이러한 식으로 노쇠하여 가고, 전쟁과 사고와 질병을 피한다 하더라도 결국에는 노령으로 죽게 되고, 이것은 사람과 사람에 따라 별 차이 없는 속도로 진행되어서 65세에서 80세 사이에서 죽게 될 가능성이 많다는 사실은 우리 모두가 알게 되는 대단히 유쾌하지 못한 발견 중의 하나이다. 어떤 사람들은 그보다 일찍 죽게 되고, 또 소수의 사람들은 그보다 더 오래 살아서 90세나 100세가 될 수도 있다. 그러나 그럴 가능성은 많지 않고, 우리가 아무리 운이 좋고 아무리 체격이 건장하다 해도 얼마나 오래 살까 하고 희망하는 데에는 실질적으로 한계가 있다.

365 다른 곳에서 무슨 일이 일어나고 있는지를 우리는 모른다. 그러나 우주에 우리보다 더 나은 존재가 없다는 것은 사실이 아닌 것 같다. 지혜가 늘어남에 따라 우리의 생각들은 공간적, 시간적으로 더 넓은 시야를 획득한다. 어린아이는 분 단위로 살고, 소년은 하루 단위로 살며, 본능적인 성인은 1년 단위로 산다. 또 역사의식에 고취된 사람은 시대 단위로 산다. 스피노자는 우리가 분 단위, 하루 단위, 연 단위 또는 시대 단위가 아닌 영원 속에 살기를 원했다. 이것을 배우는 사람들은 그렇게 함으로써 미친 듯 날뛰는 성격의 불행을 떨치고 엄청난 재앙의 힘으로 다가오는 광기의 성향을 막을 수 있음을 알게 될 것이다. 스피노자는 생애의 마지막 날을 그를 초대한 주인에게 재미있는 일화들을 이야기하며 보냈다. 그는 '자유인은 죽음에 대해 거의 생각하지 않으며 그의 지혜는 죽음이 아닌 삶에 대한 명상이다'라고 이야기하였다. 그리고 자신의 죽음에 이르러 이 교훈을 실천하였다. 내가 뜻하는 바는, 무지의 독재에서 자유로워진 사람은 감정이 없을 것이라는 말이 아니라, 그와 반대로 개인적 걱정거리들에서 벗어나지 못한 사람보다 그가 우정과 자비와 동정심을 더 많이 느끼게 될 것이라는 말이다.

366 활동이 없으면 행복해지기가 불가능하지만, 그 활동이 지나치거나 반감을 사는 유형일 경우에 행복해지는 것은 역시 불가능하다. 활동은 그것이

매우 분명하게 바람직한 목표로 방향을 설정하고 그 자체가 욕구에 반하지 않을 때에 유쾌해진다. 개는 토끼를 완전히 지칠 때까지 뒤쫓아 가면서 그 시간 동안 줄곧 행복할 것이지만, 만약에 그 개를 쳇바퀴 위에 올려놓고 반 시간 후에 맛있는 음식을 준다면 그 음식을 받을 때까지 행복하지는 않을 것이다. 왜냐하면 개는 그 시간 동안 통상적인[자연스러운] 활동에 참여한 것이 아니기 때문이다. 우리 시대의 어려움들 중 하나는, 복잡한 현대사회에서 행해져야 할 일들 중에서 사냥에서 보는 자연스러움을 지니는 일이 거의 없다는 것이다. 그 결과로, 기술이 진보된 사회에서 대부분의 사람들은 그들의 행복을 생계를 꾸려가는 일 밖에서 찾아야 한다. 그리고 만약에 하는 일이 기운을 소진시키는 일일 경우 그들의 즐거움은 수동적인 성향을 지닐 것이다. 축구 구경을 하거나 영화를 보러 가는 것은 나중에 만족을 거의 주지 못하고 창의적인 욕구를 결코 만족시키지 못한다. 활동적인 선수들의 만족은 전혀 다른 종류의 것이다.

367 문명화된 사회가 있은 이후로 인류는 두 가지 다른 종류의 문제에 직면해 왔다. 한편으로는 자연력을 장악하고, 그리고 연장과 무기를 만들어 내는 데 필요하고 유용한 동식물을 만들어 내도록 자연을 장려하는 데 필요한 지식과 기술을 습득해야 하는 문제가 있어 왔다. 현대 세계에서 이 문제는 과학과 과학 기술에 의해 다루어지며, 또한 지금까지의 경험을 통해 보면 이 문제를 적절히 다루기 위해서는 좁은 범위의 전문가들을 많이 훈련시킬 필요가 있다. 그러나 첫 번째 문제보다 덜 명확하고 어떤 사람들한테는 중요하지 않은 것으로 잘못 인식되고 있는 두 번째의 문제가 있는데, 내 말은 자연력에 대한 우리의 운용력을 어떻게 하면 가장 잘 이용하느냐 하는 문제이다. 여기에는 민주주의 대 독재 정치, 자본주의 대 사회주의, 국제 정부 대 국제 무정부, 자유로운 사유 대 권위주의적 교리 등의 중대한 문제들이 포함된다. 그러한 문제에 대해 실험실은 어떠한 결정적인 지침도 주지 못한다. 그러한 문제를 푸는 데 가장 큰 도움을 주는 지식은 현재뿐만 아니라 과거에 있어서 인간의 삶을 널리 조사하고, 역사에 나타난 모습대로 불행이나 만족의 근원을 잘 이해하는 것이다.

368 산업화의 삶이라는 조직에서 공장이 노동자들의 생리 상태와 정신 상태에 미치는 영향은 완전히 무시되어 왔다. 근대 산업은 개인이나 개인의 집단이 가능한 한 많은 돈을 벌 수 있도록 최소의 비용으로 최대의 효과를 얻어내는 개념 위에 기초를 두고 있다. 근대 산업은 기계를 돌리는 인간들의 본성에 대한 아무 생각도 없이, 공장에 의해서 부과된 인위적인 생활 양식이 개인과 그 후손에 미치는 영향을

전혀 고려하지 않고서 팽창되어 왔다. 대도시들은 우리들을 전혀 염두에 두지 않고 건설되어 왔다. 마천루의 형태와 크기는 1평방피트당 최대의 수입을 확보하려는 필요성에 전적으로 의지하고 있고, 또한 입주자들에게 그들의 기호에 맞는 사무실과 아파트를 제공한다는 요성에 전적으로 의지하고 있다. 이로 인하여 너무 많은 사람들이 한꺼번에 몰려 북적대는 엄청나게 큰 건물들이 지어지게 되었다. 문명화된 사람들은 그러한 생활 방식을 좋아한다. 그들은 자신들이 거처하는 주택의 안락함과 진부한 사치를 즐기고는 있지만, 그들은 삶의 필수 요소들을 빼앗기고 있음을 인식하지는 못한다. 현대의 도시는 괴물 같은 건축물과 매연과 석탄의 분진과 유독성 가스로 가득 차고, 택시와 화물 자동차와 버스가 내는 소음에 찢기며, 엄청난 군중들이 떼지어 모여드는 어둠침침하고 비좁은 거리로 구성이 되어 있다. 분명히 이 현대 도시는 그곳에 살고 있는 주민들의 이익을 위해 설계된 것은 아니다.

369 스포츠는 국가들 사이의 우호 관계를 만들어 내고, 따라서 만약에 세계의 모든 민족들이 축구 경기나 크리켓 경기에서 만날 수만 있다면 전쟁터에서 만나고 싶은 마음은 없어질 것이라고 사람들이 말하는 것을 들으면 나는 언제나 놀란다. 우리가 구체적인 예(가령 1936년 올림픽 경기)를 통하여 국제적인 스포츠 경기가 증오의 난장판을 가져오는지 알 수는 없다고 하더라도, 그럴 수 있다는 것을 일반적인 원칙을 통하여 추론해 볼 수는 있을 것이다.
　오늘날 행해지고 있는 거의 모든 경기는 경쟁적이다. 여러분은 이기기 위하여 경기를 하며, 이기기 위하여 최선을 다하지 않으면 경기는 거의 의미가 없다. 마을의 푸른 들판에서 편을 갈라 경기하고 지역적 애국심[애향심]의 감정이 끼어들지 않으면, 단지 즐거움을 느끼고 운동을 할 목적으로 경기를 할 수는 있다. 그러나 위신의 문제가 끼어들고, 당신과 (당신이 속한) 더 큰 편이 경기에 지면 불명예스러운 일이 된다고 느끼자마자 가장 야만적인 투쟁 본능이 생겨나게 된다. 학교 대항 축구 시합에서 경기를 해 본 사람이면 누구나 이 점을 알고 있다. 국제적인 수준에서 보면 스포츠는 솔직히 말해 모의 전투이다. 그러나 중요한 점은 선수들의 태도가 아니라 관중들의 태도이다. 또한 관중들 뒤에서 스스로 차츰차츰 흥분하여 이 얼토당토않은 시합에 분노를 터뜨리고, 어쨌든 (경기가 진행되는) 짧은 시간 동안이나마 달리고, 뛰어오르고, 볼을 차는 것이 국가적 우월성을 시험하는 것이라고 심각하게 믿는 국가들의 태도가 문제다.

370 우리 몸에 의해 흡수되며 가장 널리 퍼져 있고 위험한 물질 중의 하나가 '스트론티움 90'이라는 것은 잘

알려진 사실이다. 그것은 뼛속에 쌓이고 적혈구와 백혈구가 만들어지는 적색골수 세포로 그 광선을 분출한다. 방사선이 너무 많을 때 대부분의 경우 치명적인 골육병[백혈병]이 그 결과로 나타난다. 재생기관의 세포가 이에 특히 민감하다. 비교적 미약한 방사선조차도 치명적인 결과를 가져올 수 있다. 인체 밖의 방사선뿐만 아니라 체내 방사선의 가장 불길한 면은 수년의 세월이 지나서야 흉악한 결과들이 나타난다는 점이다. 사실 이 나쁜 결과들은 첫 세대 또는 둘째 세대가 아닌 그 다음 세대에 나타난다. 앞으로 수세기에 걸쳐 세대마다 정신적으로나 육체적으로 결손을 지닌 아이들이 계속해서 증가하는 추세로 나타나게 될 것이다. 수천 명의 아이들이 가장 심각한 정신적, 육체적 결손을 지닌 채 태어날지도 모르는 가능성에 대비해야 하는 우리의 책임을 무시해서는 안 된다. 우리가 그러한 가능성을 알지 못했다고 나중에 이야기해 보아야 결코 변명이 될 수 없다. 불구의 몸으로 아이가 태어나는 순간에 접해 보지 못했거나, 그 아이의 어머니가 처량하게 우는 것을 보지 못한 자들만이 핵 실험의 위험은 별것이 아니라고 감히 주장할 수 있을 것이다. 유명한 프랑스 생물학자 겸 유전학자인 장 로스탕은 핵 실험을 계속하는 것을 "미래에 대한 범죄"라고 부른다. 미래에 대한 이 범죄를 막는 일은 여성의 특별한 책임이다. 여성들은 자신들의 목소리가 들리도록 이 범죄에 반대하는 목청을 높여야 한다.

371 인류가 처음으로 글을 쓰는 법을 배운 근동 지방에서 5천 년 전에 일어난 일들을 우리는 책을 읽어서 알 수 있다. 그러나 지금도 세계의 어떤 지역에는 글을 쓸 줄 모르는 사람들이 있다. 그들이 자신들의 역사를 보존할 수 있는 유일한 방법은, 그것을 한 세대의 이야기꾼들로부터 다른 세대의 이야기꾼들에게 전해져 내려오는 전설인 역사 이야기로 바꾸어 이야기하는 것이다. 이 전설들은 그렇게 오래 전에 살았던 사람들의 이주에 관하여 우리들에게 무엇인가를 이야기해 줄 수 있기 때문에 유용하지만, 누구도 자신이 행한 일들을 기록할 수는 없었다. 지금은 태평양에 떠 있는 여러 섬에 흩어져 살고 있는 폴리네시아 종족들의 먼 조상들이 어디에서 왔는지 인류학자들은 의문을 갖는다. 이 종족들의 역사 이야기는 그들 중 몇몇 종족이 2천 년 전에 인도네시아에서 왔다는 점을 알려 준다. 그러나 오늘날 우리의 모습과 비슷한 모습을 한 첫 번째 종족은 너무 오래 전에 살아서 그들의 역사 이야기조차도, 만약에 그러한 것들이 있었다고 해도, 잊고 존재하지 않는다. 따라서 고고학자들은 첫 번째 '현대인'이 어디서 유래하였는지를 알아내는 데 도움이 될 역사도 전설도 갖지 못하고 있다. 그러나 다행히 고대인들은 돌로 연장, 특히 부싯돌을 만들어

냈는데, 그것은 이것이 다른 것들보다 만들기 쉽기 때문이다. 그들이 나무나 동물 가죽들을 이용했을 수도 있지만 이러한 것들은 다 썩어 없어졌다. 돌은 썩지 않으며, 따라서 오래 전에 돌로 만든 연장들은 그것을 만든 사람들의 뼈가 흔적도 없이 사라지고 없음에도 불구하고 아직도 남아 있다.

372 전 서구 사회의 지식계층의 삶이 점점 두 개의 정반대 집단으로 나뉘고 있다고 나는 믿는다. 내가 지식계층의 삶이라고 말할 때는 우리의 실용적인 삶의 상당 부분을 포함한다는 뜻이다. 왜냐하면 가장 심오한 의미에서 두 집단이 구분될 수 있다고 시사할 사람이 나는 결코 아니기 때문이다. 두 개의 양극 집단은 그 한쪽 끝에 문학가들이 있고 또 다른 한 끝에는 과학자들, 가장 대표적으로는 물리학자들이 있다. 양 그룹 사이에는 상호 불이해의 넘을 수 없는 한계가 있는데 가끔은, 특히 젊은이들 사이에서, 적대감과 혐오감이 존재하고, 무엇보다도 이해의 부족이 존재한다. 그들은 상대에 대해 이상하게도 왜곡된 인상을 가지고 있다. 그들의 태도는 매우 달라서 정서적인 측면에서만 보더라도 공통의 장을 그다지 찾을 수 없다. 비과학자들은 과학자들을 건방지고 허풍이 센 것으로 생각하는 경향이 있다. 그들은 과학자들은 천박스럽게 낙천적이고 인간의 조건을 깨닫지 못하고 있다는 뿌리 깊은 믿음을 가지고 있다. 한편 과학자들은 문학가들이 전혀 선견이 없고 동료의 문제에 특히 관심이 없으며, 깊은 의미에서 반 지성적이고, 예술과 사고를 현재의 순간[실존의 면]에만 국한시키려 안달하고 있다고 믿고 있다. 양자에게는 각각 전적으로 근거 없는 것은 아닌 무엇인가가 있다. 그것은 모든 것을 파괴하는 성질을 띠고 있으며 그것의 상당 부분은 위험한 (상호) 불이해 위에 기초하고 있다.

373 산업화가 가져온 가장 중요한 결과 중의 하나는 여성 고용으로 인해 가정이 붕괴되었다는 점이다. 여성 고용은 두 가지 결과를 가져왔는데, 한편으로는 여성이 남성으로부터 경제적으로 독립하게 되어 남성의 예속물이 더 이상 아니라는 점이고, 또 다른 한편으로는 여성들 스스로가 아이들을 양육하기가 어렵게 되었다는 점이다. 일부일처 가족 전통이 모든 주요한 산업국에서 대단히 강하여, 산업화가 가정에 미친 영향은 그것이 모습을 드러내기까지 오랜 시간이 걸렸다. 기독교가 아직 흔한 미국에서는 지금도 그 영향력은 모습을 거의 드러내지 않았다. 그러나 유럽 전체에서는 이미 시작된 가정 붕괴의 과정은 전쟁 때문에 엄청나게 가속화되었는데, 이것은 여성들이 정부 직책이나 군수품 공장이나 농지에서 일자리를 잡기가 쉬워졌기 때문이다. 지금까지의 경험으로 미루어 볼 때, 보통의 여성은 경제적으로

독립할 수 있게 되면 구식의 결혼 제약에 복종하거나 한 남자에게 충실하지는 않을 것이다. 우선은 전통적인 도덕률을 옹호하는 자들에 의해 부과되는 제약과 은폐들은 이렇게 나타난 변화의 정도를 약간은 모호하게 해 놓았다. 그러나 시간이 경과함이 따라 변화는 더욱 커질 것인데, 그것은 변화가 산업화의 본질적인 경향에 속하기 때문이다. 산업화 이전의 사회에서 부자들은 자신들의 아내를 재산으로 취급하였고, 가난한 사람들은 그들이 하는 일의 협동자로 보았다. 여성 농부들은 어려운 농사일을 많이 하고, 여성 근로자들은 지금까지 자신들의 시간을 가사나 아이들의 양육에 다 바쳐 왔다. 이렇게 하여 도시나 시골에서 가정은 하나의 경제 단위가 되었다.

374 오늘날의 부모들은 자신들의 어린 자식들을 위해 옛날에 그렇게 한 것보다 훨씬 적은 일을 해야 하고 가정은 작업장의 성격을 훨씬 덜 띠게 되었다. 옷은 기성복으로 사 입을 수가 있고, 빨래는 세탁실에서 할 수가 있고, 먹을 것은 이미 요리되고, 통조림으로 만들어져 있고, 빵은 이미 구워져서 빵 장수가 집까지 배달해 주며, 우유가 문간에 (매일 아침) 배달되고, 식사는 식당이나, 작업장의 매점이나 학교의 식당에서 할 수가 있는 상황에 이르렀다.

아버지가 자신의 생업이나 또 다른 일들을 집에서 하는 경우는 오늘날에는 드물게 되었고, 따라서 자신들의 아버지가 작업장에서 일을 하는 모습을 설령 본다 해도, 보는 경우는 극히 드물다. 사내 자식들은 따라서 아버지의 직업을 계승하도록 훈련을 받는 경우가 거의 없고, 도시에 가면 꽤 여러 가지 직업들 중에서 하나를 선택할 수가 있으며, 이것은 딸들의 경우에도 마찬가지이다. 젊은 노동자들은 종종 상당한 돈을 벌게 되고 이내 경제적으로 독립하게 되었다는 감정을 얻게 된다. 섬유 산업 분야에서는 어머니들이 작업장에 나가는 것이 관례화되어 버렸고, 이러한 상황은 매우 널리 퍼져서 일하는 엄마는 어린이의 가정생활에서 이제는 드문 현상이 아니다. 왜냐하면 기혼 여성이 일자리에 고용된 숫자가 지난 25년 동안에 두 배 이상으로 늘어났기 때문이다. 어머니가 돈을 벌고 조금은 나이가 든 자식들이 상당한 임금을 벌어들이고 있음으로, 아버지는 금세기 초엽에만 하더라도 아직은 누리고 있던 가정에서 영향력이 센 존재가 거의 되지 못하고 있다. 어머니가 일을 하게 되면 경제적인 이득은 생기지만, 만약에 어머니들의 고용으로 인하여 아이들이 학교에서 돌아왔을 때 맞이해 줄 어머니가 집에 없게 된다면 아이들은 대단히 귀중한 무엇을 잃게 되는 것이다.

375 한 나라가 산업화의 초기 단계에 있을 때 경제 조직이 소수에 의해 운용되는 독재적 성격을 띠고,

50

더 선진화된 국가로부터 많은 것을 빌려오지 못하면 대다수 국민은 매우 가난해질 수밖에 없음은 거의 필연적인 것 같다. 우선 가난의 문제를 들어 보자. 한 나라가 아직은 산업화가 되지 못한 경우 그 생산 방식은 고도로 효율적일 수 없고, 보통은 생존의 수준을 넘어서서 커다란 흑자를 생산해 내지 못한다. 그러한 나라에서 산업 개발을 향한 운동의 첫째 효과는 수많은 근로자들을 즉각적으로 생산이 가능한 작업 분야에서 뽑아내 철도를 건설하거나 기계를 만드는 일에 투입하거나, 또는 기계를 사올 수 있거나 강철레일 같은 물건을 제조하는 다른 나라에 그들의 농작물을 수출하는 것이다. 그 결과는 처음에는 분배할 수 있는 소비재의 양이 줄어든다는 것이다. (나라가 아직은 산업화가 되지 않은 연유로) 국민들에게 나눠 줄 것이 많지 않기 때문에, (소비재) 축소의 결과는 일반 근로자들에게 심각한 가난을 가져다줄 것이다. 이것을 피하는 유일한 길은 산업화를 아주 느리게 진행하거나 선진국들로부터 많이 차입을 하는 것이다. 후자의 방법은 선진국과의 관계가 우호적일 때 보통 채택되는 방편이다. 그러나 러시아의 경우처럼 적대 관계로 인해 차입이 불가능할 때에는 엄청난 가난 또한 매우 느린 속도의 산업화라는 선택의 여지만 남아 있다.

376 18세기 자본주의 제창자들에 의하면 이상적인 자본주의 사회는 시장의 한 부분을 점하기 위해 경쟁하는 많은 소기업으로 구성되는 것이라고 하였다. 이 사회에서 정부는 도로를 건설하고 유지·보수하며, 외교 정책을 수행하고, 국가 방위에 대비하며, 법을 집행하는 것과 같은 여러 가지 공공기능을 수행하는 작은 역할을 하게 된다. 미국의 많은 초기 지도자들에 의해 지지를 받은 최소한의 정부라는 이 자유 자본주의 개념에서 보면, 정부는 자유에 대한 주요한 위협으로 간주되었다. 이 견해에 의하면 자신이 원하는 대로 사업을 하는 자유는 양심의 자유와 언론의 자유에 연관되어 있었다. 이상적인 정부는 "밤의 파수꾼"—현존하는 재산 분배의 감시자—으로서 기능을 발휘하였다.

19세기 초에 들어와서 자유방임[규제되지 않은]의 자본주의는 사회를 정치적 탄압의 독재와 관료체제의 통제, 질식할 것 같은 전통에서 해방시키리라고 널리 믿어졌다. 자본주의는 정부로부터 하등의 의식적인 지시도 받지 않고 엄청난 부를 지닌 새로운 세상, 그리고 더욱 효율적이고 생산적인 경제를 창조해 낼 것이라고 많은 이론가들이 생각하였다. 가능한 최대의 이득을 얻으려 시도하는 과정에서 누구나 부를 창조해 내고 이것은 사회 전체에 이득을 줄 것이라고 믿었다. 다른 말로 해서 자기본위의 정신이 사회의 목표에 봉사할 것 같았다. 이와 같은 이상적인 자본주의 세계에서 개인은 사회적 신분, 피부 색깔,

성별 또는 종교라는 비경제상의 기준이 아니라 시장에서 그들의 기술이 갖는 가치인 자신들의 장점에 따라 평가되는 것이었다.

나름대로는 자본주의는 거의 즉시 성공하였다. 이 새로운 경제 제도는 재화의 생산과 분배를 혁신하였고 세계 무역을 촉진하였으며, 오래되고 종종은 억압적인 전통과 사회의 장벽을 무너뜨렸다. 자본주의라는 경제적 자유와 민주주의라는 정치적 자유는 수많은 사람들에게 완벽한 한 동아리를 이루었다.

377 인간들 사이의 경제적 관계뿐만 아니라 개인적 관계도 이 같은 소외의 성격을 띤다. 그 관계는 인간으로서 관계 대신에 사물 간의 관계라는 성격을 띤다. 그러나 인간이 도구가 되고 소외되어 버리는 이 사조의 아마도 가장 중요하고 가장 황폐한 경우는 개인이 자기 자신과 맺는 관계일 것이다. 인간은 상품을 팔 뿐만 아니라 자신을 팔고 자신이 상품이 되는 것을 느낀다. 육체노동자는 그의 육체 에너지를 팔고, 기업가, 의사, 사무직 근로자는 자신들의 "개성"을 판다. 자신의 생산품과 용역을 팔기 위해서는 그들의 개성을 지켜야 한다. 이 개성은 기분 좋은 것이어야 하고 그 외에도 그 소유자는 여러 가지 다른 요구 조건을 충족시켜야 한다. 즉 자신의 특수 위치가 요구하는 데 따라서 에너지, 솔선수범, 이것, 저것, 또는 그 밖의 것들을 가져야 한다. 다른 어떤 상품의 경우처럼 이 사람의 독특한 특질들, 심지어 그들의 존재 바로 그것까지도 값을 결정하는 것은 시장이다. 만약에 어떤 사람이 제공하는 특질이 쓸모가 없으면 그는 전혀 쓸모가 없다. 마치 한 물품이 이용 가치가 있을지 몰라도 팔리지 않으면 전혀 가치가 없듯이. 따라서 자신감, 즉 "자신에 대한 확실한 느낌"은 다른 사람들이 그 사람을 어떻게 생각하느냐의 표시일 뿐이다. 시장에서 인기가 있고 성공한 것과는 상관없이 자신의 가치를 확신하는 것은 그 사람이 아니다. 그를 찾는 자가 있다면 그는 상당한 존재이며, 만약 인기가 없다면 그는 단순히 별 볼 일 없는 존재이다. 자기 존중이 개성의 성공에 의존하는 것은, 현대인에게 인기가 이렇게 커다란 중요성을 갖는 이유이다. 어떤 사람이 실질적인 문제에서 앞으로 나아가느냐 아니냐의 문제뿐만 아니라 그가 자기존중을 계속 유지할 수 있느냐 아니냐, 혹은 열등감의 심연으로 떨어지느냐 아니냐의 문제는 이것에 달려 있다.

378 자유민주주의 개념은 약 300년 전에 정치사상 속으로 처음 들어왔는데, 그때는 왕의 권한과 시민의 권리에 대해 유럽에서 큰 논쟁이 한창이던 시기였다. 17~8세기의 군주들은 자신들이 "신권"으로 통치한다고 주장하였으나 초기 자유민주주의자들은 다른 유형의 정치사회를 마음에 그리고 있었다.

피통치자들의 동의에 기초를 둔 사회를 옹호하는 것 외에도 그들은 기본 인권, 시민들 사이의 평등, 압제 정부에 항의하고 반대할 수 있는 권리를 이야기하기 시작하였다.

그러나 군주 제도를 비난하는 이들은 결코 (어떤 의미에서도) 평등주의자들은 아니었다. 그들 중 많은 사람들은 소수의 잘사는 중류 계층의 동의에만 기초를 둔 정부를 원하였다. 모든 시민의 동의에 기초를 둔 사회를 기꺼이 옹호하고자 하는 자들은 극소수였다. 모든 사람이 정치적인 삶의 운명을 형성하는 데 (자신의) 목소리를 가져야 한다는 개념은 너무 급진적이어서 거의 생각해 볼 수 없는 것이었다. 지난 2세기 동안 민주주의를 얻기 위한 많은 투쟁들은 다음의 이슈에 직접적으로 초점이 모아졌다. 즉 피통치자들의 동의에 기초를 둔 정부는 누구의 동의를 구해야 하는가?

이 근대 민주주의의 이상들은 자본주의로 알려진 새로운 사회 경제제도와 제휴하여 발전되었다. 17~8세기의 성장하는 중류 계층들은 물건을 사고 팔고, 부를 축적하고, 그리고 정부의 간섭 없이 사업을 할 수 있는 완전한 자유를 얻기를 원하였다. 많은 관찰자들은 개인의 권리와 개인의 잠재력을 강조하는 자본주의가 발흥한 바로 그 이유 때문에 민주주의가 가능했다고 주장하여 왔다. 자본주의자들은 정부의 간섭에서 벗어나 사적인 삶의 한 부분을 개척해 나갈 수 있는 개인적 인권을 옹호하면서 정부의 권한을 제한하려고 고투하였다. 그러나 이러한 노력들이 민주주의의 이상들이 자리 잡을 수 있는 분위기를 만들어 내는 데 기여하였지만, 자본주의 경제 체계와 민주주의 정치 체계가 동시에 발전됨으로써 오늘날까지 지속되고 있는 문제들과 긴장들이 만들어졌다는 점에 유념해야 한다.

379 얄궂게도 거의 보편적인 호소력을 지닌 대의명분들— 예를 들어 깨끗한 공기와 안전한 소비재 등의 확보를 촉진하기 위한 운동들—은 종종 조직화하기가 가장 어렵다. 몇몇 관찰자들은 많은 사람이 공유하는 관심은 예상되는 지지자들의 상상력을 거의 잡지 못하고 따라서 조직을 통한 성공은 그들의 눈을 벗어난다고 주장한다. 그러한 운동에 몰두하고 있는 집단의 잠재적 구성원들에게는 그 집단에 참여하는 것이 어떻게 많은 차이를 가져올지를 내다보기가 어려울지 모른다. 다시 말하면 널리 퍼진 공적 이슈를 다루는 이익집단에 참여함으로써 얻는 보상보다는 그 집단에 참여하여 정보를 얻는 데 들어가는 비용이 보통 더 크다는 것이다. 그럼에도 불구하고 그러한 이익 집단들은 실제로 존재하고 종종 성공한다.

작은 문제에 초점을 맞추는 이익 집단들은 이와는 대조적으로, 단단한 지지를 얻을 수 있다. 하나의 특정한 공공정책에 직접적으로 영향을 입는 사람들은

조직을 꾸릴 강한 동기를 지니고 있기 때문이다. 예를 들어 안경 판매에서 경쟁을 허용하는 규정들이 제안되었다고 가정해 보자. 소비자들은 그러한 규정으로부터 이득을 얻을 것이지만, 그들의 대부분은 그러한 규정들이 자신들에게 어떻게 영향을 미칠지에 대해 흐릿한 생각만 가지고 있을 것이다. 그러나 안경 판매업자들은 결국 자신들로 하여금 안경 값을 내리도록 강요하게 될 규정에 반대하는 로비를 하기 위하여 조직을 결성할 것이다. 여기에서 우리는 이익 단체 정치라는 고질적인 문제를 보게 된다. 많은 사람들에게 미비하게 영향을 미치는, 거의 모두가 공유하는 이익은, 소수의 사람들에게 더 깊숙하게 영향을 미치는, 작은 문제에 초점을 맞춘 이익들에 비해 조직화된 반응을 얻을 가능성이 더 적다.

대부분의 이익 단체 활동이 지니는 은밀한 성격으로 부터 하나의 관련된 문제가 유래하는데, 그것은 영향력 추구의 과정이 종종 대중들에 의한 면밀한 조사가 이루어지지 않은 채 숨겨진다는 점이다. 이익 단체가 하는 로비는 압력을 가한 팔 비틀기보다 훨씬 더 은밀하게 파고들어가는 삼투성을 닮는다. 비평가들은 이 아늑한 움직임이 민주주의 행사에 대단히 중요한 공개적 토론을 막는다고 책망하면서 그것을 비난한다.

380 가장 기초적이고 솔직한 민주주의의 개념은 순수한 다수 지배의 개념이다. 이것은 대다수의 국민들이 특수한 정책 또는 지배자들에게 자신들의 동의를 주는 것을 의미한다. 국민들은 직접적으로 또는 국민의 이름으로, 통치하도록 선출된 대표자들을 통해서 그렇게 할 수 있다. 그러나 다수 지배를 통한 민주주의는 무리 없이 실현 가능하고 공정하며, 공평한 정치 제도를 가져다주는가? 예를 들어 다수는 일정한 종교와 정당들을 불법화시킬 결정을 내릴 수 있는가? 다수는 커다란 부를 가진 소수의 재산을 뺏을 수 있는가? 다수는 조리 있고 분별 있는 방식으로 정부를 운용할 수 있는가? 이러한 것들은 단순한 정의만으로 해답을 줄 수 없는 문제들이다. 그러나 이 문제들은 고대 그리스에서 시작된 이래로 다수 지배를 통한 민주주의에 대해 계속해서 던져진 바로 그 문제들이다.

다수 지배와 연관된 문제들이 처음으로 상당히 부각된 것은 아테네에서였다. 고대 아테네의 민주주의는 제비뽑기로 선출된 입법부의 형태를 가지고 있었는데, 이는 어느 시민이라도 봉사하도록 요청받을 수 있음을 의미하였다. 또한 민중법정이 있었는데 그 구성원들 역시 제비뽑기로 선출되었다. 공공정책의 기본 이슈들은 시민들이 경청하고 참여하며 마지막으로는 그 이슈들을 결정하는 투표를 하는 입법부에서 토의되었다. 아테네에서 다수 지배를 옹호하는 자들은 이 제도를 시민들이 정치적

결정 과정에서 자신의 목소리를 내도록 허용하는 방편으로 보았다. 다른 어떠한 조처도—민주 개혁 이전에 아테네에서 종종 있었던 경우처럼—권력을 부자나 출생 신분이 높은 사람들의 손에 배타적으로 놓을 것이라고 그들은 주장하였다. 민주주의의 신봉자들에게 아테네의 정치 제도는 국민을 무작위로 선출함으로써 사람들을 모으고 민중의 일에 합리적인 방식으로 관심을 갖게 할 수 있음을 보여 주었다. 어떤 사람들은 또한 아테네식의 (민주주의) 경험은 법을 만들고 집행하는 데 참여하는 사람들이 법을 더 잘 지키게끔 할 수 있음을 보여 주었다고 주장하였다. 민주주의는 보다 헌신적인 시민을 형성하는 데 기여하였다.

381 (A) eluded

쿼터백이 팔을 들어 공을 던졌다. 풀백이 공을 잡고서 태클을 피해 골라인을 향하여 돌진하였다. 그가 운동장의 모든 수비수들을 피해 이리저리 빠져나가는 것은 정말 멋진 질주였다.

quarterback (미식축구의) 쿼터백 **hurl** 던지다 **fullback** (미식축구의) 풀백 **grab** 움켜쥐다 **tackle** 태클 **avoid** 피하다 **defensive** 수비의 **elude** 피하다 **distil** 증류하다 **impair** 상하게 하다

382 (D) really does not exist

자유의 본질은 이론적 권리로서 그것의 존재가 아니라, 오히려 이 권리를 행사할 수 있는 가능성에 있다. 어떤 한 사람의 생계가 어느 일이나 닥치는 대로 움켜잡아야 할 만큼 변변치 못하다면, 그는 (그 일을) 선택하거나 망설일 기회 모두를 거부당하게 된다. 그럴 경우 그의 자유는 실제로 존재하지 않는다.

theoretical 이론적인 **right** 권리 **consist in** ~에 달려 있다 **exercise** 행사하다 **subsistence** 생계, 생존 **meager** 변변찮은 **seize** 잡다 **present oneself** 나타나다 **inalienable** 분리할 수 없는 **bargain** 흥정[거래]하다

Key Structure
so meager as to require ~ : ~을 요구할 만큼 변변치 못하다

383 (B) fortify

금세기에 지진으로 인하여 백만 명이 목숨을 잃었다고 전문가들은 말한다. 만약에 수십 억 명도 더 되는 주민들로 넘쳐나는 계획성 없이 퍼져 나가는 수십 개의 도시들을 강화하는[지진에 견디어내게끔 하는] 주요한 조치들을 취하지 않는다면, 다음 세기에는 지진 한 번에 백만 명을 잃게 되어 사망자가 10배나 될지도 모른다고 그들은 덧붙인다.

expert 전문가 **death** 사망자 **unless** 만약에 ~하지 않는다면 **sprawl** (도시 등이) 계획성 없이 퍼지다 **teem with** ~으로 가득 차다 **adorn** 장식하다 **fortify** 강화하다 **outshine** 능가하다 **uncover** 열다, 노출시키다

Key Structure
1. 10 times as many deaths : 10배나 많은 사망자
2. expected to teem with ~ : ~으로 가득 찰 것으로 예측되는

384 (B) mercy

증거가 소송 의뢰인에게 매우 불리하여 변호사는 배심원들이 그에게 분명히 유죄로 판결을 내릴 것이라고 생각하였다. 그는 그 의뢰인에게 자신의 유죄를 시인하고 판사의 재판을 받아 관대한 판결을 희망하도록 충고하였다.

client 소송 의뢰인 **jury** 배심원 **guilty** 유죄의 **plead** (법정에서 피고가 유죄·무죄라고) 답변하다 **trial** 재판 **judge** 판사 **appeal** 호소 **mercy** 자비, 관대함 **conviction** 신념 **acquittal** 무죄(방면)

385 (A) ugliness

산업 혁명이 가망이 없을 정도로 매력이 없고 영감을 주지 못하는 세상을 남겨 놓았다고 말하는 사람들이 있다. 그들의 말에 의하면, 현대의 예술가는 어려운 선택의 문제에 직면해 있는데, 그것은 그가 환상의 세계로 퇴각하든지 아니면 현실 세계에 직접 부딪쳐 자신의 예술에 세상의 추한 모습을 반영해야 하는 문제이다.

uninspiring 영감을 주지 못하는, 지루한 **be faced with** ~에 직면하다 **retreat** 퇴각하다, 되돌아가다 **fantasy** 환상 **reflect** 반영하다 **ugliness** 추함 **splendor** 호화, 웅장함

Key Structure
either he must ~ or he must... : ~하거나 아니면 …해야 한다

386 (C) subservient to authority

고대 아시아의 국가들은 절대군주제였다. 따라서 권위에 대한 복종은 정치적이며 사회적인 삶의 지배 원리였다. 그러나 고대 희랍인들은 공화주의 도시 국가를 형성하였는데, 이 국가에서는 사람들이 정부에 대하여 발언권을 갖고 약간의 자유를 가졌다. 그들은 신하가 아니라 시민이었다. 그들의 의무는 법을 지키는 것이지, 권위에 복종하는 것이 아니었다.

ancient 고대의 **absolute monarchy** 절대군주제 **obedience** 복종 **authority** 권위 **ruling principle** 지배 원리 **republican** 공화제의 **subject** 신하 **subservient** 복종하는

387 (B) In addition

비타민은 세 가지 주된 방법으로 음식에서 유실된다. 첫째로, 어떤 비타민들은 물에 녹는다. 채소를 물에 넣고 요리하면, 비타민이 물속에 녹아든다. 만약에 이 물을 버리면 비타민이 유실된다. 게다가 열, 빛, 산소도 몇몇 비타민들을 변화시킨다. 채소를 요리하면, 열이 몇몇 비타민을 변하게 한다. 이렇게 되면 이 비타민들은 더 이상 건강에 도움이 되지

않는다. 예를 들어, 그레이프프루트(자몽)를 끓이면, 비타민 C가 약간 파괴된다. 마지막으로 사람들은 비타민이 가장 많이 들어 있는 식물의 주된 부분을 버린다. 일례로, 밀가루를 가공 처리하면, 비타민이 매우 풍부한 맥아가 유실된다.

dissolve 녹다, 용해되다   oxygen 산소   grapefruit 그레이프프루트   flour 밀가루   process 가공 처리하다   wheat germ 맥아(麥芽)

388 (A) disappear

모든 인류 문명은 각각 그 자체가 영속하고 안정된 세계라고 여긴다. 우리가 박물관에서 보는 유물 하나하나가 이것을 증명한다. 자신의 기술로 이 물품들을 만들어 낸 사람은 그것들이 사라질 것이라는 점을 알았겠으나, 그들의 문화가 사라진다는 것이 생각할 수 없는 일이었을 것이다.

permanence 영속, 영원함   stability 안정(성)   item 물품   craftsmanship 솜씨, 기능   inconceivable 생각하지 못한   renowned 유명한

389 (A) affront

모든 사회에는 시간 엄수에 대한 자체의 사회적 관습을 결정하는 나름대로의 시간 개념이 있다. 어떤 문화권에서는 약속을 지킬 때에 약속 시간보다 일찍 또는 정각에 오라고 기대된다. 만약에 늦게 오면, 존경받지 못할 행위로 여겨지거나 기다리는 사람에게는 개인적인 모욕으로 간주된다.

punctuality 시간 엄수   disrespectable 존경받지 못할   affront 모욕(= insult)   adoration 숭배   laudation 칭찬   deference 경의, 존중

Key Structure ▶

be early and on time for appointments : 약속 시간보다 일찍 또는 시간에 맞추어 오다

390 (B) a new attitude toward his problems

최고의 상담은 스스로를 특정한 문제의 해결에만 국한하는 상담이라기보다는 오히려 문제들이 발생할 때 그것들을 해결할 수 있는 능력을 제공하는 사고와 행동의 습관을 가르쳐 주는 상담이다. 상담의 목표는 상담 받는 개인에게 자신의 문제에 대한 새로운 태도를 제공하는 것이다.

specific 특정한   attitude 태도   foresee 예견하다   insight 통찰력   technique 기술

Key Structure ▶

1. not that which ~ but rather that which... :
   not A but B 구문. that은 선행사로 counseling을 지칭함.

2. confine itself to ~ : 스스로를 ~에 국한시키다

391 (C) worries

복제 아기에 관한 매우 의심스러운 이야기들과 마찬가지로, 줄기세포를 이종 교배한다는 생각은, 정책 입안자들이 생식 복제의 금지를 넘어서서 결국은 치료용 복제도 또한 금지시킬지 모른다는 걱정들을 몇몇 연구자들 사이에 불러일으키고 있다.

clone baby 복제 아기   species-crossing 이종 교배   stem cell 줄기세포   spark 자극하다, 불러일으키다   ban 금지   rule out 제외하다   therapeutic 치료의   ecstasy 황홀경, 무아의 경지

392 (A) despite

수많은 사람들이 세계화와 이라크에 대한 미국의 정책에 항의하여 토요일에 피렌체 시내를 행진하였다. 많은 사람이 모여들었음에도 불구하고 작년에 제노바에서 있었던 8개국 정상 회담을 망친 것과 같은 폭력은 전혀 없었다.

protest 항의   globalization 세계화   turnout (집회 등의) 참석자 수   mar 망쳐놓다, 훼손하다   Group of Eight summit 8개국 정상 회담   despite ~에도 불구하고(= in spite of)   stem from ~에서 생기다

393 (C) regenerate

모든 어린아이가 알고 있듯이, 도마뱀의 꼬리는 잘라내어도 놀랍게도 다시 자라난다. 불행히도 사라지거나 손상을 입은 기관과 신체의 부분들을 재생하는 능력이 인간에게는 대부분 사라졌다.

lop off 자르다, 베다   missing 사라진   damaged 손상을 입은   regenerate 재생하다   compensate 보상하다

394 (D) unexplored

젊은 탐험가들은 절망할 필요가 없다. 오늘의 세계 지도 위에 비어 있는 여백이 거의 남아 있지 않지만, 대양의 깊은 바다에, 열대 우림의 오지에, 그리고 외계(우주)의 아주 먼 곳에도, 지도에 표시될 수 있는, 탐험이 이루어지지 않은 땅이 아직은 남아 있다.

despair 절망   blank 빈 공간   realm 국토, 영역   depth 깊은 곳   remote 멀리 떨어진   recess 깊숙한 곳   rain forest 열대 우림   reach 구역, 손이 미치는 곳   outer space 외계, 우주   inhabit 거주하다

395 (B) shallow roots

그 사람의 집은 4에이커의 땅 위에 자리 잡고 있었고 그의 평생의 목표는 그것을 숲으로 만드는 것이었다.

그는 "수고 없이는 소득도 없다"는 원예학파 신봉자이지만 새 나무에 결코 물을 주지 않았다. 그 이유를 물어보았을 때, 그는 나무에 물을 주면 뿌리가 얕게 자란다고 말하였다. 물을 주지 않은 나무는 수분을 찾아 뿌리를 깊게 내린다고 그는 말하였다.

horticulture 원예   water 물을 주다   moisture 수분, 습기   shallow 얕은   trunk 줄기

396 (C) intertwined – futile

자연과 인간 환경은 정반대의 대립 속에 서 있지 않다. 오히려 어찌할 수 없을 정도로 서로 얽혀 있다. 따라서 자연과 문화를 구분하는 것은 쓸모없는 짓이다.

diametric 정반대의, 대립적인   opposition 반대, 대립   instead 그 대신에   inexorably 냉혹하게, 가차없이   consequently 따라서   futile 쓸모없는   intertwined 서로 얽혀 있는

397 (D) forestalls – basic

정중함의 퇴보는 대중 매체나 일상적인 대화에서도 점점 비탄의 대상이 되어 왔다. 정중함은 사회적 관계에서 잠재적인 불쾌함을 미리 막는다. 정중함이 없다면 일상의 사회적 교류는 역겹고 가끔은 위험할 수도 있다. 따라서 정중함은 사회생활의 기본적인 덕목인 것 같다.

decline 하강, 퇴보   civility 정중함   lament 비탄, 탄식   media 매체   potential 잠재적인   nasty 역겨운   hazardous 위험한   momentous 중요한   forestall 미리 막다, 기선을 제압하다

398 (A) Habit

낯선 일들은 우리가 너무나 잘 알고 있는 일들보다 이해하기에 더 쉽다. 하나의 일이 더 가깝고, 더 일상적이며, 더 친숙할수록, 그것을 이해하거나 그것이 실제로 발생하는 사건이라는 것을 깨닫는 데에서 겪는 어려움은 더욱 커진다. 습관은 우리를 둘러싸고 있는 일들에 대해 우리가 자동적으로 반응을 하도록 만든다.

everyday 일상적인   comprehend 이해하다   take place 발생하다   automatically 자동적으로

Key Structure

1. those we know too well : 우리가 너무나 잘 알고 있는 일들 (those = the things)
2. causes us to react ~ : 우리가 ~ 반응을 하도록 만들다

399 (D) succeed in taking

옷은 우리를 극단적인 날씨에서 보호하고, 어느 정도의 정숙함을 제공해 준다. 또한 중요한 것은 옷이 그것을 입은 사람의 개성과, 태도와 사회적 신분에 대한 정보를 전달하는 방식이다. 어떤 전문가들은 다른 사람들에 비해 옷이 전달하는 신호에 더 민감하지만 첫인상을 형성하는 데 있어서 옷을 조금이라도 고려하는 데 성공하는 사람은 매우 적다.

extreme 극단적인 상황   modesty 정숙함   transmit 전달하다   professional 전문가   sensitive 민감한

Key Structure

take clothes into account at all : 옷을 조금이라도 고려하다

400 (B) were chosen

당신은 암모기가 누구를 물 것인지 어떻게 결정하는지 아는가? 모기는 꽤 까다로워서 희생물을 조심스럽게 고른다. 처음에 모기는 촉수를 사용하여 희생물을 찾는다. 이 촉수로 당신 몸의 습도와 체온과 땀 속에 들어 있는 화학 성분을 잰다. 만약에 찾아낸 것이 마음에 들면 모기는 물게 된다. 그러나 당신이 별로 마음에 들지 않으면 물지 않는다. 다음번에 모기에 물렸을 경우 당신이 선택된 자라는 것을 기억하라.

bite 물다, 쏘다   victim 희생자   sensor 촉수   moisture 습기, 습도   chemical substance 화학 성분   sweat 땀   appeal to 마음에 들다   insecticide 살충제

401 (B) subjectively, not objectively

우리 모두는 우리 자신의 취향과, 우리 자신의 직업과, 우리 자신의 편견으로 색칠된 안경을 쓰고 삶을 살아간다. 우리는 주관적으로 보며 객관적으로 보지 못한다. 우리는 우리가 볼 수 있는 것을 보며, 보이도록 존재하는 것을 보지 못한다. 우리가 진리라고 하는 다면적인 것에 대하여 잘못된 추측을 매우 많이 하고 있는 것은 이상한 일이 아니다.

spectacles 안경   calling 직업   prejudice 편견   prismatic 다채로운, 다면적인

402 (D) express their opinion about everything

사람은 혀는 하나를 가지고 태어나지만 눈은 두 개를 가지고 태어난다. 그것은 그들이 말하는 것보다 두 배 더 많이 보아야 하기 때문이다. 그러나 사람들의 행동을 보면 그들이 하나의 눈과 두 개의 혀를 가지고 태어나지 않았나 하는 생각이 든다. 왜냐하면 보는 것이 가장 적은 사람들이 말을 가장 많이 하고, 아무것도 깊이 들여다보지 않은 사람들이 모든 일에 대해 자신의 견해를 피력하기 때문이다.

observe 관찰하다   see into 깊이 들여다보다

in order that they should see twice as much as they say : 그들이 말하는 양보다 보는 양이 두 배가 되도록 하기 위해

403 (C) impossible to predict

중세 시대에는 라틴어가 아닌 영어가 배움과 지식의 언어가 되리라고 누구도 예견하지 못했다. 18세기에, 심지어 1950년대에는 누구도 프랑스어가 아닌 영어가 국제 외교의 첫 번째 언어가 되리라고 예견하지 못했다. 한 언어의 미래는 예측이 불가능하다.

foresee 예견하다   the Middle Ages 중세 (시대)
diplomacy 외교   predict 예측하다

404 (D) come up with

그 프로젝트는 문제에 봉착하였다. 예상보다 비용이 많이 들었고 끝내려면 시간이 너무 오래 걸렸다. 디자인팀은 새로운 계획을 내놓아야 한다고 결정을 내렸는데, 그렇지 않으면 그 프로젝트가 취소될 수도 있었기 때문이다.

cost 비용이 들다   go back on 돌아가다   put up with 참다   do away with 제거하다   come up with 제안하다

otherwise = if they did not come up with it (it = a new plan)

405 (A) the easy way isn't always the best way

인생은 선택으로 가득 차 있다. 우리는 종종 어떤 일을 쉽게 하느냐 어렵게 하느냐를 선택하게 된다. 불행하게도 우리는 거의 언제나 쉬운 방법을 선택하게 되는데, 그것이 단지 더 쉽다는 이유 때문이다. 예를 들어, 우리는 거의 언제나 제일 쉬운 임무를 맡고, 제일 쉬운 일자리를 택하고, 파티에서 말 건네기 제일 쉬운 사람을 찾으려고 한다. 그러나 이러한 선택이 언제나 최고의 선택은 아니다. 가끔은 제일 어려운 방법을 선택하면 얻는 것이 더 많을 수도 있다. 가장 어려운 임무를 택함으로써 더 많은 것을 배울 수도 있다. 파티에서 접근하기 어려워 보이는 사람에게 말을 거는 것을 택함으로써 우리는 새 친구를 사귀는 결과를 가지게 되기도 한다. 간략하게 줄여 말하면, 쉬운 길이 언제나 최선의 길은 아니다.

assignment 과제, 임무, 업무   unapproachable 접근 불가능한   end up ~로 귀결되다

406 (C) fortitude

고대나 현대의 어떠한 영웅도 죽음에 대한 당당한 경멸과 혹독한 고통을 견디어 낸 불굴의 정신을 지닌 아메리칸 인디언을 능가할 수는 없다.

surpass 능가하다   lofty 당당한, 위엄 있는   sustain 견디다   affliction 고통, 재난   condemnation 비난   fortitude 불굴의 정신   disaster 재앙

407 (B) organic

농부들은 과일과 채소를 인공적으로 익히기 위해 화학 물질을 사용한다. 그러나 요즘 몇몇 농부들은 화학 물질을 사용하지 않는 예전의 방식으로 농산물을 재배한다. 우리는 이 농산물을 유기농산물이라고 부른다.

chemical 화학 물질   artificially 인공적으로   ripen 익다   produce 농산물   organic 유기농의, 유기체의   environmental 환경의   uncontaminated 오염되지 않은

408 (A) colonial

만약에 교과서가 여고생들에게 식민지 미국 시대부터 현재까지 여성들이 지위의 상승과 정치적 참여를 위한 동등한 기회를 가져왔다고 가르친다면, 그들은 미국 역사에서 여성의 위치를 어떻게 이해할 수 있을까?

upward mobility 신분 상승 이동   colonial 식민(지)의   savage 야만(인)의   prehistoric 선사 (시대)의

409 (B) justify

공익사업 지도자들은 여러 가지 종류의 에너지원 중에서 어느 것을 개발해야 할지를 결정하면서 수익성을 기초로 자신들의 방에서 남몰래 결정을 내리면서도, 공개적으로는 자신들이 낮아진 요금 체계와 높아진 안전성을 기초로 결정을 했다고 정당화한다.

utility industry (철도, 전력, 수도 등) 공익사업   in the privacy of their room 그들의 방에서 남몰래   profitability 수익, 이득   rate (전기, 수도) 요금   justify 정당화하다   replicate 반복하다   underwrite 승낙하다, 서명하다

410 (A) cursory

비행기 추락 사고에 대해 공식적인 조사가 보여 주는 바에 따르면, 지상 근무원들의 근무 일정이 너무 여유가 없어서 그들은 그 불운의 비행기가 이륙하기 전에 예비 점검을 대단히 피상적인 것 이상으로 시행할 수 없었다.

official 공식적인   investigation 조사   crash 추락   reveal 폭로하다, 드러내다   ground crew 지상 근무원   preflight 비행[출발] 이전의   ill-fated 불운한 운명의

aircraft 비행기 prior to ~ 이전의 takeoff 이륙
cursory 피상적인 preemptory 선점하는 repetitive
반복적인 thoroughgoing 철두철미한

411 (C) superficial

월즈는 원예학에 관해 피상적인 지식을 가지고
있었지만, 그 유명한 식물학자에게 난초 가꾸는 것에
대해 충고를 해 주겠다고 계속 주장을 하여 (그들을)
초대한 주인을 매우 난처하게 만들었다.

horticulture 원예학 persist in 고집하다 orchid
난 eminent 유명한 botanist 식물학자 host
(손님을 초대한) 주인 genuine 진정한 profound 깊은
superficial 피상적인

Key Structure ▶

to the great embarrassment of their host :
주인이 커다란 난처함을 느끼게끔

412 (D) at odds with

지금쯤은 누구나 미국식의 비용이 엄청나고, 냉방
장치가 에너지를 잡아먹는 폭식가라는 것을 알 것이다.
그것은 생산된 총 전력량의 약 9퍼센트를 소비한다.
단지 편안함만을 위해 그렇게 많은 전력을 소비하는
사치는 특히 미국적이고, 에너지 부족을 위협하는
시대에 범국민적인 희생이 필요하다는 최근의 모든
말과도 현저히 상반된다.

enormous 엄청난 glutton 폭식가 extravagance
사치, 낭비 strikingly 현저하게, 두드러지게 rhetoric
미사여구, 수사법 menace 위협하다 in conformity
with ~과 일치하여 compatible with 양립할 수 있는,
조화로운 at odds with ~와 상반되는

413 (B) taking your own turn

대화를 나누는 사람이 둘 이상이면, 그것은 테니스
경기의 복식 경기나 배구 경기와 같다. 줄을 서서
기다리는 것은 있을 수 없다. 제일 가까이 있는 사람
이나 움직임이 제일 빠른 사람이 공을 치고, 뒤로
물러서면 다른 사람이 (넘어오는) 공을 받아칠 것이다.
누구도 당신에게 차례를 주기 위해서 경기를 중단하지
않는다. 당신은 스스로의 차례를 잡아야 할 책임이
있는 것이다.

doubles 복식 경기 turn 차례

Key Structure ▶

There's no waiting in line.
= It is impossible to wait in line.

414 (C) intercultural

시간은 문화적, 사회적, 그리고 개인적 삶의 핵심
체계이다. 사실상 어떠한 일도 어떠한 종류의 시간의
틀을 벗어나서 일어날 수는 없다. 이종 문화 간의
관계에서 나타나는 하나의 복잡한 요소는 문화마다
유형이 독특한 그 자체의 시간의 틀이 있다는 점이다.

core 핵심적인 frame 틀 complicating 복잡한
unique 독특한 indigenous 토착의

Key Structure ▶

except in some kind of time frame : 어떤 종류의
시간의 틀을 벗어나서

415 (A) proliferated

개인용 컴퓨터의 이용과 구입이 쉬워짐에 따라,
더 많은 가구가 인터넷상으로 World Wide
Web(www)에 연결되고 있다. 이렇게 되자 개인은
세계 어느 곳이든 다른 컴퓨터 이용자와 즉시 연결이
가능하게 되었다. World Wide Web상에 올라와 있는
정보는, 한때는 도서관과 기록 보관소에 있었던 많은
것들이 이제는 인터넷에서 찾아볼 수 있을 정도로
확장되었다.

availability 이용 가능성 affordability 구입 가능성
household 가정, 가구 be wired to ~에 연결되다
instantaneous 즉각적인 archive 기록(공문서) 보관소
proliferate 급격히 늘다 relinquish 포기하다 traverse
횡단하다 undermine 손상시키다

Key Structure ▶

1. to the point where ~ : ~에 이를 정도로
2. much of what once was in ~ archives : 한때는
도서관과 기록 보관소에 있었던 것 중 많은 양이

416 (D) creed

힌두교는 창시자도 예언자도 없다. 그것은 특정한
교회 구조를 가지고 있지 않으며, 또한 한 권위자에
의해 정의된 일련의 믿음의 체계도 가지고 있지
않다. 힌두교에서는 사고의 방식보다는 삶의 방식이
강조된다. 인도의 전 대통령이었던 라다크리슈난은
언젠가 "힌두교는 강령이라기보다는 문화에 더
가깝다."라고 말한 적이 있다.

founder 창시자 prophet 예언자 cf. prophesy 예언하다,
prophecy 예언 authority 권위자 legend 전설 creed
강령, 신조

417 (B) less traumatic

이제 막 졸업을 한 대학생에게는, 신용 거래를 하거나,
예산을 짜거나, 물건 구입할 시 무엇을 구해야 하고
누구에게서 사야 할지 같은 그러한 문제와 부딪칠 때,
"현실 세계"가 머무르기에 무서운 곳일 수도 있다.

만약에 사람들이 일상생활의 이러한 영역을 다루는 교육을 받았다면 이 "현실 세계"에 들어가는 것은 덜 충격적일지 모른다. 이것을 성취하는 데에 대학보다 더 나은 곳이 있을까?

a newly graduated 갓 대학을 졸업한   scary 무서운
purchase 구입   traumatic (정신적으로) 충격적인
dynamic 동적인   overwhelmed 압도된

Key Structure ▶

whom to purchase it from
= from whom to purchase it

418 (A) position

신생아로서 당신은 부모와 관계를 형성하고, 그 후에 자라나면서 동기들과 관계를 형성한다. 심리학자들에 의하면 당신의 출생 순서는 당신의 부모와 동기들이 당신에게 반응을 보이고 또 다루는 방법에 영향을 미친다고 한다. 다시 말해서, 당신과 당신 가족들은 가족 안에서의 당신의 위치에 따라 정해진 방식으로 처신하는 것이다.

newborn 신생아   sibling 동기(형제, 자매)   birth order 출생 순서   depending on ~에 의존하여   significance 중요성   identity 신원

419 (D) flourished

우리 선조들이 서로 의사소통을 하는 방법을 터득한 후에 일련의 기나긴 놀라운 발전이 시작되었다. 고대 이집트인들, 미노아인들, 희랍인들, 마야족들, 그리고 아프리카의 베냉족들과 같은 민족들에게서 창의성이 번성하게 되었다. 근대의 기계 시대가 시작되기 오래 전에 우리 조상들은 수학, 기계, 예술 및 문학에서 정교한 기술과 체계를 이미 개발해 냈다.

ancestor 선조, 조상   creativity 창의력, 창의성   Minoan (고대 크레타 지역의) 미노아인   the Benin 베냉족
sophisticated 정교한, 세련된   flourish 번창하다

420 (B) credited

레오나르도는 가장 유명한 작품들을 그린 후에, 다른 꿈에 시간을 더 많이 들이기 시작하였다. 공병학 전문가로서 레오나르도는 그것들이 가능하리라고 꿈꾸어지기 훨씬 전에 초기 탱크와 비행기 설계도를 그렸다. 그는 또한 첫 번째 낙하산을 설계하고 첫 번째 엘리베이터를 만든 공로를 인정받고 있다.

work (예술) 작품   military engineer 공병학 전문가
parachute 낙하산

Key Structure ▶

be credited with : ~의 공로를 인정받다

421 (C) only study on their own

스터디 그룹이라고 불리기도 하는 학습팀은 수업 시간에 공부할 읽기 자료를 토론하고, 시험공부를 같이 하고, 또 학생들의 성적을 올리기 위한 다른 일들을 할 목적으로 정기적으로 만나는 학생들의 모임이다. 한 조사가 보여 주는 바에 의하면, 수업 시간 외에 만나서 같이 공부하는 학생들이 혼자서 공부하는 학생들보다 성적이 더 좋다고 한다.

on a regular basis 정기적으로   class reading 수업 시간에 공부할 읽기 자료   introverted 내성적인, 내향적인
attentive 주의 깊은

422 (D) diversity

우리가 현대 예술의 셀 수 없이 많은 학파들, 수많은 예술가들, 그리고 예술을 표현하는 여러 가지 유형의 수단들을 고려해 볼 때, 우리는 예술이 다양성을 반영한다고 주장하는 사람들의 의견에 공감하게 된다.

countless 셀 수 없을 정도로 많은   school of modern art 현대 예술 학파   multiplicity 다수   sympathize with ~에 공감하다   uniformity 획일성   inertia 관성, 타성   cornerstone 초석   diversity 다양성

423 (B) In addition

콤팩트디스크[CD]가 카세트테이프보다 더 비싸지만, 많은 음악 애호가들은 CD를 사는 것을 좋아한다. 첫 번째 이유로는 발달된 녹음 기술 덕분에 CD의 음질이 카세트테이프의 음질보다 더 우수한 것으로 여겨지고 있기 때문이다. 게다가 CD는 카세트테이프보다 수명이 긴데, 카세트테이프가 10년 정도의 수명을 가지고 있는데 반하여 CD는 25년의 수명을 가지고 있다.

prefer 선호하다   superior to ~보다 더 나은   due to
~ 덕분에   life span 수명

424 (A) the cold shoulder

대부분의 사람들은 대학 학위가 그럴듯한 직업을 보장하는 것으로 간주한다. 그리고 경제가 호황이었던 1990년대 후반에 대부분 대학 졸업생들은 졸업 후 여러 개의 일자리 제안을 받았다. 그러나 2002년도 졸업생들은 불과 몇 년 전에 선배들을 채용하였던 열정적인 회사들이 금년 졸업생들에게는 냉담함을 보인다는 것을 배우고 있다. 무엇 때문에 일자리가 부족하고 졸업생들은 이것에 대해 어떻게 대처하고 있는가?

guarantee 보장   decent 고상한, 반듯한   grad 졸업생
(= graduate)   diploma 학위   embrace 채용하다
give ~ the cold shoulder ~에게 냉담한 태도를 보이다
berth 직장, 취직자리   blank cheque 백지 수표, 무제한의 자유   the thumbs up 격려, 찬성 (엄지를 들어서 보이므로)

PART 4
Sentence Completion

425 (C) innocent

절도에 의해 또는 인터넷 상의 무법자들의 웹사이트에서 입수된 신용카드 번호가 포르노 사이트에 접속하기 위해서 사용되고 있고, 그래서 선량한 사람들이 비용을 청구 받고 있다. 이 엄청난 사기는 아마도 은행들의 부주의 결과로 나타난 것이며, 현재 운영되고 있는 신용카드가 전자 상거래에 적합하지 않을 가능성을 제기한다.

credit-card number 신용카드 번호 theft 절도 anarchist 무법자, 무정부주의자 access 접속하다, 접근하다 be charged 비용을 부담하다 fraud 사기 negligence 부주의, 태만 electronic commerce 전자 상거래 persecuted 박해 받은

Key Structure

credit-cards as currently operated
= credit-cards as they are currently operated

426 (A) tolerance

여러 해 동안 카페인은 고혈압을 유발시키는 것으로 생각되었다. 그러나 새로운 연구 조사에 의하면, 이 자극제가 처음에 혈압의 급격한 상승을 유발하지만, 보통은 카페인에 대한 내성이 빨리 생겨서 커피가 (고혈압 상승에) 별로 영향을 미치지 않는다고 한다.

be linked to ~에 연관되다 hypertension 고혈압 stimulant 자극제 initially 처음에 blood pressure 혈압 tolerance to ~에 대한 내성 antagonism 반항심 addiction 중독, 몰두 cf. drug addict 약물 중독자 vulnerability 취약성, 상처받기 쉬움

427 (B) deserted

당신이 사람이 살지 않는 지역에 들어가거나, 밤에 너무 늦게 혼자서 돌아다니지 않으면 대부분의 도시 거리들은 안전하다. 더 안전하고 안락함을 원한다면, 몇몇 관광 안내소가 제공하는 지도에 자세하게 표시된 보행로를 따라가면 된다.

mapped-out 지도에 자세하게 표시된 walking route 걸어서 다니는 길, 보행로 deserted area 버려진[사람이 살지 않는] 지역

428 (A) imitating

어떤 인류학자들은 몇몇 원숭이들에게 초보적인 수화를 가르쳐 왔다고 주장하는데, 회의론자들은 원숭이들이 조련사들을 단지 모방하는 것이라고 주장한다.

anthropologist 인류학자 claim 주장하다 ape 원숭이, 유인원 rudimentary 초보적인 sign language 수화,

몸짓 언어 skeptic 회의론자, 회의적인 imitate 모방하다 condone 용서하다, 관대히 봐주다 instruct 가르치다 acknowledge 인정하다

429 (C) dose

당신은 타이레놀 한 병으로 간을 해칠 수도 있고 죽을 수도 있다. 아스피린을 너무 많이 복용하면 위장 출혈을 야기한다. 과도한 리튬은 갑상선과 신장을 손상시킨다. 요점은 얼마만큼의 약을 복용하는가가 중요하다는 것이다. 의학에 이런 격언이 있다. 독약이 되느냐 아니면 치료약이 되느냐의 차이는 복용량이라고.

wreck 망치다, 해치다 gastrointestinal 위장의 bleeding 출혈 lithium 리튬(가장 가벼운 원소) thyroid 갑상선 kidney 신장, 콩팥 saying 격언, 속담 dose 1회분, 복용량(= dir) content 내용물

Key Structure

1. The point is that ~ : 요점은 ~이다
2. how much you take of a drug
   = how much of a drug you take

430 (A) pay less attention to quality

우리들 대부분은 너무 많이 믿는 것의 위험을 깨닫고 있다. 그러나 우리는 종종 너무 적게 믿는 것의 위험을 과소평가한다. 아이가 모든 것을 완벽하게 하도록 도움을 주거나, 아이를 어떠한 위험으로부터도 보호하려고 하는 부모는 아이의 책임을 감소시키고 아이가 믿을 만한 사람이 될 가망성을 줄인다. 만약에 다른 누군가가 언제나 그렇게 한다면, 왜 아이는 길을 건너기 전에 양쪽 방향을 쳐다보아야 하는가? 직원을 너무 면밀하게 감독을 하는 고용주에게도 같은 이야기가 적용된다. 어떤 공장에서는 품질 관리 검사관을 추가로 투입한 것이 생산직원들이 품질에 주의를 덜 기울이게 되는 원인이 되었다.

underestimate 과소평가하다 protect 보호하다 risk 위험 responsibility 책임 diminish 줄이다 likelihood 가망성 be worthy of ~의 가치가 있다 supervise 감독하다 quality control 품질관리 inspector 검사관, 검열관 pay attention to ~에 주의를 기울이다 compete 경쟁하다

Key Structure

The same is true of : ~에도 같은 논리가 적용된다

431 (B) all but

잠과 마찬가지로 언어는 물질이 아니라 과정이다. 실제적으로 이 점은 모든 사람에게 알려져 있지만, 그 이론의 공식화는 거의 불가능하다.

substance 물질 process 과정 in practice 실제로
(= in reality) defy 무시하다, 도전하다 formulation
형식화, 공식화 anything but 결코 ～이 아니다(= never)
all but 거의(= almost)

432 (C) proponents

예산안 공청회에서는 조세 증대를 옹호하는 사람
들이나 반대하는 사람들 모두 다 자신의 견해를 진술할
수 있다.

budget hearing 예산안 공청회(심의, 청문회) opponent
반대자 auditor 회계 감사관, 감사역 con 반대(론자)
proponent 찬성자, 옹호자 subscriber 가입자

433 (D) prudent

등산에는 많은 위험이 따른다. 그래서 등산가는
언제나 주의를 기울여야 한다. 조심성 없는 등산가는
곧 사고를 당한다. 등산은 참으로 신중한 사람에게
알맞은 것이다.

mountain-climbing 등산 involve 포함하다 risk
위험(= danger) alert 기민한, 주의를 기울이는 reckless
무모한, 분별없는(= careless) bold 용감한, 대담한
(= brave) prudent 신중한

434 (A) the revolt

현대의 작곡가들은 이러한 종류의 리얼리즘에 대해
강력한 반발을 보여 왔다. 사실상 이러한 반발은
금세기 초의 먼 과거에서 시작되었다.

contemporary 동시대의, 현대의 reaction 반응
realism 리얼리즘, 사실주의 revolt 반발, 반항

435 (B) preventive

최근 수십 년 동안 생물학 연구에서 발달된 새로운
지식과 새로운 기술은 인간이 질병을 알아내고 확실한
치료와 예방책을 취할 수 있는 희망을 서서히 제공하기
시작하였다.

technique 기술 research 연구, 조사 decade 10년
cf. score 20 definitive 결정적인 therapeutic 치료의
drastic 격렬한, 철저한 preventive 예방하는, 방지하는
repressive 억압하는 rigorous 엄한, 혹독한

436 (B) creation

산업 혁명 이래 줄곧 기술의 변화는 대량 실업의
두려움과 직면하게 되었다. 그러나 급속한 기술의
진보는 일자리를 파괴하기는커녕 일반적으로 높은
비율로 일자리를 만들어 내게 되었다.

massive unemployment 대량 실업 far from -ing
～하기는커녕 be accompanied by ～이 뒤따르다
deprivation 박탈 derision 경멸, 조소(거리)

437 (A) reality

오늘날 미국에 흑인들이 급증하게 된 것은 자유와
평등을 목전의 현실로 만들고자 하는 깊고 정열적인
결심에서 우러나오게 된 것이다.

upsurge 고조, 급증 passionate 열정적인 here and
now 목전의, 당장의

438 (C) transformed

개인으로 하여금 현 형태의 사회 제도를 받아들이게끔
하는 사회화의 힘은 쉽게 깨지거나 변형되지 않는다.

social institution 사회 제도[기구] mend 고치다,
수정하다(= repair)

439 (A) persuasive

그가 사람들을 자신의 사고방식대로 바꾸는 데 성공한
것은 주로 기존 질서를 설득력 있게 비판한 결과였다.

convert 전환시키다, 개종하다 existing order 현존하는
질서, 기존 질서 persuasive 설득력 있는 substantial
실질적인 indiscreet 무분별한

440 (B) intricate

인간의 인지 구조를 진지하게 조사해 보면 인간
이라는 유기체의 삶에서 발달하는 육체적 구조와
마찬가지로 불가사의하고 복잡한 것으로 판명된다.

cognitive system 인지[의식] 구조 investigate
조사하다 intricate 복잡한, 난해한

Key Structure

1. when seriously investigated
   = when they are seriously investigated
2. no less marvelous and intricate than
   = as marvelous and intricate as

Section 2 연습문제

441 (D) the common man is likely to suffer in the long run

역사가 기록되기 시작하면서부터, 성공적으로 정부를 통제해 온 사람들은 그 통제권을 궁극적으로는 이기적으로 사용하게 되었다. 따라서 정치적, 경제적 전문가들에 의해 운용되는 정부에서는 보통 사람은 결국 손해를 입게 될 것 같다.

maintain 유지하다(= keep up) eventually 결국, 궁극적으로는 hence 따라서, 고로 layman 문외한 be relieved of ~을 면제받다 in the long run 결국

442 (C) aided communications between their countries

새로이 개설된 대서양 횡단 케이블을 통해 전달된 첫 번째 메시지 중의 하나는 미국 대통령과 영국 여왕 사이에 이루어졌다. 양국의 지도자는 이제 케이블이 양국 사이의 통신 교환에 도움을 주게 된 것을 기뻐하였다.

transatlantic cable 대서양 횡단 케이블 diplomatic corps 외교단(團)

443 (B) practical information

로마 제국의 지리학자들은 세계의 특수 지역에 관한 정보를 편찬하는 데 주로 종사하였다. 지구의 크기나 지구가 태양계의 나머지 것들에 대해 갖는 관계를 이론화하는 데에 관심을 보이지 않은 것은 로마인들이 실용적인 지식을 강조했다는 점을 반영하는 것이다.

be engaged in ~에 종사하다 compilation 편찬, 편집 theorize 이론화하다, 체계화하다 dimension 용적, 크기 the solar system 태양계 reflection 반영, 반사 astronomy 천문학 metaphysical speculation 형이상학적 고찰, 사색

444 (C) agricultural

아메리칸 인디언들은 미 대륙 평원을 돌아다니면서 자신들이 이용 가능한 천연자원을 매우 조금만 사용하였다. 인디언들은 몇 년 동안 자신들이 이미 보존해 온 것들을 먹고살게 될 수밖에 없으리라고 예상한 것 같다. 왜냐하면 그들은 농업에 종사하지 않았기 때문이다.

wander 배회하다 sparingly 절약하여, 인색하게 natural resource 천연자원 anticipate 예상하다, 기대하다 be compelled to ~을 강요받다(= be forced to) live on ~을 먹고살다 previously 예전에, 이미 conserve 보존하다

445 (A) defense

정부는 적의 침략으로부터 이 국가를 지키는 것이 그들의 의무인 육군과 해군의 유지를 위한 대비책을 마련하였다. 이 대비책은 시민들로 하여금 국가 방어에 자신의 시간을 선뜻 내주지 않고서도 어느 정도의 안전을 누릴 수 있게 해 준다.

provision 대비책 maintenance 유지 aggression 침략 a measure of 어느 정도의 give of 선뜻 내주다

Key Structure

whose duty it is to ~ aggression :
it은 가주어, to 이하는 진주어, whose duty는 보어 역할.

446 (B) could no longer maintain their equilibrium

수세기를 통해 숲은, 화재나 다른 소동들이 가끔 일시적으로 이 균형을 뒤집어엎기는 하지만, 자연과의 균형을 유지할 수 있었다. 그러나 인간이 쟁기와 도끼와 소떼를 동반하고 등장했을 때, 숲은 그 평정[균형]을 더 이상 유지할 수 없게 되었다.

disturbance 소동, 걱정거리 temporarily 일시적으로 upset 뒤집어엎다 come into the picture 등장하다 plow 쟁기 equilibrium 평형, 균형 raw material 원료 compete 경쟁하다

447 (B) there are more of them

민주주의 국가에서는 모든 시민은 평등해야 한다고 이야기되고, 다수의 의지가 최고다. 따라서, 가난한 자들이 더 많기 때문에 가난한 자들은 부자들보다 더 많은 힘을 갖게 된다.

the majority 다수 supreme 최고의 wicked 사악한

448 (A) famine and starvation

비교적 최근에 이르기까지, 상업[무역]은 운송의 불충분함 때문에 지리적으로 제약을 받았다. 단지 사치품과 희귀한 상품만이 먼 지역 사이에 교환되었다. 인간은 자신이 처한 직접적인 환경에 의존하여서, 한 특정 지역에서의 흉작은 기아와 아사로 이어졌다.

transportation 운송, 수송 inadequacy 부적합, 불충분 luxury goods 사치품 rare articles 희귀한 상품 crop failure 농작물 수확의 실패 famine 기아 starvation 아사, 기아 importation 수입

449 (B) intelligent

외모로 판단할 수는 없다. 어색한 모습과 느리고 육중한 움직임 때문에 곰은 미련하다는 평판을 얻었다. 그러나 동물원 사육사들 사이에서는 그들이

다루는 모든 동물 중에서 곰이 가장 영리한 축에
긴다는 데 의견이 일치하고 있다.

appearance 외모, 외양 **clumsy** 솜씨 없는, 서투른
ponderous 육중한, 묵직한 **stupidity** 우둔함, 어리석음

450 (A) a sudden and arbitrary creation of new hypotheses

가설은 역사를 통해서 이해되어야 한다. 왜냐하면
가설들은 갑작스러운 창조의 산물이라기보다는
점진적인 진화의 결과이기 때문이다. 우리가 어떤
개념의 과정을 따라가게 될 경우, 우리는 느리며
점진적인 변화의 모습을 보게 되겠지만 새로운 가설이
불쑥 변덕스럽게 생성되는 것을 보지는 못할 것이다.

hypothesis 가설 *pl.* **hypotheses** **progressive**
점진적인 **arbitrary** 변덕스러운(= capricious) **the
ancients** 고대인 **predecessor** 선구자

451 (D) insincerity

만약 어떤 사람이 다수결에 의한 결정에 찬성하지
않는다면 침묵을 지키는 게 정당한 일이 될 것이다.
왜냐하면 그 사람이 순교자적인 역할을 하고 싶지
않다는 것은 이해될 수 있는 일이기 때문이다. 그러나
그가 그러고 싶지도 않은 동의를 표하는 것은 변명이
안 되는[용서받지 못할] 일이다. 불성실한 언행은
정당화되지 못한다.

the majority decision 다수결에 의한 결정 **martyr**
순교자 **inexcusable** 변명이 안 되는 **voice assent**
찬성[동의]을 표하다 **justification** 정당성 **dissent** 불찬성
insincerity 불성실

452 (D) what you want

이웃 사람과 단순히 보조를 맞추기 위해 특별히
갖고 싶은 마음도 없는 온갖 종류의 물건을 사려고
스스로에게 부담을 지우는 것은 어리석은 일이다.
자신의 개인적 기분에 따라 원하는 것만을 사면서
돈을 쓰면 훨씬 더 큰 기쁨을 맛보게 될 것이다.

keep pace with ∼와 보조를 맞추다 **whim** 기분, 마음,
변덕 **bargain** 염가품 **necessities of life** 생활필수품

453 (D) played an astonishing part

미신이 지식에 의해 대치되기 전에는 실제로 국가의
운명이 가끔 일식에 의해 변화된 적도 있었다. 역사는
천체들의 움직임이 놀라운 역할을 한 한 분야이다.

superstition 미신 **be replaced by** ∼에 의해 대치되다
eclipse of the sun 일식 **celestial body** 천체
disturbance 소란, 방해

454 (B) equal rights for all

민주주의를 반대하는 사람들은 현대의 복잡한
문명이 정부를 관장하고 있는 사람 측에게 전문화된
지식을 요구한다고 주장한다. 그들은 단지 소수의
혜택 받은 사람들만이 요구되는 자질을 갖추고
있고, 민주주의에서는 통제권이 선거구민들의 손에
놓여 있기 때문에 모든 사람의 평등권은 배제된다고
이야기한다.

opponent 반대자 **contend** 주장하다 **call for** 요구하다
on the part of ∼의 편에[측에] **a favored few** 혜택
받은 소수의 사람들 **electorate** 선거구민 **preclude**
제외하다, 배제하다(= exclude) **deference** 복종, 맹종

455 (A) a basis for further operations

과학은 정체된 관점 또는 역동적인 관점 어느
쪽에서도 볼 수 있다. 정체된 관점에서 보면 과학은
우주를 설명하고 있다고 여겨지는 지식의 체계이며,
반면 역동적인 성향을 지닌 사람에게 과학은
오늘날의 지식 상태가 미래의 작동을 위한 기초가
되는 끊임없는 활동을 의미한다.

static 정체된, 정지된 **dynamic** 역동적인 **descriptive
of** ∼을 설명하는(= describing) **whereas** 한편, 반면에(=
while) **orientation** 성향, 기질 **incorporated** 병합된

456 (B) individual problems

그 연극 비평가는 그 연극이 인기가 없을 것이라고
주장하였는데, 그 이유는 연극이 사랑을 다루어서가
아니라 두 극중 인물 서로 간의 사랑을 다루었기
때문이다. 그리고 그의 말을 빌리면, 자기 나라
사람들은 개인적인 문제에 대해서는 관심을 잃었다고
한다.

critic 비평가 **deal with** 다루다 **character** 인물

457 (B) what time it was

로빈의 가족은 시계가 없었다. 로빈은 아버지가
시계를 하나 샀으면 하고 바랐는데, 그 이유는 그가
종종 학교에 늦었기 때문이었다. 그가 고의로 학교에
늦는 것은 아니었다. 그러나 그것은 매일 아침 집을
나설 때 정확한 시간을 몰랐기 때문이었다.

intentionally 고의로, 의도적으로(= on purpose, by
design)

Key Structure

upon leaving home = when he left home

458 (A) its variety of beautiful flowers

아이오와 주의 63%가 넘는 가정이 자신의 집을 소유하고 있으며 아파트보다는 개인 주택에서 살고 있다. 정원과 공원을 위한 공지도 많다. 사실 아이오와 주에 대해 특기할 사항 중 하나는 아름다운 꽃이 다양하게 있다는 점이다.

notable 특기할 만한, 주목할 만한 traffic congestion 교통 정체 industrialization 공업화, 산업화

459 (A) capitalists

정치 투쟁의 소란에 휘말려드는 것은 인간만이 아니다. 거의 모든 개미 사회에서도 준비성 많은 이웃 개미들이 축적해 놓은 꿀더미를 보고 분개하면서 그 이웃을 자본주의자로 몰아 공격하는 공산주의식 불평분자가 있다.

the human species 인류 turmoil 소란, 혼란 (= tumult) strife 분쟁, 갈등 malcontent 불평분자, 불평자 resentful of ~을 분개하는 hoard 저장물, 보고 provident 준비성이 많은 accumulate 축적하다 capitalist 자본주의자 petty thief 좀도둑 manufacturer 제조업자 unionist 노동조합원

460 (D) found in combination

미학 이론이 많지 않은 데 대하여 제시된 하나의 설명은, 이러한 이론을 만들어 내는 사람은 예술에 대한 열정을 지녀야 하고 동시에 그것에 대한 객관적 호기심의 태도를 기꺼이 취해야 한다는 것이다. 이러한 특질이 통합되어 나타나는 것을 거의 찾아볼 수 없기 때문에 우리에게는 미학 이론이 거의 없다.

sparsity 희박함, 드묾 aesthetics 미학 possess 소유하다 assume an attitude of ~의 태도를 취하다

461 (C) superior status

상류층은 산업적인 직업에 종사하지 않고 그 대신 자신들의 삶을 커다란 명예가 따르는 직업에 바치는 것이 야만스러운 사회의 법칙이다. 그들이 성직자의 지위를 갖든 무사의 지위를 갖든, 그들의 구별되는 직업은 우월한 신분에 대한 사회적인 표현이다.

barbarian 야만인(의) engage in 종사하다 A is attached to B A가 B에 덧붙여지다 priest 성직자, 목사 warrior 무사 distinctive 구별이 되는 patriotism 애국심 superior 우월한

462 (A) mythology and legend

고대에는 지중해와 그 주변 지역은 지구상에서 잘 알려진 유일한 지역이었다. 그러나 친숙한 지역과 낯선 지역 사이의 경계는 모호하고 정확하지 않았다. 11세기의 역사가들이 당시 알고 있던 세계 지리의 외곽에 접근해 갔을 때, 그때까지 알려진 사실은 신화와 전설 속으로 묻히게 되었다.

the Mediterranean Sea 지중해 comprise 구성하다 globe 지구 vague 모호한 contemporary 당대의, 동시대의 fade into ~으로 사라지다 mythology 신화 legend 전설 extensive 대단위의 migration 이주, 이민

463 (D) biography

우리는 글 속에 나오는 사건이 우리 자신의 삶에서 일어나는 것으로 생각할 때 우리가 읽는 것에서 대단한 감동을 받게 된다. 우리가 읽는 내용이 어떤 한 특정인의 삶에 있었던 사건들을 다루게 될 때 우리는 우리의 삶과 우리가 읽는 것을 가장 쉽게 비교할 수가 있다. 바로 이러한 이유로 나는 전기를 읽도록 권장하고자 하는 것이다.

narrated 이야기된, 전달된 draw parallels between A and B A와 B를 비교하다 encourage 권장하다 narration 설화

464 (A) the alliance continues

이 세상에 너무 많은 지식을 쏟아 놓는 것은 위험하다는 태도는 일반적이다. 문학 속에 파고드는 파우스트의 이야기는 지식을 지닌 인간과 어둠의 힘 사이에 존재하는 유대 관계에 대한 널리 퍼지고 오래된 믿음에 대한 증거이다. 이 믿음은 이 동맹 관계가 지속되는 한 계속될 것이다.

flood A with B A에게 B를 쏟아 놓다 permeate 침투하다, 스며들다 age-long 영속하는, 오래된 bond between A and B A와 B의 유대 관계 persist 지속되다 alliance 동맹 (관계) superstition 미신

465 (C) perished

새로 태어난 아기가 딸이어서 기분이 상한 왕은 신하 한 사람을 시켜 아기를 숲 속에 가져다 버리도록 명령하였다. 아기는 숲 속에서 완전 외톨이가 되었다. 울어 보았지만 새들만이 아기의 울음 소리를 들었다. 얼마 시간이 지나자 아기는 매우 쇠약해졌다. 사실 사냥꾼에 의해 구조되지 않았더라면 아기는 죽어 버렸을 것이다.

rescue 구조하다 befriend 친구가 되다 perish 사라지다 survive 살아남다

Key Structure

had she not been ~ = if she had not been ~

466 (A) by the piece

근로자에게 임금을 지불하는 일반적인 방법에는 두 가지가 있다. 하나는 일한 분량에 따라 지불하는 것인데, 그럼으로써 그의 임금은 그의 기술에 의존하게 된다. 또 다른 하나는 시간당 또는 주당 지불하는 것이다. 기계가 생산에 매우 자주 제약을 가하는 이 기계화의 시대에서는 일한 분량에 따라 임금을 지불하게 되면 전혀 고무적인 가치가 나타나지 않게 될지도 모른다.

by the piece 일한 분량에 따라   **mechanization** 기계화
incentive 자극적인, 고무하는

467 (B) contradiction

단지 두 가지 선택의 길이 있을 뿐이다. 즉 우주는 유한하든지 무한할 것이다. 우주가 끝이 없다는 것은 믿을 수 없는 것처럼 보이지만 우주의 한계를 상상하는 것도 그와 마찬가지로 어려운 일이다. 이 두 가지 선택의 방안 중에서 하나는 사실임에 틀림이 없지만, 어느 것도 사실일 수는 없는 것 같다. 우주에 대한 우리의 개념은 모순으로 시달리고 있다.

alternative 선택의 방안, 대안   **incredible** 믿을 수 없는   **be plagued by** ∼에 시달리다   **legend** 전설, 범례   **contradiction** 모순   **fallacy** 잘못된 생각

468 (A) increased

우리는 새로운 설명력 있는 생각들을 환영하는데, 그 생각들은 예전 생각들의 압제로부터 우리를 자유롭게 해 주기 때문이다. 그러나 아마 우리는 우리가 선택할 수 있는 여분의 설명 가능성들을 가지고 있는지 모른다. 만약에 이 가능성 중에서 하나만이 옳다고 할 때, 이 커다란 선택의 범위는 이론가들에게는 당혹스러운 것이 될지도 모른다. 왜냐하면 그가 실수할 수 있는 가능성이 증가하기 때문이다.

free ∼ from... ∼를 …에서 벗어나게 하다   **despotism** 압제, 전제(= tyranny)   **surplus** 잉여, 나머지   **disconcerting** 당황스럽게 하는, 당혹시키는(= embarrassing)   **eliminate** 제거하다

469 (D) improving crops

옛날 농부들은 유전 법칙에 대해 아무것도 알지 못하였으나, 그들은 가장 좋은 열매에서 씨를 받아 뿌림으로써 작물의 질을 개선하였다. 그 결과는 다양하게 나타났지만, 그러한 계속된 씨앗 선택으로 인해 작물은 거친 옛 작물과 많이 달라졌다. 눈으로 보고 씨앗을 택하는 방식은 작물 개선의 방법으로 지금도 이용되고 있다.

the laws of heredity 유전 법칙   **sow** 씨 뿌리다

fertilization 비옥하게 만들기

470 (A) manageable

초기 미국인들은 급속도로 변화하는 세상에 살았다. 거의 매일 모든 것들이 진보의 길을 따라 움직이는 것처럼 보였다. 그러나 삶은 아직 그렇게 복잡하지 않아서 그들은 계속되는 변화 속에서도 영광스럽게 번영을 누릴 수 있었다. 그들은 삶에 심취하면서도 그 삶에 압도되지는 않았다. 역사는 빨리 움직이고 있었지만, 다룰 만하였다.

uncomplicated 복잡하지 않은   **prosper** 번영하다
gloriously 영광스럽게   **be immersed in** ∼에 몰두하다
be overwhelmed by ∼에 압도당하다   **stagnant**
침체된, 정체된   **incomprehensible** 이해할 수 없는
dynamic 역동적인

471 (A) administrators

많은 대학 교수들이 강의실을 떠나 학장이나 학부장이 된다. 이러한 새로운 직책은 보통 재정적으로 더 많은 보수가 따르지만, 돈만이 직업을 바꾸는 유일한 이유는 아니다. 현대의 교육제도는 대학에서 인정받는 일의 주된 부분이 행정가에게 돌아가는 그러한 양태로 구성되어 있다.

rewarding 보수가 따르는   **financially** 금전적으로,
재정적으로   **administrator** 행정가   **faculty members**
교수진   **trustee** 이사

472 (B) grow native plants

열대 지방의 채소는 온대 지방에서 자란 채소보다 맛이 덜하다. 열대 지방에서는 가장 좋은 토종을 선택하여 재배하는 일이 없었고, 온대 지방에서 개발된 맛좋은 채소들은 열대 지방에서는 좋은 종자를 만들어 내지 못한다. 좋은 채소를 기르려고 하는 열대 지방의 정원사는 토종 작물을 길러야 한다.

tropical 열대 지방의   **palatable** 맛이 좋은   **native**
variety 토종, 재래종   **horticulture** 원예(법)   **temperate**
zone 온대 지방

473 (C) taking its temperature

물이 끓는 온도가 모든 고도에서 다 똑같은 것은 아니다. 섭씨 100˚는 해수면을 기준으로 물이 끓는 온도이다. 18,000피트 높이에서는 물은 섭씨 83˚에서 끓는다. 따라서 산에 오르는 사람들은 물이 끓는 온도를 재서 대략적인 고도를 측정해 볼 수 있다.

boiling point 끓는 온도, 비등점   **altitude** 고도, 높이
sea level 해수면   **approximation** 근사치   **vapor**
수증기

474 (A) peculiar to that economy

고전 경제학자들의 잘못 중의 하나는 자신들의 국가 경제에서 추출한 경제 법칙이 어디에서나 보편적으로 유용하리라고 가정한 것이었다. 역사학파는 이것에 반기를 들고 각 사회는 그 경제에 특수한 규칙성을 지닌 채 작용하는 그 자신 특유의 경제를 발전시킨다는 점을 보여 주려고 하였다.

classical economist 고전 경제학자 **universal validity** 보편적인 유용성 **extracted from** ~에서 추출된 **the historical school** 역사학파 **peculiar** 독특한

475 (C) the number of skilled workers is decreasing

경영 측면에서 더 큰 문제점 중의 하나는 숙련공을 찾는 일이다. 숙련공과 비숙련공 사이의 임금의 차이는, 숙련공들이 보다 긴 훈련 기간을 필요로 한다는 점에도 불구하고 점점 줄어들고 있다. 따라서 숙련공의 숫자가 줄어들고 있는 것은 아주 당연한 일이다.

management 경영진 **skilled worker** 숙련공 **the pay differential** 임금 차이

476 (B) raise the temperature of the water

물 한 냄비를 난로 위에 올려놓으면 끓기 시작할 때까지 물은 점점 뜨거워진다. 그러나 일단 물이 끓고 나면, 그 온도는 물의 비등점에 고정된 채 지속된다. 냄비를 난로 위에 그대로 놓아두면, 난로의 열기가 더해져서 물을 증기로 발산시키는 역할을 한다. 그러나 물의 온도를 높이지는 않는다.

pan 냄비, 접시 **boil away** steam 물을 증기로 발산하다

477 (B) were not making large salaries

설문지를 돌린 지난번 300명의 학생들 중에서 200명이 응답을 해 왔고, 그중 175명은 금전적으로 성공했다고 이야기하였다. 이 장밋빛 모습은, 만약에 300명 모두가 설문지에 응답을 해 왔다면 달라졌을지도 모른다. 왜냐하면 응답을 하지 않은 100명의 학생들이 많은 월급을 받지 못하고 있을 가능성이 충분히 있기 때문이다.

questionnaire 설문지 **monetarily speaking** 금전적으로 이야기해서 **rosy picture** 장밋빛 모습 **overall** 전반적인

Key Structure ▶

had all three hundred filled out ~
= if all three hundred had filled out ~

478 (D) her team will be better next time

운동 경기에 선수로 뛰지 않는 학생들도 그 경기에 성원을 보냄으로써 자기 팀의 사기를 유지시키는 것은 대학생의 의무이다. 응원 시합도 운동 경기와 마찬가지이다. 예일대학 팀이 하버드대학 팀보다 터치다운을 더 많이 성공시킬 수 있지만, 만약 하버드대학 응원자들이 예일대학 응원자들보다 더 크고 더 오래 성원을 하면, 승리는 하버드대학의 것이고, 그 팀은 다음에는 더 잘하게 될 것이다.

collegiate 대학생의 **nonparticipant** 참여하지 않은 자 **keep up the morale** 사기가 틀어지지 않게 하다 **cheer** 성원하다 **cheering contest** 응원 시합 **touchdown** (미식축구의) 터치다운 **supporter** 지지자 **yell** 고함지르다 **rooter** (열광적인) 응원자

Key Structure ▶

Parallel to the athletic contest ~.
= The cheering contest is parallel to the athletic contest. 응원 시합도 운동 경기와 닮았다.

479 (C) ideas about life

어느 사회고 인간 생활의 기준은 인간이 삶에 대해 가지고 있는 믿음에 의해 결정된다. 어느 때고 삶의 수준[질]은 사회가 인간이 살아가는 방법을 측정하고 비교하는 가치라고 하는 저울에 의해 결정된다. 한 사회의 삶의 기준이 변화하게 될 때, 우리는 그 사회 구성원들이 삶에 대한 생각을 바꾸었다고 추론할 수 있다.

scale 저울, 자 **alter** 바꾸다, 변경하다 **infer** 추론하다 **efficiency** 능률, 유효

480 (A) rationality of the ideas

건설적인 독서는 여러분이 읽고 있는 것에 반응을 나타내고 적응하는 것을 포함한다. 여러분이 읽는 것 모두를 맹목적으로 받아들이지 말고, 또한 작가의 생각이 여러분의 생각과 다르다고 해서 비판하지 마라. 논리와 그것을 지탱하는 증거의 관점에서 여러분이 읽는 바를 숙고해 보라. 작가의 생각을 받아들이느냐 거부하느냐 하는 점을 합리적인 생각을 기초로 결정하라.

constructive 건설적인 **adjust to** ~에 적응하다 **blindly** 맹목적으로 **critical** 비판적인 **weigh** 숙고하다 **evidence** 증거 **rationality** 합리성 **critic** 비평가

Key Structure ▶

1. so critical as to ~ : ~할 만큼 비판적이다
2. base A on B : A의 기초를 B에 두다

481 (A) deciphered

고대 이집트의 글이 수천 년 동안 보존되어 오긴 했지만, 우리는 약 150년 전까지만 해도 그것을 읽을 수 없었다. 나폴레옹 시대의 프랑스는 1798년 이집트를 공격했다. 로제타에 몇몇 군사 장치를 설치하던 중 프랑스인들은 같은 내용이 상형 문자와 희랍어로 함께 새겨진 돌을 파내게 되었다. 희랍어를 열쇠로 하여 지루한 수시간에 걸친 노력 끝에 상형 문자가 판독되었다.

military works 군사 장치[시설] uncover 벗기다, 파내다 inscribe 새기다 hieroglyphics 상형 문자, 그림 문자 tedious 지루한, 싫증나는 decipher 판독하다, 해독하다 destroy 파괴하다, 부수다 copy 복사하다, 복제하다

482 (B) individual plants

멘델의 시대 이전에 유전을 연구한 사람들은 성공하지 못했다. 왜냐하면 그들은 연구 범위에 모든 세대의 동식물, 모든 종의 동식물을 포함했기 때문이었다. 그들은 그렇게 많은 수의 개체들을 단지 약식으로만 연구할 수 있었다. 멘델은 자신의 연구를 한 가지 식물 속에서 발견되는 특정한 특징들을 연구하는 데만 국한시켰다. 그는 그보다 앞서 연구한 사람들이 실패한 부문에서 성공을 거두었는데, 그것은 그가 개별적인 식물 연구에 만족하였기 때문이었다.

heredity 유전 summarily 약식으로 confine A to B A를 B에 국한시키다 predecessor 선구자, 앞서 간 사람 successive 연속적인 vertebrate 척추동물

483 (D) lands across the ocean

16세기에 프랑스가 해외 식민지 정책에 적극적인 역할을 하지 못한 것을 설명하기란 어렵지 않다. 프랑스는 16세기 전반부에 신대륙으로부터 동떨어져 있었고 관심도 갖지 않았다. 16세기 후반부에는 종교 전쟁에 휘말려 있었다. 이 종교 분쟁이 해결되고 나서야 비로소 프랑스 국민은 그들의 정력을 바다 건너 땅에 쏟을 수가 있었다.

overseas enterprises 해외 식민지 정책 direct A to B A를 B에 쏟다 reformation 개혁

Key Structure ▶

Only after ~ did... :
~하고 나서야 비로소 …하다 (강조 · 도치 구문)

484 (D) new football coach

대학은 이미 가지고 있는 기능에 덧붙여 또 하나의 기능을 갖게 되었는데, 그것은 운동 경기라는 형태로 대중을 즐겁게 하는 기능이다. 대학 생활의 이 특수한 면에 대한 대중의 관심은 대학 교육 활동의 그 어느 것보다도 크다. 대학 총장이 누구로 임명되었느냐 하는 것에 대해서보다 새로운 축구 코치가 누가 되었느냐에 더 많은 시선이 쏠려 있다.

entertainment 오락, 즐겁게 하기 appointment 임명 physical education 체육 enrollment 등록

Key Structure ▶

1. another = another function : 또 다른 기능
2. that of ~ = the function of ~

485 (C) run out of the danger zone

화재에서 대부분의 참사자들은 연기 질식에 의해 야기되었다. 연기 중의 일산화탄소는 현기증을 유발하고 결국에는 쓰러지게 한다. 자신을 보호하기 위해서는, 언제나 화재 현장에는 유독 가스가 존재한다는 가정 하에서 행동하라. 호흡 활동의 증가는 흡입되는 유독 가스의 양도 증가시키게 되므로 숨을 많이 쉬지 않는 것이 중요하고, 위험 지역에서 재빨리 빠져나오는 것이 제일 안전한 일이다.

fatality 참사자 asphyxiation 질식(= suffocation) carbon monoxide 일산화탄소 cf. carbon dioxide 이산화탄소 dizziness 현기증 eventual 궁극적인 collapse 쓰러짐, 붕괴 poisonous gas 유독 가스 inhale 흡입하다, 숨을 들이쉬다 stimulate 자극하다

486 (C) combining known techniques

발명품들은 여러 각도에서 볼 수 있다. 첫째로 발명가가 지닌 영감의 결과로 볼 수도 있고, 둘째로 이미 존재하는 기술과 도구를 재결합하여 얻은 결과로 볼 수도 있다. 새로이 나타나는 기술과 도구의 놀라운 모습 중의 하나는 자주, 똑같은 기술이 두 사람에 의해서 거의 같은 시기에 발견된다는 사실이다. 이러한 상황은, 발명품이 이미 알려진 기술을 결합하는 것이라는 면에서 보면 가장 잘 이해될 수 있다.

angle 각도 inspiration 영감 recombine 재결합하다 amazing 놀라운, 굉장한 feature 모습 ; simultaneous 동시의

487 (B) the whole population

남성들은 사회를 생산이라는 관점에서 보는 경향이 많은 데 반하여 여성들은 사회를 사람들이 생계를 꾸려나가는 장소로서뿐만 아니라, 모든 사람들이 훌륭한 삶을 얻고 즐기는 장소로 본다. 이것이 바로 여성들이 교육, 어린이와 가족의 삶, 공공의 건강 등의 문제에 관심을 갖는 이유이며, 또한 여성이 전 인류의

복지를 위해 기능을 발휘할 수 있는 가장 나은 환경을 얻기 위한 작업에 참여하도록 기대되는 이유이다.

count on 기대하다, 의지하다(= rely on) participate in 참여하다, 참가하다(= take part in) welfare 복지, 후생 underprivileged 혜택을 받지 못하는 delinquent 태만한

488 (A) so that we can be like everybody else

광고는 그 상품을 소유함으로써 우리가 남의 시선의 중심이 되고 동료들의 부러움을 살 것이라는 점을 우리에게 확신시키려는 노력을 통하여 어떤 상품에 대해 갖고 싶어하는 욕망을 만들어 내려고 자주 추구한다. 이것은 젊은이들의 마음을 움직이는 힘인데, 그것은 성숙이란 것이 자신의 대등한 사람들과 함께 살아가는 능력에 기초하기 때문이다. 우리가 다른 사람과 거의 같아질 수 있도록 하기 위해 광고는 우리에게 여러 상품들을 원하도록 만든다.

advertising 광고 convince 확신하다 adolescent 청년기의, 젊은이의 maturity 성숙(도) equal 동등한 사람, 동배(同輩)

489 (B) the expressions on his parents' faces

제스처는 신체의 의미 있는 움직임, 특히 얼굴의 움직임이다. 제스처는 말에 의해 전달되는 내용 외에 또 그것을 넘어서 감정과 기분을 표현하는 데에 이용된다. 연인들은 많은 말로 사랑을 표시할 수 있지만, 그들의 말보다는 제스처가 보다 많은 것을 전달한다. 마찬가지로 부모가 (말로) 자식에게 위협을 가하기는 하지만 눈치 빠른 아이는 그 위협을 부모님의 얼굴 표정에 견주어 볼 것이다.

over and above 덧붙여(= in addition to) transmit 전달하다 convey 전달하다 in like manner 마찬가지로 threaten 위협하다 a knowing child 약삭빠른 아이

Key Structure

those transmitted by words : 말로써 전달되는 그것들 (those = the feelings and moods)

490 (D) the rewards of good conduct

얼마 전까지만 해도, 선생님들은 엄하게 규율을 지키는 사람으로 기대되었다. 학급에서 지켜야 할 많은 규칙을 하나라도 어기면 정해진 처벌이 있었다. 물론 선생님이 효과적인 수업을 하기 위해서는 행실이 바른 학급을 지도해야 되겠지만, 선생님은 좋은 행실을 만들어 내는 보다 긍정적인 방법을 채택하게 되었다. 선생님은 왜 학생들의 행실이 좋지 않은지를 이해하려 하고, 좋은 행실에는 보상이 따른다는 점을 강조함으로써 질서 있는 학급을 유지하려고 노력한다.

disciplinarian 엄격한 사람, 규율을 지키는 사람 violation 범법 행위, 어김 well-behaved class 행실이 좋은 학급 foster 기르다 obedience 복종 reward 보상, 보답

491 (C) the words came from the man who wrote them

말은 그것을 사용한 사람의 감정을 정확히 반영한다는 점에서 거울과 같다. 말은 슬픔에 찬 작가의 눈물과 행복에 찬 작가의 미소를 반영한다. 이 반영의 기초는 글을 쓰는 기교나 문체, 그 자체에 있는 것이 아니다. 왜냐하면 글로 표현된 말은 만약 그것을 쓴 사람에게서 나온 것이 아니면 눈물도 미소도 또한 어떠한 다른 감정도 드러내 보이지 않을 것이기 때문이다.

mirror 거울 reflect 반영하다 mechanics 기교, 기법 (= technique) as such 그 자체, 그것만으로는 unless ~이 아니면(= if ~ not) emotion-laden 감정이 깃든

492 (A) importance of sunlight

인간이 지닌 비합리적이고 무의식적인 동기들을 계속 중시함으로써 어떤 비관론자들은 모든 가치에서 합리성을 제거해 버리게 되고, 사실 그것의 존재까지도 부인하게끔 되었다. 물론 새로운 발견들이 인간 행동의 적절한 이론으로 나타나야 하지만, 인간 삶의 꽃이 어두운 토양 속에 뿌리박고 있다는 발견이 어떤 면으로도 햇빛의 중요성을 부인하지는 못한다.

irrational 비합리적인 unconscious 무의식적인 pessimist 비관론자, 염세주의자 strip A of B A에게서 B를 빼앗다 refute 반박하다 erosion 부식

493 (B) experience anguish

우리는 자유롭게 숨 쉬도록 용인될 때 만족의 감정을 특별히 느끼지 않는다. 그러나 숨 쉬는 것에 제약을 받을 때, 우리는 분명히 불쾌감을 겪게 된다. 생각도 마찬가지이다. 자유롭게 흘러 논리적인 결론에 이르는 생각들에 대해서는 반응이 없다가도, 생각이 어려움에 둘러싸이게 될 때 우리는 고통을 느끼게 된다.

restrain 제약하다 be beset by ~에 둘러싸이다(= be surrounded by) shallowly 얕게, 피상적으로 anguish 번민

494 (D) from the last paragraph to the introduction

잡지는 책처럼 앞표지부터 뒷표지까지 순서대로 읽게 되어 있다. 그러나 잡지를 읽는 많은 사람들이 정기 간행물[잡지]을 뒤에서부터 거꾸로 손가락으로

넘기며 보는 유해한 습관을 갖게 되었다. 그러한 사람들이 4페이지짜리 이야기를 마지막 문단에서 첫 문단으로 거꾸로 멍하게 읽고 있는 것이 종종 목격된다.

in the order 순서대로   segment 부분   pernicious 유해한, 치명적인   thumb backward through periodicals 정기 간행물을 손가락으로 거꾸로 넘기다 absent-mindedly 멍하니, 정신이 나간 듯   skim 건성으로 읽다   paragraph 문단

495 (B) a succession of races or nations

어떤 교묘한 책략을 쓴 결과로 특정한 한 집단의 인간, 민족 또는 국가가 세계의 전략적인 위치를 점령할 수도 있다. 그들은 지구상의 어느 지역을 지배하게 될 때까지 이 위치를 강화할 수도 있다. 그러나 그들은 새로운 민족 또는 국가에 의해 대치되므로 그들의 지배는 단지 일시적일 뿐이다. 인간 역사 활동의 중심지는 서로 다른 여러 종족과 국가들에 의해 번갈아가며 점령당해 왔다.

maneuver 교묘한 책략[조치](= manoeuvre)   strategic 전략적인   temporary 일시적인   be superseded by ~에 자리를 빼앗기다, ~에 대치되다   concurrently 동시에

496 (B) each culture borrows from a preceding one

미국은 토착 문화가 없어서 예술과 문학의 형태를 유럽에 크게 빚지고 있다고 자주 이야기되고 있다. 그러나 유럽에 있어서도, 오랜 시간에 걸쳐 나타난 동화 현상이 토착적인 독창성으로 잘못 불리고 있다. 더욱 거슬러 올라가 보면, 로마인들의 문화는 필연적으로 그리스인들의 문화에서 유래한 것이었다. 변하지 않는 역사 발전의 유형에 따라서 개별적인 각 문화는 앞선 문화에서 차용하고 있다.

indigenous 토착의, 고유한   be in debt to A for B A에게 B를 빚지다   assimilation 동화(同化) inevitably 필연적으로   in accordance with ~에 따라 notoriously 악명 높게   unperceptive 둔한   pinnacle 정상, 봉우리

497 (A) dissolution

지난 세기에 서구 학자들은 더 이상 존재하지 않는 문명권들의 역사를 밝히는 일뿐만 아니라 현존하는 다른 문명권의 구조를 이해하고 설명하기 위하여 많은 일을 하였다. 그 모든 경우에 있어서 학자들은, 문명권마다 서구 문명과 접하게 될 때 부패[붕괴]의 상태에 이르렀고, 경우에 따라서는 소멸에 이르게 되었다는 점을 알아내게 되었다.

illuminate 밝히다, 조명하다   extant 현존하는, 남아

있는   decay 붕괴, 부패   dissolution 해체, 소멸, 용해 rejuvenation 회춘, 원기 회복

498 (D) either a madman or a criminal

어린아이 시절부터 인간은 물질적 소유에 대한 자신의 권리와 자신의 문화권의 사회적, 종교적 의식[의례]에 대하여 뿌리 깊은 태도를 개발한다. 이 영역에서 그는 이성적이라기보다는 감성적으로 생각한다. 현재의 철도 체계가 변화를 가함으로써 개선될 수 있다는 점을 기꺼이 인정하려는 많은 사람들은 현재의 경제 체계나 우리 사회의 관습에 변화가 있어야 한다고 제안한 사람을 마치 미치광이나 범인쯤 되는 것으로 생각하려 할 것이다.

right to ~에 대한 권리   possessions 소유물 practices 의식, 예식   realm 영역   enlightened 개화된, 계몽된   old-fashioned 구식의   criminal 범인

499 (C) vastly different

현미경 기술이 개선되기 전에는 과학자들은 물질을 비교적 큰 단위로만 연구할 수 있었고, 이 단위 각각에는 많은 개별적인 분자가 들어 있었다. 보다 커다랗고 관찰 가능한 단위를 구성하고 있는 이 작은 구조물의 움직임에 대하여 어떠한 예측도 할 수 없었다. 왜냐하면 이 분자라는 구조물들이 똑같은 법칙을 따른다는 확신은 없었기 때문이었다. 마찬가지로 오늘날 군중의 행위를 보고 개개인 인간의 행위를 예언하는 것은 불가능하다. 왜냐하면 두 가지 수준의 행동을 지배하는 규칙은 완전히 다른 것 같기 때문이다.

refinement 개선, 세련   microscopic 현미경의 molecule 분자   prediction 예언, 예보   assurance 확신   the two levels of action 두 수준의 행위(즉 군중의 행위와 개인의 행위)   virtually 실제로   identical 동일한 consistent 일관된

500 (A) uniformity of opinion is developed

어떤 한 사람이 여론의 풍조를 효과적으로 반대하고 자기 자신의 견해와 다른 견해가 자신의 사고 속으로 들어오는 것을 막아낸다는 것은 실질적으로 불가능한 일이다. 만약 이와 같은 반대되는 견해가 널리 알려지는 경우, 이 견해들은 반드시 모든 개인에게 자극제가 되고 그는 그 견해들이 정당한 것인가를 스스로에게 물어보아야 한다. 해답의 성질은 문제의 성질에 의해 결정이 된다. 그 개인은 자기 자신이 그 견해들에 반대하기 위해서 자신과 반대 입장을 가진 자의 견해에 나타난 방향을 따라 사고하고 있음을 곧 알게 될 것이다. 얼마 가지 않아 그 개인은 반대

입장을 가진 자가 얼마 전까지 지니던 견해들을 이제는 자신이 지니고 있음을 알게 된다. 아직은 그 자의 최근 이야기에 반대하고는 있지만. 바로 이런 방식으로 여러 가지 견해가 통일되어지는 것이다.

virtually 실질적으로   **the climate of opinion** 여론(의 풍조) *cf.* **climate** 사조, 풍조   **intrusion** 침범   **be publicized** 알려지다   **stimuli** 자극제 *sg.* stimulus   **before long** 얼마 가지 않아   **uniformity of opinion** 견해의 획일성   **adversary** 적, 상대(= opponent)

Key Structure ▸

1. the intrusion into his own thinking of opinions contrary to his own
   = the intrusion of opinions contrary to his own into his own thinking
2. Thus it is that ~ = It is thus that ~ :
   이렇게 하여 ~된다 (It ~ that 강조 구문)

501 (D) what you're called

잭 로즈만이 직원 2명인 회사를 설립하고서 컴퓨터 프로그래머가 긴급히 필요해서 첫 직원을 고용한 후의 일이었다. 그 사람이 로즈만의 사무실에 들러 말하기를 "덧붙여 말해둘 게 있는데 잭, 저의 직함이 무엇이죠?" 로즈만은 그에게 말했다. "있잖아! 나는 회장이고 자네는 회장을 보좌하는 직책이라 할 수 있지."

약 일주일 이내에 그 새 직원은 "회장 보좌역"이라고 새겨진 명함을 만들어서 손님들에게 돌렸다.

로즈만은 이런 그의 행동에 놀랐고, 이 일로 인해 자신의 비즈니스 관행이 영향을 받았다고 말했다. 이제 그는 장미가 이름만 달리 불리고 향기는 매한가지이더라도, 사람들은 자신들의 직함에 매우 신경을 쓴다고 믿는다. 비즈니스를 연구하는 학자들도 이에 동의한다.

"당신의 자아상은 당신이 무슨 일을 하는가와 어떻게 불리고 있는지에 달려 있다. 단순히 직함을 바꾸는 것일지라도 그것이 당신의 자아와 인격에 영향을 미친다."라고 로드 아일랜드, 브리스톨에 있는 로저 윌리엄 대학의 직업연구소 소장인 패트릭 레너헌은 말했다. 그는 경력에 자아가 관련되는 것을 연구해 왔는데, 많은 사람들이 돈보다는 오히려 좋은 직함을 원한다는 것을 발견했다. 이것은 아마도 직함이 직업에 대한 만족도를 증가시켜 주기 때문일 것이다.

urgently 긴급하게, 다급히   **drop by** 들르다   **incidentally** 부수적으로, 우연히, 덧붙여 말하자면   **I'll tell you what.** 있잖아!   **hand out** 나누어 주다, 분배하다   **self-concept** 자아상(= self-image)   **affect** 영향을 미치다, 작용하다   **would rather A than B** B보다는 차라리 A하다

Section 1 어법 문제

502 (C) uncritical → uncritically

우리의 교양 교육이 대다수에게 미치는 영향력은 대단하여서 우리는 조금은 무비판적으로 다음을 받아들여 온 경향이 있다. 첫째로 자유는 좋은 것이라는 점, 둘째로 자유를 소유하면 우리의 행복이 증가하리라는 점이다. 그러나 언제나 조금만 생각해 보면 이 두 명제의 어느 것도 자명한 것이 아니라는 점을 알기에 충분했을 것이라고 이야기해도 당연할 것이다.

general education 교양 교육, 일반 교육 uncritically 무비판적으로 self-evident 자명한

구문

1 On most of us the effect of our general education
= The effect of our general education on most of us
2 A has been such that ~ :
A는 ~할 정도로 대단하였다, A는 매우 대단해서 그 결과 ~하였다
  • such that = so great that
3 the possession of it is likely to increase our happiness
그것의 소유는 우리의 행복을 증가시킬 가능성이 많다
  • it = liberty
4 It may well be said that ~ :
~라고 말하는 것도 당연하다
5 a moment's consideration should have been sufficient to ~
= if we had considered for a moment, it should have been sufficient to ~
조금만 생각해 보았다면 ~하기에 충분했을 것이다
  • should는 가정법을 나타내는 조동사.
6 neither of these propositions is self-evident
이 (두) 명제들 중 어느 것도 자명하지는 않다
  • either나 neither는 둘 중의 어느 하나를 가리키며 보통은 단수 동사가 나옴.

해설

동사 believe를 꾸미는 부사이므로 uncritically로 고친다.

503 (B) is → be

과거에는 인간은 생존을 위하여 종종 피차의 공포라는 굴레로 결속되어 있었다. 오늘날 우리의 생존은 우리의 공동의 굴레가 공유된 지식이기를 요구하고 있다. 개선된 이해가 예전의[오래된] 적대 관계를 반드시 묻어 버리지는 않겠지만, 오해가 그러한 적대 관계에 기여하리라는 것은 분명하다. 따라서 국가들 사이에서처럼, 우리가 국민들 간의 소통과 이해와 협력을 증진시키는 것이 중요하다.

be bound together 결속되다, 같은 운명체가 되다 survival 생존 bond 유대 관계, 굴레 mutual fear 상호[피차] 공포 shared knowledge 공유된 지식 not necessarily 반드시 ~은 아니다(부분 부정) antagonism 적대 관계 contribute (to) ~에 기여하다 communication 소통, 교제 cooperation 협력

구문

1 Our survival requires that our common bond be shared knowledge.
우리의 생존은 우리의 공동의 유대 관계[굴레]가 공유된 지식이기를 요구한다.
  • require의 종속절인 that절에는 가정법 현재 동사인 원형동사를 써야 함. require, command, propose, suggest, order, be important, 등등.
2 be certain to ~ : 틀림없이 ~하다
3 It is important that we increase communication ~
소통과 ~를 증진시키는 것이 중요하다
  • It is important 뒤에도 require처럼 가정법 현재 동사인 동사 원형을 써야 한다. 따라서 increase는 현재시제 동사라기보다는 원형동사로 볼 수 있음.
4 as among nations 국가들 사이에서처럼
= as it is important that we increase communication, understanding and cooperation among nations

해설

주절의 동사가 require인 경우, 종속절인 that절에는 의미상 당위성을 표현하는 가정법 현재 동사인 원형동사를 써야 한다.

504 (C) be up → being up

사람이 보통 잠들어 있는 시간에는 체온이 떨어진다. 체온이 떨어지면 사람은 쌀쌀함을 느끼게 된다. 이것이 바로 잠자는 사람을 덮어 주어야 하는 이유이다. 낮에 활동하고 밤에 자는 것에 습관이 든 사람은, 온밤을 자지 않고 (일을 하고) 있는 경우에도 밤에 체온이 떨어지게 된다. 밤에 일하고 낮에 자는 사람은 잠을 자든 자지 않든 낮에 체온이 떨어지게 된다.

temperature of the body 체온 asleep 잠들어 있는 feel chilly 냉기를 느끼다 be up (일어나) 활동하다 stay up all night 온밤을 자지 않고 보내다

구문

1 be accustomed to -ing(동명사) :
~하는 것에 익숙해져 있다
2 be up during the day and sleep at night
낮에 활동하고 밤에 자다

해설

be accustomed to + -ing : ~에 익숙해져 있다, 습관이 되어 있다
  • to는 부정사를 동반하는 말이 아니고 전치사이므로 그 뒤에 (동)명사가 와야 함. (sleeping의 -ing 형태에 유의.)

505 (A) We are impossible → It is impossible for us

산업화의 이득과 폐해에 대하여 대차 대조표를 작성하는 것은 불가능하다. 산업화의 폐해나 이득이 증가하는지 아니면 줄어드는지에 대한 의견이 일치하지 않을 것이기 때문이다. 어떤 열성분자들은 산업화와 문명화를 동일시할 것이다. 그러나 대다수의 사람들은 그(산업화) 결과가 좋기도 하고 나쁘기도 하다는 점을 인정할 것이다. 세계 거의 모든 지역에서 산업화는 물질문명의 진보, 생활 수준의 향상, 그리고 서민층의 정치권력 증대를 의미해 왔다.

draw up (문서를) 작성하다　balance-sheet 대차 대조표　good and ill 이득과 폐해　as to ～에 관하여(= about, concerning, regarding)　enthusiast 열성분자, 광신자　both good and bad (동시에) 좋기도 하고 나쁘기도 하다　advance (in) ～의 진보　a rise (in) ～의 향상　political power 정치권력　the humble classes 서민층

구문

1 There would be no agreement ~ : 의견의 일치가 없을지 모른다
　• would는 추측이나 가정의 뜻을 나타냄.
2 identify industrialization and civilization : 산업화와 문명화를 동일시하다
　• identify A and B = identify A with B

해설

impossible, easy, difficult, hard, tough 등의 형용사는 어떤 행위를 하는 것이 어렵거나 불가능하다는 뜻이므로 사람을 주어로 쓸 수 없다.
cf. He is impossible to please.에서 He는 please의 목적어이던 him이 주어로 나온 것이므로 올바른 문장임.
(→ It is impossible to please him.)

506 (E) to be stripped of → stripped of

문화적 요소들의 전파와 관련하여 가장 중요한 요인 중의 하나는 그 요소들이 한 문화권에서 다른 문화권으로 거의 전적으로 형태적인 면에서만 전해진다는 점이다. 다시 말하여, (문화를) 빌려 오는 사회는 보통은 본래의 문화적 배경을 이해하지 않은 채 행동의 특정한 유형을 자신이 터득한 대로 본떠 온다는 점이다. 따라서 새로운 요소는 객관적인 모습의 수준에서 전파되어 들어오고, 본래의 배경 속에서 그것이 지녔던 대부분의 의미와 연상되는 내용들이 제거된 채로 그것을 받아들이는 사회에 들어온다.

diffusion (문화 등의) 확산, 전파　transfer 이전하다　exclusively 전적으로, 오로지　apprehend 터득하다. (직관으로) 감지하다　association 연상(되는 내용)

구문

1 (The new element) … comes into the receiving culture stripped of ~
(새 요소가) ～이 제거된 채로 들어온다
　• 수동분사 stripped of ～는 comes의 보어로 쓰였음.
2 stripped of most of the meanings 대부분의 의미들이 제거된
　• strip A of B : A에게서 B를 빼앗다[제거하다]
　→ (수동형) A is stripped of B: A가 B를 뺏기다

해설

수동분사 stripped of B는 그 자체가 형용사처럼 comes의 보어로 쓰였으므로 부정사를 쓸 이유가 없다.

507 (E) rapid-changing → rapidly-changing

전 세계 사람들이 여가라는 새로운 자유가 갖는 무한한 가능성들을 깨닫기 시작하였다. 특히 이것은 고도로 발달된 기술을 가진 나라에서 그러하다. 현대적 기술, 단축된 근로일, 길어진 주말, 조기 은퇴, 그리고 나아진 건강은 사람들에게 예전에 가졌던 것보다 더 많은 자유 시간을 주었다. 그러나 이러한 시대에 오직 학생들만이 여가 시간을 얻지 못하였다. 그들은 급속하게 변화하는 세상에 보조를 맞추고 미래에 대비하기 위해 그전 어느 때보다 더 오래 더 열심히 공부해야 하기 때문이다. 학생의 삶은 늘 노력은 많이 하지만 여가 시간은 거의 없는 그런 삶이었고, 아마 앞으로도 그럴 것이다.

countless 셀 수 없을 정도의　highly-developed technology 고도로 발달된 기술　retirement 은퇴　keep up with ～에 보조를 맞추다　rapidly-changing 빠른 속도로 변화하는

구문

1 This is especially true in ~ : ～에서 특히 사실이다
2 one of much effort = a life of much effort

해설

현재분사 changing은 동사적인 성질을 유지하고 있으므로 부사인 rapidly의 꾸밈을 받아야 한다.

508 (A) turned over → has turned over

저는 이제 52년의 군 생활을 마칩니다. 이 세기[20세기]로 들어서기도 전에 제가 육군에 입대한 것은 제가 소년 시절에 키운 희망과 꿈을 실현하기 위해서였습니다. 제가 웨스트포인트 연병장에서 충성을 맹세한 이후로 강산도 여러 번 변하였고 꿈들이 사라진 지 오래이지만, 아직도 저는 그 당시 가장 인기 있었던 병영가(兵營歌) 중 하나의 후렴을 잊지 않고 있는데, 그것은 "노병은 결코 죽지 않는다. 단지 사라져 갈 뿐이다."라고 매우 당당하게 선언하고

있었습니다. 그리고 그 노래의 노병처럼 저는 군 생활을 마치고 이제 사라져 갑니다. 신이 자신의 임무를 보도록 빛을 주신 것처럼 자신의 임무를 다하려고 힘쓴 노병으로서... 안녕!

military service 군(대) 생활 the turn of the century 세기의 도래(여기에서는 20세기를 일컬음) fulfillment 성취 boyish hopes and dreams 소년 시절의 희망과 꿈들 turn over 바뀌다, 뒤집어지다 take the oath (충성의) 맹세를 하다 the plain at West Point (미국의 육군사관학교인) 웨스트포인트 연병장 refrain (노래의) 후렴 barrack ballad 병영가, 군가(군의 막사에서 부르는 노래) proclaim 선언하다, 선포하다 fade away 사라져 가다

구문 ▶

1 The world has turned over many times since I took the oath on the plain at West Point
내가 웨스트포인트 연병장에서 충성을 맹세한 이후로 강산이 여러 번 변했습니다
• 종속절 since 이하의 동사가 과거시제(took)이므로 주절의 동사는 현재완료형(have + p.p.)이 되어야 함.

2 the dreams have long since vanished
= it is long since the dreams vanished
꿈들이 사라진 지 오래이다

3 as God gave him the light to see that duty
신이 그에게 자신의 임무를 보도록 빛을 주신 바처럼
• as는 모습, 양태를 나타내는 접속사.

해설 ▶

종속절(since...)에 과거 동사(took)가 쓰였으므로, 주절에는 현재완료형 동사가 와야 한다.

509 **(D) of understanding and appreciating → to understand and appreciate**

현대문학들은 고전 작품들에 엄청나게 많은 빚을 지고 있는데, 그 본보기들은 그리스 작품들보다는 라틴 작품들인 경우가 훨씬 더 많다. 이것이 현대문학뿐만 아니라 현대어들에도 적용된다는 것은 분명하다. 이 언어들에는 고전어들에서 유래한 단어들의 수가 엄청나게 많고 대부분은 라틴어에서 온 것들이다. 우리의 현대어들과 문학들이 진 빚은 너무나 심오하여 대단히 많은 작품들과 어휘들이 라틴어를 모르면 이해와 감상이 안 될 지경이다. 고대 로마인들이 그리스인들에게 빚진 것 못지않게 우리도 로마인들에게 빚지고 있는 것이다.

innumerable 엄청나게 많은, 무수한 debt 빚 classical writing 고전 작품 obvious 분명한 contain 포함하다 huge 거대한 classical language 고전어(그리스어와 라틴어) indebtedness 빚짐(debt → indebt → indebtedness) profound 심오한, 깊은 appreciate 이해하다 Latin 라틴어(고대 로마제국의 언어. 이탈리아어, 프랑스어, 스페인어, 포르투갈어, 루마니아어 등이 여기에서 나온 언어들임)

구문 ▶

1 the greater part of them = most of them
그들 대부분

2 We owe to the Romans scarcely less than the Romans owed to the Greeks.
고대 로마인들이 희랍인들에게 빚진 것 못지않게 우리도 로마인들에게 빚지고 있다.
• owe A to B : A를 B에 빚지다, A가 있는 것은 B 덕택이다
• scarcely less : 거의 마찬가지로, 거의 뒤지지 않게(no less와 거의 비슷한 뜻)

해설 ▶

impossible이라는 형용사는 부정사와 함께 쓰인다.
Very large parts of them are impossible to understand and appreciate ~
= It is impossible to understand and appreciate very large parts of them ~

510 **(B) unchallenging → unchallenged**

우리 사회의 많은 인사들은 사람들이 더 열심히 일하도록 시키는 가장 좋은 방법은 그들의 이윤이나 급료를 올려 주는 것이라고 느끼고 있다. 자신의 물질적 소유물을 늘리기를 원하는 것이 다름 아닌 "인간의 본성"이라고 이들 인사들은 생각한다. 이러한 유의 독단은 우리가 다른 나라들에 대하여 아는 것이 없다면 문제되지 않고 통용될지도 모른다. 그러나 어떤 사회에서는 이윤이라는 동기가 효과적인 유인책은 아니라는 것이 밝혀졌다. 백인들과 접촉하고 난 후에 멜라네시아 군도의 트로브리앙 섬의 주민들은 진주조개 채취 잠수를 통하여 어마어마하게 부자가 될 수도 있었다. 하지만 그들은 자신들의 당장 필요한 것들을 충족시킬 정도로만 일하고자 하였다.

profit 이윤, 이득 wage 임금, 급료 material possessions 물질적 소유(물) dogma 독단 the profit motive 이익이라는 동기 effective 효과적인 incentive 유인책 Melanesia 오스트레일리아 북동쪽에 이어져 있는 남태평양의 섬들을 일컫는 용어 cf. Polynesia 하와이, 사모아, 타히티, 뉴질랜드 등의 여러 섬을 일컫는 명칭 fabulously 어마어마하게 pearl diving 진주조개를 채취하기 위해 바다에 뛰어드는 것 immediate wants 당장 필요한 것들

구문 ▶

1 get people to work harder 사람들을 더 열심히 일하게 시키다
• get는 사역의 뜻을 지니고 있지만 아직은 목적격보어에 to부정사를 가짐.

2 This sort of dogma might well go unchallenged
이러한 종류의 독단은 문제되지 않고 통용될지 모른다
• might well ⓥ 당연히 ~하다 (might는 가정법 동사)
• go unchallenged (상황이) 제지받지 않고 지속되다

3 could have become fabulously rich
진주조개 채취 잠수를 통하여 어마어마하게 부자가 될 수도 있었다

• 가정법 과거완료 구문으로 과거에 있을 수 있었던 일의 반대 상황을 표현.

4 only long enough to ~ : ~할 정도의 시간만

해설

go unchallenged : 독단이 제지되지 않고 진행되는 것이므로, 수동의 뜻을 지닌 과거분사 unchallenged를 써야 한다. unchallenged는 go의 보어 역할.

511 **(D) be resulted from → result from**

내 나이 15세쯤 되던 때에 내가 관찰한 것 중의 하나로 나에게 인상 깊었던 것은 사회의 모든 계층, 아마도 특히 상류층에 일어날 것 같은 일이다. 사람들에게 나타나는 고통이나 고민은 사랑하는 사람의 죽음, 중병, 극도의 가난, 자연재해 등 피할 수 없는 불행보다 근본적으로 피할 수 있는 불행으로부터 야기되는 경우가 더 많다는 생각이 들었다. 불행의 대부분은 친구와의 사소한 불화나 마음의 갈등에서 생기는 것 같다. 이 불행은 상당 부분 충족되지 않은 욕구나 헛된 야망, 혹은 일반적으로 말해서 그릇된 가치관에서 나오는 것이다. 가난하지도 않고 몸이 아프지도 않은데 자신이 비참하다고 느끼는 사람들이 많고, 자신들의 허영심만이 다쳤을 뿐인데 몹시 기분 상해하는 사람들도 있다.

observation 관찰 ⓥ observe   all strata of society 모든 사회 계층   stratum 계층 *pl.* strata   avoidable evil 피할 수 있는 불행   catastrophes occurring in nature 자연재해, 천재지변   petty 작은, 사소한   feuding 불화(를 빚는)   one's fellow man 동료   inner conflict 내적[심적] 갈등   a large extent 상당 부분   frustrated desire 좌절된 욕구   vain ambition 헛된 야망   a false sense of value 잘못된 가치관   miserable 비참한   physically ill 육체적으로 병든   badly injured 몹시 상처 입은   nothing but 단지(=only)   vanity 허영심

구문

1 It struck me that ~ : ~라는 생각이 들었다
  • It은 가주어, that ~ 이 진주어
  • strike - struck - struck 때리다
2 be caused more often by A than by B : B보다 A에 의해 더 자주 야기되다
3 unavoidable ones such as ~ : ~과 같은 피할 수 없는 불행들
  • ones = evils, 부정대명사

해설

result는 수동형이 없는 자동사이다.

Section 2 내용 흐름 파악 문제

512 **(B) due to → in spite of / despite**

가택 침입의 절반 정도는 열린 채 또는 잠그지 않은 채로 남겨둔 문이나 창문을 통하여 이루어진다. 그리고 우리들의 반복되는 경고에도 불구하고 주부들은 외출할 때 여전히 신문과 우유병을 문간 계단에 쌓이도록 놔두거나 "월요일까지 집을 비움"이라는 쪽지를 문에 붙여 놓아 자신의 부재를 널리 알린다.

by way of ~을 통하여(= by means of)   unfastened 잠그지 않은   due to ~ 덕분에   warning 경고   housewife 가정주부   advertize 광고하다   accumulate 쌓이다   doorstep 문간 계단   notice 쪽지

구문

1 Something like half the entries into houses are made 가택 침입의 절반 정도가 이루어진다
  • something like = about
2 doors and windows which have been left open or unfastened
  열린 채 또는 잠그지 않은 채로 남겨둔 문이나 창문
3 by leaving newspapers and milk bottles to accumulate
  신문이나 우유병을 남겨두어 쌓이도록 놔두어서

해설

우리의 반복되는 경고에도 불구하고 문이나 창문을 열어놓은 채 주부들이 집을 비운다는 내용이므로, due to를 in spite of 또는 despite로 고친다.

513 **(E) smallness → vastness**

정말로 현명한 사람들은 겸손만큼 마음의 태도로 적합한 것이 없다는 것을 깨달을 것이다. 가장 위대한 사상가들은 자신들의 무지를 늘 가장 깊숙하게 인식하고 있었다. 다른 사람들보다 더 넓은 빛의 범위를 보는 한편, 그들은 또한 주변의 어둠이 갖는 더 넓은 범위도 보았다. 그들이 알았던 것은 그들에게 알려지지 않은 것의 방대함을 확신시킬 따름이었다.

the truly wise 진정으로 현명한 사람들 *cf.* the wise 현명한 사람들   be conscious of ~을 의식하다   ignorance 무지, 무식   behold 보다   a wider circle of light 빛의 더 넓은 영역   surrounding darkness 주변의 어둠

구문

1 there is no attitude of mind so fitting as that of humility 겸손만큼 마음의 태도로 적합한 것이 없다
2 convinced them of the vastness of what remained unknown   알려지지 않은 것의 방대함을 그들에게 확신시킬 따름이었다
  • convince A of B : A에게 B를 확신시키다
  • what remained unknown 알려지지 않은 채로 남아 있던 것

514 (D) who will live in the future

기억을 통하여 인간은 과거에 얻은 지식과 경험을 유지한다. 인간은 자기보다 먼저 살아온 사람들에게서 배울 수 있도록 자신이 이룩한 발자취들에 대한 기록을 보존한다. 따라서 어느 한 세대가 성취한 인간의 편안함을 향하는 모든 발전은 새로운 세대가 그 위에다 (무언가를) 쌓아올릴 수 있는 건설의 토대가 된다.

preserve 보존하다   records 기록(물)   step in progress 진보의 발자취   foundation 토대, 기초

구문 ▶

1 man keeps alive the knowledge and experience
  인간은 지식과 경험을 유지한다
  • 원래는 keeps the knowledge and experience alive의 5형식 문장임.
2 so that he can learn from those who ~
  ~한 사람들에게서 배울 수 있도록
3 whatever advance toward human comfort has been achieved by one generation
  = any advance toward human comfort that has been achieved by one generation
  어느 한 세대에 의해 성취된 인간의 편안함을 향하는 모든 발전
  • 이 복합관계대명사절은 becomes의 주어 역할을 하고 있음.
4 the foundation on which a new generation may build 새로운 세대가 그 위에다 건설을 해나가는 토대

해설 ▶

인간은 자기보다 먼저 살아온 사람들에게서 배우는 것이므로, 앞으로 올 미래의 사람들에게서 배운다는 것은 논리에 맞지 않는다.

515 (D) however → therefore / consequently

우리는 그것이 훨씬 더 중요한 미래의 이익을 달성하지 못하도록 할 수 있음에도 불구하고, 당장의 쾌락을 주는 일을 하고 싶은 유혹을 종종 느낀다. 과식과 과음은 나중에 우리의 직무 수행을 불가능하게 하거나, (맡은 바) 일을 좋은 결과로 이끌지 못하게 하는 무절제의 명백한 본보기들이다. 따라서 절제는 비록 우리에게서 멀리 있을지 모르지만, 더 큰 이익을 성취하는 데에 방해가 될 수도 있는, 당장의 쾌락의 유혹을 거부할 수 있는 습관적인 능력이라고 정의될 수 있을 것이다.

immediate pleasure 당장의 쾌락   overeating 과식 overdrinking 과음   obvious 분명한   intemperance 무절제   subsequent inability 뒤따르는 무능력

discharge one's obligations 의무를 이행하다   resist 거부하다   interfere (with) ~을 방해하다, 참견하다

구문 ▶

1 be tempted to ~ : ~하고 싶은 유혹을 받다
2 prevent A from -ing: A가 ~하는 것을 막다
3 of much greater importance = much more important : 훨씬 더 중요한
4 A results in B: A가 B라는 결과를 낳다
5 greater, though more remote, goods
  = greater goods, though they are more remote
  (이루기에) 멀지 모르지만 더 큰 이익들

해설 ▶

앞에 나오는 이야기를 결론적으로 정리하는 말을 이끌고 있으므로 therefore, consequently 등 인과관계를 나타내는 접속부사가 와야 한다.

516 (C) either → neither

역사는 끝이 없으니 나는 미래를 예측할 수 있는 체하지 않겠다. 그러나 역사는 위쪽으로 나아가는 진보의 계속되는 흐름의 하나라는 학설에 대해, 내가 전반적인 불신을 되풀이하는 것은 가치 있는 일이라고 생각한다. 혹은 역사가 반복 가능한 일련의 순환이라고 주장하는 아리스토텔레스, 비코, 니체의 더 오래된 역사관에 대해서도 마찬가지다. 나는 역사가 그렇게 단순하다고 믿지 않기 때문에 이 두 견해 어느 것도 받아들이지 않는다. 사실, 우리가 역사라는 복합체 전체를 통틀어 생각해 보면 역사가 무엇인가에 대한 어떤 적절한 상징을 이끌어낼 수는 없다고 믿는다. 우리가 할 수 있는 일은 역사의 어떤 단편들을 고려해 보는 일일 것이다.

pretend to ~인 체하다   worth while 가치 있는 reiterate 반복하다   general disbelief in ~에 대한 전반적인 불신   doctrine 학설, 주장 progress onward and upward 전진하며 위쪽으로 나아가는 진보 Vico, Giovanni Battista 비코(1668~1744, 이탈리아의 철학자 · 법학자)   Nietzche, Friedrich Wilhelm 니체(1844~1900, 독일의 철학자)   a series of repeatable cycles 반복 가능한 일련의 순환   adequate 충분한, 적절한 phase 단편(斷片), 국면

구문 ▶

1 I accept neither of these views
  나는 이 두 견해 어느 것도 받아들이지 않는다
2 history is as simple as that
  역사는 그처럼 단순하다
3 if we take the whole complex of history
  역사라는 복합체 전체를 통틀어 생각하면

해설 ▶

글쓴이는 윗글에 나타난 역사에 대한 두 가지 견해를 다 받아들이지 않고 있으므로 either를 neither로 고쳐야 한다.

PART 5
Reading Comprehension

517 **(D) reluctant to hear → eager[willing] to hear**

동화는 우리에게 흥미를 준다. 왜냐하면 그 속에서는 사람들이 신기한 일들을 쉽게 해내고, 숲이나 땅 밑에 숨어 기다리다가 나타나서는 사람들에게 도움을 주기도 하고 방해하기도 하는 온갖 종류의 크고 작은 피조물이 존재하는 세계의 모습들이 그려져 있기 때문이다. 그리고 마법은 매우 적은 수단들과, 분명히 매우 어울리지 않는 재료를 가지고 매우 많은 일을 성취해 내기 때문에 우리를 즐겁게 한다. 마찬가지 방식과 마찬가지 이유로 사람들은 늘 영웅들의 이야기를 듣고 싶어 하는데, 영웅들이란 다름 아닌 커다란 어려운 일들을 극복하고, 커다란 장애물을 뛰어넘어 모든 종류의 방해에도 불구하고 경주에서 승리한 자들이다.

fairy tale 동화, 꾸며낸 이야기 **marvellous** 신기한, 믿어지지 않는 **with ease** 쉽게(= easily) **hinder** 방해하다 **creature** 피조물 **lurk** 숨어 기다리다 **so apparently inadequate** 분명히 매우 부적절한 **be reluctant to** ~하기 망설이다 **overcome** 극복하다 (= get over) **obstacle** 장애물 **win the race** 경주에서 승리하다 **discouragement** 용기를 꺾는 일, 방해(물)

구문
1 accomplish so much with means so few
   매우 적은 수단으로 매우 많은 것을 이루다
   • so much는 accomplish의 목적어 역할을, so few는 means를 꾸미는 역할을 함.
2 in spite of all kinds of discouragement
   모든 종류의 방해(물)에도 불구하고

해설
'우리가 동화와 마법 이야기를 듣고 즐거워하는 것처럼, 사람들은 영웅들의 이야기를 듣고 기뻐하기를 갈망한다'는 내용이므로 reluctant to hear는 잘못된 것이다.

518 **(E) easiest → chief**

현대 세계에서 신속히 움직이는 사건들의 흐름이 중요하므로 우리는 정보를 잘 갖추고 있을 필요가 있다. 사회적, 경제적, 정치적으로 의미심장한 문제들은 모두가 진지하고 열린 마음의 연구를 요구하지만, 그 어느 때보다도 더 높은 수준의 독자의 계몽을 요구한다. 지식을 증진시키려면 사람은 늘 더 많이 배우고, 더 많이 연구하고, 더 많이 사유해야 한다. 독서는 이것을 성취하는 데에 도움을 준다. 대학에서 거의 85퍼센트에 해당하는 공부가 독서를 필요로 한다. 사실 그렇지만, 만약에 발전이 공부를 통해서 온다면, 아마도 독서는 학생의 학문적 진보를 이루는 주요한 수단일 것이다.

the fast-moving stream of events 신속히 움직이는 사건[일들]의 흐름 **imperative** 반드시 해야 하는, 긴요한

significant 중요한, 의미심장한 **more than ever before** 그 어느 때보다도 더 **reader enlightenment** 독자들을 계몽시키는 일 **reason** 사유(思惟)하다, 추론하다 **involve** 포함하다, 요구하다, 관련되다 **means to academic progress** 학문적 발전을 이루는 수단

구문
1 The importance of ~ makes it imperative that...
   ~의 중요성이 (that 이하)를 긴요하게 만든다
   • imperative가 당위성을 나타내는 형용사이므로 that 이하의 we be well informed에서 동사 원형을 씀. (가정법 현재)
2 all demanding serious and open-minded investigation
   = though all (of them) demand serious and open-minded investigation
   그것들 모두가 진지하고 열린 마음의 연구를 요구하지만 (즉, 그것들을 연구하기 위해서는 진지하고 열린 마음의 연구가 요구되지만)
3 Reading helps accomplish this
   = Reading helps to accomplish this
   • to가 없는 경우에는 도움이 보다 직접적인 것임을 의미함.
4 as it certainly does 사실 그렇지만
   • 내용은 progress comes through study를 나타냄.

해설
학문의 발전이 사실 공부를 통해서 오기 때문에 독서가 그것을 이루는 <u>주요한</u> 수단이지만, 그것이 가장 쉬운 수단이라는 말은 아니다.

519 **(E) the declining interest → the growing interest**

순회도서관의 성장은 문학의 확산에 도움을 주었다. 책값이 대다수 주민들의 구매력에 비해 매우 높던 시절에 순회도서관은 중요한 사회 기관이었다. 이 순회도서관은 독서에 취미를 갖게 된 사람들에게 그것들이 아니었다면 접할 수 없었을 책들에 접근할 수 있는 길을 제공하였다. 순회도서관은 독서에 대한 관심과 구매력 사이의 간격을 줄이는 데에 도움이 되었다. 최초의 순회도서관은 1740년 런던에서 개관하였고, 경쟁자들이 런던뿐만 아니라 지방들에서도 빠르게 나타났다. 18세기 말까지 약 1,000개의 순회도서관이 전국에 걸쳐 설립되었다. 그들의 빠른 성장은 독서에 대한 관심이 늘어나고 있었음을 입증해 준다.

circulating library 순회도서관 **aid** 도움을 주다 **expansion** 확산, 확장 (ⓥ expand) **purchasing power** 구매력 **social invention** 사회 기관 **furnish** 제공하다 **access to** ~로의 접근 **rival** 경쟁자 **spring up** 생겨나다, 솟아나다 **provincial** 지방 **as well** 마찬가지로, 역시 **dot** 점을 찍다 **dotted the country** 전국에 산재하다 **testify to** ~을 입증하다

76

구문 ▶

1 at a time when ~ : ~하던 시절에
   • when은 시간의 관계부사.
2 They furnished those who had acquired a taste for reading with access to ~
   • furnish A with B: A에게 B를 제공하다
   • those who had acquired a taste for reading 독서에 취미를 갖게 된 사람들
   • access to ~ : ~에 대한 접근
3 books (which would have been) otherwise out of their reach
   그들(순회도서관)이 아니었다면 접할 수 없었을 책들
   • otherwise = if it had not been for them
   • (...have been) out of their reach : 그들의 접근 밖에 있었을(즉, 접근이 불가능했을)

해설 ▶

순회도서관의 빠른 성장은 독서에 대한 관심이 늘어나고 있었음을 입증해 주는 것이므로 declining(줄어드는)은 맞지 않다. 반대의 의미를 지니는 growing으로 바뀌어야 한다.

520 (B) less →more

예술은 예술가의 마음과 그 마음이 주변 세계와 맺는 관계를 반영하는 거울이다. 우리가 현재 알고 있듯이 세계는 매우 복잡한 경험의 하나가 되었다. 정치적, 사회적 발달 과정에서 세계는 기록된 역사상 다른 그 어느 시기에서보다도 지난 40년간에 더 심대한 변화를 겪었고 더 많은 재난에 의해 뒤흔들렸다. 우리 세대의 문학에서 이러한 변화들의 흔적을 약간이라도 찾지 못한다면 참으로 이상한 일이 될 것이다. 오늘날의 작가는 더 이상 상아탑에 안주하지 않는다. 작가는 그가 살아가는 세상의 일부이며, 세상에 대한 자신의 고양된 인상을 전달함에 있어서 언제나 새로운 표현의 형태와 적절한 기법을 추구하고 있는 것이다. 혼란을 더 혼란스럽게 만들지 않고, 오히려 명백한(겉으로 드러난) 혼돈에서 상상의 통일성과 질서와 조화를 찾는 것이 그의 중심 목표이다.

the world around him 자기 주변의 세계 far-reaching 먼 범위까지 미치는, 심대한 trace 흔적 dwell in ~에 거주하다 ivory tower 상아탑(실사회와 격리된 사상, 예술 세계; 대학) convey 전하다 heightened impression 고양된 인상 adequate technique 적절한 기법 imaginative unity 상상의 통일성(통일된 상상) order 질서

구문 ▶

1 as we know it now
   우리가 현재 그것을 알고 있듯이(있는 바로는)
2 be shaken by ~ : ~에 의해 흔들리다
3 at almost any other period in recorded history
   역사상 다른 그 어느 시기에도
4 It would be strange indeed not to ~

= It would be strange if he should not ~ :
~하지 못한다면 참으로 이상한 일이 될 것이다 (가정법 과거 구문)
5 not to make ~ , but to win : not A but B 구문
6 make confusion more confused
   혼돈을 더 혼란스럽게 만들다 (5형식 동사 구문)

해설 ▶

문맥상 지난 40년 동안 세계는 역사상 어느 시기보다도 더 심대한 변화를 겪었고 더 많은 재난에 의해 뒤흔들렸다는 내용이므로 less를 more로 고쳐야 한다.

521 (A) the lower classes →the ruling classes

지난 세기의 중반에 이르기까지 역사가의 주된 관심과 일반 대중의 주된 관심은 공히 그 정치와 헌정의 역사, 정치적 사건, 전쟁, 왕조, 그리고 정치 제도와 그것의 발전에 놓여 있었다. 따라서 본질적으로 역사는 지배 계급에 대하여 관심을 표현하였다. '자, 이제 유명한 인물들을 찬양합시다.'라는 것이 역사가의 표어였다. 역사가는 대중의 알려지지 않은 삶과 활동을 조사하는 것을 좋아하지 않았는데, 그러나 실은 그 대중들의 꾸준한 노력에 의해 세계의 번영이 이룩되었고, 그 대중들은 역사가가 찬양하는 유명한 인물들이 만든 정치와 헌법이라는 큰 건축물의 숨겨진 기초였다. 보통 사람들을 논하는 것은 역사의 위엄에 어울리지 않는 일이었나 보다.

lie in ~에 놓여 있다(= consist in) constitutional history 헌정(憲政)의 역사 dynasty 왕조(王朝) political institution 정치 제도 substantially 본질적으로 lower class 하층 계급 cf. ruling class 지배 계급 motto 표어, 좌우명 care to ~하는 데에 관심을 갖다 obscure 모호한, 알려지지 않은 the great mass of humanity 대중 toil 노고, 수고 edifice 큰 건물, 조직 rear 기르다, 만들다 beneath the dignity of history 역사의 권위 아래에 있는(즉, 권위에 어울리지 않는)

구문 ▶

1 the chief interest of the historian and of the public alike
   역사가와 일반 대중의 관심사는 공히
   • A and B alike = both A and B 구문
2 history concerned itself with
   = history was concerned with
   역사는 ~에 관심을 표현하였다
3 upon whose slow toil was built up the prosperity of the world
   그들(대중)의 꾸준한 노력 위에 세계의 번영이 이룩되었다
4 (the great mass of humanity) who were the hidden foundation of the political and constitutional edifice
   정치와 헌법이라는 큰 건축물의 숨겨진 기초였던 (대중)
5 the political and constitutional edifice (that was) reared by the famous men

유명한 인물들이 만든 정치와 헌법
6 the famous men (that / whom) he praised
그(역사가)가 칭찬하는 유명한 인물들
7 To speak of the ordinary people would have been beneath the dignity of history.
= If he were to speak of the ordinary people, it would have been beneath the dignity of history.
보통 사람들을 논하는 것은 역사의 위엄에 어울리지 않는 일이었을 것이다.
• 가정법 과거완료 구문 (would have been의 형태에 유의)

해설

이 글의 골자는, 지난 세기 중반까지 역사가와 일반 대중이 공히 정치와 헌정의 역사, 정치적 사건, 전쟁, 왕조 및 정치 제도와 그 발전에 주된 관심을 두었기 때문에, 역사는 본질적으로 지배 계급에 대하여 관심을 표현하였다는 내용이다. 따라서 (A) the lower classes는 글의 흐름에 맞지 않다.

Section 3 장문 독해 기출문제

522 1. (A) 2. (D) 3. (B) 4. (C)

만약에 당신이 ⓐ미국 교육에 미치는 기업의 영향이 얼마나 침투력이 강한지를 알고 싶으면, 이웃에 있는 학교에 한번 가 보면 된다. 식당에 들어가 보면 학교 점심을 공급하는 패스트푸드 업체인 Taco Bell, Arby's, Subway의 음식 포장지를 아마 보게 될 것이다. 3학년 학생들은 Tootsie Rolls를 세는 것으로 수학을 배우고 있을지도 모른다. 과학의 교과 과정이 Dow Chemical, Dupont, 또는 Exxon에서 당연하게 오고 있을지도 모른다. 거기에서 끝나지 않는다. 미국의 교육은 큰 산업이 되었다. 투자 은행회사인 EduVentures에서 붙인 용어인 교육산업은, 미국에서 6,300억 내지 6,800억 달러 정도의 가치가 있다고 평가된다. 공개적으로 거래되는 교육 분야 회사들의 주식 가치는 다우존스 평균보다 두 배나 빠르게 성장하고 있다. Lehman Brothers와 Montgomery Securities 같은 종합 증권 회사들은 교육산업에 투자할 벤처 자본을 찾아다니는 전문가를 두고 있다.

Heritage Foundation, Hudson and Pioneer Institutes와 같은 보수적인 싱크탱크에 근무하는 분석가들은 교육의 문제들이 비효율적이고 비대해진 학교관료들에게서 나온다고 말한다. 보수주의자들은 증표(영수증)와 공적/사적 계획들을 가리키면서 '학교의 선택'에 대해 이야기한다. 자유시장주의자들은 많은 부모와 코드를 맞추면서 학생 가족들은 특히 도시의 학군에서 당연히 누려야 할 선택권을 갖지 못하고 있다고 지적한다. ⓑ그러나 진보 성향의 학교 운동가들에 의하면, 교육의 문제들은 그 뿌리가 수십 년에 걸쳐 존재해 온 불평등한 학교기금에 있다고 한다. 학군의 재정이 재산세를 통해 이루어지는 한, 가난한 도시 지역의 어린이들은 도시 외곽의 (부유한) 학교 아이들과 같은 수준의 교육을 결코 받을 수 없을 것이라고 말한다. 특히 도심 지역의 학교에서 학교 재원의 커다란 불균형은 기업들이 그 차이(그리고 자신들의 호주머니)를 채우는 문을 열어 주고 있다.

take a tour of ~을 찾아가 보다 wrapper (햄버거 등을 싸는) 겉포장지 Taco Bell / Arby's / Subway 미국의 패스트푸드 체인 회사명 Tootsie Rolls 미국의 초콜릿 캔디 curricula 교과 과정 Dow Chemical / Dupont / Exxon 미국의 화학과 정유회사명 term coined by EduVentures EduVentures가 지은 이름(용어) billion 10억 stock value 주식 가치 brokerage firm 종합 증권 회사 Lehman Brothers / Montgomery Securities 미국 증권 관련 회사명 analyst (시장)분석가 think tank 싱크탱크(고급 두뇌 집단) stem from ~에서 유래하다 bloated 팽창된, 비대하여 비효율적인 bureaucracy 관료 집단 conservative 보수주의자 voucher 증표, 영수증

strike a chord with ~와 코드를 맞추다   deserve
자격이 있다   school district 학구, 학군   progressive
진보적인   property tax 재산세   disparity 불균형

1 grow twice as fast as the Dow Jones Average
   다우존스 평균치보다 두 배나 빠르게 성장하다
   • 배수사 as 원급 as ~ 구문
2 decades of unequal school funding
   수십 년에 걸쳐 존재해 온 불평등한 학교기금
3 as long as school districts are financed through
   property taxes 학군들이 재산세를 통해 재정 지원을
   받는 한

1 이 글은 미국 교육산업의 문제를 다룬 글이다.
2 윗글에는 (A), (B), (C)의 내용이 언급되어 있지만 (D)의
   내용은 없다.
3 '미국 교육에 미치는 기업의 영향이 얼마나 침투력이
   강한지를'의 영어 표현으로 올바른 것은 (B)이다.
   이 구조를 이해하기 위해서는 평서문의 구조를 잘 알아야
   한다. 위의 우리말을 평서문 형태로 고치면 '미국 교육에
   미치는 기업의 영향은 매우 침투력이 강하다'가 된다. 이것을
   영어로 옮기면, corporate influence in U.S. education
   is very pervasive이다. 이것을 감탄문 형식으로
   바꾸면 how pervasive corporate influence in U.S.
   education is가 된다.
4 빈칸 ⓑ 앞에는 보수주의자(conservative)들의 교육
   문제에 대한 견해가 언급되어 있고, 그 뒤에는 진보주의자
   (progressive)들의 견해가 기술되어 있다. 이 두
   견해들은 서로 상반되므로, 빈칸 ⓑ에는 However가
   들어가야 한다.

523 **1. (B)   2. (A)   3. (B)**

이동 전화가 전기통신에서 점차 주목을 받음에 따라,
우리는 주요한 통합 효과가 통신 사업자들에게서
통신 판매자들에게로 퍼져나갈 것으로 예측한다.
세계화로 인해 숫자는 더 줄어들고 덩치는 더 커진,
다국적 유무선 통신 서비스 사업자가 나타날 것이다.
기존의 전기통신 사업자들은 전기통신 무대에서의
신규 진입자들에 대비하고 있다. 그들은 이 신규
진입자들이 폭넓은 서비스를 앞세워 시장 점유율을
얻기 위해 경쟁할 것으로 예상한다. 케이블통신
회사들이 기존 전기통신 업체들에 직접적인 위협을
가할지도 모른다. 그러나 케이블 회사들 앞에 놓인
장애물은, 그들이 규모가 작고 여러 기술들이 고도로
맞물린 사업체인 경향이 있어서 튼튼한 전기통신
업체를 개발하기 위해 필요한 투자를 유치하지 못할
수도 있다는 점이다. 케이블 회사들의 대차 대조표는
투자자들이 보기에 매력적이지 않은 경향이 있다.
왜냐하면 케이블 회사들이 높은 성장을 보여 주고
있지만 높은 투자가 있어야 가능하고, 또한 그들의
경영 기술이 허약하기 쉽기 때문이다. 전화 회사들과

경쟁하여 믿을 만하고 장기적으로 존재할 수 있는
회사가 되기 위해서는, 케이블 회사들은 양방향
대화형 서비스를 제공하기 위해 그들의 케이블 망을
어떻게 업그레이드하거나 제작할지에 기민한 신경을
써야 할 것이다. 한편, 전기통신 회사들은 높은 이득을
누리고 있지만 성장이 더디어, 경쟁에서 필연적으로
나타나는 이익 감소에 대비해야 할 것이다. 그들은
경쟁에 민첩하게 반응하거나 새로 생기는 기회들을
효과적으로 이용함에 있어 대비가 서투른 관료
문화에 종종 방해를 받기도 한다.

take center stage 주목을 받다, 각광받다   consolidation effect 통합 효과   operator 운용자   vendor
판매자   lead to ~을 가져오다(= bring about)   fixed
and mobile services 유무선 통신 서비스   incumbent
현직의   entrant 신입자   arena 무대, 마당   market
share 시장 점유(율)   pose a direct threat to ~에
직접적인 위협을 주다   highly geared businesses 고도
기술들이 같이 맞물린 사업체들   balance sheet 손익
계산서, 대차 대조표   credible 신용할 만한   long-term
competitor 오랜 기간 버티는 경쟁자   astute 기민한
inevitable 필연적인   erosion 부식, 쇠퇴   ill-equipped
to ~할 준비를 제대로 갖추지 않은   nimbly 민첩하게,
재빠르게   emerging 새로이 생겨나는

1 engineer their cable networks to accommodate
   two-way interactive services
   양방향 대화형 서비스를 제공하도록 그들의 케이블 망을
   제작하다
   • engineer는 5형식 동사로 쓰임: V + O + O.C.
2 They are often hindered by bureaucratic cultures
   = Bureaucratic cultures often hinder them
   • 이때 bureaucratic cultures는 기존의 회사들이 갖는
     관료 문화를 지칭함.

1 이 글은 전기통신 시장에서 나타날 전기통신 회사들과
   케이블 회사들 간의 첨예한 경쟁을 다룬 글이다.
2 이 문제의 답은 맨 마지막 문장에 있다. 전기통신 회사들이
   지닌 관료적인 행태를 빨리 수정하지 않으면 경쟁에서
   이길 수 없다는 뜻이 내재되어 있다.
3 (B)는 오히려 기존의 전기통신 회사들의 속성이다.

524 **1. (A)   2. (B)   3. (C)**

스타일은 어떤 면에서 보면 주체성이다. 즉 자기
인식이며 자기 이해(자각)이다. 당신이 스스로의
모습을 분명히 표현하기 전까지는 스타일을 가질 수
없다. 그리고 스타일은 신체적으로나 정신적으로 몸에
딱 맞아 편안함을 느끼는 안전성을 요구한다. 물론
모든 지식처럼, 자각은 당신이 나이가 들고 발전함에
따라 최신의 내용으로 새로워져야 한다. 스타일은
지속적인[발전하는] 자기 평가를 취한다.

스타일은 또 다른 면에서 보면 개성이다. 영혼이며, 기백이며, 태도이며, 기지이며, 창의성이다. 그것은 한 사람이 원하는 모든 분위기를 표현하려는 욕구와 자신감을 요구한다. 그러한 변화의 성질은 필요할 뿐만 아니라 인간으로서 한 개인의 독특한 복합성을 반영한다. 사람들은 자신의 현재 모습이고 싶어 하고 그 모습으로 보이기를 원한다. 그렇게 되기 위해서는 스타일은 진정한 자신의 모습과 개인으로서의 성격과 개성을 반영해야 한다. 그것보다 덜한 어느 것도 그냥 걸치는 의상에 지나지 않아 보인다.

마지막으로, 스타일은 또 다른 면에서 패션이다. 수많은 옷을 가지고 있으면서도 스타일은 눈곱만큼도 없는 경우가 있을 수 있다. 반대로 옷은 몇 벌 안 되면서도 많은 스타일을 지니는 경우도 가능하다. 패션은 우리가 스타일을 표현하는 방법이지만, 스타일리시하기 위해서는 의상에 의존할 필요가 생각보다는 덜하다. 그것이 바로, 수세대에 걸쳐 여성들이 선을 별로 뽐내지 않으면서도 비율에서는 매우 완벽하여 자신을 표현하는 행위들에서 가장 세련되게 사람을 돋보이게 하는 의상인 조그마한 검은 드레스를 갈망해 온 이유가 된다.

one part 일면에서 보면, 일부분은 **identity** 정체성 **self-awareness** 자기 인식 **self-knowledge** 자각 **articulate a self** 스스로의 모습을 분명히 드러내다 **feel at home** 편안함을 느끼다 **be updated** 최신 정보로 새로워지다 **evolve** 발전하다 **ongoing** 발전하는, 지속적인 **self-assessment** 자기 평가 **verve** 기백, 힘 **inventiveness** 창의력 **variability** 변화성 **reflection** 반영 **work** 효력이 발생하다 **ounce** 온스(무게 단위로 1/16 파운드, 약 30g) **in the way of** ~의 면에서 **covet** 갈망하다 **garment** 의상, 의류 **unassuming** 겸손한, 젠체하지 않는 **foil** 은박, 돋보이게 하는 것

구문

1 **whatever mood one wishes** 어떠한 것이든 한 사람이 원하는 모든 분위기
2 **variability is not only necessary but a reflection of ~** 변화는 필요할 뿐만 아니라 인간으로서 한 개인의 독특한 복합성의 반영이다
 • not only A but (also) B 구문
3 **anything less appears to be ~** 그보다 덜한 것은 무엇이나 ~처럼 보인다

해설

1 스타일은 진정한 자신의 모습과 개인으로서의 특징과 개성을 반영해야 하는 것이며, 그 이하가 되면 그냥 걸치고 다니는 옷에 불과하다는 뜻이므로, 정답은 (A).
2 첫 문단에 "style requires security—feeling at home in one's body, physically and mentally"를 보면, '의복은 몸에 맞아야 한다', 즉 '불편해서는 안 된다'는 추론이 가능하다.
3 본문은 옷을 어떻게 입느냐에 따라 사람의 스타일이 달라지는 것을 세 가지 측면에서 보고 있다. 따라서

'스타일은 가식(pretentiousness), 사치(extravagance), 변경(alteration)이 아닌 의복의 전달(conveyance: 입는 방식)과 관련이 있다'고 말할 수 있다.

525 **1. (C)　2. (B)　3. (A)**

개개의 문화는 양심의 소리, 즉, 마음속 자아비판의 목소리를 감지한다. ⓐ그러나 서구 기독교 문명은, 말하자면, 스테로이드가 마음에 걸린다. 우리의 죄의식은 비교적 극단적이고, 우리 문화의 원죄와 타락한 상태 때문에 우리는 우리 존재 자체에 대해 죄의식을 느낀다. 서구 문화의 뱃속에는 우리가 가치 없는 존재라는 느낌이 있다. 이러한 느낌이 왜 그곳에 있을까?

내재하는 이 모든 자기 증오는 우리가 문명화되는 데에 대해 지불하는 비용이다. 다수의 이득을 보호하는 매우 잘 조직된 사회에서 우리는 매일 우리의 자연스러운 충동을 억제해야 한다. 우리는 언제나 스스로의 이기적이고 공격적인 충동을 억눌러야 한다. 그리고 우리는 성인으로서 그 일에 너무 익숙해져 있어서 그것을 언제나 눈치 채지 못하는 것이다. 그러나 내가 나의 충동에 따라 행동하는 버릇이 있다면, 나는 커피숍에서 정교하게 거품을 낸 모카가 든 ⓑ혼합 음료를 주문하는 내 앞에 서 있는 사람들을 규칙적으로 죽일지도 모른다. 사실 나는 줄을 서서 기다리는 것을 상관하지 않지만, 카운터를 내려치고 완력을 써서 사람들을 내 앞에서 쫓아내고 싶은 것이다. 그러나 자연스레 생겨나는 그러한 공격성으로부터 나를 막아 주는 조그마한 갈등이 내 마음속에서 일어나고 있다. 그리고 그것이 모닝커피라면—얼마나 자주 당신이 누군가를 대중교통 수단을 타고 가다 목 졸라 죽이고 싶겠는가 생각해 보시라.

conscience 양심 **self-criticism** 자아비판 **have conscience on** ~이 마음에 걸리다 **comparatively** 비교적, 상대적으로 **original sin** 원죄 **fallen status** 타락한 상태 **belly** 배, 내부 **internalized self-loathing** 내재화된 자기 증오 **the cost we pay for** ~에 대해 우리가 지불하는 비용 **many** 많은 사람들(뒤에 명사가 없이 단독으로 쓰인 경우, 보통 '사람들'을 이야기함) **refrain from** ~을 삼가다 **repress** 억누르다 **aggressive** 공격적인 **urge** 충동 **in the habit of** ~하는 버릇이 있는 **elaborate whipped-cream mocha concoction** 정교하게 거품을 낸 모카가 든 혼합 음료 **in a queue** 줄을 서서 **storm** 세게 내려치다 **muscle people out of my way** 완력으로 사람들을 내 앞에서 쫓아내다 **strangle** 목 졸라 죽이다 **public transportation** 대중교통 수단

구문

1 But Western Christian culture has conscience on steroids, so to speak. 〔직역하면〕 그러나 서구 기독교 문명은, 말하자면, 스테로이드가 마음에 걸린다.

→ 〔비유적으로〕 스포츠맨들이 금지된 스테로이드를 사용하는 것은 불법이고, 그래서 '서구 문명은 우리들에게 그러한 일에 죄의식을 느끼도록 한다'는 뜻.

2 we are so accustomed to it as adults that ~
우리는 성인으로서 그 일에 너무 익숙해져 있어서 그 결과 ~한다

3 if I was in the habit of acting on my impulses
  • 여기 if절에는 were를 쓰는 것이 원칙이지만 미국인들은 was를 자주 씀. (가정법 과거 동사)

해설

1 '양심'이라는 개념은 첫 문단의 첫 문장과 둘째 문단의 첫 문장에서 설명하고 있다. conscience = internal self-criticism = internalized self-loathing

2 ⓐ의 의미는 위 〔구문 1〕 참조. 이 물음에 대한 답은 바로 뒤 문장 "Our sense of guilt is comparatively extreme, and, with our culture of original sin and fallen status, we feel guilty about our very existence."에서 찾을 수 있다.

3 ⓑ concoctions는 '혼합 음료'라는 뜻.
  cf. (B) glade 숲속의 빈터, (C) convolution 나선형 물체, (D) drove 대군중

526 1. (C)   2. (B)   3. (C)   4. (C)

이 점을 근거로 볼 때, 미덕과 합치되는 행동은 근원적으로 즐거운 것이어야 한다. 그리고 확실히 그 행동들은 고상하기도 하고 선하기도 하는데, 만약에 선한 사람에 대한 판단이 어떤 기준이라면, 둘 다 높은 수준으로 그래야 한다. 왜냐하면 그는 우리가 말한 것처럼 행동을 판단할 것이기 때문이다. 따라서 행복은 사물의 최고의 것이며, 동시에 최고로 고상하고 최고로 즐거운 것이라는 이야기가 뒤따른다. 왜냐하면 우리의 최선의 행동들은 이 모든 속성을 가지고 있기 때문이다. 그리고 우리가 행복이 있다고 이야기할 때 그것은 우리의 최선의 행동에, 아니면 그중 하나에 있는 것이다. ⓐ그럼에도 불구하고, 행복은 명백히 외부의 물건을 마찬가지로 요구한다. 왜냐하면 적절한 장비가 없이는 고상하게 행동하기가 불가능하거나 적어도 쉽지는 않기 때문이다. 친구, 부, 정치적 영향력 같은 도구를 통해야만 이루어지는 행동들이 많이 있다. 그리고 다시 그것이 없으면, 좋은 출생 신분, 멋진 자식들, 그리고 잘생긴 모습 등과 같은 지고한 행복을 ⓑ해치게 되는 것들도 있다. 왜냐하면 생긴 모습이 역겹거나, 태생이 좋지 않거나, 외롭거나, 자식이 없는 사람은 행복한 사람의 요구 조건을 맞추지 못한 것이고, 더구나 몹쓸 자식들이나 친구들을 가진 자나, 죽음으로 참된 친구를 잃어버린 사람은 더욱 더 행복한 사람의 요구 조건을 맞추지 못한 것이기 때문이다. 그러면, 우리가 말한 것처럼 행복은 외적인 번영을 추가로 요구하는 것처럼 보이고, 이것은 어떤 사람들로 하여금 행복을 '행운'과 동일시하게끔 이끌었는데, 이것은 마치 다른 사람들이 행복을 미덕으로 잘못 동일시하는 반대의 실수를 했던 것과 마찬가지이다.

on this ground 이 이유로 볼 때(= for this reason)   in conformity with ~과 합치하는   intrinsically 본질적으로   consist in ~에 놓여 있다(= lie in)   plainly 명백히   mar 해치다   felicity 지고한 행복   good birth 좋은 가정에서 태어나는 것   comeliness 예쁜 모습, 잘생김   repulsive 역겨운   ill-born 잘못 태어난   solitary 고독한   requirements 요구 조건   external prosperity 외적인 번영

구문

1 It follows, therefore, that ~
따라서 ~라는 이야기가 (자연스럽게) 귀결되어 나온다

2 it is in our best activities, or in the best one of them, that we say happiness consists
  • it ~ that ... 강조 구문으로, 원래의 표현은 we say happiness consists in our best activities, or in the best one of them

3 there are some things, again, the lack of which must mar felicity
= there are some things, again, and the lack of them must mar felicity
  • which는 앞의 some things를 가리키는 관계대명사.

4 still less does one who ~   ~한 사람은 더욱 그러하다

5 identify it with "good fortune"
그것(행복)을 '행운'과 동일시하다

해설

1 본문의 첫 부분에 이 문항에 대한 답이 있다.
On this ground, actions in conformity with virtue must be intrinsically pleasant. And certainly they are good as well as noble
→ 이 문장에 action, virtue, pleasant 등이 나옴에 유의하면 문제의 답이 나온다. 따라서 이 기준에 어긋나는 것은 (C)이다.

2 이 문항의 답은 happiness seems to require the addition of external prosperity, and this has led some to identify it with "good fortune"에서 찾을 수 있다. 작가는 행복이나 행운이 외적인 번영을 요구한다고 보는 사람이 있다고 이야기하고 있다.

3 빈칸 ⓐ 앞에서는 행복이 우리의 선한 행동에서 나오는 것이라고 하여 내적 행복을 이야기하는 데 반하여, 빈칸 ⓐ 뒤의 이야기는 외부의 물건도 행복을 주는 요소 중의 하나라는 이야기를 하고 있으므로, 앞뒤의 이야기를 대조시켜 연결하는 Nevertheless가 필요하다.
빈칸 ⓑ에는 '해치다', '망치다'라는 부정의 뜻을 지닌 단어가 들어가야 한다. 왜냐하면 바로 뒤에 '생긴 모습이 역겹거나, 태생이 좋지 않거나, 외롭거나, 자식이 없는 사람은 행복한 사람의 요구 조건을 맞추지 못한 것이다'라는 말이 나오기 때문이다.

4 이 문항의 답은 비교적 쉽게 찾을 수 있다. good fortune으로 여겨지는 것들은 good birth, fine children, and personal comeliness 등이다. 여기에 속하지 않는 것은 (C) love for justice이다.

527 1. (B)   2. (D)   3. (A)

화재 사고에 대한 경험이 있는 사람들과의 수많은 면담에서 연구자들이 알아낸 중요한 내용 중의 하나는 실제로 화재가 발생했는가를 깨닫는 데에 관련된 문제들이다. 화재는 흔한 경험이 아니기 때문에 사람들은 화재의 초기 징조들을 화재가 아닌 다른 것으로 해석하는 설명을 거의 다 받아들인다는 것이다. 예를 들어, 한 호텔 화재 사고에서 투숙객들은 우지끈 소리와 펑펑거리는 소리들을 듣고 그것을 기물 파괴범들의 소행으로 치부하고서, 문이 꽉 잠겼나를 확인하고 TV를 다시 시청하였다고 한다. 이와 비슷하게 화재경보기가 흔히 훈련이나 시험 가동, 오작동쯤으로 인식되고 있음을 한 연구가 보여 주고 있다. 사실, 화재일 가능성이 있다는 증거에 접해서 거의 모든 사람이 (그것에 대해) 더 많은 이유를 찾는다. 한 연구자는 "화재를 다른 것으로 오인하는 데에는 강한 사회적 오점이 연루되어 있다."고 말한다. 그래서 사람들은 (경보기 소리를 듣고) 급히 거리로 뛰쳐나가거나 잘못된 것일 수도 있는 경보에 소방대를 불러서 웃음거리가 되는 것을 꺼린다. 화재가 발생한 것이 분명히 확인된 경우에도 문간으로 즉시 달려가는 행위는 거의 볼 수가 없다. 화재라는 비상상태에서 사람들은 나중에 적절하지 못했던 것으로 여기게 되는 일들을 하는 것이다.

cracking and popping noises 우지끈 소리와 펑펑거리는 소리들   put A down to B A를 B로 축소하다   make sure 확인하다   drill 훈련   malfunction 오작동   social stigma 사회적 오점(사회적으로 매장하는 등의 행위)   be reluctant to ~하기를 꺼리다   make a fool of oneself 바보짓을 하다. 웃음거리가 되다   rush out into the street 거리로 뛰쳐나가다   fire brigade 소방대. 소방대

구문 ▶

1 hundreds of interviews with people (who are) involved in fires
화재 사고에 대한 연루된(경험이 있는) 사람들과의 수많은 면담
2 put it down to vandals at work
기물 파괴범들의 소행으로 치부하다
3 faced with evidence of a possible fire
화재일 가능성이 있다는 증거에 접해서
4 what may be a false alarm 잘못된 것일 수 있는 경보
5 things (that) they afterwards see to have been inappropriate
나중에 적절하지 못했던 것으로 여기는 일들

해설 ▶

1 이 글은 화재 사고를 경험한 사람들이 화재에 대하여 나타내는 반응을 기술한 것이다. 사실 전달에 해당하므로 '정보전달적(informative)'이라고 할 수 있다.
2 화재 사고에 직면하면 사람들은 그것이 화재인지 아닌지 더 알고 싶어 한다.

3 화재경보 등에 사람들의 반응이 느린 이유는 빨리 대처하여 남의 웃음거리가 될까 봐이다.

528 1. (C)   2. (D)

우선 과학의 정의를 내리는 것이 도움이 될 것 같다. ①현재로서는 과학은 인류가 자신의 환경을 이해하고 조절하기 위해 해 온 의식적인 노력이라고 받아들일 수 있다. 이렇게 되면 논의의 범위가 넓어지게 되고, 누구도 자연의 여러 가지 측면에 따라 이루어져야 하는 (과학의) 잡다한 분야를 알고서 놀라지 않을 것이다. 대다수의 사람들은 과학을 천문학, 물리학, 화학, 생물학과 같은 주제의 관점에서 생각한다. 이것들은 분명히 최고로 발달한 분야들이지만 우리가 그것들을 깊게 생각해 보면 그것들도 결국 많은 소분야로 나누어진다는 것을 알게 된다. 물리학은 당연히 운동이나, 열, 빛, 소리, 자기(磁氣), 전기, 그리고 물질의 일반적인 속성에 관한 연구와 같은 여러 모습들로 ②세분화된다. 그러나 ③이런 세부적인 분류에도 불구하고 개개의 주제 내에서는 밀접한 일관성이 있음이 발견되고, 이 주제들 사이에 많은 연관성과 상호 간의 응용 작용도 있다. 다시 말하면 일반적으로 받아들여지는 과학 연구들의 전체적인 범위가 같이 얽혀 있으며, 한 분야에서 잘 확립된 내용은 다른 모든 분야로 확신 있게 전달된다는 것이다.

for the present 현재로서는, 당장은   conscious effort 의식적인 노력   lay a very wide net 범위를 넓히다   multifarious 가지각색의, 잡다한   in terms of ~면에서   astronomy 천문학   in turn 결국   magnetism 자기(磁氣)   consistency 일관성, 정합성(整合性)   hang together 같이 매달려 있다

구문 ▶

1 we can take it to mean ~
• take A to mean B : A가 B를 뜻하는 것으로 받아들이다
2 divides itself into = is divided into
3 what is well established in one division
한 분야에서 잘 확립된 내용
4 s confidently carried over into all the others
다른 분야에도 확신 있게 전달된다

해설 ▶

1 Despite of all such divisions에서 despite는 of를 동반하지 않는 단독 전치사이므로 (C)가 정답이다.
2 이 글은 과학의 여러 분야 사이에 존재하는 밀접한 관계를 논한 글이므로 정답은 (D)이다.

529 1. (E)   2. (D)   3. (A)

모든 종류의 기술의 발달 속도가 너무 빠르고 맹렬해서 인류는 그것에 적응할 시간을 갖지 못하였다. 그

결과는 우리가 오늘날 목격하고 있는 혼란으로, 이 혼란은 우리의 물질세계뿐만 아니라 정신세계까지도 뒤흔들고 있다. 후자의 경우를 먼저 살펴보면, 산업, 상업, 재정 분야의 방식과 기계들의 성장이 매우 무모하고 무자비하여 큰 회사들이 그들을 ①번창하게 했어야 할 바로 그 행위들에 의해 망해 버렸다. 극단적인 삶의 기계화는 개인과 사회의 행복의 샘을 망쳐 버렸다. 오늘의 정치가들이 풀어야 할 가장 큰 문제는 산업과 노동의 인간화이지만, 한 세기나 지속되어 온 기술의 무자비함과 무절제한 탐욕이라는 악을 원상태로 되돌리기가 쉽지 않을 것이다. 어느 경우이든 문제는 매우 어려운데, 그것은 이론적인 해결책만을 찾아내는 것만으로는 충분하지가 않기 때문이다. 우리는 편견들을 극복하고 잘못된 목적을 되돌리고 헛된 이상들의 베일을 벗겨야 한다. ②더구나 경제 문제들은 거의 국제적인 수준의 문제가 되어 버려서 사회악들은 국제적인 기준 위에서가 아니면 완전히 치유할 수도 없을 것이다.

drastic 격렬한, 맹렬한, 급격한 adjust oneself to ~에 적응하다 chaos 혼란, 혼돈 witness 목격하다 upset 뒤집다 the latter 후자, 뒤의 것 reckless 무모한 merciless 무자비한 excessive 지나친 mechanization 기계화 poison 망치다 well 샘 statesman 정치가 humanization 인간화, 인성 undo 원상태로 돌리다 ruthlessness 냉혹함 unrestrained greed 절제되지 않은 욕망 exceedingly 지나치게 uncover 찾아내다, 벗기다 social ill 사회악

구문

1 the very activities which should have made them prosperous 번창하게 했어야 할 바로 그 행위들
2 except on an international basis 국제적인 기준 위에서가 아니라면

해설

1 위의 (구문 1) 참조.
2 본문 중에 The greatest problem which the statesmen of our time have to solve is the humanization of industry and labor에 유의하면 답이 나온다.
3 이 글은 너무 빠르고 맹렬하게 진행된 기술의 발달로 인해 인류가 겪게 되는 두 가지 혼란인 물질세계와 정신세계의 혼란 중에서, 우선 물질세계의 혼란을 기술하는 글이다. 따라서 다음 문단은 정신적 혼란과 그것의 해결책 제시에 대한 이야기가 될 것으로 예상해 볼 수 있다.

530 **1. (A) 2. (B) 3. (D)**

1859년에 생물학자 찰스 다윈은 「종의 기원」을 출간하였는데, 그것은 17세기에 갈릴레오와 뉴턴에 의한 과학적인 발견들의 내용이 야기한 사고의 혁명만큼 급진적이고 파급 효과가 큰 사고의 혁명을 가져올 책이었다. 19세기 중엽의 대다수 사람들은 성경에 기록된 창조설을 말 그대로 받아들였는데, 그 창조설에 의하면 모든 형태의 생명체들은 약 6,000년 전에 단 일주일이라는 기간 동안 이 세상에 생겨났다. 다윈은 자기보다 앞선 연구자들을 뛰어넘었다. 수년에 걸쳐 앞서 간 과학자들의 연구 내용을 공부하고 자신만의 자료를 수집하고 분석함으로써, 그는 지구의 나이에 대한 예전의 결론에 동의했을 뿐만 아니라 모든 생명체가 한 번에 태어난 것이 아니라 복잡한 (생명의) 형체들이 단지 적자만이 생존하는 커다란 생존 경쟁에서 살아남아 진화하였다는 결론을 내렸다. 많은 사람들이 종교의 가르침과 새로운 생물학의 발견들 사이에 실질적인 갈등은 없다는 점을 궁극에는 알게 되었지만, 다윈의 연구 업적은 많은 사람들을 자신의 종교적 믿음에 대한 의구심을 갖게끔 하는 초기의 효과를 가지고 있었다. 어떤 사람들은 계속하여 의문의 상태에 머물러 있었고, 또 다른 사람들은 의심을 넘어 절망에 이르기도 하였다. 그리고 믿음을 위해 과학을 포기하거나, 과학을 위해 믿음을 포기하는 사람들도 있었다.

Origin of Species 종의 기원 radical 급진적인 far-reaching (영향력이) 멀리 미치는 literally 말 그대로 account 설명 evolve 진화하다 struggle for existence 생존 경쟁 the fittest 가장 잘 적응하는 자들 eventually 궁극적으로는, 실제로는 conflict 갈등 initial 초기의 despair 절망 react 반응하다 renounce 포기하다

구문

1 a book that was to produce ~ ~을 가져올 책
　• 'be+to부정사' 용법 중 예정을 나타냄.
2 that brought about in the seventeenth century by ~ ~에 의해 17세기에 이룩된 그것
　• 지시대명사 that = a revolution in thought
3 according to which 그런데 그것에 의하면
　• 관계대명사 which = the account of Creation given in the Bible
4 he not only agreed with ~ but concluded...
　그는 ~에 동의하였을 뿐만 아니라 …라는 결론을 내렸다
　• not only A but (also) B 구문
5 instead of all forms of life appearing at once
　모든 생명체 형태가 한 번에 나타나는 대신에
　• appearing은 동명사로 all forms of life가 의미상의 주어

해설

1 ① far-reached → far-reaching '영향력이 멀리까지 미치는'이라는 뜻의 능동 표현이 요구된다. 즉 현재분사형(-ing)이 필요하다.
2 이 글은 다윈의 진화론이 끼친 영향에 관한 내용이므로 정답은 (B)이다.
3 결국 다윈의 진화론으로 대변되는 생물학적 발견은 궁극적으로는 종교의 가르침과 크게 어긋나지 않는다는

PART 5
Reading Comprehension

것을 많은 사람들이 알게 되었다는 문장에서 정답이
(D)라는 것을 유추할 수 있다.

531 1. (A) 2. (D)

사람들이 매일의 삶에서 접하는 공기와 물에는
모든 종류의 미생물이 가득하다고 오랫동안 알려져
왔다. ①고맙게도, 이 미생물들 대부분은 유순하며,
불미스러운 놈들은 보통 어떤 해도 주지 않고
배수관을 통하여 씻겨 내려간다. 그러나 언제나 그런
것은 아니다. 한 연구 팀의 보고에 의하면 샤워를
하는 것이 어떤 사람들에게는 해가 될 수 있다고
한다. 그들은 미국 9개 도시의 45곳에서 샤워꼭지
안에 쌓이는 얇은 미생물 막을 채집하고 그 안에 들어
있는 유전자 물질을 분석하였다. ②놀랍게도, 그들은
몇몇 샘플에서 호흡기 질환을 유발할 수 있는 고도로
응축된 병원균을 발견하였다. 이것은 수도꼭지에서
나오는 물에서 발견되었는데, 그것을 연무질로
바꾸거나 들이마시지 않으면 해가 되지 않은 채로
머무른다. 이것(연무질로 바꾸거나 들이마시는 것)은
바로 세균이 든 물을 고압으로 샤워꼭지로 강제로
내보낼 때 생기는 현상이다. 조그마한 입자들을
들이마시면 그것들이 폐로 들어가서 감염을 일으킬
수 있다. 이것이 주의를 요하는 원인이 될까?
건강한 사람들은 괜찮지만, 손상된 면역 체계를
가진 사람들이나 노인들처럼 폐질환의 위험이 있는
사람들은 예방조치를 할 필요가 있다. 표백제로 샤워
꼭지를 청소하는 것은 별 효과가 없는데, 왜냐하면
병원균이 새 물과 함께 또 나타날 것이기 때문이다.
미생물이 잘 들러붙는 플라스틱 샤워꼭지를 금속으로
교체하는 것이 더 나을 것이다.

encounter 만나다 micro-organism 미생물 benign
유순한, 해가 없는 unsavory 맛없는, 불미스러운
drain 배수구 biofilm 미생물 막[층] build up 쌓다
showerhead 샤워꼭지 genetic material 유전자 물질
high concentrations of a microbe 고도로 응축된
미생물 respiratory illness 호흡기 질병 tap water
수돗물 bug-laden water 세균이 든 물 infection 감염
compromised 손상된 immune system 면역 체계
pulmonary diseases 폐질환 take precaution 예방
조치를 강구하다 bleach 표백제 bug-prone 미생물이 잘
달라붙는

구문

1 Not always, though. = But it is not always so.
그러나 언제나 그런 것은 아니다.
2 unless turned into an aerosol and inhaled
= if it is not turned into an aerosol and inhaled
그것을 연무질로 바꾸거나 들이마시지 않으면
3 those with a compromised immune system
손상된 면역 체계를 가진 사람들

4 Cleaning showerheads with bleach will not do
표백제로 샤워꼭지를 청소하는 것은 별 효과가 없다
• do = be effective
5 metal ones = metal showerheads

해설

1 빈칸 ①의 다음에 우리가 매일 접하는 미생물의 대부분이
해가 되지는 않는다는 설명이 뒤따르므로, '감사하게도',
'다행스럽게도'와 같은 긍정적 표현의 부사가 와야 한다.
빈칸 ②의 뒤 문장을 통해 채집하여 분석된 물질에서
예상치 않은 물질이 발견되었다는 것을 알 수 있다. 또한
본문 셋째 문장에 Not always, though.라 하였으므로
평상시의 상황과는 반대의 내용이 올 것을 쉽게 짐작할
수가 있다.
2 본문의 내용과 일치하는 것은 (D) '샤워꼭지에서 고압으로
병원균을 강제로 내보내면 해롭게 된다.'이다.
cf. (A) '나이 든 사람이 샤워를 자주 해서는 안 된다'는
말은 본문에 없다.
(B) 수돗물에 들어 있는 미생물은 cardiovascular
illness(심장혈관 병)가 아닌 pulmonary disease
(폐질환)를 일으킬 가능성이 크다.
(C) '건강한 사람만이 금속 샤워꼭지를 쓰라'는 말은
없다.

532 1. (D) 2. (C)

1960년 이래로 세계의 육류 생산량은 4배로 증가하여
연 2억8천만 톤 이상을 생산하기에 이르렀다.
부유한 나라들의 모든 국민이 오늘 고기 먹는 것을
끊겠다고 맹세한다고 해도, 소비는 계속해서 솟구칠
것이다. (ⓐ) 이 이유 때문에 최근에 진지한 환경
계획[입안]자들은 육류 산업을 없애는 쪽이 아닌
그것을 녹색화하는 쪽으로 초점을 맞추어 왔다.
소고기, 돼지고기, 또는 닭고기를 만드는 것은 환경을
피폐화하는 과정이 될 수 있다. (ⓑ) 그리고 동물의
단백질 중에서, 소고기 1kg을 생산하는 데에는
닭고기 1kg을 생산하는 것보다 7배나 넓은 농장이
필요하고, 돼지고기 1kg을 생산하는 것보다 15배의
땅이 필요하다. 그러나 과학자들과 목축업자들과
녹색운동가들은 이 폐해를 억제할 수 있다고
확신하고 있다. 생산 및 공급의 모든 연쇄 과정을
조정하고, 가축을 기르고 사육하는 방식을 바꾸고,
현대 유전학을 통해 더 청정한 소를 기름으로써.
(ⓒ이 노력은 동물 자체에서 시작된다.) 소가 먹이를
먹을 때 소의 위에서는 부산물로 메탄가스가 나온다.
소들은 풀은 아주 잘 먹지만, 대부분의 기업화된
가축 농장에서 소에게 먹이는 콩과 옥수수는 소의
위장에 과도한 가스를 분출시켜 배에 이상한 소리가
나게 한다. (ⓓ) 이것과 싸워 이기기 위해서 몇몇
농장들은 콩과 옥수수 중심의 먹이를 없앰으로써
소의 건강을 증진시키고 우유 생산량을 늘리며
메탄가스 배출을 줄일 수 있다는 것을 알았다. 그

대신에 그들은 소들에게 예전식의 알팔파[목초]를 주었는데, 그것은 영양분들과 좋은 지방산으로 가득하다.

quadruple 4배가 되다 swear off meat 맹세코 고기 먹는 것을 끊다 soar 솟구치다, 급속으로 증가하다 serious 진지한 focus on ~에 초점을 맞추다 eliminate 제거하다 the meat industry 육류 산업 environmentally devastating process 환경을 피폐화하는 과정 herder 목축업자, 목동 green group 녹색운동가 curb 억제하다 all along the supply chain 생산 및 공급의 모든 연쇄 과정에서 methane 메탄가스 byproduct 부산물 soybean 콩 bovine 소의 rumble with excess gas 과도한 가스 분출로 이상한 소리가 나다 boost 촉진시키다 the herds 소떼들 emission 배출, 분출 alfalfa 알팔파(목초) be packed with ~으로 가득 채워지다 nutrient 영양소 benign 좋은, 온화한 fatty acids 지방산

구문

1 Even if everyone in the rich nations <u>swore</u> off meat today, consumption <u>would</u> continue to soar.
부유한 나라들의 모든 국민이 오늘 고기 먹는 것을 끊는다고 맹세해도 소비는 계속해서 솟구칠 것이다.
• 가정법 과거 구문

2 serious environmental planners have recently focused not on eliminating the meat industry but on turning it green
진지한 환경 계획(입안)자들은 육류 산업을 없애는 쪽이 아닌 그것을 녹색화하는 쪽으로 최근에 초점을 맞추어 왔다
• focus <u>not</u> on A <u>but</u> on B

3 to make a kilogram of beef takes seven times more farmland than is needed to produce a kilo of chicken
소고기 1kg을 생산해 내는 데에는 닭고기 1kg을 생산해 내는 것보다 7배나 넓은 농토가 필요하다
• 주어는 to make a kilogram of beef, 동사는 takes, 목적어는 seven times more farmland than~ 임에 유의.
• than is needed~에서 than은 주어로 쓰인 유사 관계대명사.

4 the way we farm and feed livestock
우리가 가축을 기르고 먹이를 주는 방식

해설

1 본문의 내용과 일치하는 것은 (D)이다. '소고기 1kg을 생산해 내는 데에는 닭고기 1kg을 생산해 내는 것보다 7배나 넓은 농장이 필요하고, 돼지고기 1kg을 생산해 내는 것보다 15배의 땅이 필요하다.'라고 언급되어 있으므로 돼지고기 1kg을 생산하는 데에 가장 작은 땅이 필요하다.
cf. (A) 실제 상황이 아닌 가정이다.
(B) 이와 반대로 메탄가스는 환경에 해롭다.
(C) 소들은 풀은 잘 먹지만, 콩과 옥수수는 소의 위장에서 과도하게 가스를 분출하게 하여 배에 이상한 소리가 나게 한다.

2 본문의 빈칸 ⓒ 바로 앞에서 '모든 생산 및 공급 과정에서 연쇄적으로 조절을 하고 가축을 기르고 먹이를 주는 방식을 바꾸고, 현대 유전학을 통하여 더 청정한 소를 기름으로써 이 폐해를 줄일 수 있다'고 했으므로, 그 방편의 하나인 The effort starts with the animals themselves.는 빈칸 ⓒ에 들어가야 한다.

PART 5
Reading Comprehension

Section 4 장문 독해 연습문제

533 1. (A) 2. (D) 3. (C)

대다수 미국의 포크 송은 수입품이다. 그것들은 정착민들이 가지고 들어왔으며, 새로운 생활 환경에 영향을 받고, 예전과 다른 현장과 배경을 반영하게끔 변화되었으나, 아직도 그들의 본래의 모습들을 보여 주고 있다. 다른 제목을 달고 불리며, 다른 일단의 인물들을 칭송하는 노래들인 버몬트의 스토리 중심 노래와 애팔래치아 산맥 지역의 산(山) 노래들은 대부분이 〈Barbara Allen〉, 〈The Hangman's Song〉, 〈The Two Sisters〉, 그리고 〈Lord Randal〉과 같은 잉글랜드와 스코틀랜드 발라드[민요]를 개작한 것이다. 그러나 아마도 최고라고 꼽을 수 있는 몇몇 미국 발라드는 토박이 미국산으로, 표현이 활달한 만큼 주제도 독창적이다. 지역에서 일어난 일 또는 당시 사람들의 믿음에 대한 보고 형태로 시작되거나, 단순히 (어린이들을 위한) 놀이 노래로서 시작된 발라드는 전 국민의 삶의 일부가 되었다. 그중 가장 발랄한 다섯 개는 역시 가장 인기 있기도 한데, 그것은 〈Dixie〉, 〈My Old Kentucky Home〉, 〈Frankie and Johnny〉, 〈Casey Jones〉, 그리고 〈John Henry〉이다. 대다수 포크 송과는 달리 이들 노래 중 적어도 두 곡은 누가 만들었는지 알려져 있다.

folk song 포크 송[민요] **importation** 수입품(다른 데에서 가져온 물건) **celebrate** 축하하다, 칭송하다 **character** 인물, 사람 **story song** 이야기식의 노래 **Vermont** 버몬트(미국 동부 뉴잉글랜드 여섯 주 중의 하나로 애팔래치아 산맥의 위쪽 꼭대기에 위치함) **mountain tunes** 산(山) 노래 **the Appalachians** 애팔래치아 산맥(미국과 캐나다 동부에 있는 산맥 이름) **largely** 주로, 대부분 **adaptation** 개작(改作) **genuinely** 진짜로 **native** 토박이(의) **local event** 지역에서 일어난 일 **current** 현존하는, 유행하는 **merely** 단지 **play song** (주로 어린이용) 놀이 노래 **vivid** 생생한, 발랄한

구문

1 Brought over by the settlers, ~ = Though they were brought over by the settlers, ~
   정착민들에 의해 유입되었지만
2 as original in subject as they are lively in expression
   표현이 활달한 만큼 주제도 독창적이다

해설

1 genuinely = truly / honestly / in fact
2 Beginning as reports of local events or current beliefs or merely as play songs에 답을 찾는 힌트가 있다.
3 이 글의 중심 내용은 '미국의 포크 송은 외국에서 들여온 옛 발라드의 개작들이 많지만, 몇몇 최고의 것들은 미국에서 쓰인 토착의 포크 송이라고 할 수 있다.'이다.

534 1. (C) 2. (A) 3. (C)

조지 워싱턴이 젊은 시절에 쓴 노트 중 몇 개가 아직도 존재하는데, 그것들을 보면 그가 라틴어를 약간 배워 알고 있었으며, 좋은 처신의 기본적인 요소들을 몸에 익혔고, 영문학도 어느 정도는 읽었음을 알 수 있다. 학창 시절에 그는 오로지 수학에만 관심이 있었던 것 같다. 그가 받은 교육은 신사로서 받아야 할 교육으로는 짧고 매우 불완전한 것이었으며 그것은 그가 받을 정규 교육의 모든 것이었다. 왜냐하면, 그 당시 버지니아의 다른 젊은이들과는 달리 그는 버지니아 주 수도인 윌리엄즈버그에 소재한 윌리엄메리 대학에 진학하지 않았기 때문이다. 그러므로 지적인 준비나 힘의 면에서 워싱턴은 존 애덤스, 토머스 제퍼슨, 제임스 매디슨 같은 초기의 다른 대통령들과 매우 극명한 대조를 이룬다. 후년에 워싱턴은 아마도 자신의 지적 훈련의 부족함에 관해 후회했을지도 모른다. 그는 공적인 대담이나 일상의 실용적인 문제들과 관계가 없는 토론을 편안해 하지 않았다. 또한 그는 프랑스어를 말하는 법을 결코 배운 적이 없어서 프랑스를 방문하는 것을 거부했는데, 그것은 프랑스의 정치가들과 직접 대화를 할 수 없어 당황해 할지도 몰라서였다. 그래서 제퍼슨, 애덤스와는 달리 그는 유럽에 결코 가 보지 못했다.

care for 좋아하다, 관심을 갖다 **formal education** 정규 교육 **be embarrassed at** ~에 당황해하다 **statesman** 정치인

구문

1 His was a brief and most incomplete education
   그가 받은 교육은 짧고 매우 불완전한 교육이었다
   • His = His education (소유대명사가 명사를 대신하는 독립적인 용법으로 쓰인 것)
2 the formal education he was to have
   그가 받을 수 있는 모든 정규 교육
3 In terms of intellectual preparation and power
   지적인 준비나 힘의 면에서 (보면)
4 A is in sharp contrast with B : A는 B와 극명한 대조를 이룬다
5 He never felt comfortable in formal debate
   그는 공적인 대담을 편안해 하지 않았다
6 inasmuch as he never learned to speak French
   프랑스어를 말하는 법을 결코 배운 적이 없어서

해설

1 embarrassed = perplexed / ashamed
2 마지막 문장에 이 문제의 힌트가 있다.
3 대학에 진학하지 않은 워싱턴이 받은 교육은 매우 짧고 제한적이었고 이것이 그의 후년의 삶에서 큰 불리함으로 작용하였다.

535 1. significance 2. less 3. (A) 4. (C)

우리는 시가 시인과 같은 민족이며 같은 언어를 쓰는 사람들에게는 가치가 있지만 다른 언어를 사용하는 사람들에게는 그렇지 않을 수 있다는 점에서 다른 모든 예술과는 다르다고 말한다. 음악과 미술조차도 지역적이고 민족적인 특색을 가지는 것이 사실이지만 외국인들의 이 예술들에 대한 감상의 어려움은 (시의 경우보다는) 훨씬 덜하다. 반면에, 산문들은 모국어로 쓰였을 때 중요성을 가지지만 그것을 번역의 과정에서 잃게 된다는 것이 사실이다. 하지만 (번역된) 시를 읽을 때보다는 소설을 번역본으로 읽을 때 잃는 것이 훨씬 적다는 것을 우리 모두는 느끼고 있으며, 어떤 종류의 과학을 다룬 작품을 번역하는 경우에는 잃는 것이 사실상 없을 수도 있다. 시가 산문보다 상당히 더 지역적이라는 점은 유럽 언어들의 역사에서 찾아볼 수 있다. 중세 시대 내내 (오늘에서 거슬러) 수백 년 전에 이르기까지 라틴어는 철학, 신학, 그리고 과학의 언어였다. 언어를 문학에 사용하려는 개개의 국민들의 충동은 시와 더불어 시작되었다. 시란 감정과 정서를 표현하는 것과 주로 관계가 있다는 점과, 생각은 일반적이지만 감정과 정서는 개별적인 것이라는 점을 깨달을 때 이는 지극히 당연한 것으로 보인다. 한 외국어로 느끼는 것보다는 그 언어로 생각하는 것이 더 쉽다. 따라서 시보다 더 명백하게 민족적인 예술은 없는 것이다.

observe 소견을 진술하다, 목격하다 local and racial character 지역적이며 민족적인 색채 appreciation 감상 on the other hand 반면에, 다른 한편으로 prose writing 산문 significance 중요성, 가치 scientific work 과학을 다룬 작품 virtually 실제로 nil 무(無), 영(零) theology 신학(神學) impulse 충동 literary use 문학에 사용하는 것 stubbornly 완강하게, 분명하게

구문

1 in having a value for ~ : ~을 위한 가치를 가진다는 점에서
2 for no other = for no other people
3 which is lost in translation
   그런데 그것(중요성)은 번역의 과정에서 잃게 된다
4 read a novel in translation 소설을 번역본으로 읽다
5 A has primarily to do with B : 기본적으로 A는 B와 관계가 있다
6 no art is more stubbornly national than poetry
   시보다 더 명백하게 민족적인 예술은 없다

해설

1 which는 significance를 받는 관계대명사.
2 소설을 번역본으로 읽을 경우, 시를 번역본으로 읽을 때보다 잃는 것이 더 적다.
3 nil = nothing
4 이 글의 마지막 두 문장 속에 답이 있다.

536 1. (C)   2. (D)   3. (B)

미국에서의 대량 생산, 대중들의 욕구나 취향을 표준화하여 생산을 표준화[규격화]하기 위한 광고의 이용, 그리고 이에 뒤따른 생산 비용의 ①저하와 임금의 인상, 이 모든 것들은 순수하게 물질적 관점에서 미국인들의 생활 규모에 엄청난 상승을 만들어 내었다. 관세 장벽으로 인하여 쪼개지지 않는 1억 이상의 인구가 있으며, 대부분의 원자재가 국내에서 생산이 되고, 이상하게도 개성이 부족하면서 다른 사람들처럼 똑같은 생활을 하고 똑같은 것을 갖기를 기꺼이 원하는 국민이 있어서, 산업 지도자들은 표준화된 생산이라는 자신들의 이상을 실현할 수 있었다. 그러나 이러한 결과의 성취는 유럽인들이 아직도 절대 중요하다고 생각하고 있는 몇몇 가치의 ②합락을 야기했다. 교양 있는 유럽인이 다른 무엇보다도 앞서 원하는 것은 개성적인 사람이 되는 것, 일과 놀이에서 자신만의 독특한 개성을 표현할 수 있는 것이다. 광대한 대륙 전역에 걸친 미국인의 삶이 지루하게도 ③똑같다는 점은 유럽인을 오싹하게 한다. 뉴욕에서 샌프란시스코까지 3,000마일을 여행하면서 대부분 같은 종류의 사람들만 만나거나, 똑같은 만화와 연합하여 공동으로 제공되는 뉴스난만을 읽고, ④자신의 일[장사] 이야기만 지루하게 하고 똑같은 도시 건축물만을 본다면, 그 여행이 무슨 소용이 있겠는가?

mass-production 대량 생산 advertising 광고 standardize 표준화[규격화]하다 consequent 뒤따라 나타나는 lowering 하락, 저하 production cost 생산 비용 wage 임금(賃金) immense 엄청난 scale 규모 raw material 원료 produce at home 국내에서 생산되다 singularly 이상하게도, 드물게 lacking in individuality 개성이 결여된 more than willing to 기꺼이 ~하려 하다 of vital importance 매우 중요한(=vitally important) unique personality 특유의 개성 dreary 지루한 appall 오싹하게 하다 comic strip 만화 syndicated news column 연맹에 의해 공동으로 제공되는 뉴스난 talk the same "shop" 각자 자기 장사 이야기만 지루하게 하다 city architecture 도시 건축물

구문

1 from the purely material standpoint
   순수하게 물질적 관점에서 볼 때
2 With a population of over ~, with most ~, with a people ~, the leaders of industry...
   • with에 의해 이끌리면서 (마치 분사구문처럼) 부사구 기능을 하는 전치사구가 3개 있고, 각각은 뒤의 주어(the leaders of industry)의 상태를 나타냄.
3 undivided by tariff barriers 관세 장벽으로 인하여 분할되지 않는(미국이 50주로 구성되어 있지만 각 주간에는 관세 장벽이 없는 한 나라임을 말함)
4 A has brought about the surrender of certain values A가 몇몇 가치의 합락을 가져왔다

87

5 Of what use (is it) to travel three thousand miles
3,000마일을 여행해 본들 무슨 소용인가?

해설

1 ①대량 생산은 생산 비용을 낮추는(lowering) 결과를
가져왔다.
②표준화된 생산의 실현으로 인해 유럽인들이 매우
중요시하는 가치의 포기(surrender)가 나타났다.
③대량의 표준화된 생산은 삶이 지루하도록 똑같은
모습(sameness)을 갖게 하였다.
2 talk the same "shop" : 자신의 일(장사) 이야기만
지루하게 하다
3 유럽인들은 미국 생활의 지루하고 단조로움이 개성을 잃은
재미없는 삶이라고 보았다.

537 **1. abounded   2. exhaustion   3. (D)   4. (B)**

백인들이 처음으로 미국 대륙에 왔을 때, 그들은
무시무시한 가치를 지닌 엄청난 양의 천연자원을
발견하였다. 대륙의 큰 지역을 숲이 덮고 있었고,
이후에 믿지 못할 정도로 많은 양의 가스와 석유,
여러 광물이 발견되었다. 매우 비옥한 땅도 그 크기가
엄청났으며, 숲, 대초원, 시냇물, 강들은 야생의
생물들이 ①가득하였다. 자원이 매우 풍부하여서
그것은 결코 고갈될 것 같아 보이지 않았다.
그래서 농지를 만들기 위해 숲들이 파괴되었으며,
목초지와 대초원들이 경작되고 써레질되었다.
신생공업국(미국)에 공급하기 위해 엄청난 양의
광물들과 석유가 소비되었다. 거의 모든 강가에는
제조 공장, 제분소, 전력 회사가 들어섰다. 식량과
재미를 위해 동물과 새들이 죽임을 당했다.
얼마 가지 않아 (이러한 행위들의) 결과가 분명하게
나타났다. 홍수로 인해 매년 수백만 달러에 해당하는
피해가 발생했고, 매우 비옥한 땅이 씻겨나가거나 큰
먼지바람을 일으키며 사라져 버렸다. 겉으로 보기에는
고갈될 것 같지 않은 기름과 광물들이 ②고갈의
징후를 보였고, 강은 공장과 가정에서 나온 오물과
쓰레기로 가득 찬다. 많은 강들이 물고기가 살기에
적합하지 않게 되었으며 여러 종의 새들이 사라지고
몇몇 동물들이 멸종될 찰나에 있었다. 장래에는
목재도 부족하게 될 것이라고 예측되었다. 그래서
몇몇 보존 프로그램이 세워지기 시작하였는데, 그것은
미국인들이 그 프로그램들의 중요성을 깨달았기
때문이다. 그들은, 만약에 현재뿐만 아니라 미래의
미국인들이 미국이라는 나라의 유산인 천연자원을
공유하기를 바란다면, 그것들이 (③없어서는 안 되는)
것이라고 진지하게 믿었다.

natural resources 천연자원   tremendous 엄청난,
무시무시한   mineral 광물(질)   a great abundance
of 엄청난 양의   fertile soil 옥토(沃土)   prairie 대초원
abound with ~로 가득하다   wild life 야생의 동식물

be used up 고갈되다   make way for 길을 트다
farmland 농지   grassland 목초지   plow 경작하다,
갈다   harrow 써레질하다, 이랑을 파다   mill (바람, 물
등을 이용한) 제분소, 제조 공장   power company 전력
회사   be washed away 씻겨나가다   be blown
up 바람에 날아가다   in great clouds 큰 구름 덩어리
모습으로   inexhaustible 고갈될 줄 모르는, 무궁무진한
exhaustion 고갈   dirt and waste 오물과 쓰레기
unfit 부적합한   species 종(種)   on the verge of
disappearing 사라질 찰나에 있다   timber shortages
목재 부족   preservation program 보존 계획   set up
세우다(= establish)   indispensable 없어서는 안 되는,
절대로 필요한   heritage 유산

구문

1 Forests, prairies, streams, and rivers abounded
with wild life.
숲, 대초원, 시냇물, 강들은 야생의 생물들이 가득하였다.
 • A abound with B: A가 B로 가득 차다
2 So vast were the resources that it seemed ~
= The resources were so vast that it seemed ~
3 The seemingly inexhaustible oil and minerals
겉으로 보기에는 고갈될 것 같지 않은 기름과 광물들
4 if future, as well as present, Americans were to
share in the resources
만약에 현재뿐만 아니라 미래의 미국인들이 미국이라는
나라의 유산인 천연자원을 공유하기를 바란다면
 • 가정법 과거 구문, be+to부정사 : ~하고자 한다면

해설

1 A abound with B: A가 B로 가득 차다
 • abound는 자동사이므로 수동형 be abounded로
 쓰일 수 없음.
2 명사형이 필요하므로 exhaustion으로 바꾼다.
3 천연자원 보존 프로그램이 반드시 필요하다는 내용이다.
4 제분소와 전력 회사의 부족은 자연의 과도한 이용의
결과로 나타난 현상은 아니다.

538 **1. (E)   2. (D)   3. 도구에 적용되는 이야기는 직업에도
마찬가지로 적용되었다.   4. (B)**

어떤 사람이 옛 시대의 상황에 갑자기 던져지는
경우, 그는 필연적으로 많은 것들을 알게 된다. 그는
자신이 사용하는 도구들의 잊힌 용도를 재발견하고,
그 도구들을 원시 시대에 분류되던 대강의 범주로
그것들을 보는 법을 배우게 된다. 원시인이 사냥할
때 사용하던 날카로운 돌도끼는 물건을 자르는 데
사용하던 것과 거의 다르지 않았지만 더 개화된
문화권들에서는 "무기"와 "도구"가 각각 더 특화된
도구로 발달되어감에 따라 그것들에 대한 구분이
나타나게 되었다. 그리하여 18세기 영국에서는 (소총,
권총 같은) 화기(火器)가 주로 무기로 사용되었다.
그러나 식민지 시대에, 기습 공격을 해 오는 야만의
토인들로부터 자신과 가족을 보호해야 하고 종종

식탁에 오를 고기를 사냥하여야만 했던 오지에 살고 있던 미국인에게는, "무기"와 "도구"의 구분은 역시 별 의미가 없었다. Ⓐ 도구에 적용되는 이야기는 직업에도 마찬가지로 적용되었다. 원시 시대의 상황 하에서 여러 가지 방식으로 상처나 질병을 치료하는 자들, 즉 기도문[주문]을 중얼거려 치료하는 자, 칼을 써서 치료하는 자, 그리고 여러 가지 약재를 섞어 지어 치료하는 자들 사이에 거의 구분(분업화)이 없었던 것 같다. 그러나 18세기 영국에서는 이 모든 일이 구분이 되어서 그 일 하나하나가 이미 서로 다른 집단의 고유한 전유물이 되었다. 미국에서는 이러한 분업화를 유지하기가 어려웠을 것이고 그래서 상처 치료사가—가끔은 법률가나 총독이나 성직자가—이 모든 여러 가지 다른 일들을 혼자서 다 수행하였다.

plunge into ~ 안으로 뛰어들다　inevitably 필연적으로, 반드시　forgotten use 잊힌 용도　crude 조잡한, 거친　category 범주　primitive age 원시 시대[사회]　sharp stone 날카로운 돌도끼　developed culture 발전된 사회　specialized implement 특화된 도구　colonial America 식민지 미국　backwoodsman 오지인(奧地人)　raiding savage 기습 공격을 해 오는 야만의 토인　shoot meat for his table 식탁에 오를 고기를 사냥하다　practice the different modes of healing and curing 여러 가지 방식으로 상처나 질병을 치료하다　mutter the prayer 기도문[주문]을 외다　the man who insert the knife 칼로 상처를 치료하는 사람(수술하는 사람)　mix the medicine 여러 가지 약재를 섞어 약을 짓다　private preserve 고유한 전유물

구문

1　What was true of implements was also true of occupations.
　도구에 적용되는 이야기는 직업에도 마찬가지로 적용되었다.
　• A is true of B : A는 B에 적용된다
2　there seem to have been few distinctions
　= it seems that there were few distinctions
　거의 구분(분업화)이 없었던 것 같다
3　In America such distinctions would have been difficult to preserve
　미국에서는 이러한 분업화를 유지하기가 어려웠을 것이다
　• would have been은 가정법 과거완료 표현

해설

1　'전문 분야에 쓰이는 도구'는 그 자체가 전문화하는 역할을 하는 능동의 의미가 없으므로 a specialized implement라고 써야 한다.
2　문화적으로 발달이 되지 않은 18세기 미국에서는 유럽과 달리 한 사람이 여러 가지 일을 모두 담당하였기 때문에, 직업을 분화하여 전문화하기가 어려웠다.
3　A is true of B : A는 B에도 적용된다
4　18세기 유럽은 미국보다 더 발달되고 직업이 분화된 사회였다.

539　1. (C)　2. (A)　3. of　4. (D)　5. reduced, of

굶주림은 세상의 많은 사람들에게 상존하는 동반자가 되고 있다. 수백만의 사람들이 충분히 먹을 식량을 갖지 못하며 매년 6천5백만이 넘는 인구가 세계 식량 생산량의 어느 정도를 나누어 갖기를 바란다. 농부들이 더 많은 식량을 생산해 왔으나 많은 나라에서 오랫동안 있어 온 심각한 영양실조를 바로잡을 만큼 충분히 생산하지는 못하였다. 더 부유하고 ① 더 잘 먹는 나라에서는 식량 생산이 더 빠른 속도로 증가해 오고 있으나, 가난한 나라들에서는 (오히려) 뒤처져 왔다. 사실, 식량 공급량과 인구 성장 사이의 균형을 유지하는 것은 많은 나라에서 이루기가 매우 어려운 일이다. 비가 정상적으로 내리지 않거나 불규칙한 다른 기후 변화들이 한 해 안에도 식량 공급의 위기를 초래할 수 있고, 그래서 식량 공급이 더 나은 나라들로부터 식량을 선적해 오는 일들은 현존하는 낮은 영양 수준을 유지하기 위해서라도 필요한 것이다. 날씨가 좋으면 많은 나라들이 일시적으로나마 이용할 수 있는 식량이 늘어날 것이다. ② 그러나 빠른 인구 성장 때문에, 현재의 영양 수준을 유지하려 한다면, 생산의 증가가 끊임없이 요구된다. 많은 나라가 인구가 매우 많고, 인구 성장률이 매우 높아서 그 결과 매년 수많은 인구가 늘어나고 식량 공급량을 늘리는 문제도 따라서 큰 것이다. 만약에 영양 수준이 건강하고 정상적인 신체 활동을 할 정도로 일반적으로 받아들여지는 적정 수준에 이르려 한다면, 개발도상국의 식량 생산은 인구 증가보다 더 빨리 늘어나야 할 것이고, 그렇지 않으면 국제 무역을 통하여 필요한 식량을 확보하기 위한 비식량 분야의 생산이 충분히 늘어나야 한다. 인구 성장률의 감소는 이런 나라들의 인구의 영양 수준을 개선하는 데 있어서 가장 중요하다.

ever-present 상존(常存)하는　companion 동료, 동반자　under-nutrition 영양실조　better-fed countries 더 잘 먹고사는 나라들(feed - fed - fed)　lag behind 뒤처지다　climatic irregularity 불규칙한 기후　crisis 위기 pl. crises　shipment 선적(船積)　prevail 현존하다. 세력을 떨치다　normal physical activity 정상적인 신체 활동　secure 확보하다　reduction of the rates of population growth 인구 성장률의 감소

구문

1　if current levels of nutrition are to be maintained
　현재의 영양 수준이 유지되려면
　• be+to부정사 : ~하고자 한다면 (의도를 나타내는 표현)
　cf. If nutrition is to be brought up to~도 같은 구조를 지닌 표현임.
2　is of primary importance = is primarily important
　가장 중요한

PART 5
Reading Comprehension

해설

1 better-fed countries = countries which are fed better 더 잘 먹고사는 나라들
2 앞에 나온 내용과 어긋나는 내용이 뒤따르므로 반대의 의미를 지닌 접속사를 써야 한다.
3 of primary importance = primarily important 매우 중요한(이때 of는 '본질적인 속성'을 나타내는 전치사)
4 narrow : 이루기가 쉽지 않은(= difficult), 범위가 좁은(= limited)
5 인구의 성장 속도가 줄지 않으면, 식량 생산의 증가는 별 의미가 없다.
   • of help 도움이 되는(= helpful)
     of+추상명사 = 형용사

540 1. (D) 2. (C) 3. (B) 4. (D) 5. (A) 6. (E)

40여 년의 열성적인 활동의 삶을 살면서 헨리 소로가 추구해 온 단 하나의 일은 만족스러운 삶을 제공할 것으로 간주되는 경제적인 삶을 찾아내는 것이었다. 콩코드 벌판을 이리저리 돌아다니는 일에 모험이라는 점에서 높은 가치를 부여하였던 그의 하나의 관심사는 부(富)의 진정한 의미를 탐구하는 것이었다. 그가 경제학의 문제라고 이해하였던 바에 따르면 그에게 열려 있는 해결 가능한 방법은 세 가지였는데, 그것은 스스로를 이용하여 (문제를) 풀어 보는 것, 다른 사람들을 이용하여 풀어 보는 것, 아니면 그 문제를 최소의 분모로 축소하는 것이었다. 첫 번째의 방법은, 아침이 되어 큰 모험을 해야 할 시점에 자신을 답차(踏車) 속에 가두는 일로 거의 불가능한 일이었다. 자신의 친구들을 이용하는 방법은 사회적 양심에 민감한 소로에게는 더욱더 큰 부당 행위로 보였다. 금욕을 유지한 자유 상태가 그에게 물질적 행복이 있는 노예 상태보다는 나아 보였고, 그래서 그는 월든 호수로 이주하는 데에 만족하고 "삶의 필수적인 사실들에만 직면하고 삶이 가르치고자 한 것들을 알아보는" 수준 높은 생활에 착수하였다. 그는 다른 사람들이 오두막집을 짓고 홀로 살아야 한다는 점을 옹호하지 않았다. 그는 삶의 가장 좋은 방식에 관하여 자신의 의견을 독단으로 주장하고 싶지 않았으며 개개인이 스스로 그 방식을 터득해야 한다는 것이 그의 생각이었다. 그러나 그는 만족스러운 삶을 살아야 한다는 것에는 적극적으로 관심을 가졌다. (물질적 행복이 주가 되는) 낮은 수준의 경제생활로부터 그가 벗어나는 이야기는 그가 자신의 삶에서 얻고자 한 즐거움의 한 단편(斷片)이고, 「Walden」은 그것(단편)을 기록한 위대한 책이다. 「Walden」은 자연에 대한 찬양이라기보다는 삶에 대한 찬양의 책으로, 월든 호수에서 보낸 2년의 삶의 기록이다. 그러나 그 책은, 그가 분명하게 그러한 목적을 부인하고 있지만, 또한 사회를 비판한 책이다. 경제생활의 진정한 본질을 고려하면서, 러스킨의 의견에 동조하여, 그는 하나의 물건을 얻는 데 드는 비용은 당장이나 또는 궁극적으로 그것을 얻기 위해 필요한 삶의 양이라는 결론을 내렸다. 「Walden」에서 소로는 "유일한 부(富)는 삶이다."라는 표제를 상세히 설명하고 있다.

Thoreau, Henry David 헨리 데이비드 소로 (1817~1862, 미국의 초절(超絶)주의 시인, 수필가) odd 나머지, 남짓 rambling 산책, 소요(逍遙) exploit oneself 스스로를 대상으로 이용하다 lowest denominator 최소의 분모(본질적 요소) imprison oneself 스스로를 가두다 treadmill 답차(踏車: 비유적으로 '단조로운 일') infidelity 부정한 행위(= unfaithfulness, adultery, disloyalty) freedom with abstinence 금욕을 유지한 자유 상태 serfdom 노예 상태(= slavery) material well-being 물질적 행복 Walden Pond 월든 호수(미국 매사추세츠 주, 콩코드 시에 있는 호수. 이름은 pond이지만 둘레를 빠른 속도로 걷는 데 1시간이 걸리는 큰 호수로, 모래사장이 있어서 수영도 하고 보트도 탈 수 있다. 「Walden」은 소로가 이곳에서 2년간 살면서 적은 삶에 대한 책이다.) set about 착수하다 advocate 옹호하다 live isolated 홀로 떨어져 살다 dogmatize 독단을 펴다 emancipation 해방(= liberation) the lower economics 낮은 수준의 경제생활(여기서는 삶의 만족이 없이 물질적인 것이 주가 되는 생활을 뜻함) romance 즐거움의 감정 in praise of ~을 칭찬하는 social criticism 사회 비판 as well 또한, 역시 explicit 분명한 denial 부인, 부정 in exchange for ~과 교환하여 in the long run 궁극적으로 elaborate 자세히 설명하다 the text 표제

구문

1 an economy calculated to provide a satisfying life 만족스러운 삶을 제공할 것으로 여겨지는 경제적인 삶
2 one concern that gave to his ramblings in Concord fields a value of high adventure ~
   = one concern that gave a value of high adventure to his ramblings in Concord fields
   콩코드 벌판을 이리저리 돌아다니는 일에 높은 모험 가치를 부여하였던 하나의 관심사
3 As he understood the problem of economics, ~
   그가 경제학의 문제라고 이해하였던 바에 따르면
4 when the morning called to great adventure
   아침이 되어 큰 모험을 하려고 떠나야 할 시점에
5 see what it had to teach
   그것[삶]이 가르치고자 한 것들을 알아보다
   • had to가 must의 뜻을 갖는 조동사가 아님에 유의할 것.
6 each must settle that for himself
   개개인이 스스로 그 방식을 터득해야 한다
   • that = the best mode of living
7 But that a satisfying life should be lived, he was vitally concerned.
   = But he was vitally concerned that a satisfying life should be lived.
8 with Ruskin 러스킨의 의견에 동조하여

1 이 글은 '소로의 삶의 철학'에 관한 이야기이다.
2 소로의 삶의 주된 목표는 '만족할 만한 경제적인 삶을 찾는 것'이었다.
3 첫 문장의 forty-odd years of <u>eager</u> activity에서 힌트를 얻을 수 있다.
4 따라서 소로가 찾아낸 하나의 해결책은 소박한 삶(simple life)을 사는 것이었다.
5 마지막에서 두 번째 문장을 보면 알 수 있다.
6 infidelity = unfaithfulness 부정(不貞), 배신

20년 동안 검증된 영문 독해 베스트셀러!

독해에 꼭 필요한 구문 분석으로 더욱 빠르고 정확하게!

◆ 대학편입, 공무원시험 등을 위해 엄선한 540편의 지문 수록

◆ 4단계 독해 연습: 단문 ➡ 중문 ➡ 장문 ➡ 실전 문제

◆ 영문 독해에 필요한 고급 핵심 문법

◆ 효율적인 독해 연습을 위한 단어와 주요 어구 해석

〈NEXUS 영문독해연습 501 플러스〉 4th Edition, 이렇게 달라졌다!

더욱 높아진 지문의 완성도

독해 지문의 내용을 한층 더 업그레이드하여 더욱 명확하게 지문 파악이 가능하며, 어떤 영어 시험이라도 대비할 수 있도록 했다.

우리말 번역 & 모범 답안 분리

우리말 번역과 모범 답안 부분을 따로 분리하여 책속의 책으로 넣어 더욱 편리하게 모범 답안과 번역/해설을 확인할 수 있다.

독 해 · 문 법 · 작 문 을 한 번 에 완 성 하 는

NEXUS 영문 독해연습 501＋ 플러스

ENGLISH READING PRACTICE

4th Edition